Paul Insel

BEHAVIORAL MEDICINE:
Changing Health Lifestyles

Other books from Banff International Conferences on Behavior Modification available from Brunner/Mazel

Behavior Modification and Families (Banff VI)
Behavior Modification Approaches to Parenting (Banff VI)
The Behavioral Management of Anxiety, Depression and Pain (Banff VII)
Behavioral Self-Management: Strategies, Techniques and Outcome (Banff VIII)
Behavioral Systems for the Developmentally Disabled: I. School and Family Environments (Banff IX)
Behavioral Systems for the Developmentally Disabled: II. Institutional, Clinic and Community Environments (Banff IX)

BEHAVIORAL MEDICINE:
Changing Health Lifestyles

Edited by

PARK O. DAVIDSON, Ph.D.
Department of Psychology
and
SHEENA M. DAVIDSON, M.S.N.
School of Nursing

University of British Columbia,
Vancouver, British Columbia

BRUNNER/MAZEL, *Publishers* • New York

Library of Congress Cataloging in Publication Data
Main entry under title:

Behavioral medicine.

Includes bibliographies and indexes.
1. Behavior therapy. 2. Mental health. 3. Health
I. Davidson, Park Olof, 1937- II. Davidson,
Sheena M. [DNLM: 1. Behavior therapy—Congresses.
2. Life style—Congresses. W3 BA203 10th 1978 /
WM425 B215 1978b]
RC489.B4B4374 616.8'914 79-14944
ISBN 0-87630-200-2

Published by
Brunner/Mazel, Inc.
19 Union Square
New York, New York 10003

MANUFACTURED IN THE UNITED STATES OF AMERICA

Preface

This is one in a continuing series of publications sponsored by the Banff International Conferences on Behavior Modification. The conferences are held each spring in Banff, Alberta, Canada, and serve the purpose of bringing together outstanding behavioral scientists to present and discuss data related to emergent issues and topics in the field of behavior modification. Thus, the International Conferences, as a continuing event, have served as an expressive "early indicator" of the developing nature and composition of behavioristic science and scientific application.

Distance, schedules, and restricted audiences preclude wide attendance at the conferences. Consequently the publications have equal status with the conferences proper. They are not, however, simply publications of the papers presented at the conferences. Major presenters at the Banff Conferences are required to specifically write a chapter for the forthcoming book, separate from their informal presentation and discussion at the conference itself.

The original conference, held in 1969, had as its theme "Ideal Mental Health Services". The policy consciously adopted at that conference, and followed ever since, was to identify for each year's theme those behavioral researchers who could best identify the state of the art. In 1969 the conference faculty were Nathan Azrin, Ogden Lindsley, Gerald Patterson, Todd Risley and Richard Stuart!

The conference topics for the first five years were as follows:

1969: I. Ideal Mental Health Services
1970: II. Services and Programs for Exceptional Children and Youth
1971: III. Implementing Behavioral Programs for Schools and Clinics
1972: IV. Behavior Change: Methodology, Concepts, and Practice
1973: V. Evaluation of Behavioral Programs in Community, Residential and School Settings

Beginning in 1974, the Banff Conference books have been published by Brunner/Mazel and the interested reader may obtain copies of these earlier publications from the publisher. The conference topics and faculty were:

1974: VI. BEHAVIOR MODIFICATION AND FAMILIES

Frances Degen Horowitz
Todd R. Risley,
Hewitt B. Clark and
Michael F. Cataldo
Elaine A. Blechman and
Martha Manning
L. Keith Miller,
Alice Lies,
Dan L. Pettersen and
Richard Feallock
John B. Conway and
Susan L. Kreutzer
Paul M. Rosen
Lief Terdal,
Russell H. Jackson and
Ann M. Garner
Bradley D. Bucher
Stephen M. Johnson,
Orin D. Bolstad and
Gretchen K. Lobitz
Sander Martin,
Stephen Johnson,
Sandra Johansson and
Gail Wahl
Martha E. Bernal,
Leo F. Delfini,
Juell Ann North and
Gerald R. Patterson
John A. Corson
Victor A. Benassi and
Kathryn M. Larson
Robert F. Peterson

and

BEHAVIOR MODIFICATION APPROACHES TO PARENTING

Donald R. Green,
Karen Budd,
Moses Johnson,
Sarah Lang,
Elsie Pinkston and
Sara Rudd
Barbara Stephens Brockway and
W. Weston Williams
Edward R. Christophersen,
James D. Barnard,
Dennis Ford and
Montrose M. Wolf
Buell E. Goocher and
David N. Grove
Merihelen Blackmore,
Nancy Rich,
Zetta Means and
Mike Nally
Virginia Tams and
Sheila Eyberg
Karen E. Kovitz
Barclay Martin and
Craig Twentyman
Wallace L. Mealiea, Jr.
Martin E. Shoemaker and
Terry L. Paulson
Joe H. Brown
A. M. Gamboa, Jr.,
John Birkimer and
Robert Brown
Margaret Steward and
David Steward
Peter D. McLean
W. Doyle Gentry
Allison Rossett and
Todd Eachus

1975: VII. THE BEHAVIORAL MANAGEMENT OF ANXIETY, DEPRESSION AND PAIN

Donald Meichenbaum and
Dennis Turk
Ernest G. Poser
Peter McLean
Peter Lewinsohn,
Anthony Biglan and
Antonette M. Zeiss
Wilbert E. Fordyce

1976: VIII. Behavioral Self-Management: Strategies, Techniques and Outcomes

Frederick H. Kanfer
Gary E. Schwartz
Todd R. Risley
Marvin R. Goldfried
G. Alan Marlatt and
Janice K. Marques
William R. Miller
Richard R. Bootzin
Richard M. McFall
Carol Landau Heckerman and
James O. Prochaska
Peter Suedfeld
Lynn Buhler and
Reta McKay
Richard B. Stuart
Frances Phillips,
Jackie Hooper,
Cathy Batten,
Molly Dexall,
Dave Beamish,
Tom Pollok and
Gordon McCann
Albert J. Stunkard

1977: IX. Behavioral Systems for the Developmentally Disabled: I. School and Family Environments

R. L. Schiefelbusch
Kern A. Olson and
Max W. Rardin
Stephen I. Sulzbacher and
Kathleen A. Liberty
Hyman Hops,
Hill M. Walker and
Charles R. Greenwood
Edward R. Christophersen and
Bobby W. Sykes
Robert G. Wahler,
George Leske and
Edwin S. Rogers
Gerald M. Kysela,
Kathleen Daly,
Martha Doxsey-Whitfield,
Alex Hillyard,
Linda McDonald,
Susan McDonald and
Julie Taylor
Sander Martin and
Bruce Graunke

and

Behavioral Systems for the Developmentally Disabled: II. Institutional, Clinic, and Community Environments

Todd R. Risley and
James Favell
Richard P. Swenson,
Tom Seekins and
Chrys Anderson
Timothy Plaska and
Gregory Ragee
H. Robert Quilitch
Michael F. Cataldo and
Dennis C. Russo
Eric Trupin,
Lewayne Gilchrist,
Roland D. Maiuro and
Gayle Fay
Dean P. Inman
Gary Martin and
Angela Pallotta-Cornick
Steven P. Schinke
G. Thomas Bellamy,
Dean P. Inman and
Robert H. Horner

The Banff Conferences have been more than places at which theories and research data are presented and discussed. They have stimulated planning and research in selected areas, and have helped to bring together policy makers, program administrators, researchers, and clinicians in an effort to stimulate the adoption in practical settings of many of the programs that have been discussed during the conference proceedings. Many people have devoted their energies and talents to the continued success of the Banff Conferences. Primarily, of course, we must acknowledge the guest faculty who develop, present, and discuss topics found in this volume. The staff and resources of the Banff Centre, which has been the site of the conferences, have also contributed greatly to their success. Other members of the conference Planning Committee need to be singled out for their substantial help and guidance. They are Drs. Gus Hamerlynck and Dick Stuart, and Ms. Donna Fraser who both helps in the planning and oversees every aspect of the administration of the conferences. My special thanks to Ms. Suzanne Vaughan for managing program correspondence and for editorial assistance.

Editing of this volume was supported in part by Canadian National Health Grant 1213-9-13.

P.O.D.

Contents

Introduction

Ten years ago when we were planning the first Banff Conference, we tried to speculate about where the relatively new field of behavior modification would have its major impact over the next decade. In the late sixties it appeared that behavioral principles were finding their most obvious application in the educational system. But it seemed to us that the real frontier for behavioral intervention that needed to be developed was the mental health field, and we asked our first faculty to address the question of how behavior modification principles might fit into ideal mental health services.

When planning our tenth conference we considered the possibility of redoing Banff I, and asking the question of how behavioral principles might fit into mental health services over the next ten years. Suggested answers to this question appeared to be routine or idiosyncratic—and, in either case, dull. Behavioral principles have become so much a part of most mental health services that many of the major questions remaining tend to be ones of detail. What was seen as a frontier ten years ago is now a highly cultivated field (although a few weeds have shown up in the harvest!).

When we asked the question: "Are there any applied behavioral frontiers for the 1980s?" the answer we came up with was both affirmative and exciting. One of the major challenges emerging for the coming decade is the application of behavioral principles to problems of physical health and illness. Suggestive evidence that this is a frontier is shown in the fact that there is not even an agreed upon name for this new field. Many labels have been used—sometimes interchangeably; health psychology, medical psychology, psychosomatic medicine, and behavioral medicine are examples. There have been some recent attempts to differentiate these labels (cf., Schwartz & Weiss, 1977; Lipowski, 1977). While the issue seems far from settled, some distinctions are worth noting. Psychosomatic medicine has traditionally emphasized etiology and pathogenesis of physical disease, whereas behavioral medicine has focused more on behavioral approaches to the treatment and prevention of physical disease. It was our feeling that the term "behavioral medicine" most closely captured the subject matter of the present volume, and the chapter authors concurred in this opinion. Probably the most useful definition of behavioral medicine is the one developed at the recent Yale Conference on Behavioral Medicine:

> "Behavioral medicine" is the field concerned with the development of behavioral science, knowledge and techniques to the understanding of physical health and illness and the application of this knowledge and these techniques to diagnosis, prevention, treatment and rehabilitation (Schwartz & Weiss, 1977).

The term behavioral medicine is starting to appear in a number of articles and books. There is a new *Journal of Behavioral Medicine* and a Society of Behavioral Medicine is being organized in the fall of 1978. The term is also being adopted as a new name for various departments and laboratories.

The tremendous increase in research publications in the field of biofeedback (Butler, 1978, contains 2300 citations) sometimes creates the erroneous impression that this self-regulation technique constitutes the major component of behavioral medicine. As the Yale Conference definition clearly indicates, however, this is far too narrow a perspective of what the behavioral sciences can contribute to understanding physical health and illness. We feel that a major contribution will be made by behavioral scientists to the development of health lifestyle change programs and to research endeavors relevant to these kinds of programs. An increased awareness of two factors has contrived to make health lifestyle programs extremely important to our health delivery system (Lalonde, 1974). The first factor is an increased understanding that faulty habits, behaviors, and lifestyles may be important causal components of many physical disorders, and that correcting these faulty behaviors reduces the risk associated with these disorders. The second factor is that refined behavioral technology is currently available to be put into programs for correcting these faulty behaviors. Effective development of such programs could result in impressive savings in the escalating costs of our health delivery system. The chapters in the present book describe some of the best current technology and research for health lifestyle change, as well as indicating promising leads for future developments. Some of the chapter authors, in the process of describing their own programs, discuss general theoretical and research problems current to this area of behavioral medicine. Other authors provide interesting insights into the practical problems of developing and delivering health lifestyle change services.

There are several recurring themes among the various chapters that are worth noting. Perhaps most interesting in comparison with the state of the art at the time of Banff I a decade ago is the general move away from a Skinnerian operant theory of behavior to Bandura's (1977) social learning theory of behavior. This reorientation is reflected in the first chapter of the book by Wilson, who deals with some of the current theoretical problems and conceptual models that affect our design of health lifestyle programs. Consistent with this social learning perspective is an increased emphasis on cognitive factors in behavior change. The emphasis on cognitive factors in a number of the chapters of this book does not simply reflect obsequiousness to the current fashion of cognitive behavior modification, but arises more from the importance of self-management for successful health lifestyle change. One of the important issues that Wilson raises regarding health lifestyle programs is that their success must be judged more by their ability to maintain behavior change rather than simply initiate it. (Stuart, in his chapter, elaborates on some of the practical problems involved in maintenance of behavior change.) This emphasis on the importance of maintenance is the second major theme that runs through a number of the chapters. Wilson also draws our attention to the important issues of consumer satisfaction, treatment acceptability, and adherence to treatment, as factors that may have to be considered much more carefully in health lifestyle change programs than in other kinds of behavioral interventions.

A third major theme, discussed in Chapter 2 by Roskies and Lazarus and in Chapter 3 by Schachter, is the critical role that stress and the management of stress play in the field of behavioral medicine in general, and in health lifestyle change in particular. Roskies and Lazarus draw our attention to the extensive changes that have occurred in the theoretical conceptualization of the nature of stress since the time of the early research studies on stress in psychosomatic medicine. Their chapter attempts to build a bridge between the theoretician/researcher and the clinical therapist in conceptualizing stress and the management of stress. While Roskies and Lazarus place a very heavy emphasis on cognitive factors in understanding how stress operates in health lifestyle change, Schachter, in his inimitable way, reminds us that all of these cognitions, behaviors, and lifestyles exist in what is basically a biological organism. Schacter focuses his discussion on the relationship of stress to the problem of cigarette smoking, and concludes that the effects of stress on smoking can best be understood in purely biochemical terms. Schachter suggests that this is probably the case for many of the presumed psychological correlates of smoking, and that smoking may be an example of a behavior for which conventional psychological modes of analysis and thought are particularly inappropriate and misleading. Pomerleau in the next chapter reviews the widely divergent models of smoking, and suggests some research strategies to test these divergent models. Milsum, in his chapter on stimulating lifestyle change through health hazard appraisal, emphasizes the interdisciplinary needs of behavioral medicine and details the role that lifestyle plays as a major factor in disease and premature death. He describes in detail the Health Hazard Appraisal and how to use it to quantify risks to individuals' health, together with information on the lower levels of risk that could be expected if lifestyle changes were made by the individual.

The theme of importance of maintenance for health lifestyle change is developed by Stuart in the context of weight control programs. As with the previous five chapters, Stuart's chapter raises a number of important theoretical issues, but he goes beyond these to deal with some of the practical problems of service delivery for health lifestyle change, and supplies recommendations for improvement in the long-term effects of behavioral intervention programs. The next three chapters deal with primary and secondary preventive programs for health lifestyle change. Peterson, Hartmann, and Gelfand, in their chapter *Prevention of Child Behavior Disorders,* remind us that many health lifestyle problems begin in childhood and, therefore, that primary prevention strategies should begin with this age group as well. They describe the general strategies for prevention programs and review the literature on behaviorally based preventive interventions. Using examples such as their study on preventing the stress experienced by hospitalized children, they describe the steps required to mount a prevention program. Cormier, Prefontaine, MacDonald, and Stuart discuss the problems involved in promoting good health practices in adolescents and young adults, and describe a pilot project of a broad-band preventive program to improve student health practices. In doing so, they examine the problems of delivering lifestyle change services *before* risk factors associated with any particular problem develop. Alden gives us an example of a secondary preventive strategy in the treatment of alcohol abuse. She discusses in detail the importance of self-management, which is the fourth recurrent theme of this book.

Not all behavioral programs are automatically successful in promoting health lifestyle change. Peter Nathan's chapter includes a frank and revealing discussion of the problems and frustrations involved in implementing a novel health lifestyle change program and what can be learned from the failure of such a program. Nathan outlines the current state of knowledge for behavioral treatment of alcoholism. Roskies reviews the literature on coronary-prone (Type A) behavior patterns and outlines the factors that need to be considered in developing a treatment program for these individuals.

The programs described in chapters 6 through 11 are all programs that are essentially designed for individuals or specific small groups. The next three chapters discuss health lifestyle change programs that are designed to be implemented through mass media in the community at large. Keir and Lauzon make the point that health lifestyles involve increasing desirable behaviors and not just eliminating undesirable behaviors. While they focus on the importance of physical fitness, they describe a number of interesting and novel media education programs that were designed to promote physical fitness as a component of healthy lifestyles. Since they recognize the importance of modeling as an effective behavioral intervention, they demonstrated during the Conference itself the "fitness break" described in their chapter. As a matter of fact, a preview of their chapter prior to the Conference enabled us to implement most of their conference behavior recommendations that we had not already incorporated. We can report, from our follow-up evaluations, both consumer satisfaction and treatment acceptability for such things as fitness breaks and refreshment breaks as opposed to the more usual coffee breaks. In introducing these changes into the Conference a subtle point was made by Keir and Lauzon, and that is that lifestyle change behaviors are not just performed in some therapeutic environments, but have to be incorporated in non-aversive ways into the routines of our daily living. Maccoby and Alexander, in their chapter on the use of media in lifestyle programs, describe their involvement in one of the largest scale primary prevention programs for health lifestyle change (the Stanford Heart Disease Prevention Program). In their account of this attempt to reduce cardiovascular disease they describe many of the problems and procedures of developing a mass media educational program. Best continues this discussion with a description of his mass media therapeutic program for control of smoking, and how the various models of self-control can be translated from the individual therapy environment to the community's television screens. These three chapters all serve to underline the very large scale to which some health life-style programs must be designed, and they alert the reader to the fact that there are many different and unique problems in working with programs at this scale that don't occur in behavioral medicine programs that are designed for individuals in controlled hospital environments.

The chapter by Davidson attempts to draw together the final major theme running through most of these studies, and that is the perceived importance of evaluation to the long-range success of health lifestyle change programs. Davidson discusses a number of conceptual problems in evaluating lifestyle change programs and outlines some evaluation strategies for such programs. The final chapter in the book, *Determinants of Relapse* by Marlatt and Gordon, reminds us that all lifestyle programs have their failures, but points out that we can do more than just shake our heads in sorrow when clients relapse back into their unhealthy lifestyle patterns. Marlatt notes the similarity in relapse patterns across behavior problems, and develops a theoretical model of the relapse process which has very important implications for both prevention and treatment of relapse, and consequently for improving maintenance of lifestyle change.

The reader will note that none of these chapters can or should represent the final word on what is a rapidly developing field of research and practice. They do attempt to reflect the current state of the art, including its inconsistencies, unanswered questions, and rapid development. As such, it is hoped that this book will serve as a stimulus to those individuals who are just entering the field of behavioral medicine, and wish to know where it's been and perhaps where it's going in relation to health lifestyle programs. As much as possible, we have attempted to include practical and applied guidelines and procedures for those who are attempting to develop, or working on the front line of, health lifestyle change programs.

REFERENCES

Bandura, A. *Social learning theory.* Englewood Cliffs, NJ: Prentice Hall, 1977.

Butler, F. *Biofeedback: A survey of the literature.* New York: IFI/Plenum Data Co., 1978.

Lalonde, M. *A new perspective on the health of Canadians.* Ottawa: Information Canada, 1974.

Lipowski, Z.J. Psychosomatic medicine in the seventies: An overview. *American Journal of Psychiatry,* 1977, *134,* 233-244.

Schwartz, G.E., & Weiss, S.M. What is behavioral medicine? *Psychosomatic Medicine,* 1977, *39,* 377-381.

Contributors

LYNN ALDEN
Department of Psychology,
University of British Columbia

JANET ALEXANDER
Institute for Communication Research,
Stanford University

J. ALLAN BEST
Department of Kinesiology,
University of Waterloo

AUREA CORMIER
Department of Home Economics,
University of Moncton

PARK DAVIDSON
Department of Psychology,
University of British Columbia

DONALD P. HARTMANN
Department of Psychology,
University of Utah

DONNA M. GELFAND
Department of Psychology,
University of Utah

JUDITH R. GORDON
University Counseling Center,
University of Washington

SANDY KEIR
Fitness and Amateur Sport Branch,
National Health and Welfare,
Canada

RICHARD LAUZON
Fitness and Amateur Sport Branch,
National Health and Welfare,
Canada

RICHARD S. LAZARUS
Department of Psychology,
University of California, Berkeley

NATHAN MACCOBY
Institute for Communication Research,
Stanford University

HELEN MACDONALD
Department of Nutrition,
Calgary General Hospital

G. ALAN MARLATT
Department of Psychology, University of Washington

JOHN H. MILSUM
Division of Health Systems, University of British Columbia

PETER E. NATHAN
Graduate School of Applied and Professional Psychology, Rutgers University

LIZETTE PETERSON
Department of Psychology, University of Utah

OVIDE F. POMERLEAU
Center for Behavioral Medicine, Hospital of the University of Pennsylvania

MARIELLE PREFONTAINE
Department of Home Economics, University of Moncton

ETHEL ROSKIES
Department of Psychology, University of Montreal

STANLEY SCHACHTER
Department of Psychology, Columbia University

RICHARD B. STUART
Graduate School of Social Work, University of Utah

G. TERENCE WILSON
Graduate School of Applied and Professional Psychology, Rutgers University

BEHAVIORAL MEDICINE: Changing Health Lifestyles

1
Cognitive Factors in Lifestyle Changes: A Social Learning Perspective

G. TERENCE WILSON

Each year, in editing the *Annual Review of Behavior Therapy,* Cyril Franks and I attempt to characterize the previous year's progress in terms of some overridingly influential or controversial development. In our most recent volume (Franks & Wilson, 1977), we had little hesitation in designating 1976 as the Year of Cognition for the theoretician and practitioner alike. Cognitive approaches to behavior modification are riding the crest of a wave of popularity. Even a cursory review of the recent literature in clinical behavior therapy readily reveals that like the Scarlet Pimpernel, cognitions seem to be here, there, and everywhere—and, some would add, just as elusive. Some of the important referents of what is now loosely called "cognitive behavior therapy" include Beck's (1976) book on *Cognitive Therapy,* Ellis and Grieger's (1977) anthology on rational-emotive therapy, Meichenbaum's (1977) text on *Cognitive Behavior Modification,* and the emergence of a new journal, *Cognitive Therapy and Research* (Mahoney, 1977a). Packed houses at conferences, an increasing demand for workshops and clinical training, and a report that rational-emotive therapy now enjoys a wider professional following than client-centered therapy (Garfield & Kurtz, 1976) are further indications of the current Zeitgeist of our changing times.

To many, this recent burst of enthusiasm for cognitive approaches to behavior modification represents a conceptual renaissance that heralds a new era of therapeutic progress. Some view the current fascination with cognitive factors in therapy as the means of facilitating a long-awaited integration of the traditional psychodynamic approach (especially the ego-analytic methods) with behavior therapy. Still others regard the emphasis on cognitive and self-regulatory functions not as a rapprochement between rival theoretical positions but as a distinctly new hybrid or genuine dialectic synthesis that transcends the limitations of both traditional psychodynamic and behavioral approaches (Kanfer, in press; Mahoney, 1977b). Predictably, the cognitive connection has received a less than enthusiastic and even hostile reception in some quarters of the behaviorally committed. For example, Wolpe (1976) has severely criticized what he refers to as "cognitive exclusivism" and has branded as "malcontents" those who espouse it. A malcontent is defined as "a critic of (behavior therapy) whose criticisms stem from misunderstandings of one or more of its basic premises" (p. 109). Cognitive exclusivism is identified with the principles and procedures of rational-emotive therapy (Ellis, 1970) and self-instructional training (Meichenbaum, 1977). According to Wolpe, cognitive therapy is merely a subclass of behavior therapy that cannot alter conditioned autonomic habits that are elicited directly by external stimuli.

Those who espouse an operant conditioning model clearly eschew any resort to cognitive constructs in their explanations of psychological functioning (Catania, 1975; Skinner, 1977). From this perspective, developments in cognitive behavior therapy are, at best, seen as nothing new or merely mischievous in introducing semantic confusion into previously precise, operationally defined behavioral formulations (Biglan & Kass, 1977; Rachlin, 1977). At worst, they are rejected as an unfortunate return to crypto-mythological models and mentalistic psychotherapy. For example, Observer (1977), the anonymous but clearly radical behaviorist commentator in the *Psychological Record,* objects to the alleged resurgence of mentalism or "current reversionary thinking." As (s)he sadly laments, "What makes this backtracking movement so damaging is that it is propagated at a time when psychology is capable of becoming genuinely observational and experimental and therefore genuinely progressive."

The view presented here is that the emergence of cognitive behavior therapy as referred to above is not a recent conceptual breakthrough of paradigmatic significance. The major shift in behavior therapy from a radical behavioristic or simplistic S-R psychology dominated by a reliance upon animal conditioning models to more complex, cognitive formulations of behavior was formally ushered in by Bandura's (1969) influential text. During the latter part of the 1960s several developments had emphasized the limiting nature of a strict conditioning approach and resulted in an explicit concern with cognitive mediating processes in the theory and practice of behavior therapy. Among some of the more seminal sources of this expansion of behavioral assessment and modification to incorporate the role of cognitive factors were the contributions of Davison (1969), Kanfer and Phillips (1970), Lang (1969), Lazarus (1971), Mischel (1968), and Peterson (1968). As I have argued elsewhere (Wilson, 1978b), the recent advances in cognitive-behavioral therapy that have been spearheaded by Beck (1976), Mahoney (1977a), Meichenbaum (1977) and others are best seen as important extensions and clinically significant applications that are consistent with the existing conceptual model and empirical foundations of social learning theory (Bandura, 1969; 1977b). It is also proposed that this focus on cognitive factors is well-grounded in contemporary scientific psychology (Bower, 1977; Brewer, 1974) and of fundamental importance in enhancing the efficacy and applicability of behavioral treatment methods (Franks & Wilson, 1978). It is no longer a question of whether we can afford to introduce cognitive concepts within the scientific analysis of behavior; both developments within experimental psychology and the reality of clinical practice suggest that we cannot afford *not* to pay serious attention to cognitive processes in human behavior. The inferential leap from overt behavior to unobservable private events must be made.

The remainder of this chapter is organized along the following lines. First, social learning is briefly described, the thesis being advanced that this is where we might look in making the inferential leap.* Second, the pros and cons of going beyond the behavioristic bounds of operant conditioning principles and procedures are discussed. This is followed by a summary evaluation of the empirical status of the more prominent cognitive-behavioral methods. Thereafter, the vital issues of generalization and maintenance of behavioral change and adherence to treatment programs aimed at altering lifestyles are addressed in some detail.

Social Learning Theory

There are several advantages in placing the cognitive behavior ther-

*There will be those, of course, who might conclude that this insistence on making the inferential leap results in the searching for a soft place to land.

apies within the broader perspective of social learning theory* (Bandura, 1977b).

An Integrative Theory of Psychological Change

The various current conceptual models of behavior therapy can each be said to place primary emphasis on one dimension of psychological functioning to the relative neglect of the others. Thus applied behavior analysis focuses almost exclusively on overt behavior; Wolpe's neobehavioristic S-R counterconditioning approach is directed towards autonomic or emotional habits; and the cognitive therapists, of course, are preoccupied with the primary causal role of maladaptive thought patterns. One of the advantages of social learning theory is that it integrates these three regulatory systems of antecedant, consequent, and mediational influence in a comprehensive yet testable framework.

Bandura's (1969, 1977b) social learning analysis has not only emphasized the importance of cognitive mediating processes in the regulation of behavior, but has also provided a theoretically consistent interpretation of the mechanisms of classical and operant conditioning in more cognitive terms (Wilson & O'Leary, in press). In this interpretation, for example, classical conditioning is no longer viewed as an automatic reflexive process; rather conditioned responses are seen as self-activated on the basis of learned expectations. Similarly, reinforcement is not an automatic strengthener of behavior but a source of information and incentive that governs behavior. Antecedent and consequent external events significantly influence behavior but this influence appears to be mediated largely by internal cognitive processes. These cognitive processes help determine what is attended to, how it is centrally processed, whether it will be remembered, and how it affects future actions. Those who classify therapies arbitrarily as either "behavioral" or "cognitive" help perpetuate a simplistic dichotomy (e.g., Ledwidge, 1978). What is required is a specification of the treatment procedures employed in any form of therapy, as well as an analysis of their likely mechanisms of psychological change.

---

*Rotter (1954) earlier used the term social learning theory and has been justly credited as an important historical influence in the development of a cognitive-behavioral view in clinical psychology (cf. Mahoney & Arnkoff, 1978). However, Bandura's (1977a, 1977b) social learning theory is distinctly different and widely accepted as one of the most significant influences on contemporary cognitive-behavioral treatment approaches.

Behavioral Procedures versus Cognitive Processes

In this connection, a crucially important assumption of social learning theory is that while cognitive mechanisms are increasingly used to explain the acquisition and regulation of abnormal behavior, the most powerful methods of behavior change are increasingly shown to be those that are performance-based. The significance of this distinction between treatment *procedure* and theoretical *process* must be underscored. By ignoring the role of cognitive processes, strict behavioristic approaches needlessly delimit the scope and efficacy of their treatment methods. By failing to emphasize the superior efficacy of behavioral methods in altering cognitive processes, cognitive therapists run the risk of overlooking some of the most effective therapeutic techniques yet developed and returning therapy to a verbal, interview-based model of treatment in opposition to which behavior therapy was originally developed. Although the more cautious cognitive therapists are aware of this danger (e.g., Mahoney & Arnkoff, 1978), recognition of the primacy of behavioral methods is far from evident in much of the rapidly emerging literature on cognitive behavior therapy. In Ellis's (1970) rational-emotive therapy, for example, abnormal behavior is viewed as nothing but a question of irrational, maladaptive cognitions. Moreover, the treatment methods emphasized most heavily in rational-emotive therapy are cognitive in nature—verbal persuasion, rational argument and logical reasoning. Similarly, attribution therapy is a cognitive form of treatment in which an attempt is made to modify cognitions directly using verbal interaction as the instrument of change (Johnson, Ross, & Mastria, 1977).

It is imperative that as the conceptual and empirical bases of behavior therapy are broadened to incorporate cognitive factors, the hard won behavioral gains of the last 20 years not be sacrificed. These behavioral advances include the development of specific, replicable treatment methods; the use of direct behavioral measures of treatment outcome; and, most importantly, an active, intervention-oriented approach to psychological problems. These characteristics that have been at the core of all behavioral approaches are particularly pertinent to considerations of healthy lifestyles and how to help people achieve them. Medical science has now advanced to the point where we know numerous things that would result in healthier, happier lifestyles if only people would heed informed advice. Instead of generating endless, impotent theories about *why* people engage in self-defeating actions and unhealthy lifestyles, behavior therapy has provided practical and effective techniques for *how* positive lifestyle changes can be made.

Reciprocal Determinism as a Causal Model of Human Behavior

Another salient feature of social learning theory is its roots in a reciprocal determinism model of causal processes in human behavior (Bandura, 1978). In rejecting the psychoanalytic model of largely autonomous psychic forces, some behavior modifiers sought refuge in a similarly unidirectional causal model of another kind—radical behaviorism. The radical behaviorism of the Skinnerian or strict operant approach is essentially a unidirectional causal model because the environment is held to be the ultimate determinant of behavior. As Skinner (1971) bluntly put it, "A person does not act upon the world, the world acts upon him" (p. 211). Although the operant approach is often described as an interactionist position, true interdependence among person variables, behavior, and the environment requires that the person be the agent as well as the object of environmental change. The importance of self-directed change is a distinguishing characteristic of the reciprocal determinism model. In the unidirectional operant analysis there cannot be self-control, only environmental control of apparent self-directed behavior (cf. Rachlin, 1974). In terms of the social learning model, psychological functioning involves a continuous interdependence among behavior, mediational processes, and external events. The relative weight of these separate but interactive influences will vary across individuals and situations. Acceptance of this reciprocal determinism model highlights the fact that healthy lifestyles will not be achieved simply as a function of altering our physical and social environment. Needed environmental changes will necessarily be coupled with the active involvement of individuals in their own self-directed programs of behavioral change. As a model of causal processes in human behavior, reciprocal determinism, as it is argued below, promises to be a more useful means of making sense of the complex interpersonal interactions that take place in psychological therapies (cf. Wilson & Evans, 1976).

Behaviorism and Beyond

The social learning analysis described here is an unabashedly inferential and mediational approach to understanding and modifying human behavior. While its cognitive concepts might draw criticism from behavior therapists within the neobehavioristic S-R tradition, it must be remembered that this type of therapy has always been inferential and mediational in nature. Central to Wolpe's (1958, 1973) seminal contributions, such as systematic desensitization, has been an unshakeable reliance on the hypothetical construct (by definition, unobservable, and on the evidence, unsupported) of reciprocal inhibition. Consider as another example Mowrer's (1960) heavily influential two-factor theory of avoidance learning, long a fundamental building block in conditioning explanations of the acquisition and maintenance of anxiety-related disorders and the commonly accepted basis of most behavioral anxiety reduction methods like desensitization, flooding, and response prevention (Wilson & Davison, 1971). According to Mowrer's formulation, which was logically related to Freud's second theory of anxiety, an underlying anxiety drive (classically conditioned autonomic responses) directly mediated instrumental avoidance behavior. Two-factor theory has now been largely discredited as an adequate explanation of the maintenance and modification of neurotic disorders (Bandura, 1977b; Rachman, 1976b). Specific cognitive alternatives to two-factor theory have been proposed that appear to fare far better with the available experimental evidence (Bandura, 1977a; Seligman & Johnston, 1973). Acknowledging the importance of cognitive factors in neurotic disorders, Eysenck (1976b) has suggested that a revised conditioning theory is the equal of cognitive theory in accommodating the relevant data. However, the value of Eysenck's new conditioning model in predicting or explaining recent treatment findings can be seriously questioned (cf. Bandura, 1977a, 1978; Wilson, 1978d). Finally, diverse covert conditioning techniques are usually considered to be part of the behavior therapist's armamentarium of treatment methods. The explicit mediational model from which they are derived has been shown to be conceptually inadequate (Mahoney, 1974).

In contrast to the battered neo-Hullian infrastructure of many behavior therapy techniques, it is considerably more difficult to justify the abandonment of the non-mediational operant conditioning approach to behavior change. Operant conditioners, for example, have been openly critical of the S-R mediational model and have put forward an alternative account of avoidance learning that dispenses with the underlying construct of fear or anxiety and that is based solely on observable environmental contingencies (cf. Herrnstein, 1969). Theoretically consistent, parsimonious, successful in having generated a demonstrably effective (albeit limited) technology of applied behavior change, and eminently teachable to professionals and non-professional treatment personnel alike, the virtues of the operant conditioning approach to behavior modification are impressive (Brigham & Catania, in press; Ullmann & Krasner, 1975). What then is the case for adopting the more inclusive and inevitably more complicated cognitive social learning approach?

In making the argument for going beyond the clearly demarcated conceptual boundaries of operant conditioning, it is necessary to clarify some basic assumptions of operant conditioning. For example, a typical misunderstanding is evident in the following assertion by Zifferblatt and Hendricks (1974) in their advocacy of the use of applied behavior analysis to improve family planning programs: "No inference to personality, history, or unobservable conflicts is made (in applied behavior analysis). Instead the events that generate or maintain behavior are to be found in the immediate environment. . .In other words, *behavior is a direct consequence of here-and-now external stimulus events*" (emphasis added). However, neither applied behavior analysis nor operant conditioning holds that behavior is always under current environmental control. The failure to recognize that behavior is often free of immediate external control would be, as Fodor (1975) has charged, to "deny the indisputable." Operant conditioning is not guilty on this score.

Contemporary theorists within operant conditioning and radical behaviorism reject the notion that a cause must be in temporal contiguity with its effect (cf. Lacey & Rachlin, 1978; Staddon, 1973). Confronted with behavior that is apparently unexplained by current observable events, the operant conditioner infers past environmental events to be the causal variables. As Rachlin (1977) has put it, "If observed events in the past are usually correlated in certain ways with events in the present, it should be sufficient to infer such events even when they are not observed. If a subject in an experiment is instructed on Day 1 to make response X on Day 2, the cause of response X, when it is observed, need not be attributed to anything inside the subject's head, but directly to events on the previous day. There is nothing logically wrong with supposing that events on Day 1 directly cause events on Day 2 without supposing a chain of intermediary events (in the mind or the nervous system or elsewhere)" (p. 373). In short, antecedent influences on behavior are said to include both current external events and the person's past history of environmental interaction. Moreover, the effects of consequent events are governed by a revised law of effect. Unlike earlier formulations that stressed the necessity of immediate, temporally contiguous reinforcement, the correlation-based law of effect of what is called molar behaviorism emphasizes an aggregate effect of consequent events over time (Baum, 1973). As a result, faulting operant conditioning for an inability to account for reactions to subjectively perceived versus physically "real" stimuli, or for the easily observed lack of impact of many immediate environmental events on behavior are not necessarily fatal criticisms. Indeed, it would seem virtually impossible to disprove operant conditioning principles in the light of these recent theoretical revisions.

The point to be emphasized here is that the operant conditioning approach is unquestionably inferential. However, Rachlin (1977) argues that this operant model involves inference without mediation. In assessing alternative conceptual models of human behavior, therefore, the issue, as Mahoney (1977b) points out, is not *whether* to make inferences but *what* sort of inferences to draw. Rachlin opts for inferences about past observable events as opposed to current cognitions in explaining behavior on two counts: a) while both are speculative, he suggests that the latter are at least potentially observable and suggest methods of assessment and modification short of brain surgery; and b) he concludes that the therapeutic methods that are described in cognitive terms (e.g., cognitive restructuring) are essentially identical to what non-cognitive behavior therapists routinely do. Taking this analysis further, Rachlin argues that the semantics of translating current cognitions into past events are nontrivial and will influence the formulation of therapeutic strategies.

Justifying an appeal to a cognitive mediational model of behavior requires the rebuttal of this analysis. It is proposed here that in practice, the accommodating construct "history of environmental interaction" has proved to be no more observable than present cognitions. Moreover, the focus on a cognitive social learning theory has led to innovative methods of assessment and modification that were not prompted by the operant conditioning model. This is the critical point. Heuristic value is the criterion that provides the acid test of the relative merits of competing theories in contemporary behavior therapy. The seminal influence of operant conditioning on the development of behavior therapy need hardly be emphasized here. However, it may be that the heuristic value of traditional classical and operant conditioning learning principles has reached its asymptote. Fresh theoretical leads are required (cf. Wilson, 1978b). For example, the therapeutically effective uses of vicarious observation methods, including covert, symbolic, and live modeling, were derived not from operant conditioning, but from social learning theory with its emphasis on cognitive mediating processes. Treatment methods that depend upon visual imagery and cognitive transformations of external events can be explained away as instances of the instructional control of behavior. Yet it was a commitment to a mediational model of behavior that initially resulted in the development of these methods of "instructional control" (Wilson & O'Leary, in press). The fact that some procrustean maneuver may be engaged in to accommodate these methods within the post hoc parsimony of an operant framework is less important than the failure of this conceptual scheme to generate such techniques. Several other treatment methods and strategies that are derived from social learning theory are discussed in greater detail below.

It is suggested here that operant conditioning as it is presently formulated is sufficiently elastic to accommodate virtually any empirical finding, albeit if often on a post hoc basis that is unacceptable to nonoperant theorists (cf. Davison, 1969). In their original rejection of psychoanalysis as a scientific approach, behavior therapists hammered away at the point that Freudian theory was irrefutable—it could explain everything and hence nothing (cf. Eysenck & Rachman, 1965). Reference was made repeatedly to Popper's (1963) criterion of falsifiability as the defining characteristic of scientific method. If a theory could specify experimental conditions under which it could be disconfirmed, it was scientific; if not, it was pseudo-scientific. This does not mean that operant conditioning is an unscientific approach to behavior modification. For that matter, it must be acknowledged that it is far from impossible to generate plausible social learning interpretations of most findings. Rachman (1976a), for example, has suggested that the social learning explanation of the effects of modeling may not meet the criterion of refutability. What is required is a broader view of what constitutes a scientific approach.

Citing the views of the philosopher Lakatos, Eysenck (1976a) has pointed out that all scientific theories have developed amidst anomalies and some apparently irrefutable tenets. As a more realistic and persuasive alternative to Popper's criterion, Eysenck proposes that the presence of a progressive research program that yields important and novel predictions and facts is the hallmark of a scientific approach. Such progressive research programs are to be contrasted with degenerating research programs in which theories are devised to account for known facts. Marxism and psychoanalysis, with their inability to predict new facts successfully and their defensive preoccupation with explaining away empirical contraindications, are two prominent examples of degenerating programs of research. Unquestionably, conditioning theories have generated some bold and novel predictions, led to the discovery of important facts, and have spurred the development of a wide range of effective treatment methods. They continue to be useful in many areas of behavior modification. Certainly they are not part of a degenerating research program. In discussing the ubiquity of reinforcement contingencies in operant analyses of behavior, Skinner (1966) noted the resemblance to the equally ubiquitous Marxist concept of the class struggle and the Freudian notion of the Oedipal conflict. However, he pointed out that the operant conditioner is in a position to search effectively for the causes of behavior and was demonstrably successful in clarifying the relationship between behavior and its environmental consequences. However, the argument here is that the value of conditioning theories in sparking therapeutic innovations may have peaked and that alternative theoretical analyses are needed to restore the full vigor and momentum of a progressive program.

Science and Semantics

Rachlin (1977) emphasizes that the semantic translation of current cognitions into past external events has implications for what behavior modifiers do. Both Catania (1975) and Goldiamond (1976) have criticized the use of social learning terms such as *self*-reinforcement on the grounds that this "selfy" talk will muddy the clear conceptual waters of behaviorism and lead us astray in our search for causal variables. In objecting to any departure from the operant argot, Catania (1975) observes that "the language of behavior has consequences." Precisely! The consequences, however, are different from those hypothesized by Catania and they are of fundamental importance to the successful application of behavioral procedures in the real world.

Evaluation of any approach to lifestyle change must take into account not only the efficacy of specific treatment methods but a variety of other considerations including the acceptability of procedures to potential consumers (Kazdin & Wilson, 1978a). Yet the term "behavior modification" has become a term to which considerable opprobrium is often attached. The very language of stimuli, responses, and reinforcements that Catania refers to may critically interfere with the implementation of applied programs in community settings (Reppucci & Saunders, 1974). In keeping with their own mechanistic metaphors stressing total external control of behavior, behavior modifiers have been viewed as impersonal and mechanistic (Woolfolk, Woolfolk, & Wilson, 1977). This language of control is undesirable. As Bandura (1975) observes, "it generates needless public alarm (and) may encourage coercion in those who interpret it literally."

Finally, the language of control is unnecessary and inaccurate.* The jargon of behavior therapy can be humanized without compromising scientific accuracy provided that clear operational definitions are pro-

*This position can be contrasted to Skinner's (1971) insistence that "Nothing is to be gained by using a softer word (than control)."

vided. Abandoning the use of terms that convey an image of people automatically shaped by environmental forces and that exaggerate the presumed unidirectional power of "behavior shapers" (therapists?) to change behavior is also consistent with good psychology (cf. Wilson & Evans, 1976). This point is discussed in greater detail below.

Evaluating the Efficacy of Cognitive-behavioral Methods of Psychological Change

Therapeutic change and alteration of lifestyles will be facilitated by incorporating an emphasis on cognitive factors in intervention programs. It is beyond the scope and purpose of this chapter to review the many sources of evidence bearing on the efficacy of a cognitive-behavioral approach (but see Franks & Wilson, 1978; Mahoney & Arnkoff, 1978). However, some comments on the issues and strategies involved in the evaluation of cognitive-behavioral methods are in order.

There is little to be gained by comparing arbitrarily defined categories of "cognitive" versus "behavioral" methods as Ledwidge (1978) has recently done. Conducted within the box score tradition of treatment outcome evaluation (cf. Luborsky, Singer, & Luborsky, 1975), Ledwidge's review predictably resulted in a numerical count indicating few if any differences between the competing categories of techniques. A previous review of comparative outcome studies of behavioral and cognitive methods, among other methods, by Smith and Glass (1977) arrived at a similar conclusion. Suffice it to note here that this sort of global evaluation strategy inevitably ignores or minimizes the methodological adequacy of individual studies—and to refer the reader to a detailed critique by Kazdin & Wilson (1978b) and Rachman & Wilson (in press).

Another problem is the fact that many treatment methods are multifaceted, consisting of behavioral, affective, and cognitive components. As such they defy compartmentalization into simple categories. Beck's (1976) cognitive therapy is a case in point. Despite the name, it is a deliberate amalgam of explicit behavioral methods (e.g., graded in vivo behavioral assignments) and cognitive restructuring strategies (e.g., decentering and distancing). Then there is the previously emphasized point that behavioral *procedures* might be effective because they produce changes in cognitive *processes* that govern behavior (Bandura, 1977a). A more useful approach to evaluation would entail a detailed analysis of methods in which the contribution of specific treatment components is assessed.

In terms of a social learning analysis, behaviorally-based treatment methods would be predicted to be more effective than those that rely upon purely symbolic (imagery or verbal) operations (cf. Bandura, 1977a). The evidence tends to bear out this prediction. Participant modeling is a performance-based method that has been shown to be significantly more effective in eliminating phobic behavior than either symbolic modeling or imaginal systematic desensitization (Bandura, Blanchard, & Ritter, 1969; Blanchard, 1970) or covert modeling (Thase & Moss, 1976). Similarly, Rachman and Hodgson (in press) have pointed to the superiority of performance-based treatment over imaginal and vicarious methods in the modification of obsessive-compulsive disorders. Other studies have shown the superiority of performance-based treatment over imaginal desensitization (Crowe, Marks, Agras, & Leitenberg, 1972; Sherman, 1972) and imaginal flooding (Emmelkamp & Wessels, 1975; Stern & Marks, 1973). Finally, both Kockott, Dittmar, and Nusselt (1975) and Mathews et al. (1976) reported that sexual dysfunction was most effectively treated by a Masters and Johnson-type program that relied on directed practice in vivo as opposed to imaginal systematic desensitization. However, evidence that Beck's combined cognitive-behavioral therapy is not only more effective than strictly behavioral methods (Shaw, 1977; Taylor & Marshall, 1977) but also pharmacotherapy (Rush, Beck, Kovacs, & Hollon, 1977) provides support for the importance of cognitive factors in psychological change.

Therapeutic techniques such as systematic desensitization that have traditionally been dubbed as behavioral have been compared to cognitive methods that rely on covert verbal operations. From a social learning perspective there is little a priori reason to expect substantial differences in outcome efficacy between these sets of techniques, both of which involve symbolic induction procedures. With few exceptions —verbal cognitive restructuring methods appear to be especially effective in the treatment of text anxiety (e.g., Holroyd, 1976)—this has proved to be the case (cf. Ledwidge, 1978; Wilson, 1978b). Lastly, cognitive restructuring methods that systematically employ well-established induction procedures such as modeling, rehearsal, and corrective feedback for the modification of specifically targeted self-instructions would be expected to be superior to the unsystematic verbal methods of conventional psychotherapy. The growing evidence attesting to the efficacy of Meichenbaum's (1977) self-instructional training and Goldfried's

(1977) rational restructuring therapy (essentially the same as rational-emotive therapy) indicates that this expectation is being confirmed.

Generalization and Maintenance of Treatment-Produced Change

Evaluation of treatment outcome must distinguish among the initial induction of therapeutic change, its generalization to the natural environment, and its maintenance over time. It is important to distinguish among these different phases of treatment since they appear to be governed by different variables and require different intervention strategies at different times. For the most part, behavioral research and therapy have been directed towards producing initial treatment changes and the study of the processes of generalization and maintenance has lagged behind. Thus impressive effects of biofeedback training on psychophysiological disorders in the laboratory tend to dissipate when the client returns to his or her natural environment. Weight loss, for example, has been consistently shown in the short term, but demonstrations of long-term maintenance of weight loss are conspicuously lacking in the literature. As a result there has been a disturbing but growing tendency for some mental health professionals to reject behavioral methods prematurely when in fact the applied research necessary to develop effective maintenance strategies has hardly begun (cf. Franks & Wilson, in press). It is not overstating the case to assert that there is no more important task confronting behavioral investigators than the development of effective strategies of generalization and maintenance (Agras, Kazdin, & Wilson, in press). In the next two sections of this chapter some of the contributions of a social learning analysis to the problems of generalization and maintenance are briefly discussed.

In a recent refinement of his social learning theory, Bandura (1977a) has proposed that psychological treatment methods are effective because they increase the client's expectations of *personal efficacy.* Efficacy expectations reflect the individual's subjective estimate that (s)he has the capacity to cope successfully with a threatening situation. They are differentiated from *outcome expectations* that are defined as the client's belief that a particular action will result in a certain outcome. Efficacy expectations are based on four major sources of information: behavioral performance (e.g., participant modeling), vicarious experience (e.g., symbolic modeling), physiological arousal (e.g., systematic desensitization), and verbal persuasion (e.g., traditional psychotherapy).

Efficacy expectations are said to play a decisive role in the initiation, generalization, and maintenance of coping behavior. In an experimental test of the theory, snake phobic subjects received treatments designed to create differential levels of efficacy expectations and relate them to behavioral change (Bandura, Adams, & Beyer, 1977). The three treatment methods were participant modeling, symbolic modeling, and a no treatment control group. Predictably, participant modeling produced significantly stronger efficacy expectations of coping successfully with the phobic object and more generalized behavioral changes than symbolic modeling. The latter resulted in greater expectations of personal efficacy and behavioral change than the control condition. The degree of behavioral change was closely related to an increase in efficacy expectations. The greater the increase in self-efficacy, the greater the reduction in phobic behavior. Consistent with the theory, increases in efficacy expectations were predictive of behavioral change irrespective of whether they were induced by participant or symbolic modeling methods.

Generalization of Behavioral Change

Expectations of self-efficacy also generalize to other situations and help explain the process of generalized behavioral improvement. In the Bandura et al. (1977) study, for example, generalization of treatment effects was assessed at posttreatment by exposing subject to snakes that were either similar or dissimilar to the snake used in treatment. Strength of efficacy expectations predicted subsequent approach behavior towards similar and dissimilar snakes equally well. Subjects' past behavioral performance during treatment successfully predicted posttreatment approach behavior towards the similar but not the dissimilar snake. This predictive superiority of efficacy expectations over simple overt past behavior shows that treatment-produced improvement cannot be explained solely on the basis of specific behavioral cues or stimulus similarity but is attributable to enhanced personal control or efficacy.

Traditionally, generalized behavioral change has been explained on the basis of the learning principles of stimulus and response generalization. These well-known principles were derived from animal conditioning research in the laboratory and have been developed into a technology for generalization in applied behavior analysis (Stokes & Baer, 1977). However, it has always been difficult to account adequately for the generalization of behavior change in one specific situation to radically different situations solely on the basis of stimulus and response similarity. For example, Bandura, Jeffery, and Gajdos (1975) showed that after snake phobic subjects had been successfully treated using participant modeling, they coped more effectively both with fears of other animals and with their own social anxieties. Bandura (1977a) suggests that the mediating process in this type of generalization is an increase in self-efficacy. As one of the subjects in the Bandura et al. (1975) study said, "The biggest benefit to me of the successfulness of the treatment was the feeling that if I could lick snakes, I could lick anything. It gave me the confidence to tackle, also successfully, some personal stuff."

Efficacy expectations are not automatically increased as a result of the successful behavioral performance of a formerly threatening task. Self-attribution of increased personal mastery is a necessary element in the development of strong self-efficacy. Unlike earlier extrapolations from attribution theory, however, successful self-attribution of therapeutic change does not demand an ambiguously structured treatment process or preclude the use of powerful therapeutic techniques. In the treatment of phobic clients with participant modeling, for example, gradually withdrawing the supportive presence of the therapist and ensuring that the client engages in self-directed rehearsal of non-fearful approach behavior results in the attribution of treatment change to a sense of personal competence that generalizes to other situations (Bandura et al., 1975). In its present form, self-efficacy theory does not permit precise predictions about generalization. An increased sense of personal efficacy is assumed to be a necessary but not always a sufficient condition for the sort of quantum leap in generalization that is frequently observed following a key therapeutic event. The precise manner in which this occurs and the boundary conditions of the generalized changes produced by alterations in self-efficacy remain to be investigated.

It is often assumed that the alteration of cognitions will result in greater cross-situational generalization of treatment change than the modification of specific behavioral responses. Glass, Gottman, and Shmurak (1976), for example, suggest that self-instructional training produces greater transfer effects to non-therapeutic situations than a behavioral skills training program in the modification of heterosexual anxiety. Other studies have failed to replicate this finding (Thorpe, 1975). On the basis of a post hoc analysis of the data of their study comparing self-instructional training with systematic desensitization, Meichenbaum, Gilmore, and Fedoravicius (1971) suggested that desensitization was more effective with specific, monosymptomatic phobias whereas self-instructional training was more effective with more generalized and abstract anxiety disorders. This hypothesis was disconfirmed by Goren (1975) who found that systematic desensitization and self-instructional training were equally effective in producing significantly improvement over control groups in the treatment of both snake phobias (a highly focused specific fear) and test anxiety (an abstract fear). Meichenbaum (1973) predicted that techniques mediated by verbal cognitive processes would produce superior across-different-target behaviors to methods based on visual imagery—and reported an initial experimental confirmation of this notion. Although generalization effects have been obtained in other applications of self-instructional training (Meichenbaum & Cameron, 1973), O'Leary (1977) has recently reported that improvement on laboratory tasks as a function of self-instructional training did not generalize to the classroom situation.

Theoretically, there is no reason why treatment-produced changes in specific self-statements should have greater generalizability than the modification of overt behaviors. It may be predicted, however, that to the extent that self-instructional (or any other cognitive restructuring technique) alters a more fundamental cognitive mediating process such as self-efficacy (for example) increased generalization will be the result.

Maintenance of Therapeutic Improvement

The problem of maintaining therapeutic improvement, i.e., reducing the risk of relapse, besets all forms of psychological treatment, including behavior therapy. Behavioral attempts to solve this problem thus far have been sketchy and inconsistent at best.* Most maintenance methods have been based on extensions of the principles of conditioning. They include the use of intermittent reinforcement schedules, overlearning, increasing the number of conditioned stimuli associated with a response, lengthening the response chain, and fading the magnitude and frequency of the maintaining reinforcers (Atthowe, 1973; Eysenck & Rachman, 1965). These procedures are all derived from laboratory studies with animals. Subsequent research has shown that these procedures delay extinction (i.e., facilitate maintenance of behavioral change) because they obscure discriminability between acquisition and extinction conditions (Bandura, 1969). However, humans have infinitely greater symbolic and discriminatory capabilities. The increased awareness of

---

*A timely "lifestyle" change for applied behavioral researchers would be to direct their energies to the development of effective maintenance strategies instead of concentrating almost exclusively on demonstrating short-term treatment effects (cf. Agras et al., in press). Some suggestions for facilitating such a "lifestyle" change are offered by Emery and Marholin (1977) and Wilson (1978c).

contingencies between events that this entails usually negates the effects of variables such as intermittent reinforcement in increasing resistance to extinction (relapse) unless the contingency relationships are obscured for one or other reason (cf. Bandura, 1969). The result is that the practical value of these typical conditioning means of enhancing maintenance is very limited.

Another behavioral strategy for facilitating posttreatment maintenance has been the use of booster sessions. Despite positive findings from uncontrolled clinical applications in the treatment of alcoholism and sexual deviance, the results from controlled experimental evaluations have been mixed in the case of obesity and negative with regard to cigarette smoking (see Franks & Wilson, 1978, for a more detailed discussion of the empirical status of booster sessions).

Consistent with the underlying philosophy of operant conditioning, other behavioral maintenance strategies have involved attempts at reprogramming the natural environment (cf. Atthowe, 1973; Walker & Buckley, 1972). Arranging for some source of environmental support for newly acquired behaviors is often indispensable if maintenance is to be obtained, especially in the case of what Atthowe (1973) has called the "marginal man"—the ex-mental hospital patient, the ex-convict, or the former chronic alcoholic. Yet the massive socio-political changes that this strategy calls for are often out of the question. Moreover, as the above discussion of reciprocal determinism as a causal model of human behavior indicated, restructuring external environments alone (without due concern for the ineluctably intimate relationship between the individual's behavior, cognitions, and the environment) is simplistic.

Self-control methods have been used to promote maintenance of treatment effects. For example, following an effective token reinforcement program with disruptive children, Turkewitz, O'Leary, and Ironsmith (1975) first made reinforcement contingent on accurate self-ratings of behavior. The requirement that these self-ratings be accurate was then gradually eliminated after which all back-up reinforcers were faded. Treatment effects were maintained under these self-control conditions. Of theoretical importance is the fact that this adherence to self-determined performance standards was maintained despite the fact that the children knew that they could ignore performance contingencies and reward themselves freely with impunity. The children verbalized the understanding that they could "be bad" when the external consequences were withdrawn. This demonstration of self-control despite the discrimination of altered reinforcement contingencies suggests the importance of hitherto neglected cognitive processes in treatment-produced maintenance effects.

Cognitive Processes in Treatment Maintenance

Attribution Theory. The first extension of cognitive principles to the maintenance of behavior change involved attribution theory. Simply stated, it was argued that to the degree that clients attribute therapeutic improvement to themselves as opposed to some external agent such as a drug, posttreatment maintenance will be facilitated. For example, Davison, Tsujimoto, and Glaros (1973) treated insomniacs with a combination of a mild sleep-inducing drug and self-produced relaxation. Following treatment the drug was discontinued and half the subjects were informed that they had received an optimal dose of the drug; the other half were told that the dosage had been too weak to have had a significant effect. Subjects in this latter group, who attributed success in sleeping better to their own efforts at relaxation, showed superior maintenance of improvement compared to subjects in the drug-attribution condition.

Social Learning Theory. A significant practical limitation on the use of attribution therapy such as that employed by Davison et al. (1973) is the necessity of creating a relatively weak, ambiguous treatment effect so that the client can be persuaded to attribute improvement to his or her own efforts. Fortunately, such deception is unnecessary. In terms of social learning theory, self- versus external-attributional processes are one source of cognitive appraisal that influences the nature and strength of judgments about self-efficacy (Bandura, 1977a). Attributions of improvement to external factors that might short-circuit durable treatment effects can be minimized by emphasizing self-directed rehearsal of therapeutic gains. For example, Bandura et al. (1975) produced significant reductions in phobic behavior using a powerful behavioral treatment method (participant modeling). Thereafter they allowed subjects to engage in self-directed mastery experiences in which they approached the feared object without any external prompting or support. As a result subjects presumably not only were able to make a self-attribution of behavior change, but they also strengthened existing efficacy expectations based on their behavioral performance in approaching the feared object.

Social learning theory emphasizes that necessary social skills and adequate external incentives are fundamental to long-term maintenance of treatment effects. In addition, however, since efficacy expectations are assumed to influence the effort and persistence with which an individual engages in coping behavior in the face of adversity following treatment, self-efficacy may play a decisive role in maintenance.

Consider, for example, the treatment of alcoholism, one of a class of addictive disorders that is notorious for a high relapse rate. The sudden, often devastating return to uncontrollable drinking by a former alcoholic who had been abstinent for a period of months or even years is a relatively common and perplexing occurrence. The "loss of control" construct, with its emphasis on a hypothetical physiological addictive process that is triggered by one or two drinks and that unleashes involuntary and compulsive drinking, is widely accepted as an explanation of alcoholic relapses. Over the past few years, however, a number of lines of experimental evidence have seriously challenged the validity of the disease model of alcoholism and the notion of "loss of control" as a physiologically-based addictive process in the speculative Jellinek (1960) sense (e.g., Nathan & Marlatt, 1978; Pomerleau, Pertschuk, & Stinnet, 1976).

Alternative cognitive-behavioral interpretations of these relapse phenomena have been outlined by Marlatt (in press) and Wilson (in press a). These investigators note that in most treatment approaches the alcoholic is virtually indoctrinated in the belief that (s)he is suffering from an irreversible disease. The alcoholic learns that (s)he is qualitatively different from non-alcoholics, that (s)he is uniquely vulnerable to the addictive effects of alcohol, and that recovery hinges upon life-long abstinence. In terms of self-efficacy theory, the alcoholic's efficacy expectations about coping with alcohol are reduced to zero. Negative outcome expectations are created stressing the certainty of a return to addictive drinking in the event of any deviation from strict abstinence. A self-fulfilling prophecy may be developed—first drink then drunk. As an alcoholic, the client almost inevitably has positive outcome expectations about alcohol, such as its perceived power to reduce tension, increase feelings of control, enhance sexual responsiveness and others (Marlatt, 1978; Wilson, 1977). In addition, few treatment programs teach alcoholics appropriate self-regulatory and behavioral skills with which to resist the innumerable social pressures or to cope with the sources of anxiety or frustration that are often associated with relapse. Chaney, O'Leary, and Marlatt (1978) have shown that social skills training geared to helping alcoholics cope more effectively with socio-psychological situations in which they are at high risk for relapse significantly improves maintenance of sobriety.

This combination of factors leaves the alcoholic extremely vulnerable to the potentially deleterious effects of a drinking transgression. The significance of this lies in the fact that a majority of alcoholics seen in abstinence-oriented therapy, including those who are successfully treated, engage in sporadic posttreatment drinking (cf. Armor, Polich, & Stambul, 1976; Orford, Oppenheimer, & Edwards, 1976). It is suggested here that it is not so much the actual ingestion of alcohol during the posttreatment abstinence period that may be responsible for relapse but the meaning that the act of drinking has for the client. Given the likely deficits in specific behavioral coping strategies, a drastically diminished sense of personal mastery, and outcome expectations that predict relapse, the client may well react to transgression by interpreting his or her drinking as further proof of a lack of personal control. The client may fail to persist in constructive attempts to cope with the inevitable psychological pressures that are the fate of the former alcoholic and "blow" the entire treatment program. In variously related theoretical developments, the cognitive concepts of an "abstinence violation effect" (Marlatt, 1978), "cognitive claustrophobia" (Mahoney & Mahoney, 1976), and the "counter-regulatory effect" (Polivy, 1976) have been proposed to account for sudden relapses in addictive disorders.

Several explicit treatment maintenance strategies follow logically from the social learning analysis of relapse outlined above (cf. Wilson, 1978 a). Briefly, realistic efficacy expectations that are based on authentic personal control are best created using performance-based methods similar to those that have yielded success in the treatment of phobias (Bandura, 1977a) and obsessive-compulsive disorders (Rachman & Hodgson, in press). This treatment approach would involve exposing the client to specific, high risk stimuli that were associated with alcohol abuse in his or her natural environment. The consumption of alcohol under carefully structured circumstances would be one source of high risk stimulation. Its purpose is to minimize the negative consequences of any posttreatment drinking mishap and to ensure that the client returns to the treatment program strictures as rapidly as possible. This strategy is adaptable to either abstinence or controlled drinking as treatment goals.

Maintenance strategies that rely on symbolic operations include the imaginal rehearsal of coping reactions to high risk situations. Lazarus (1978) has described what he terms "emotional fire drills" to attenuate or preclude the adverse psychological impact of "future shock." Stress-inoculation training is a coping strategy in which potential psychological stresses are anticipated and neutralized through the use of self-instructional training, guided imagery, and relaxation training (Meichenbaum, 1977). The sense of all these maintenance strategies is summarized in the old saying; forewarned is forearmed.

The preceding analysis is speculative. Although clinical observations and uncontrolled case reports provide support for the predictions that have been generated, the necessary experimental tests remain to be carried out. Few existing studies bear directly on the hypothesized role of personal efficacy in the maintenance of treatment-produced outcome. In a study of the effects of relaxation methods on alcohol consumption in heavy drinkers, Marlatt and Marques (1977) found no differences among meditation, progressive relaxation, or an attention-placebo condition at a seven week follow-up. All three conditions, however, produced a significantly greater decrease in alcohol consumption than no treatment. The three treatment conditions were associated with a shift towards internal locus of control on the Rotter (1966) scale whereas the no treatment control group showed no change. In interpreting these findings Marlatt and Marques (1977) argue that the locus of control changes indicate an increase in perceived control that mediated a decrease in drinking. However, other equally plausible interpretations of these correlational data are possible.

There is little reason to expect that the internal-external locus of control construct will be useful in refining a cognitive-behavioral analysis of the maintenance of treatment effects. Despite numerous attempts, locus of control scores have not been shown to be associated with treatment-produced weight loss (Tobias & MacDonald, 1977; Weiss, 1977), nor do they predict success in cigarette smoking cessation programs (Abrams & Wilson, in press; Danaher, 1977). It is not clear why the situation should be any different for problem drinking. Finally, it is questionable whether an increase in internality on the Rotter scale can be accurately interpreted as an increase in perceived power or control. In this connection more specific measures of self-efficacy—a construct that is directly related to perceived control—might provide a better test of the hypothesized relationship between perceived control and the effective treatment of addictive disorders.*

Adherence to Treatment Regimens

In a commentary on the inadequacies of the biomedical model in accounting for the psychosocial problems related to health care, Fabrega

*Several psychological benefits of *perceived* control over life situations have been reported (cf. Perlmuter & Monty, in press). However, durable therapeutic effects are obtained only to the extent that perceived control is based on actual behavioral control even though the relationship between the two is not necessarily isomorphic (Wilson, in press d).

(1975) made the following point: "in a rather basic sense, medical practitioners, regardless of their culture, have to persuade people to do such things as take medicines, alter personal habits, agree to submit to dangerous procedures, acknowledge negative personality attributes, modify their relations with others, accept and reorient to bodily constraints, return for a follow-up visit, comply with and participate in formally structured ('ritualistic') exchanges, check and report on bodily functions, and so forth" (p. 972). Fabrega's concern about how to persuade people to do things that are in their own best health interests is part of the wider problem of treatment adherence. This includes entering into treatment, following instructions, implementing therapeutic prescriptions, and terminating treatment.

Adherence is also of crucial significance for behavioral interventions. Behavior therapy is a directive, intervention-oriented approach in which clients are asked to *do* things in and out of therapy sessions. Non-adherence to these behavioral prescriptions is usually the blue-print for therapeutic failure. For example, if clients self-monitor daily caloric intake they will usually lose weight. The problem is that they often cease self-monitoring and consequently regain weight. What behavioral supervisor has not had the experience of a student therapist complaining about the effective treatment program (s)he has designed if only the client would cooperate and do the techniques! In the enthusiasm of extending behavioral procedures to improve adherence to medical treatment regimens (part of what has come to be labeled behavioral medicine) it would be well to bear in mind the fact that adherence to psychological interventions is still a neglected and imperfectly understood problem.

The first behavioral attempts at increasing adherence to medical regimens have consisted of relatively narrow applications of operant conditioning procedures such as positive reinforcement, shaping, and contingency contracting (e.g., Zifferblatt, 1975). For some individuals who show no resistance to external direction these are extremely useful procedures. However, in line with the position taken throughout this chapter, it is argued that a broader conceptual framework and a more flexible array of treatment strategies are required if more effective methods for improving adherence are to be developed.

Improving Adherence: Some Social Learning Strategies

Effective solutions to the problem of adherence will have to recognize the reciprocal determinism causal model of human behavior. A lopsided model in which behavior is viewed as under total external control will impede progress. Contrary to the views of some proponents and opponents of behavior modification alike, the notion of unilateral therapist control over the client is largely a myth (Wilson & Evans, 1976). It is difficult if not impossible to change people's behavior without some minimum degree of active cooperation of their part, and blatant attempts at influence that are inspired by unidirectional thinking will usually be counter-productive. The explicit recognition of self-regulatory capacities and of the limited role of automatic behavioral change is called for. Although the therapist's influence is considerable, (s)he is more accurately seen not as a controller but as a consultant who needs the client's active participation in the treatment and maintenance processes.

Resistance or Counter Control

Cognitive-behavioral conceptualizations of the adherence problem and suggestions for combating what is usually referred to as "resistance" or "counter control" have been discussed by Davison (1973), Mahoney (1974), and Wilson and Evans (1976, 1977). In short, non-adherence should not necessarily be construed as volitional. The individual may be unable rather than unwilling to comply with instructions. Similarly, the task demands may be impractical given the current psychological state of the client; instructing an obese client to count calories continually might be too demanding because of interfering anxieties and depression. Fear of social disapproval and guilt may often counteract the therapist's instigative influence. The client's motivation to perform assigned tasks is sometimes diminished by anticipation of failure. A history of prior failures, leading to minimal or negative outcome expectations, may also undermine adherence. If the client does not possess the necessary behavioral repertoire, direct training and rehearsal of assignments are required. A carefully graded approach can help overcome competing negative influences in the client's natural environment. Prompting the client to make a specific statement of interest or commitment to a well-defined task increases the probability of compliance. One method of obtaining commitment is to draw up a formal contract; another is to offer a pair of equally important therapeutic assignments that the client is asked to choose between (Mahoney, 1974). To the extent that clients perceive themselves as having *choice* it is possible that what Brehm (1966) has called psychological reactance is reduced. Reactance is assumed to be aroused when individuals perceive their choices as being restricted or threatened by an external authority. In a related proposition, Johnson and Matross (1977) argue that clients will be less resistant to influence they attribute as deriving from themselves rather than from the therapist. Instead of directly rewarding or punishing clients, the therapist, by providing expertise and direction within a problem-solving discussion, might foster self-attribution of influence and thereby increase adherence.

Trust and the Therapeutic Relationship

A not uncommon reason for the lack of therapeutic progress or treatment adherence concerns a client's feelings about the therapist. The therapist's ability to create a trusting relationship—in which the client can share personally distressing material without fear of being criticized or hurt by the therapist—is fundamental. Trust facilitates communication, open discussion of problems, and makes it easier for the therapist to provide constructive feedback (cf. Johnson & Matross, 1977). Not surprisingly, Dunbar and Stunkard (in press) in their review of the literature of adherence to medical regimens conclude that "better adherence tends to be elicited by the clinician who is warm and empathetic, engages in social conversation. . . .(and) active interchange, gives specific and individualized instructions, shows continuing interest. . .and demonstrates genuine concern." Although the development of trust has received no formal attention in the behavioral literature, Johnson and Matross (1977) describe some specific procedures for building trust in a cooperative problem-solving situation such as behavior therapy.

The Role of Expectations

As discussed above, efficacy expectations are assumed to influence the persistence with which the client will continue to try to cope constructively with stressful life events. Such efficacy expectations have obvious significance for adherence. Also, by fostering in the client realistic outcome expectations of ultimate success, the therapist may bridge the gap between the immediate, often taxing, actions required and eventual improvement (Mischel, 1974). It is a well-established fact that immediate consequences control behavior more effectively than delayed consequences. Consider the individual who is asked to take an unpleasant drug that may produce unwanted side effects in order to control elevated blood pressure that will increase the risk of a heart attack in the future. The prospect of dire consequences in the future as a result of non-adherence is unlikely to overcome the more powerful controlling influence of the immediate negative drug-induced consequences unless specific behavioral measures are taken to bring the individual's behavior under the influence of the long-term—and in a very basic sense more important—contingencies. Creating appropriate outcome expectations is one facet of a social learning approach to this problem of prompting asymptomatic patients to engage in medically relevant actions.

Another benefit of encouraging appropriate outcome expectations is the elicitation of positive emotional states, such as hope, which can help counteract feelings of demoralization and helplessness. One way of reducing demoralization is by having the client relabel or reinterpret the reasons for his problem. Reviewing the medical adherence literature, Blackwell (1976) notes that alarming or unexpected side effects seem to reduce adherence to drug regimens. However, effective management of side effects by a physician who is reassuring and gives more hope for benefit appears to minimize their negative impact.

Since it is the case that clients usually enter treatment with expectations not only about outcome but also of what the treatment process will entail, incongruities between what they expect and what they experience may reduce adherence or even result in termination (cf. Baekelund, Lundwall, & Kissin, 1975). Dunbar and Stunkard (in press) note that adherence is diminished in those individuals whose expectations about their medical regimen are not congruent with their experience of it. In this connection, Goldfried and Davison's (1976) practical suggestions for how the broad-spectrum behavior therapist can attempt to "shape" expectations that are congruent with therapy might be instructive for those who are faced with the task of improving adherence.

Structuring the Treatment Process

Adequate comprehension and recall of therapeutic information are necessary although not sufficient conditions for treatment adherence. Yet there is evidence indicating that many routine descriptions of treatments do not result in satisfactory comprehension and recall of information and instruction (Dunbar & Stunkard, in press). Proper cognitive processing of necessary information is facilitated by deliberately structuring the treatment experience for the client. Thus Goldfried and Davison (1976) recommend giving clients an explanation of the development, maintenance, and modification of their problems, a persuasive rationale for the specific treatment methods to be employed, a description of the procedural steps involved, and the client's own responsibilities in actively participating in the treatment. This latter point is important as it not only strengthens the clients' attribution of change to their own efforts but helps define the client role they are expected to assume. The sparse data that exist suggest that this sort of structuring of information increases adherence (cf. Dunbar & Stunkard, in press).

According to Blackwell (1976) and Dunbar and Stunkard (in press), perhaps the single most important determinant of adherence is the degree of complexity of the treatment regimen. This appears to be especially true if the treatment involves lifestyle changes, e.g., the long-term modification of eating habits. This consistent finding should give behavior therapists pause for thought. Current behavioral treatment approaches are characterized by their multifaceted nature (cf. Azrin, 1977; Lazarus, 1976). Behavioral weight control programs, for example, are very intrusive in nature, requiring numerous alterations in food-related behavior (e.g., Stuart & Davis, 1972). Examination of most behavioral outcome studies shows that these complex and demanding programs are typically administered over periods ranging from approximately four to 16 weeks. In retrospect, it seems highly unlikely the individuals in these programs could assimilate so many behavioral changes in so short a time span.* The relative absence of convincing evidence of adequate adherence in behavioral treatment studies of obesity (Jeffery, Wing, & Stunkard, 1978; Wilson, 1978c) is probably no coincidence. Obviously, complicated clinical disorders demand multifaceted treatment programs if therapy is to come to grips with the relevant maintaining variables. However, the question of whether multifaceted treatment packages are always preferable to simpler interventions is not easily answered at this juncture (cf. Franks & Wilson, 1977). What can be confidently asserted, however, is that complex treatment regimens should be introduced gradually and due time allowed for their different components to "take."

Consumer Satisfaction or Treatment Acceptability

As noted earlier in this chapter, evaluation of treatment methods must take into account not only their efficacy but also their acceptability to

---

*Furthermore, treatment administration is usually didactic with few serious attempts to ensure that program participants have implemented initial techniques before administering the next set of procedures. This practice raises the possibility that one reason Stuart's (1967) unprecedented results have never been replicated is that at least some of his procedures have not been replicated either.

the people who are going to use and or receive them. Ideally, efficacy and acceptability would coincide. Yet this is not always the case. Thus Kazdin and Wilson (1978a) have pointed out that faced with particularly intrusive treatments, consumers are likely to seek alternative and less drastic methods even if this involves a sacrifice in treatment efficacy. Satisfaction with treatment, which is not the same as quality of care, is said to affect adherence rates (Dunbar & Stunkard, in press).

From a practical point of view, this fact places a premium on those treatments that are both effective *and* acceptable to clients. The selection of treatment methods must take the likelihood of implementation and adherence into consideration. In those instances where two or more treatments are equally effective but one is preferred, the latter is definitely the treatment of choice. For instance, Marlatt and Marques (1977) found that meditation and progressive relaxation training were equally effective in reducing heavy alcohol consumption. However, the fact that meditation seemed to be performed more easily and preferred by most subjects would recommend it as the means of teaching relaxation skills to problem drinkers who are similar to Marlatt and Marques' subjects. Similarly, Green (1978) found that self-monitoring of caloric intake prior to eating was no more effective than post-prandial self-monitoring. Since independently obtained estimates indicated that pre-monitoring resulted in particularly poor adherence compared to post-monitoring, the latter would be the preferred procedure.

Conclusion

The thrust of this chapter has been to argue for a social learning approach to therapeutic attempts to alter unhealthy lifestyles. Unlike the non-mediational operant conditioning approach, social learning theory emphasizes the cognitive mediation of behavior. In contrast to a unidirectional causal model of human behavior, social learning theory is geared to a reciprocal determinism model in which behavior is not always a direct consequence of external environmental events. It is suggested that the social learning approach is more heuristic and more acceptable in trying to understand and effect lifestyle changes.

A social learning approach distinguishes among three treatment phases: the initial induction of behavior change, its generalization to other situations, and its maintenance over time. The development of effective strategies for facilitating generalization and maintenance of change has lagged far behind demonstrations of short-term treatment effects. Similarly, the nature of adherence to treatment prescriptions —medical and behavioral—has been relatively ignored in behavior therapy. The present chapter suggests that social learning theory provides a useful conceptual analysis of these processes and points towards practical strategies for increasing generalization, maintenance, and adherence.

In conclusion, the sense of this chapter can be summarized by describing the image of human functioning on which the social learning analysis presented here is based. It is an image that we shall ignore or oversimplify to our cost in assisting people to alter unwanted lifestyles. As Mischel (1977) put it:

> This image is one of the human being as an active, aware problem-solver, capable of profiting from an enormous range of experiences and cognitive capacities, possessing great potential for good or ill, actively constructing his or her psychological world, and influencing the environment but also being influenced by it in lawful ways—even if the laws are difficult to discover and hard to generalize. It views the person as so complex and multifaceted as to defy easy classifications and comparisons on any single or simple common dimension, as multiply influenced by a host of interacting determinants, as uniquely organized on the basis of prior experiences and future expectations, and yet as rule-guided in systematic, potentially comprehensible ways that are open to study by the methods of science. It is an image that has moved a long way from the instinctual drive-reduction models, the static global traits, and the automatic stimulus-response bonds of traditional personality theories (p. 253).

REFERENCES

Abrams, D.B. & Wilson, G.T.: Self-monitoring, reactivity, and cigarette smoking. *Journal of Consulting and Clinical Psychology,* in press.

Agras, W.S., Kazdin, A.E., & Wilson, G.T.: *Behavior therapy: Towards an applied clinical science.* San Francisco, CA: Freeman, in press.

Armor, D.J., Polich, J.M., & Stambul, H.B.: *Alcoholism and treatment.* Santa Monica, CA: The Rand Corporation, 1976.

Atthowe, J.M.: Behavior innovation and persistence. *American Psychologist,* 1973, *28,* 34-41.

Azrin, N.H.: A strategy for applied research: Learning based but outcome oriented. *American Psychologist,* 1977, *32,* 140-149.

Baekeland, F., Lundwall, L., & Kissin, B.: Methods for the treatment of chronic alcoholism: A critical appraisal. In R.J. Gibbins, Y. Israel, H. Kalant, R.E. Popham, W. Schmidt, & R.G. Smart (Eds.), *Research advances in alcohol and drug problems.* (Vol. 2). Toronto: Addiction Research Foundation, 1975, Pp. 247-327.

Bandura, A.: *Principles of behavior modification.* New York: Holt, Rinehart & Winston, 1969.

BANDURA, A.: The ethics and social purpose of behavior modification. In C.M. Franks & G.T. Wilson (Eds.), *Annual review of behavior therapy: Theory and practice.* (Vol. 3). New York: Brunner/Mazel, 1975.

BANDURA, A.: Self-efficacy: Toward a unifying theory of behavioral change. *Psychological Review,* 1977, *84,* 191-215(a).

BANDURA, A.: *Social learning theory.* Englewood Cliffs, NJ: Prentice-Hall, 1977 (b).

BANDURA, A.: The self system in reciprocal determinism. *American Psychologist,* 1978, 33, 344-358.

BANDURA, A., BLANCHARD, E.B., & RITTER, B.: The relative efficacy of desensitization and modeling approaches for inducing behavioral, affective, and cognitive changes. *Journal of Personality and Social Psychology,* 1969, *13,* 173-199.

BANDURA, A., JEFFERY, R.W., & GAJDOS, E.: Generalizing change through participant modeling with self-directed mastery. *Behaviour Research and Therapy,* 1975, *13,* 141-152.

BANDURA, A., ADAMS, N.E., & BEYER, J.: Cognitive processes mediating behavior change. *Journal of Personality and Social Psychology,* 1977, *35,* 125-139.

BAUM, W.M.: The correlation-based law of effect. *Journal of the Experimental Analysis of Behavior,* 1973, *20,* 137-153.

BECK, A.T.: *Cognitive therapy and the emotional disorders.* New York: International Universities Press, 1976.

BIGLAN, A., & KASS, D.J.: The empirical nature of behavior therapies. *Behaviorism,* 1977, *4,* 1-15.

BLACKWELL, B.: Treatment adherence. *British Journal of Psychiatry,* 1976, *129,* 513-531.

BLANCHARD, E.B.: The generalization of vicarious extinction effects. *Behaviour Research and Therapy,* 1970, *8,* 323-330.

BOWER, G.: Cognitive psychology and behavior modification. Invited address, Association for Advancement of Behavior Therapy, Atlanta, Georgia, December 9, 1977.

BREHM, J.W.: *A theory of psychological reactance.* New York: Academic Press, 1966.

BREWER, W.F.: There is no convincing evidence for operant or classical conditioning in adult humans. In W.B. Weimer & D.S. Palermo (Eds.), *Cognition and the symbolic processes.* Hillsdale, NJ: Lawrence Erlbaum Associates, 1974.

BRIGHAM, T., & CATANIA, A.C.: *Handbook of applied behavior research: Social and instructional processes.* New York: Halsted Press, in press.

CATANIA, A.C.: The myth of self-reinforcement. *Behaviorism,* 1975, *3,* 192-199.

CHANEY, E.F., O'LEARY, M.R., & MARLATT, G.A.: Skill training with alcoholics. *Journal of Consulting and Clinical Psychology,* 1978, *46,* 1092-1096.

CROWE, M.J., MARKS, I.M., AGRAS, W.S., & LEITENBERG, H.: Time-limited desensitization, implosion and shaping for phobic patients: A cross-over study. *Behaviour Research and Therapy,* 1972, *10,* 319-328.

DANAHER, B.G.: Rapid smoking and self-control in the modification of smoking behavior. *Journal of Consulting and Clinical Psychology,* 1977, *45,* 1068-1075.

DAVISON, G.C.: Appraisal of behavior modification techniques with adults in institutional settings. In C.M. Franks (Ed.), *Behavior therapy: Appraisal and status.* New York: McGraw-Hill, 1969.

DAVISON, G.C.: Counter-control in behavior modification. In L.A. Hamerlynck, L.C. Handy, & E.J. Mash (Eds.), *Behavior change: Methodology, concepts, practice.* Champaign, IL: Research Press, 1973.

DAVISON, G.C., TSUJIMOTO, R., & GLAROS, A.: Attribution and the maintenance of behavior change in falling asleep. *Journal of Abnormal Psychology,* 1973, *82,* 124-133.

DUNBAR, J.M., & STUNKARD, A.J.: Adherence to medical regimen. In R. Levy, B. Rifkind, B. Dennis, & N. Ernst (Eds.), *Nutrition, lipids, and coronary heart disease.* New York: Raven Press, in press.

ELLIS, A.: *Reason and emotion in psychotherapy.* New York: Stuart, 1962.

ELLIS, A.: *The essence of rational psychotherapy: A comprehensive approach to treatment.* New York: Institute for Rational Living, 1970.

Ellis, A., & Grieger, R.: *Handbook of rational psychotherapy.* New York: Springer, 1977.

Emery, R.E. & Marholin, D.: An applied behavior analysis of delinquency: The irrelevancy of relevant behavior. *American Psychologist,* 1977, *32,* 860-873.

Emmelkamp, P.M.G., & Wessels, H.: Flooding in imagination vs. flooding *in vivo:* A comparison with agoraphobics. *Behaviour Research and Therapy,* 1975, *13,* 7-15.

Eysenck, H.J.: Behaviour therapy—dogma or applied science? In P. Feldman & A. Broadhurst (Eds.), *The experimental bases of behaviour therapy.* New York: Wiley, 1976 (a).

Eysenck, H.J.: The learning theory model of neurosis—a new approach. *Behaviour Research and Therapy,* 1976, *14,* 251-268(b).

Eysenck, H.J., & Rachman, S.: *Causes and cures of neuroses.* London: Routledge & Kegan Paul, 1965.

Fabrega, H., Jr.: The need for an ethnomedical science. *Science,* 1975, *189,* 969-975.

Fodor, J.A.: *The language of thought.* New York: Cromwell, 1975.

Franks, C.M., & Wilson, G.T.: *Annual review of behavior therapy: Theory and practice, Vol. IV.* New York: Brunner/Mazel, 1976.

Franks, C.M., & Wilson, G.T.: *Annual review of behavior therapy: Theory and practice, Vol. V.* New York: Brunner/Mazel, 1977.

Franks, C.M., & Wilson, G.T.: *Annual review of behavior therapy: Theory and practice, Vol. VI.* New York: Brunner/Mazel, 1978.

Garfield, S.L., & Kurtz, R.: Clinical psychologists in the 1970's. *American Psychologist,* 1976, *31,* 1-9.

Glass, C.R., Gottman, J.M., & Shmurak, S.H.: Response-acquisition and cognitive self-statement modification approaches to dating-skills training. *Journal of Counseling Psychology,* 1976, *23,* 520-526.

Goldfried, M.R.: The use of relaxation and cognitive relabeling as coping skills. In R.B. Stuart (Ed.), *Behavioral self-management.* New York: Brunner/Mazel, 1977.

Goldfried, M.R., & Davison, G.C.: *Clinical behavior therapy.* New York: Holt, Rinehart & Winston, 1976.

Goldiamond, I.: Self-reinforcement. *Journal of Applied Behavior Analysis,* 1977, *9,* 509-514.

Goren, E.: A comparison of systematic desensitization and self-instruction in the treatment of phobias. Unpublished Masters Thesis, Rutgers University, 1975.

Green, L.: The temporal and stimulus dimensions of self-monitoring in the behavioral treatment of obesity. *Behavior Therapy,* 1978, *9,* 328-341.

Herrnstein, R.J.: Method and theory in the study of avoidance. *Psychological Review,* 1969, *76,* 46-69.

Holroyd, K.A.: Cognition and desensitization in the group treatment of test anxiety. *Journal of Consulting and Clinical Psychology,* 1976, *44,* 991-1001.

Jeffery, R.W., Wing, L., & Stunkard, A.J.: Behavioral treatment of obesity: The state of the art 1976. *Behavior Therapy,* 1978, *9,* 189-199.

Jellinek, E.M.: *The disease concept of alcoholism.* New Brunswick, NJ: Hillhouse Press, 1960.

Johnson, D.W. & Matross, R.P.: Interpersonal influence in psychotherapy: A social psychological view. In A.S. Gurman & A.M. Razin (Eds.), *Therapist's handbook for effective psychotherapy: Empirical assessment and multidisciplinary approach.* New York: Pergamon Press, 1977.

Johnson, W.G., Ross, J.M., & Mastria, M.A.: Delusional behavior: An attributional analysis of development and modification. *Journal of Abnormal Behavior,* 1977, *86,* 421-426.

Kanfer, F.H.: Self-management: Strategies and tactics. In A.P. Goldstein & F.H. Kanfer (Eds.), *Maximizing treatment gains: Transfer-enhancement in psychotherapy.* New York: Academic Press, in press.

Kanfer, F.H., & Phillips, J.S.: *Learning foundations of behavior therapy.* New York: Wiley, 1970.

Kazdin, A.E., & Wilson, G.T.: Criteria for evaluating psychotherapy. *Archives of General Psychiatry,* 1978, in press (a).

KAZDIN, A.E., & WILSON, G.T.: *Evaluation of behavior therapy: Issues, evidence and research strategies.* Cambridge, Mass: Ballinger, 1978 (b).

KOCKOTT, G., DITTMAR, F. & NUSSELT, L.: Systematic desensitization of erectile impotence: A controlled study. *Archives of Sexual Behavior,* 1975, *4,* 493-500.

LACEY, H.M. & RACHLIN, H.: Behavior, cognition and theories of choice. *Behaviorism,* 1978, *6,* 177-202.

LANG, P.J.: The mechanics of desensitization and the laboratory study of fear. In C.M. Franks (Ed.), *Behavior therapy: Appraisal and status.* New York: McGraw-Hill, 1969.

LAZARUS, A.A.: *Behavior therapy and beyond.* New York: McGraw-Hill, 1971.

LAZARUS, A.A.: *Multimodal behavior therapy.* New York: Springer, 1976.

LAZARUS, A.A.: *In the mind's eye.* New York: Rawson, 1978.

LEDWIDGE, B.: Cognitive behavior modification: A step in the wrong direction? *Psychological Bulletin,* 1978, *85,* 353-375.

LUBORSKY, L., SINGER, B., & LUBORSKY, L.: Comparative studies of psychotherapies: Is it true that everyone has won and all must have prizes? *Archives of General Psychiatry,* 1975, *32,* 995-1008.

MAHONEY, M.J.: *Cognition and behavior modification.* Cambridge, Mass: Balinger, 1974.

MAHONEY, M.J.: Cognitive therapy and research: A question of questions. *Cognitive Therapy and Research,* 1977, *1,* 1-5 (a).

MAHONEY, M.J.: Reflections on the cognitive-learning trend in psychotherapy. *American Psychologist,* 1977, *32,* 5-13 (b).

MAHONEY, K., & MAHONEY, M.J.: Cognitive factors in weight reduction. In J.D. Krumboltz & C.E. Thoresen (Eds.), *Counseling methods.* New York: Holt, Rinehart & Winston, 1976.

MAHONEY, M.J., & ARNKOFF, D.: Cognitive and self-control therapies. In S.L. Garfield & A.E. Bergin (Eds.), *Handbook of psychotherapy and behavior change* (2nd ed.). New York: Wiley, 1978.

MARLATT, G.A.: Craving for alcohol, loss of control, and relapse: A cognitive-behavioral analysis. In P.E. Nathan & G.A. Marlatt (Eds.), *Alcoholism: New directions in behavioral research and treatment.* New York: Plenum Press, 1978.

MARLATT, G.A., & MARQUES, J.K.: Meditation, self-control, and alcohol use. In R.B. Stuart (Ed.), *Behavioral self-management: Strategies, techniques and outcome.* New York: Brunner/Mazel, 1977.

MATHEWS, A.M., BANCROFT, J., WHITEHEAD, A., HACKMANN, A., JULIER, D., BANCROFT, J., GATH, D., & SHAW, P.: The behavioral treatment of sexual inadequacy: A comparative study. *Behaviour Research and Therapy,* 1976, *14,* 427-436.

MEICHENBAUM, D.H.: Cognitive factors in behavior modification: Modifying what clients say to themselves. In C.M. Franks & G.T. Wilson (Eds.), *Annual review of behavior therapy: Theory and practice.* New York: Brunner/Mazel, 1973, 416-431.

MEICHENBAUM, D.H.: *Cognitive Behavior Modification.* New York: Plenum, 1977.

MEICHENBAUM, D.H., & CAMERON, R.: Training schizophrenics to talk to themselves: A means of developing attentional controls. *Behavior Therapy,* 1973, *4,* 515-534.

MEICHENBAUM, D.H., GILMORE, J., & FEDORAVICIUS, A.: Group insight vs. group desensitization in treating speech anxiety. *Journal of Consulting and Clinical Psychology,* 1971, *36,* 410-421.

MISCHEL, W.: *Personality and assessment.* New York: Wiley, 1968.

MISCHEL, W.: Processes in the delay of gratification. In L. Berkowitz (Ed.), *Advances in experimental social psychology* (Vol. 7). New York: Academic Press, 1974.

MISCHEL, W.: On the future of personality assessment. *American Psychologist,* 1977, *32,* 246-254.

MOWRER, O.H.: *Learning theory and the symbolic processes.* New York: Wiley, 1960.

NATHAN, P.E., & MARLATT, G.A.: *Alcoholism: New directions in behavioral research and treatment.* New York: Plenum, 1978.

OBSERVER: Concerning cognitive reversionism in psychology. *The Psychological Record,* 1977, *2,* 351-354.

O'Leary, S.G.: Behavioral treatment for hyperactive children. Paper presented at Association for Advancement of Behavior Therapy, Atlanta, Georgia, December 1977.

Orford, J., Oppenheimer, E., & Edwards, G.: Abstinence or control: The outcome for excessive drinkers two years after consultation. *Behaviour Research and Therapy,* 1976, *14,* 409-415.

Perlmuter, L.C., & Monty, R.A.: *Choice and perceived control.* Hillsdale, NJ: Lawrence Erlbaum, in press.

Peterson, D.R.: *The clinical study of social behavior.* New York: Appleton-Century-Crofts, 1968.

Polivy, J.: Perception of calories and regulation of intake in restrained and unrestrained subjects. *Addictive Behaviors,* 1976, *1,* 237-244.

Pomerleau, O., Pertschuk, M., & Stinnett, J.: A critical examination of some current assumptions in the treatment of alcoholism. *Journal of Studies on Alcohol,* 1976, *37,* 849-867.

Popper, K.R.: *Conjectures and refutations.* London: Routledge & Kegan Paul, 1963.

Rachlin, H.: Self control. *Behaviorism,* 1974, *2,* 94-107.

Rachlin, H.: A review of M.J. Mahoney's *Cognition and Behavior Modification. Journal of Applied Behavior Analysis,* 1977, *10,* 369-374.

Rachman, S.: Observational learning and therapeutic modeling. In M.P. Feldman & A. Broadhurst (Eds.), *Theoretical and experimental bases of the behaviour therapies.* New York: Wiley, 1976(a).

Rachman, S.: The passing of the two-stage theory of fear and avoidance: Fresh possibilities. *Behaviour Research and Therapy,* 1976, *14,* 125-131(b).

Rachman, S.: The conditioning theory of fear-acquisition: A critical examination. *Behaviour Research and Therapy,* 1977, *15,* 375-388.

Rachman, S., & Hodgson, R.: *Obsessions and compulsions.* Englewood Cliffs, NJ: Prentice-Hall, in press.

Rachman, S. & Wilson, G.T.: *The effects of psychotherapy.* Oxford: Pergamon Press, in press.

Reppucci, N.D., & Saunders, J.T.: Social psychology of behavior modification: Problems of implementation in natural settings. *American Psychologist,* 1974, 29, 649-660.

Rotter, J.B.: *Social learning and clinical psychology.* Englewood Cliffs, NJ: Prentice-Hall, 1954.

Rotter, J.B.: Generalized expectancies for internal versus external control of reinforcement. *Psychological Monographs,* 1966, *80,* 61 (Whole No. 609).

Rush, A.J., Beck, A.T., Kovacs, M., & Hollon, S.: Comparative efficacy of cognitive therapy and pharmacotherapy in the treatment of depressed out-patients. *Cognitive Therapy and Research,* 1977, *1,* 17-37.

Seligman, M.E.P., & Johnston, J.: A cognitive theory of avoidance learning. In J. McGuigan & B. Lumsden (Eds.), *Contemporary approaches to conditioning and learning.* New York: Wiley, 1973.

Shaw, B.F.: Comparison of cognitive therapy and behavior therapy in the treatment of depression. *Journal of Consulting and Clinical Psychology,* 1977, 45, 543-551.

Sherman, A.R.: Real-life exposure as a primary therapeutic factor in the desensitization treatment of fear. *Journal of Abnormal Psychology,* 1972, *79,* 19-28.

Skinner, B.F.: Operant behavior. In W.K. Honig (Ed.), *Operant behavior: Areas of research and application.* New York: Appleton-Century-Crofts, 1966.

Skinner, B.F.: *Beyond freedom and dignity.* New York: Alfred A. Knopf, 1971.

Skinner, B.F.: Why I am not a cognitive psychologist. *Behaviorism,* 1977, *5,* 1-10.

Smith, M.L. & Glass, G.V.: Meta-analysis of psychotherapy outcome studies. *American Psychologist,* 1977, *32,* 752-760.

Staddon, J.E.R.: On the notion of cause, with applications to behaviorism. *Behaviorism,* 1973, *1,* 25.

Stern, R., & Marks, I.: Brief and prolonged flooding. *Archives of General Psychiatry,* 1973, *28,* 270-276.

STOKES, T.F., & BAER, D.M.: An implicit technology of generalization. *Journal of Applied Behavior Analysis,* 1977, *10,* 349-368.

STUART, R.B.: Behavioral control of overeating. *Behaviour Research and Therapy,* 1967, *5,* 357-365.

STUART, R.B., & DAVIS, B.: *Slim chance in a fat world.* Champaign, Ill.: Research Press, 1972.

TAYLOR, F.G. & MARSHALL, W.L.: Experimental analysis of a cognitive-behavioral therapy for depression. *Cognitive Therapy and Research,* 1977, *1,* 59-72.

THASE, M.E., & MOSS, M.K.: The relative efficacy of covert modeling procedures and guided participant modeling on the reduction of avoidance behavior. *Journal of Behavior Therapy and Experimental Psychiatry,* 1976, *7,* 7-12.

THORPE, G.L.: Desensitization, behavior rehearsal, self-instructional training and placebo effects on assertive-refusal behavior. *European Journal of Behavioural Analysis and Modification,* 1975, *1,* 30-44.

TOBIAS, L.L., & MACDONALD, M.L.: Internal locus of control and weight loss: An insufficient condition. *Journal of Consulting and Clinical Psychology,* 1977, *45,* 647-653.

TURKEWITZ, H., O'LEARY, K.D., & IRONSMITH, M.: Generalization and maintenance of appropriate behavior through self-control. *Journal of Consulting and Clinical Psychology,* 1975, *43,* 577-583.

ULLMANN, L.P., & KRASNER, L.: *A psychological approach to abnormal behavior* (2nd ed.). Englewood Cliffs, NJ: Prentice-Hall, 1975.

WALKER, H.M., & BUCKLEY, N.K.: Programming generalization and maintenance of treatment effects across time and across settings. *Journal of Applied Behavior Analysis,* 1972, *5,* 209-224.

WEISS, A.R.: Characteristics of successful weight reducers: A brief review of predictor variables. *Addictive Behaviors,* 1977, *2,* 193-202.

WILSON, G.T.: Alcohol and human sexual behavior. *Behaviour Research and Therapy,* 1977, *15,* 239-252.

WILSON, G.T.: Booze, beliefs, and behavior: Cognitive processes in alcohol use and abuse. In P.E. Nathan & G.A. Marlatt (Eds.), *Alcoholism: New directions in behavioral research and treatment.* New York: Plenum Press, 1978(a).

WILSON, G.T.: Cognitive behavior therapy: Paradigm shift or passing phase? In J.P. Foreyt & D. Rathjen (Eds.), *Cognitive behavior therapy: Research and application.* New York: Plenum Press, 1978(b).

WILSON, G.T.: Methodological considerations in treatment outcome research on obesity. *Journal of Consulting and Clinical Psychology,* 1978, *46,* 687-702(c).

WILSON, G.T.: Perceived control and the theory and practice of behavior therapy. In L.C. Perlmuter & R.A. Monty (Eds.), *Choice and perceived control.* Hillsdale, NJ: Lawrence Erlbaum, in press (d).

WILSON, G.T.: The importance of being theoretical. Comments on Bandura's "Self-efficacy: Toward a unifying theory of behavioral change." In H.J. Eysenck & S. Rachman (Eds.), *Advances in Behaviour Research and Therapy,* 1978, *1,* 217-230(d).

WILSON, G.T., & DAVISON, G.C.: Processes of fear reduction in systematic desensitization: Animal studies. *Psychological Bulletin,* 1971, *76,* 1-14.

WILSON, G.T., & EVANS, I.M.: Adult behavior therapy and the therapist-client relationship. In C.M. Franks & G.T. Wilson (Eds.), *Annual review of behavior therapy: Theory and Practice, Vol. IV.* New York: Brunner/Mazel, 1976.

WILSON, G.T., & EVANS, I.M.: The therapist-client relationship in behavior therapy. In A.S. Gurman & A.M. Razin (Eds.), *Therapist's handbook for effective psychotherapy: Empirical assessment and multidisciplinary approach.* New York: Pergamon Press, 1978.

WILSON, G.T., & O'LEARY, K.D.: *Principles of behavior therapy.* Englewood Cliffs, NJ: Prentice-Hall, in press.

WOLPE, J.: *Psychotherapy by reciprocal inhibition.* Stanford: Stanford University Press, 1958.

WOLPE, J.: *The practice of behavior therapy.* New York: Pergamon Press, 1973.

WOLPE, J.: Behavior therapy and its malcontents—II. Multimodal eclecticism, cognitive exclusivism and "exposure" empiricism. *Journal of Behavior Therapy and Experimental Psychiatry,* 1976, *7,* 109-116.

WOOLFOLK, A.E., WOOLFOLK, R.L., & WILSON, G.T.: A rose by any other name. . .: Labeling bias and attitudes toward behavior modification. *Journal of Consulting and Clinical Psychology,* 1977, *45,* 184-191.

ZIFFERBLATT, S.M.: Increasing patient compliance through the applied analysis of behavior. *Preventive Medicine,* 1975, *4,* 173-182.

ZIFFERBLATT, S.M., & HENRICKS, C.G.: Applied behavioral analysis of social problems: Population change, a case in point. *American Psychologist,* 1974, *29,* 750-762.

2

Coping Theory and the Teaching of Coping Skills

Ethel Roskies
and
Richard S. Lazarus

There is mounting belief among research and clinical workers that how people cope with stress is even more important to overall morale, social functioning and somatic health than the frequency and severity of the stress episodes themselves (Coelho, Hamburg, & Adams, 1974; Goldfried, 1977; Goldfried & Goldfried, 1975; Meichenbaum, 1977; Murphy & Moriarty, 1976). This is partially the result of accumulating empirical evidence linking coping to outcome; we shall examine some of these data shortly. Much more important, however, this belief signals a profound restructuring of our assumptions concerning stress in human existence and the relationship between stress and pathology. The shift in emphasis from stress to coping can best be understood as part of a much broader change in *Zeitgeist.*

Writing of this paper was supported in part by research grants from the National Institute on Aging (AG 00002) and the National Cancer Institute (CA 19362). The work by Ethel Roskies was done during a sabatical leave spent as a Visiting Scholar at the University of California, Berkeley, partially supported by a Canada Council League Fellowship.

Traditionally, stress has been viewed as a state of emergency to be contrasted with the smooth flow of everyday adaptation. Cannon, one of the early pioneers, actually used the term "emergency reactions" to denote the physiological changes he observed in animals during stress situations. Current definitions of stress also highlight the emergency flavor of the concept by categorizing stress as a situation in which routine or automatic responses are inadequate (cf. White, 1974). Not surprisingly, therefore, early stress theory and research implicitly equated stress with the *unusual* by studying extreme situations in the field (Baker & Chapman, 1962; Bettelheim, 1960; Bowlby, 1961; Grinker & Spiegel, 1945; Janis, 1951; Lindemann, 1944) or by bringing very noxious stimuli into the laboratory (Frankenhaeuser & Kareby, 1962; Frankenhaeuser & Patkai, 1964; Funkenstein, King, & Drolette, 1956; Furer & Hardy, 1950; Lazarus, Speisman, Mordkoff, & Davison, 1962; Levi, 1965; Selye, 1950). The aim in both cases was to investigate how these exceptional situations disrupted "normal" behavioral, physiological and emotional functioning.

In contrast to stress researchers, clinicians have, in the past, emphasized the endogenous sources of stress, rather than external, causal or precipitating events. But they, too, shared the assumption that stress constituted an abnormal state, a deviation from the norm. In the orthodox Freudian view, for instance, the major source of neurotic disturbance is unresolved infantile conflicts and the aim of therapy is to resolve these conflicts. Although Freud himself was careful to caution that psychoanalysis could not remove "normal" unhappiness, the myth of the fully analyzed person devoid of conflict exerted a powerful influence.

This view of stress as an unusual state is no longer tenable. Our society is changing, and we are also viewing it differently. Social critics point to the rapidly accelerating rate of change and to the decreasing number of situations for which routine or habitual responses are adequate (Toffler, 1970). Life-span psychologists no longer view the adult years as a calm moratorium between the vicissitudes of adolescence and old age, but depict them instead in terms of change, conflict and challenge (Levinson, 1978; Lowenthal, Thurnher, & Chiriboga, 1975). Even social institutions like marriage, which traditionally have provided structure and stability for human relationships, are being buffeted by changing norms to the point where they no longer provide even the myth of a safe harbor of routine and habit. To confront harm, threat or challenge in a manner which taxes or exceeds our adaptive capacities is no longer viewed as the fate of only the particularly vulnerable, or those exposed to an exceptional set of circumstances, but instead as part of the "average expectable environment." Just as on the political scene, the concept of peace has given way to classifications of degree of strife, so in psychology one can no longer speak of the complete absence of stress, but only of variations in its intensity and quality.

But if all of us are stressed, not all of us are troubled or sick. The figures on the number of cardiac, cancer, alcohol-related and automobile accident deaths per year are dramatic, as are those on mental illness and the use of tranquilizers. What these figures can lead us to forget, however, is the large number of people who manage to lead reasonably productive, satisfying lives. Even under the extreme conditions of the concentration camp, not all succumbed (Dimsdale, 1974) and some of the survivors show surprisingly few signs of pathology (Antonovsky, Maoz, Dowty, & Wijsenbeek, 1971). In seeking to explain immunity to the diseases of adaptation, Selye (1974) has recently begun to distinguish between good and bad stress, or eustress and distress, as he calls them. The more relevant distinction, we suggest, is between effective and ineffective coping.

Although coping is usually regarded in a positive light, there are at least three ways in which *ineffective coping* can add to the risk of illness or death (cf. Lazarus, Cohen, Folkman, Kanner, & Schaefer, in press). The first is by direct damage to tissue. The person who copes with job stress or marital dissatisfaction by drinking, smoking, overeating and reckless driving may not only further damage the social relationships which are a source of trouble, but is also increasing his or her general or specific vulnerability to disease. The second way is more indirect and involves the harmful physiological disturbances that may be a consequence of mobilization. Sympathetic arousal, including elevations in blood pressure and massive hormonal activity, may provide the laid-off worker with the extra energy necessary to seek a new job, or to rearrange his or her finances or household while unemployed (Kasl, Gore, & Cobb, 1975). Whatever the contribution of this type of physiological mobilization to coping, however, it is also related in epidemiological studies to hypertension (Ostfeld, 1967; Syme, 1977) and other diseases (cf. House & Jackman, in press). The third way in which coping may increase risk of illness is by interfering with adaptive behaviors that could help to preserve life or well-being. Denying that a suspicious breast lump might signal cancer (Katz, Weiner, Gallagher, & Hellman, 1970), or a chest pain a heart attack (Hackett & Cassem, 1975; Von Kugelgen, 1975), is likely to effectively reduce immediate emotional distress, but at the cost of interfering with the seeking of medical care that might save or prolong life.

Effective coping is also a potent influence on health. For instance, in their study of patients with advanced cancer, Weisman and Worden (1975) focused on the difference in coping strategies between those patients who survived longer than expected on the basis of the severity of the disease and those whose outcomes were unexpectedly poor. Patients who could maintain active and mutually responsive relationships were likely to live longer, while lack of such relationships was associated with decreased morale and shorter longevity.

Further support for the positive influence of effective coping, even under unfavorable circumstances, is provided by the study of Aldrich and Mendkoff (1963) of aged persons moved from one institution to another. This type of move constitutes a life-threatening situation in that it is usually followed by a sharp rise in mortality rates. While the psychotic and the depressed elderly in this sample fared most poorly, as expected, both those who accepted the move philosophically and those who resisted it angrily had lower than expectable mortality rates. Thus, effective coping can positively influence even the most severe criterion of adaptation, namely, survival itself.

This recent conceptualization of stress as prevalent but not necessarily pathogenic has led to an increasing interest in coping by stress researchers and clinicians in the past few years. Stress researchers have increasingly been seeking to understand the types of coping used to manage stress and the relation between coping patterns and outcome. Clinicians, on the other hand, who deal with people seeking help because of inability to cope adequately, have been attempting to alleviate their clients' distress by "teaching" them more adequate coping skills.* Both approaches, however, have had to struggle with the same fundamental questions: 1) What functions does coping serve and what are the rules governing the emergence and manifestations of coping?, and 2) How and why do people differ in coping patterns and how are these variations related to outcome?

In seeking answers, the trends in stress research and clinical therapy have been complementary in some respects, divergent in others. Except for a few scattered cross-references, however, the two trends have tended

---

*The psychotherapeutic approach most closely identified with the explicit teaching of coping skills is that of the cognitive behavior therapists (Beck, 1976; Goldfried, 1977; Goldfried & Goldfried, 1975; Mahoney, 1974; Meichenbaum, 1977) and their predecessor, Ellis (1962). While there are obvious differences in substance and style distinguishing them, their basic assumptions are sufficiently similar to permit us to treat them for the purposes of this paper as a group. All serve on the Editorial Board of the recently established journal of *Cognitive Therapy and Research.*

to develop relatively independently. Our purpose here is to build a bridge between theory and research on coping and its current clinical counterparts. Ideally, such cross-fertilization will help both disciplines become more effective in using what we already know and in tackling the many things still to be learned about coping.

A Process-oriented Model of Stress and Coping

For coping to become an integral part of stress research, it was first necessary to develop a transactional theoretical model of stress broad enough to encompass the person as an active shaper of the stress experience as well as a responder to a demanding environment. Earlier models tended to view stress simplistically, either as an external condition generating turbulence (stressor) or as the turbulent response itself (stress response), and to postulate a linear cause-effect relationship between the two. This S-R model did not provide a means for exploring and explaining individual differences in reaction. The goal was to uncover universal relationships and any exceptions were embarrassments (see Lazarus & Cohen, 1976).

Nevertheless, empirical studies continued to produce fresh evidence that the relationship between stimulus and response varied considerably in different people. Examples of this are legion (see Lazarus, 1966; Lazarus, Deese, & Osler, 1952) but a very simple study will serve as an illustration. In measuring students' reactions to an impending college examination, Mahl (1949) found that two of his eight subjects did not show the expected increase in secretion of hydrochloric acid (HCL). Moreover, each of the two nonresponders was deviant for a different motivational reason, one because he had already been accepted into the medical school of his choice, and the other because his expectations did not go beyond attaining a gentlemanly C.

One solution to this lack of correspondence between stimulus and response is to introduce some classification of individuals by personality trait or type, for example, possession of a distinctive mode of defense or motivational pattern, using this as an intervening variable to account for the differences in response to the same stimulus. In this way the S-R linear model is transformed into an S-O-R linear model (Lazarus & Cohen, 1976). Even this revised model, however, is inadequate in explaining the empirical data.

For instance, because of the evidence linking the rushed, aggressive, competitive Type A behavior pattern to increased risk of coronary heart disease, a number of recent studies have attempted to explore differences in response to challenge between people classified as Type A and the more relaxed, easygoing Type Bs (Dembroski, MacDougall, & Shields, 1977; Friedman, Byers, Diamant, & Rosenman, 1975; Glass, 1977). The results highlight the complexity of the interaction between the predisposed person and the environment in evoking the Type A behavior pattern. Individuals with the predisposition to Type A behavior do create much of their own stress by appraising a problem as a challenge where others do not. For instance, the same puzzle that aroused no more than mild interest and effort in a group of Type B men was responded to, behaviorally and physiologically, as an intense challenge by a comparable group of Type A men (Friedman et al., 1975). This tendency to maximum effort, however, is not completely independent of the situation. If in the course of doing a task, Type As come to believe that they cannot effectively control the course of events, then they may actually give up faster than Type Bs. Where the task demands are perceived as challenging but not overwhelming, however, Type As will work longer and harder than Type Bs (Glass, 1977). A static personality characteristic alone is no more adequate than a stimulus alone in explaining these complex variations in response.

The inadequacy of a static model, even one including organismic variables, is particularly well highlighted in longitudinal studies of stress response. For instance, there are at least three studies in the literature which seek to follow parents through the crisis engendered by the severe illness, deformity or impending death of a child (Davis, 1963; Friedman, Chodoff, Mason, & Hamburg, 1963; Roskies, 1972). Each of these studies comes from a different discipline and each deals with a very different population. Yet, the conclusion common to all three studies is that over a period of months and years, parental reaction to this severe stress was neither rigidly fixed nor randomly fluctuating. Instead, the shift in reactions can best be conceptualized as a series of stages, each of which reflected a delicate and changing balance between the characteristics of the external situation and the meaning the parent attributed to these events. Even a parent with a consistent tendency to denial behaved very differently at the moment when the doctor first broached the possibility of hospitalization for suspected polio and the day two years later when the child returned home in a wheelchair. At the moment of initial suspicion the tendency towards minimization was likely to be expressed in the hope that the sore throat and fever were no more than the symptoms of a common cold. Two years later, the same tendency was channeled into the conviction that with sufficient physiotherapy the child would continue to make progress. One more year later it might be expressed in still another form, the hope for an eventual cure for polio (Davis, 1963). The static model, regardless of its comprehensiveness, cannot adequately encompass this type of dynamic interplay between the person and the environment.

Lazarus (1966; Lazarus, Averill, & Opton, 1970; Lazarus & Launier, in press) attempted to overcome the shortcomings of traditional stress theory by postulating a transactional model that emphasizes cognitive appraisal and coping as process. According to this view, stress is no longer a static interaction between certain properties of the stimulus and certain properties of the organism, but instead is conceptualized as an ongoing transaction and relationship, encompassing a whole series of stimulus, response, altered stimulus, altered response, and so on. Central to this process is the way in which the individual continuously *appraises* what he or she is experiencing and uses this understanding of what is happening to shape the future course of events. Appraisal is basically an evaluative perception or judgment. The occurrence or anticipation of a given event is stressful and generates emotional reactions because the person *construes* it both as important to his or her well-being and as taxing his or her resources. The type of coping response made is again based on *evaluation* of the best available way to achieve the outcome which is *judged* as most desirable or least harmful. The static S-O-R linear model has been replaced by a dynamic, cognitive one (cf. Folkman, Schaefer, & Lazarus, in press).

This new model radically alters the direction of the cause-effect relationship between stress and coping. Coping is no longer simply a response to an event that *has* happened, but instead, has become an active force in shaping what *is* happening and what *will* happen. In an illustrative study of maternal reaction to the birth of a thalidomide child (Roskies, 1972), an attempt was made to isolate the factors that led the attending physicians to diagnose some neonates as deformed but intelligent, while others with similar limb deficiencies were classified as monsters. It soon became clear that the mother's behavior on the days following birth was a key determinant. Those mothers who asked to see and feed their babies were far more likely to be assured by the physician of the child's normal intelligence and encouraged to take the child home to rear, while those who refused to see the child more often received the diagnosis of monster and the recommendation of institutionalization. The degree to which the mother's coping behavior could influence the situation is illustrated by the case of one extremely distraught mother whose husband was then advised that the child could be "helped to die."

Coping, then, is not only engendered by a disturbance in the person-environment relationship but also, in turn, is anticipatory and helps to shape the future course of this relationship.

The altered cause-effect relationship between stress and coping also extends to the person's initial evaluation of the situation as potentially stressful or not and thereby also to the emotional response. What is judged to be stressful depends not only on the taxing qualities of the environment as appraised, but also, and equally as important, on the appraised strength and suitability of the available resources to meet these demands. The requirements of giving a speech, meeting strangers, or driving a car in heavy traffic are unlikely to arouse more than mild degrees of apprehension, pleasure or annoyance in the person who is experienced, competent and confident in these situations. The same requirements are likely to be sources of considerable stress for the inexperienced, incompetent or timid. The appraisal of excessive demands, therefore, is equally the appraisal of inadequate resources. Beliefs about one's capacity to cope relate back to one's original appraisal of stress and constantly affect the flow of cognitive and emotional activity.

In sum, from its humble beginnings as a footnote to stress theory, the concept of coping has grown to occupy a central place in current theoretical models of stress and emotion. Coping is a reaction to stress, but also a shaper of the stress experience, and in determining whether or not a given event will be evaluated as potentially stressful, the appraisal of the person's coping resources is as important as the appraisal of the environment. Coping and stress are but two faces of the same coin and any model of stress must also be viewed as a model of coping.

In contrast to the stress researchers, the cognitive therapists have favored innovations in therapeutic techniques more than theoretical models. With a few notable exceptions (Bandura, 1977 a, b; Ellis, 1962), most of the theory building on the clinical side has come after the empirical work, and has focused on the specific problem of maladaptive coping, rather than on stress and coping in general (Beck, 1976; Goldfried, 1977; Goldfried & Goldfried, 1975; Mahoney, 1974; Meichenbaum, 1977). Their understanding of maladaptive or ineffective coping, however, is consistent with and complementary to the Lazarus model. According to their view, the common factor in the diversity of complaints brought to the therapist (e.g., social anxiety, phobias, text anxiety) is the person's feeling of being in one or more threat-harm-challenge situations which cannot be handled adequately. The "problem" is created by the person's self-appraised inadequacy in *managing important aspects of the environment in a manner satisfactory to that person and/or sig-*

nificant others. Human distress is not attributed solely to traumatic events (past or present), or to a structural inadequacy of the person, but to a sensed lack of competence in handling specific and significant person-environment transactions. As in the Lazarus model, cognitive evaluation, coping, and transactional processes are, at least implicitly, of primary importance in understanding emotional reactions and maladaptive outcomes.

A Taxonomy of Coping

For coping to be systematically studied, either in the laboratory or in the clinic, we must not only have a theoretical rationale, but, equally as important, a method for classifying and describing what we observe. For the stress researcher, a concrete and detailed set of descriptive categories is an essential prerequisite both for intra-individual and inter-individual comparison. For the clinician seeking to assess and treat the coping of a specific client, it is equally essential to have a general reference scheme against which to contrast the individual case. Unfortunately, a widely accepted and used taxonomy of coping does not yet exist. Some efforts at classification have been made and used in stress research (Folkins, 1970; Haan, 1969, 1977; Lazarus, 1975; Murphy & Moriarty, 1976; Pearlin & Schooler, 1978; Weisman & Worden, 1975), but we are still a long way from a system that adequately covers the ground.

Coping Processes

The major shortcoming of most of the classification schemes proposed to date is that they have dealt with traits, as in the concept of coping style or built-in hierarchies of defense mechanisms (Haan, 1977; Menninger, 1954; Vaillant, 1977), and do not describe coping processes as they actually occur in life stress (cf. Cohen & Lazarus, 1973). We have many measures of coping traits in stress research (Moos, 1974), but few of how a person actually handles a particular harm, threat or challenge (Lazarus & Cohen, 1976).

Lazarus and Launier (in press) have recently attempted to develop a classification scheme for coping processes. In this scheme, strategies are divided both according to the mode used (direct action, action inhibition, information search and intrapsychic modes) and the function they serve (problem-oriented vs. palliative regulation of the emotional response). While this classification scheme is superficially very simple, it is comprehensive enough to encompass a wide variety of stressful transactions including planning a holiday, dealing with the chronic irritation of a nagging supervisor, handling adolescent turmoil, and coming to terms with serious illness or death of a loved one. Each of the major coping modes (i.e., direction action, action inhibition, information search and the intrapsychic mode) is also sufficiently broad to encompass a large range of discrete acts. In confronting the stress of having to write a scientific paper, for example, possible direct actions are as varied as preparing an outline, phoning a friend for solace, having a snack to keep up one's strength, carefully sharpening six pencils to exactly the right point, and eventually sitting down and painfully writing the first draft; while intrapsychic modes can vary from forgetting the date on which the paper is due to rehearsing mentally what one is going to write.

The introduction of function into the scheme (coping can be problem-oriented or palliative) provides a way of dealing with the complexity inherent in most patterns of coping used by optimally effective or adequate persons. For instance, there has been a tendency to downgrade intrapsychic, palliative modes because of their traditional association with pathology and self-deception (cf. White, 1974). It is debatable, however, whether palliation is necessarily a second-best coping function, and we shall examine this in greater detail below when we discuss the evaluation of coping adequacy. More to the point is that intrapsychic modes can be used for problem-solving as well as palliative ends. As the cognitive behavior therapists have so vividly demonstrated in the past few years, changing how a person thinks and feels in a situation can constitute an extremely effective form of problem-solving. In some cases this intrapsychic adjustment may even be sufficient in itself to remove a transaction from the harm-threat-challenge category. The person who is able to apply Ellis' (1962) strategy of cognitive relabeling, and thus meet a criticism from a colleague with the thought that one cannot be expected to be approved of by everybody all the time, is not only reducing his or her own discomfort, but actually changing the transaction's appraised significance, thereby changing the way he or she will greet the colleague on their next encounter.

In other stressful encounters, regulation of disruptive emotions through intrapsychic efforts or drugs may constitute a necessary prelude to the implementation of task-oriented problem-solving action. For example, in treating a case of chronic anger, Novaco (1977) used relaxation and cognitive relabeling to reduce the anger, but also added assertion training to help the patient attain his goals in a more effective manner.

Similarly, Linehan, Goldfried, and Goldfried (1977) have recently shown that a combination of rational restructuring (intrapsychic) and behavior rehearsal (direct action) was more effective than either alone in facilitating appropriate assertive behavior in women. Coping with any major threat or challenge usually involves an amalgam of many diverse coping acts performed over time and in multiple contexts.

The Freudian concept of "acting out" serves to remind us also of the converse, that direct action can be used for palliative as well as instrumental ends. In the case of chronic anger described by Novaco, the patient's direct actions of verbal and physical assaults on his children may have served to vent his anger and frustration, but were hardly likely to change the troubled relationships with his co-workers and supervisors that were the source of much of his distress. Less obviously palliative is the pace of frantic activity maintained by the Type A individual. It has been suggested, however (Glass, 1977), that this activity may be more directed toward warding off feelings of anxiety over lack of mastery than toward solving a specific problem. Some confirmation for this hypothesis is provided by the observation of Suinn, Brock, and Edie (1975) that Type A patients often experience a rise in anxiety when they try to slow down.

The details of the classification scheme proposed by Lazarus and Launier (in press) will probably undergo further refinement as they are tested in actual research use. What is important is that we use this or similar classification schemes to study coping *processes*, both in a wide variety of populations and in the same persons confronting different stressful transactions. Observation of many types of people in varied stressful encounters is necessary if we are to build a picture of the range of coping patterns used by "normal" people, and their consistency or variability across stressful situations and over time. To order these data on coping processes in a fashion permitting useful intra-individual or inter-individual comparisons, some effort at classification and description is essential.

Coping Resources

If coping modes or strategies are conceptualized as the currency expended in a specific stress transaction, coping resources constitute the bank account from which this currency is drawn. Our present knowledge of this banking system is severely limited. We know in a general way that a strong positive balance is positively related to favorable outcome. What we do not know is how deposits are made (the development of coping resources) or funds withdrawn when needed (the transformation of resources into specific coping processes). Unfortunately, these are the very questions that are most relevant to a theoretical and clinical understanding of coping.

At least six categories of resources have been identified (Folkman et al., in press), some existing within the person (health/energy, morale, problem-solving skills, system of beliefs) and some that can be drawn from a cooperative environment (social support, material resources). Of these, social support has been most explored, although such research is still in its infancy. Recent studies have shown that close, positive relationships facilitate good health and morale, particularly in times of crisis (Berkman, 1977; Cassel, 1976; Cobb, 1976; Kaplan, Cassel, & Gore, 1973).

The powerful impact of this resource is dramatically illustrated by the changing rate of coronary heart disease in Roseto, an Italian-American community in Eastern Pennsylvania. This community was initially selected for study in the early 1960s because of its unusually low mortality rate for coronary heart disease (CHD), in spite of the high prevalence of risk factors such as a diet with a large amount of animal fat, smoking, and lack of exercise. In the initial report on the town, it was hypothesized that the unusually strong social support available to the inhabitants (close family and community ties, lack of social competitiveness) might be responsible for the unexpectedly favorable outcome by counteracting the negative effects of any stress experienced (Bruhn, 1965). Continuing reports since 1963 show the erosion of this social structure and the accompanying rise in death rate from myocardial infarction. By 1975, Roseto had not only been "Americanized" socially, but it had also achieved a mortality rate closely resembling that of the United States at large (Bruhn & Wolf, 1978).

Fascinating as this community case history may be in demonstrating the importance of social support, it raises more questions than it answers about the combination of social conditions and personal skills that facilitates the development and maintenance of social networks and their use, or, alternatively, makes it difficult for them to exist or to be used. In the case of Roseto, the inhabitants appeared to inherit their social networks on the basis of kinship and geographical ties, and as these weakened so did the networks. On the other hand, some people are able to use a high level of personal skill to develop and maintain adequate social networks in spite of geographical and social mobility. Under what circumstances do people best learn and use these skills? To what degree can nontraditional structures (e.g., intentional families, the use of working relationships as a social network) be creatively used to replace traditional ones? Our ability to understand and help people who lack a given resource requires a much greater knowledge than we currently possess of the manifold ways in which "normal" people acquire and replenish resources. Only the detailed study of these nonclinical populations will help develop a normative scheme that will serve as a reference point for specific case studies or interventions.

The other vital area in which our understanding of coping resources is limited is in delineating how they are used to produce more effective coping patterns and a more favorable outcome. It is possible that possession of a resource limits the number of transactions that are appraised as stressful or the intensity of distress experienced. For instance, the man who loses his job but is surrounded by a loving wife and a close circle of friends and family may be less distressed initially than an isolated individual in the same situation because the retention of the roles of husband, father and friend limit the threat to his sense of self-worth, while the belief that friends will lend money if necessary provides a psychological buffer against the economic threat of unemployment. Alternatively, social support may not cushion the initial shock, but may help the person deal with it more effectively. The willingness of spouse and friends to listen to the unemployed worker's fear and anger can provide a much needed catharsis, while their suggestions of possible job openings may hasten the process of actually finding a new job. Any or all of these functions of social support systems may apply in a given situation.

To date, there have been only a few scattered attempts to explore the mechanisms through which resources affect coping and outcome (Nuckolls, Cassel, & Kaplan, 1972). Bloom's (1978) study of the psychological adjustment of 133 women following mastectomy is one of these pioneer efforts. Her results indicate that adjustment to mastectomy is a two-stage process. Women with greater resources (more social support and fewer life changes) are likely to cope better in terms of sleeping, eating, drinking, and worrying. This, in turn, leads to higher self-esteem and less mood disturbance. Coping resources, therefore, seemingly affect outcome not only by regulating feeling and hence behavior, but also in the reverse sequence. Greater resources may permit us to function with less behavioral disruption and, in maintaining habits, we also avoid mood disturbance. Obviously, this provocative hypothesis deserves further investigation.

The Evaluation of Coping Adequacy

The core issue in any discussion of coping is the evaluation of the adequacy of coping. We are interested in coping because we believe that effective coping positively influences morale, social functioning and health, while ineffective coping has equally powerful negative effects. Both the study and treatment of coping, therefore, are properly based upon the ability to distinguish effective from ineffective coping.

To date neither the clinicians nor the researchers have seriously addressed themselves to this issue. The clinicians have largely avoided the problems of evaluation by treating adequacy as if it were self-evident. Faced with a female student distressed by the insensitivity of her boyfriend, the solution is to help her via assertion training to express her needs more clearly and forcefully. Similarly, the text-anxious student requires help to write exams more competently and comfortably. It is assumed that the remedy is inherent in the problem and the therapist's job is simply to supply the means to help the client reach these self-evident goals.

These assumptions do not, of course, stand up to close scrutiny. The choice of training in assertion skills as a means of improving a female student's relationship with her boyfriend is as much a product of the women's movement as of any necessary relationship between the perceived problem and the suggested solution. Even within the American cultural context, there are geographical regions and subcultures where the Total Women approach, in contrast to assertion training, would constitute the normative view of adequate coping for this type of situation. Similarly, for certain test-anxious students withdrawal from the course might be a better strategy than seeking to overcome the anxiety. Clinicians continuously make these value judgments in assessing clients and choosing appropriate treatment goals and strategies. Value judgments are indeed inherent in the evaluation of coping adequacy (Goldfried, 1976; Lazarus, 1976). Unfortunately, the criteria by which these evaluations are made are rarely explicit.

To the degree that researchers have tackled the problem of adequacy, they too have used predetermined standards, usually of outcome, by which to judge coping adequacy. Cancer patients who live longer than expected (Weisman & Worden, 1975), college students who report many stressful life events but few illnesses (Marx, Garrity, & Somes, 1977), and medical corpsmen in Vietnam who do not show the expected elevation in stress hormones (Bourne, Coli, & Datel, 1966) are all presumably coping adequately. Apart from the theoretical difficulties involved in linking a complex outcome to a single cause, there is the practical disadvantage that in many instances the time lag between the coping act and the expected outcome is far too long (it can vary from a millisecond to a lifetime) to make long-term outcome sufficient as the sole criterion. For research as well as clinical purposes, we require explicit criteria for on-the-spot assessment of coping adequacy in a given situation.

The Evaluation of Coping Episodes

The first problem to be confronted in seeking to establish criteria for coping adequacy is to delineate the unit of behavior to be evaluated. "Coping styles" or "coping dispositions" assume a stability in coping behavior that may not be present. A single coping act, on the other hand, is too fragmentary an element in what we conceptualize as a complex pattern of coping in an ongoing person-environment transaction taking place over time. For the purposes of the field research projects the second author and his associates are currently conducting, the notion of coping episodes has been developed to demarcate the unit of analysis. If the global process of coping with a recurring or chronic stress is viewed as a novel, then episodes are the chapters in the story. They begin with a precipitating event (externally or internally generated) that pushes stress to the forefront of consciousness and end when the feeling or situation changes, either temporarily or permanently. Within each coping episode a person may use one or more coping modes to achieve the desired change(s) in the stressful transaction. A good indicator of the natural end of a coping episode is the ability of the person to turn his or her attention to other things (cf. Horowitz, 1976), and the cessation of the stress-linked emotion.

The problem remains, however, of establishing criteria by which to evaluate the resolution of one of these coping episodes. One of the more adequate operational definitions is that provided by Silber and his associates (1961 a, b). According to this view, coping behavior can be evaluated along two dimensions: a) the effectiveness with which a task is accomplished, and b) the cost of this effectiveness to the individual. In a recent paper (Folkman et al., in press) this definition is further refined by separating the notion of cost into two components: a) the physiological cost of harmful disturbance in bodily homeostasis and b) the psychic cost of violation of value integrity. Decisions and evaluations become difficult in those situations where there is a lack of congruence between these components. There is also the possibility of conflict between immediate and long-term outcomes, a good example of which is "grief work," the status of which changes greatly depending on how long we wait to evaluate its effectiveness.

The instrumental effectiveness of a coping strategy is probably the easiest dimension to evaluate. Even here, however, it is possible to find transactions in which the task demands are sufficiently ambiguous to make evaluation a difficult task. For instance, Hennig and Jardin (1977) report that middle-level women executives are likely to master the technical details of their specific jobs far more thoroughly than their male counterparts. By most standards, therefore, the women would be judged as more competent and hence more likely to be promoted. In fact, the reverse is true. The woman's involvement in and identification with her specific job may actually constitute a barrier to promotion while, conversely, the male's lack of such identification serves to increase the perception of him as mobile and hence promotable.

The possibility that effective instrumental action may have harmful somatic effects has received considerable attention in recent psychosomatic and epidemiological literature. The assembly line worker paid on a high incentive piecework basis may rise to the challenge by increasing production significantly, but is also likely to show increased physiological wear and tear in the form of feelings of fatigue and increased stress hormone production (Levi, 1972). The Type A behavior pattern is another example of a relatively stable coping pattern that often leads to instrumentally effective coping strategies, particularly in the occupational sphere (cf. Howard, Cunningham, & Rechnitzer, 1977; Mettlin, 1976) but also doubles the risk of CHD (Rosenman, Jenkins, Brand, Friedman, Straus, & Wurm, 1975).

Souls are currently less fashionable than bodies and much less attention has been paid to the conditions under which a coping action may be instrumentally and physiologically effective, may even save life itself, but at the same time damage the person's own value integrity or the welfare of the group in which he or she lives. A dramatic example a few years ago was a group of survivors of a plane wreck who eventually were forced to resort to cannibalism as the sole means of maintaining life until help arrived. This action did save their lives, but a book one of them wrote (Read, 1975) some time later clearly manifested their continuing and perhaps unresolvable conflict concerning the price of their survival.

Most of the moral choices we confront are far less dramatic, but their effects can be almost as strong. Levinson and his colleagues (Levinson, Darrow, Klein, Levinson, & McKee, 1974) have used the term "the dream" to describe the vision of the future, usually in an occupational context, characteristic of their male subjects in early adulthood. Twenty years later the cases of severe mid-life crisis observed in some of these men were often precipitated by the reactivation of this dream and the individual's sense that he had betrayed or compromised it. Objectively rated occupational success was no protection against the anguish of the violated dream.

Our discussion of coping adequacy has centered on conflicts between the problem-solving effectiveness of coping and other values. There are situations, however, where there is little the person can do to alter the damaging course of events, and the regulation of emotional distress (e.g., through toleration, minimization, denial, avoidance, acceptance) may be the best possible bargain that he or she can negotiate with the environment. As Lieberman (1977) has pointed out, in certain situations simply maintaining homeostasis, or not breaking down, may constitute the upper limits of successful coping. In general, our moral approval for this form of coping is reserved for those who are permanently removed from the battle because of severe handicap, completely debilitating illness, or impending death. The rest of us, including most of the ill, are expected to make problem-solving efforts. In fact, one of the conditions for being permitted to assume the sick role in our society is that we actively strive to become healthy, or actively collaborate with professional dispensers of health care should our own efforts prove insufficient (Parsons, 1958).

It is tempting to speculate, however, about the value of accepting temporary helplessness and seeking instead to reduce affective distress by all available means, including denial. Such a period of purely palliative coping may provide a necessary moratorium in which strength can be gained, or the situation allowed to change, until the person is once more able to attempt instrumental action (Hamburg & Adams, 1967). The potential value of temporarily abandoning problem-oriented coping is illustrated by the course of patients experiencing a myocardial infarction. Initial denial of symptoms can cause delay in seeking medical care and may have fatal consequences (Hackett & Cassem, 1975). During the period of rehabilitation, the patient is also required to make active coping efforts to return to work, resume a social and sexual life, and so on, if he or she is not to develop a "cardiac neurosis" (Wynn, 1967). In contrast, during the patient's stay in the coronary care unit the use of denial as a major coping mode is correlated with increased chances of survival (Hackett, Cassem, & Wishie, 1968). The situations one encounters when studying or teaching coping are usually less clear-cut, but it is worth keeping in mind that "giving up," if it is accompanied by maintenance of morale, can literally help the individual to live to fight another day (Klinger, 1975).

In contrast to the Western emphasis on confronting problems head on, many Eastern cultures place much greater value on the ability to bend with the wind, as in the Aesop fable of the oak and the reed. For instance, in discussing the much lower rate of coronary heart disease in Japan, compared to Western countries with an equivalent rate of industrialization, Matsumoto (1970) has suggested that Japanese social arrangements may account for this difference. In particular, he emphasizes the institutionalized ways in which workers can vent frustration and anger with their work situations, without any expectation or necessity that change will occur. It is possible that the distress observed by clinicians is as much the result of the person's belief that there is an obligation to resolve problems, as the inability to find satisfactory palliative coping strategies.

After examining the various dimensions on which coping adequacy can be rated, we are still left with the problem of integrating these separate ratings into a global judgment. We may have to accept the impossibility of the task and agree to live, as does the coping person, with a multidimensional rating scheme. To the degree that a unifying factor could override these disparate elements, it probably is expressed in the meaning which the person gives to the resolution of a specific coping episode in the context of general goals and values. Visotsky, Hamburg, Goss, and Lebovitz (1961) have defined truly functional coping as that which not only lessens the immediate impact of stress, but also allows the person to maintain some sense of self-worth and unity with the past and future, some overall meaning (Dimsdale, 1974; Frankl, 1963) on which the person can count.

The Competent Coping Person

One can safely assume that all people can cope adequately with at least some stressful transactions and that all people are likely to fail under some circumstances. We also tend to assume, and observation of family, friends and co-workers provides support for this, that people vary widely in the number and type of encounters they can competently handle. Beyond these categorical statements, however, we know remarkably little about the continuum of coping adequacy along which individuals range. The aim of clinical intervention is to develop competent coping persons, but even here the ideal has not been the subject of careful study.

The major reason for our limited knowledge of the individual who copes competently is the same as the one that has confronted us throughout this paper: We lack data on how nonclinical populations handle a variety of stressful transactions over time. Trait measures and typical studies of coping assume that people will use the same coping strategies regardless of the situation. Clinical studies of coping, in contrast, often center on the specific encounters with only passing mention, if any, of how the person copes with other ongoing stresses, or coped with previous ones. We don't know the degree to which competent coping is purely situation-specific, or the degree to which it constitutes a trait and, if so, the characteristics and correlates of this trait.

One issue of theoretical and clinical relevance concerns the relative advantages of broad vs. narrow repertoires of coping. Do people who perform in an above average fashion use one or two strategies in a particularly successful fashion, or are they likely to vary them within situations and across situations? Most of the data on this point come from rehabilitation literature tending to show that a narrowed repertoire of strategies produced by physical limitations need not be a barrier to above average competence. Helen Keller is a particularly illustrious example, but there are many other less well known handicapped people who, in Goffman's term (1963), have "professionalized their handicap" by serving as models of successful coping. Yet, according to Pearlin and Schooler (1978), "having a particular weapon in one's arsenal is less important than having a variety of weapons," reminding us that data based on clinical populations may not be generalizable to nonclinical populations.

Even the most highly developed repertoire of coping skills is useless unless the person is able to mobilize it when needed. Murphy (1974) has identified "the capacity to mobilize resources under stress, to be strained and yet still to be able to pull up extra energy" (p. 95) as one of the fundamental prerequisites of resilience. But there is no simple correspondence between level of resources, initiative and persistence in coping. One is frequently confronted by the paradox of people with apparently limited resources who manifest this "extra energy," while those with apparently far superior resources do not. Schwartz and Gottman (1976) have provided empirical support for this view with the finding that clients with apparently deficient social interactions often possessed the necessary social skills, but were unable or unwilling to use them when needed.

One factor that has received little attention, but which may play a significant role in coping is the value which the person attaches to a particular coping mode. We touched on this briefly in the discussion of instrumental vs. palliative coping. People may be reluctant to use palliative coping modes if they consider these less moral or valued, and therapists are apt to be equally reluctant to advise them to do so, even though palliation may be the most effective coping mode available in certain contexts. Similarly, subcultural groups within our society may refuse to use or be uncomfortable with strategies that do not conform to their standards of appropriate behavior. The sexual stereotypes of the dependent woman and the strong silent man have left their imprint in the reluctance of some women to use aggressive problem-solving skills, and some men to use social support. As we seek to understand and treat the coping strategies of different segments of the population, we will probably also have to explore the impact of values.

In discussing the values assigned to coping, we have moved from what the competent coping person does to what he or she thinks. The cognitive behavior therapists have highlighted the importance of the appraisal of one's own competence as a determinant of stress and how it is dealt with. It is not enough to possess the skills of a competent coping person; one must also believe one has them. This notion has been formalized in Bandura's (1977a) definition of self-efficacy:

> In this conceptual system, expectations of personal mastery affect both initiation and persistence of coping behavior. The strength of people's convictions in their own effectiveness is likely to affect whether they will even try to cope with given situations. At this initial level, perceived self-efficacy influences choice of behavioral settings. People fear and tend to avoid threatening situations they believe exceed their coping skills, whereas they get involved in activities and behave assuredly when they judge themselves capable of handling situations that would otherwise be intimidating.
>
> Not only can perceived self-efficacy have directive influence on choice of activities and settings, but, through expectations of eventual success, it can affect coping efforts once they are initiated. Efficacy expectations determine how much effort people will expend and how long they will persist in the face of obstacles and aversive experiences. The stronger the perceived self-efficacy, the more active the efforts. Those who persist in subjectively threatening activities that are in fact relatively safe will gain corrective experiences that reinforce their sense of efficacy, thereby eventually eliminating their defensive behavior. Those who cease their coping efforts prematurely will retain their self-debilitating expectations and fears for a long time (pp. 193-194).

The Teaching of Coping Skills

Methods of teaching coping skills explicitly constitute the unique contribution of the cognitive behavior therapists to the area of coping (Goldfried, 1977; Goldfried & Goldfried, 1975; Mahoney, 1974; Meichenbaum, 1974, 1977). Stress researchers have observed effective and ineffective coping in a wide variety of situations, but only the clinicians have sought to transform maladaptive coping strategies into more adaptive ones. Somewhat paradoxically, therefore, the clinicians have provided the main opportunities for the experimental manipulation of coping.

All psychotherapies seek to help the person feel more comfortable. What distinguishes the clinical teaching of coping skills is the attempt to go beyond this goal and, in addition, to help the person to function adequately despite discomfort. The aim of this type of training is not to attain an absence of conflict or a state of nirvana, or even socially acceptable behavior, but rather to increase competence in mastering stressful encounters and tolerating distress. For example, the ideal is not the student who takes the exam without experiencing any anxiety whatsoever, but the one who can control anxiety, and even harness it to improve performance.

Competence, as defined by the cognitive behavior therapists, is very close to Bandura's (1977 a, b) notion of self-efficacy. The client must not only possess the skills necessary to confront a given task but, equally crucial, possess the belief in his or her capacity to accomplish the task. This cognitive component is not simply a therapeutic version of positive thinking. Rather, the cognitions that facilitate coping are those which help the person recognize the difficulties in the situation, internal (My palms are sweating) as well as external (This exam is tough), but also facilitate proper attribution (It's pretty normal to be a bit aroused during an exam and this may actually help me to do better) and remedial action (Slow down, take a deep breath and make a plan for this essay). If psyching oneself constitutes a necessary part of the coping process, it does not constitute the whole. On the contrary, effective behavior is the major criterion of adequacy. All types of training procedures provide for *in vivo* practice in which clients test their skills in relatively simple situations and then move on to more difficult challenges and threats.

It is in the area of specific techniques rather than assumptions that one finds the greatest differences among the cognitive behavior therapists. Nevertheless, as Meichenbaum (1977) points out, there are certain common treatment components that underlie the many different coping-skills programs. The components include: (1) teaching the client the role of cognitions in producing the problem (e.g., derogatory thoughts about the way the encounter is handled); (2) training in the self-monitoring of maladaptive self-statements and behaviors; (3) training in the fundamentals of problem-solving (e.g., problem definition, anticipation of consequences, evaluating feedback); (4) modeling and rehearsal of effective self-statements, attention-focusing skills and positive self-evaluation; (5) training in specific coping skills such as relaxation and assertiveness, and (6) *in vivo* behavioral assignments that become increasingly demanding.

Such coping-skills training approaches have been successfully applied in a number of different problem areas (cf. Meichenbaum, 1977). These include speech anxiety (Meichenbaum, Gilmore, & Fedoravicius, 1971), test anxiety (Sarason, 1973), phobias (Meichenbaum & Cameron, 1972; Tori & Worell, 1973), anger (Novaco, 1975), social incompetence (Christensen, 1974; Glass, Gottman, & Shmurak, 1976; Kazdin, 1973; Shmurak, 1974), alcoholism (Sanchez-Craig, 1975, 1976), social withdrawal in children (Gottman, Gonso, & Rasmussen, 1974), and laboratory and clinical pain (Turk, 1975, 1976; Levendusky & Pankratz, 1975). Extensions of this approach to nonclinical populations are just beginning, but there are reports of training programs for surgical patients (Langer, Janis, & Wolpe, 1975), law enforcement officers (Novaco, in press), nurses making the transition from the school setting to the work one (Benner, 1974), and Type A managers (Roskies, Spevack, Surkis, Cohen, & Gilman, 1978).

Considering the fact that most of the work in this area has been done in the last ten years, the number of techniques developed and the variety of problems treated attest to a high degree of creative ferment. Moreover, in contrast to much clinical work, the therapeutic research on training in coping skills has been characterized by careful attention to design and a serious attempt to evaluate outcome (cf. Linehan, Goldfried, & Goldfried, 1977). To date, however, the work has been restricted to very specific target symptoms or problems, and whole areas of major life crisis or severe chronic stress have been largely untouched. As Meichenbaum (1977) tongue-in-cheek points out, the plural pronouns and phobias that constituted the favorite doctoral dissertation topics of the fifties and sixties have been replaced by assertion training in the seventies. Even within the limited areas treated, only beginning attempts to measure durability and generalizability of results (Glass et al., 1976; McFall & Twentyman, 1973; Meichenbaum & Cameron, 1973) exist. There have been few attempts to build in generalizability by developing coping strategies explicitly designed to be used in a broad range of contexts (e.g., D'Zurilla & Goldfried's work on problem-solving, 1971, and Suinn & Richardson's work on anxiety management, 1971), but the success of these efforts remains to be verified.

Building a Bridge between Coping Theorists and Those Who Teach Coping Clinically

In examining some of the key issues involved in understanding how coping is used to manage or minimize stress, we touched on the many similarities between the Lazarus model and the approach of the cognitive behavior therapists. Now we should like to close this discussion with a more systematic analysis of conceptual overlaps and divergences, and then to consider some theoretical and research needs common to both. Let us look first at the overlaps.

Overlaps in Approach

Most notable of the convergences between the two approaches is the joint emphasis on the central role of *cognitive processes* in stress transactions, both in shaping the person's emotional response to the situation and in determining the coping strategies that will be used to manage it. Ellis' (1962) analysis of dysfunctional emotional reactions makes the key role of cognition very clear, and all the cognitive behavior therapists discussed in this paper have been heavily influenced by this view. For Ellis, both the inappropriate emotional response and the maladaptive behavior depend on the person's faulty interpretation of a transaction, which, in turn, is derived from a system of irrational beliefs. The task of rational-emotive therapy is to get the individual to change such beliefs, thereby altering the interpretation (Lazarus' word for interpretation is appraisal) of stressful disorders. Thus, belief systems exert their influence by shaping cognitive appraisal, and emotion is a response to this appraisal. This shared view of the fundamental importance of interpretation or appraisal constitutes a natural bridge between the cognitive behavior therapists and the cognitive theorists of emotions, as exemplified by the similarities in the formulations of Beck (1976) and Lazarus.

A second similarity in outlook is the joint emphasis on *coping* or stress management, rather than on the stressful situation itself. As we have seen in the Lazarus scheme, coping plays as important a role in determining the stress response as does the stimulus itself. The cognitive behavior therapists also place the main emphasis on coping, and use it as the point of intervention in their handling of stress-related disorders. In their treatment scheme, the client not only needs to modify his or her appraisal of a given person-environment relationship, but also to learn to manage it more effectively, for example, by expressing his or her needs to others more clearly and forcefully, by becoming a better interpreter of others' needs, by controlling exaggerated or inappropriate emotional responses, and by tolerating a certain level of distress and ambiguity.

Third, both approaches share a common concern with *process* or dynamics as opposed to structure or traits. Clinicians have traditionally sought to understand the problem or symptom for which the client seeks help by examining concrete examples of what the person actually does, feels or thinks in a specific situation. To better understand the behavior in the specific situation, the therapist will broaden his or her inquiry to include more general personality characteristics, needs and values, but the emphasis remains on how these evolve and shift in the course of a constantly changing person-environment transaction. It is this focus on the fluid elements in human behavior, rather than on that which is fixed, that provides the ideological basis for using therapeutic intervention to help the person purposefully change in a growth-enhancing way.

Fourth, and related closely to the above, is a joint emphasis on *intra-individual* as opposed to inter-individual comparisons. By intra-individual comparison, we mean the study of the same individual as he or she manifests multiple facets of personality in a variety of settings. This, of course, is the way clinicians traditionally function. Researchers using this approach speak of it as an ipsative or ipsative-normative view, as opposed to a strictly normative one (Broverman, 1962; Lazarus, in press; Lazarus & Cohen, 1976; Marceil, 1977). Much of coping research has been of the purely normative type, but Lazarus and his associates have consistently emphasized the need to supplement this knowledge by detailed study of how the same people concurrently and consecutively manage a series of chronic, intermittent and acute stresses. It is important to understand not only similarities and differences in coping between people, but also within the same person across situations and over time.

Fifth, the two approaches share the belief that coping involves both what people think and do in stressful transactions, rather than merely what they do. The coping theorist is interested in the way changes in self-statements reflect the person's reappraisal of his or her situation as feedback comes both from the evolving person-environment transaction and from the intrapsychic adjustments (e.g., denial, avoidance, intellectual detachment) used to regulate the emotion. The clinician, in addition, actively seeks to produce changes in faulty or stereotyped self-statements (cf. Meichenbaum, 1977). Both agree that what people *say to themselves* is an essential component of the way they manage stressful situations.

Sixth, there is agreement that both exogenous *and* endogenous factors are involved in problems of adaptation. To reach this common meeting ground, the coping theorists and the clinicians have each had to abandon the extreme intrapsychic and extreme environmentalist positions that at times have characterized their respective fields. The early Holmes and Rahe work and the psychosomatic theories of Dunbar and Alexander are examples of the environmental and intrapsychic poles, respectively, in stress research, while operant conditioning in the strict Skinnerian sense and orthodox Freudian analysis represent their therapeutic equivalents. In contrast to these extremes, we think the best approaches in the stress field and in the clinical world attempt to integrate both the vulnerability of the individual and the provocative role of the social environment as determinants of dysfunctional responses. The transactional perspective recently used by Coyne (1976 a, b) in his work on depression is a case in point. Researchers and clinicians seem increasingly ready to deal with both inner and outer forces, and this is an exciting prospect.

Divergences in Approach

The major divergences, as we see them, stem from differences in the immediate objectives of therapists and theoreticians-researchers. Therapists must center their attention on treating the specific person who is seeking help, and this focus on the individual makes it difficult to build general principles. The stress researcher, in contrast, uses paradigms designed to establish general principles, but often settles for a superficial rather than in-depth categorization of the individuals composing the population under study. Both would benefit from the blending of their respective styles into an ipsative-normative approach, and both can make substantial contributions to the development of this approach. Clinical in-depth methods of interview and observation permit the detailed analysis of coping process, while the experimental tradition provides the sampling techniques and the systematization of procedures and analyses that are often absent in the clinical setting.

The second major difference is the range of coping behaviors which each observes. Clinicians, by the very nature of their work, deal exclusively with self-referred or other-referred failures in coping. The result is that they must teach "normal" coping without really knowing very much about how, and how adequately, most people in the community actually cope. Researchers, in contrast, are more likely to observe adequate or optimal functioning, but may lack the clinician's opportunities to study maladaptive coping in depth and to explore its responsiveness to therapeutic intervention. For a comprehensive understanding of coping, we must observe the full range of coping failures and coping successes.

Theoretical and Research Needs Common to Both

The clinical work on teaching coping skills raises the exciting possibility of not only being able to explain and predict outcome, but of also being in a position to improve it. Therapeutic interventions that can change maladaptive coping strategies into effective ones may prove to be the most powerful clinical tool yet devised for treating and even preventing stress-related disorders. In order to fulfill this promise, however, the clinicians must grapple with the same unresolved questions that currently confront researchers.

We see three major needs at the present time. First we must have a system of describing, measuring and evaluating coping. The necessity for developing these measures is obvious on the research side, but we believe that they would also benefit the clinician. In clinical work, the person must be compared with him or herself from one time to another (say, before and after therapy), and across encounters so that we can tell in what contexts he or she is doing well or poorly. There is no substitute for a classificatory scheme, both to measure and compare persons and situations as to patterns of coping, and to measure and compare coping adequacy. One of the major objectives of our research at Berkeley is to develop methods of describing coping and to relate these descriptions to adaptational outcome. Progress in this area would help us in testing both theoretical concepts and treatment techniques.

Second, we need to know more about the development of coping strategies, especially how ineffective and effective patterns arise and are changed. As implied above, we do not know much about which patterns work or fail, in what ways, under what conditions, with what costs and in what kind of persons. Although these may be identified as basic research questions, they also relate very closely to the practical concerns of treatment. Without answers to such questions, our attempts to help people cope better will always remain at the level of stumbling in the dark.

Third, we need treatment paradigms that recognize the important role of individual variations in commitments, values, styles of thinking and living, belief systems, and special hidden agendas. From the coping theorist's standpoint, it seems unlikely that the same patterns of coping can be successfully used by everyone. Limitations are set by the environmental conditions of life and by personality variations. To date, the cognitive behavior therapists have largely avoided this problem in their therapy research studies (though probably not in their clinical practices) by all too often restricting samples to homogeneous groups of college students. As Mahoney (1977) has recently pointed out, however, clinical responsibilities go beyond snake phobics and unassertive college sophomores. If the clinical work on teaching coping skills is to avoid sterility and triviality, it must develop principles of treatment broad enough to encompass many different kinds of people confronting many different kinds of stress situations. Clinical work provides a fertile ground for observing these variations and developing hunches to be tested; the research approach is needed to test these hunches in a systematic manner.

In describing these unmet needs in coping theory and practice, our intention is not to prove the superiority of one approach over the other. On the contrary, the major thrust of this paper has been to show how both the theoreticians and clinicians have contributed to our current understanding of coping and how each group individually possesses *some* of the concepts and techniques that will permit us to advance this knowledge further. Even more important, we believe that many of the unresolved questions are of vital concern to both and may best be resolved by combining procedures derived from each. The potential for collaboration need not remain merely a pious hope. Little more than terminology and separate journals keep theoreticians and teachers of coping apart. Surely, we can learn to cope effectively with these relatively minor obstacles to cross-fertilization.

REFERENCES

Aldrich, C. K., & Mendkoff, E.: Relocation of the aged and disabled: A mortality study. *Journal of the American Geriatric Society,* 1963, *11,* 185-194.

Antonovsky, A., Maoz, B., Dowty, N., & Wijsenbeek, H.: Twenty-five years later. *Social Psychiatry,* 1971, *6,* 186-193.

Baker, G. W., & Chapman, D. W. (Eds.): *Man and society in disaster.* New York: Basic Books, 1962.

BANDURA, A.: Self-efficacy: Toward a unifying theory of behavioral change. *Psychological Review,* 1977, *84,* 191-215. (a)

BANDURA, A.: *Social learning theory.* Englewood Cliffs, N.J.: Prentice-Hall, 1977. (b)

BECK, A.: *Cognitive therapy and emotional disorders.* New York: International Universities Press, 1976.

BENNER, P.: Reality testing a reality shock program. In M. Kramer (Ed.), *Reality shock: Why nurses leave nursing.* St. Louis: C. V. Mosby, 1974, pp. 191-215.

BERKMAN, L.: Social networks, host resistance and mortality: A follow-up study of Alameda County residentsm Unpubli hed doctoral dissertation, School of Public Health, University of California, Berkeley, 1977.

BETTELHEIM, B.: *The informed heart.* New York: The Free Press of Glencoe, 1960.

BLOOM, J. R.: Social support, coping and adjustment to mastectomy. Paper presented at the International Congress on Cancer, Buenos Aires, Argentina, October, 1978.

BOURNE, P. G., COLI, W. M., & DATEL, W. E.: Anxiety levels of six helicopter ambulance medics in a combat zone. *Psychological Reports,* 1966, *19,* 821-822.

BOWLBY, J.: Process of mourning. *International Journal of Psychoanalysis,* 1961, *42,* 317-340.

BROVERMAN, D. M.: Normative and ipsative measurement in psychology. *Psychological Review,* 1962, *69,* 295-305.

BRUHN, J. G.: An epidemiological study of myocardial infarction in an Italian-American community. *Journal of Chronic Disease,* 1965, *18,* 353-365.

BRUHN, J. G., & WOLF, S.: Update on Roseto, PA: Testing a Prediction. Paper prepared for the annual meeting of the American Psychosomatic Society, Washington, D.C., March 31-April 2, 1978.

CASSEL, J.: The contribution of the social environment to host resistance. *American Journal of Epidemiology,* 1976, *104,* 107-123.

CHRISTENSEN, C.: *Development and field testing of an interpersonal coping skills program.* Toronto: Ontario Institute for Studies in Education, 1974.

COBB, S.: Social support as a moderator of life stresses. *Psychosomatic Medicine,* 1976, *38,* 300-314.

COELHO, G. V., HAMBURG, D. A., & ADAMS, J. E. (Eds.): *Coping and adaptation.* New York: Basic Books, 1974.

COHEN, F., & LAZARUS, R. S.: Active coping processes, coping dispositions and recovery from surgery. *Psychosomatic medicine,* 1973, *35,* 375-389.

COYNE, J. C.: Depression and the response of others. *Journal of Abnormal Psychology,* 1976, *85,* 186-193. (a)

COYNE, J. C.: Towards an interactional description of depression. *Psychiatry,* 1976, *39,* 28-40. (b)

DAVIS, F.: *Progress through polio.* Indianapolis: Bobbs-Merrill, 1963.

DEMBROSKI, T. M., MACDOUGALL, J. M., & SHIELDS, J. L.: Physiologic reactions to social challenge in persons evidencing the Type A coronary-prone behavior pattern. *Journal of Human Stress,* 1977, 3 (No. 3), 2-9.

DIMSDALE, J. E.: The coping behavior of Nazi concentration camp survivors. *American Journal of Psychiatry,* 1974, *131,* 792-797.

D'ZURILLA, T. J., & GOLDFRIED, M. R.: Problem solving and behavior modification. *Journal of Abnormal Psychology,* 1971, *78,* 107-126.

ELLIS, A.: *Reason and emotion in psychotherapy.* New York: Lyle Stuart, 1962.

FOLKINS, C. H.: Temporal factors and the cognitive mediators of stress reaction. *Journal of Personality and Social Psychology,* 1970, *14,* 173-184.

FOLKMAN, S., SCHAEFER, C., & LAZARUS, R. S.: Cognitive processes as mediators of stress and coping. In V. Hamilton and D. M. Warburton (Eds.), *Human stress and cognition: An information-processing approach.* London: Wiley, in press.

FRANKENHAEUSER, M., & KAREBY, S.: Effect of meprobamate on catecholamine excretion during mental stress. *Perceptual and Motor Skills,* 1962, *15,* 571-577.

FRANKENHAEUSER, M., & PATKAI, P.: Catecholamine excretion and performance during stress. *Perceptual and Motor Skills,* 1964, *19,* 13-14.

FRANKL, V.: *Man's search for meaning.* New York: Washington Square Press, 1963.

FRIEDMAN, M., BYERS, S. D., DIAMANT, J., & ROSENMAN, R. H.: Plasma catecholamine response of coronary-prone subjects (Type A) to a specific challenge. *Metabolism,* 1975, *24,* 205-210.

FRIEDMAN, S. B., CHODOFF, P., MASON, J. W., & HAMBURG, D. A.: Behavioral observations on parents anticipating the death of a child. *Pediatrics,* 1963, *32,* 610-625.

FUNKENSTEIN, D. H., KING, S. H., & DROLETTE, M. E.: *Mastery of stress.* Cambridge, Mass.: Harvard University Press, 1956.

FURER, M., & HARDY, J. D.: The reaction to pain as determined by the galvanic skin response. *Proceedings of the Association for Research in Nervous Diseases,* 1950, *29,* 72-89.

GLASS, C., GOTTMAN, J. M., & SHMURAK, S. H.: Response acquisition and cognitive self-statement modification approaches to dating skills. *Journal of Counseling Psychology,* 1976, *23,* 520-526.

GLASS, D. C.: *Behavior patterns, stress and coronary disease.* Hillsdale, N.J.: Erlbaum, 1977.

GOFFMAN, E.: *Stigma: Notes on the management of spoiled identity.* Englewood Cliffs, N.J.: Prentice-Hall, 1963.

GOLDFRIED, M. R.: Taking stock of behavior therapy for better or worse. Paper presented at the annual meeting of the American Psychological Association, Washington, D.C., September, 1976.

GOLDFRIED, M. R.: The use of relaxation and cognitive relabeling as coping skills. In R. B. Stuart (Ed.), *Behavioral self-management: Strategies, techniques and outcome.* New York: Brunner/Mazel, 1977, pp. 82-116.

GOLDFRIED, M. R., & GOLDFRIED, A. P.: Cognitive change methods. In F. H. Kanfer & A. P. Goldstein (Eds.), *Helping people change.* New York: Pergamon, 1975, pp. 89-116.

GOTTMAN, J., GONSO, J., & RASMUSSEN, B.: Social interaction, social competence, and friendship in children. Unpublished manuscript, Indiana University, 1974.

GRINKER, R. R., & SPIEGEL, J. P.: *Men under stress.* New York: McGraw-Hill, 1945.

HAAN, N.: A tripartite model of ego functioning values and clinical research applications. *Journal of Nervous and Mental Disease,* 1969, *148,* 14-30.

HAAN, N.: *Coping and defending: Processes of self-environment organization.* New York: Academic Press, 1977.

HACKETT, T. P., & CASSEM, N. H.: Psychological management of the myocardial infarction patient. *Journal of Human Stress,* 1975, 1 (No. 3), 25-38.

HACKETT, T. P., CASSEM, N. H., & WISHIE, H. A.: The coronary-care unit: An appraisal of its psychologic hazards. *New England Journal of Medicine,* 1968, *279,* 1365-1370.

HAMBURG, D. A., & ADAMS, J. E.: A perspective on coping: Seeking and utilizing information in major transitions. *Archives of General Psychiatry,* 1967, *17,* 277-284.

HENNIG, M., & JARDIN, A.: *The managerial woman.* New York: Doubleday, 1977.

HOROWITZ, M. J.: *Stress response syndromes.* New York: Aronson, 1976.

HOUSE, J. S., & JACKMAN, M. F.: Occupational stress and health. In P. Ahmed & G. Coelho (Eds.), *Toward a new definition of health: Psychosocial dimensions.* New York: Plenum Medical Book Co., in press.

HOWARD, J. H., CUNNINGHAM, D. A. & RECHNITZER, P. A.: Work patterns associated with Type A behavior: A managerial population. *Human Relations,* 1977, *30,* 825-836.

JANIS, I. L.: *Air war and emotional stress.* New York: McGraw-Hill, 1951.

KAPLAN, B. H., CASSEL, J. C., & GORE, S.: Social support and health. Paper presented at the American Public Health Association Meetings, San Francisco, November 9, 1973.

KASL, S. V., GORE, S., & COBB, S.: The experience of losing a job: Reported changes in health, symptoms and illness behavior. *Psychosomatic Medicine,* 1975, *37,* 106-122.

KATZ, J. L., WEINER, H., GALLAGHER, T. G., & HELLMAN, L.: Stress, distress and ego defenses. *Archives of General Psychiatry,* 1970, *23,* 131-142.

KAZDIN, A.: Covert modeling and the reduction of avoidance behavior. *Journal of Abnormal Psychology,* 1973, *81,* 87-95.

KLINGER, E.: Consequences of commitment to and disengagement from incentives. *Psychological Review,* 1975, 82, 1-25.

LANGER, E., JANIS, I., & WOLPE, J.: Reduction of psychological stress in surgical patients. *Journal of Experimental Social Psychology,* 1975, *11,* 155-165.

LAZARUS, R. S.: *Psychological stress and the coping process.* New York: McGraw-Hill, 1966.

LAZARUS, R. S.: The self-regulation of emotion. In L. Levi (Ed.). *Emotions: Their parameters and measurement.* New York: Raven Press, 1975, pp. 47-67.

LAZARUS, R. S.: *Patterns of adjustment* (3rd ed.). New York: McGraw-Hill, 1976.

LAZARUS, R. S.: Research strategy for the study of psychological and social factors in hypertension. *Journal of Human Stress,* in press.

LAZARUS, R. S., AVERILL, J. R., & OPTON, E. M., JR.: Toward a cognitive theory of emotion. In M. Arnold (Ed.), *Feelings and emotion.* New York: Academic Press, 1970, pp. 207-232.

LAZARUS, R. S., & COHEN, J. B.: The study of stress and coping in aging. Paper presented at the 5th WHO Conference on Society, Stress and Disease: Aging and Old Age, Stockholm, Sweden, June 14-19, 1976.

LAZARUS, R. S., COHEN, J. B., FOLKMAN, S., KANNER, A., & SCHAEFER, C.: Psychological stress and adaptation: Some unresolved issues. In H. Selye (Ed.), *Guide to stress research.* New York: McGraw-Hill, in press.

LAZARUS, R. S., DEESE, J., & OSLER, S. F.: The effects of psychological stress upon performance. *Psychological Bulletin,* 1952, *49,* 293-317.

LAZARUS, R. S., & LAUNIER, R.: Stress-related transactions between person and environment. In L. A. Pervin & M. Lewis (Eds.), *Perspectives in interactional psychology.* New York: Plenum, in press.

LAZARUS, R. S., SPEISMAN, J. C., MORDKOFF, A. M., & DAVISON, L. A.: A laboratory study of psychological stress produced by a motion picture film. *Psychological Monographs,* 1962, 76:34 (Whole No. 553).

LEVENDUSKY, P., & PANKRATZ, L.: Self-control techniques as an alternative to pain medication. *Journal of Abnormal Psychology,* 1975, *84,* 165-169.

LEVI, L.: The urinary output of adrenalin and noradrenalin during pleasant and unpleasant emotional states: A preliminary report. *Psychosomatic Medicine,* 1965, *27,* 80-85.

LEVI, L.: Stress and distress in response to psychosocial stimuli. *Acta Medica Scandinavia,* 1972, 191, Suppl. 528.

LEVINSON, D. J.: *The seasons of a man's life.* New York: Knopf, 1978.

LEVINSON, D. J., DARROW, C. M., KLEIN, E. B., LEVINSON, M. H., & MCKEE, B.: The psychosocial development of men in early adulthood and mid-life transition. In D. F. Ricks, A. Thomas, & M. Roff (Eds.), *Life history research in psychopathology,* Vol. 3. Minneapolis: University of Minnesota Press, 1974, pp. 243-259.

LIEBERMAN, M. A.: Adaptive processes in later life. In N. Datan & H. W. Reese (Eds.), *Life-span developmental psychology.* New York: Academic Press, 1977, pp. 135-159.

LINDEMANN, E.: Symptomatology and management of acute grief. *American Journal of Psychiatry,* 1944, 101, 141-148.

LINEHAN, M. M., GOLDFRIED, M. R., & GOLDFRIED, A. P. Assertion therapy: Skill training or cognitive restructuring. Unpublished manuscript, 1977.

LOWENTHAL, M. F., THURNHER, M., & CHIRIBOGA, D. *Four stages of life.* San Francisco: Jossey-Bass, 1975.

MAHL, G. F.: Anxiety, HCL secretion and peptic ulcer etiology. *Psychosomatic Medicine,* 1949, *11,* 30-44.

MAHONEY, M.: *Cognitive and behavior modification.* Cambridge, Mass.: Ballinger, 1974.

MAHONEY, M.: Cognitive therapy and research: A question of questions. *Cognitive Therapy and Research,* 1977, *1,* 5-17.

MARCEIL, J. C.: Implicit dimensions of idiography and nomothesis: A reformulation. *American Psychologist,* 1977, *32,* 1046-1055.

MARX, M. B., GARRITY, T. F., & SOMES, G. W.: The effect of imbalance in life satisfactions and frustration upon illness behavior in college students. *Journal of Psychosomatic*

Research, 1977, 21, 423-429.

MATSUMOTO, Y. S.: Social stress and coronary heart disease in Japan: A hypothesis. *Milbank Memorial Fund Quarterly,* 1970, *48,* 9-36.

McFALL, R. M., & TWENTYMAN, C. T.: Four experiments on the relative contributions of rehearsal, modeling and coaching to assertion training. *Journal of Abnormal Psychology,* 1973, *81,* 199-218.

MEICHENBAUM, D.: *Cognitive behavior modification.* Morristown, N.J.: General Learning Press, 1974.

MEICHENBAUM, D.: *Cognitive behavior modification: An integrative approach.* New York: Plenum, 1977.

MEICHENBAUM, D., & CAMERON, R.: An examination of cognitive and contingency variables in anxiety relief procedures. Unpublished manuscript, University of Waterloo, 1972.

MEICHENBAUM, D., & CAMERON, R.: Training schizophrenics to talk to themselves: A means of developing attentional controls. *Behavior Therapy,* 1973, *4,* 515-534.

MEICHENBAUM, D., GILMORE, B., & FEDORAVICIUS, A.: Group insight vs. group desensitization in treating speech anxiety. *Journal of Consulting and Clinical Psychology,* 1971, *36,* 410-421.

MENNINGER, K.: Regulatory devices of the ego under major stress. *International Journal of Psychoanalysis,* 1954, 35, 412-420.

METTLIN, C.: Occupational careers and the prevalence of coronary-prone behavior. *Social Science and Medicine,* 1976, 10, 367-373.

MOOS, R. H.: Psychological techniques in the assessment of adaptive behavior. In G. V. Coelho, D. A. Hamburg, & J. E. Adams (Eds.), *Coping and adaptation.* New York: Basic Books, 1974, pp. 334-399.

MURPHY, L. B.: Coping, vulnerability and resilience in childhood. In G. V. Coelho, D. A. Hamburg, & J. E. Adams (Eds.), *Coping and adaptation.* New York: Basic Books, 1974, pp. 69-101.

MURPHY, L. B., & MORIARTY, A. E.: *Vulnerability, coping and growth.* New Haven: Yale University Press, 1976.

NOVACO, R. W.: *Anger control: The development and evaluation of an experimental treatment.* Lexington, Mass.: Heath, 1975.

NOVACO, R. W.: Stress inoculation: A cognitive therapy for anger and its application to a case of depression. *Journal of Consulting and Clinical Psychology,* 1977, *45,* 600-608.

NOVACO, R.: A stress-inoculation approach to anger management in the training of law enforcement officers. *American Journal of Community Psychology,* in press.

NUCKOLLS, K. B., CASSEL, J., & KAPLAN, B. H.: Psychosocial assets, life crisis and the prognosis of pregnancy. *American Journal of Epidemiology,* 1972, *95,* 431-441.

OSTFELD, A. M.: The interaction of biological and social variables in cardiovascular disease. *Milbank Memorial Fund Quarterly,* 1967, *45,* 13-18.

PARSONS, T.: Definitions of health and illness in the light of American values and social structures. In E. G. Jaco (Ed.), *Patients, physicians and illness.* Glencoe, Ill.: The Free Press, 1958, pp. 165-188.

PEARLIN, L. I., & Schooler, C.: The structure of coping. *Journal of Health and Social Behavior,* 1978, *19,* 2-21.

READ, P. P.: *Alive.* New York: Avon, 1975.

ROSENMAN, R. H., JENKINS, C. D., BRAND, R. J., FRIEDMAN, M., STRAUS, R., & WURM, M.: Coronary heart disease in the Western Collaborative Group Study: Final follow-up experience of 8½ years. *Journal of the American Medical Association,* 1975, *233,* 872-877.

ROSKIES, E.: *Abnormality and normality: The mothering of thalidomide children.* Ithaca: Cornell University Press, 1972.

ROSKIES, E., SPEVACK, M., SURKIS, A., COHEN, C., & GILMAN, S.: Changing the coronary-prone (Type A) behavior pattern in a non-clinical population. *Journal of Behavioral Medicine,* 1978, 1, 201-217.

SANCHEZ-CRAIG, M.: A self-control strategy for drinking tendencies. *Ontario Psychologist,*

1975, 7, 25-29.

SANCHEZ-CRAIG, M.: Cognitive and behavioral coping strategies in the reappraisal of stressful social situations. *Journal of Counseling Psychology,* 1976, *23,* 7-12.

SARASON, I.: Text anxiety and cognitive modeling. *Journal of Personality and Social Psychology,* 1973, *28,* 58-61.

SCHWARTZ, R. M., & GOTTMAN, J. M.: Toward a task analysis of assertive behavior. *Journal of Counseling and Clinical Psychology,* 1976, *44,* 910-920.

SELYE, H.: *The physiology and pathology of exposure to stress.* Montreal: Acta, 1950.

SELYE, H.: *Stress without distress.* Philadelphia: Lippincott, 1974.

SCHMURAK, S.: Design and evaluation of three dating behavior training programs utilizing response acquisition and cognitive self-statement modification techniques. Unpublished doctoral dissertation, Indiana University, 1974.

SILBER, E., COELHO, G. V., MURPHY, E. B., HAMBURG, D. A., PEARLIN, L. I., & ROSENBERG, M.: Competent adolescents coping with college decision. *Archives of General Psychiatry,* 1961, *5,* 517-527. (a)

SILBER, E., HAMBURG, D. A., COELHO, G. V., MURPHY, E. B., ROSENBERG, M., & PEARLIN, L. I.: Adaptive behavior in competent adolescents. *Archives of General Psychiatry,* 1961, 5, 354-365. (b)

SUINN, R. M., BROCK, L., & EDIE, C. A.: Letters to the Editor: Behavior therapy for Type A patients. *American Journal of Cardiology,* 1975, 36, 269.

SUINN, R. M., & RICHARDSON, F.: Anxiety management training: A nonspecific behavior therapy program for anxiety control. *Behavior Therapy,* 1971, 2, 498-510.

SYME, S. L.: Psychosocial determinants of hypertension. Paper presented at Hahnemann College's Fifth International Symposium on Hypertension, San Juan, Puerto Rico, January 9-12, 1977.

TOFFLER, A.: *Future shock.* New York: Random House, 1970.

TORI, C., & WORELL, L.: Reduction of human avoidant behavior: A comparison of counterconditioning, expectancy and cognitive information approaches. *Journal of Consulting and Clinical Psychology,* 1973, 41, 269-278.

TURK, D.: Cognitive control of pain: A skills training approach for the treatment of pain. Unpublished Master's thesis, University of Waterloo, 1975.

TURK, D.: An expanded skills training approach for the treatment of experimentally induced pain. Unpublished doctoral dissertation, University of Waterloo, 1976.

VAILLANT, G.: *Adaptation to life.* Boston: Little, Brown, 1977.

VISOTSKY, H. M., HAMBURG, D. A., GOSS, M. E., & LEBOVITZ, B. Z.: Coping behavior under extreme stress. *Archives of General Psychiatry,* 1961, 5, 423-443.

VON KUGELGEN, E.: Psychological determinants of the delay in decision to seek aid in cases of myocardial infarction. Unpublished doctoral dissertation, University of California, Berkeley, 1975.

WEISMAN, A. D., and WORDEN, J. W.: Psychosocial analysis of cancer deaths. *Omega: Journal of Death and Dying,* 1975, 6, 61-75.

WHITE, R. W.: Strategies of adaptation: An attempt at systematic description. In G. V. Coelho, D. A. Hamburg, & J. E. Adams (Eds.), *Coping and adaptation.* New York: Basic Books, 1974, pp. 47-68.

WYNN, A.: Unwarranted emotional distress in men with ischaemic heart disease. *Medical Journal of Australia,* 1967, 2, 847-851.

3

Urinary pH and the Psychology of Nicotine Addiction

STANLEY SCHACHTER

There was a time when graduate students in clinical psychology at the University of Minnesota were required to take a course in neuroanatomy. Since this was a course designed for graduate students in physiology and medical students, the psychologists were barely prepared for the material, worked like dogs, moaned and groaned about it and generally did miserably. Like it or not, though, generations of Minnesota clinicians took this year of neuroanatomy. Since the department at that time was known for its work in clinical psychometrics and was also more than sympathetic to the principles of operant psychology, I, as a new faculty member at Minnesota, never quite understood what this biological requirement was all about. I finally decided that Paul Meehl and Stark Hathaway had a suspicion that sooner or later it was all going to turn out that schizophrenia and anxiety neurosis had nothing to do with Mamma or with impoverished environments or psychodynamic complexities but would all be due to some unpronounceable chemical which was either in excess or in deficiency at some inaccessible spot in the brain. And, I suspect that Meehl and Hathaway simply wanted to be sure that their students could, at least, understand what had wiped them out even if they could do nothing about it.

I am indebted to Julian Hochberg and to Don Hood for their critical reading of this paper.

I don't think that the clinicians are alone in their forebodings, for this biological "boogie man" is probably an occasional nightmare visitor to most of us, particularly those who work with patients or who work on a class of "real" phenomena such as eating or drinking or mood states. On the one hand when one is in a super-psychological state of mind, I suppose that one tends to say to oneself, "Of course it's biological. What isn't and so what? This biological machine operates in an unpredictable environment and unless you know how the stimulus field is perceived and interacts with the individual's learning history you'll be able to predict nothing but trivia even from an exquisite knowledge of the machinery." On the other hand, when you're immersed in stimulus control or cognitive structures or psychodynamics and find that with all of this intellectual baggage you've been able to cure nothing, if that's your concern or, if you prefer experiments, that the best you've done is account for 20% of the variance, I think you incline to despair and conclude that it's all some lousy chemical in some pulpy, fleshy, slimy place.

The Minnesota clinicians' uncertainties highlight one of the peculiarities of the field. The psychologist's subject is a machine, a biological machine of guts and glands and fluids; yet the psychologist's explanatory systems and theories by and large have little, if anything, to do with the machinery. Certainly few of the dominant conceptual schemes in the field, whether learning theory or psychoanalysis or theories of cognitive functioning, pay more than lip service to the machinery proper. Given the current state of biological knowledge as it relates to most aspects of behavior, this state of affairs is probably both inevitable and desirable. It would be preposterous and pretentious to attempt to understand a political attitude or the course of a love affair or a sociometric choice in biological terms.

Eventually, perhaps, in some encyclopedic utopia, even such matters will be reducible to biological terms, but for now clearly we are more likely to achieve understanding, insight and useful predictions on such subjects by forgetting biology entirely. Despite these truisms, however, it shall be the contention of this paper that for certain sharply delimited subjects matters, this utopian future is imminent and that for such subject matters, the continued use of purely psychological explanatory concepts is erroneous and misleading and can lead to the complete misunderstanding of a phenomenon.

I shall attempt to document this contention by considering cigarette smoking—a behavior that almost everyone would agree involves both biological and psychological components. On the one hand, the smoker is a junkie. He's hooked, addicted—whatever those words mean physiologically, he's got it. Some place, there is some set of cells that, when depleted, initiates signals to smoke.

On the other hand, almost any smoker can convince you and himself that there are major psychological components to smoking. They will convince you that smoking calms them, that they smoke more when they're anxious; that smoking helps them work; that they smoke more at a party and so on. In short, smoking serves some psychological function; it does something positive for the smoker and this is the reason he smokes. This emphasis on the functional properties of smoking is at the heart of virtually every serious psychological attempt to understand smoking. Presumably nicotine or tar or some component of the act of smoking is so gratifying that despite the well-publicized dangers the smoker is unwilling or unable to give up the habit. Undoubtedly the ultimate eulogy of the act is Marcovitz's (1969) suggestion that "as a psychological phenomenon, smoking is comparable to the ritual of the Eucharist. There the communicant incorporates bread and wine and in so doing symbolically introjects the Lord Jesus Christ. This is a conscious process, with the hope of identification, of attaining some of the attributes of Jesus. Similarly, the smoker incorporates the smoke introjecting in an unconscious fantasy some object which will confer on him its magic powers" (p. 1082). Among these magic powers, smoking serves to "delimit the body image in the quest for the sense of self," to "relieve the unconscious fear of suffocation" and as "proof of immortality." Though no one has matched Marcovitz's panegyric, almost all attempts to account for the habit have assumed that it does something positive for the smoker. And this is an assumption that is shared by the smoker himself, for questionnaire study after study (e.g. Coan, 1973; McKennell, 1973; Tomkins, 1968) indicates that heavy smokers report that cigarettes relax them or stimulate them, put them at ease, give them something to do with their hands, and so on. In short, for both the psychologist and the smoker, the act of smoking is functional; it does something for the smoker and this is the reason he smokes. In this paper, I shall concentrate on just one of the presumed motivations for smoking. Smokers widely report that they smoke more when they are tense, anxious or upset and they also report that smoking calms them. Smoking, then, serves a respectable psychological function and this presumably is one of the motivations for and explanations of smoking under stress.

Before worrying about interpretations of these facts, let us make sure that they are facts. First, does smoking increase with stress? The available evidence indicates that indeed it does, if the stress is fairly intense. In two almost identical experiments, Schachter, Silverstein, Kozlowski, Herman and Liebling (1977) and Schachter, Silverstein and Perlick (1977) manipulated stress within the context of experiments presumably designed to measure tactile sensitivity. In high stress conditions, such sensitivity was measured by the administration, sporadically over an experimental hour, of a series of intense, quite painful shocks. In low stress conditions, the shocks were a barely perceptible tingle. Between the testing intervals, the subjects, all smokers, were free to smoke or not as they pleased. In both studies, the subjects do smoke considerably more in high than in low stress conditions. This effect may be limited to fairly intense stressors, for Glad and Adesso (1976) found no effects on smoking when they attempted to manipulate anxiety by giving subjects the impression that their opinions of X-rated films were about to be evaluated.

Turning to the effects of smoking on stress, we ask next, does smoking reduce stress? The answer appears to be that it depends upon how you look at it. Silverstein (1976), in a modification of an experiment designed by Nesbitt (1973), attempted to answer the question by measuring how much electric shock a subject was willing to take within the context of a study of tactile perception. The procedure required that electrodes be attached to a subject's fingers, that he be exposed to a series of shocks of gradually increasing voltage and that he report when he could first feel the shock, next when the shock first became painful and finally when the shock became so painful that he could no longer bear it. Silverstein assumes that the more anxious and tense the subject, the less pain he will be willing to tolerate. There were four experimental groups—smokers who smoked either high or low nicotine cigarettes during the experiment or who did not smoke at all during this time and a group of non-smokers who did not smoke.

The results of this experiment are presented in Figure 1. The ordinate plots the number of shocks the subjects endured before calling it quits. It is clear that smokers take more shocks when they are smoking high nicotine than when smoking low nicotine cigarettes than when not smoking. Given this pattern one has a choice of interpretations: either nicotine decreases anxiety or lack of nicotine increases anxiety. The choice depends, of course, on the position of the group of non-smokers who, as can be seen in the figure, take virtually the same number of shocks as smokers on high nicotine. It would appear then that smoking is not anxiety reducing but, rather, that no smoking or insufficient nicotine is, for the heavy smoker, anxiety increasing.*

Precisely the same pattern of results emerges in a study of irritability

---

*In the Nesbitt (1973) study, non-smokers also took significantly more shocks than did deprived smokers but, unlike Silverstein's findings, the non-smokers took fewer shocks

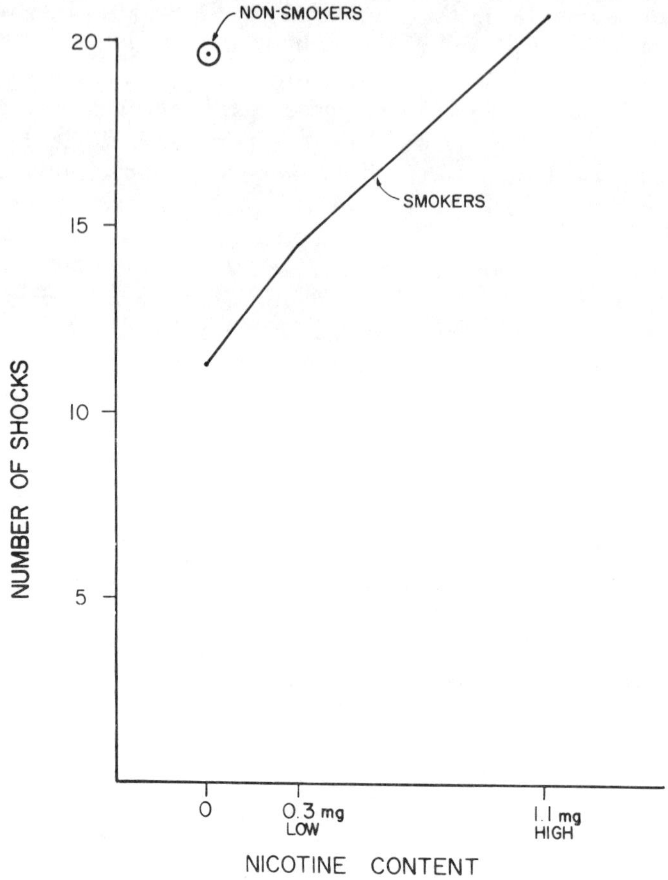

FIGURE 1. The effects of nicotine on tolerance of shock.

conducted by Perlick (1977). Within the context of a study of aircraft noise, subjects watching a television drama rated how loud and how annoying they found each of a series of simulated over-flights. During

---

than smokers of high nicotine cigarettes. This difference between the two experiments is almost certainly explained by procedural differences. Nesbitt's study was couched as a study of the effects of smoking on GSR and his non-smoker subjects (1) knew that following testing they would be required to smoke two cigarettes and (2) were required to puff at an unlit cigarettes while thresholds were being taken. Both of these factors would almost inevitably make non-smokers uneasy. In contrast, as far as the subjects knew, Silverstein's experiment had nothing to do with smoking and no unlit cigarettes were used.

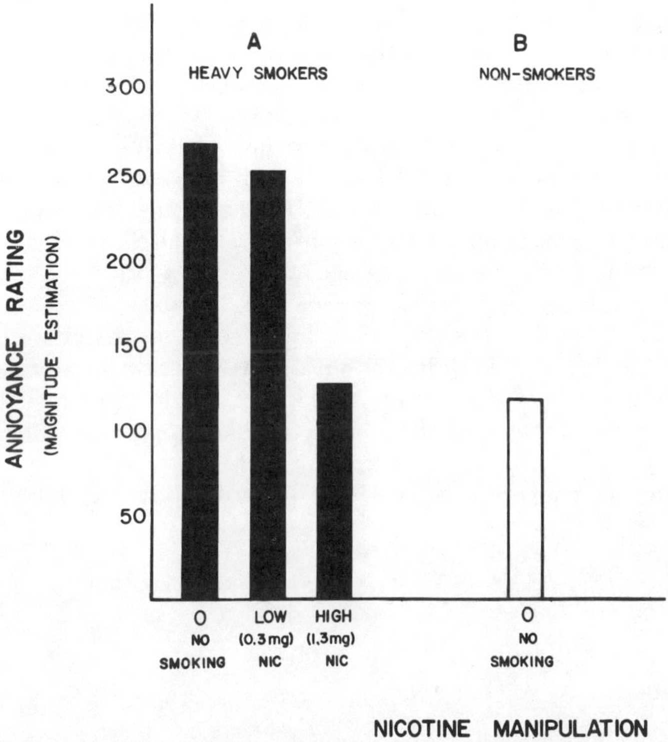

FIGURE 2. The effects of nicotine on irritability.

the experimental session, heavy smoking subjects were permitted ad lib smoking of high nicotine cigarettes in one condition, of low nicotine cigarettes in another condition and, thanks to a large "No Smoking" sign, were prevented from smoking in a third condition. Finally, there was a control group of non-smokers. The results are presented in Figure 2 where it can be seen that smokers on high nicotine cigarettes were markedly less irritated by this series of obnoxious noises than were smokers restricted to low nicotine cigarettes or prevented from smoking. However, these high nicotine smokers were neither less nor more irritated than the group of non-smokers. Again it would appear that smoking doesn't make the smoker less irritable or vulnerable to annoyance; non-smoking or insufficient nicotine makes him more irritable.

This same pattern appears to be characteristic of psychomotor as well as emotional behavior. Heimstra, Bancroft and DeKock (1967) examined the hypothesis that smoking facilitates driving performance by comparing ad-lib smokers, deprived smokers and non-smokers in a six hour simulated driving test. On a variety of measures of tracking and vigilance, ad-lib smokers did neither better nor worse than non-smokers but did markedly better than deprived smokers.

Again and again, then, one finds the same pattern—smoking doesn't improve the mood or calm the smoker or improve his performance when compared with the non-smoker. However not smoking or insufficient nicotine makes him considerably worse on all dimensions.* Given this persistent fact, how, then, to account for the fact that the smoker smokes more when he is stressed? One can, obviously, account for the generally debilitating effects of no or low nicotine by assuming that the deprived smoker is in withdrawal but this assumption alone cannot account for the effects of stress on smoking rate unless one assumes that stress, in some fashion, depletes the available supply of nicotine. And this hypothesis, of course, can account for this pattern of data only if it is the case that the smoker, an addict, is smoking to keep nicotine at a constant level.**

Nicotine as Addiction

Though almost everyone would probably agree that cigarette smok-

---

*There is, of course, one alternative interpretation of this consistent pattern. Rather than indicating withdrawal, it is conceivable that people who become smokers are by nature more frightened of shock, more irritated by noise and worse drivers than people who never become smokers, and that for such people smoking is indeed calming and does improve psychomotor performance. Though nothing short of a longitudinal study could unequivocally settle the matter, it should be noted that there have been a formidable number of studies that compared smokers and non-smokers on virtually every personality dimension imaginable. Smith (1970) in his review of this extensive literature concludes that the *only* variables which, with reasonable consistency, discriminate between smokers and non-smokers are extraversion and anti-social tendencies. And, even on these variables, the differences are all quite small. To this writer, it seems particularly unlikely that selection rather than withdrawal can account for the numerous painful consequences of not smoking or inadequate nicotine, for to accept this interpretation requires that he concede that he was a thoroughly rotten, miserable human being before taking up smoking and would become so again were he to give up the habit.

**Another way of phrasing this same conclusion is that the heavy smoker gets nothing out of smoking. He smokes only to prevent withdrawal. I freely admit that this is a perverse conclusion to reach about a habit that is quite as costly and universally pervasive as smoking but the existing data for humans don't encourage any other conclusion. Though my colleagues and I have found occasional hints that smoking may do something for the smoker when compared to the non-smoker (Nesbitt, 1973; Silverstein, 1976), in general, these differences have been small and usually seem explainable by some procedural artifact. In addition, Heimstra et al. (1973) have presented tentative evidence that smokers

ing, with nicotine or some nicotine metabolite as the active agent, is addicting, the evidence in support of this assumption is puzzlingly inconsistent. On the assumption that one manifestation of addiction is the regulation of nicotine intake, studies of the matter have either preloaded subjects with varying amounts of nicotine or have manipulated the nicotine content of the available cigarettes and measured the effects on smoking. There have been at least ten such studies on human subjects with results varying from no indication of regulation to one study which appears to indicate exquisitely precise control of nicotine intake. At one extreme, Finnegan, Larson and Haag (1945) and Goldfarb, Jarvik and Glick (1970) supplied subjects with several weeks' worth of cigarettes of varying nicotine content and checked daily cigarette consumption. Though both studies did find some subjects who regulated—i.e. smoked substantially more low than high nicotine cigarettes—the groups of subjects as a whole failed to demonstrate regulation. In sharp contrast, Ashton and Watson (1970) observed subjects smoke high and low nicotine cigarettes under controlled conditions and found evidence of precise regulation in that their subjects puffed considerably more at low than at high nicotine cigarettes and, via this mechanism, extracted almost the same amount of nicotine from the two kinds of cigarettes. Between these extremes Frith (1971) and Russell, Wilson, Patel, Cole and Feyerabend (1973) find reasonably good evidence of nicotine regulation and Herman (1974), Jarvik, Glick and Nakamura (1970), Johnston (1942), Kozlowski, Jarvik and Gritz (1975) and Lucchesi, Schuster and Emley (1967) find a tendency for smokers to regulate nicotine intake but, at best, crudely and imprecisely.

Though there is probably no single, simple reconciliation of this spectrum of diverse results, one suggestion may partially account for the general failure to find conclusive evidence for the precise regulation that might be expected from the addiction hypothesis. There are smokers who don't inhale; there are "smokers" who simply toy with the habit, smoking an occasional cigarette at parties and meetings; and, most im-

---

may have somewhat less mood fluctuation than non-smokers and there have been numerous studies suggesting that smoking may affect one or another psychomotor or mental ability but, in general, these have all been quite small effects and inconsistent from study to study (Larson, Haag, & Silvette, 1961, pp. 572-75). It should be noted, however, that almost all studies of the matter have used long-time heavy smokers as subjects. It may be that in the early stages of the smoking habit, there are indeed major gratifications and effects, that the smoker gradually adapts to these effects and by the time smoking no longer does anything for him he is thoroughly addicted.

TABLE 1
The Effects of Nicotine Content on Smoking

Subject Characteristics					*Smoking Behavior*		
					Cigs/day on:		
Subject	Age	Sex	No. yrs. a serious smoker	No. cigs/day self-report	Low (0.3 mg) Nic	High (1.3 mg) Nic	% Increase High Nic to Low Nic
J.A.	52	F	30	30	31.25	21.50	+45.3
S.S.	37	F	22	40	55.00	40.50	+35.8
R.R.	38	F	19	40	42.50	30.75	+38.2
R.S.	43	F	27	20	22.75	20.00	+13.8
D.R.	47	F	29	40-45	70.75	58.75	+20.4
R.A.	50	M	40	30	30.25	26.25	+15.2
J.E.	52	M	33	33	48.00	44.25	+ 8.5
Mean	45.6		28.6	33.6	42.93	34.57	+25.3

portantly, there are undoubtedly many smokers, sensitive to the health hazards, who deliberately inhibit smoking by such devices as imposing an upper limit on daily consumption, scheduling smoking, restricting smoking to particular occasions and so on—all devices intended to lower consumption and which would tend to mask such behavioral manifestations of addiction as tracking nicotine content. To the extent that such people are subjects in studies of regulation, one should expect that the manipulation of level of nicotine would have weak effects on smoking behavior.

In an attempt to eliminate such subjects, Schachter (1977) deliberately selected a group of subjects who satisfied the following criteria:

a) By self-report, the subject currently smoked at least a pack a day and had smoked at this level for many years.
b) By self-report, the subject was trying neither to cut down nor to limit his smoking.
c) If the subject had ever attempted to quit, he reported great difficulty and suffering.
d) By self-report, the subject exhibited "regular" smoking behavior, i.e. smoked about the same amount each day, began smoking in the morning and continued regularly throughout the day, etc.

The salient characteristics of each of these subjects are presented on the left side of Table 1, where it can be seen that they all had smoked a pack or more a day for at least 19 years. For the course of the experiment, these subjects agreed to smoke only the experimenter's cigarettes and on alternating weeks each subject was presented with cartons of specially prepared and packaged cigarettes which contained either 1.3 mg of nicotine per cigarette or 0.3 mg of nicotine per cigarette.* At bedtime, the subjects noted the number of cigarettes smoked.

Obviously, there was an inherent and deliberate circularity in the design of this study. I was simply asking do smokers who, by one set of criteria—behavioral self description—appear to be addicted, behave in an addicted fashion on a totally independent criterion—nicotine regulation. The effects of the nicotine manipulation are presented on the right side of Table 1. Obviously, the manipulation had a strong and consistent effect on these long-time heavy smokers, for each of them smoked more low than high nicotine cigarettes. On the average, there was a 25% increase (p. <.01) of smoking accompanying the manipulation of nicotine content.

It does appear, then, that heavy, long-time smokers do regulate nicotine. Given that the manipulation involved a four-fold difference in nicotine content while smoking increased only 25%, it would appear to be at best crude and imprecise regulation. There is, however, reason to believe that nicotine regulation is considerably more precise than these data suggest. First, several studies (Ashton & Watson, 1970; Herman, 1974; Schachter, Silverstein & Perlick, 1977) report that smokers puff more at low than at high nicotine cigarettes—clearly a mechanism for increasing nicotine intake. Second, given the range of nicotine content in this study, precise regulation was virtually impossible. For example, a subject who normally smoked 2 packs a day of 1.3 mg nicotine cigarettes would have to smoke almost 9 packs a day of our low nicotine cigarettes to get her customary dose of nicotine. Under these circumstances, virtually any theory of addiction would predict withdrawal for the subjects on low nicotine cigarettes. Though unfortunately no systematic provision was made in this study to measure withdrawal, there is dramatic anecdotal evidence, that the subjects who were the worst regulators in this study were in states of marked irritability and explosive emotionality while on the low nicotine cigarettes. Supporting this observation, Perlick (1977) and Silverstein (1976) have both demonstrated experimentally that heavy smokers on low nicotine cigarettes are markedly more anxious and irritable than such smokers on high nicotine cigarettes.

It does appear, then, that heavy smokers do adjust smoking rate so

---

*Most of the currently popular cigarette brands have a nicotine content varying between 1.0 and 1.3 mg.

as to keep nicotine at a roughly constant level. To account for this fact, one may suppose that there is an internal machine of sorts—one which detects the level of nicotine and regulates smoking accordingly. To begin consideration of the nature of such regulation let us review some of the basic facts about the metabolic fate and excretion of nicotine. As summarized by Goodman and Gilman (1958):

> Nicotine is readily absorbed not only from the oral and gastrointestinal mucosa and from the respiratory tract but also from the skin. . .nicotine is chemically altered in the body, mainly in the liver but also in the kidney and lung. The fraction of nicotine which escapes detoxication is completely eliminated as such in the urine along with the chemically altered forms. The rate of excretion of the alkaloid is rapid and increases linearly with the dose. . . When the urine is alkaline, only one fourth as much nicotine is excreted as when the urine is acid; this is explained by the fact that nicotine base is reabsorbed from an alkaline urine (p. 622).

The effects of the acidity, or the pH, of the urine on the rate of excretion of unchanged nicotine suggests, given that smokers appear to regulate nicotine, that the pH of the urine may affect the rate of smoking. Whether an effect of any consequence is to be anticipated, however, depends on the proportion of unchanged nicotine which is excreted. One can make reasonably accurate estimates from the work of Beckett and his associates. Beckett, Rowland and Triggs (1965) have shown that subjects who smoke 20 cigarettes a day excrete an average of 1.0 μg nicotine per minute under normal conditions, 5.0 μg nicotine per minute when the urine was made acidic by the oral administration of ammonium chloride and 0.1 μg after oral administration of the alkalizer sodium bicarbonate. In another study, Beckett and Triggs (1967) have demonstrated that smokers whose urine has been maintained acidic excrete in unchanged form about 35% of known quantities of nicotine that have been administered either by intravenous injection, inhalation of nicotine vapor or smoking. Putting these facts together, it appears reasonable to estimate that the proportion of nicotine which will be excreted in unchanged form will vary with the manipulated acidity of the urine as follows:

urine is:	*% nicotine excreted:*
acid	35
normal	7
alkali	< 1

TABLE 2
The Effects of Vitamin C, Acidulin and Placebo on Cigarette Smoking

Condition	Cigarettes smoked per day	Mean % change from Placebo
Vitamin C	26.7	+19.8
Placebo	23.1	—
Acidulin	28.1	+20.9
Comparison	*p* value	
Vitamin C vs Placebo	< .05	< .05
Acidulin vs Placebo	< .01	< .01

Obviously, the exact proportions will vary with the precise pH of the urine. However, one thing seems clear: given the quite low proportion of unchanged nicotine which is excreted under normal or placebo conditions, increasing the alkalinity of the urine can at best have trivial effects on plasma level nicotine while increasing the acidity of urine can potentially have substantial effects on plasma level nicotine. If, then, one assumes first, that changes in urinary pH are reflected in circulating nicotine and second, that the amounts smoked vary with changes in plasma level nicotine, it should be expected that experimentally increasing the acidity of the urine will increase the amounts smoked.

To test this guess, Schachter, Kozlowski and Silverstein (1977) manipulated urinary pH by, in alternate weeks, administering to a group of 13 smokers substantial daily doses of placebo or of the acidifying agents vitamin C (ascorbic acid) and Acidulin (glutamic acid hydrochloride). The subjects were given cartons of their favorite cigarettes and kept count of the amount they had smoked each day of the study. The effects of these manipulations on smoking are presented in Table 2 where it can be seen that acidification is accompanied by increased smoking. During the period in which they were taking either of two different acidifying agents, subjects smoked 20% more cigarettes than during the time they were taking a corn starch placebo.

It should be specifically noted that in keeping with the magnitude of the pharmacological effects (Haag & Larson, 1942; Beckett, Rowland & Triggs, 1965; Beckett & Triggs, 1967), this 20% increase is not a large experimental effect. On the basis of our estimates of nicotine excretion from the work of Beckett and his colleagues one would expect, at best, roughly a 30% increase in smoking with even a strongly effective aci-

TABLE 3
The Effects of Academic Stress on Urinary pH

Subject	pH on: Stress Day	Control Day	Stress-Control
A. Colloquium Talk			
E.G.	5.50	6.35	−0.85
H.T.	5.70	5.95	−0.25
M.C.	6.70	6.90	−0.20
H.K.	5.50	6.20	−0.70
S.S.	5.40	6.45	−1.05
B. Ph.D. Oral Defense			
E.D.	5.40	7.10	−1.70
A.L.	6.00	6.20	−0.20
C. Ph.D. Comprehensive Examination			
B.S.	5.85	5.80	+0.05
I.S.	5.20	5.70	−0.50
D.P.	5.40	5.70	−0.30
All subjects (Mean)	5.67	6.24	− .57

difying manipulation which ours was not. It seems clear that of the body's two chief mechanisms for disposing of nicotine, enzymatic breakdown and urinary excretion of unchanged nicotine, the urinary excretion route plays by far the lesser role in the confirmed smoker. Nevertheless, acidification does affect smoking behavior and this finding does at least raise the possibility that it may be useful to invoke this bit of pharmacological machinery in order to understand some of the presumed psychological and situational determinants of smoking rate. Conceivably, events that stimulate smoking may do so via their action on urinary pH.

In order to learn if this guess had any merit as a possible explanation of the stress-smoking relationship, Schachter, Silverstein et al. (1977) examined the effects of a variety of academic stressors on pH. In one study, subjects urinated immediately before an obviously stressful event such as delivering a colloquium lecture or taking Ph.D. oral or compre-

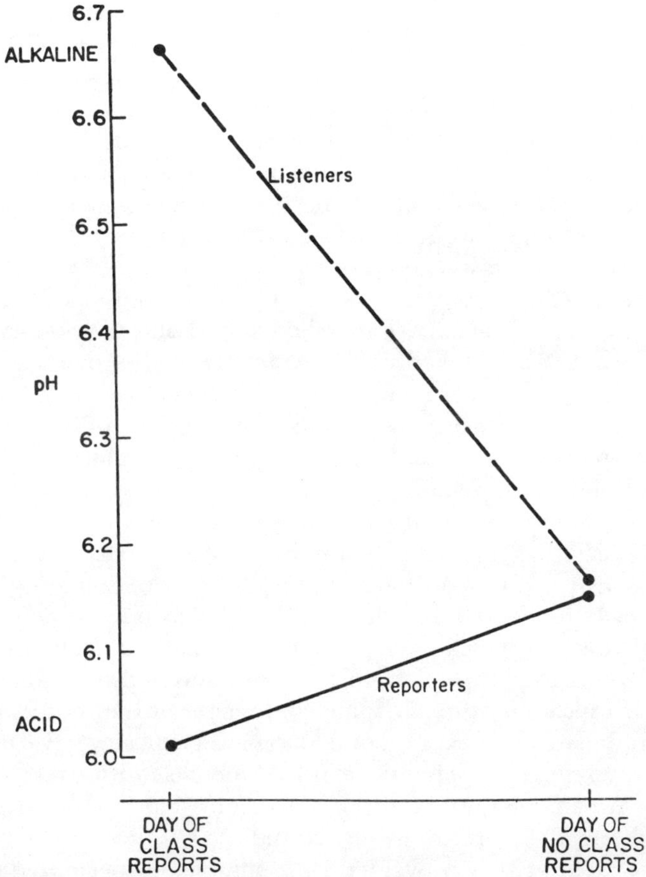

FIGURE 3. The effects of academic stress on urinary pH.

hensive examinations. And, for control purposes, these same subjects urinated at precisely the same time on routine, non-stressful days. The results are presented in Table 3 where it can be seen that for 9 of 10 subjects, the urine was considerably more acidic on stress than on control days.

Precisely the same pattern is manifest in the urine of the undergraduate members of a seminar that normally was an intense, trying affair involving oral quizzing on assigned reading, enforced student participation in class discussion and so on. On the experimental day, things were probably more trying than usual for half of the class and considerably less so for the other half. Nine of the 20 students had been assigned to read highly technical material and prepare 10-15 minute oral reports for class. For most of these students, this was the first time in college that they had been called upon to give an oral report. The remaining members of the class had no assignment and no reading; they were simply expected to provide an audience for the reporters.

An hour before class each of the students urinated and, following instructions, brought his urine to class. And, on a control day which was a business-as-usual class with no reporters or listeners, they did the same thing. The effects of these events on pH can be seen in Figure 3 where it is evident that on the experimental day, the urine of students assigned to give reports was markedly more acidic than that of those students who for that day simply composed an audience ($p < .05$). In marked contrast, on a regular class day when both groups of students had equally good reason to be tense, pH for the two groups of subjects was virtually identical (interaction $p < .05$).

It does appear, then, that stress, at least of the sort endemic to academic life, acidifies the urine,*—a finding which at least encourages the exploration of a pharmacological interpretation of smoking behavior.

To review the line of argument so far: It has been widely reported that smoking increases with stress and that smoking is calming —observations that appear to go hand in hand and to support the assertion that nicotine or tar or some component of the act of smoking is anxiety reducing. The experimental facts are peculiarly at variance with this interpretation. Smoking does indeed increase with stress but smoking smokers are neither more nor less calm than a control group of non-smokers. They are, however, considerably calmer than groups of smokers who are either prevented from smoking or permitted to smoke only low nicotine cigarettes. This fact can be interpreted as indicating that smoking isn't anxiety reducing but that not smoking or insufficient

---

*It should be emphasized that I do not believe that pH changes are a quick and easy index of any sort of stress at all. In the data reported in this paper, an acid urine is associated with the chronic, long-duration sort of stress associated with preparing for and worrying about a public lecture or an important examination. In our experiments, Schachter, Silverstein and Perlick (1977) succeeded in lowering pH over the course of an experimental hour during which a subject was repeatedly shocked. Silverstein (1976) using a similar procedure failed to lower pH when the subject was shocked for only a 5 minute period and then urinated immediately thereafter. Similarly a 10 minute horror film had little effect on pH. It may be that only chronic and intense stress effects pH. Alternatively, it may be that pH changes do accompany acute manipulations of stress but for many possible reasons such changes are simply not reflected in urine samples taken immediately after the stressful event.

nicotine is anxiety increasing. In effect, the smoker smokes more during stress because of budding withdrawal symptoms and not because of any psychological property of nicotine or of the act of smoking. Such an interpretation is plausible if one assumes that the smoker smokes in order to keep nicotine at some constant level and that there is something about the state of stress that depletes the body's supply of nicotine. A variety of studies have been described which, via the effects of urinary pH on the rate of nicotine excretion, suggest a biochemical mechanism that could account for this set of facts.

Though this elegant juxtaposition of facts makes almost irresistible the conclusion that the smoker's mind is in the bladder, obviously we are hardly yet in a position to rule out psychological explanations of smoking. Though "anxiety reduction" seems, by now, a particularly unsatisfactory explanation of the stress-smoking relationship, innumerable other purely psychological explanations are still conceivable. Ferster (1970), for example, has attempted to explain the relationship in these terms:

> With the increase in emotional symptoms there is frequently a major cessation in most of the ongoing repertoire the person might engage in. With such a temporary decrease in the frequency in most of the items in a person's repertoire, the relative importance of even the minor reinforcers increases enormously. Thus the relative position of smoking in the entire repertoire is increased considerably when other major items of the repertoire are depressed. Smoking becomes something to do when no other behavior is appropriate (page 99).

In short, though the effect of pH on nicotine elimination is a well established pharmacological fact, it may have little, if anything, to do with the effects of stress on smoking, for it is certainly conceivable that stress, with or without accompanying pH changes, will affect smoking rate. In order to learn if pH changes are a necessary and sufficient explanation of the stress-smoking relationships, it is clear that we must experimentally pit the mind against the bladder and this Schachter, Silverstein and Perlick (1977) attempted to do in an experiment which independently manipulated stress and the pH of the urine. If it is correct that pH changes are a necessary part of the machinery, we should expect more smoking in high than in low stress conditions when pH is uncontrolled and no difference between the two conditions when pH is experimentally stabilized. If, on the other hand, pH changes are irrelevant to the smoking-stress relationship, there should be more smok-

TABLE 4
The Effects of the Manipulations on Urinary pH

		Mean pH:			No. of subjects whose pH:		
Condition	N	Pre-stress	Post-stress	Pre-post	Decreased	Stayed same	Increased
High Stress-Placebo	12	6.00	5.83	−0.17	8	3	1
Low Stress-Placebo	12	5.99	6.13	+0.14	4	1	7
High Stress-Bicarbonate	12	6.08	7.44	+1.36	0	0	12
Low Stress-Bicarbonate	12	6.20	7.01	+0.81	2	1	9

ing in high than in low stress conditions no matter what the state of the urine.

In this study, too, stress was manipulated by use of electric shock. In fact, the experiment already described on the relationship of stress to smoking (Schachter, Silverstein et al., 1977) was replicated with one major modification—in one pair of conditions the high or low stress manipulation began 50 minutes after subjects took a placebo; in the other conditions 50 minutes after subjects had taken 3 grams of bicarbonate of soda—an agent virtually guaranteed to quickly elevate urinary pH and for a time to stabilize it at highly alkaline levels. In Table 4, note first the effects of the manipulation on urinary pH. Examining first the two placebo conditions, it will be noted that pH decreases in the High Stress condition ($p = .02$) and tends to increase in the Low Stress condition. In the two bicarbonate conditions, in sharp contrast, pH increased markedly from the beginning to the end of the experiment and the stress manipulation has had absolutely no effect on pH. If anything, the pH of High Stress bicarbonate subjects has increased more than the pH of Low Stress bicarbonate subjects.

Next we note that on a variety of self-report measures the manipulation of stress was highly successful in both the placebo and bicarbonate conditions. Obviously, then, the conditions necessary to pit the psychological against the pharmacological explanation of the effects of stress on smoking have been established. Subjects in High Stress conditions are considerably more tense than are subjects in Low Stress conditions, whether they have taken a placebo or bicarbonate. In the placebo conditions, however, where pH is uncontrolled, stress acidifies, whereas in the bicarbonate conditions, it does not.

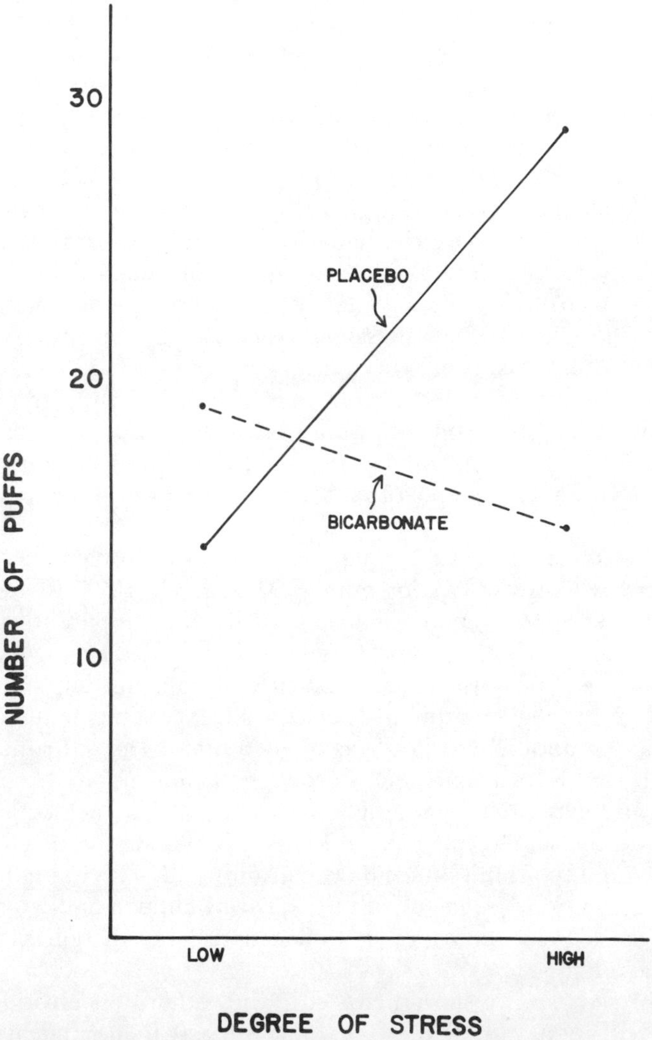

FIGURE 4. The effects of sodium bicarbonate and placebo on smoking under stress.

The effects of these manipulations on smoking are presented in Figure 4, which plots the mean number of puffs taken by subjects in each condition once the stress manipulation had begun. It is clear that with placebo, there is considerably more smoking in high than in low stress conditions, while with bicarbonate stress has absolutely no effect on smoking (interaction $p < .01$). It does appear, then, that smoking under stress has nothing to do with psychological, sensory or manipulative needs that are presumably activated by the state of stress but is explained by the effects of stress on the rate of excretion of nicotine. The smoker under stress smokes to replenish nicotine supply, not to relieve anxiety.

Given these facts, a formidable case can be made for a purely pharmacological, addictive view of cigarette smoking. It must be admitted, however, that satisfactory though such a mechanistic view of smoking may be for understanding the behavior of many, perhaps most, smokers, the apparent exceptions to such a model are maddeningly various. There are smokers (see Schachter, 1977) who do not track nicotine content. Though it is known (Isaac & Rand, 1972) that plasma nicotine level is zero on awakening, there are smokers who find cigarettes distasteful in the morning and do not light up their first cigarette before lunchtime. Though withdrawal is a necessary component of virtually any model of addiction, some orthodox Jewish smokers, forbidden to smoke on the Sabbath, report that they can do so without a qualm. And so on.

Just how to cope with such blatant exceptions is problematic. Perhaps it is necessary to invent typologies (e.g., McKennell, 1973; Russell, 1974; Tomkins, 1968) to accommodate the distressing apparent variety of smokers, but I find this an unsatisfying scientific stratagem. As a working hypothesis, I propose instead that virtually all long-time smokers are addicted and suggest that many, perhaps all, exceptions to an addiction model can be understood in terms of such notions as self-control, concern with health, restraints, etc. Certainly all smokers are aware of the dangers and expense of smoking. To the extent that such concerns are prominent, the smoker probably inhibits his smoking by such devices as imposing an upper limit on his daily consumption, scheduling his smoking, and so on—devices intended to lower consumption and which would tend to mask such behavioral manifestations of addiction as tracking nicotine content.

If this is correct, we should expect to find other, less obvious indications of addiction and, of these, I would suggest that withdrawal is the key. Obviously anyone can give up smoking, limit his daily intake or restrict smoking to particular times or occasions if he is willing and able to put up with the withdrawal syndrome. If it is correct that virtually all long-time smokers are addicted, it should be anticipated that smokers who don't smoke in the morning will be more irritable at that time of day than in the afternoon; that smokers who restrain their smoking will be more volatile people than heavy smokers, and so on. To test such expectations, Perlick (1977), in the experiment described earlier, com-

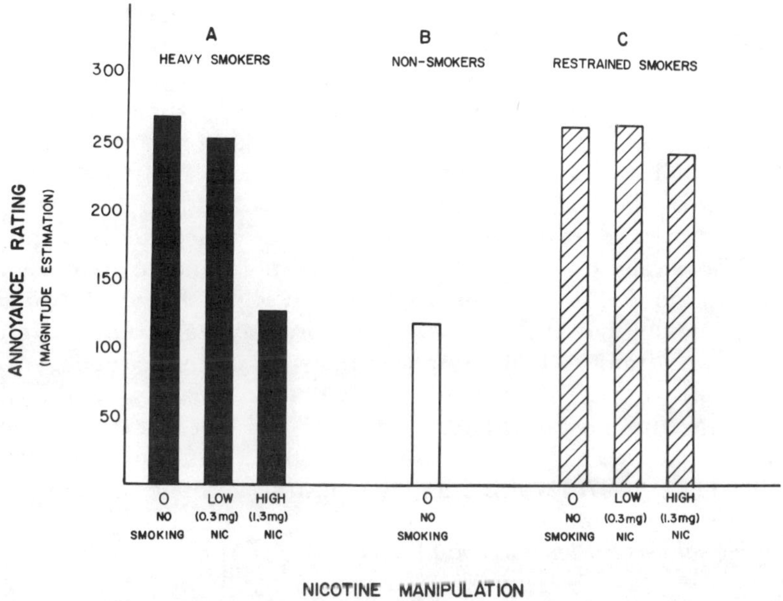

FIGURE 5. The effects of nicotine deprivation on the irritability of heavy smokers, non-smokers and restrained smokers.

pared a group of heavy, unrestrained smokers to a matched group of highly restrained smokers, mostly former heavy smokers who on a variety of indices indicated that they were deliberately and successfully attempting to cut down, though not eliminate, smoking by a combination of devices such as smoking cigarettes only half way, smoking very low nicotine cigarettes, counting daily intake and the like. On the average, these restrained smokers reported smoking at a rate less than half of their former level. As described earlier, all subjects rated how annoying they found the noise of each of a series of simulated aircraft over-flights while, depending on condition, they were either prevented from smoking or permitted ad lib smoking of high or of low nicotine cigarettes. It should be noted first that in the conditions where they were permitted to smoke, restrained former heavy smokers smoked only half as much as did current heavy smokers. They behaved in the laboratory, then, as they report they do in life. The effects of these manipulations on the two groups of smokers are presented in Figure 5. As noted earlier, the extent to which heavy, unrestrained smokers were annoyed depends on the nicotine manipulation. When they did not smoke or smoked very low nicotine cigarettes, they were markedly more annoyed than when they smoked high nicotine cigarettes. The restrained, former heavy smokers stand in fascinating contrast, for they were chronically annoyed—as they should be—even in the high nicotine condition where they are still getting considerably less nicotine than in former days was their want. In other tests of the same hypothesis, Perlick (1977) demonstrates that such restrained smokers eat more than do heavy smokers when given free access to candy and also do worse at a proofreading task requiring concentration. Restrained smokers appear to be chronically more irascible, to nibble more and to have poorer concentration than unrestrained smokers. It is possible to control and restrict smoking but at a price—and the price appears to be a chronic state of withdrawal.* It does appear that one of the exceptions to a purely addictive view of smoking is no exception. I suspect that this shall be the case with most of these exceptions** and that by taking account of withdrawal we can understand those studies (Finnegan et al., 1945; Goldfarb et al., 1970) which fail to demonstrate nicotine regulation.

Psychological versus Pharmacological Explanation of Smoking

Let us review our conclusions so far. For the confirmed smoker:

(1) The psychological and probably the sensory and manipulative gratifications of smoking are illusory. Serious smokers smoke to prevent withdrawal.
(2) Smokers regulate nicotine intake.
(3) Variations in smoking rate, which customarily have been interpreted in psychological terms, seem better understood as an attempt to regulate nicotine.
(4) Apparent exceptions to a regulatory model of smoking seem understandable in terms of withdrawal. The smoker who fails to regulate suffers withdrawal.

Given these facts, one is faced with a formidable question which reduced to essentials is this—so where's psychology? What's with the oral

---

*One alternative interpretation of these data must be considered. It is conceivable that naturally irascible people are more likely to restrain their smoking. If so, these results could be attributable to self-selection rather than withdrawal. Acutely aware of this possibility, Perlick (1977), compared these groups on numbers of personality and demographic variables and found no differences between the two groups.

**With one exception—there are a small number of long-time, light smokers who give no evidence of nicotine regulation (Schachter, 1977) and no indication of withdrawal when deprived of nicotine (Perlick, 1977). What to make of such cases is, at this time, equivocal but by standard criteria of addiction they do appear to be genuinely non-addicted smokers.

dependency needs or the habit strength or the misattribution if, as seems to be the case for stress, it all depends on the hydrogen ion concentration in the urine? Obviously, this has been an openly reductionist attempt to explain some of the effects of psychological variables without making use of the conceptual equipment of psychology. I believe that in the case of stress the attempt has been successful, for, given the facts outlined, attempts to formulate the stress-smoking relationship in terms of oral dependency needs (Marcovitz, 1969), or of attribution theory (Nesbitt, 1973; Schachter, 1973) or of learning theory (Ferster, 1970; Hunt, 1970) seem unnecessary, ad hoc constructions. Smoking increases with stress because that is the way the biological machine is built and it makes as much sense to ask psychodynamically, cognitively or functionally, why does the smoker smoke more under stress, as it does to ask why psychologically does the car speed up when I press on the accelerator.

There is also, it should be added, reason to suspect that not only stress but many of the presumed psychological determinants, both situational and characterological, of smoking behavior may also be reducible to these elementary biochemical terms. For example, virtually all smokers agree that they smoke more at parties than at other times—a self-observation which is supported in data gathered by Silverstein, Kozlowski and Schachter (1977). These same authors also have found in two independent studies that parties markedly increase urinary acidity. This is true for non-smokers as well as smokers—a finding which indicates that it is not smoking which is the cause of acidity and which makes somewhat more plausible the guess that the urinary pH mechanism may also be responsible for the party-smoking relationship.*

As a final example of a plausible reductionist possibility, it has several times been reported (Eysenck, Tarrant, Woolf, & England, 1960; Coan, 1973) that extraversion is positively correlated with amounts smoked. The more extraverted the smoker, the greater the average daily consumption of cigarettes. Obviously one can conceive of numerous psychological explanations of this relationship but the findings on parties, pH and smoking do at least raise the possibility that this relationship too may be reducible to these biochemical terms. This possibility becomes even more cogent when we note that Schachter, Kozlowski and Silverstein (1977) have found that chronic urinary pH (as estimated from 21

*An equally plausible and equally reductionistic interpretation of this relationship may lie in the effects of party-going on nicotine metabolism. There is evidence that alcohol acidifies the urine (Eggleton, 1946) and there is also evidence that alcohol can affect the rate of metabolism of many drugs (Lieber, 1976).

urine samples obtained from each of 14 subjects over a 7 day period) is negatively correlated with the amount smoked. The more chronically acidic the urine is, the greater the daily consumption of cigarettes. If further work does demonstrate that extraversion, whether in smokers or non-smokers, is associated with urinary acidity, the reductionistic explanation of this relationship between an abiding personality characteristic and a behavior acquires considerable plausibility.

Even if one grants the plausibility of these various reductionistic speculations, it seems only reasonable by now to ask: What more do we know now about smoking? Though this attempt to reduce presumably complex psychological processes to the bladder has much the charm of pricking overinflated balloons, have my colleagues and I done anything more really than demonstrate that cigarette smoking is an addiction—hardly a novel conclusion—and simply elaborated the fashion in which known metabolic and excretory mechanisms mediate the action of presumed psychological determinants of smoking? I don't think that we have, but I do think that this reductionistic exercise is a long overdue foray into the impact of the offal rather than the psyche on behavior.

REFERENCES

Ashton, H., & Watson, D. W.: Puffing frequency and nicotine intake in cigarette smokers. *British Medical Journal,* 1970, *3,* 679-681.

Beckett, A. H., Rowland, M., & Triggs, E. G.: Significance of smoking in investigations of urinary excretion rates of amines in man. *Nature,* 1965, *207,* 200-201.

Beckett, A. H., & Triggs, E. G.: Enzyme induction in man caused by smoking. *Nature,* 1967, *216,* 587.

Coan, R. W.: Personality variables associated with smoking. *Journal of Personality and Social Psychology,* 1973, *26,* 86-104.

Eggleton, M. G.: Urine acidity in alcohol diuresis in man. *Journal of Physiology,* 1946, *104,* 312-320.

Eysenck, H., Tarrant, M., Woolf, M., & England, L.: Smoking and personality. *British Medical Journal,* 1960, i, 1456-1460.

Ferster, C. B.: Comments on paper by Hunt and Matarazzo. In W. A. Hunt (Ed.), *Learning mechanisms in smoking.* Chicago: Aldine, 1970.

Finnegan, J. K., Larson, P. S., & Haag, H. B.: The role of nicotine in the cigarette habit. *Science,* 1945, *102,* 94-96.

Frith, C. D.: The effect of varying the nicotine content of cigarettes on human smoking behaviour. *Psychopharmacologia,* 1971, *19,* 188-192.

Glad, W., & Adesso, V. J.: The relative importance of socially induced tension and behavioral contagion for smoking behavior. *Journal of Abnormal Psychology,* 1976, *85,* 119-121.

Goldfarb, T. L., Jarvik, M. E., & Glick, S. D.: Cigarette nicotine content as a determinant of human smoking behavior. *Psychopharmacologia,* 1970, *17,* 89-93.

Goodman, L. S., & Gilman, A.: *The pharmacological basis of therapeutics.* New York: MacMillan, 1958.

Haag, H. B., & Larson, P. S.: Studies on the fate of nicotine in the body. I: The effect of pH on the urinary excretion of nicotine by tobacco smokers. *Journal of Pharmacology and Experimental Therapeutics,* 1942, *76,* 235-239.

HEIMSTRA, N. W., BANCROFT, N. R., & DEKOCK, A. R.: Effects of smoking upon sustained performance in a simulated driving task. *Annals of the New York Academy of Sciences,* 1967, *142,* Art. 1, 295-307.

HERMAN, C. P.: External and internal cues as determinants of the smoking behavior of light and heavy smokers. *Journal of Personality and Social Psychology,* 1974, *30,* 664-672.

HUNT, W. A. (Ed.): *Learning mechanisms in smoking.* Aldine, 1970.

ISAAC, P. F., & RAND, M. J.: Cigarette smoking and plasma levels of nicotine. *Nature,* 1972, *236,* 308.

JARVIK, M. E., GLICK, S. D., & NAKAMURA, R. K.: Inhibition of cigarette smoking by orally administered nicotine. *Clinical Pharmacology and Therapeutics,* 1970, *11,* 574-576.

JOHNSTON, L. M.: Tobacco smoking and nicotine. *Lancet,* 1942, *2,* 742.

KOZLOWSKI, L. T., JARVIK, M. E., & GRITZ, E. R.: Nicotine regulation and cigarette smoking. *Clinical Pharmacology and Therapeutics,* 1975, *17,* 93-97.

LARSON, P. S., HAAG, H. B., & SILVETTE, H.: *Tobacco.* Baltimore: Williams & Wilkins, 1961.

LIEBER, C. S.: The metabolism of alcohol. *Scientific American,* 1976, *234,* 25-33.

LUCCHESI, B. R., SCHUSTER, C. R., & EMLEY, G. S.: The role of nicotine as a determinant of cigarette smoking in man with observations of certain cardiovascular effects associated with the tobacco alkaloid. *Clinical Pharmacology and Therapeutics,* 1967, *8,* 789-796.

MARCOVITZ, E.: On the nature of addiction to cigarettes. *Journal of the American Psychoanalytic Association,* 1969, *17,* 1074-1096.

MCKENNELL, A. C.: A comparison of two smoking typologies *(Research Paper 12).* London: Tobacco Research Council, 1973.

NESBITT, P. D.: Smoking, physiological arousal, and emotional response. *Journal of Personality and Social Psychology,* 1973, *25,* 137-145.

PERLICK, D.: The withdrawal syndrome: Nicotine addiction and the effects of stopping smoking in heavy and light smokers. Unpublished doctoral dissertation, Columbia University, 1977.

RUSSELL, M. A. H.: The smoking habit and its classification. *The Practitioner,* 1974, *212,* 791-800.

RUSSELL, M. A. H., WILSON, C., PATEL, U. S., COLE, P. V., & FEYERABEND, C.: Comparison of effect on tobacco consumption and carbon monoxide absorption of changing to high and low nicotine cigarettes. *British Medical Journal,* 1973, *4,* 512-516.

SCHACHTER, S.: Nicotine regulation in heavy and light smokers. *Journal of Experimental Psychology: General,* 1977, *106,* 5-12.

SCHACHTER, S.: Nesbitt's paradox. In W. L. Dunn (Ed.), *Smoking behavior: Motives and incentive.* Washington, D.C.: V. H. Winston, 1973.

SCHACHTER, S., KOZLOWSKI, L. T., & SILVERSTEIN, B.: Effects of urinary pH on cigarette smoking. *Journal of Experimental Psychology: General,* 1977, *106,* 13-19.

SCHACHTER, S., SILVERSTEIN, B., KOZLOWSKI, L. T., HERMAN, C. P., & LIEBLING, B.: Effects of stress on cigarette smoking and urinary pH. *Journal of Experimental Psychology: General,* 1977, *106,* 22-30.

SCHACHTER, S., SILVERSTEIN, B., & PERLICK, D.: Psychological and pharmacological explanations of smoking under stress. *Journal of Experimental Psychology: General,* 1977, *106,*31-40

SILVERSTEIN, B.: An addiction explanation of cigarette-induced relaxation. Unpublished doctoral dissertation, Columbia University, 1976.

SILVERSTEIN, B., KOZLOWSKI, L. T., & SCHACHTER, S.: Social life, cigarette smoking, and urinary pH. *Journal of Experimental Psychology: General,* 1977, *106,* 20-23.

SMITH, G. M.: Personality and smoking: A review of the empirical literature. In W. A. Hunt (Ed.), *Learning mechanisms in smoking.* Chicago: Aldine, 1970.

TOMKINS, S.: A modified model of smoking behavior. In E. F. Borgatta & R. R. Evans (Eds.), *Smoking, health and behavior.* Chicago: Aldine, 1968.

4

Why People Smoke: Current Psychobiological Models

OVIDE F. POMERLEAU

Smoking is a major public health problem. As the conclusions of the recent Third World Conference on Smoking and Health (1977) indicate, cigarette smoking continues to be a source of concern in the United States and many other countries. The harmful effects of the habit have been well documented: Smokers have been found to have higher death rates than non-smokers from coronary heart disease, from various bronco-pulmonary diseases and from carcinoma—especially of the lung (Borgatta & Evans, 1968; Hammond, 1962; U.S. Public Health Service, 1971, 1973, 1974). While there is evidence that health risks associated with smoking can be reduced by quitting (American Heart Association, 1970; Hammond & Garfinkel, 1969) and though information on the dangers of smoking has been widely disseminated to physicians and to the public at large, the effects on the reduction of cigarette consumption have been disappointing (Auger, Wright & Simpson, 1972; O'Keefe, 1971).

The author acknowledges with gratitude the assistance of David Adkins in the preparation of the manuscript.

At present, the understanding of the behavioral, physiological, and psychological reasons for smoking leaves much to be desired. Relatively little scientific information is available in some critical areas such as initiation of smoking (e.g., Gritz, 1977) while a large number of loosely related facts has been accumulated in other areas such as the physiological effects of nicotine (e.g., Stephens, 1977). In general, experimental findings have yet to be integrated into a cohesive theoretical framework for explaining the phenomenon.

With respect to treatment, Bernstein (1969), who exhaustively reviewed the work of the 60s, was forced to conclude that "very little in the way of useful knowledge [had] been contributed beyond the rather elementary observations that smoking behavior is widespread and becoming more so, that it is very likely unsafe, and that it is incredibly resistant to long-term modification" (p.437). Because of new developments in behavioral research based on social learning theory (Bandura, 1969), however, more recent reviews of smoking treatment have been somewhat more encouraging (Bernstein & Glasgow, 1979). Among the more promising behavioral approaches have been aversive smoking procedures (e.g., rapid smoking programs; Lichtenstein & Penner, 1977) and stimulus control (e.g., multicomponent positive reinforcement programs; Pomerleau, 1979; Pomerleau & Pomerleau, 1977). While these approaches have yielded sustained abstinence of about 33 percent in follow-ups a year or more after the start of treatment (which compares favorably with 14 percent for non-behavioral treatments such as the Five Day Plan; Thompson & Wilson, 1966) and a recidivism rate of about 50 percent (which compares favorably with 70 to 80 percent recidivism rates reported for non-behavioral clinics; Hunt & Bespalec, 1974), the results still leave considerable room for improvement (Pomerleau, 1978). A major limitation of past clinical research—both behavioral and non-behavioral—has been that it has tended to rely on a trial and error approach rather than being based on a scientific analysis of smoking behavior.

The purpose of this chapter is to review some of the work that has been done on three models of smoking and to explore some of the implications for basic and applied research as well as treatment and social policy. A major premise of the present approach is that adequate elucidation of the mechanisms which control smoking requires a combination of behavioral, physiological, and cognitive exploration and that special attention should be given to the interrrelationships among the levels of analysis. The discussion will focus principally on those variables which contribute to the maintenance of smoking and to the difficulty of quitting—central issues in the understanding of smoking.* Among the major unresolved problems to be examined specifically are: a) the role of nicotine as a reinforcer in smoking, b) the role of stimulus control in the regulation of smoking behavior, c) smoking as a positive reinforcer, a negative reinforcer, or both, and d) the contribution of conditioned craving or withdrawal to the overdetermination of the habit.

Facts about Smoking

As Jarvik (1977) indicates, remarkably little is known about why cigarette smoking is among the most popular and persistent habits of the age. What is known biologically can be summarized fairly succinctly.

> The first stimuli that the smoker perceives from a cigarette are its visual characteristics, and upon lighting it he can see the smoke, feel the warmth and smell the aroma. Upon inhaling the smoke he feels it in his mouth and some of it is deposited on his buccal and nasal mucous membranes where the nicotine is rapidly absorbed (though less so if the pH is acid than alkaline). Tars which may have been deposited upon his fingers are also deposited on his teeth and mucous membranes. Taste and smell are stimulated and so are pain receptors in the pharynx, larynx, trachea and bronchii.
>
> As the smoker inhales the smoke into his lungs the respiratory epithelium is coated with fine particles and droplets from the smoke. The nicotine and carbon monoxide paralyze the cilia but increase the secretion of mucous, and coughing is likely to occur. All of these stimuli, so unpleasant to the novice, come to be reinforcing to the habitual smoker and are incorporated as part of the "feel" of smoking.
>
> The inhaling smoker takes a deep breath of smoke to enable the smoke particles to reach his alveoli and he may hold this breath for several seconds. The duration of inspiration determines how much of the nicotine and other constituents will be absorbed into the lungs and vascular circulation during each breath. Then he exhales the remaining smoke, some of it through his nose, some of it through his mouth. In the meanwhile, his face and head are surrounded by a halo of smoke. The main purpose of all this activity appears to be to get nicotine into the blood and particularly into the brain as quickly as possible (Jarvik, 1977, p.123).

---

*Because of a lack of scientific information on the subject, very little can be said about initiation at present; the problem is clearly important, however, for a better understanding may lead to the development of more effective methods of prevention.

Though a large number of smoke products, including various "tars" and carbon monoxide, are taken in (Schmeltz & Hoffman, 1976), the acute actions of inhaling a cigarette are largely attributable to the alkaloid, nicotine. The direct effects of the drug are to stimulate nicotine cholinergic receptors, and its indirect effects, the release of catecholamines. Peripheral effects are largely due to release of epinephrine and norepinephrine (Cryer, Haymond, Santiago & Shah, 1976). Easily observed reactions include increased heart rate, vaso-constriction, and elevated blood pressure (Stephens, 1977) as well as increased cardiac output and stroke volume (Frankl, Friedman & Soloff, 1966). Skin temperature decreases (Agué, 1973), along with skeletal muscle tone and a depression of the patellar reflex (Domino, 1973). Nicotine has been shown to produce an alerting pattern in the EEG (decreased alpha production) and behavioral arousal (Larson & Silvette, 1975); it increases secretion of saliva, inhibits stomach contractions, and delays gastric emptying (Russell, 1976). Nicotine stimulates the emetic chemoreceptor trigger zone in the medulla and, in novice smokers or in large doses, causes nausea and vomiting. Various hypothalamic and pituitary hormones are also stimulated (Volle & Koelle, 1975).

Animal research indicates that monkeys will self-administer nicotine intravenously (Deneau & Inoki, 1967) and can be trained to smoke nicotine-containing cigarettes (Yamagita, Ando, Oinuma & Ishida, 1974). Nicotine facilitates conditioned-avoidance behavior as well as positively-reinforced behavior in rats (Armitage, Hall & Morrison, 1968) and has been found to reduce social or pain-induced aggression in both animals and humans (Silverman, 1971; Hutchinson & Emley, 1973).

The role of nicotine as the principal reinforcer for smoking continues to be a subject of some controversy. While no one has shown that carbon monoxide intoxication is pleasurable, the possibility that tar may be reinforcing is not so easily dismissed, especially since the tar and nicotine content of cigarettes tends to covary. One study in which tar and nicotine in cigarettes were dissociated (Goldfarb, Gritz, Jarvik & Stolerman, 1976), suggested that the number of cigarettes smoked was related to nicotine rather than tar content, but the importance of the interaction remains to be determined.

According to Jarvik (1977), much of the evidence for the role of nicotine as the primary reinforcer in cigarette smoke is circumstantial. Smokers clearly prefer cigarettes with nicotine than without (Goldfarb, Jarvik & Glick, 1970), but they will smoke nicotine-free cigarettes grudgingly for a while. The fact that smoking such cigarettes is not sustained, despite the usual cues for smoking, suggests that the other variables are secondary reinforcers which extinguish when nicotine—the primary reinforcer—is not present.

Attempts to study the role of nicotine directly have produced conflicting results. Preloading nicotine, by having subjects smoke or chew nicotine-containing gum before testing, did reduce subsequent puffing (Kozlowski, Jarvik & Glick, 1975; Kumar, Cooke, Lader & Russell, 1977; Lucchesi, Schuster & Emley, 1967); moreover, administering the nicotine "antagonist," mecamylamine, increases smoking rate (Stolerman, Goldfarb, Fink & Jarvik, 1973). On the other hand, Kumar et al. (1977) were unable to demonstrate a dose-response effect on subsequent smoking when nicotine preloading was administered intravenously. In addition, the fact that lettuce cigarettes with added nicotine were as unacceptable as non-nicotine cigarettes also seems to undermine the nicotine-only hypothesis (Jarvik, 1977). Jarvik (1977) concludes, therefore, that nicotine is a necessary but not sufficient condtion for smoking behavior to occur and to be sustained. Clearly, more research will be needed to settle the issue of whether nicotine functions as the primary reinforcer or as a "reinforcing co-factor" with another substance, possibly tar.

Tars and carbon monoxide contribute to the chronic effects of smoking on health. Jarvik (1977) points out that the effects on the skin mucous membranes, stomach, heart, circulation, respiratory system, and other organ systems are all undesirable, but the onset of pathophysiological changes is so subtle and insidious that the smoker is usually not aware of their existence or has habituated to them (as in the case of coughs and hoarseness). Jarvik further observes that even severe diseases in which the onset is gradual, such as emphysema or thromboanginitis obliterans, have a negligible impact on smoking; acute myocardial infarction, however, is much more likely to result in prompt cessation.

Smoke particles are accumulated in the oral cavity, esophagus, and lungs and, after decades of smoking, smokers are more prone to carcinoma in these organs than non-smokers. Atherosclerotic changes are also found frequently in the cardiovascular system of smokers; the mechanisms may be the result of interactions among several factors, including anoxemia following carboxyhemoglobin formation by carbon monoxide, increases in platelet adhesiveness, and the effects of catecholamine release by nicotine (Jarvik, 1977).

While there is considerable overlap between smokers and non-smokers in personality, cigarette smokers tend to be impatient, somewhat more angry, and more easily bored (Larson & Silvette, 1975). Eysenck (1973) has proposed that the smoker is an extroverted person functioning at less than an optimal level of arousal. Such a view is not inconsistent with observations that smokers drink more coffee than non-smokers (Thomas, 1973) and that they smoke more when bored than when aroused (Fuller & Forrest, 1973). Dividing smokers into those who said they smoked to reduce tension and those who smoked to alleviate boredom and increase arousal, Myrsten, Anderson, Frankenhauser & Elgerot (1975) found that on a monotonous task, arousal smokers performed better and tension smokers showed no significant difference from baseline; on a task characterized by high tension the reverse was found, with tension smokers doing better and arousal smokers showing no difference from the baseline. Studying the orienting response in the EEG, Friedman, Horvath and Meares (1974) reported that smoking facilitates habituation to irrelevant stimuli; thus smoking seems to provide a barrier (or "smoke screen") against distracting stimulation.

When smokers stop smoking, they experience a wide variety of symptoms (Jaffe & Jarvik, 1977). Smoking-cessation symptoms include craving for tobacco, irritability, restlessness, dullness, sleep disturbances, gastro-intestinal disturbances, anxiety, and impairment of concentration, judgment, and psychomotor performance (Shiffman & Jarvik, 1976). The onset of symptoms may occur within hours or days after quitting and may persist from a few days to several months. Additional objective signs include a decrease in heart rate and blood pressure, increased REM sleep, and slower rhythms in the EEG (Knapp, Bliss & Wells, 1963; Kales, Allen, Preston & Tan, 1970; Itil, Ulett, Hsu, Klingenberg & Ulett, 1971). Spontaneous jaw clenching (i.e., increased Masseter potentials) lasting for several weeks has been correlated with verbal reports of irritability (Hutchinson & Emley, 1973).

While the above suggest a number of possible mechanisms to explain the persistence of smoking and the difficulty of quitting, integrating these various findings into a testable model involving behavioral, physiological, and cognitive elements has been difficult. At present, three models are of sufficient scope to make substantial contributions toward the formulation of a comprehensive overview of smoking. These three models are the social learning, nicotine addiction, and opponent process models.

The Social Learning Model

Social learning theory has functioned less as a formal explanatory model of smoking and more as a methodological approach with an associated intervention technology. As Bernstein and Glasgow (1979) point out, the impetus for using behavior modification techniques was based upon the belief that research procedures which operationalize definitions, emphasize well-controlled empirical research, and are derived from concepts formed in the experimental laboratory, will provide valuable practical and theoretical knowledge—a position justified by previous contributions in the management of other difficult problems in human behavior (e.g., Bandura, 1969; Leitenberg, 1976; Rimm & Masters, 1974).

Behavior modification is derived from basic research on animal learning by Pavlov and Skinner (Skinner, 1953) and emphasizes the control of antecedent and consequent environmental events (stimuli) in determining behavior (Brady, 1979). Social learning theory represents an extension of behavior modification to situations which involve interpersonal activity and incorporates the added explanatory concepts of imitation and social reinforcement (Bandura, 1969).

A social learning explanation of smoking proceeds along the following general lines. The habit is acquired under conditions of social reinforcement, typically through peer pressure. Initially the inhalation of smoke is aversive but after sufficient practice, habituation (or tolerance) occurs, and the behavior begins to provide sufficient positive reinforcement in its own right to be sustained independently of social reinforcement and now generalizes to situations other than the one in which it was originally acquired.

Discrimination between situations in which smoking is punished socially and those in which it is either ignored or favorably received is learned and various circumstances (both external and internal) now control smoking. By virtue of being associated with smoking, some situations (e.g., an empty cigarette pack, an annoying telephone call) may serve as conditional stimuli (CSs) which elicit covert responses that increase the likelihood of smoking (e.g., physiological changes or discomfort, perceived as craving). The same situations can also serve as discriminative stimuli (S^Ds) setting the occasion for the reinforcement provided by smoking. Moreover, stimuli which are preparatory for the act of smoking (e.g., the sight of a cigarette) can function as secondary reinforcers for behaviors preceding them (e.g., a full cigarette pack) and also as discriminative stimuli for behaviors which follow them (e.g., lighting the cigarette), forming a linked chain of responses (i.e., a smoking ritual). Thus, the successful termination of the overt act of smoking requires the extinction of most or all of the conditional stimuli, secondary reinforcers, and discriminative stimuli which make up the habit.

The emotional events which can influence smoking are potentially quite numerous. If smoking is seen, in part, as an avoidance/escape response to aversive withdrawal states, then, hypothetically, by a process of stimulus generalization, other dysphoric states (e.g., anger, tension, boredom) may also serve as discriminative stimuli for smoking. Similarly, response generalization may occur in which the smoking ritual serves as a temporary escape (coping response) from various aversive situations (smoking as a response which provides relief). Smoking can be seen, therefore, as a generalized primary and secondary reinforcer providing both positive and negative reinforcement over a remarkably wide array of life situations.

Smoking may also be difficult to modify because of its ability to provide immediate reinforcement—nicotine from an inhaled cigarette reaches the brain in seven seconds, which is twice as fast as intravenous administration from the arm. Furthermore, the habit is tremendously overlearned: at ten puffs per cigarette, the pack-a-day smoker gets more than 70,000 nicotine "shots" in a year—a frequency unmatched by any other form of drug taking (Russell, 1977). While most smokers recognize that sustained smoking can lead to a variety of unpleasant events, ranging from bronchitis to lung cancer, the ultimate aversive consequences of smoking (though potentially of great magnitude) are delayed and, therefore, have less influence over ongoing smoking behavior than immediate consequences—a situation common to a number of self-management problems (Pomerleau, Bass, & Crown, 1975). Also, unlike alcohol and many other drugs of dependence, not only does smoking not impair performance but it may even enhance the capacity of normal people to work and to socialize—thus, there are few immediately noticeable negative consequences (Russell, 1977). Furthermore, for many smokers, the unpleasant consequences of smoking develop so gradually that habituation probably occurs (Jarvik, 1977).

As Lichtenstein (1977) has observed, to a large extent, behavioral researchers have assumed relationships between environmental events and smoking. Treatment practices have been based on the general theory rather than on specific research on smoking behavior. Thus, part of the promise of social learning theory has been fulfilled—and several behavioral concepts have generated new standards of effectiveness in the treatment of smoking—but there has not been a corresponding contribution to the understanding of smoking in its own right.

The Nicotine Addiction Model

Schachter (1978) among others (e.g., Jarvik, 1977; Russell, 1977) has proposed that smoking is an escape response to nicotine withdrawal in an addictive cycle: an internal regulatory mechanism is implied which detects the level of nicotine and keeps it within characteristic limits by regulating the frequency of smoking. Much of the evidence in support of the theory comes from a series of innovative experiments conducted by Schachter and his associates over a ten year span, which are reviewed by Schachter in Chapter 3.

The Schacter experiments suggest that the smoker regulates nicotine levels under widely varying conditions, implying a mechanism (possibly a central "nicostat" or the integration of various peripheral drug effects of nicotine) which senses nicotine and provides the impetus for directed behavior. While the model is straightforward and plausible, critical tests have yet to be performed. Particularly, direct measurements of changes in nicotine titer and of the withdrawal state have not been attempted. Also, among variables not adequately explained by the model are: a) the role of stimulus control at different stages of the habit, b) individual differences in smoking behavior (light or occasional smokers versus heavy or chronic smokers), and c) the mechanism(s) by which relapse occurs following pharmacological withdrawal.

The Opponent Process Model

The opponent process theory of acquired motivation propounded by Solomon (Solomon & Corbit, 1973, 1974; Solomon, 1977) uses data derived from animal experimentation—particularly Pavlovian conditioning and shock-avoidance studies—to explain a number of phenomena in the addiction field, including smoking (Ternes, 1977). The model postulates central nervous system (CNS) mechanisms which operate homostatically to reduce significant departures (either positive or negative) from affective equilibrium. Reduction in affective intensity occurs through the activation of an opposing process, brought into action when hedonic or emotional states are aroused. Events capable of producing an imbalance are typically unconditional stimuli (UCSs) or primary reinforcers. In opponent process terminology, a UCS is an affect-arousing stimulus capable of eliciting primary affective processes (UCRs) called *a*-processes. An *a*-process may reflect either pleasant or unpleasant affect depending on the UCS that elicited it. The elicitation of the *a*-process triggers a *b*-process, an opposite affective response. The *a*-process closely tracks the input variable (the UCS) and does not show much habituation during the UCS presentation; the *b*-process, however, is more sluggish than the *a*-process and is slower to peak or to return to baseline following the termination of the UCS. Since the hedonic tone or state reflects the algebraic sum of the two opponent processes at a given point in time, a biphasic pattern is predicted: thus, initially at UCS onset, when $a>b$, the affective state is dictated by the *a*-process and A state dominates; later at UCS offset, when $a<b$, the affective state reflects the *b*-process and B state dominates. These processes are nonassociative and are not based on conditioning or learning.

Parameters which affect the growth of the *b*-process include intensity of UCS, duration of UCS, interval between UCS presentations, and frequency of UCS presentations. The opponent process theory postulates that the *b*-process will be strengthened through use and weakened through disuse. In the case of addictive substances, the intensifying of withdrawal symptoms with repeated drug use is taken to reflect an enhancement of the B state; the corresponding decrease in pleasure associated with drug taking is seen as the result of the inhibitory influence of the *b*-process on the A state. Increasingly larger doses of the drug are thus required to produce pleasure. Under this formulation, a major requirement for maintaining the addictive cycle is that the interval between UCS presentations be short enough to anticipate the complete decay of the *b*-process; stimulus presentations exceeding this critical interval do not contribute to the growth of the *b*-process, and thus the *a*-process, being relatively unopposed, continues to engender a strong A state. Going back to addictive substances as an example, if the user takes the drug infrequently, the likelihood of addiction is low and drug taking is more likely to be positively reinforced (taken for pleasure) rather than negatively reinforced (taken to escape withdrawal symptoms).

These concepts are related to cigarette smoking in the following general terms. First, cigarettes must contain substances which provide pleasure (initiate the *a*-process) during early use. There may be some aversive effects on the first few occasions but these should be offset by the drug effect or by other reinforcers (possibly social reinforcers such as peer pressure); if they are not, the act of smoking will not be repeated. As cigarette consumption continues, the opponent *b*-process becomes strengthened: the pleasurable A state weakens while the aversive B state and withdrawal intensify. Because the *b*-process is the opponent of the *a*-process, the best way of getting rid of the B state is to use the substance that produces the A state. Smoking as an operant is thus positively reinforced by producing pleasure and negatively reinforced by terminating withdrawal, setting up an addictive cycle. As the *b*-process is further strengthened, still larger amounts of tobacco have to be smoked to offset a decrease in the pleasurable A state—the phenomenon of tolerance.

Stimuli associated with smoking (CS_As), such as a pack of cigarettes and the sight of matches, should elicit a brief conditioned (pleasurable) A state at stimulus onset and a conditioned (unpleasant) withdrawal B state at stimulus offset. Stimuli associated with the B state (CS_Bs), such as an empty cigarette pack, no stores, empty pockets, "no smoking" signs, should elicit conditioned craving or withdrawal. An important implication is that as the smoking habit becomes well established and the *b*-process becomes stronger, CS_As elicit a brief conditioned state which is pleasant but then is followed by more extended conditioned craving which is added to the pre-existing, intensified (withdrawal) B state; similarly, CSBs directly elicit conditioned craving, which adds to the discomfort of withdrawal. A further implication is that as CSBs become stronger, they may become more anticipatory, and so, redosage and restimulation intervals become shorter, until an asymptote is reached. Should the smoker quit, the CSBs and the *b*-process should weaken eventually through disuse, but unfortunately the CSAs and the A state increase in strength correspondingly—thus, if a cigarette is smoked after a period of abstinence, the pleasurable component has increased to the original level, and the resumption of the addictive cycle is facilitated.

The explanations of the opponent process model are consistent with subjective reports by former smokers: after a brief acquisition stage in which smoking was sufficiently aversive to require extrinsic reinforcement, smokers report that smoking was pleasurable for a while (*a*-process>*b*-process) but, in time, more cigarettes were consumed (tolerance) and the pleasure of smoking was overshadowed by the discomfort of not smoking (*a*-process<*b*-process). Also, after abstaining for a few weeks, relapsing smokers indicate that craving decreased but that when cigarette smoking was resumed, the first few seemed very strong and were highly pleasurable (*a*-process>*b*-process). While the opponent process model has not been tested in formal research on cigarette smoking yet, conditioning studies in the animal laboratory provide support for its basic constructs, including opposed A and B states (Katcher et al., 1969) and conditionability (Rescorla & LoLordo, 1965).

The greatest amount of relevant research has been done in the area of opiate addiction. Among the major tenets of the opponent process model is that drug self-administration produces opposed *a*- and *b*-processes. In the case of opiates, the states reported initially are immediate intense pleasure followed by sedation. After repeated dosage, a smaller pleasurable immediate response is followed by highly disagreeable withdrawal symptoms. The presence of a pleasurable drug state and an aversive withdrawal state has been confirmed clinically in humans using subjective, behavioral, and physiological measures (O'Brien, Testa,

O'Brien & Greenstein, 1976); in animals, reports of operant strengthening of behavior which produces the drug state (positive reinforcement) and of behavior which terminates the withdrawal state (negative reinforcement) along with physiological concomitants are interpreted as consistent with the human findings (Schuster & Thompson, 1969).

While the growth of tolerance with repeated drug administration has long been recognized as a characteristic of the opiates (Maurer & Vogel, 1967), it has not been as widely recognized that a major feature of addictive substances is that the withdrawal B state must be sufficiently prolonged (critical decay duration) so that instrumental self-dosing provides both relief from aversive craving (the B state) and pleasure from consumption (A state). Moreover, consistent with the assumptions of the opponent process model, evidence suggests that the phenomena of addiction are the result of both associative and non-associative processes (Wikler & Pescor, 1967; Weeks & Collins, 1968).

The conditionability of opiate drug states has been well established in animals and humans. Stimuli associated with the pleasurable drug state (A state) have been shown to function as secondary positive reinforcers (Davis & Smith, 1976) as well as to restore ongoing instrumental responding in a manner analogous to administration of the primary reinforcing drug (Thompson & Schuster, 1964). Conditioned withdrawal (B state) has also been demonstrated in numerous studies on physically dependent animals and people: A previously neutral stimulus paired with an opiate antagonist (which precipitates the withdrawal syndrome) becomes an aversive CS—suppressing instrumental responding, functioning as a secondary negative reinforcer, or eliciting both physiological and subjective manifestations of the abstinence syndrome (Goldberg, 1976; O'Brien et al., 1976; Wikler, 1976).

The demonstration of conditionability has important implications for understanding opiate-addiction relapse in humans, for environmental stimuli may precipitate conditioned craving even after an extended abstinence period has ended physical dependence (O'Brien et al., 1976). Wikler (1965) has even proposed that relapse in the detoxified addict should be expected if conditioned craving is not extinguished as part of therapy. The opponent process model predicts a biphasic response (A state followed by B state) to the presentation and removal of stimuli associated with drug taking during acquisition; later in the addiction process when tolerance is large, however, the dominant conditioned effects should be those of craving or withdrawal (B state predominates). In a general way, this prediction is consistent with research on heroin addicts by O'Brien (1977) showing that slides of drug taking paraphernalia (the "works") elicit "compensatory" physiological responses (craving or B state) which are opposite in direction to the drug response (A state).

The opponent process model has the potential of providing a comprehensive framework for smoking, for it takes in both associative and non-associative factors in combining elements from the social learning and nicotine regulation models. In addition, the concept of hedonic regulation using opposed states and of the conditionability of these states—measurable at both the cognitive and physiological levels—has clear implications for experimentation. The model's major shortcoming at present is that it remains untested in the smoking area.

Toward a General Theory of Smoking

While not necessarily as extensively elaborated, a number of other theories and models have been promulgated to explain smoking and related phenomena. The development, maintenance, and modification of smoking have been seen from the perspective of models emphasizing affective, behavioral, motivational, personality, and pharmacological variables (Bernstein & Glasgow, 1979) as well as multidimensional attempts (Glad, Tyre & Adesso, 1976; Mausner, 1973).

The three models chosen for detailed review here were selected because, taken together, they seem to be the most suitable for integrating into a comprehensive framework and for providing a general theory. While there are some inconsistencies and contradictions among them, the formulations are sufficiently explicit to enable the differences to constitute testable hypotheses.

Current issues needing resolution include the following. Schachter's nicotine addiction model implies that the day-to-day regulation of smoking is more under the control of pharmacological variables than of environmental stimuli (Schachter, Chapter 3); the relative contribution of these sets of variables, however, remains to be determined. The extent to which smoking reduces anxiety is not fully settled either: Hutchinson and Emley (1973) emphasize nicotine's ability to function as a tranquilizer, since it decreases aggression as well as conditioned suppression, and they speculate that the difficulty of training animals to smoke under ordinary conditions is because a background of aversive stimulation is needed to provide motivation to use smoking for anxiety relief. The pharmacological primacy of nicotine implied by Schachter's model has yet to be unequivocally established also (e.g., Kumar et al., 1977). Clearly additional research needs to be directed toward these issues.

Similar problems arise for the opponent process model. For example, Wikler (1973) has argued that certain responses associated with chronic drug use, such as tolerance or conditioned withdrawal, are counter-adaptions serving to protect the organism by acting in a direction opposite the normal drug effect. The opponent process model is stated in sufficiently general terms to incorporate these observations if certain (untested) assumptions are made: Wikler's observations emphasize the dominant drug-negative B state; in the opponent process interpretation, the initial drug-positive *a*-process (and thus the pleasurable A state) is still operative but may be so brief and attenuated that it goes undetected. Clearly, a closer examination of the time course for the response to drugs at different stages of acquisition will be needed to settle this issue. Moreover, Siegel (1975, 1977) has shown that the stimuli which constitute the ritual of (repeated) drug injection can elicit conditioned reactions which increase tolerance to the drug; extinction of these conditioned reactions using a series of saline injections results in decreased tolerance. The implication is that tolerance is influenced by or is the result of compensatory *associative* processes and is not simply a pharmacological (non-associative) phenomenon. While opponent process theory can be modified to accommodate these findings also, by defining them as the manifestations of stimuli which serve as conditioned B state elicitors, the relative contribution of associative and non-associative factors cannot be specified at present. Also if tolerance is basically an associative process, the problem of explaining why certain drugs produce tolerance while others do not will also have to be dealt with.

Suggestions for Basic Research

The three models presented can be used to provide a general framework and theory for research. Since smoking consists of a complex interaction between overt behavior, autonomic responses, and subjective states, parallel measurements on the three levels of functioning should be made. To get at these processes, measures should be taken of smoking behavior (specifying variables such as puff frequencies and duration, depth of inhalation, nicotine drawn from a standard cigarette, etc.), of major physiological variables (e.g., cardiovascular changes, relevant biochemical activity including cholinergic, catecholamine, and nicotine changes), and cognitive variables (e.g., hedonic states and subjective desire to smoke at different points in time). The tremendous number of variables known to affect smoking suggests that investigating smoking in a laboratory situation using a standard preparation might be a useful strategy, initially. While such an approach might seem artificial to some, enhancing experimental control by restricting extraneous variables has been productive for other difficult problems (e.g., in alcoholism, Nathan & O'Brien, 1971). If successful, subsequent research can be conducted in increasingly complex, naturalistic settings. The following are some of the questions which can be addressed in the context of the general theory.

a) Most physiological models assign a central role to nicotine in the regulation of smoking. As a preliminary step, the issue can be explored in habitual smokers by studying the relationship between the act of smoking, subjective desire, and nicotine levels in the body under different conditons of deprivation. Implementation could involve presenting a cigarette at regular (short) intervals and measuring blood nicotine levels and craving, while noting on which trials cigarettes were or were not smoked. Nicotine excretion rates could also be shifted using drugs (or stress) to provide further modulation of physiological, behavioral, and subjective responses, thus replicating and extending previous work in this area. The demonstration of nicotine regulation by direct measurement might lead to further exploration of other important biochemical variables, such as catecholamines, and might stimulate additional activity on the elucidation of a central regulatory mechanism (the "nicostat"). The delineation of a relationship between nicotine levels and physiological activity, such as cardiovascular changes, might also suggest a new line of experimentation using cigarette smoking to study how patterns of autonomic activity are perceived and influence behavior (Mandler, Mandler & Uviller, 1958; Schwartz, 1977).

b) The social learning model assumes that smoking behavior is subject to stimulus control. A number of experiments can be devised to test this hypothesis. A direct approach would be to measure behavioral, physiological, and subjective responses in simulated smoking situations. (A good example is provided in a recent study by Griffiths, Bigelow & Liebson, 1976, on the relationship between smoking and drinking by alcoholics). One way of approaching the problem might be to provide the opportunity to smoke a cigarette at regular intervals under different conditions consisting of visual (e.g., slides of places associated with smoking), auditory (sounds of people lighting up at a cocktail party), and olfactory stimuli (the smell of cigarette smoke) as well as social stimulation (being offered a cigarette). It is important to note that the chain of behavior which constitutes the smoking ritual for a particular smoker has not been studied experimentally—determination of how different components function as a unit might have important theoretical and practical implications. The extent to which smoking is a learned phenomenon is an important question: A series of experiments could be conducted on the question of conditioning in tolerance, for instance. While addicting non-smokers is ethically unacceptable, habitual smokers not intending to quit could be asked to abstain for varying periods of time. The intensity of their physiological and subjective responses could be compared before quitting and after different abstinence intervals. With sufficiently cooperative subjects (who were willing to restrict their smoking to the laboratory), the conditioned tolerance hypothesis (Siegel, 1977) might be tested in smokers. For example, three groups of smokers could be trained to smoke under artificial conditions using a cigarette dispensing machine—one group could then abstain entirely for a period of time, while a second group would also abstain but would be exposed to extinction trials using the smoking machine, and a third group would simply continue smoking during the same interval. Conditioned tolerance would be supported if less tolerance occurred in subsequent testing, in the group undergoing extinction; pharmacological tolerance would be suggested if *both* non-smoking (abstaining) groups exhibited less tolerance than the smoking group.

c) The nicotine addiction model holds that smoking is an escape response to nicotine withdrawal and is thus a negative reinforcer; on the other hand, both positive and negative reinforcing functions are hypothesized for smoking in social learning theory and the opponent process model. Using a preparation similar to that suggested for investigating conditioned tolerance, the problem could be studied in addicted smokers by asking them to undergo a period of abstinence followed by re-addiction. The opponent process model predicts that in the original addiction phase, the resultant pleasurable A state (the initial response to smoking) is weak and the dysphoric B state (the delayed response) is strong; in the early re-acquisition phase, however, the resulting A state should be stronger and the B state weaker. The demonstration of physiologically different states, correlated with pleasant and/or unpleasant affect, would provide implicit support for the idea that smoking involves both positive and negative reinforcement. Further definition on a behavioral level could be attempted by pairing one stimulus with the physiological manifestation of the A state and another with the B state; the reinforcing value of these stimuli could be tested objectively by determining which stimulus the subject would work to present (defining a secondary positive reinforcer) or to remove (a secondary negative reinforcer).

d) The opponent process model emphasizes the role of associational variables such as conditioned craving in explaining the difficulty of quitting cigarettes. As in previous examples, conditioning variables might be studied profitably by measuring behavioral, physiological, and subjective responses in the laboratory. A straightforward approach to the problem might involve presenting a stimulus associated with smoking (e.g., a "smoking permitted" sign, prior to and during the smoking of a cigarette) and a stimulus never associated with smoking (a "no smoking" sign). Opponent process theory makes a number of detailed predictions: Presentation of the stimulus associated with smoking should elicit physiological and subjective A states—conditioned satiation—and the offset, a B state—conditioned craving. The stimulus never associated with smoking should elicit only conditioned craving at the onset followed by a gradual return to baseline at the offset. The procedure also provides a test for the counteradaption model (Wikler, 1973), which predicts that *all* conditioned responses should be craving or withdrawal states (B states). Understanding the conditions under which conditioned craving does or does not occur may lead to the development of procedures for its modification—a development with important implications for the maintenance of non-smoking following treatment.

Implications for Applied Research, Treatment, and Social Policy

The paradigms for research just discussed can be used to ask questions with immediate practical consequences as well. Thus, the suggestion that nicotine plays a major or dominant role in the regulation of smoking raises the issue of the appropriateness of trying to get people to smoke low tar, low nicotine cigarettes: As Schachter (1978) put it, low tar, *high* nicotine cigarettes might be safer because fewer cigarettes would be smoked. This question could be pursued in the laboratory using the preparations described above, by comparing ad libitum smoking of cigarettes with high and/or low tar and nicotine. A careful description of the number of cigarettes smoked and the number of puffs per cigarette, backed up with quantitative determinations of nicotine, carbon monoxide, tars, and other smoke products ingested, might provide more exact information than is currently available from surveys of smoking in the natural environment.

Similarly, a greater understanding of the stimulus control of smoking, including the limits of such control, could be very valuable. From the point of view of reinforcing consequences, the growing emphasis on the social unattractiveness of smoking (e.g., the non-smoker's rights movement) has clear justification because it provides more immediate reinforcement for quitting than is obtained when the focus is limited to the health consequences of the habit; the effects of such an approach on the decision to quit smoking, however, have yet to be studied formally. Social learning theory has produced major improvements in the short-term modification of smoking behavior, but it has not devoted sufficient attention to the problem of sustaining non-smoking (Pomerleau, 1978). Very little is known about the activities which might serve as suitable replacements for smoking: For example, the possibility that smoking provides positive reinforcement suggests rewarding activities—such as exercise, hobbies, etc.; smoking as negative reinforcement suggests the inculcation of coping behaviors—deep breathing or muscle relaxation exercises to deal with anxiety or tension. Various substitute activities have been proposed (Bernstein & Glasgow, 1979), but, perhaps because outcome research is so difficult and time consuming, none have received full experimental corroboration to date. A more productive approach might come out of an experimental analysis of smoking behavior, in which the degree to which alternative patterns could be substituted for smoking (behaviorally, physiologically, psychologically) was determined in the laboratory under more controlled conditions.

Finally, demonstrating conditioned craving on an experimental basis may provide an entirely new approach to the old problem of recidivism. If therapy modifies only the overt act of smoking (an operant) for a given smoker, without extinguishing the various eliciting stimuli for covert responses (physiological and cognitive respondents), then, at the end of therapy, that person will continue to be plagued by conditioned craving and withdrawal symptoms—even after pharmacological withdrawal is complete—and thus will be more likely to relapse and resume smoking (e.g., the "negative affect" smoker in Pomerleau, Adkins, & Pertschuk, 1978). Preliminary support for the idea is provided in the area of alcoholism by Kennedy (1971), who demonstrated that patients who exhibited pupillary dilation in response to the smell of a favorite beverage, just prior to discharge from a treatment program, were much more likely to relapse within six months than patients who did not show this response. If a similar result for smoking were demonstrated, the next step would be to conduct outcome studies comparing a standard smoking-cessation treatment with augmented therapy in which autonomic responses were extinguished in a simulated environment or modified directly using biofeedback. The expected result should be a demonstrably lower rate of recidivism for smokers exposed to augmented therapy.

Conclusion

The present review has suggested that the integration of three models for smoking—the social learning, nicotine addiction, and opponent process models—may provide a more rational basis for treatment and a more comprehensive framework for generating and evaluating research hypotheses. While the formulation subsumes data from various clinical and research areas and seems to offer some promise of internal consistency as a unified general theory, the final measure of its adequacy must be the productivity and usefulness of the treatment and experimentation which it stimulates.

REFERENCES

Ague, C.: Smoking patterns, nicotine intake at different times of day and changes in two cardiovascular variables while smoking cigarettes. *Psychopharmacologia,* 1973, *30,* 135-144.

American Heart Association: *Report of the Inter-Society Commission for Heart Disease Resources,* Vol. 42, 1970.

Armitage, A., Hall, G., & Morrison, C.: Pharmacological basis of the tobacco smoking habit. *Nature,* 1968, *217,* 331-334.

Auger, T., Wright, E., & Simpson, R.: Posters as smoking deterrents. *Journal of Applied Psychology,* 1972, *56,* 169-171.

Bandura, A.: *Principles of behavior modification.* New York: Holt, Rinehart, & Winston, 1969.

Bernstein, D.: Modification of smoking behavior: an evaluative review. *Psychological Bulletin,* 1969, *71,* 418-440.

Bernstein, D. & Glasgow, R.: Smoking. In O. F. Pomerleau & J. P. Brady (Eds.), *Behavioral medicine: Theory and practice.* Baltimore: Williams and Wilkins, 1979.

Borgatta, E. & Evans, R. (Eds.): *Smoking, health, and behavior.* Chicago: Aldine Publishing Co., 1968.

Brady, J. V.: Learning and Conditioning. In O. F. Pomerleau and J. P. Brady (Eds.), *Behavioral medicine: Theory and practice.* Baltimore: Williams and Wilkins, in press.

Cryer, P., Haymond, M., Santiago, J., & Shah, S.: Norepinephrine and epinephrine release and adrenergic meditation of smoking-associated hemodynamic and metabolic events. *New England Journal of Medicine,* 1976, *295,* 573-577.

Davis, W. & Smith, S.: Role of conditioned reinforcers in the initiation, maintenance and extinction of drug behavior. *The Pavlovian Journal of Biological Science,* 1976, *142,* 222-236.

Deneau, G. & Inoki, R.: Nicotine self-administration in monkeys. *Annals of the New York Academy of Sciences,* 1967, *142,* 277-279.

Domino, E.: Neuropsychopharmacology of nicotine and tobacco smoking. In W. Dunn, (Ed.), *Smoking behavior: Motives and incentives.* Washington: Winston, 1973.

Eysenck, H.: Personality and the maintenance of the smoking habit. In W. Dunn (Ed.), *Smoking behavior: Motives and incentives.* Washington: Winston, 1973.

Frankl, W., Friedman, R., & Soloff, L.: Cardiac output, blood pressure, and free fatty acid responses to smoking in the non-basal state. *American Journal of Medical Science,* 1966, *252,* 39-44.

Friedman, J., Horvath, T., & Meares, R.: Tobacco smoking and a stimulus barrier. *Nature,* 1974, *248,* 455-456.

Fuller, R. & Forrest, D.: Behavioral aspects of cigarette smoking in relation to arousal level. *Psychological Reports,* 1973, *33,* 115-121.

GLAD, W., TYRE, T., & ADESSO, V.: A multidimensional model of cigarette smoking. *American Journal of Clinical Hypnosis,* 1976, *19,* 82-29.

GOLDBERG, S.: Conditioned behavioral and physiological changes associated with injections of a narcotic antagonist in morphine-dependent monkeys. *The Pavlovian Journal of Biological Science,* 1976, *11,* 203-221.

GOLDFARB, T., JARVIK, M., & GLICK, S.: Cigarette nicotine content as a determinant of human smoking behavior. *Psychopharmacologia* (Berl.), 1970, 17, 89-93.

GOLDFARB, T., GRITZ, E., JARVIK, M., & STOLERMAN, I.: Reactions to cigarettes as a function of nicotine and "tar." *Clinical Pharmacology and Therapeutics,* 1976, *19,* 767-772.

GRIFFITHS, R., BIGELOW, G., & LIEBSON, I.: Facilitation of human tobacco self-administration by ethanol: a behavioral analysis. *Journal of the Experimental Analysis of Behavior,* 1976, *25,* 279-292.

GRITZ, E.: Smoking: The prevention of onset. In M. Jarvik, J. Cullen, E. Gritz, T. Vogt, & L. West. (Eds.) *Research on smoking behavior* (NIDA Research Monograph #17). Rockville, Md.: National Institute on Drug Abuse, 1977.

HAMMOND, E.: The effects of smoking. *Scientific American,* 1962, *207,* 39-51.

HAMMOND, E. & GARFINKEL, L.: Coronary heart disease, stroke, and aortic aneurism. *Archives of Environmental Health,* 1969, *10,* 167-182.

HUNT, W. & BESPALEC, D.: An evaluation of current methods of modifying smoking behavior. *Journal of Clinical Psychology,* 1974, *30,* 431-438.

HUTCHINSON, R. & EMLEY, G.: Effects on nicotine on avoidance, conditioned suppression and agression response measures in animals and man in smoking behavior: motives and incentives. In W. Dunn (Ed.), *Smoking behavior: Motives and incentives.* Washington: Winston, 1973.

ITIL, T., ULETT, G., HSU, W., KLINGENBERG, H., & ULETT, J.: The effects of smoking withdrawal on qualitatively analyzed EEG. *Clinical Electroencephalography,* 1971, *2,* 44-51.

JAFFE, J. & JARVIK, M.: Tobacco use and the tobacco use disorder. In *Psychopharmacology: A review of progress, 1967-1977.* Proceedings of the American College of Neuropsychopharmacology, 1977.

JARVIK, M.: Biological factors underlying the smoking habit. In M. Jarvik, J. Cullen, E. Gritz, T. Vogt, & L. West. (Eds.), *Research on smoking behavior* (NIDA Research Monograph #17). Rockville, Md.: National Institute on Drug Abuse, 1977.

KALES, J., ALLEN, C., PRESTON, T., & TAN, T.: Changes in REM sleep and dreaming with cigarette smoking and following withdrawal. *Psychophysiology,* 1970, *7,* 347-348.

KATCHER, A., SOLOMAN, R., TURNER, L., LOLORDO, V., OVERMIER, J. & RESCORLA, R.: Heart rate and blood pressure responses to signalled and unsignalled shocks: effects of cardiac sympathectomy. *Journal of Comparative and Physiological Psychology,* 1969, *68,* 163-174.

KENNEDY, D. A.: Pupilometrics as an aid in the assessment of motivation, impact of treatment, and prognosis of chronic alcoholics. Unpublished dissertation, University of Utah, 1971.

KNAPP, P., BLISS, C., & WELLS, H.: Addictive aspects in heavy cigarette smoking. *American Journal of Psychiatry,* 1963, *119,* 966-972.

KOZLOWSKI, L., JARVIK, M. & GRITZ, E.: Nicotine regulation and cigarette smoking. *Clinical Pharmacology and Therapeutics,* 1975, *17,* 93-97.

KUMAR, R., COOKE, E., LADER, M., & RUSSELL, M.: Is nicotine important in tobacco smoking? *Clinical Pharmacology and Therapeutics,* 1977, *21,* 520-529.

LARSON, P. & SILVETTE, H.: *Tobacco: Experimental and clinical studies III.* Baltimore, Md.: Williams and Wilkins, 1975.

LEITENBERG, H. (ED.): *Handbook of behavior modification and behavior therapy.* Englewood Cliffs, N. J.: Prentice-Hall, 1976.

LICHTENSTEIN, E.: Current approaches: I. Social learning. In M. Jarvik, J. Cullen, E. Gritz, T. Vogt & L. West. (Eds.) *Research on smoking behavior* (NIDA Research Monograph #17). Rockville, Md.: National Institute on Drug Abuse, 1977.

LICHTENSTEIN, E. & PENNER, M.: Long-term effects of rapid smoking treatment. *Addictive Behaviors,* 1977, *2,* 109-112.

LUCCHESI, B., SCHUSTER, C., & EMLEY, G.: The role of nicotine as a determinant of cigarette smoking frequency in man, with observations of certain cardiovascular effects associated with the tobacco alkaloid. *Clinical Pharmacology and Therapeutics,* 1967, *8,* 789-796.

MANDLER, G., MANDLER, J., & UVILLER, E.: Autonomic feedback: the perception of autonomic activity. *Journal of Abnormal and Social Psychology,* 1958, *56,* 367-373.

MAURER, D. & VOGEL, M.: *Narcotics and narcotic addiction.* Springfield, Ill.: Charles C Thomas, 1967.

MAUSNER, B.: An ecological view of cigarette smoking behavior. *Journal of Abnormal Psychology,* 1973, *81,* 115-126.

MYRSTEN, A., ANDERSON, F., FRANKENHAUSER, M., & ELGEROT, A.: Immediate effects of cigarette smoking as related to different smoking habits. *Perceptual and Motor Skills,* 1975, *40,* 515-523.

NATHAN, P. & O'BRIEN, J.: An experimental analysis of the behavior of alcoholics and non-alcoholics during prolonged experimental drinking. *Behavior Therapy,* 1971, *2,* 455-476.

O'BRIEN, C.: Psychobiology of addiction. In J. P. Brady, J. Mendels, M. Orne, & W. Rieger, *Psychiatry: Areas of promise and advancement.* New York: Spectrum, 1977.

O'BRIEN, C., TESTA, T., O'BRIEN, T., & GREENSTEIN, R.: Conditioning in human opiate addicts. *The Pavlovian Journal of Biological Science,* 1976, *11,* 195-202.

O'KEEFE, M.: The anti-smoking commercials: A study of television impact on behavior. *Public Opinion Quarterly,* 1971, *35,* 242-248.

POMERLEAU, O. F.: Strategies for maintenance: The problem of sustaining abstinence from cigarettes. Paper presented at the International Conference on Smoking Cessation, New York, June, 1978.

POMERLEAU, O.F.: Commonalities in the treatment and understanding of smoking and other self-management disorders. In N. Krasnegor (Ed.), *Behavioral approaches to analysis and treatment of substance abuse* (NIDA monograph series). Rockville, M.D.: National Institute on Drug Abuse, 1979.

POMERLEAU, O. F., ADKINS, D., & PERTSCHUK, M.: Predictors of outcome and recidivism in smoking-cessation treatment. *Addictive Behaviors,* 1978, *3,* 65-70.

POMERLEAU, O. F., BASS, F., & CROWN, V.: The role of behavior modification in preventive medicine. *New England Journal of Medicine,* 1975, *292,* 1277-1282.

POMERLEAU, O. & POMERLEAU, C.: *Break the smoking habit: A behavioral program for giving up cigarettes.* Champaign, Ill.: Research Press, 1977.

RESCORLA, R. & LOLORDO, V.: Inhibition of avoidance behavior. *Journal of Comparative and Physiological Psychology,* 1965, *69,* 406-412.

RIMM, D. & MASTERS, J.: *Behavior therapy.* New York: Academic Press, 1974.

RUSSELL, M.: Smoking and nicotine dependence. In R. Gibbons et al. (Eds.), *Research advances in alcohol and drug problems,* Vol. 3. New York: Wiley, 1976.

RUSSELL, M.: Smoking problems: An overview. In M. Jarvik, J. Cullen, E. Gritz, T. Vogt, & L. West. (Eds.) Research on smoking behavior (NIDA Research Monograph #17). Rockville, Md.: National Institute on Drug Abuse, 1977.

SCHACHTER, S.: Pharmacological and psychological determinants of smoking. *Annals of Internal Medicine,* 1978, *88,* 104-114.

SCHMELTZ, I. & HOFFMAN, D.: Chemical studies on tobacco smoke XXXVIII. The physiochemical nature of cigarette smoke. In E. Wynder, D. Hoffman, and G. Gori (Eds.), *Modifying the Risk for the Smoker,* Volume I. Proceedings of the 3rd World Conference on Smoking and Health, New York, June 2-5, 1975. (DHEW Pub. #NIH76-1221: 13-34, 1976).

SCHUSTER, C. & THOMPSON, T.: Self-administration of and behavioral dependence on drugs. *Annual Review of Pharmacology,* 1969, *9,* 483-502.

SCHWARTZ, G.: Biofeedback and patterning of autonomic and central processes: CNS-cardiovascular interactions. In G. Schwartz & J. Beatty (Eds.), *Biofeedback: Theory and research,* New York: Academic Press, 1977.

SHIFFMAN, S. & JARVIK, M.: Smoking withdrawal symptoms in two weeks of abstinence. *Psychopharmacologia,* 1976, *50,* 35-39.

SIEGEL, S.: Evidence from rats that morphine tolerance is a learned response. *Journal of Comparative and Physiological Psychology,* 1975, *89,* 498-506.

SIEGEL, S.: Morphine tolerance acquisition as an associative process. *Journal of Experimental Psychology: Animal Behavior Processes,* 1977, *3,* 1-13.

SILVERMAN, A.: Behavior of rats given a "smoking dose" of nicotine. *Animal Behavior,* 1971, *19,* 67-74.

SOLOMON, R. L.: An opponent-process theory of acquired motivation: IV the affective dynamics of addiction. In J. Maser & M. Seligman (Eds.), *Psychopathology: Experimental models.* San Francisco: W. H. Freeman, 1977.

SOLOMON, R. & CORBIT, J.: An opponent-process theory of motivation: II Cigarette addiction. *Journal of Abnormal Psychology,* 1973, *81,* 158-171.

SOLOMON, R. & CORBIT, J.: An opponent-process theory of motivation: I Temporal dynamics of affect. *Psychological Review,* 1974, *81,* 119-145.

SKINNER, B. F.: *Science and human behavior.* New York: Macmillan, 1953.

STEPHENS, R.: Psychophysiological variables in cigarette smoking and reinforcing affects of nicotine. *Addictive Behaviors,* 1977, *2,* 1-7.

STOLERMAN, I., GOLDFARB, T., FINK, R., & JARVIK, M.: Influencing cigarette smoking with nicotine antagonists. *Psychopharmacologia,* 1973, *28,* 247-259.

TERNES, J.: An opponent process theory of habitual behavior with special reference to smoking. In M. Jarvik, J. Cullen, E. Gritz, T. Vogt, & L. West (Eds.), *Research on smoking behavior* (NIDA Monograph #17). Rockville, Md.: National Institute on Drug Abuse, 1977.

THIRD WORLD CONFERENCE ON SMOKING AND HEALTH: In J. Steinfeld et al. (Eds.), *Smoking and health* (Vol. 2). Washington: Department of Health Education, and Welfare, 1977.

THOMAS, C.: The relationship of smoking and habits of nervous tension. In W. Dunn (Ed.), *Smoking behavior: Motives and incentives.* Washington: Winston, 1973.

THOMPSON, T. & SCHUSTER, C.: Morphine self-administration, food-reinforced and avoidance behavior in rhesus monkeys. *Psychopharmacologia,* 1964, *6,* 267-279.

THOMPSON, D. & WILSON, T.: Discontinuance of cigarette smoking: "Natural" and with "therapy." *Journal of the American Medical Association,* 1966, *196,* 1048-1052.

VOLLE, R. & KOELLE, G.: Ganglionic stimulating and blocking agents. In L. Goodman & A. Gilman, (Eds.), *The pharmacological basis of therapeutics* (5th ed.). New York: Macmillan, 1975.

UNITED STATES PUBLIC HEALTH SERVICE: *Health consequences of smoking.* Washington: U.S. Government Printing Office, 1971, 1973, 1974.

WEEKS, J. & COLLINS, R.: Patterns of intravenous self-injection by morphine-addicted rats. In A. Wikler (Ed.), *The addictive states.* Baltimore, Md.: Research Publishers Association on Nervous and Mental Disease, Vol. 46, 1968.

WIKLER, A.: Conditioning factors in opiate addictions and relapse. In D. Wilner & G. Kassebaum (Eds.), *Narcotics.* New York: McGraw-Hill, 1965.

WIKLER, A.: Dynamics of drug dependence. *Archives of General Psychiatry,* 1973, *28,* 611-617.

WIKLER, A.: Symposium on conditioning and addiction. *The Pavlovian Journal of Biological Science,* 1976, *11,* 191-194.

WIKLER, A. & PESCOR, F.: Classical conditioning of a morphine abstinence phenomenon, reinforcement of opioid-drinking behavior and "relapse" in morphine addicted rats. *Psychopharmacologia,* 1967, *10,* 255-284.

YAMAGITA, T., ANDO, K., OINUMA, N., & ISHIDA, K.: Intravenous self-administration of nicotine and an attempt to produce smoking behavior in monkeys. In *Report of the thirty-sixth Annual Scientific Meeting, Committee on Problems of Drug Dependence.* Washington: National Academy of Sciences, 1974.

5

Lifestyle Changes for the Whole Person: Stimulation Through Health Hazard Appraisal

JOHN H. MILSUM

INTRODUCTION

Lifestyle has rather suddenly become a major focus of public concern as evidence of its major contribution to our health problems has mounted. Furthermore, it has become clear that we cannot buy our way to better health by simply feeding more money into the acute care medical system and conveniently ignoring the need for lifestyle change.

Lifestyle change to achieve better individual health is intimately related to behavior modification, and also to many other areas ranging from medical practice to personal relations. Consequently, many professional groups see key roles for themselves in this newly important area. For example, since lack of exercise has been established as a major risk factor for cardiovascular disease, physical educators have been encouraged to develop not only fitness clinics, but also wide-ranging plans which inevitably involve other professional areas, such as nutrition. Equally, nutritionists note that health depends upon all cells being continuously well nourished, and thus tend to see nutrition as the core subject of another equally broad focus. Extending the list of risk factors, we readily include stress, cigarette smoking, excessive alcohol consumption, and obesity, all of which are of prime interest to physicians, psychiatrists, and clinical psychologists. Indeed, all health and allied professions become involved when further risk factors are included.

Each profession is correct in believing that it should be involved in lifestyle change. However, no single group has by itself all the knowledge, expertise, and facilities to tackle the whole problem of lifestyle change in an integrated way. Yet when individuals are being counseled for change, each must be treated as a whole rather than as a set of related but separable functions, if real progress is to be made. Therefore, the aim of this chapter is to explore some avenues for such a holistic approach to man, his behavior and its change, using as a point of departure the currently available system called Health Hazard Appraisal.

Modeling the Dynamics of Behavioral Change and Health/Illness

Our lifestyle represents a complex outcome of many personal, interpersonal, environmental, and societal factors which arise not only from our present situation but also from our life history and heredity. Any lifestyle changes we make will therefore inevitably involve our individual Gestalt, both as a present condition, and as a dynamic historical process. In this historical process, the concept of *threshold for change* plays an important part, for we are typically exposed to many different messages before we accumulate enough awareness, appreciation, or concern in order to reach the threshold at which we actually initiate change.

Brown (1976) has developed a qualitative model for behavioral change, in relation to personal risk reduction, which involves five components at different stages of motivational receptivity. These five stages are arranged in a hierarchical manner such that the earlier ones must be fulfilled before each next one becomes possible. In ascending order the stages are:

(1) *Awareness* of risk; the person must be aware that the current behavior is harmful;
(2) *Acceptance* of this knowledge of risk, as applying personally;
(3) *Integration* of the knowledge into the personal self-image; for example "I *could* undertake an exercise program";
(4) *Effort* toward change; a decision to change or modify behavior, with the beginning of an effort to change; and

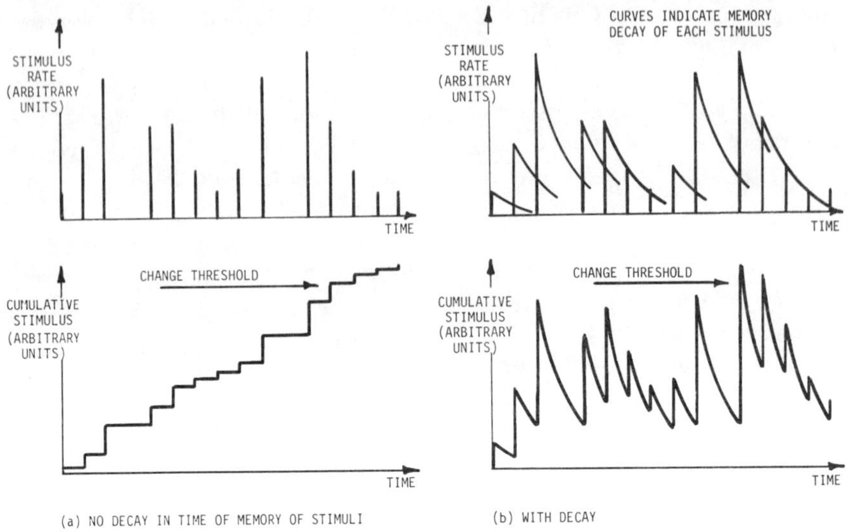

FIGURE 1. Models for accumulation in memory of change stimuli, with threshold for change decision.

(5) *Application* of knowledge to produce actual change; that is, personal application of the acquired knowledge with actual change of lifestyle.

In this paper, we are concerned with behavior change in relation to reduction of health risks. It is therefore interesting to note that an accumulating-and-threshold model also applies to the related but inverse process of becoming sick following a sufficient accumulation of Life Change Units (LCU), as shown by Holmes and Rahe (1967). Figure 1 suggests alternative mathematical models for this process since the way in which the accumulation functionally occurs is not yet conceptually understood. Holmes and Rahe use simple addition of the values of the individual units as shown in Figure 1(a), in order to arrive at the cumulative effect of the stimuli for onset of illness. However, we could plausibly expect a decay in both our conscious and subconscious awareness of an individual event as the event recedes in time. The simple memory-decay model suggested in Figure 1(b) uses an exponential decay in time of the effect of each successive stimulus, so that greatest importance is attached to the most recent events.

In order to postulate the effect of accumulation in relation to threshold for change we must first digress to consider the effects of opposing

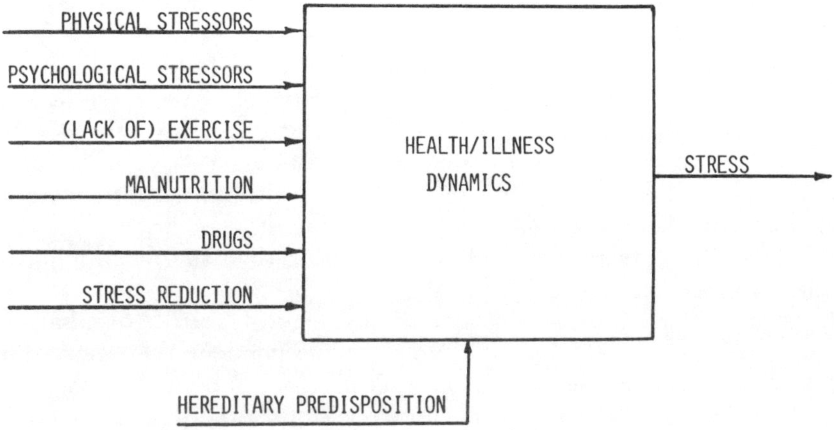

FIGURE 2. Multifactorial health/illness dynamics.

forces in this context. Lewin (1938) has stated that human behavior is always in dynamic equilibrium between opposing forces. The "driving forces" push for change while the "restraining forces" resist. For example, when the force of vehicular weight occurs on a bridge, a corresponding opposing force is generated in the structure, otherwise the structure collapses. However, since the equilibrium is generally "dynamic," the opposition and cancellation are not always perfectly matched, and transient movements or even oscillations may occur, in which dominance alternates between the opposing forces. Further, if the driving force reaches a sufficiently high value for short periods, then the resisting force can be briefly overwhelmed, with structural deformation resulting. These descriptions are suggestive of the corresponding situation in human behavior.

Comparison with another model for health/sickness may be useful. The Life Change Units (LCU) previously mentioned constitute only one of the forces or "stressors" typically operating on the human. Figure 2 represents a more general model in which four major "stressors," or factors tending to produce stress, are included, namely:

physical stressors—for example the major pollutants emitted from automobiles, including carbon monoxide, heat, rubber particles, and asbestos particles;
psychological stressors—including the Life Change Units;
malnutrition—which is highly prevalent in developed countries, although not most importantly as underfeeding; and
lack of exercise—a most pervasive stressor in energy-rich countries.

Many other stressors could be included, according to one's viewpoint or the particular purpose of the analysis. The basic point in this multifactorial model is that the stressors combine, in some fashion, to produce a total "stressor" effect. The net effect in producing stress in the human then depends on the extent to which these stressors are cancelled by available stress-reduction or coping mechanisms.

However, the method for combining the different components to characterize their total effect is not self-evident. It seems more likely that a multiplicative-type relation is operating than simply an additive one. This becomes more obvious in the case of combining "risk factors" for a particular disease—as is done in the Health-Hazard-Appraisal system to be discussed. If the risk factors are independent, then their combined risk will be the result of multiplying component risks. This multiplicative model may clarify why some of the otherwise inexplicable "last straw" phenomena occur. Thus, it often seems that for highly stressed individuals a small additional stressful stimulus can produce an inappropriately large response, quite out of accord with a typical "dose-response" relation (as compared to the response to the same amount of stimulus when the individual is less stressed).

Returning to the Life-Change-Units hypothesis, that model assesses the probability of a person's becoming hospitalized in some period (typically 8 months) after the LCU have been accumulated for a longer initial period (typically 2 years). One interesting statistic is that the accumulation of 350 LCUs corresponds approximately to a 50% probability of illness. The probability figure is, of course, based on group experience and tells us nothing about the likelihood of any particular person becoming ill. Clearly it is for the individual case that we become concerned and want to know more about his or her health determinants in terms of stress management and coping mechanisms.

Continuing then to the model of Figure 1, we see that, in terms of field theory, the diagram represents only the effects of the "driving forces," and in terms of the health/illness model, it represents the stressors. Change is conceived of as resulting from a threshold type phenomenon when the stressor variable has built up to a sufficiently high level. This model implicitly represents, by a threshold, the net effect of the resistive forces and the stress-reduction mechanisms beyond which maintenance of the equilibrium, as in health, is not possible. However, it would be simple enough to generalize the model to include the resistive forces or stress-reduction mechanisms explicitly. Thus for each time unit the net effect of the two opposing forces would be found, noting that in some periods this might be negative. The accumulative process, with or without decay, would then proceed as before.

In this regard, it is interesting to compare Selye's (1975) concept of the General Adaptation Syndrome for stressors. This syndrome comprises three stages, namely:

> *alarm reaction:* during which a higher level of stress is initiated in the system following the occurrence of a stressful stimulus;
> *resistance:* during which adaptation to the stimulus establishes a new equilibrium at some higher level of stress; and
> *exhaustion:* when the resistance cannot be maintained, and irreversible pathological results occur.

It will be recognized that while the various models just described have features in common, they are not isomorphic. At present it would not seem possible to suggest confidently any universally-representative model. However, it undoubtedly will have to contain most or all of the following features:

> dynamic effects of opposing forces, with time decay of the effects (memory, hysteresis);
> non-linear combinations of some component forces;
> different thresholds for different individuals, with statistical norms for groups being permissable; and
> adaptation and feedback.

The result of these features is that the various factors in an individual's life often interact inextricably. Furthermore, in the development of behavior, adaptation involves feedback, which in turn means that the closed-loops make it difficult, if not impossible, to distinguish cause from effect, or stimulus from response in any satisfactory way. Hence it would seem clear that an integrated view must be taken when considering lifestyles and techniques for stimulating change in them. This unfortunately may not be the case in many specific "anti-risk" programs aimed at behavior modification, such as quitting smoking, quitting drinking, undertaking exercise programs, losing weight, wearing seatbelts, managing and reducing stress, achieving balanced nutrition, or a host of others. Since the particular technique of Health Hazard Appraisal attempts just such a comprehensiveness, we shall now use it as an example of an integrated approach to behavioral modification.

A Framework for Health Hazard Appraisal

Health Hazard Appraisal is a system designed for prevention of illness and promotion of health through the stimulation of lifestyle change. It is both prospective and comprehensive in its viewpoint, since as many risks to the individual's health as possible are quantitatively estimated, together with information on the lowered levels of risks that could be expected if certain recommended lifestyle changes were made by the individual. It inherently incorporates the concept that future good health depends importantly upon current habits, and upon any decisions to change them which are made today.

In order to stimulate motivation for behavioral change in people, it is important that there be good evidence to establish that changes made in lifestyle will, in fact, result in reduced risk. Evidence suggestive of this is being gathered on a broad front, but, unfortunately, in our society it is ethically very difficult, if not impossible, to perform the appropriate critical epidemiological experiments. Specifically, such experiments would involve randomly-assigned test and control groups followed over a sufficiently long period of time, probably up to 30 years, in which the individuals in the test group were randomly assigned specific lifestyle changes to follow, with the evidence ultimately appearing in terms of changed mortality rates. Actually, even these experiments would not be ideal, since forced responses by the individual, without genuine internal motivation for the lifestyle changes prescribed, would probably not produce these changes. On the other hand, the typical current test situation in which individuals self-select themselves into the test groups by volunteering to undertake the desired lifestyle changes is not consistent with basic experimental protocol, since this self-selection process invalidates the random assignment considered necessary for a mechanistic model of simple cause-effect, or stimulus-response relationship.

Some work has recently begun to appear which monitors a large number of individuals over a decade or more, while accepting their own self-selection of lifestyle. Most notable in this regard is the study of Breslow and his colleagues (cf. Belloc & Breslow, 1972; Belloc, 1973). They monitored a randomly-selected sample of almost 7,000 persons, which was representative of the general adult population of a typical Californian urban community. At the time of publication, the survey had lasted for 5½ years, but it has been continued and further results are expected soon. They monitored seven specific individual health practices, namely: non-smoking; weight being close to desirable standards for height; moderate alcohol consumption; 7-8 hours of sleep regularly; regularity of eating breakfast; seldom snacking between meals; and frequent vigorous physical activity. Each of these health practices seemed to be equally important, so that a "health practice score" between 0 and 7 could be generated by counting the number of health practices that an individual followed. A striking inverse relation emerged between this health practice score and mortality rate, especially for men. Furthermore, this relation was independent of income level and physical health status. The data could be presented in many different forms, one appropriate measure being that of average life expectancy. Specifically, men reporting 6 or 7 good health practices at age 45 had an average life expectancy 11 years greater than that of men reporting 3 or less. For women the corresponding increase was somewhat less (7 years) but this difference merely brings the average life expectancy of such males and females closer together, since on average women outlive men by some 7 years.

In a working document entitled "A New Perspective on the Health of Canadians," Lalonde (1974) and his staff at the Department of National Health and Welfare in Canada, have contributed thoughtfully on the subject of striking an appropriate balance between the need for public action to achieve lifestyle change and the unsettled scientific state of the epidemiological evidence for benefits of lifestyle change. This document has attracted widespread international attention and some extended quotes seem appropriate.

> The spirit of enquiry and skepticism, and particularly the Scientific Method, so essential to research, are, however, a problem in health promotion. The reason for this is that science is full of "ifs," "buts," and "maybes" while messages designed to influence the public must be loud, clear and unequivocal. To quote I Corinthinans Chapter XIV, Verse 8: "If the trumpet give an uncertain sound, who shall prepare himself to the battle?"
>
> The scientific proof underlying the cause-and-effect relationships between, on the one hand, environment and lifestyle and, on the other, sickness and death, is fraught with disagreement. . . . we can find scientists on both sides of the following questions:
>
> Does exercise lessen the likelihood, or abate the severity, of coronary artery disease?
> Is obesity an important contributory factor to sickness and death?
> Does marijuana have any serious long-term effects?
> Does ingestion of high levels of fatty foods and cholesterol increase the likelihood of coronary-artery disease?
> Is frequent self-medication, particularly with over-the-counter drugs, bad? . . .
>
> Faced with conflicting scientific opinions of this kind, it would be easy for health educators and promoters to sit on their hands; it certainly makes it easy for those who abuse their health to find a ready "scientific" excuse.
>
> But many of Canada's health problems are sufficiently pressing

> that action has to be taken on them even if all the scientific evidence is not in.
>
> The scientific community, then, needs to make special efforts to resolve some of the debates on health-related questions of the environment and lifestyle. Until it does. . . the following hypotheses. . . now appear sufficiently valid to warrant taking positive action:
>
> (1) It is better to be slim than fat.
> (2) The excessive use of medication is to be avoided.
> (3) It is better not to smoke cigarettes.
> (4) Exercise and fitness are better than sedentary living and lack of fitness.
> (5) Alcohol is a danger to health, particularly when driving a car.
> (6) Mood-modifying drugs are a danger to health unless controlled by a physician.
> (7) Tranquility is better then excess stress.
> (8) The less polluted the air is, the healthier it is.
> (9) The less polluted the water is, the healthier it is.
>
> . . . major health problems lie before us and we must move ahead with programs on precepts such as the foregoing. The scientific "yes, but" is essential to research but for modifying the behaviour of the population it sometimes produces the "uncertain sound" that is all the excuse needed by many to cultivate and tolerate an environment and lifestyle that is hazardous to health (pp. 57-58).

Dever (1975) has used the concept of four "health fields" from the Lalonde document, namely lifestyle, environment, human biology, and the system of health care organization, to estimate the percentage allocation of mortality attributable to each field for various major causes of mortality. Specifically, the five top causes of mortality are diseases of the heart, cancer, cerebro-vascular disease, motor vehicle accidents, and all other accidents, together accounting for 70% of total deaths. For each of these, lifestyle is attributed the largest single percentage allocation of mortality, with the amount ranging from 37% for cancer, to 69% for motor vehicle accidents. Indeed, when averaged over all causes of death, the percentage allocations are 43% for lifestyle, 27%for human biology, 19% for environment, and 11% for the system of health care organization. Clearly lifestyle is becoming widely recognized as a major factor in disease and premature death.

None of these data quoted above rigorously proves any cause/effect relationship between improvement in lifestyle and reduction of mortality. Thus, it is not possible to guarantee any given individual who is currently rated as high-risk for a particular cause of mortality because of high values of component risk factors, that appropriate changes of lifestyle will, in fact, reduce his risk factors and result in a greater life expectancy. Nevertheless, it would seem prudent to advise individuals that such lifestyle changes would probably be beneficial. In any case, the most important issue for individuals in regard to being motivated for lifestyle change may not be that of future life expectancy but rather that of more immediate freedom from illness. Again it is impossible, at present, to give absolute assurance that morbidity will decrease and therefore quality of life increase, but nevertheless the circumstantial evidence and the subjective anecdotal experiences of many people are so strongly suggestive, that it would appear imprudent and irresponsible not to consider this in the absence of contrary evidence.

It is in this context that Health Hazard Appraisal becomes a significant tool for influencing individuals by making them *aware* and *accepting* of their risks and by stimulating them to *integrate* this knowledge so that they can respond with an *effort* toward change.

Health Hazard Appraisal (HHA)—Methodology, Data, Interpretation, and Counseling

Health Hazard Appraisal (HHA) is a tool to help health professionals increase their practice of the prevention of illness and promotion of health. HHA originated at the Methodist Hospital of Indiana in Indianapolis (Robbins & Hall, 1970; Sadusk & Robbins, 1968) some ten years ago, and is fairly widely available in the United States and Canada. It arose from the philosophy of prospective medicine, which anticipates the likelihood of diseases developing in a person and recommends changes through which the person could expect to reduce this likelihood. However, reduction of risk does not guarantee that disability or premature death will not occur for a particular individual. In general, the goal is primarily to promote a healthy life by preventing death and disability *due to reducible risk,* and could be stated succinctly as "to add life to our years, rather than years to our life." The emphasis is that the HHA is applied well in advance of the onset of disease and therefore typically in advance of the time when traditional medical care is called for. It is not basically a screening tool for existing disease and indeed preexisting disease conditions, together with operations, etc., typically invalidate the risk assessments. Figure 3 illustrates six stages in the natural history of a disease, using heart attacks as a particular example, showing especially the time phases during which HHA is applicable.

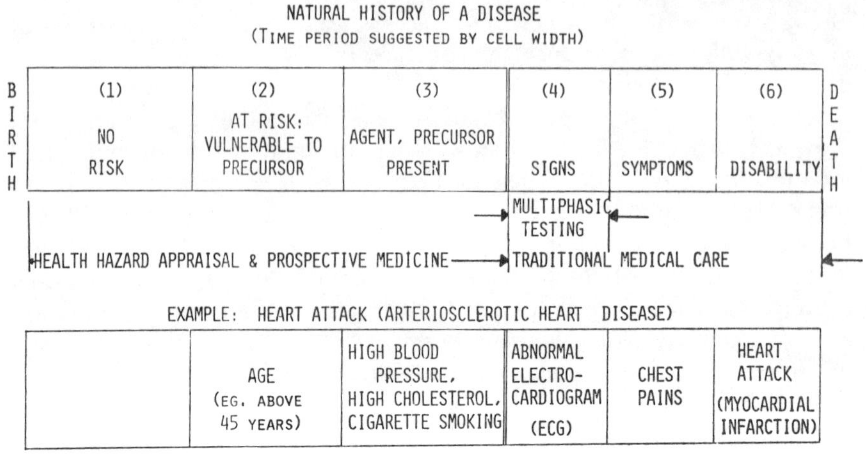

FIGURE 3. Health Hazard Appraisal and natural history of disease.

HHA tries to be comprehensive in its concern for the individual's total risk, without fragmentation due to the imposition of specialty considerations. The individual is treated as a whole person, living in a complex social setting, with concern being given to total risk whether this arises from physiological, environmental, psychological, or social areas.

Table 1 illustrates the diversity of the risk factors for a few important causes of death, while Figure 4 shows how the total risk of dying in the next 10 years varies as a function of age for both females and males. Table 2 shows in addition the breakdown of mortality into major causes of death, illustrating in particular how accidental or violent deaths are responsible for most of the mortality in the young, whereas in later years the major killers are due to physiological or patho-physiological breakdowns.

The HHA Process

The patient or client fills out the relatively simple questionnaire, largely concerning lifestyle patterns, past history, and a few clinical measures (see Table 3). Generally people are able to complete this form themselves, except for the questions on systolic and diastolic blood pressures and fasting blood cholesterol levels. Typically the forms are then computer processed, although they can be done manually (Robbins & Hall, 1970). The computer print-out typically involves about three pages and its results are discussed by the health professional with the client, either individually or in groups. There are ideally two phases to this:

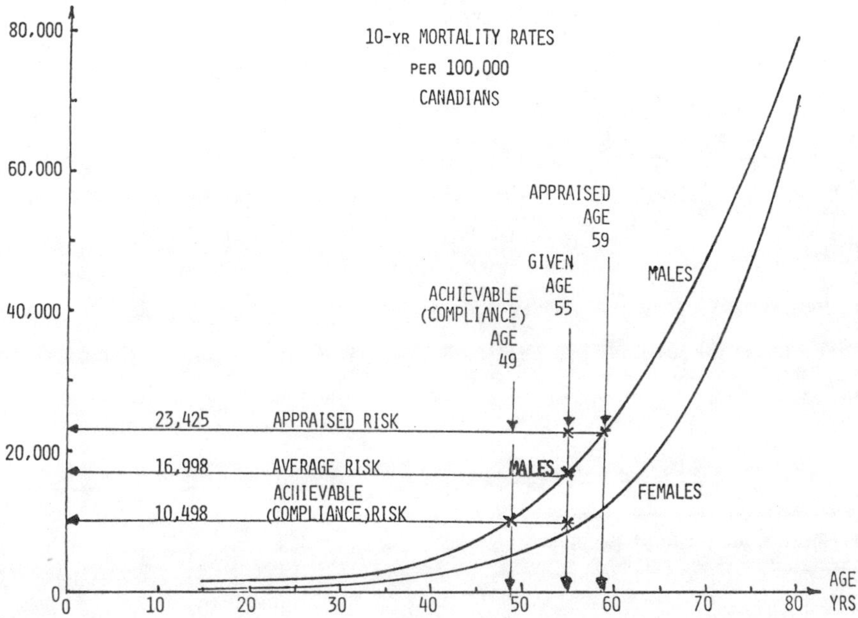

FIGURE 4

interpretation of the meaning of the risk appraisal numbers in each case; and

counseling in order to encourage each patient/client to make some commitment for lifestyle change, with one or more follow-up sessions automatically scheduled if feasible.

Important points are:

(1) *Teachable Moment*—The primary long-term importance of HHA may reside in the fact that it creates a "teachable moment" when a health professional as counselor and a patient as client come together to discuss comprehensively the person's health condition, and the risks to which he is exposing himself, with a view to developing a contract for lifestyle change. Such possible changes can be discussed in regard to their potential efficacy, with due respect for the client's present beliefs, reservations, prejudices, etc., in such a way that a decision to contract for change is fundamentally reserved for the clients themselves.

(2) *Self-Responsibility*—The client is encouraged to accept self-responsibility for his/her health as completely as possible and helpful. The "*3C model*" of client, counselor, and contract emphasizes this aspect in comparison with the more traditional "*3P model*" of patient, physician, and

TABLE 1

Risk Factors	*Major Disorders*
Increased Smoking Habits Blood Cholesterol Elevated Blood Pressure Elevated Presence of Diabetes Family History of Diabetes Overweight Lack of Exercise Family History of Ischemic Heart Disease	Arteriosclerotic Heart Disease (Heart Attack)
High Annual Mileage Seat Belt Non-Usage Increased Alcohol Habits Drugs and Medications (Influencing Driving)	Motor Vehicle Accidents
Increased Alcohol Habits History of Bacterial Pneumonia Presence of Emphysema/Bronchitis Increased Smoking Habits	Pneumonia
Rectal Polyp Rectal Bleeding Ulcerative Colitis Proctosignoidoscopy Not Done	Cancer of the Intestine and the Rectum
Pap Smear Not Done Early Age of Intercourse (Higher Risk)	Cancer of the Cervix

prescription. Of course, adoption of self-responsibility by the client implies that the counselor may need to accept a choice of lifestyle change by the client that the counselor would not consider best; for example the client may not be prepared to tackle the areas of greatest risk at this time, but rather only some relatively trivial areas. However, the acceptance of self-responsibility may be a long process, involving many phases during which considerate counseling provides an important contribution.

(3) *Exemplar concept*—An important factor seems to be the attitude of the health professional to the value of healthful lifestyles as exhibited by his or her own conditions and habits, and these are often only too visible during the interaction between the client and the counselor. The "exemplar" is able to show the way to his/her clients and therefore more likely to stimulate a client to lifestyle change. The old stereotype of the

TABLE 2
Canadian Ten-Year Mortality Rates per 100,000,
by Age, Sex and Major Disease Groups

	Female 15 yrs	Male 15 yrs	Female 45 yrs	Male 45 yrs	Female 75 yrs	Male 75 yrs
Motor Vehicle Accidents	225	734	117	322		
Suicide (and Homicide)	63	214	145	302		
Accidental, poisoning, drowning, firearms, fires, falls	42	223			683	
Stroke	15	13	266	309	8,459	8,522
Pneumonia	15	16		104	1,726	2,651
Tumors, lymph and leukemia	36	32	70	111		
Breast cancer			516		1,084	
Heart attack and other heart disease			496	2,784	19,363	25,358
Cancer of ovary, cervix			167		1,827	
Lung cancer			122	477		2,181
Cirrhosis of liver			122	316		
Cancers: stomach, intestine, pancreas, prostate			196	301	1,340	6,204
Chronic bronchitis and emphysema				106		2,208
Diseases of arteries, capillaries and high blood pressure					3,299	2,911
Diabetes					1,516	1,231
Others	186	338	1,454	2,132	8,979	12,197
Total	572	1,581	3,771	7,264	48,276	63,467

health professional dispensing wisdom, advice, and instructions, based upon superior scientific knowledge and experience, is neither completely valid nor useful in this new context. If the health professional is to be useful in catalyzing lifestyle change and activating the patient, it is essential that the patient perceive that the counselor indeed cares for, values, and practices health-inducing precepts personally. These ideas are pointedly expressed in the following anonymous poem:

> I'd rather see a sermon than hear one any day,
> I'd rather one should walk with me than merely tell the way;
> The eye's a better pupil and more willing than the ear,
> Fine counsel is confusing, but example's always clear; . . .
> I soon can learn to do it, if you'll let me see it done,
> I can watch your hands in action, your tongue too fast may run;
> The lectures you deliever may be very wise and true,
> But I'd rather get my lessons by observing what you do;
> For I may misunderstand the high advice you give,
> But there's no misunderstanding how you act and how you live.

TABLE 3
Health Hazard Appraisal

NAME ____________________

ADDRESS ____________________

____

Processed by:
Division of Health Systems
Health Sciences Centre
Univ. of BC, Vancouver V6T 1W5
228-5776

PLEASE RECORD THE MOST APPROPRIATE RESPONSE BY WRITING THE CODE NUMBER IN THE COLUMN ON THE RIGHT HAND SIDE OF THE PAGE

TO BE COMPLETED BY ALL PARTICIPANTS:

SEX	(1) male	(2) female			
AGE	(in years)				
HEIGHT—without shoes					Ft. / Ins.
WEIGHT—IN POUNDS—naked					
FRAME	(1) small	(2) medium	(3) large		
ALCOHOL HABITS (Drinks per week, on average. Include apertifs, wine, beer, etc.)	(1) 41 or more (5) 1-2	(2) 25-40 (6) stopped	(3) 7-24 (7) never drank	(4) 3-6	
USE OF DRUGS THAT MAY INFLUENCE DRIVING	(1) excess	(2) moderate	(3) none		
SERIOUS DEPRESSION recent, non-menstrual, e.g., disabling	(1) often	(2) seldom or never			
CURRENT SMOKING HABITS OR HEAVIEST AMOUNT SMOKED IN LAST 5 YEARS (FOR EX-SMOKER, MARK HEAVIEST AMOUNT SMOKED IN YEAR BEFORE QUITTING, EXCEPT AFTER 10 YRS OR MORE NON-SMOKING). (If cigarettes and pipes/cigars, mark only code for cigarettes)	CIGARETTES — (PACKS/DAY) (1) 2 + (2) 1 - 2 (3) 1/2 - 1 (4) 1/2 or less:	PIPES/CIGARS (No./Day) (5) 5+ or any inhaled (6) 4 or less not inhaled	NON-SMOKERS (7) do not smoke (or have stopped for more than 10 years)		

TABLE 3 (*continued*)

STOPPED SMOKING	Mark number of years stopped.* (Mark 0 if still smoking, or non-smoker, or stopped for more than 10 years).		*If stopped less than 1 year mark 1.		
MILES DRIVEN PER YEAR	(as driver and/or passenger in private motor vehicle) (in thousands of miles)				
SEAT BELT USAGE (percentage of time)	(1) 10% or less	(2) 10-24%	(3) 25-74%	(4) 75-100%	
CRIME RECORD	(1) crimes involving possible injury	(2) crimes with no possible injury	(3) not involved		
WEAPONS CARRIED	(1) yes	(2) none			
EXERCISE PER DAY	(1) not much (SEDENTARY under 5 flights of stairs or less than 1/2 mile of walking	(2) some (LOW MODERATE) 5-15 flights of stairs or 1/2-1-1/2 miles of walking	(3) fairly active (HIGH MODERATE) programmed exercise 4 times/wk. or 15-20 flights of stairs or 1-1/2 miles of walking	(4) very active (VIGOROUS) greater than fairly active	
SERIOUS PNEUMONIA (Bacterial)	(1) have had	(2) never had			
HEART ATTACK	PARENTS DIED OF HEART ATTACK BEFORE AGE 60: (1) both parents	(2) one parent	PARENTS DIED UNDER AGE 60 (of other causes), or STILL ALIVE BELOW AGE 60 (3)	NONE OF THESE (4)	
FAMILY HISTORY OF SUICIDE (blood relative)	(1) yes	(2) no			
FAMILY HISTORY OF DIABETES (blood relative)	(1) yes	(2) no			
DO YOU HAVE DIABETES?	(1) yes - no treatment	(2) yes - under treatment	(3) do not have		
RECTAL DISORDERS (history of disease other than piles/hemorrhoids)	growth: (1) yes	(2) no			
	bleeding: (1) yes	(2) no			
annual rectal examination (proctosigmoidoscopy)	(1) yes	(2) no			

TABLE 3 (*continued*)

TO BE COMPLETED BY FEMALES ONLY: — RECORD ALL ANSWERS IN THIS COLUMN

SOCIAL-ECONOMIC STATUS	(1) low (2) average (3) high	
JEWISH (Less risk of cervical cancer)	(1) no (2) yes (if both parents Jewish)	
AGE OF STARTING INTERCOURSE	(1) under 20 (2) 20-25 (3) over 25 or never	
PAPSMEAR	(1) have not had (2) 1 neg. in 5 yrs (3) 1 neg. in 1 yr (4) 3 neg. in 5 yrs or annual	
ABNORMAL VAGINAL BLEEDING IN LAST YEAR (note: not normal menstruation)	(1) yes (2) no	
FAMILY HISTORY OF BREAST CANCER	(1) Mother or sister had breast cancer. No self exam. (2) Mother or sister had breast cancer but patient examines breasts regularly and has periodic examinations by physician. (3) Neither mother nor sister had breast cancer. No self exam. (4) Neither mother nor sister had breast cancer but patient examines breasts regularly and has periodic examination.	

TABLE 3 (*continued*)

TO BE COMPLETED BY PARTICIPANT AS MUCH AS POSSIBLE, OR BY PHYSICIAN/NURSE

SYSTOLIC BLOOD PRESSURE*	(in mm.)	
DIASTOLIC BLOOD PRESSURE*		
CHOLESTEROL LEVEL*	(1) 280 mg% or over (2) 220-279 mg% (3) 219 mg% or less; Give level if known	
RECORD OF EMPHYSEMA OR BRONCHITIS	(1) yes (2) no	
ULCERATIVE COLITIS	(1) Had for 10 years (2) less than 10 years (3) do not have	
CHRONIC RHEUMATIC HEART DISEASE	(1) murmur/no treatment (2) murmur/treatment (3) history/no murmur/or treatment (4) history/no murmur/treatment (5) no history/no murmur	
CHRONIC RHEUMATIC HEART DISEASE (SIGNS OR SYMPTOMS)	(1) no (2) yes	

*LEAVE BLANK IS UNKNOWN. ANALYSIS WILL BE PERFORMED BY ASSUMING NORMAL VALUES.

DATE QUESTIONNAIRE COMPLETED:

(4) *Follow-up and Community Resources*—The effectiveness of HHA in stimulating behavioral change is often increased if follow-through facilities or services can be made available, for example, by the client's becoming involved with appropriate anti-risk programs or community resources in relation to such areas as quitting smoking, reducing alcohol consumption, increasing exercise and losing weight, in which the client expresses concern for lifestyle change.

(5) *Sensitizing the Health Professional*—Frequent repetition in looking at a comprehensive set of risk factors tends to imbue the health professional with a much more urgent sense of the pervasiveness of unhealthy lifestyles and their combined bad effect upon most individuals. In consequence, many health professionals will themselves become concerned

TABLE 4
Health Hazard Appraisal Analysis

THE UNIVERSITY OF BRITISH COLUMBIA
- - - HEALTH HAZARD APPRAISAL - - -

THE RISK REGISTRY DATA HAVE BEEN ANALYSED AND THE RESULTS ARE SUMMARIZED BELOW AS THEY RELATE TO THE 12 MOST FREQUENT CAUSES OF DEATH FOR FEMALES AGED 53.

AVERAGE (COL.1) AVERAGE CHANCES OF DYING PER 100,000 WITHIN 10 YRS. FROM SPECIFIC CAUSES. BASED ON CAUSES OF DEATH, CANADA, 1971, (STATISTICS CANADA CATALOGUE 84-2031).
APPRAISAL (COL.2) CHANCES OF DYING PER 100,000 WITHIN 10 YRS. BASED ON RISK REGISTRY INFORMATION.
COMPLIANCE (COL.3) CHANCES OF DYING PER 100,000 ASSUMING MODIFICATION OF CERTAIN RISK FACTORS.*

RANK	CAUSE OF DEATH	CHANCES OF DYING PER 100,000 COL.1 AVERAGE	COL.2 APPRAISAL	COL.3 COMPLIANCE
1	HEART ATTACK	1577	1975	557
2	BREAST CANCER	769	769	769
3	STROKE	600	479	240
4	INTESTINAL CANCER INCL. RECTUM	466	466	139
5	CANCER OF OVARY TUBE BROAD LIGT.	244	244	244
6	LUNG CANCER **	225	450	359
7	DIABETES	210	145	113
8	CIRRHOSIS OF LIVER	187	374	187
9	CANCER OF THE CERVIX	155	77	15
10	MOTOR VEHICLE ACCIDENTS	153	336	152
11	CHRONIC RHEUMATIC HEART DISEASE	150	1	1
12	SUICIDE	136	136	136
	ALL OTHER CAUSES	2638	2638	2638
	ALL CAUSES OF DEATH	7510	8090	5550

GIVEN AGE: 53 APPRAISED AGE: 53.9 COMPLIANCE AGE: 49.5

FOR HEIGHT 67 INCHES AND MEDIUM FRAME, 148 LBS. IS APPROXIMATELY 13% OVERWEIGHT ---- DESIRABLE WEIGHT IS 131 LBS.

--- COMPLIANCE ---

THE COMPLIANCE CHANCES OF DYING (COL.3) ARE BASED UPON THE ASSUMPTION THAT FACTOR(S) ARE MODIFIED AS FOLLOWS

EXERCISE	FROM	LOW	TO	EXERCISE PROGRAM
SMOKING	FROM	STILL SMOKES 20+	TO	STOPPED SMOKING
ALCOHOL	FROM	7-24/WEEK	TO	3-6/WEEK
PAPSMEAR	FROM	NEG. IN 1 YR.	TO	ANNUAL IN FUTURE
WEIGHT	FROM	148 LBS.	TO	131 LBS.
SEATBELT	FROM	10-24%	TO	75-100%
PROCTO	FROM	NOT HAD IN PAST YEAR	TO	ANNUAL IN FUTURE

* *

N.B. (1) Papsmear frequency should be referred to physician's discretion.
(2) Proctosigmoidoscopy probably not jusitifed if under middle-age; - at physician's discretion.

TABLE 4 (*continued*)

CAUSE OF DEATH	CONTRIB. CHARACTER.	APPRAISAL AS SUBMITTED	APPRAISAL ACTUAL RISK	APPRAISAL COMPO. RISK	COMPLIANCE AS COMPLIED	COMPLIANCE APPLIED RISK	COMPLIANCE COMPO. RISK
HEART ATTACK	BL.PRESS	120/ 80	0.4/0.4		120/ 80	0.4/0.4	
	CHOLESTR	220-278	1.0		220-279	1.0	
	DIABETES	NOT DIABETIC	1.0		NOT DIABETIC	1.0	
	WEIGHT	148	1.0		131	0.9	
	EXERCISE	LOW	1.0		EXERCISE PROGRAM	0.8	
	SMOKING	STILL SMOKES 20+	1.9		STOPPED SMOKING	1.1	
	FH/HEART	NO	0.9	1.25	NO	0.9	0.35
BREAST CANCER	FH/BREST	FH + SELF-EXAM	1.0	1.00	FH + SELF-EXAM	1.0	1.00
STROKE	BL.PRESS	120/ 80	0.4/0.4		120/ 80	0.4/0.4	
	CHOLESTR	220-279	1.0		220-279	1.0	
	DIABETES	NOT DIABETIC	1.0		NOT DIABETIC	1.0	
	SMOKING	STILL SMOKES 20+	1.4	0.80	STOPPED SMOKING	1.0	0.40
INTESTINAL CANCER INCL. RECTUM	POLYP	HAS NOT HAD	1.0		HAS NOT HAD	1.0	
	PROCTO	NOT HAD IN PAST YEAR	1.0		ANNUAL IN FUTURE	0.3	
	RCTBLOOD	NO BLOOD IN STOOL	1.0		NO BLOOD IN STOOL	1.0	
	ULCERCOL	HAS NO SYMPTOMS	1.0	1.00	HAS NO SYMPTOMS	1.0	0.30
LUNG CANCER **	SMOKING	STILL SMOKES 20+	2.0	2.00	STOPPED SMOKING	1.6	1.60
DIABETES	WEIGHT	148	0.8		131	0.6	
	FH/DIAB	NO	0.9	0.59	NO	0.9	0.54
CIRRHOSIS OF LIVER	ALCOHOL	7-24/WEEK	2.0	2.00	3-6/WEEK	1.0	1.00
CANCER OF THE CERVIX	AGE/MAR	TEENAGE	1.0		TEENAGE	1.0	
	PAPSMEAR	NEG. IN 1 YR.	0.5		ANNUAL IN FUTURE	0.1	
	SOCIO/EC	AVERAGE	1.0		AVERAGE	1.0	
	JEWISH	NO	1.0	0.50	NO	1.0	0.10
MOTOR VEHICLE ACCIDENTS	ALCOHOL	7-24/WEEK	2.0		3-6/WEEK	1.0	
	MIL/YEAR	12000	1.2		12000	1.2	
	SEATBELT	10-24%	1.0		75-100%	0.8	
	DRUG/MFD	NONE	1.0	2.40	NONE	1.0	1.00
CHRONIC RHEUMATIC HEART DISEASE	RH:FEVER	NO R.F. + NO MURMUR	0.1		NO R.F. + NO MURMUR	0.1	
	RH:S/U/S	NO SYMPTOMS	0.1	0.01	NO SYMPTOMS	0.1	0.01
SUICIDE	DEPRESS	SELDOM OR NEVER	1.0		SELDOM OR NEVER	1.0	
	FH/SUICD	NO	1.0	1.00	NO	1.0	1.00

* Risk factors adapted from "How to Practice Prospective Medicine", Drs. Robbins and Hall, Methodist Hospital of Indiana.

** Lung cancer risk decreases steadily and reaches non smoker level 10 years after stopping.

Table 4 (*continued*)

```
APPRAISAL GRAPH FOR ABCD0007                    - - - BODYCHECK - - -            RUN ON APR 7, 1978

TOTAL REDUCIBLE RISK 4.5 YRS - - - CHRONOLOGICAL AGE 53 YEARS - - - APPRAISED AGE 53.9 YRS - - - ACHIEVABLE AGE 49.5 YRS

CAUSE OF DEATH                    PERCENT RISK RELATED
                                  TO THE AVERAGE CDN
                                     (100.0 IS AVG)     0         1         2         3         4         5         6
                                                        +.........+.........+.........+.........+.........+.........+
                                                        +         +
                                                        +         +
HEART ATTACK                            125.24          +===WEESSSSSSS
                                                        +===WEESSSSSSS
                                                        +===WEESSSSSSS
                                                        +===WEESSSSSSS
                                                        +===WEESSSSSSS
                                                        +         +
BREAST CANCER                           100.00          +==========
                                                        +==========
                                                        +         +
STROKE                                   79.83          +====SSSS +
                                                        +====SSSS +
                                                        +         +
INTESTINAL CANCER INCL. RECTUM          100.00          +===PPPPPPP
                                                        +         +
LUNG CANCER **                          200.00          +================SSSS
                                                        +         +
DIABETES                                 69.05          +======WW +
                                                        +         +
CIRRHOSIS OF LIVER                      200.00          +==========AAAAAAAAAA
                                                        +         +
CANCER OF THE CERVIX                     49.68          +=YYYY    +
                                                        +         +
MOTOR VEHICLE ACCIDENTS                 219.61          +==========AAAAAAAAAABB
                                                        +         +
CHRONIC RHEUMATIC HEART DISEASE           0.67          +=        +
                                                        +         +
SUICIDE                                 100.00          +==========
                                                        +         +
                                                        +.........+.........+.........+.........+.........+.........+
OTHER (NOT GRAPHED)                     100.00
                                        ------
TOTAL                                   107.72


LEGEND        A - ALCOHOL              B - SEATBELT                D - DIABETES        E - EXERCISE
              H - BLOOD PRESSURE       M - DRUGS/MEDICATIONS       P - PROCTO/EXAM.    S - SMOKING
              W - WEIGHT               X - BREAST SELF-EXAM        Y - PAPSMEAR        = - IRREDUCIBLE
-----------------------------------------------------------------------------------------------------------------------

* Risk factors adapted from "How to Practice Prospective Medicine", Drs. Robbins and Hall, Methodist Hospital of Indiana.

** Lung cancer risk decreases steadily and reaches non smoker level 10 years after stopping.

N.B.  Smoking here affects 3 causes of death, and contributes much greater total risk than others; next is Alcohol.
```

to improve their own health risks and hence ultimately to become the exemplars noted above.

A Possible Format for an Interpretation/Counseling Session with the Client

This session may represent the first occasion on which the client has ever been able to review his/her health risk status as a whole. It may, therefore, represent a teachable moment at which behavioral change will be undertaken. However, it is important to accept that such willing change may not necessarily be in the areas of greatest risk, and that the most important thing in lifestyle change seems to be getting started.

Then as the person subsequently begins to note positive changes in health and attitudes to life, further change is often undertaken naturally and the whole process may become "addictive." However, this is the most optimistic scenario, and in many cases there may be need for much support before lifestyle change is commenced, in accordance with the five-stage model of behavioral change, discussed earlier.

The following material in quotes suggests a possible format for presentation, which may be helpful and efficient in transmitting information and ideas to patients and clients (Milsum, 1978). Of course, all counselors will evolve the most suitable formats for themselves as experience with HHA increases.

"Health Hazard Appraisal (HHA) is designed to illustrate the importance of your lifestyle in determining your health risks (your health-risks are self-imposed, and consequently it is at least partly your responsibility to deal with them).

"HHA is based on the concept of risk. A risk is a chance or probability, the likelihood of something occurring. However, being at high risk of some event (injury, disease, or death) does not necessarily mean that it will happen, while being at low risk does not mean that the event can not occur. An estimate of risk is not a prediction.

"Your personal health risks are determined by comparing you to the average population of people your own age and sex—in particular by using Canadian death statistics. Naturally, we would like to compare you on the basis of 'health statistics,' but unfortunately only death statistics are accurately kept. The emphasis of the appraisal is not intended to be on an absolutely accurate numerical statement of your risks, but on the general extent to which you are above, at, or below the average for your age and sex. Of course, the Canadian average does not represent best health, and it is both desirable and usually possible for you to move to lower risk than average. The following notes refer directly to your computer print-out." (See Table 4 for an example.)

(The HHA print-out should now be viewed together and discussed.) "In general there are three patterns of appraisal:

(i) "*I.M.Hirisk.*" This person is readily exemplified by the sedentary, middle-aged worker whose risks are twice or more times the average risk. Such risks can, however, occur at any age in either sex. The result will be an "Appraised Age" (see below) of some five to ten years greater than the "Actual Age." The "Achievable Age," which can be reached by following the recommendations, may still be significantly higher than the "Actual Age," often indicating high "irreducible" risks* such as family histories and such occupational risks as high mileage. This person needs special attention and follow-up to get started on some lifestyle changes and to maintain them.

(ii) *"I.N.Dulgent."* This person has an aggregate risk somewhat above average, and therefore an Appraised Age perhaps up to five years above Actual. However, Achievable Age is probably slightly below Actual, and the person should be counseled to try to achieve this.

(iii) *"E.X.Emplary."* This person is living at very low risk and has very few recommendations to change lifestyle. Appraisal Age is below Actual by 5-10 years, and very close to the Achievable. Congratulations are in order, with emphasis on the desirability of maintaining, and improving if this seems desired, the present good status.

(Table 4) Page 1—*"Column 1—Average"* "In order to compare you to the normal population, the risk levels of the twelve major causes of death for your age and sex are identified. The risks for the many possible remaining causes are summed beneath, and then the total risk for all causes of death are given. Thus in the first column, the average number of deaths expected per 100,000 people within the next ten years, for each cause, are given—the Canadian Average. Notice again that this is a *ten-year* risk.

"The top 12 causes of mortality typically account for from one-half to three-quarters of your total risk of dying. Any other single cause of death usually accounts for less than one percent of your total risk.

"The average risks of death are low when you are young (around one chance in 100 at age 15), but climb with age, as shown in Figure 4. For youths, "violent" deaths are predominant, in particular car accidents and suicide (Table 2), while from middle-age on "degenerative" deaths, especially heart attack, cancer, and stroke predominate. Both "violent" and "degenerative" types are at least partly due to bad lifestyle habits. Females have much lower total risks than males at all ages."

(Table 4) Page 1—*"Column 2—Appraisal"* "The second column presents your individual appraisal figures. Again, the figures represent the chances

---

*Note that not all these risks are genuinely "irreducible," for example mileage, depression, and cholesterol level. At present HHA does not specifically recommend changes, however.

of dying per 100,000 within the next ten years, and are determined from your answers on the appraisal questionnaire. The appraisal figures are determined by estimating risk factors which alter the average values of Column 1. The details and rationale used for estimating the risk multipliers are presented on the next page."

(Table 4)—*"Column 3—Compliance"** "The third column presents your lesser chances of dying, assuming some improvement of risk factors by your adopting the recommendations listed at the foot of the page."

Page 1—*Material below the appraisal columns* "Immediately below the three columns, three *ages* are specified: Given (Actual); Appraised; Achievable (Compliance). These ages provide another way of appreciating your appraised and achievable risks in comparison with the average Canadian. As indicated on the curve for total death risk versus age (Figure 4), your Appraised Age is that age at which an average Canadian has the same risk as you. Thus a lower Appraised Age than Actual is desirable. Similarly, your Achievable Age is that lower risk age which you can reach by adopting the lifestyle-change recommendations.

"The recommendations are developed from your answers on the questionnaire. Since only the "Top 12" death risks for your age and sex group have been considered, there may be some further useful recommendations which have not been included because they do not reduce the risk for these diseases, and we can discuss this."

(Each recommendation should be noted and commented on. Discuss the statement on the person's height, weight, and frame size, derived from the Metropolitan Life Tables. Note that the figures are processed in the computer for *height with shoes* and *weight with clothes.* Sometimes the improvements due to following recommendations do not appear very large, but even small gains may be more significant than the numerical factors indicate. Since young people may have low risks, they may be given greater motivation toward lifestyle change by considering their appraisal for middle-age (e.g., 45) assuming continuation of their present lifestyle, when heart attack, stroke, and cancer deaths predominate (Table 2).)

"Behavior change is easier to accomplish when you begin as early as

---

*Compliance Age is also called Achievable Age.

possible, and the potential gains are greater. Also, since the figures given are for death, they represent only a small part of the total disease entity—the tip of an iceberg of sickness—and consequently, we can assume that the advantages in reduced risk would be more significant than actually presented by mortality figures alone. Thus, although your total risk of dying is small, indicating a favorable chance of living, small alterations in these risks can still have favorable results in terms of your sickness, with its associated disease and disability."

(In some cases it is useful to indicate that the program is designed to be in an educational format. Thus the program is not intended to give an absolutely accurate estimate of one's risk of dying, although every attempt is made to be accurate and informative. Emphasize that although the recommendations may appear rather commonplace, these issues keep coming up because they are important.)

(Table 4) Page 2—"On this page your individual risk factors (multipliers) have been related to the major causes of death. The left column shows those causes of death for which specific information is available in the risk registry, together with the listing of 'contributing characteristics' or risk factors for each cause of death. The middle columns contain the appraisal figures with the 'actual risk' multipliers being given in the center of this column for each contributing characteristic. The overall or 'composite risk' factor is calculated from these, and is used to generate column 2 on page 1 for each cause of death.

"The right-hand columns contain the achievable figures in the same format. The achievable composite risk factors on the right-hand side of the column similarly produce column 3 on the first page."

(Table 4) Page 3—"Page 3 summarizes *graphically* much of the data already *tabulated* on the first two pages. Again the left-hand column presents the diseases for which specific appraisal information is available.

"The actual depth (vertically) of each band on the graph, representing one cause of death, indicates the relative importance of this cause for your age and sex group. A wide band thus indicates that the disease causes proportionately more deaths compared with narrower bands. Presenting the diseases in this way helps place them in perspective. Thus a recommendation associated with a disease of significant importance for your age and sex group should preferably be considered more seriously than one for a disease of lower significance. The horizontal length of the bar indicates your percentage risk related to the average Canadian risk for your age and sex group. On the graph itself the average Canadian risk (100% or 1) is shown by the vertical line of '+' marks below the number 1. To the left is below average and to the right is above average. It is important to appreciate that the graph gives a percentage of risk related to the average, and *not a percentage of certainty that a disease event will occur.* The letters on these bar graphs indicate the amounts by which the risks can be reduced given your adoption of the corresponding recommendations, which appear in full on page 1. You can initially obtain the largest risk reduction by adopting those recommendations which have the largest number of corresponding letters on the graphs.

"The symbol '=' represents those risks considered "irreducible" by this HHA program, that is, for which no known risk reduction programs can be numerically estimated at present. This does not mean that through good lifestyle habits you may not reduce them further—for example, we all know that the following are important: regular meals of good foods providing balanced nutrition, with little in-between snacking; reduction of stress; and regular sleep (usually 7-8 hours preferred).

"Please note also that recommendations do not imply that you must bring the new condition about immediately. You should instead tackle change only on a gradual basis so that your body and state-of-mind have time to adjust."

(Where appropriate, aspects such as nutrition and stress may merit a major share of the discussion. For some recommendations, such as for blood pressure, it would be desirable to repeat HHA when the suggested improvement has been achieved, since the recommendation does not call for full reduction to 120/80. The program does not make a recommendation to reduce elevated cholesterol level (above 280), and this is left to your discretion. Your discretion should also be applied with "Depression" and "Mileage" (no recommendations given), papsmear and proctosigomoidoscopy (yearly tests discretionary on advice of physician are recommended).

Effectiveness of Health Hazard Appraisal

Health Hazard Appraisal is a relatively new tool for lifestyle modification and has not yet received adequate funding for evaluative research. Such research should ideally be continued for a number of years,

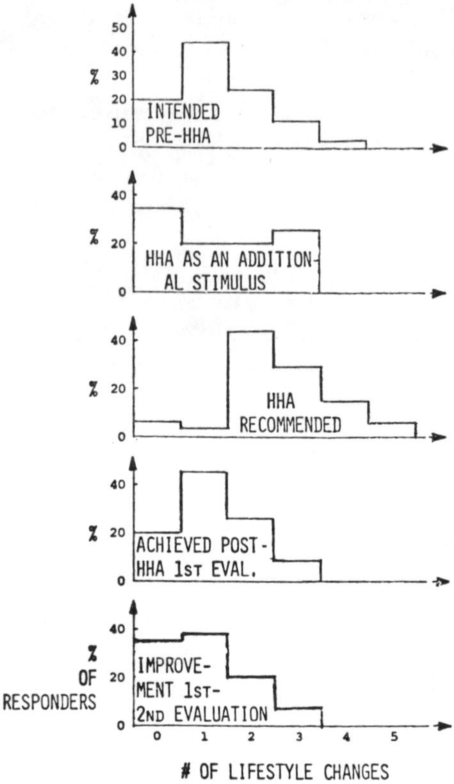

FIGURE 5. Frequency of lifestyle changes—second evaluation; total number of responses—35.

as in the study by Belloc and Breslow (1972) and Belloc (1973). However, most evaluative projects reported so far have been of short duration, typically with follow-up occurring within the range of three to eighteen months after administration of HHA and counseling (Dunton & Rasmussen, 1977; Leppink & deGrassi, 1977; Milsum, Laszlo, & Prince, 1976; Lauzon, 1977; Shires, Hennen, & Bell, 1977; Warner, 1977). Most studies do not have a control group, but rather do a "before-and-after" study on volunteer groups of subjects. Typically, the results are expressed in terms of reduction in appraised age relative to chronological age, over the interval of the follow-up study. It should be noted that the data are acquired by a repeated self-assessment through filling out the HHA questionnaire for a second time, and are therefore subject to possible bias. Typically, the results show that an average appraised "age reduction" of around one year is achieved, corresponding usually to about one behavioral change.

We carried out a small evaluative study in a Community Health Center (Milsum, Laszlow, & Prince, 1976) which illustrates some of the aspects of behavioral change discussed earlier. Over a six-month follow-up period the clients were asked, in regard to major precursors or risk factors, whether:

(1) they had intended to make changes in that area before taking HHA;
(2) HHA had acted as an additional stimulus to them for making change:
(3) HHA had recommended change in this area;
(4) they had achieved change in this area following the first evaluation;
(5) improvement had occurred between the initial and the follow-up evaluation.

The data for this study are shown in histogram form in Figure 5. Several interesting features emerged. First, there are significant percentages ranging from 20-35 percent of clients who had: (1) not intended lifestyle change, (2) had not been stimulated to change, and (3) had not achieved lifestyle change. In comparison there were only 5 percent for whom HHA did not recommend any lifestyle changes.

The profiles of the histograms for changes that were intended before Health Hazard Appraisal and those that were achieved after the first evaluation are very similar, while that for changes recommended by HHA is also similar except that it is shifted to the right in Figure 5 by approximately one more lifestyle change. Thus achievement seems to match declared previous intention fairly well, but does not reach the level recommended by HHA. Nevertheless, the interesting point emerging in the second histogram from the top is that HHA was reported by approximately two-thirds of the group as being an additional stimulus for lifestyle change. This would support the hypothesis discussed earlier that some stimuli may still serve an important role in the multi-stage process leading to behavioral change even though they may not be the final trigger producing it.

In regard to specific lifestyle risk-factors, our study found that HHA was particularly reported as a stimulus for lifestyle change in the four areas of exercise pattern, body weight, seatbelt usage, and alcohol usage. The results from the other referenced studies (Dunton & Rasmussen, 1977; Lauzon, 1977; Leppink & deGrassi, 1977; Shires, Hennon, & Bell,

1977; Warner, 1977) are somewhat mixed, although there is general agreement that HHA tends to be effective in reduction of alcohol consumption and of weight, but not very effective in changing smoking behavior. The results for exercise are very inconsistent. Generally there is significant improvement in screening procedures (papsmear, breast self examination, and rectal examination) although the (rectal) proctosignoidoscopy is controversial, as indeed are regular annual check-ups.

The better-designed evaluations have typically assigned subjects to one of three treatment groups, namely: (1) a control oroup with no HHA; (2) the test group with HHA being administered and interpreted; and (3) HHA administration with interpretation and, in addition, a counseling regimen (cf. Lauzon, 1977). In general, and perhaps not surprisingly, counseling emerges as the most important feature in stimulating behavioral change.

Health Hazard Appraisal as a System

HHA is emerging as a major tool for promoting improved lifestyles and individual responsibility for health, in a counseling framework. We have, therefore, developed an integrated system involving three major areas of activity as shown in Figure 6: (1) educational programs for HHA; (2) methodological and technological improvement of the computerized system; (3) research involving statistical and epidemiological analyses using an accumulating anonymous data base.

An important feature of the educational program has been the development of a full-day interprofessional workshop offered to health professionals. Apart from the obvious core content, this workshop emphasizes the development of appropriate techniques for acting as a counselor for lifestyle change in a client-counselor setting, with a "contract" as an important goal. Participants are also encouraged to consider the potential importance of their own influence as exemplars.

Since HHA will not remain a fixed instrument, we have tackled the methodological and technological development of a computerized modular system which can flexibly accommodate changing ideas of its form and content, epidemiological risk, and presentation of output material. Further, as enough information becomes available to incorporate major missing areas (such as nutrition and stress), these should also be incorporated into the system.

The third significant aspect has been the molding of HHA data into a structured data base containing the data input from the questionnaires

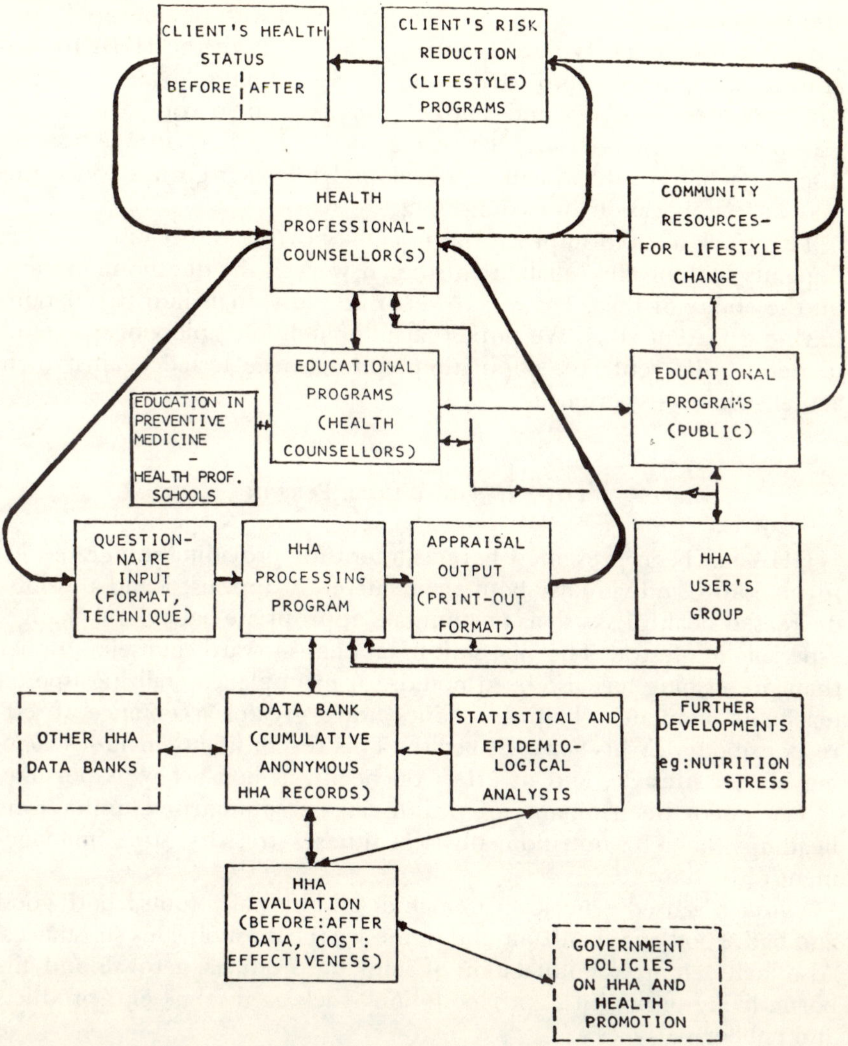

FIGURE 6. Information flow diagram for Health Hazard Appraisal system.

and selected results generated by the HHA computation. The structure ensures anonymity of individual records. This data base provides opportunities for epidemiological evaluation of lifestyles and their changes over time. Further, simulation modeling can be started to evaluate the sensitivity of life-expectancy patterns to changes in lifestyles, and to check the reliability of the risk factors currently provided. Provision will also be made for linking the HHA information with demographic and environmental data. We are evaluating the ability of the HHA to separate the population into various lifestyle groupings, for example, in correlation of drinking and smoking habits, and in comparison of a group of "impaired drivers" with a matched control group. We hope to discover what "profiles" can be developed for such groups, since this may have implications for counseling.

This work aims to improve the reliability of HHA, because its value depends both on the reliability of the answers to the questionnaire and on the ability of these answers to separate individuals into populations having different risks. We hope that ultimately the ability of questions to define different risk populations may also be tested against their actual sickness experience.

Toward the Whole Person

HHA has been presented here as a tool for providing integrated information to individuals about their currently-appraised and possibly-decreased health risks so as to stimulate appropriate behavioral change, especially in lifestyle. The vital shift in emphasis toward counseling rather than prescribing has also been noted, for example, capitalizing upon a teachable moment to help the client toward greater acceptance of self-responsibility for his/her own health. This responsibility includes viewing his/her lifestyle, and its effect on health as holistically as possible.

The major determinants of health can be summarized under four headings, namely: nutrition, physical fitness, stressors, stress management/reduction.

Nutrition is used generically to include all physical "inputs," both good and bad. Food and drink, air and water are the most obvious substances. Also included are the inhalation of smoking products, aerosols and airborne living organisms, and "pollution" such as gasoline end-products and rubber particles.

Physical Fitness is used generically to include all physical work "outputs," including physical work and exercise. Clearly physical inputs and outputs must be balanced for good health.

Stressors are used generically for pressures at the psychological-emotional level, such as the Life Change Units, and for the more detailed stressors encountered each day (family relations, work pressures, examinations, emotional experiences, etc.).

Stress Management/Reduction is used generically to describe the various

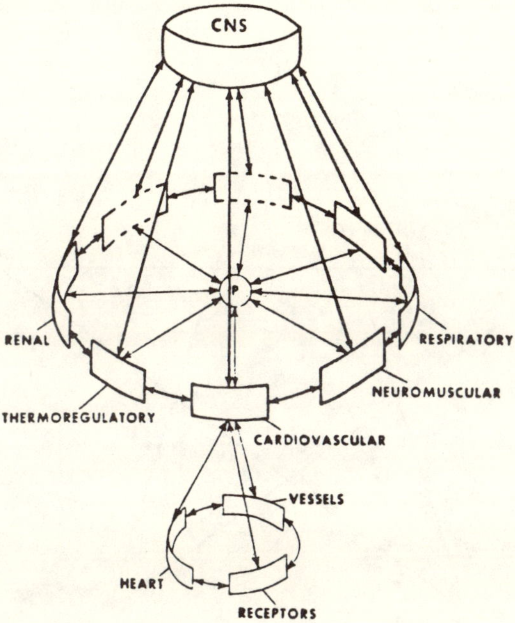

Physical interactions between physiological functions are represented by point P

FIGURE 7. The multihierarchical system constituting an organism.

individual techniques for coping with the tendency for stress levels to increase under the effect of stressors. Included are quiet, aloneness, recreation, dancing, sports, relaxation (both informal and formal; the latter by progressive muscular relaxation, desensitization, autogenic training, etc.), meditation and prayer.

Stressors and Stress Management/Reduction therefore primarily include the interplay of forces at the emotional and psychological levels, and in part at the social level. In terms of the World Health Organization definition of health, the three areas of "physical, mental, and social well-being" are therefore covered by these two levels. But are these levels sufficient for a person's whole needs? Clearly not, according to Maslow (1962), since we have a hierarchy of needs, moving upwards, through successively pre-requisite sets of physical and emotional D-needs (defi-

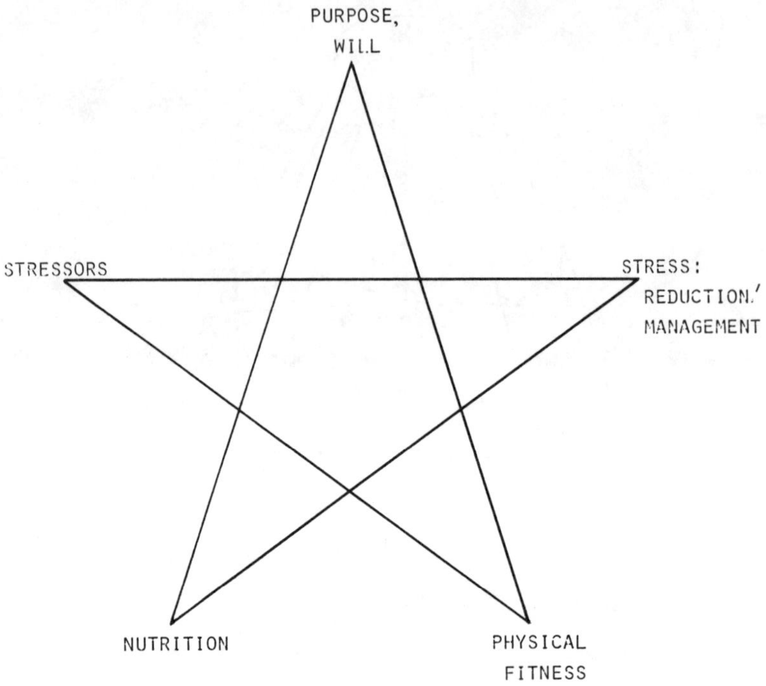

FIGURE 8. Determinants of individual health.

ciency) to the "intrinsic values of being," the B-needs (being) which involve sense of purpose, self-actualization, and peak experiences.

From a systems-analytic viewpoint, we are led to argue for the necessity of purpose in order to maintain our full health. We each comprise hierarchical sets of subsystems (as suggested in Figure 7 for the cardiovascular system, Milsum & Roberge, 1973). Each subsystem, at each level, is typically characterized by a feedback control configuration, for which a "set-point" or "system purpose" is necessary (Milsum, 1966); for example, blood pressure, cardiac output, and blood distribution pattern in the cardiovascular system. Typically, these set-points are set by the system at a higher level in the hierarchy, which in so doing must coordinate and optimize a larger set of interacting subsystems. The central nervous system, representing our mind-brain as the summit of this hierarchy, must then even more crucially have its own sense of purpose, in order meaningfully to achieve the continuous setting, balancing, and harmonizing of these manifold dependent systems.

What must be added to our schema then is a sense of meaning and purpose to produce and sustain will—the will to survive, learn, maintain, recover, generate, procreate, and ultimately to face our physical death. To this point, Jung (1959) asserts that the conscious denial of our deep instincts results in uprootedness, disorientation, and neurotic restlessness. Further, a "restlessness begets meaninglessness, and the lack of meaning in life is a soul-sickness whose full extent and full import our age has not yet begun to understand" (p. 233).

A fifth point, for purpose and will, therefore completes the five-pointed star shown in Figure 8, the pentacle by which man has classically been symbolized. The star then represents the three successive hierarchical levels of the physical, mental (emotional, psychological, intellectual), and spiritual (meaning, purpose, will).

Ultimately our health and our lifestyles depend upon our deepest beliefs. While these beliefs may not always be fully accepted by our conscious reason, they will nonetheless exert their influence, in harmony if possible, but in discord if necessary. For our complete health, therefore, it is vital to establish basic harmony between our emotional, intuitive, and spiritual upwellings on the one hand and our psychosomatic science on the other.

REFERENCES

BELLOC, N.B.: Relationship of health practices and mortality. *Preventive Medicine,* 1973, *2,* 67-81.

BELLOC, N.B. & BRESLOW, H.: Relationship of physical health status and health practices. *Preventive Medicine,* 1972, *1,* 409-421.

BROWN, S.: Issues related to developing criteria for the evaluation of risk reduction. *Proceedings of 12th Meeting of the Society of Prospective Medicine,* 1976, 66-70.

DEVER, G.E.A.: *An epidemiological model for health policy analysis.* Atlanta, Georgia: Georgia Department of Human Resources, 1975.

DUNTON, S. & RASMUSSEN, W.: Comparative data of risk reduction, 1975-1977. *Proceedings 13th Meeting Society of Prospective Medicine,* 1977, 111-119.

HOLMES, T.H. & RAHE, R.H.: The Social Readjustment Rating Scale. *Journal of Psychosomatic Research,* 1967, *11,* 213-218.

JUNG, C.G.: The soul and death. In H. Feifel (ed.), *The meaning of death.* New York: McGraw-Hill, 1959.

LALONDE, M.: *A new perspective on the health of Canadians.* Ottawa: Information Canada, 1974.

LAUZON, R.R.J.: A randomized controlled trial of the ability of HHA to stimulate appropriate risk reduction behavior. *Proceedings 13th Meeting Society of Prospective Medicine,* 1977, 102-103.

LEPPINK, H.B. & DEGRASSI, A.: Changes in risk behaviour: a two year follow-up study. *Proceedings 13th Meeting Society of Prospective Medicine,* 1977, 104-107.

LEWIN, K.: Brief reviews of learning theories. *Health Education and Behavioural Science,* Third Party Associates, 45-57, 1938.

MASLOW, A.: *Towards a psychology of being,* New York: D. Van Nostrand Co., 1962.

MILSUM, J.H.: *Biological control system analysis.* New York: McGraw-Hill, 1966.

MILSUM, J.H.: *Introductory manual on Health Hazard Appraisal.* Division of Health Systems, Report #HS-78-01, University of British Columbia, 1978.

MILSUM, J.H., LASZLO, C.A., & PRINCE, P.R.: A pilot evaluation of introducing Health Hazard Appraisal in a community health center environment. *Proceedings 12th Meeting Society of Prospective Medicine,* 1976, 92-102.

MILSUM, J.H. & ROBERGE, J.A.: Physiological regulation and control. In R. Rosen (Ed.), *Foundations of mathematical biology, Volume III, Supercellular Systems.* New York: Academic Press, 1973, 1-95.

ROBBINS, L.C. & HALL, J.H.: *How to practice prospective medicine.* Indianapolis: Methodist Hospital of Indiana, 1970.

SADUSK, J.F. & ROBBINS, L.C.: Prosposal for Health Hazard Appraisal in comprehensive health care. *Journal of American Medical Association,* 1968, *203,* 106-110.

SELYE, H.: *The stress of life.* New York: Signet Books, 1975.

SHIRES, D.B., HENNEN, B.K., & BELL, G.: BODYCHECK: measuring precursors and factors influencing compliance. *Proceedings 13th Meeting Society of Prospective Medicine,* 1977, 99-101.

WARNER, H.L.: Health Hazard Appraisal—an instrument for change. *Proceedings 13th Meeting Society of Prospective Medicine,* 1977, 120-123.

6

Weight Loss and Beyond: Are They Taking It Off and Keeping It Off?

Richard B. Stuart

Recent reviews have concluded that behavioral interventions offer a better promise of weight loss by the obese than do alternative psychological and medical methods (e.g., Leon, 1976; Stuart, 1975; Stunkard, 1975; Stunkard & Mahoney, 1976). Summarizing the sentiments of many of these reviews, Beller concluded her unusually thoughtful and provocative commentary with the observation that:

> Where it has been systematically compared to other more conventional programs, behavior therapy can be demonstrated to outperform other popular approaches by an impressive margin (1977, p. 266).

However, as many have observed "Almost any fat person can lose weight: few can keep it off" (Schachter & Rodin, 1974, p. 1). Therefore, the *maintenance of weight loss is a mandatory criterion* in the evaluation of the behavior-therapy approach. Unfortunately, in many studies, the longer term results of this approach have not equaled the immediate outcomes. While Leon (1977) found the long-term results satisfactory, others have found them wanting. For example, Stunkard concluded his presentation at the Eighth Banff International Conference on Behavior Modification by noting that behavioral treatments "have been no more effective than traditional ones" (1977, p. 349). In the same vein, Mahoney and his collaborators noted that:

> We have begun to describe behavioral procedures as *more* effective rather than *very* effective, our typical weight loss as *modest* rather than impressive, and our outcomes as variable rather than consistent (Mahoney, Rogers, Straw, & Mahoney, 1977, p. 1).

Was Stunkard's (1975) early heralding of the emergence of behavioral technology as a "landmark in the treatment of obesity" (p. 210) an accurate assessment, or was it an error which later experience has helped to reveal? It is the contention of this author that behavior therapy remains the *best available alternative for the promotion of weight loss, and that when properly administered the techniques also yield highly acceptable long-term results.* In support of this contention, it will be argued that many of the failures of clients to maintain their loss of weight are attributable to poorly conceived and executed interventions. Six flaws in treatment planning and delivery will be reviewed, three of which commonly lead to "trivial" behavior-therapy outcomes, and three of which commonly lead to inadequate results. Long-term results of behavioral treatments for the overweight will be examined as support for continued optimism about the potential of the behavioral approach. Finally, several suggestions will be made in the hope that they might contribute to the design of research which will yield increasingly positive outcomes.

Six Sources of Failure in Behavior Therapy

When treatment goals and/or methods are poorly chosen, clients have little opportunity to achieve meaningful therapeutic results. When well-chosen goals and methods are delivered poorly, it is reasonable to expect a high rate of attrition before the end of intervention and a rapid relapse when treatment has been concluded. Trivial treatment outcomes often stem from any of three all-too-frequent limitations:

(1) Acceptance of negative change goals;
(2) Failure to manage both the antecedents and consequences of the target behavior; and
(3) Utilization of "direct" rather than "indirect" intervention strategies.

Insufficient or short-lived treatment results often result from:

(4) Failure to attend to the requirements of effective service delivery;
(5) Failure to collect and/or to properly utilize data that reflect therapeutic progress; and
(6) Failure to provide a technology that is needed in the maintenance of therapeutic gains.

Because all of these limitations can be observed in the literature which evaluates the effectiveness of behavioral strategies for controlling overeating, each will be discussed prior to assessing this literature specifically.

Negative Change Goals (Response Suppression)

The selection of negative change targets is a problem for several reasons: First, achievement of these target goals almost always involves the use of aversive techniques, such as punishment, the loss of positive reinforcement, or extinction. Utilization of these techniques requires a degree of environmental control rarely achieved outside the laboratory (Azrin & Holz, 1966). Their utilization also often leads to reactions ranging from disenchantment with the intervenor, whose influence is thereby weakened, to direct attacks against the intervenor or others. In addition, when negative strategies of behavioral influence are employed, these methods are often imitated by those who come under their influence (e.g., Gelfand, Hartmann, Mahan, & Lamb, 1975)—an illustration of negative modeling.

As a second limitation, use of response-decreasing procedures does not offer the intervenor any means of controlling the emergent, alternative behaviors. As Kazdin (1975) observed, "extinction may effectively decrease the behavior, but it does not ensure that a desirable behavior will replace the (one) that has been eliminated" (p. 187). This may explain the observation that many subjects whose treatment emphasizes "giving up" a behavior, like smoking, frequently develop alternative problematic behaviors like overeating when their smoking is suppressed (Belloc & Breslow, 1972).

Finally, the use of response-suppression procedures also conflicts with a philosophical tenet of behavior therapy: the belief that treatment should help to increase rather than to diminish the range of satisfactions in the daily lives of clients. Violation of this principle is seen in some of the early studies in which extinction was used to quell operant crying by toddlers and preschool-age children (e.g., Hart, Allen, Buel, Harris, &

Wolf, 1964) despite the fact that it has been learned that children of mothers who *do* attend to their crying, cry *less* over time than do those of mothers who do not attend to these bids for attention (Bell & Ainsworth, 1972). Rather than minimize parent-child contact, it would seem far more humane to begin intervention by strengthening parental attention to children's constructive social behavior, possibly relying upon extinction as a secondary method (e.g., Etzel & Gewirtz, 1967).

Unfortunately, many of the efforts to modify eating behavior are more oriented toward the suppression of problem eating than toward the development of more constructive means of securing needed pleasures in living. For example, covert sensitization (Horan, Baker, Hoffman, & Shute, 1975; Cautela, 1972) and use of aversive stimuli, such as cigarette smoke (Morganstern, 1974), noxious odors (Foreyt & Kennedy, 1971), or electric shock (e.g., Wijesinghe, 1973), have been used in efforts to suppress eating behavior. It can be argued that selection of positive change goals offers the advantages of being more readily accomplished, more risk free, more philosophically acceptable, less subject to the possibility of "symptom substitution" (Cahoon, 1968; Stuart, 1975; Stunkard & Rush, 1974), and more likely to be successful in the long run.

Rather than suppressing problem behavior which would, in effect, create a behavioral void, behavioral interventions should be aimed at developing constructive behaviors. At a critical moment in the middle stage of treatment, the client, in ideal circumstances, should be confronted with an intriguing approach-approach conflict which poses a choice between the habitual problem behavior and a new alternative action. With therapeutic help, the client will then ideally choose the new alternative, which offers a higher level of reinforcement with a lower level of expected adverse consequence. In that way the therapist preserves some control over the emergent behavior, and the general level of satisfaction in the client's life is improved rather than impoverished.

Incomplete Planning

Many of the behavior-control programs published under the banner of behavior modification have been woefully inadequate in planning some of the more obvious intervention essentials. While virtually all writers have noted the importance of modification of the balance between energy intake and energy expenditure as a means of weight control, and while program participants have been found to rate the importance of food plans above that of the behavioral interventions

(Stuart & Mitchell, in press), very few behavioral researchers specify prescriptions for food-intake and energy-expenditure requirements. Because these critically important independent variables are uncontrolled, many of the treatments come close to being ethically irresponsible, and comparison of results across treatment is apt to show a predictable but avoidable rate of therapeutic failure.

In addition to omitting eating and exercise prescriptions from their planning, behavior modifiers often fail to specify recommendations for control of the contingencies of eating. Without energy-balance prescriptions, clients run the risk of adopting plans that neutralize the potential benefits of behavior change; without prescription of specific antecedent and consequent control of eating behavior, they are exposed to the risk of needless frustration in their self-management efforts. Indeed, complete instruction in the management of personal environments is as important for adults who would manage their weight as it is for children whose home and school social behavior is the target of concern (e.g., Herman & Tramantana, 1971). Neglect of this comprehensive planning can result in lamentable iatrogenic treatment effects.

As an illustration, Mann (1972) sought to use contingency contracting as a primary intervention technique for managing problem eating, much as Tighe and Elliott (1968) used it in their efforts to control smoking behavior. To this end, Mann asked his clients to deposit valued objects that would be returned as contingencies for their attainment of weekly weight-loss goals. To achieve these goals the clients were free to choose their own methods, with the strong possibility that they would overuse diuretics, laxatives, and self-starvation in desperate attempts to reach their weekly weight-loss goals. A far more prudent and benign treatment strategy would have included instructions for healthful means of promoting weight loss, providing contingencies for compliance with these changes rather than for their presumed weight-loss effects (e.g., Harris & Hallbauer, 1973).

Direct as Opposed to Indirect Therapeutic Planning

A variety of accelerating and decelerating techniques have been advocated for use in the service of direct efforts to control problem eating. Positive changes have been sought through the use of client-provided (e.g., Mahoney, 1974) and therapist-provided (e.g., Dinoff, Rikard, & Colwick, 1972) positive reinforcements. Negative change goals have been sought through the aversion methods mentioned earlier. All of these procedures, and others like them, have in common one major limitation:

They seek to control eating behavior without changing the forces that maintain the *urge to eat.* This places the client in the painful dilemma of either foregoing the pleasure of eating and experiencing the stress of an unfulfilled urge or of yielding to the urge and suffering the immediate psychological and longer range health consequences of self-indulgence. Faced by this choice, many clients doubtless choose the more immediately gratifying alternative.

This direct approach is much in keeping with the Protestant Ethic which stresses the virtue of working now for reward later, and little in common with the Buddhist belief that "suffering ends when craving ceases" (Mikulas, 1978, p. 62). It implies that suffering may be a necessary dimension of all constructive change, but it essentially ignores much of our understanding of the hedonistic dimension of much human behavior. Rather than bucking the tide in our efforts to find constantly higher levels of satisfaction and lower levels of stress, behavior modifiers would do well to build this realization into their models of intervention by adopting an *indirect model of intervention.* Simply stated:

> The principle of indirection requires two stages of therapeutic planning: (1) an effort should be made to modify the conditions that create and maintain the urge to behave in problematic ways; and (2) an effort should be made to promote alternative positive actions when the problem urge is under control.

Figure 1 summarizes some of the sources of the urge to emit problem behaviors that would require change if these behaviors are to be successfully replaced. For example, if overeating is Mr. Jones' prime concern, his urge to overeat might be prompted by any of at least six different factors: (1) physiologically he might be hypoglycemic and therefore crave carbohydrates at frequent intervals; (2) he might have highly established habitual routines in which eating is a link in a behavioral sequence, like entering his office in the morning, getting coffee and a snack, and then beginning his work for the day; (3) he may believe that he "cannot work without eating," a cognition that surely prompts excessive eating; (4) he may feel chronically bored, lonely, tense, or angry—all emotions he has learned to quell with food; (5) important people in his life may urge him to overeat and disparage his efforts at self-management; and (6) food may be carelessly available throughout his home and work environments, so that the physical prompts to eat are ever present. Unfortunately, most intervenors would advise Mr. Jones to eat more wisely—a direct approach; few would help him reduce his urge to eat before dealing with eating per se—the indirect approach.

Recognition of the many interrelated sources of influence that control

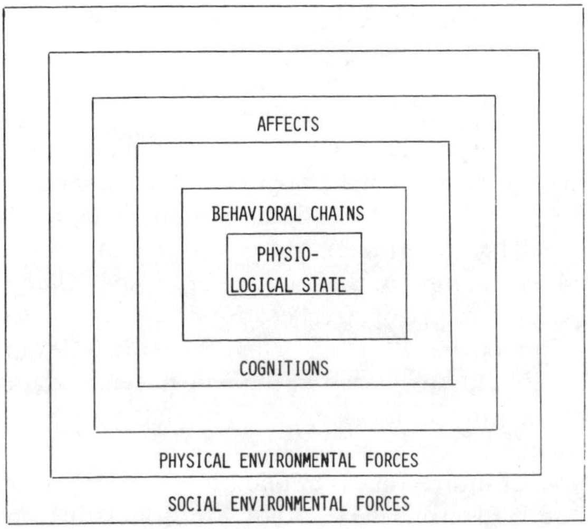

FIGURE 1. Forces that can strengthen problem behavior.

both positive and problem behaviors is not new either within (e.g., Brown, 1972; Lazarus, 1971) or beyond (e.g., Dembroski, 1977) behavior modification. However, the so-called "broad spectrum" approaches in both psychology and preventive health efforts have traditionally sought direct rather than indirect goal attainments. In contrast, the present proposal calls for an order effect in the planning of change in human behavior in which preparatory steps promote a series of intrapersonal, interpersonal, and situational changes before secondary efforts are made to achieve the target changes.

The model presented in Figure 1 makes no assumptions as to which sources of behavior are the most powerful, nor does it address the question of the sequences in which the varied influences come into play. Application of the principle does, however, require several important considerations:

(1) Change may or may not be necessary in all of the identifiable sources of behavior.
(2) Clients, themselves, are the best sources of information about the idiographic basis of their own problem urges.
(3) It is often desirable to undertake efforts to simultaneously change aspects of several sources of the problem urge.
(4) Because it is rarely, if ever, possible to totally eradicate a high-strength problem urge, clients should be taught means to *avoid* some stressors and to *escape* from those that cannot be avoided.

Because intervention should, of course, be as parsimonious as possible, the level of treatment needed must be determined empirically for each client. Because individual expression of general laws is always to be expected, client-supplied detail is almost always needed in the development of viable treatment plans. Because clients are more willing to work on some aspects of their behavior than on others, it is prudent to suggest several changes in order to increase the likelihood that, at least, some changes will be undertaken. Moreover, making several suggestions for changes gives meaning to the concept of lifestyle change that is basic to successful intervention. Finally, because time-bound intervention programs cannot anticipate all of the client's future relevant life experiences, training should be offered in the two-stage avoidance-and-escape planning that will enable the client to formulate later self-management strategies as needed.

The principle of indirection is applied in a five-step procedure: First, positive change goals are selected. For Mr. Jones this would mean an effort to "make constructive food decisions" rather than to "cut down on problem eating," or to be "more physically active" rather than "to overcome pathogenic inactivity." Next, the forces that create and maintain the urge to behave in problem ways are functionally analyzed. Mr. Jones might need medical help in restoring his glycogen balance, or may require assistance in developing behavioral routines to help him avoid rather than seek out contact with food; for example, changing some of his self-referent ideas, modifying experiences that lead to problematic emotions, gaining more constructive social support from others, and managing his life space in more constructive ways. Third, steps are instigated to achieve many of these changes. The fourth step is the planning of direct efforts to achieve the target change, which, in the case of Mr. Jones, calls for specific plans for the modification of eating and activity patterns. Finally, these planned energy-balance manipulations are carried out.

Techniques of Service Delivery

It has been suggested that three technologies are needed in the effective delivery of behavior-change services: a technology of focal behavior change; a technology of maintaining this change; and a technology for delivering both sets of services (Stuart, 1972). With this tripartite requirement in mind, it is clear that the most well-conceived change and maintenance-of-change strategies might be little more than the intervenor's good intentions if they are not presented in a manner that captivates the clients' interests and mobilizes their desires to change.

Effective service delivery is a complex process that involves many careful choices: First, intervenors must be selected for their capacity to have maximum impact upon clients. Unfortunately, decades of psychotherapy research have not identified any specific set of therapist characteristics that necessarily facilitate greater client gains. Indeed, it has been observed that some clients would probably do well with any therapist, some only with therapists who are like them, some only with therapists who are different from them, and some would probably not be helped by any therapist (Meltzoff & Kornreich, 1970). Nevertheless, it is important to make an effort to assess the effectiveness of therapists of varying characteristics, particularly in light of the long-standing observation that both lay people and professionals have been shown to be effective in the delivery of human services (e.g., Goldstein, 1972; Strupp & Bergin, 1969).

In the weight-management literature, psychiatrists (e.g., Currey, Malcolm, Riddle, & Schachte, 1977; Jeffrey, Wing, & Stunkard, 1978; Levitz & Stunkard, 1974; Penick, Filion, Fox, & Stunkard, 1971), nutritionists (Paulsen, Lutz, McReynolds, & Kohrs, 1976), social workers (Currey et al., 1977), professional psychologists (Hall, Hall, Hanson, & Borden, 1974; Romanczyck, Tracey, Wilson, & Thorpe, 1973), psychology graduate students (Hagen, 1974; Harris, 1969; Harris & Hallbauer, 1973), psychology undergraduate students (Jeffrey, 1974; Ost & Gottestam, 1976) and lay leaders (Levitz & Stunkard, 1974; Stuart, 1977a; Stuart & Guire, in press) have all served in therapeutic capacities. Given the fact that clients who participate in these studies are solicited from college campuses (e.g., Hagen, 1974; Harris, 1969; Wollersheim, 1970), the general community (e.g., Mahoney, 1974; Penick et al., 1971, Stuart, 1977b; Stuart & Guire, in press) and medical settings (e.g., Currey et al., 1977), the blend of client and therapist characteristics may indeed interact in a way that influences the probability of successful treatment outcome.

While there is some evidence that professional leaders may out-perform lay leaders working with professional materials (Levitz & Stunkard, 1974), there is more abundant evidence that lay leaders, working with or without professional materials, in self-help settings generally achieve better results than professionals (Ashwell, in press; Ashwell & Garrow, 1973; Gartner & Riessman, 1977; Stuart, 1977b, Stuart & Mitchell, in press; Williams & Duncan, 1976a, 1976b). Stuart (1977b) has noted that self-help groups offer at least ten distinct advantages over professional programs: (1) They are more likely to define behaviors as problems, while professionals are more likely to label participants as problems. (2) They are less restrained and thereby cultivate greater faith in their methods than do many professionals. (3) They provide more varied opportunities for social contact with sympathetic listeners to encourage new behaviors. (4) They are usually conducted by leaders who have themselves conquered the problem and thereby serve a valuable modeling function. (5) They have few, if any, gating mechanisms, so members can join or leave their groups without suffering the indignities often associated with professional diagnosis and labeling. (6) They more effectively "normalize" and "destigmatize" the target behaviors because the behaviors are or have been common among all members of the group. (7) They are more likely to develop a unique argot and various ritualized practices that help reinforce members' sense of belonging to a change-oriented organization. (8) They generally use more effective techniques of social marketing—of informing potential members about their offerings —perhaps because they are not bound by restrictions that limit professional advertising. (9) They generally have a modest fee for service which allows members to meet the responsibility of payment for service received without recourse to third-party payment. (10) This contributes to the final and perhaps most important of all of the advantages: participants in self-help groups are more likely than professional clients to feel they have achieved something for themselves. As will be suggested later, this self-attribution may be a major contributor to members' abilities to maintain the changes made during their active treatment.

In addition to selecting therapists with optimal characteristics, attention should be paid to the nature of the nonfocal interactions between therapists and clients. For example, Frank (1961, 1962) observed that effective therapists create a neutral environment in which expressions of feelings are facilitated and offer clients a rationale for restructuring their understanding of their distress and the possible remedies available to them. Luborsky (1976) has suggested that the relationship that mediates therapeutic change passes through two stages: one in which the therapist is perceived as supportive and helpful, followed by the formation of an alliance that is change-oriented. In the same vein, Lorr (1965), among others, stressed the importance of therapist assertiveness, understanding, acceptance, and encouragement as key change-producing skills. Lieberman (1976) has outlined several skills required of effective therapeutic group leaders: the capacity to enhance group cohesiveness; skill in directing the intra-group behavior of members;

skill in defining objectives; skill in accomplishing tasks; and skill in building the group as a context for social comparison that can neutralize extra-group forces which might subvert change.

Beyond the details of therapist-member interaction, selection of the format of group services can also be expected to interact with behavior-change technology in mediating outcomes of varying degrees of success. For example, groups may be didactic, interactional, or a balance of both; they may be highly structured or informal in their operation. These and other structural considerations that have been enumerated by Rose (1977) may all serve to enhance or to thwart therapeutic progress, and all must be taken into account in evaluating the effects of any service offering. Unfortunately, many researchers fail to report these essential details when publishing their results, and when they are reported, reviewers of weight-management literature tend not to take them into account.

Evaluation of On-line Results

In their recent book, Mahoney and Mahoney (1976b) built the monitoring of intervention results into a superstructure for their entire method. In this regard, they are exemplary in their commitment to the use of data as a basis for the constant monitoring of therapeutic effects. Indeed, this kind of monitoring and the accountability it implies are core dimensions of the ethical practice of behavior modification (Association for Advancement of Behavior Therapy, 1977). Unfortunately, this use of data is more the exception than the rule in studies evaluating behavioral interventions with the overweight.

Therapists need at least two different kinds of information: They must know whether or not their clients are complying with the instigations for behavior change that are the essence of the intervention; and they must know what effect this compliance has on the target behavior as well as upon related behaviors.

Several investigators have made attempts to evaluate the extent to which clients do, in fact, make use of the instigations they are offered during their behavior therapy. Unfortunately, most of these assessments appear to be made at the conclusion of treatment rather than as a dimension of the ongoing assessment of therapeutic progress (e.g., Horan & Johnson, 1971; Stuart & Mitchell, in press; Wollersheim, 1970; Yates, in press). The results of these assessments can offer therapists systematic information about their clients' compliance with instigations and guide them in determining which techniques do and do not tend to be acceptable to clients.

In the context of studies of self-monitoring effects (e.g., Kazdin, 1974), much has been written about the way in which these compliance data can be collected, and it has been recognized for several years that positive self-monitoring (i.e., tracking successes rather than failures in performance) is the most effective approach (e.g., Gottman & McFall, 1972; Mischel, Ebbeson, & Zeiss, 1973). Recently a new force has been added to this recommendation with the finding that those who were experimentally instructed to monitor failures:

> a) evidenced greater devaluation of their performance relative to an ideal standard; b) lowered their self-reward rates over time; c) associated anxiety somewhat with performance (specifically for low- and medium-ability subjects); and d) solved problems least accurately (Kirschenbaum & Karoly, 1977, p. 1123).

Just as it has been shown that change goals should be positive, it is now clear that the assessment of progress toward these goals should also be positive. Once again behavioral interventions are inconsistent in their approach; many stress monitoring weight rather than the behaviors expected to produce weight change; and researchers are more likely to ask their clients to report failures than successes.

Measures of compliance, unless they are achieved through social monitoring, are naturally subjective; measures of effect, while more objective, are subject to their own problems—requiring assessment of clients' weight changes as well as measures of the psychological and other related impacts of the interventions.

In a thoughtful review of the weight-measurement problem, Feinstein (1974) noted that several different approaches have been tried. The most obvious approach is reporting the number of pounds lost—a problem in that a 20-pound loss by a 300-pound man may or may not be comparable to a 10-pound loss by a 150-pound woman. The rate of weight loss, found by dividing pounds lost by weeks of treatment, has also been used. This method suffers from the limitation that more weight is lost at the start of treatment due to fluid loss associated with dietary change, a fact leading to a strong bias favoring shorter duration treatments. A third method is the "performance index" developed by Jolliffe and Alpert (1951). This index is calculated by dividing actual weight loss by anticipated weight loss. Unfortunately, however, anticipated loss must be subjectively determined, and this approach takes no notice of the attainment or failure to attain goal weight. The fourth method cited by Feinstein is the Trulson criteria (Trulson, Walsh, & Caso, 1947) which measures success in meeting tabulated expectations of weight loss by persons with differing starting weights. As with the arbitrary anticipated loss advocated by Jolliffe and Alpert, the expected losses in the Trulson criteria are also subjectively and not empirically determined. Feinstein (1959) offered a fifth method in the development of his "reduction index," in which the amount of weight lost is multiplied by a factor comprised of the initial weight divided by the amount of surplus weight times the target weight by 100. Finally, Mahoney and his colleagues (Mahoney et al., 1977) have suggested use of a "fat-loss index" obtained by dividing fat lost by the percent of excess fat. Fat, in turn, is measured by skinfold calipering which the authors found to correlate very well (approximately .80) with the more sophisticated and expensive hydrostatic, ultrasonic, and radiographic densitometry methods of fat assessment.

With this range of alternatives from which to choose, researchers are offered a variety of methods for assessing treatment outcome. Currently the Feinstein Index is the most widely accepted method beyond reporting simple weight loss (Stuart, 1975). To this method should be added assessment of changes in skinfold density using the equation developed by Durnin and Womersley (1974), as recommended by Mahoney and his associates. Were all investigators to adopt these methods, consumers of the weight-control literature would find it far easier to compare outcomes in efforts to select the interventions most likely to be successful in promoting weight changes by their clients.

While all investigators include in their designs some measure of weight and/or fat loss, few address the collateral issue of the psychological and social concomitants of weight management. Herman and Mack (1975) speculated that compliance with weight-control measures may be the cause of considerable psychological stress, while Stunkard and Rush (1974) believe this reaction can lead to clinical levels of depression, which could result from the psychosomatic strain inherent in efforts to resist the relentless urge to eat. If this is true, reduction of eating urges prior to or in association with management of eating behavior should reduce this tendency. Using the Lublin Depression Adjective Check List (1967), Stuart and Jacobson (in press) measured the depression levels of adults who joined Weight Watchers classes, with measurement repeated after five and ten weeks of class attendance. While initial depression levels were within the "clinical" range for both men and women, after five weeks all participants reported depression levels that were well within normal range on the Lublin scale. While this is a measure of "state" depression, it does give some information about the general mood level of respondents. In the same vein, Mahoney et al. (1977) found statistically significant positive change in both the anxiety and depression levels of their subjects. Use of mood measurement would therefore seem to be an important addition to any evaluation package designed to better understand the general impact of the intervention. If the behavior-change techniques are adopted at too high a personal price, it is natural to expect that they will be quickly dropped when the social support of the treatment situation is withdrawn.

The Problem of Incomplete Service

There is a natural history in every therapeutic intervention. The roots of the intervention are the forces that influence the client's decision to seek help. The traditional model suggests a four-step sequence in this decision making process: (1) a belief in personal susceptibility to a problem; (2) followed by perception of the seriousness of this possible affliction; (3) which leads to an evaluation of the potential costs and rewards of alternative actions; that (4) promotes a readiness to respond to a cue to act (National Heart and Lung Institute, 1977). It is prudent to recognize that the decision making is *not* complete when treatment contacts are initiated, and that at various times during intervention, clients reassess their motivation to persist. Therefore, early stages of intervention should be devoted to efforts to consolidate the commitment to action. While efforts have been made to use fear arousal as a motivational tool prior to and at the start of weight-control treatments, these efforts have generally not met with success (e.g., Ley, Whitworth, Woodward, & Yorke, 1977), and it is probably wiser to stress the potential benefits of an improved quality of life, the joy of self-mastery, and greater social, occupational, and recreational opportunities associated with successful weight management.

Understanding the nature of the disorder is a pre-requisite to the remaining stages of treatment: delivery of the focal technology, preparation of the client to cope with the potential of an immediate relapse (see Chapter 16 by Marlatt and Gordon), and reinforcement of continued application of the focal procedures and/or their adaptation to shifting demands as a function of life and situational changes during the life-long maintenance phase of the program. The adequacy with which these intervention, relapse-inoculation, and maintenance phases are completed depends in large measure upon the adequacy with which certain theoretical issues are resolved.

The soundness of the theory of obesity that underlies treatment efforts is a good predictor of the probable effectiveness of these efforts. Many writers have noted an apparent homeostatic mechanism in weight regulation in infrahuman and human species. Miller (1977) observed that "there is extreme power to the weight-regulatory mechanism" (p.3), and Stunkard (1977) considers "the evidence for regulation in animals of normal weight (to be) clear and unequivocal" (p. 318). In other words, when animals are artificially fattened by injecting them with insulin, which permits fat to enter adipocytes for storage, they will fatten, only to lose their excess weight when injections are terminated (Hoebel & Teitelbaum, 1966). In the same vein, when animals are fasted and lose weight, they regain this weight as rapidly as it was lost when *ad libitum* feeding is resumed (Hamilton, 1969). Comparable results have been found for humans. For example, Sims, Goldman, Gluck, Horton, Kelleher, and Rowe (1968) fed prison inmates 8,000 calories per day for 40 weeks in order to produce up to a 25% weight gain and noted that normal weight was established when normal eating opportunities were restored. For both animals and humans, then, there appear to be natural upper and lower weight limits, and exceeding these limits seems to create a problem of homeostatic balance. This imbalance, in turn, appears to result in pressure to restore the original weight, whether above or below the present weight. Therefore, anyone who deviates from this natural homeostatically-regulated individual weight range can be expected to experience physiologically mediated pressure to return to a point within that range.

Hirsch and Knittle (1970) of the Rockefeller Institute contend that this optimal individual weight range is determined by the number of fat cells available for fat storage during early infancy. Unfortunately, difficulty in reliably measuring cell number (Bray, 1976) coupled with inconsistencies in the potency of age of onset of obesity in predicting weight change (see later discussion) weaken confidence in this theory. Another theory has been advanced by Nisbett (1972), who conceives of a hypothalamic "set point" for the metabolic regulation of weight. While it can be demonstrated that rats with ventromedial hypothalamic lesions behave like obese humans in certain respects, they behave differently in some important ways. These rats also behave differently from genetically obese Zucker rats, thus weakening confidence in Nisbett's theory. Herman and Mack (1975) have argued for acceptance of the belief that the overweight have a psychologically and physiologically mediated pressure to restrain their eating so that it falls within clearly delineated boundaries. While heuristically appealing, their Restrained Eating Scale has not predicted weight management in several studies in which its explanatory power was explored (e.g., Cormier, Prefontaine, MacDonald & Stuart, Chapter 8; Stuart & Guire, in press). Other theories offered to explain this weight regulation tendency include thermogenesis, genetics, hormonal balance, and the habitual level of physical activity (Bray, 1976; Garrow, 1975), but none of these theories is supported by convincing evidence that would lead to its acceptance to the exclusion of other theories. While such explanations may still be theoretical, the fact of resistance to long-term weight change must be taken as one of the realities of the effort to modify human body weight.

Despite the difficulty in selecting an etiological model, two things are clear: obesity has homeostatic implications; and those who are overweight do appear to develop lifestyle adaptations supportive of the consumption of more energy than is needed to support the energy demands of daily living. Therefore, treatment of obesity must take into account its probable biological, psychological, and lifestyle implications. Unfortunately, the assumption apparently implicit is most behavioral treatment programs is that obesity is a transitory condition and therefore treatable through relatively simplistic, highly time-constrained interventions. Scientific investigators have, in effect, offered participants in their research an implied promise that they can be "fat-free forever" by participating in a short course in behavioral self-management. Sadly, while the promise can be glibly made, its delivery is controverted by all that we currently know about the complexity of the problem of obesity.

Rather than offering promises of short routes to long-term effectiveness, researchers who respect the problems of the obese should make two dramatic departures from the approach seen most often in the literature:

> First, treatment should be extended through the entire difficult process of the attainment of goal weight. Second, service should be offered through a maintenance period to bolster resistance to the inexorable pressures to return to the original weight.

If indeed there is a biological homeostatis that must be overcome in the loss of weight and its maintenance, then certainly the overweight would require long-term help in combating biological pressures toward fatness. Beller (1977) poignantly phrased the problem faced by the formerly fat as follows:

> Hunger is the dieter's ghost at the feast. Except in rare cases, there would have been no problem with weight gain to begin with unless the dieter's physiology and/or his psyche had not condemned him to a chronic nagging hunger that went to bed with him at night and woke up with him in the morning for the better part of his

> life. This kind of hunger is a problem that is obviously not going to go away with dieting (p. 273).

Unfortunately, the format of services offered to the overweight pay little heed to the depth of the dieter's dilemma. The modal studies that have appeared in print have been the work of psychology graduate students whose thesis and dissertation data must fit into a two-semester time frame. Therefore, treatments of as little as two (e.g., Thorn & Boudewyns, 1976), four (e.g., Mahoney, Moura & Wade, 1973; Romanczyk et al., 1973), and eight to twelve weeks (e.g., Hall, 1972;, Hall et al., 1974; Harris, 1969; Harris & Hallbauer, 1973; Penick et al., 1971; and Wollersheim, 1970) are the norm in the literature. Only rarely have interventions lasting six months or longer been reported (e.g., Currey et al., 1977; Stuart, 1967, 1971; Stuart & Guire, in press; Stuart & Mitchell, in press). Therefore, few, if any, of the participants in most of these studies have been helped through treatment to reach their goal weight. Instead, investigators relied on the implicit power of their technologies to teach participants the self-management skills believed necessary for successful goal attainment. Sadly, there is no empirical support for this hope and/or promise, and, indeed, respect for the homeostatic hypothesis would argue strongly against acceptance of this belief. Quite to the contrary, one could make a very strong case for the argument that the challenges of the early stages of weight loss when new self-regulation habits must be learned—reinforced by the novelty of self-discovery and typically a large amount of social support from significant others—are very different from the later challenges when the once-new habits are now familiar, when significant others have lost interest in the client's progress, and when it is realized that, in fact, there are no easy answers in a battle that may well last for life. Like the weight loser whose hopes of quick and easy methods of weight control are dashed by experience, behavioral researchers must also come to grips with the reality that weight control is a painstaking process for which great patience is needed, the experimenter's need for haste notwithstanding.

An extension of the same homostatic arguments can also support the notion that even if treatment methods do help clients reach their goal weight, maintenance of this weight requires continued intervention, at least until strengths are consolidated in combating the forces that would refatten the "noveaux thin."

Most of the more frequently cited studies in this area do not include follow-up services of any kind. As a novel approach, Mahoney et al. (1977) attempted to build maintenance programming into their basic intervention by training clients in their problem-solving model (Mahoney & Mahoney, 1976a) and expecting them to generalize this skill over the varied challenges of weight loss and weight maintenance. For reasons that will be discussed later, however, this approach did not achieve the expected level of success.

A more traditional approach is found in the work of Kingsley and Wilson (1977), who randomly assigned individual and group-treated participants to conditions in which they either did or did not receive "booster" contacts following treatment termination. Four booster sessions were offered during a 14-week posttreatment period, bringing to 12 the number of client contacts for those receiving maximal treatment. Results indicated that participants in a social-pressure condition lost an average of 6.7 pounds at the end of treatment in contrast to those in group and individual behavior therapy who lost an average of 11.5 and 12.7 pounds, respectively—a statistically significant difference. However, after one year these differences were no longer significant. Instead of the original treatment method accounting for major outcome differences, the differentiating factor was subjects' participation in booster sessions. Participants in these sessions averaged weight losses of 10.8 pounds in contrast to the 6.3 pound average loss of nonparticipants. It is possible that the booster sessions may have provided much needed social support for maintaining behavior change. This view is supported by the findings that group-served participants in the behavioral intervention condition outperformed all others, whether or not booster sessions were offered, while those in the social-pressure conditon outperformed those in individual behavior therapy when both received booster training. Together these results support the value of group format for service delivery. Given the observation of Lieberman (1975), cited earlier, that groups help members by providing social support for countering social pressures fostering relapse, booster sessions may be viewed as offering important reinforcement for efforts to resist these pressures.

In a related study, Hall et al. (1974) offered a 12-week behavioral intervention program. Following basic treatment, participants were assigned to one of three follow-up programs, the one most relevant to this discussion being six small-group booster sessions offered during a 12-week period. Treated subjects significantly outperformed those in the control group. Both at the end of treatment and after follow-up, no significant differences were found in the weight changes of those who did or did not receive booster treatment. However, participation did lead to a statistically significant advantage if the therapist who conducted the follow-up sessions was the same person who conducted the basic weight-loss sessions. These data clearly underline the importance of therapist-client matching in the prediction of favorable treatment outcomes referred to earlier.

Further support for this conclusion was found by Stuart and Guire (in press) who reported the results of a 15-month follow-up study of 721 persons who had reached their goal weights through participation in a behavioral self-management program offered by Weight Watchers. They found that the 32.6% of the members who regularly attended booster classes on a monthly basis were an average of 3.1 pounds above their goal weights, in contrast to the 43.2% who never or rarely attended these classes and averaged 13.4 pounds above goal. Moreover, when members attended classes conducted by lecturers who had helped them reach their goal weights, these members (like participants in the aforementioned study by Hall et al.), were significantly more likely to maintain or go below their goal weights.

With these findings in mind, it can be argued that when services are terminated before participants reach their target weights, or when services do not include carefully designed follow-through sessions, participants are being offered less service than they require. Unfortunately, few of the reported studies satisfy these requirements. This failure may be one of the explanations of Stunkard's (1975) observation that Stuart's (1967, 1971) early results have rarely been equaled. Too many investigators may have been trying to accomplish too much, in too little time, with too little attention to needed planning.

Long-Term Results of Behavioral Treatments for the Overweight

Some of the studies that do report follow-up data have led to negative results; some have achieved positive outcomes; and much can be learned from an analysis of both groups of studies.

In order to understand this long-term outcome literature, it is necessary to place the present research in the context of several decades of trial-and-error efforts to manage obesity. In one of the most often quoted studies in the obesity literature, Stunkard and McLaren-Hume (1959) noted that very few participants in most of the early studies lost as much as 20 pounds, and most of those who did lose weight regained their losses shortly after treatment ended. Glennon (1966) extended a similar study for several years and noted virtually no improvement in results. Craddock (1973) carried the review further still and found that from

10% to 40% of the participants in the most thoughtful studies may have lost some weight by the end of the first year of treatment, but that only between 1% and 13% of the participants maintained any of their weight loss for a period of years after treatment ended. As an illustration of one of the more optimistic findings, Craddock (1977) reviewed the histories of 157 patients he had treated, reporting that 48% "maintained significant weight loss," although only 6% were within normal weight range. As an illustration of one of the more common findings, Sohar and Sneh (1973) reported on long-term follow-up of 27 patients. They found that "in 1971, the weight of 19 of the 27 patients was close to their weight in 1957, prior to successful dieting" (p.847). Of the remaining patients, three weighted more than they did initially, while "only five succeeded in keeping their weight approximately 15% below their 1957 weight, although all five remained overweight" (p. 848). They concluded their report with the sad suggestion that,

> Obese patients who seek advice should be told that their chances to maintain the new, lower weight reached by dieting are slim, and that this can be achieved only by continuous curtailing of food intake (p. 848).

It is against this backdrop of dismal expectations that the literature evaluating the longer term effects of behavioral interventions should be studied.

The review that follows will deal only with studies that offered at least 12 weeks of basic intervention and included at least 24 weeks of follow-up data. Some of the published reports meet these criteria but omit needed information, and have been excluded from this review for that reason. Therefore, this review is offered as suggestive of the content of the results of the weight-loss and loss-maintenance literature rather than as an exhaustive summary of the results of that literature. A review of several studies reaching negative conclusions will be followed by a review of studies with more positive outcomes. Each of the studies will be assessed in light of the common problems identified above.

Studies with Negative Results

One study, which concluded that "behavior modification was either less effective than standard group methods or not significantly different" (Weisenberg & Fray, 1974, p. 413), exemplifies many of the weaknesses of the research leading to negative results. This research utilized a direct approach to the suppression of problem eating, incorporating some, but by no means all, of the standard stimulus control techniques (see: Stuart, 1978a; Stuart & Davis, 1972). Aversive techniques that were unacceptable to many of the behavior-therapy clients were included. For example, clients were asked to pose in bathing suits for "before" photos, to publicly post weight graphs, and to provide themselves with negative contingencies for compliance failures. In addition, the clients who received individualized or group nutritional counseling received instruction in exercise as well as food management, while the behavior-therapy clients received no exercise instruction. In sum, many of the planning errors likely to result in trivial outcomes are evident in this research.

A few experimental errors revealing the nonequivalence of treatment methods are also noteworthy: The nutritionist and psychologist experimenters did not explain their competence in behavior therapy; clients were not randomly assigned to the various groups; participants differed significantly in starting weights; "little gifts" were dispensed to the nutrition-and-exercise counseled clients, but not to those in the behavior-therapy groups.

Following 16 weeks of treatment, the weight losses for the behavior-therapy clients, individual dietary counseling clients, and group diet-and-exercise-counseling clients averaged 6.4, 4.4 and 16.1, respectively. This represented 11.6% of the excess weight of the behavior-therapy clients as opposed to 17.6% of the excess weight of those receiving group diet-and-exercise counseling.

The authors noted that they experienced constant difficulty in motivating the behavior-therapy clients to participate. This is taken to be an indication of the weakness of the approach, but clearly it is an analysis which overlooks striking differences between the service-delivery techniques used in the two approaches. The authors also overlook the strong probability that the inclusion of exercise techniques can significantly improve the rate of weight loss (e.g., Stuart, 1971, 1978a; Stuart & Davis, 1972; Harris & Hallbauer, 1973). Finally, the authors overlook the possible impact of their personal biases (Rosenthal, 1966), a problem magnified by the fact that the investigators were also the intervenors. In addition, the authors also appear to underestimate the importance of experience with behavioral methods, a factor that has been shown to have a significant impact upon the results of treatment by psychiatrists using these methods (Jeffrey, Wing, & Stunkard, 1978). For these reasons, data from such studies must be viewed skeptically when reviewing the general effectiveness of behavioral methods.

Other studies that reached disappointing conclusions were better designed but still suffered from some common methodological and design problems: Penick et al. (1971) assigned 32 outpatients at the University of Pennsylvania Hospital to either supportive psychotherapy or behavior therapy, both of which met weekly for two hours over a three-month period. Both groups were led by male-female professional teams, none of whom had prior experience in behavior therapy. The behavioral intervention was a direct approach at weight management using the standard stimulus-control techniques (Stuart, 1978a; Stuart & Davis, 1972), while the group psychotherapy approach used the best of the currently available techniques in that method.

At the termination of treatment, 53% of the behavior-modification recipients, as opposed to 24% of those receiving psychotherapy, lost 20 or more pounds. At follow-up six months later, 53% of the former group and 29% of the latter group recorded 20-pound weight losses. At the conclusion of their study the authors noted their results:

> showed that behavior modification, devised by a team with little experience in this modality was more effective in the treatment of obesity than was the best alternative program that could be devised by an internist with long experience in the treatment of this disorder (p. 54).

Unfortunately, this euphoria was not long-lasting. Stunkard (1977) later presented one-year follow-up data on these patient cohorts. Among the behaviorally treated patients, only three of seven who had lost more than 20 pounds maintained their losses, while five of the six who had lost less than 20 pounds continued to lose during the year following treatment. This maintenance success rate of 8 of 13 patients compared with 9 of 15 in the psychotherapy group was taken as a clear sign that the behavior-therapy recipients had lost their edge.

While it is possible to view the longer range outcome as an indication that the behavioral treatment was not superior to the psychotherapeutic approach, other explanations are also possible. The behavior-therapy program used a direct approach. It failed to carry treatment through to the point at which clients achieved goal weight and beyond into a maintenance period. Its therapists were not skilled in the techniques they applied, and the intervention was carried out in the most professionalized of all settings, a teaching hospital, where none of the advantages of the self-help approach were present (Stuart, 1977a; Stuart & Mitchell, in press; Williams & Duncan, 1976b). It is reasonable to speculate that the results might have been different if experienced therapists had used indirect methods that were extended through the entire weight-loss process in a setting that offered maximal advantage.

Many of the same limitations are seen in three other studies that reached less than satisfying conclusions. Currey et al. (1977) offered behavior therapy to small groups of medically referred patients who were seen for blocks of ten sessions in a hospital setting. In all, 87% of the 165 patients seen completed ten weeks of treatment, 30% completed 20 weeks, and 17.5% completed 30 or more weeks of treatment. At termination the results were as follows: "43% lost less than 5 kg., 28% lost 5 to 9 kg., 23% lost more than 9 kg., and 6% lost more than 18 kg." (p.2830). Of the 56 patients contacted for follow-up after 12 months, only 30% either maintained their losses or continued to lose weight. While this is not an unacceptable result given the standard of comparison for non-behavioral studies, the authors concluded that use of "behavior modification for treating obesity is simply not as good as other treatment programs" (p. 2831). Here, again, we have inexperienced professionals using a direct approach in a hospital setting. While it may be true that behavioral interventions do not stack up well against other methods, they deserve a better test than was conducted here.

In another study, Ost and Gotesdam (1976) assigned 15 Swedish patients to a behavioral program of 20 half-hour sessions distributed across 12 weeks, 15 to a condition in which they received standard doses of fenfluramine (an anorectic drug with a very low potential for abuse (Bray, 1974), and 15 to a wait-list control. Members of the behavior-therapy group lost an average of 9.4 kg. during treatment, and one year later had maintained only 4.6 kg. of this loss. Corresponding figures for the fenfluramine group were 5.8 and 0.9 kg., and for the control group 3.6 and 2.6 kg. While the behavior-therapy recipients significantly outperformed those treated with drugs or those offered no treatment, they did regain over half of their lost weight within one year. Unfortunately, this research was also subject to several limitations: The therapists were undergraduates working with an English manual (Stuart & Davis, 1972); the treatment methods were direct rather than indirect; the behavior-therapy clients who averaged 87 kg. at the start of treatment were 36.2% overweight, and although they lost approximately one-third of their excess weight, they were clearly far above their target weights when service ended. Again, a different experimental approach might have yielded a different outcome.

In the last negative result study, Mahoney et al. (1977) used the problem-solving approach (Mahoney & Mahoney, 1976a), in which clients are taught to formulate their own behavior-change plans in the hope that their skill will generalize to new situations encountered after the termination of regular treatment sessions. Great care went into the planning and execution of this study, which is unparalleled in the precision with which intervention and outcome variables were measured. Treatment lasted 26 weeks, with one group receiving weekly sessions and another meeting at three-week intervals. Follow-up data were collected after 12 months and indicated an average aggregate weight loss of only eight pounds for members of both groups.

Mahoney and his collaborators speculated that the model they used "may be very effective. . . (but) that our specific application of this model, however, was not" (p. 11). This level of self-examination is unfortunately an exception rather than the norm in the obesity outcome literature. It may be, however, that the culprit was the model of behavior modification they employed. Using a similar problem-solving mode, Perri and Richards (1977) were successful in helping students to modify smoking behavior and social patterns on dates, but not in helping students to overcome overeating. In another study (Richards & Perri, in press) they found that the problem-solving model was acceptable to students, but that it was not as highly valued as simple self-monitoring. Therefore, some doubt has been cast upon the utility of the problem-solving model as an effective means of packaging behavioral intervention services for weight loss.

In summary, it can be seen that some applications of behavior therapy do indeed reach negative or equivocal outcomes. Because of the problems common to these studies, it is not possible to clearly determine whether the fault lies with the theory or with its application. While some investigators whose results were not positive hold the theory accountable, some of the explanation for the outcomes must be placed with the particular applications used. An examination of some of the positive-outcome studies will help to identify some, but by no means all, of the factors that may contribute to success.

Positive Outcome Studies

Leon's (1977) recent review of the research reporting longer range outcome data noted 8 of 11 studies that obtained positive results. This is in contrast to Stunkard's (1977) review in which 7 of 8 studies were viewed as reaching negative outcomes. In comparing the two reviews, it is seen that they selected only 4 studies in common from among the scores of data-based papers published since 1967. It is clear that reviews can be misleading if differing standards of acceptance are used for the selection of studies for analysis, and if the analytic criteria differ among reviewers. Leon, for example, simply reported the original authors' reports of their outcomes, while Stunkard graphed pre-to-post weight differences against post-to-follow-up weight changes.

More as a means of illustrating the range of studies that have achieved positive results than as a means of documenting the case for optimism about the long-range effects of behavioral interventions, five studies that reached positive conclusions will be reviewed here. Interestingly, only one of these studies (Levitz & Stunkard, 1974) was included in both the Leon and Stunkard reviews.

In the first project, Harris and Hallbauer (1973) offered 12 weeks of behavior therapy to 20 participants (randomly selected from volunteers recruited through newspaper ads); focal treatment, which included exercise programming, to 22 of the volunteers; and a control procedure to 14 of the volunteeers. The behavior therapy included stimulus-control training as well as contingency contracting. Unfortunately, attrition rates were very high between the first session, when procedures were explained, and the second session, when experimental subjects were required to deposit money with the experimenters and to contract for its return as a contingency for weight loss.

Compared with the controls, 31% of whom did not return after learning about the dietary focus of the treatment they were offered, 39% of the behavior-therapy group and 47% of the behavior-therapy group that included exercise failed to return. These results underscore the reality of client resistance to contracting and to the inclusion of exercise in behavioral interventions aimed at weight control. Weight losses for those who did persevere in the behavior-therapy group averaged 6.9 pounds at the end of treatment and 8.8 pounds at the end of a seven-month follow-up. This compared with losses of 9.1 and 13.1 pounds at the two time periods for participants in the behavior-therapy group that included exercise, and a loss of 6.8 pounds by the controls, which was all regained by the end of the follow-up period.

While the follow-up differences are statistically significant, the authors depreciated the results. During the time of active treatment, their best performing group lost an average of slightly more than 0.7 pounds weekly. This rate of loss is quite consistent with the normal expectations as documented in the medical literature (e.g., Bortz, Worldson, Morris, & Issekutz, 1967). Moreover, the fact that the clients continued to lose after the end of treatment is a remarkable achievement in light of the fact that no booster sessions were offered.

In the next study, Levitz and Stunkard (1974) offered three months of treatment to 234 members of TOPS chapters under four different conditions: Some participated in meetings conducted by professional behavior modifiers, some in meetings conducted by chapter leaders who were concurrently receiving instructions in the use of behavioral self-management techniques; some in meetings conducted by chapter leaders who stressed nutrition education; and some in meetings conducted by chapter leaders who followed the normal TOPS program. Weight changes during the 12 weeks of treatment averaged −4.2 lbs., −1.9 lbs., −0.3 lbs., and +0.7 lbs., respectively. These differences were modest but showed that the professional behavior modifiers working in a self-help setting achieved results that were statistically significantly better than those of the lay leaders. At the 12-month follow-up, the weight loss for the professionally led group averaged 5.8 pounds, equaling half of the average weight loss of members during their three prior years of participation in the TOPS program. Perhaps more significant still is the weight gain or relapse experience of participants in the various groups. During the posttreatment year, 20% of the members in the best performing group regained some weight, as opposed to 27% of those receiving behavioral intervention from lay leaders, 77% of those who received TOPS-leader-conducted nutrition education, and 58% of those receiving normal TOPS service. Given the absence of follow-through service (consistent with the initial program), the experiences of members of the first two groups is indeed noteworthy.

In the following year, Jeffrey and Christensen (1975) published a report of the assignment of 19 subjects to a behavioral program using stimulus control and contracting (similar to that of Harris & Hallbauer, 1973), 12 subects to a "will-power" placebo intervention condition, and 12 subjects to a no-treatment control. Thirteen subjects completed the 18-week behavior-therapy program and lost an average of 16.3 pounds, in contrast to weight losses of 5.1 and 1.7 pounds, respectively, for the will-power and control subjects. Follow-up data were reported for the behavior-therapy subjects only, and these data indicated that weight losses were maintained.

In the following year, researchers at the University of Missouri (Paulsen, Lutz, McReynolds, & Kohrs, 1976) offered training in behavior-change techniques to nutritionists, who, in turn, offered a 14-week program to 54 female volunteers. Half of the women received a self-control program modeled after the work of Wollersheim (1970), with the other half receiving treatment based on the stimulus-control package designed by Stuart and Davis (1972). At the end of treatment, the former group posted losses averaging 7.3 kg. as opposed to the latter group whose losses averaged 8.4 kg. After an 18-month follow-up period, 50% of the self-control group and 80% of the stimulus-control group maintained their losses. This is a dramatic achievement, particularly in light of the unusual rigor evident in the design, execution, and data analysis in this project.

Finally, in what is the largest long-term assessment of the results of behavioral intervention published to date, Stuart and Guire (in press) collected descriptive data from 721 women who had achieved their goal weights 12 to 15 months earlier through participation in a behavioral self-management program offered in Weight Watchers classes. Lay leaders trained in behavioral self-management techniques (described elsewhere, Stuart, 1978a) met with members in groups in which members discussed both the behavior-change techniques and a food plan of some 1,350 calories. The average member had reached his or her goal weight through 31 weeks of class attendance, shedding 19% of an average 162.1 lb. starting weight. Fifteen months later, 24.6% of the women were below their goal weights, 28.9% were within 5% of their goal weights, 17.5% were from 6% to 10% above their goal weights, and the remaining 28.9% were 11 or more percent above goal.

The perplexing feature in enumerating these successful studies is that they do not appear to differ markedly from the negative outcome studies reviewed earlier. Intervention in these studies tended to be direct rather than indirect, but intervention methods were of the "stimulus-control" variety and tended to be more comprehensive than those used in the less successful ventures. Treatment durations were essentially comparable in both groups of studies, as were many details of service delivery. However, the two self-help group evaluations (Stuart & Guire, in press; Levitz & Stunkard, 1974) were among the more successful projects. Unfortunately, inconsistencies in reporting methods and results make it all but impossible to accurately discriminate between factors associated with success and those that are more predictive of failure.

Recommendations for Improving Behavioral Research

The limitations in studies of the effectiveness of behavioral techniques for controlling obesity have not gone unnoticed in the literature. Unfortunately, it is impossible to generalize across studies and to make confident predictions about which clients will derive varying amounts of benefit from participation in the behavioral interventions.

To correct this situation, Mahoney (1976) noted six common flaws in these studies, each of which can be restated as a positive recommendation: inclusion of nontreatment controls; inclusion of attention-placebo controls; accurate and complete procedural descriptions; complete reporting of outcome data for all subjects; inclusion of adequate follow-up periods; and exploration of potential contributors to change, such

TABLE 1
Factors Associated with Weight Loss and with Maintenance of Weight Loss

Factor	Best Result	No Difference	Worst Result
Male Gender	Craddock, 1973 Craddock, 1977 Stuart, 1977b	Jeffrey, Wing & Stunkard, 1978 Cormier, 1972 Musante, 1976 Stuart & Jacobson, 1979 Christakis, 1967	Glennon, 1966
High Start Weight	Ashwell, in press	Sohar & Sneh, 1973	Craddock, 1977 Glennon, 1966 Mahoney et al., 1977 Stuart, 1978a
Married	Craddock, 1973 Craddock, 1977 Christakis, 1967 Ashwell, in press	Stuart, 1977b Paulsen et al., 1976 Stuart, 1978a Currey et al., 1977	
Early Onset	Jeffrey, Wing & Stunkard, 1978	Currey et al., 1977 Stuart, 1978a Ashwell, in press	Craddock, 1973 Paulsen et al., 1976 Christakis, 1967
Youth	Hall & Hall, 1974 Stuart, 1977b	Currey et al., 1977 Paulsen et al., 1976 Glennon, 1966 Stuart, 1978a	Christakis, 1967 Ashwell, in press
Medical Reason for Loss	Craddock, 1973 Craddock, 1977	Christakis, 1967 Stuart, 1978a	
SES & Education—High	Craddock, 1973	Glennon, 1966 Christakis, 1967 Stuart, 1978a	
Unhappy, Introverted, Neurotic		Stuart, 1978a Stuart & Jacobson, 1979	Craddock, 1977
Employed	Stuart, 1977b	Stuart, 1978a	
Good Self-Concept	Stuart, 1978a Tobias & MacDonald, 1977		
Prior Eating Problems (nibble, night, unstructured)		Paulson et al., 1976	
Posttreatment Behavior Change (maintenance)	Stuart, 1978a Ost & Gotestam, 1976 Perri & Richards, 1977 Stuart, 1978a		

as beliefs and attitudes. Jeffrey (1974) argued that control groups may not be necessary in behavioral studies because of repeated observations that controls do not tend to lose weight nor to keep it off. Subjects who might have been used as controls, could, therefore, be assigned to attention-placebo control conditions. In keeping with ethical research guidelines, however, these techniques must have some potential validity, and all must be fully explained to potential subjects (Stuart, 1978b). Brevity in procedural descriptions and in detailed reporting is, in part at least, a function of the requirements of journal publication constraints. Without knowing how services were delivered, however, it is impossible to understand treatment outcome. Without information about weight changes by individual subjects, the wide variability observed by Mahoney and Mahoney (1976) and predicted by Bergin (1971) will be overlooked in reports that create an illusion of uniform effect. Follow-up periods of at least one year, and ideally two to three years, would seem to be mandatory when recognition is paid to the possible ill-effects of the so-called "yo-yo" pattern of weight gain and weight loss (Miller, 1977; Smith, Smith, Mameesh, Simon, & Johnson, 1964; Surgeon General of the United States, 1966; Walker, Lawry, Love, Mann, Levine, & Stare, 1953). Finally, measurement of a variety of dimensions of outcome has a long-standing tradition in psychological research and should surely be an integral part of this line of investigation. Unfortunately, as will be seen in Table 1, when efforts are made to associate outcome with a variety of client characteristics, the results are highly inconsistent. For example, while many variables such as gender, marital status, and age appeared not to predict outcome, they were predictors in at least some studies. Unfortunately, rather contrary results were found for several of the variables that did show predictive strength. Moreover, when several of these factors are included in multivariate designs, they tend to account for a rather small portion of the variance. For example, the standard factors such as age, marital status, employment, and area of residence accounted for only 1.1% of the variance in the Stuart and Guire (in press) study, while age of onset of obesity accounted for 2.5%, and highest-weight-ever accounted for 19.6% of the variance in maintenance results, leaving 76.8% of the variance unaccounted for. Elsewhere, Jeffrey, Wing and Stunkard (1978) also were able to account for only 25% of the variance in outcome using regression analysis, with highest-weight-ever also being the best predictor.

Modification of research designs to include these recommendations would surely improve the quality of the investigations of behavior-therapy outcomes. In the next section, some suggestions will be made for improving the quality of the programs that are tested through use of these designs.

Recommendations for Improving Therapeutic Success

Several recommendations have already been made for program changes that could be expected to improve therapeutic results. In summary, these include: (1) uniform adoption of positive change goals; (2) uniform inclusion of complete technologies for controlling both eating and exercise behaviors in all treatment programs; (3) adoption of indirect treatment methods that weaken the urge to eat before dealing directly with eating behavior; (4) utilization of the service-delivery techniques with the greatest likelihood of achieving client compliance; (5) inclusion in all studies of means through which compliance and effectiveness can be assessed during the intervention process; and (6) extension of the intervention program to include goal-weight attainment and at least early efforts to maintain that weight. The remaining suggestions are amplifications of some of the foregoing ideas.

Improving Service Delivery

Behavior modifiers have long been concerned with identifying the least demanding treatments with the greatest possible benefits. It is this consideration that may well have prompted Stunkard and Mahoney (1976) to suggest that "the effective components of behavioral treatment programs need to be isolated" (p. 61). Unfortunately, this quest for a low cost/benefit ratio has sometimes resulted in inadequate intervention programs: for example, "bibliotherapy" approaches, in which printed materials, backed up with little if any in-person contact, have been offered (e.g., Hagen, 1974; Jeffrey, Christensen, & Pappas, 1973; Thorn & Boudewyns, 1976; Tobias & MacDonald, 1977) with unimpressive results. Despite the fact that the participants in these projects tended to be the "cream of the crop"—volunteering college students with many resources for weight control and few situational constraints that would retard their progress—average weekly weight losses have been negligible. The treatment programs mentioned earlier which offer a small number of sessions are also illustrative of this tendency to place great faith in the power of an as-yet-unvalidated technology. Therefore, rather than making use of "knock-down" designs that offer less than a total push, this area still requires maximum effort research which will demonstrate that the techniques can help clients to achieve maintainable weight losses. Only when these demonstrations have been convincingly made will it be time to address the economies that may be possible through streamlining intervention packages.

Improving the Core Technology

Three dimensions of the generally accepted techniques for the management of eating behavior could be strengthened with very probable good results. First, the suggestion of Mahoney and Mahoney (1976) for improved "cognitive ecology" is certainly well taken. Elsewhere (Stuart & Guire, in press) it has been shown that cognitive factors may very well predict success in the maintenance of weight losses. Specifically, those who thought of themselves as "thin" rather than as "formerly fat" were more likely to be maintainers. So, too, were those who believed they had indeed learned new self-management skills. The weight losers in this study were not unlike the school children in another investigation (Miller, Brickman, & Bolen, 1975) who were more likely to pick up litter on the school grounds or to solve math problems correctly if they were told by teachers that they were both tidy and good at math. Thus, modified self-definitions may play an important role in maintaining long-term results.

In a recent paper, Bandura (1977) built a strong argument in support of the value of building cognitive change into behavior modification programs. He cites evidence that not just the provision of contingencies, but also awareness of the response-effect relationship influence behavior (Baum, 1973; Dawson & Furedy, 1976); that expectations of future reward can be shown to have an important impact upon behavior (Bolles, 1972); and that behavior also comes under the influence of cognitively mediated self-evaluation of ongoing response chains (Bandura, 1976). Bandura then differentiates between two different elements in a cognitive chain that parallel behavioral chains: "Efficacy expectations" are the individual's belief that he or she can do what is expected, while "outcome expectations" are beliefs that the target actions will produce the desired effects. Thus an individual might or might not believe in his or her ability to change patterns of physical activity, and then might or might not believe that these behavior changes will be reflected in altered body weight. A behavior change would therefore require both a positive self-efficacy belief and a positive outcome expectation.

Bandura believes that positive self-efficacy beliefs originate through four processes: performance accomplishments, vicarious experience, verbal persuasion, and emotional arousal. Most of these sources are operative in normal behavior change situations, but direct efforts to utilize their potential could have a potentially salubrious effect upon treatment outcome. For example, positive performance-produced feedback can go far toward building one's sense of self-efficacy while provision of small, constructive behavior change goals can contribute to this development. Vicarious experiences are provided by the opportunity to witness the success of others: group leadership by successful former members and group ceremonies in which unusual achievements by members are recognized are both means for providing these invaluable experiences. Persuasion has been an element of behavior change efforts throughout time, and while not sufficient in and of itself (Lick & Bootzin, 1975), it can prompt action that can be maintained through positive outcomes. Indeed, such persuasion may be a necessary but not a sufficient condition for the motivation of change efforts in the face of potential danger or failure. Because one's state of emotional arousal provides cues for action, creating some arousal through role-play and related means in a group setting, and then coaching self-definitional change under these aroused circumstances can serve as another learning opportunity. All of these factors are available for use in group settings but each will provide self-efficacy feelings of different magnitude (re: complexity of tasks), generality, and strength (i.e., resistance to extinction) when specific efforts are made to translate these experiences into new self-referent ideas.

In addition to taking advantage of the potential value of self-attribution of the source of change and/or belief in self-efficacy, currently used technology could also be improved by making more effective use of the family relationships of would-be weight losers and maintainers. Evidence summarized by Stuart (1978a) suggests that family experience plays a pivotal role in the creation and control of obesity among both children and adults. For example, data from the Ten-State Nutrition Survey (Garn & Clark, 1976) clearly indicate strong statistical correlations between weight status of spouses and between those of parents and children, with these correlations being much better explained by interaction than by genetics. Others (e.g., Huenemann, 1974; Crisp, Douglas, Ross, & Stonehill, 1970; Brandon, 1970) have identified some of these weight-generating interactions as sharing similar eating and exercise patterns, conflicting over food, use of food as reinforcement, and sharing misinformation about eating and its management. In light of the importance of family interaction in the promotion of obesity, it is not surprising that husband-wife and parent-child exchanges have also been shown to be barriers to weight loss, even when one member of the family is motivated to make the necessary changes (e.g., Crisp & Stonehill, 1970; McEwen, Jacobson, Battrum, Crealock, Mitchell, & McLaren, 1972; Stuart & Davis, 1972). These observations support the critical importance of mobilizing the family as a basic support system for the development of new health behaviors and motivating family members to work toward reduction of family-produced obstacles to these behavioral changes.

Four programs have already evaluated the role of spouses in efforts to manage the weight of their mates. In the first such effort, Rosenthal (1976), at the University of Connecticut, asked both husbands and wives to participate in a 27-week program aimed at promoting weight loss by the wives. Volunteers were randomly assigned to a condition in which husbands participated in eight training sessions as well as in the day-to-day efforts of their wives to manage eating and increase exercise, to a condition in which husbands offered part-time help, and to a condition in which husbands had no involvment in their wives' efforts. Results indicate that husbands who participated either on a full-time or part-time basis were similarly effective in helping their wives reach weight-loss objectives, and that both were more effective than those who remained uninvolved in their wives' efforts. Matson (1977) next presented a case report showing that self-monitoring for ten weeks produced only a three-pound weight loss in his female patient, but that positive social reinforcement by her husband produced a 39-pound loss in 19 weeks—a loss that was maintained through a 90-week follow-up. Brownell, Heckerman, Westlake, Hayes, and Monti (1977) asked the spouses of overweight wives to join their wives in weight-loss efforts. Some husbands refused, and only half of those who expressed willingness to join the effort were invited to attend intervention sessions with their mates. All three groups of wives lost weight through ten weeks of treatment; all continued weight loss through a three-month follow-up; and all maintained their losses through a six-month follow-up. At both follow-up times, however, the wives of participating husbands lost significantly more weight than did those of husbands who were either unwilling or uninvited.

In the fourth study, Saccone and Israel (1978) randomly assigned 49 subjects to one of several conditions involving the use of stimulus-control training (Stuart & Davis, 1972) and monetary reinforcement by either the therapist or significant others. In the relevant conditions, others participated in the third treatment session of an eight-meeting program. Best results (a weight loss of 13.0 pounds) were obtained when others monitored changed eating behaviors as opposed to simply monitoring weight change (6.9 pounds) or when therapists reinforced behavior (7.6 pounds) or weight (5.3 pounds) changes.

These findings about the role of family interaction in the creation and modification of behavioral patterns associated with weight problems suggest that it is important to include training in reprogramming the social environment in all weight-control programs. This can be done by either directly including spouses in the intervention meetings, with or without the presence of the overweight mate, or through training the weight loser in strategies that could be useful in redirecting food-related interactions with the mate. Intervention could also be directed toward helping the mates of those who succeed in weight loss to cope constructively with the new social, job, and recreational opportunities that altered body weight can produce.

As a third and somewhat unexplored possibility, weight losers could be offered opportunities to self-determine the sequence of behavior changes they undertake. This is uniquely possible in behavior therapy because of the explicitness and relative independence of the techniques that comprise the approach. Yates (in press) has offered a potentially valuable way to formulate plans to permit the development of these individualized approaches (see Stuart & Mitchell, in press). He asked program participants to rate on a ten-point scale the perceived difficulty and usefulness of the various treatment components, and then he produced a usefulness/difficulty ratio. He found, for example, that shopping from a list, reducing the number of eating episodes, keeping a food diary, and storing foods in "see-proof" containers all recieved relatively high ratings. In contrast, low ratings were scored for the instruction to graph weight, leave some food on the plate, and count calories. If weight losers could be asked to rate the perceived difficulty and usefulness of proposed techniques in advance of their therapeutic introduction, they could construct for themselves a hierarchy of procedures that they consider to be comparatively easy to use and of relatively high potential yield. Then, by taking these steps, they could have successful experiences that could build their belief in self-efficacy and, quite possibly, their motivation to persevere and enjoy long-range successes. Applying this possibility, Stuart and Davis (1978) have presented a framework for building personalized intervention programs by individualizing the sequence of actions taken according to a hierarchy of those that seem most achievable, while also offering the greatest potential for change.

Adapting Programs to Client Cohorts

It is obvious that all overeaters are not alike! This is clearly seen when large inter-subject differences in response to standardized weight-control programs are observed. For example, Jeffrey, Wing and Stunkard (1978) found an average loss of 11.0 pounds among their 125 subjects, but the range of weight changes extended from a gain of 7 pounds to a loss of 47 pounds. This obvious truth can be an asset or a liability for the organizer of group services for the overweight. Differences between members can contribute a range of perspectives to each meeting that can be useful in developing innovative member-produced suggestions for the solutions of one another's problems. On the other hand, the fact that members of the same group have different concerns could all but guarantee that at least some of the treatment time will be devoted to issues which are irrelevant to the concerns of at least some of the members. Because of these and related considerations, uncertainty still exists about the wisdom of forming homogeneous as opposed to heterogeneous groups (Rose, 1977).

When heterogenous groups are formed, the suggestion made above can help to individualize programs to a degree while preserving their "generic" (Jacobson, Strickler, & Morley, 1976) character. If homogeneous groups are desired, it is necessary first to define criteria for member selection and then to determine the nature of the intervention that would be most useful to each group.

As was seen in Table 1, the past ten years of very active research have failed to delineate any clear and consistent predictors of success in weight control. Nevertheless, it is reasonable to assume that certain groups face special challenges in the management of their weight. For example, mothers who must purchase and prepare food for slender family members tend to be confronted by foods they find difficult to resist. College students who must eat dormitory fare face different challenges from those who live alone and do their own cooking. Youths who have the energy for vigorous pastimes have more degrees of freedom in efforts to manage their eating urges than do the elderly. Each of these, and many similar characteristics, could be used in choosing members for homogeneous groups—once it was decided that homogeneity was desirable.

Whatever other ways may seem reasonable for subsetting clients, se-

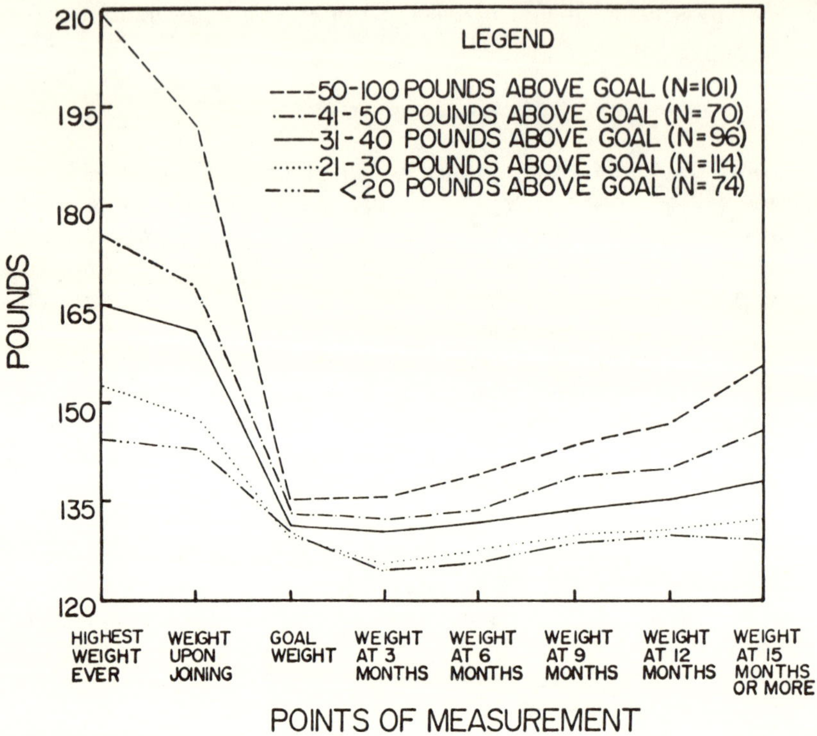

FIGURE 2. Weight changes experienced by women with different levels of highest weight ever.

lection of members according to the level of their starting weight and/or the relative level of their overweight would seem to be wise. Figure 2 portrays some of the results of the study by Stuart and Guire (in press), who found that those with relatively greater starting weights were able to maintain their goal weight for the shortest relative periods and appeared to experience a markedly faster relapse rate than those who began with lesser amounts of weight to lose.

The explanation of this result is not difficult to imagine: If overweight is an expression of varied lifestyle dimensions, then those who are 75 pounds above their desirable weight are under significantly more pressure to overeat than are those who have put on only 25 extra pounds. This means that weight loss for the very heavy would be associated with the need for greater readjustment in the psychological, physiological, and social arena than would be necessary for those with lower starting weights. For example, losers of a great many extra pounds often must learn to walk, sit, and use their bodies differently—changes that are not necessary for those who have lost smaller amounts of weight. They may have new social and employment possibilities and be faced with decision-making opportunities that did not exist before, in contrast to their lighter peers for whom weight loss does not open new doors. They also require longer periods of work before they achieve the satisfaction of goal-weight attainment, and they may need more encouragement to mobilize themselves for this long haul. Many of these issues may be better addressed in groups that are homogenous as to weight, so the extra-heavy will not suffer the embarrassment of public discussion of their special problems among the nonafflicted, and the less heavy members will not be faced with the necessity to sit through discussions that may have little personal relevance for them. If their total treatment does not take place in homogeneous settings, they could at least be offered some service in special sessions particularly targeted to their unusual needs.

Conclusion

Behavioral treatments for obesity have enjoyed a meteoric rise in popularity for several reasons. They offer a logical and explicit technology that is expected to lead to precisely measurable results. Moreover, early studies revealed that the obtainable results were positive relative to the decades of comparatively unsuccessful treatments that had been offered before. Strong statements were made about the importance of these early results, and the studies increased in range and number. Recently, close inspection of research outcomes have led some to wonder whether the early claims may not have been just another instance of what Miller (1977) termed an expression of "overoptimistic expectations, which may lead to disillusionment which could set the whole movement towards behavioral medicine back many years" (p. 1). A time of reappraisal is clearly at hand.

This questioning has arisen because, at least in some of the more frequently quoted studies, weight losses achieved during treatment have not been consistently maintained after intervention ended. It has been argued here that many of the studies have included design and execution flaws which have led to unsustainable outcomes. Many of these flaws might have been avoided if the researchers had begun with a set of assumptions including the following:

(1) Obesity is a complex disorder representing the logical impact of forces of physiological, psychological, social, and situational origin.
(2) Obesity is a lifestyle disorder that can only be overcome through a lifetime of effort.
(3) Lifestyle change can only be accomplished through the development of positive alternatives to problem behaviors, through a weakening of the motivation to emit problem behaviors, and through suppression of the problem responses.
(4) To accomplish the necessary changes, clients must be helped to master the challenges of four major stages of weight control: the decision to commit themselves to take action; management of the urge to eat followed by management of eating behavior *per se;* management of the immediate posttreatment period when relapse is imminent; and management of the extended posttreatment period when new challenges arise.

Recognition of the impact of these four assumptions leads to the requirement that services to the overweight must offer constructive interventions that are systematically evaluated as they are offered, through use of optimal techniques of service delivery over an extended period of time. So long as behavior researchers and therapists continue to regard their technology as a powerful brand of magic that is effective whether delivered in whole or in part, and so long as basic program plans omit consideration of the essential nature of the disorders that are the targets of intervention, less than satisfying outcomes will be the norm rather than the exception. It is time now to go back to basics in a continuing effort to demonstrate the power of behavioral interventions to reach goals not achievable through more traditional means, in what promises to be a highly successful effort to bring weight under lasting control.

REFERENCES

ASHWELL, M.: Commercial weight loss groups. In G. A. Bray (Ed.), *Recent advances in obesity research: 2.* London: Newman Publishing Company, in press.

ASHWELL, M., & GARROW, J. S.: A survey of three slimming and weight control organizations in the UK. *Nutrition,* 1973, *29,* 347-356.

ASSOCIATION FOR ADVANCEMENT OF BEHAVIOR THERAPY. Ethical issues for human services. *Behavior Therapy,* 1977, *8,* v-vi.

AZRIN, N. H., & HOLZ, W. C.: Punishment. In W. K. Honig (Ed.), *Operant behavior: Areas of research and application.* New York: Appleton-Century-Crofts, 1966.

BANDURA, A.: Self-reinforcement: Theoretical and methodological considerations. *Behaviorism,* 1976, *4,* 135-155.

BANDURA, A.: Self-efficacy: Toward a unifying theory of behavioral change. *Psychological Review,* 1977, *84,* 191-215.

BAUM, W. M.: The correlation-based law of effect. *Journal of the Experimental Analysis of Behavior,* 1973, *20,* 137-153.

BELL, S. M., & AINSWORTH, M.D.S.: Infant crying and maternal responsiveness. *Child Development,* 1972, *43,* 1171-1190.

BELLER, A. S.: *Fat and thin: A natural history of obesity.* N.Y.: Farrar, Straus & Giroux, 1977.

BELLOC, N. B., & BRESLOW, L.: Relationship of physical health status and health practices. *Preventive Medicine,* 1972, *1,* 409-421.

BERGIN, A. E.: The evaluation of therapeutic outcomes. In A. E. Bergin, & S. L. Garfield (Eds.), *Handbook of psychotherapy and behavior change: An empirical analysis.* New York: Wiley, 1971.

BOLLES, R. C.: Reinforcement, expectancy and learning. *Psychological Review,* 1972, *79,* 394-409.

BORTZ, W. M., WORLDSON, A., MORRIS P., & ISSEKUTZ, B.: Fat, carbohydrate, salt, and weight loss. *American Journal of Clinical Nutrition,* 1967, *20,* 1104-1112.

BRANDON, S.: An epidemiological study of eating disturbances. *Journal of Psychosomatic Research,* 1970, *14,* 253-257.

BRAY, G. A.: Pharmacological approach to the treatment of obesity. In G. A. Bray & J. E. Bethune (Eds.), *Treatment and management of obesity.* N.Y.: Harper & Row, 1974.

BRAY, G. A.: *The obese patient.* Philadelphia: W. B. Saunders, 1976.

BROWN, B. M.: The multiple techniques of broad spectrum psychotherapy. In A. A. Lazarus (Ed.), *Clinical behavior therapy.* New York: Brunner/Mazel, 1972.

BROWNELL, K. K., HECKERMAN, C. L., WESTLAKE, R. J., HAYES, S.C., & MONTI, P. M.: The effect of couples training and partner cooperativeness in the behavioral treatment of obesity. Paper presented at the Annual Meeting of the Association for the Advancement of Behavior Therapy, Atlanta, Georgia, December, 1977.

CAHOON, D. D.: Symptom substitution and the behavior therapies. *Psychological Bulletin,* 1968, *69,* 149-157.

CAUTELA, J. R.: The treatment of over-eating by covert conditioning. *Psychotherapy: Theory, Research and Practice,* 1972, *9,* 211-216.

CHRISTAKIS, G.: Community programs for weight reduction: Experience of the Bureau of Nutrition, New York City. *Canadian Journal of Public Health, 1967, 58* 499-504.

CORMIER, A.: Group versus individual dietary instruction in the treatment of obesity. *Canadian Journal of Public Health,* 1972, *63,* 327-332.

CRADDOCK, D.: *Obesity and its management.* Edinburgh: Churchill Livingston, 1973.

CRADDOCK, D.: The free diet: 150 cases personally followed-up after 10 to 18 years. *International Journal of Obesity,* 1977, *1,* 127-134.

CRISP, A. H., DOUGLAS, J. W. B., ROSS, J. M., & STONEHILL, E.: Some developmental aspects of disorders of weight. *Journal of Psychosomatic Research,* 1970, *14,* 313-320.

CRISP, A. H., & STONEHILL, E.: Treatment of obesity with special reference to seven severely obese patients. *Journal of Psychosomatic Research,* 1970, *14,* 327-345.

CURREY, H., MALCOLM, R., RIDDLE, E., & SCHACHTE, M.: Behavioral treatment of obesity: Limitations and results with the chronically obese. *Journal of the American Medical Association,* 1977, *237,* 2829-2831.

DAWSON, M. E., & FUREDY, J. J.: The role of awareness in human differential autonomic classical conditioning: The necessary-gate hypothesis. *Psychophysiology,* 1976, *13,* 50-53.

DEMBROSKI, T. M.: Clarification of the relationship between the development and modification of life-style and chronic disease: Is it possible? In National Heart and Lung Institute, *Working Conference on Health Behavior.* Washington, D.C.: U.S.D.H.E.&W. Publication No. (NIH) 77-868, 1977.

DINOFF, M., RICHARD, H. C., & COLWICK, J.: Weight reduction through successive contracts. *American Journal of Orthopsychiatry,* 1972, *42,* 110-113.

DURNIN, J. V. G. A., & WOMERSLEY, J.: Body fat assessed from total body density and its estimation from skinfold thickness: Measurements in 481 men and women aged from 16 to 72 years. *British Journal of Nutrition,* 1974, *32,* 77-97.

ETZEL, B. C. & GEWIRTZ, J. L.: Experimental modification of caretaker-maintained high-rate operant crying in a 6-and 20-week-old infant (infants tyranotearus): Extinction of crying with reinforcement of eye contact and smiling. *Journal of Experimental Child Psychology,* 1967, *5,* 303-317.

FEINSTEIN, A. R.: The measurement of success in weight reduction. *Journal of Chronic Diseases,* 1959, *10,* 439-456.

FEINSTEIN, A. R.: How do we measure accomplishment in weight reduction? In L. Lasagna (Ed.), *Obesity: Causes, consequences and treatment.* New York: Mecom Press, 1974.

FOREYT, J. P., & KENNEDY, W. A.: Treatment of overweight by aversion therapy. *Behaviour Research and Therapy,* 1971, *9,* 29-34.

FRANK, J. D.: *Persuasion and healing: A comparative study of psychotherapy.* Baltimore: The Johns Hopkins Press, 1961.

FRANK, J. D.: The role of cognitions in illness and healing. In H. H. Strupp & L. Luborsky (Eds.), *Research in Psychotherapy.* Washington, D. C.: American Psychological Association, 1962.

GARN, S. M., & CLARK, D. C.: Trends in fatness and the origins of obesity. *Pediatrics,* 1976, *57,* 443-456.

GARROW, J. W.: The regulation of body weight. In T. Silverstone (Ed.), *Obesity: Its pathogenesis and management.* Acton, Ma.: Publishing Sciences Group, 1975.

GARTNER, A., & RIESSMAN, F.: *Self-help in the human services.* San Francisco: Jossey-Bass, 1977.

GELFAND, D. M., HARTMANN, D. P., MAHAN, M. A., & LAMB, A.: Children's imitation of adults' behavior control techniques. In D. M. Gelfand (Ed.), *Social learning in childhood: Readings in theory and application.* (2nd ed.) Monterey, CA: Brooks/Cole, 1975.

GLENNON, J. A.: Weight reduction—an enigma. *Archives of Internal Medicine,* 1966, *118,* 1-2.

GOLDSTEIN, A. P.: Domains and dilemmas. In A. E. Bergin & H. H. Strupp (Eds.), *Changing frontiers in the science of psychotherapy.* Chicago: Aldine-Atherton, 1972.

GOTTMAN, J. M. & MCFALL, R. M.: Self-monitoring effects in a program for potential high school dropouts: A time series analysis. *Journal of Consulting and Clinical Psychology,* 1972, *39,* 273-281.

HAGEN, R. L.: Group therapy versus bibliotherapy in weight reduction. *Behavior Therapy,* 1974, *5,* 222-234.

HALL, S. M.: Self-control and therapist control in the behavioral treatment of overweight women. *Behaviour Research and Therapy,* 1972, *10,* 59-68.

HALL, M., HALL, R. G., HANSON, R. W., & BORDEN, B. L.: Permanence of two self-managed treatments of overweight in university and community populations. *Journal of Consulting and Clinical Psychology,* 1974, *42,* 781-786.

HAMILTON, C. L.: Problems of refeeding after starvation in the rat. *Annals of the New York Academy of Sciences,* 1969, *157,* 1004-1016.

HARRIS, M. B.: Self-directed program for weight control: A pilot study. *Journal of Abnormal Psychology,* 1969, *74,* 263-270.

HARRIS, M. B., & HALLBAUER, E. S.: Self-directed weight control through eating and exercise. *Behaviour Research and Therapy,* 1973, *11,* 523-529.

HART, B. M., ALLEN, K. E., BUEL, J. S., HARRIS, F. R., & WOLF, M. M.: Effects of social reinforcement on operant crying. *Journal of Experimental Child Psychology,* 1964, *1,* 145-153.

HERMAN, C. P., & MACK, D.: Restrained and unrestrained eating. *Journal of Personality,* 1975, *43,* 647-660.

HIRSCH, J., & KNITTLE, J. L.: Cellarity of obese and non-obese human adipose tissue. *Federation Proceedings,* 1970, *29,* 1512-1516.

HOEBEL, R. G., & TEITELBAUM, P.: Weight regulation in normal and hypothalamic rats. *Journal of Comparative Physiology and Psychology,* 1966, *61,* 189-193.

HORAN, J. J., & JOHNSON, R. G.: Coverant conditioning through a self-management application of the Premack Principle: Its effect on weight reduction. *Journal of Behavior*

Therapy and Experimental Psychiatry, 1971, *2,* 243-249.

HORAN, J. J., BAKER, S. B., HOFFMAN, A. M., & SHUTE, R. E.: Weight loss through variations in the coverant control paradigm. *Journal of Consulting and Clinical Psychology,* 1975, *43,* 68-72.

HUENEMANN, R. L.: Environmental factors associated with obesity. *Journal of the American Dietetic Association,* 1974, *65,* 480-487.

JACOBSON, G. F., STRICKLER, M., & MORLEY, W. E.: Generic and individual approaches to crisis intervention. In A. P. Goldstein & N. Stein (Eds.), *Prescriptive psychotherapies.* N.Y.: Pergamon Press, 1976.

JEFFREY, D. B.: Some methodological issues in research on obesity. *Psychological Reports,* 1974, *35,* 623-626.

JEFFREY, D. B., & CHRISTENSEN, E. R.: Behavior therapy versus 'will power' in the management of obesity. *The Journal of Psychology,* 1975, *90,* 303-311.

JEFFREY, D. B., CHRISTENSEN, E. R., & PAPPAS, J. P.: Developing a behavioral program and therapist manual for the treatment of obesity. *Journal of the American College Health Association,* 1973, *21,* 455-459.

JEFFREY, R. W., WING, R. R., & STUNKARD, A. J.: Behavioral treatment of obesity: The state of the art 1976. *Behavior Therapy,* 1978, *9,* 189-199.

JOLIFFE, N., & ALPERT, E.: The "performance index" as a method for estimating effectiveness of reducing regimens. *Postgraduate Medicine,* 1951, *9,* 106-115.

KAZDIN, A. E.: Self-monitoring and behavior change. In M. J. Mahoney & C. E. Thoresen (Eds.) *Self-control: Power to the person.* Monterey, CA: Brooks/Cole, 1974.

KAZDIN, A. E.: *Behavior modification in applied settings.* Homewood, Ill.: The Dorsey Press, 1975.

KINGSLEY, R. G., & WILSON, G. T.: Behavior therapy for obesity: A comparative investigation of long-term efficacy, *Journal of Consulting and Clinical Psychology,* 1977, *45,* 288-298.

KIRSCHENBAUM, D. S., & KAROLY, P.: When self-regulation fails: Tests of some preliminary hypotheses. *Journal of Consulting and Clinical Psychology,* 1977, *45,* 1116-1125.

LAZARUS, A. A.: *Behavior therapy and beyond.* N.Y.: McGraw-Hill Book Company, 1971.

LEON, G. R.: Current directions in the treatment of obesity. *Psychological Bulletin,* 1976, *83,* 557-578.

LEON, G. R.: A behavioral approach to obesity. *The American Journal of Clinical Nutrition,* 1977, *30,* 785-789.

LEVITZ, L. S., & STUNKARD, A. J.: A therapeutic coalition for obesity: Behavior modification and patient self-help. *American Journal of Psychiatry,* 1974, *131,* 423-427.

LEY, P., WHITWORTH, M. W., WOODWARD, R., & YORKE, R.: The effects of sidedness and fear arousal on willingness to participate in a slimming scheme. *The Health Education Journal,* 1977, *36,* 63-65.

LICK, J., & BOOTZIN, R.: Expectancy factors in the treatment of fear: Methodological and theoretical issues. *Psychological Bulletin,* 1975, *82,* 917-931.

LIEBERMAN, M.: Some limits to research on T groups. *Journal of Applied Behavioral Science,* 1975, *11,* 241-249.

LIEBERMAN, M. A.: Change induction in small groups. *Annual Review of Psychology,* 1976, *27,* 217-250.

LORR, M.: Client perceptions of therapists: A study of therapeutic relation. *Journal of Consulting Psychology,* 1965, *29,* 146-149.

LUBLIN, B.: *Manual for the Depression Adjective Check Lists.* San Diego: Educational and Industrial Testing Service, 1967.

LUBORSKY, L.: Helping alliances in psychotherapy. In J. L. Claghorn (Ed.), *Successful psychotherapy.* New York: Brunner/Mazel, 1976.

MAHONEY, M. J.: Self-reward and self-monitoring techniques for weight control. *Behavior Therapy,* 1974, *5,* 48-57.

MAHONEY, M. J.: The behavioral treatment of obesity: A reconnaissance. *Biofeedback and Self-Regulation,* 1976, *1,* 127-133.

MAHONEY, M. J., & MAHONEY, K.: Treatment of obesity: A clinical exploration. In B. J. Williams, S. Martin, & J. P. Foreyt (Eds.), *Obesity: Behavioral approaches to dietary management.* New York: Brunner/Mazel, 1976.(a)

MAHONEY, M. J., & MAHONEY, K.: *Permanent weight control: A total solution to the dieter's dilemma.* N.Y.: W. W. Norton, 1976.(b)

MAHONEY, M. J., MOURA, N. G. M. & WADE, T. C.: Relative efficacy of self-reward, self-punishment, and self-monitoring techniques for weight loss. *Journal of Consulting and Clinical Psychology,* 1973, *40,* 404-407.

MAHONEY, B. K., ROGERS, T., STRAW, M., & MAHONEY, M. J.: Results and implications of a problem solving treatment program for obesity. Paper presented at the 11th Annual Convention of the Association For Advancement of Behavior Therapy, Atlanta, Ga., Dec. 1977.

MANN, R. A.: The behavior-therapeutic use of contingency contracting to control an adult behavior problem: Weight control. *Journal of Applied Behavior Analysis,* 1972, *5,* 99-109.

MATSON, M. L.: Social reinforcement by the spouse in weight control: A case study. *Journal of Behavior Therapy and Experimental Psychiatry,* 1977, *8,* 327-329.

MCEWEN, H., JACOBSON, H., BATTRUM, E. C., CREALOCK, R. J., MITCHELL, M.N., & MCLAREN, B. A.: Experience with a hosptial based weight reduction program. *Canadian Medical Association Journal,* 1972, *107,* 43-45.

MELTZOFF, J., & KORNREICH, M.: *Research in psychotherapy.* New York: Atherton Press, 1970.

MIKULAS, W. L.: Four noble truths of buddhism related to behavior therapy. *The Psychological Record,* 1978, *28,* 59-67.

MILLER, N. E.: Behavioral medicine as a new frontier: Opportunities and dangers. In National Heart and Lung Institute, *Working Conference on Health Behavior.* Washington, D.C.: U.S.D.H.E. & W. Publication No. (NIH-77-868), 1977.

MILLER, R. L., BRICKMAN, P., & BOLEN, D.: Attribution versus persuasion as a means of modifying behavior. *Journal of Personality and Social Psychology,* 1975, *31,* 430-441.

MISCHEL, W., EBBESEN, E. B., & ZEISS, A. R.: Selective attention to the self: Situational and dispositional determinants. *Journal of Personality and Social Psychology,* 1973, *27,* 129-142.

MORGANSTERN, K. P.: Cigarette smoke as a noxious stimulus in self-managed aversion therapy for compulsive eating: Technique and case illustration. *Behavior Therapy,* 1974, *5,* 255-260.

MUSANTE, G.J. The dietary rehabilitation clinic: Evaluative report of a behavioral and dietary treatment of obesity. *Behavior Therapy,* 1976, 7, 198-204.

NATIONAL HEART AND LUNG INSTITUTE: *Working Conference on Health Behavior.* Washington, D.C.: U.S.D.H.E.&W. Publication No. (NIH-77-868), 1977.

NISBETT, R. E.: Hunger, obesity, and the ventromedial hypothalamus. *Psychological Review,* 1972, *79,* 433-453.

OST, L.G., & GOTESTAM, K. G.: Behavioral and pharmacological treatments for obesity: An experimental comparison. *Addictive Behaviors,* 1976, *1,* 331-338.

PAULSEN, B. K., LUTZ, R. N., MCREYNOLDS, W. T., & KOHRS, M. B.: Behavior therapy for weight control: Long-term results of two programs with nutritionists as therapists. *The American Journal of Clinical Nutrition,* 1976, *29,* 880-888.

PENICK, S. B., FILION, R., FOX, S., & STUNKARD, A. J.: Behavior modification in the treatment of obesity. *Psychosomatic Medicine,* 1971, *33,* 49-55.

PERRI, M. G., & RICHARDS, C. S.: An investigation of naturally occurring episodes of self-controlled behaviors. *Journal of Counseling Psychology,* 1977, *24,* 178-183.

RICHARDS, C. S., & PERRIP M. G.: Do self-control treatments last? An evaluation of behavioral problem solving and faded counselor contact as treatment maintenance strategies. *Journal of Counseling Psychology,* in press.

ROMANCZYK, R. G., TRACEY, D. A., WILSON, T., & THORPE, G. L.: Behavioral techniques in the treatment of obesity: A comparative analysis. *Behaviour Research and Therapy,*

1973, *11,* 629-640.
ROSE, S. D.: *Group therapy: A behavioral approach.* New York: Prentice-Hall, 1977.
ROSENTHAL, B.: The dieting teams. *Human Behavior,* 1976, *5,* 49.
ROSENTHAL, R.: *Experimenter effects in behavioral research.* New York: Appleton-Century-Crofts, 1966.
SACCONE, A. J., & ISRAEL, A. C.: Effects of experimenter versus significant other-controlled reinforcement and choice of target behavior on weight loss. *Behavior Therapy,* 1978, *9,* 271-278.
SCHACHTER, S., & RODIN, J.: *Obese humans and rats.* Patomic, Md.: Lawrence Erlbaum, 1974.
SIMS, E. A. H., GOLDMAN, R. F., GLUCK, C. M., HORTON, E. S., KELLEHER, P. C., & ROWE, D. W.: Experimental obesity in man. *Transactions of the Association of American Physicians,* 1968, *81,* 153-170.
SMITH, G. S., SMITH, J. L., MAMEESH, M. S., SIMON, J., & JOHNSON, B. C.: Hypertension and cardiovascular abnormalities in starved-refed swine. *Journal of Nutrition,* 1964, *82,* 173-182.
SOHAR, E., & SNEH, E.: Follow-up of obese patients: 14 years after a successful reducing diet. *The American Journal of Clinical Nutrition.* 1973, *26,* 845-848.
STRUPP, H. H., & BERGIN, A. E.: Some empirical and conceptual bases for coordinated research in psychotherapy. *International Journal of Psychiatry,* 1969, *7,* 18-90.
STUART, R. B.: Behavioral control of overeating. *Behaviour Research and Therapy,* 1967, *5,* 357-365.
STUART, R. B.: A three-dimensional program for the treatment of obesity. *Behaviour Research and Therapy,* 1971, *9,* 177-186.
STUART, R. B.: The role of social work education in innovative human services. In F. W. Clark, D. R. Evans, & L. A. Hamerlynck (Eds.), *Implementing behavioral programs for schools and clinics.* Champaign, Ill.: Research Press, 1972.
STUART, R. B.: Exercise prescription in weight management: Advantages, techniques and obstacles. *Obesity and Bariatric Medicine,* 1975, *40,* 16-24.
STUART, R. B. (ED.): *Behavioral self-management: Strategies, techniques and outcome.* New York: Brunner/Mazel, 1977 (a).
STUART, R.B.: Self-help in self-management. In R.B. Stuart (Ed.), *Behavioral self-management.* New York: Brunner/Mazel, 1977 (b).
STUART, R.B.: *Act thin: Stay thin.* New York: W.W. Norton, 1978 (a).
STUART, R.B.: Protection of the right to informed consent to participate in research. *Behavior Therapy,* 1978, *9,* 73-82 (b).
STUART, R.B., & DAVIS, B.: *Slim chance in a fat world.* Champaign, Ill.: Research Press, 1972.
STUART, R.B., & DAVIS, B.: *Slim chance in a fat world. Revised Condensed edition.* Champaign, Ill.: Research Press, 1978.
STUART, R.B., & GUIRE, K.: Some correlates of the maintenance of weight lost through behavior modification. *International Journal of Obesity,* in press.
STUART, R.B., & JACOBSON, B.: Sex differences in obesity. In E. Gomberg & V. Franks (Eds.), *Gender and psychopathology: Sex differences in disordered behavior.* New York: Brunner/Mazel, 1979.
STUART, R.B., & MITCHELL, C.: Self-help on the rise: The growing strength of peer-led programs of weight control. *Psychiatric Clinics of North America,* in press.
STUNKARD, A.J.: Presidential Address—1974. From explanation to action in psychosomatic medicine: The case of obesity. *Psychosomatic Medicine,* 1975, *37,* 195-236.
STUNKARD, A.J.: *The pain of obesity.* Palo Alto, Ca.: Bull Publishing Company, 1976.
STUNKARD, A.J.: Behavioral treatments of obesity: Failure to maintain weight loss. In R.B. Stuart (Ed.), *Behavioral self-management.* New York: Brunner/Mazel, 1977.
STUNKARD, A. J., & MAHONEY, M. M.: Behavioral treatment of the eating disorders. In H. Leitenberg (Ed.), *Handbook of behavior modification and behavior therapy.* Englewood Cliffs, N.J.: Prentice-Hall, 1976.

Stunkard, A. J., & McLaren-Hume, M.: The results of treatment for obesity: A review of the literature and report of a series. *Archives of Internal Medicine,* 1959, *103,* 79-85.

Stunkard, A. J., & Rush, J.: Dieting and depression re-examined: A critical review of reports of untoward responses during weight reduction for obesity. *Annals of Internal Medicine,* 1974, *81,* 526-533.

Surgeon General of the United States: *Obesity and health.* Washington, D. C.: U. S. Government Printing Office, 1966.

Thorn, M. E., & Boudewyns, P. A.: A behaviorally oriented weight loss program for counseling centers. *Journal of Counseling Psychology,* 1976, *23,* 81-82.

Tighe, T. J., & Elliott, R. A.: A technique for controlling behavior in natural life setting. *Journal of Applied Behavior Analysis.* 1968, *1,* 263-266.

Tobias, L. L., & MacDonald, M. L.: Internal locus of control and weight loss: An insufficient condition. *Journal of Consulting and Clinical Psychology,* 1977, *45,* 647-653.

Trulson, M., Walsh, E. D., & Caso, E. K.: A study of obese patients in a nutrition clinic. *Journal of the American Dietetic Association,* 1947, *23,* 941-946.

Walker, W. J., Lawry, E. Y., Love, D. E., Mann, G. V., Levine, S.A. & Stare, F. J.: Effect of weight reduction and caloric balance on serum lipoprotein and cholesterol levels. *American Journal of Medicine,* 1953, *14,* 654-664.

Weisenberger, M. & Fray, E.: What's missing in the treatment of obesity by behavior modification. *Journal of the American Dietetic Association,* 1974, *65,* 410-414.

Wijesinghe, B.: Massed electrical aversion treatment of compulsive eating. *Journal of Behavior Therapy and Experimental Psychiatry,* 1973, *4,* 133-135.

Williams, A. E., & Duncan, B. A.: A commercial weight-reducing organization: A critical analysis. *Medical Journal of Australia,* 1976, *1,* 781-785(a).

Williams, A. E., & Duncan B. A.: Comparative results of an obesity clinic and a commercial weight-reducing organization. *Medical Jouranl of Australia,* 1976, *1,* 800-802(b).

Wollersheim, J. P.: Effectiveness of group therapy based upon learning principles of the treatment of overweight women. *Journal of Abnormal Psychology,* 1970, *76,* 462-474.

Yates, B. T.: Improving the cost-effectiveness of obesity programs: Three basic strategies for reducing the cost per pound. *International Journal of Obesity,* in press.

7

Prevention of Child Behavior Disorders: A Lifestyle Change for Child Psychologists

LIZETTE PETERSON,
DONALD P. HARTMANN, and
DONNA M. GELFAND

By any reasonable standard, it is difficult to argue that the child mental health profession is meeting its goal of reducing the prevalence of behavior disorders. Despite the expenditure of billions of dollars,* only a small portion of children thought to be in need of mental health services actually receive help (Report of the Joint Commission, 1969). For example, the Bureau of Education for the Handicapped found that in 1970, 48% of retarded youngsters were not receiving special services; 49% of speech impaired children, and an amazing 87% of those considered emotionally disturbed were *not* receiving treatment (White, Day,

*According to the Report of the Joint Commission on Child Mental Health (1973), more than $4.3 billion is expended annually in the United States for the diagnosis and treatment of child mental health problems.

Freeman, Hartman, & Messenger, 1973). Even for those children treated, the bulk of scientific outcome data does not provide a compelling argument for the effectiveness of the treatment (Hartmann, Roper, & Gelfand, 1977).

One recommended approach for redressing the imbalance between service demand and service supply is to increase the number of service providers.* Attempts to increase the number of service providers for children have included using peer therapists (e.g., Allen, 1976), and paraprofessionals (e.g., Guerney, 1969), in addition to the professionals traditionally associated with child mental health services. But even with the increase in the number of child mental health personnel, past experience would suggest that the demand for services would probably outstrip the supply. According to Gelfand (1977):

> the provision of new treatment services and the construction of additional community mental health centers has acted to stimulate rather than to reduce the demand for services. So the faster we build centers and train therapists, the further behind we seem to get in treating existing problems. This is a race we cannot win.

If an increase in services simply results in an escalating spiral of increasing need, then it is perhaps time to review our assumptions and goals and to begin to change our focus from increasing the supply of services to decreasing need by the prevention of new cases. Perhaps we can learn what modern medicine has apparently failed to learn: Despite the tremendous recent increase in costs of specialized medical goods and services (see Kristein, Arnold, & Wynder, 1977) we are not reducing infant mortality nor are we appreciably increasing our longevity. Because of the dramatic and costly nature of specialized medical treatment procedures, it is generally not recognized that the *real* contributions to longevity and to general health have come from preventive and public health measures rather than from expensive and specialized diagnostic and treatment measures (Powles, 1973).

Our suggestion that child mental health workers refocus their attention on prevention may be greeted with some skepticism. Some critics might suggest that prevention is already highlighted because of the explicit provision for prevention in the Comprehensive Community Men-

*This apparent deficiency in the number of service providers may come as a shock to those who can recall Boring's alleged prognostication that on the basis of the current graduate enrollment trends, by the year 2000 everyone in the United States would be a psychologist.

tal Health Act. Cowen (1973) suggests that a field's conceptual stance is indicated by the sum of the activities of its constituents. If that is the case, then it is apparent that there is little correspondence between the mandate for prevention and the mandate's implementation. Far from effectively preventing behavioral disorders, we are hardly beginning to study preventive methods. Cowen (1973) found that only two to three percent of the references in the community mental health literature dealt with prevention, and many of these papers were philosophical essays rather than evaluations of preventive services. The 1974 statistics of 400 operating federally funded community mental health centers revealed that only 5.2 % of staff time was devoted to consultation and educative activities (the activities most closely associated with preventive interventions) and virtually one-half of this time was spent on secondary rather than primary prevention* (Goldston, 1977). Similarly, Wade and Baker's (1977) survey of clinical psychologists indicates that neither prevention nor activities related to prevention are indicated as significant areas of occupational specialization. A recent survey of behavior therapists (Wade, Baker, & Hartmann, 1979) suggests that this group fares little better than do other mental health workers. Prevention again was not mentioned as a category of specialization. Furthermore, the category most closely allied to prevention, that is, consultation, involved only 5.4% of professional staff time. Therapy, therapy supervision, and assessment, consumed approximately 39% of the behavior therapists' time.

It may be worthwhile to examine more closely this potentially valuable, yet elusive, preventive enterprise which may be our only viable approach to equalizing needs of and services for children. In the following sections, we will describe the primary activities required of the preventionist, and the advantages and current limitations of training in behavioral psychology for performing these activities. Next, we will describe the role of behavioral psychologists as preventionists in a variety of programs, including those for the educationally disadvantaged, for parents, and for children facing stressful experiences. Our illustrations will highlight the work done at the University of Utah with child surgery patients. Finally, we will suggest a number of examples of prevention roles for psychologists in health-related fields.

---

*Secondary prevention, a term of dubious value introduced into the prevention literature by Caplan (1964), is essentially equivalent to the more traditional word, treatment.

Mounting a Prevention Program

Mounting a successful prevention program requires attention to a series of interrelated issues. First, the preventionist must select an appropriate problem behavior for prevention. The choice of problem behavior will depend upon the availability of a cost-effective and otherwise suitable (e.g., politically acceptable) prevention techniques as well as upon the prevalence and seriousness of the problem. Some problem behaviors, even though low in rate, may be targeted because of their serious, even lethal consequences. Examples include CNS impairment which results from ingesting lead-based paints and other toxic substances, head injuries incurred in automobile accidents, childhood suicides, psychotic reactions, and genetic anomalies such as PKU and mongolism. Other less serious problems may be targeted because of their high rates of occurrence. Examples include dental caries, adverse reactions to medical treatment, and heterosexual adjustment problems in adolescents. Other high rate, but temporary and generally minor problems such as fear of water or of the barber also may be the subject of experimental prevention programs. Children at risk for developing these minor problems may function for the preventionist in a manner similar to the white rat for the experimental psychologist or the snake phobic college student for the behavior therapist. These children may provide a convenient subject population for analogue research in the development of effective prevention techniques and delivery systems.

Next, the preventionist must select a general strategy. Bloom (1968) distinguished three general strategies or approaches: community-wide, milestone, and high-risk. In the first, or community approach, all members of the community are exposed to the program. Examples include tamper-proof medicine bottles, water treatment programs to guard against bacterial infections and dental caries, and prohibitions against the use of lead-based paints. With the milestone approach, children are exposed to the prevention program at a specified period of their lives. Before this specified period or event, children are unprotected; following it, they are protected. Examples include measles vaccinations administered on the first day of school, a modeling film on contraceptives required of all ninth-graders, and driving education courses given prior to receiving a driver's license. The prevention program may be associated with a milestone event because this is a convenient means of reaching all potential participants—the milestone is a "gate" through which all participants must pass—or, the milestone itself may be associated with stressors which the program is intended to neutralize. With the high-risk approach, the focus is on identifying high-risk populations.

Examples of high-risk populations include the children of schizophrenic, depressed, or abusive parents; children who are physically disabled; and children who experience the loss of a parent through separation, death or divorce.

Heller and Monahan (1977) discuss the advantages and limitations of each of these approaches. The community and milestone methods, because of their lack of selectivity, treat many children who are not at risk, and often may most effectively reach those least in need. For example, Cook, Appleton, Conner, Shaffer, Tamkin, and Weber (1975) have charged that "Sesame Street," which was developed for the educationally disadvantaged, is watched more by the children from middle-class homes than by economically deprived children. While high-risk programs are more selective, the identification of high-risk children can pose serious difficulties. Parents or their children may resent invasion of their privacy by the project staff, and consequently may refuse to participate. Furthermore, labeling children as incipiently disordered may itself prove iatrogenic (Levine & Graziano, 1972). Sarason, Levine, Goldenberg, Cherlin, and Bennett (1966) report, for example, that school children labeled as disturbed are avoided by teachers, the very persons with whom they might otherwise experience therapeutic interactions. Whether this same consequence would occur for children labeled incipiently disturbed in prevention programs remains to be seen. In order to minimize such problems, it is most important that the strategy for prevention be carefully matched to the behavior it attempts to eliminate, and that investigators be alert to any unwanted side-effects.

Next, the preventionist must decide upon a specific intervention technique and a route for implementing the technique. Behaviorally oriented preventionists have employed a variety of intervention techniques, including stimulus-control and contingency management procedures, coping-skills training techniques, and modeling, as we shall see in more detail in our selective review of behavioral prevention programs. According to Gelfand and Hartmann (1977), there are many possible routes that may be used in implementing prevention programs for children. The physical environment may be altered to change the probability of a targeted response. For example, play areas can be constructed in a manner to promote social interactions, or cigarette vending machines may be placed in areas inaccessible to children. Alternately, one could focus on the social rather than the physical environment. In these latter programs, some attempt is made to either directly increase coping skills of children at risk or to train their caretakers (e.g., parents or teachers) in working with the children to reduce the probability of future problems. These person-oriented programs can be directed at selected, specific behaviors such as the use of automobile seat restraints, or at more generalized classes of behavior such as responses to stressful situations.

Finally, each program should be evaluated to establish its effectiveness, its cost, and any untoward effects of the intervention such as adverse effects caused by labeling. Unlike the evaluation of behavioral *treatment* programs which can be undertaken on subject samples as small as one, behavioral intervention programs will undoubtedly require large sample sizes and traditional control group designs to establish their worth. It is only by means of thorough evaluation and a solid foundation of empirical evidence that we will be able to establish an effective science of prevention.

THE RELEVANCE OF BEHAVIORAL TRAINING TO PREVENTION

We have sketched in broad brushstrokes the issues involved in undertaking a preventive intervention, and in the following section we shall examine some programs based on behavioral principles. Before examining these programs, it might be advantageous to assess the assets and limitations of behavioral approaches to determine their suitability for intervention work. Poser (1976) and Gelfand and Hartmann (1977) list a number of characteristics of behavioral approaches that contrast with earlier, less successful preventive attempts, and that should increase our likelihood of success as preventionists.

Many past programs employed influence methods and models derived from psychotherapy—methods which were of unproven success in psychotherapy, and which were no more successful in prevention. For example, the Cambridge-Somerville youth project of the 1940's (Powers & Witmer, 1951) aimed to prevent juvenile delinquency by the provision of social work counseling services. This project was a notable failure, and even produced some evidence that the treated group actually exceeded the control group on certain indices of delinquency. Nor is this an isolated case. Other types of preventive programs based upon nondirective or supportive counseling, or sensitivity training, group therapy, or traditional types of mental health consultation (see Mannino & Shore, 1975) have also been generally ineffective.* In contrast, be-

---

*Some programs may even worsen target problems. Stuart (1974), for example, reports that in comparison to control subjects not explicitly informed about drugs, children who were exposed to a 10-session fact-oriented drug program reported *increased,* rather than *decreased,* drug use.

havioral techniques are based on sound, carefully developed procedures rather than on unproven, traditional clinical procedures and hunches. Typically, behavioral techniques have gone through a series of laboratory tests or analogue conditions that insure their efficiency, or embarrassingly reveal their deficiencies.

Second, many past psychotherapy-based programs have employed complex intervention techniques which vary considerably among both clients and therapists. Thus, even if these programs were successful, it would be difficult to identify the effective treatment components and virtually impossible to replicate their procedures. In contrast, behavioral psychologists' emphasis on design structure, procedural specifications, and reliability helps to insure that the behaviorally based techniques can be characterized, and procedures as well as results can be replicated. Furthermore, component analysis is an important aspect of behavioral intervention research, so nonfunctional aspects of treatment can be excluded from the treatment package.

Third, the goals of many past programs were vague and unrealistic. For example, they aimed to prevent conditions such as maladjustment, psychosis, neurosis, character disorders, or learning disabilities. There is considerable debate whether some of these represent actual homogeneous syndromes of behavior, and there is much evidence to suggest that these disorders cannot be reliably identified. If we don't know what exactly we are trying to prevent, if we can't get adequate levels of agreement and classification, then how could anyone tell whether a program reduced the incidence of the problem? Behavioral procedures, on the other hand, are typically directed to clearly defined observable problem behaviors.

Fourth, in many cases, behavioral procedures are understandable to the client (Gelfand & Hartmann, 1968), and can either be administered by moderately trained individuals or by the client himself. Behavioral techniques meeting these requirements should be less costly than traditional intervention techniques which require substantial professional time to administer.

Fifth, in contrast to some intervention programs in which results are described in terms of statistical significance, behavioral psychologists tend to emphasize clinically significant and socially valid results (e.g., Baer, Wolf, & Risley, 1968; Kazdin, 1977). Important aspects of clinical and social significance include the durability and generalizability of the intervention effects (Baer et al., 1968; Mash & Terdal, 1977), as well as the absence of undesirable side effects (Rogers-Warren & Warren, 1977). These latter points have been recent foci of behavioral interventions.

While the durability and generalizability of results are not uniformly characteristic of all clinical behavioral research (Cochrane & Sobol, 1976; Hartmann, Roper, & Gelfand, 1977; Peterson & Hartmann, 1975), they are part of the behaviorists' creed, and hence are important aspects of graduate training as well as crucial considerations in manuscript and grant review procedures.

Other aspects of behavioral training may have far less applicability to prevention work. First, the effectiveness of behavior modifiers in treating children's behavioral disorders may be a strong disincentive for their involvement in prevention. Behaviorists may be trapped by social reinforcers stemming from their own effectiveness in much the same way as a child's newly acquired skills are trapped by the reinforcers existing in his natural environment. Also, our design training may not prepare us well for certain aspects of prevention. Effective prevention requires careful selection of target behaviors and identification of high-risk groups. This work may require some expertise in epidemiological research (e.g., Cooper & Shepherd, 1973), training which does not appear to be highlighted in behavioral programs. The evaluation of preventive interventions will almost certainly require substantial familiarity with group experimental designs, longitudinal methodology, and problems of statistical power, subject attrition, discontinuous assessment, and unreliable classifications. None of these appear to be particular strengths in behavioral training programs, and will likely require increased attention if behavioral psychologists are to make the lifestyle change from problem solvers to problem preventers.

Given these assets and limitations in the training of behavioral psychologists, how do they perform in the role of preventionists? Although not many examples of relevant activities are available, those that exist are grounds for cautious optimism.

Prevention Programs

By far the most extensively developed behavior prevention programs have been person-oriented programs directed at the educationally disadvantaged. These programs, including those guided by other than a behavioral ideology, are reviewed by Bronfenbrenner (1975), by Horowitz and Paden (1973) and by Chilman (1973). The Project Follow-Through programs sponsored by the University of Kansas and the University of Oregon (see Stallings, 1975) are examples of programs of this kind. These successful programs employ a variety of stimulus-control and contingency management procedures, and focus on traditional educational goals such as reading and arithmetic achievement. Stallings' (1975) evaluation of these two behavior programs, as well as other follow-through programs, represents a model of large-scale prevention research.

Unlike most evaluation research, Stallings included control programs as well as multiple representations of each intervention program, used procedural-reliability assessments to ensure that the various intervention programs actually did operate as they were supposed to, and included a variety of dependent variables so that the strengths and weaknesses of each program could be assessed. On some aspects, such as mathematics and reading achievement, the behavioral programs excelled; on others, such as self-direction of activities and cooperation, the less structured open-classroom programs proved stronger. Consumers could thus choose the program model that produced the behavioral results they preferred.

The teacher is a pivotal figure in school-based programs, and training teachers in behavioral management techniques is critical to the success of these programs. The Responsive Teaching Model developed by Hall and his associates (Hall & Copeland, 1972; Hall, Copeland, & Clark, 1975) is illustrative of primary as well as secondary prevention work in this area. Education in behavioral child management procedures is offered in lectures, films and discussion groups. Following the lecture presentations, small discussion groups meet with trained leaders who administer quizzes to insure that participants master the material on objective child behavior observation, reinforcement principles and their application. Participants' progress is closely monitored as they plan and carry out a behavioral training program with a child. Participants trained in these programs are taught to employ a variety of novel contingency management procedures. For example, a principal may autograph good student papers, and teachers may frequently send home notes detailing children's academic accomplishments. This program seems exceptionally promising and the evaluation of its preventive and treatment accomplishments has just begun.

A second focus of behavioral prevention has been directed at parent training. Reviews of this literature have been published by O'Dell (1974), by Tavormina (1974), and by Reisinger, Ora, and Frangia (1976). While much of this work has been directed at secondary prevention, the same methods might be used to educate prospective parents, or parents whose children are at risk for developing behavioral probems. The monograph edited by Mash, Handy, and Hamerlynck (1976) describes a number of parent training programs that hold promise. These programs typically offer parents demonstrations of behavioral child management techniques such as the use of praise and attention to reinforce children's appropriate behaviors. Because humans have been unfavorably engineered to attend to undesired behavior and to ignore good behavior, most programs try to teach parents to do the opposite—often with good results. The parents and children may also be trained to negotiate contracts which detail the reinforcements the children will receive for desirable behavior.

A number of these parent training programs (e.g., Patterson, Reid, Jones, & Conger, 1975) employ commercially available training manuals. The sizeable number of these inexpensive training manuals available to the public might be viewed as a panacea for the prevention of children's problem behaviors. Presumably, by studying these manuals, parents will learn a variety of effective child management skills, and become proficient in teaching their children personal hygiene skills, value orientations, personal responsibility and the like. However, Glasgow and Rosen (1978), in their review of behavioral self-help books, report that the "number of current child-management programs clearly exceeds the number of related validational reports" (p. 13), and that additional research will be required before these manuals can be recommended and used with confidence.

A third focus of activity is aimed at the prevention of children's fears. Again, while much of this research concerns secondary rather than primary prevention, the modeling and coping-skills training procedures used to treat children's anxieties should be applicable to their prevention as well (Gelfand, 1977). A number of recent experimental programs directed at the primary prevention of fears associated with medical and dental treatments seem particularly promising. For example, Melamed and her associates (e.g., Melamed, Hawes, Heiby & Glick, 1975) have demonstrated that providing children with filmed models of another child undergoing dental treatment can be extremely effective as a means of preventing anxiety. In their initial study, control-group children who had seen a film unrelated to dentistry *increased* their fearful and resistant behavior (e.g., crying, kicking, and refusing to cooperate) 256 percent from an initial exam to observations made during the dental treatment session. Children exposed to the experimental modeling film, however, showed a remarkable 23 percent *decrease* in their resistant behavior during the treatment session.

Poser and his associates (Poser, 1970, 1976; Poser & King, 1975) also had some success using a pre-exposure treatment with children scheduled for dental treatment. Poser's pre-exposure technique focuses on gradual exposure to a potentially fear-provoking stimulus in order to prevent or at least minimize the strength of conditioned avoidance responses. Children who had never experienced dental treatment were pre-exposed up to ten times to a dental treatment room and its related paraphernalia. In comparison to children who had not received the pre-exposure treatment, the treated subjects showed far more cooperative and less resistant behavior in their first dental treatment session.

While both modeling and pre-exposure treatments appear promising for the prevention of mono-symptomatic phobias, they are time consuming and inefficient if the goal is to inoculate children against a wide variety of fears and anxieties. Shigetomi and Barrios (1978) have argued instead for coping skills training, a set of intervention techniques that are brief and inexpensive to teach, and which provide the individual with an active skill that can be used in a variety of anxiety-eliciting life situations. Coping-skills training techniques include self-control desensitization (Goldfried, 1971), anxiety management training (Suinn & Richardson, 1971), applied relaxation (Deffenbacher, 1976), cue-controlled relaxation (Russell & Sipich, 1973), rational restructuring (Goldfried, Decenteceo, & Weinberg, 1974), and stress inoculation (Meichenbaum & Cameron, 1973). In a study, which we shall describe in some detail, a set of coping skill procedures was compared with a filmed modeling condition and a stimulus pre-exposure condition in the prevention of children's fears and anxiety related to minor surgery.

Psychological Preparation for Surgery

Research in the early 1950s described the apparently maladaptive responses of children to hospitalization. Prugh, Staub, Sands, Kirschbaum, and Lenihan (1953) reported that 92% of the children they observed experienced moderate or severe behavioral problems following surgery. Typical problems observed included: a) depressive reactions such as listlessness, apathy, and negativism; b) irritability, anger, and aggression; c) panic, crying, and screaming; d) regressive behavior such as enuresis, clinging to parents, and thumb sucking; and e) sleep and appetite disturbances (Chapman, Loeb, & Gibbons, 1956; Jensen, 1955; Jessner, Blom, & Waldfogel, 1952; Prugh et al., 1953; Skipper & Leonard, 1968; Vernon, Foley, Sipowicz, & Shulman, 1965). According to Janis (1958) and Skipper and Leonard (1968), these behavior problems adversely affect post-operative recovery in children.

Four major causes have been suggested for the distress experienced by hospitalized children: a) lack of information concerning what will happen at the hospital; b) inability to adjust to a strange environment; c) a need for emotional support; and d) the lack of control over the situation (Bowlby, Robertson, & Rosenbluth, 1952; Cassell, 1965; Haller, Talbert, & Dombro, 1967; Jackson, Winkley, Faust, & Cermek, 1952; Jessner et al., 1952; Prugh et al., 1953; Skipper & Leonard, 1968; Vernon et al., 1965).

Although these causes overlap, they can be treated as conceptually discrete entities, as a later study will indicate. In the past, there have been three major kinds of preventive therapeutic interventions for hospitalized children. The first offered information. Early research suggested that children could receive information about hospitalization through play therapy (e.g., Prugh et al., 1953) and through puppet shows (e.g., Cassell, 1965; Landes, 1973). Additional research has also indicated that information could be given to parents in order to reduce their child's anxiety (e.g., Haller et al., 1967; Landes, 1973; Skipper & Leonard, 1968).

A second form of intervention has employed a filmed coping model and thus provided not only information but also a model for adaptive responding within the hospital setting (e.g., Vernon & Bailey, 1974). Melamed and Siegel (1975) prepared a 16-minute color film which realistically portrayed a seven-year-old white boy undergoing hernia surgery. Each aspect of hospitalization, from admission to blood tests, from pre-operative injections to post-operative distress was dealt with and the child's initially hesitant and finally adaptive behavior was highlighted by the narrative portion of the film. Children who received various types of surgery and who viewed the film were signficantly less anxious than were children who received traditional forms of information from a nursing staff member.

A series of repeated interactions in which both information and support are offered has been employed in a third form of primary prevention of hospitalized children. Wolfer and Visintainer (1975) trained nurses to interact with parents and children at prespecified stress points throughout the hospitalization. Rather than giving all information on a single occasion prior to surgery, information concerning any stressful procedure was dispensed just prior to each procedure. Children and parents were told exactly what would take place and were given the opportunity to voice concerns and ask questions. An attempt was made to develop a supportive and trusting relationship between the nurse and the child patient. Wolfer and Visintainer (1975) demonstrated that nurse intervention at prespecified stress points resulted in decreased anxiety in both children and adults.

Each of these techniques has attempted to remediate the first two causes of distress in hospitalized children—that is, they have provided information concerning what procedures are to take place during hospitalization, and since most of these techniques have taken place in the hospital, they also provide the child with some familiarity with the hospital environment. However, the third cause of distress—lack of emotional support—has been dealt with only partially in the work by Wolfer and Visintainer, and even their work has not focused on the child's primary emotional support agent—the parent. The final cause, that is, lack of control, has been largely ignored.

All of the previously employed therapeutic techniques have attempted to improve the child's ability to cope with the stress associated with hospitalization and surgery. Coping and self-control have been closely associated concepts within the literature on stress management. Since it has been demonstrated that children can control their own behavior (Ballard & Glynn, 1975; Bandura & Perloff, 1967; Kanfer & Duerfeldt, 1967a, 1967b; Lovitt & Curtiss, 1969), self-control techniques might be taught prior to the onset of threatening events in order to prevent anxiety. Lizette Peterson investigated such a combination of self-control techniques with hospitalized children who were to undergo elective surgery. These behavioral techniques were compared with a filmed modeling technique previously demonstrated to be effective by Melamed and Siegel (1975).

In Peterson's experiment (1978) all subjects received standard information about the hospital routine and also were assigned to one of four cells in a 2 × 2 factorial structure (filmed modeling vs. no filmed modeling and coping vs. no coping).* The information and introduction to the hospital environment, components common to all four groups, were provided via an entertaining puppet show and a tour of the hospital. Subjects were recruited by their pediatric surgeons who invited their child-clients to attend "Big Bird's Ice Cream Party" approximately a week before their scheduled surgery. Children were randomly assigned to experimental conditions prior to each party.

Children in all four groups viewed a "Big Bird" puppet encountering all of the typical situations children encounter in a hospital. In a play scenario, the children saw "Big Bird" pack his suitcase, go to the hospital, go to the admitting office, get a blood test, receive a pre-operative in-

---

*Thanks is extended to the nursing staff of Ward 3 West, St. Marks Hospital in Salt Lake City, Utah. Their enthusiastic help and cooperation were essential to this study. Carol Shigetomi receives special gratitude for her consistently reliable and intelligent help with data collection and manuscript preparation.

jection, and recover from surgery. While this puppet show was originally designed to provide information only, it probably functioned as a stimulus pre-exposure session and provided a puppet-coping model as well. "Big Bird" provided information about hospital procedures and also concerning his initial feelings of fear and his ultimate adaptive behavior in stressful situations. In the process, and in the tour which followed, children were exposed to many of the instruments and procedures they would later experience as patients.

Children in the information-only condition viewed "Big Bird" act out all the behavioral sequences from admission to discharge. Children in the information-plus-self-coping condition went on to hear a description of techniques which "Big Bird" used whenever he drifted too far away from the calm, peaceful feelings that he had at home. Each of three coping skills techniques (relaxation, imagery, and self-talk) was described, modeled by "Big Bird," and then practiced by the children. Parents were told that they would act as the child's primary therapists and that they would train the children in the use of the procedures at home and prompt the child to use them in the hospital. Thus, both children and parents were given training in the use of coping skills. The children first learned *cue-controlled relaxation* (e.g., Russell & Sipich, 1973, 1974), in which they were taught Jacobsonian relaxation techniques, and were then instructed to concentrate on their breathing, and to pair the cue word "calm" with each exhalation. They were then trained to use *distractive imagery* (e.g., Lazarus & Abramovitz, 1962). Parent and child were asked to create an image of a place where the child would feel happy and calm, for example, a favorite picnic place in the mountains. The children were asked to make this image as vivid as possible, including sights, sounds, odors, textures, and so forth. Finally, the children were instructed in *comforting self-talk* (Meichenbaum & Goodman, 1971). They were asked to repeat two phrases either aloud or to themselves: "I will be all better in a little while," and "Everything is going to be all right."

This was the end of the narrative portion of treatment. Children receiving the filmed model then saw "Ethan Has an Operation," the film used by Melamed and Siegel (1975). After the film, all children and their parents went on a tour of the hospital in order to increase their familiarity with the hospital facilities. Then they returned to the treatment room where everyone received ice cream and cookies. Parents also received a written description of the study and their signed permission was solicited. No parent refused permission nor did any subject withdraw from the study. Finally, parents in the coping groups received a booklet describing the three coping techniques which had been presented and parents were requested to record the number of times they practiced each technique. Although the party was organized for tonsillectomy patients, party participants underwent a variety of different types of major and minor surgery. However, a random assignment to experimental conditions resulted in an unequal distribution of major surgery candidates. Data were therefore analyzed only for tonsillectomy patients. Children who had undergone previous surgery, who had been hospitalized in the last year, or who had other medical or psychological problems, were excluded from the subject sample. The final sample consisted of 66 middle-class, white, English-speaking children (35 girls and 31 boys) ages 2.5 to 10.5 with a mean age of 5.4 years.

Since anxiety is widely believed to be a multi-faceted variable (Izard, 1972; McReynolds, 1968), and many researchers (e.g., Melamed & Siegel, 1975; Wolfer, 1973) have suggested that anxiety in hospitalized children should be analyzed in terms of objective, subjective, and physiological data, a variety of blind observational, physiological, and self-report measures were employed in the present study. Briefly, several persons who were blind to the child's experimental condition observed and rated the child. The laboratory technician rated the child's anxiety, cooperativeness, and tolerance for the procedure following the blood test. The parent (who was not blind, but simply uninformed of the other experimental conditions), nurse, and a graduate student observed and rated the child's anxiety and cooperativeness on two 5-point Likert-type scales both before and after surgery. The parent, nurse, and graduate student each independently noted the number of maladaptive behaviors emitted by the child both before and after surgery.

Child self-report and parental self-report were obtained both pre- and post-operatively. Physiological measures such as pulse rate, temperature, time to first post-surgical voiding, and amount of food and liquids consumed after surgery were recorded for each child. Finally, follow-up data were obtained from parent and child two weeks following hospital discharge.

Before presenting the results, it should be emphasized that the author was not attempting to assess whether some treatment was better than no treatment in preventing or reducing children's distress. The control condition was not a no-treatment control, but was rather a minimal treatment condition. Previous research has clearly indicated that children receiving information—which the hospital tour and "Big Bird" ice cream party certainly provided—are less anxious than uninformed children (e.g., Cassell, 1965; Haller et al., 1967; Landes, 1973). The study

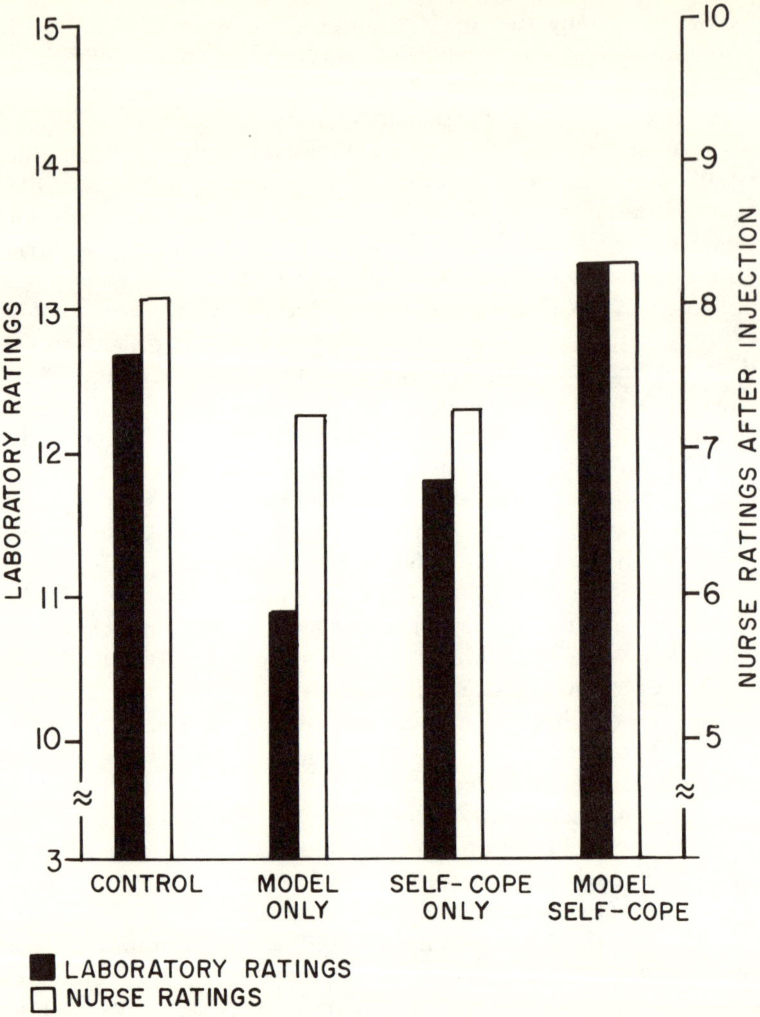

FIGURE 1. Laboratory technician and nurse ratings. Laboratory ratings are a composite of three 1-5 point ratings. Range: 3 (maximum upset) to 15 (maximum calm). Nurse post injection ratings are a composite of two 1-5 point ratings. Range: 2 (maximum upset) to 10 (maximum calm).

was instead an attempt to determine whether the addition of coping-skills training added anything to a set of techniques previously demonstrated to be effective.

Because of the variety of the independent variables used in the study, multivariate analyses were performed on clusters of variables, and only

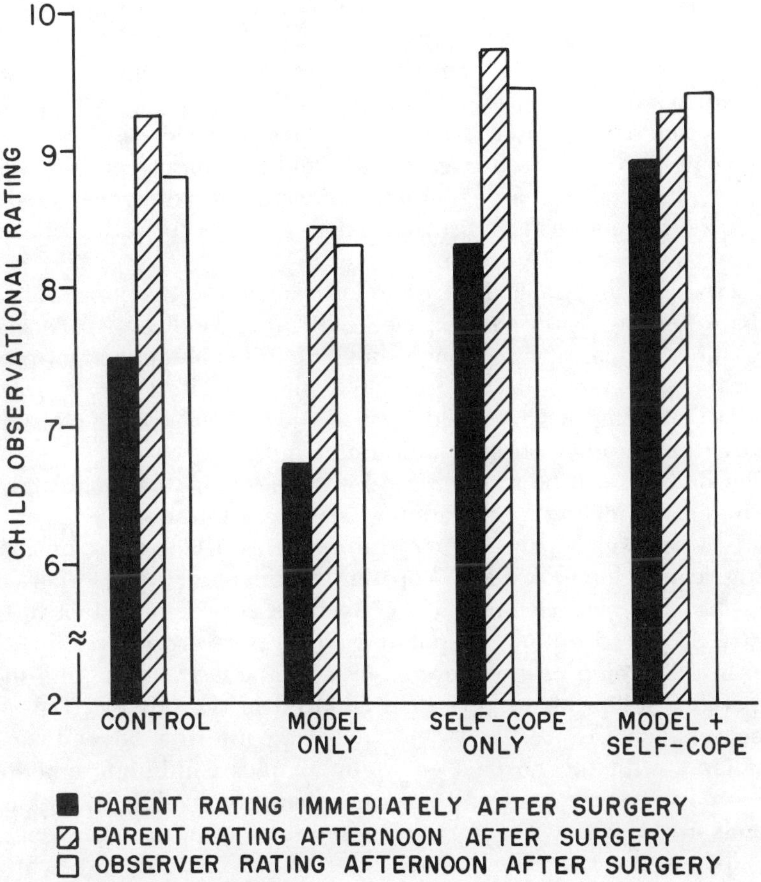

FIGURE 2. Parent and observer ratings following surgery. Scores are a composite of two 1-5 point ratings. Range: 2 (maximum upset) to 10 (maximum calm).

those clusters showing significant multivariate *F*'s are reported here. Observational measures indicated that there were signficant modeling-by-coping interactions when children were asked to endure painful procedures. Both the laboratory technician who drew blood samples and the nurses who gave the pre-operative injections rated the children in the modeling-plus-coping group as least anxious and most cooperative, with increasing anxiety and decreasing cooperativeness noted in the control group, the coping only group, and the modeling only groups, respectively (see Figure 1). Observational ratings from parents and a graduate student observer indicated that following surgery, children in the coping groups were less anxious and more cooperative than children in the other groups (see Figure 2). Moreover, parents receiving the coping instructions rated themselves as feeling more calm and competent, while parents viewing the modeling film (some of whom complained that the realistic portrayal of post-surgical discomfort was frightening) rated themselves as less calm and less competent. Two weeks following hospital discharge, parents in the coping groups also rated the hospital experience as less disturbing than the parents in the other two groups (as shown in Figure 3).

There were no reliable differences in the child's self-report measures, perhaps because approximately one half of the subjects—particularly the younger children—seemingly did not understand the self-report ratings. Finally, there was a marginally significant effect ($p < .09$) showing that following surgery, children in the coping groups ate more than children in the other groups, indicating a quicker recovery.

The findings can be summarized by three major conclusions: a) the coping-plus-modeling combination was superior to the single treatment groups whenever a painful procedure such as a blood test or a preoperative injection took place. Apparently, both observing another child behaving appropriately and having a vehicle to promote adaptive self-control produced optimal responding to invasive procedures. b) Children in the coping groups were observed to be less anxious and more cooperative following surgery than children in the other two groups. Improved behavior resulted from receiving information and an acquaintance with the hospital environment plus continuing emotional support from the parent and a sense of control over the situation. c) Parents in the coping groups rated themselves as more competent and less anxious, and rated the hospital experience as better than the parents in the other groups. The definition of the parent as primary therapist and the administration of self-control techniques to the child apparently aided the parents as well as their children.

There are many promising avenues for future research in the primary prevention of hospitalized children's distress. Modeling techniques may be improved by providing additional information concerning anticipated physical sensations for the child and by defining a supportive role for the parent. Coping procedures may be enhanced by individualizing the technique and by utilizing systematic retraining during preselected stress points, as suggested by Wolfer and Visintainer (1975). Future research will need to deal with cost-benefit considerations; the convenience and consistency of a filmed modeling approach must be compared with the easily accessible and more individualized information and self-

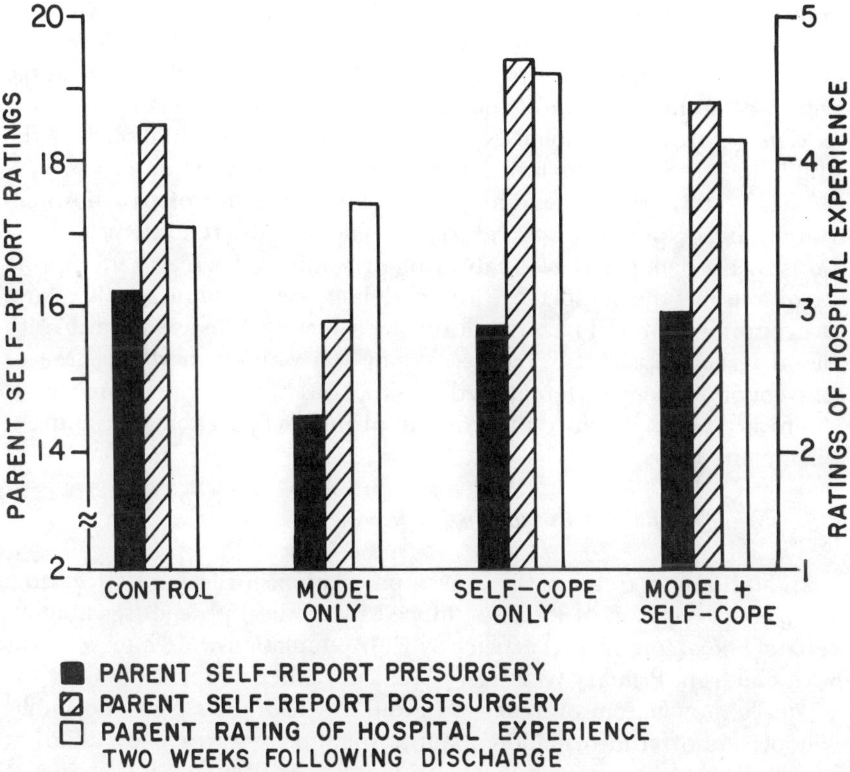

FIGURE 3. Parent ratings. Parent self-report ratings are a composite of two 1-10 point ratings. Range: 2 (maximum upset) to 20 (maximum calm). Parent ratings of the hospital experience two weeks following hospitalization are based on a single rating scale ranging from 1 (worse than I had expected) to 5 (better than I had expected).

coping approaches. Optimal combinations of techniques remain to be determined for various kinds of child surgery patients.

Primary prevention in the future not only will include simple elective surgery candidates but also may deal with critically ill, nonsurgery candidates, with emergency procedures, and with nonelective surgery for life threatening conditions. Wolfer and Visintainer (1978), for example, have begun to investigate the treatment of emergency surgery child patients. Since emergency surgical procedures differ from case to case, preparation must be highly individualized. Nurses must define stress points for each child rather than intervening at pre-arranged times and this necessitates extensive ongoing assessment of the child and his family. Wolfer and Visintainer utilize an energy conservation model, noting that if the child is not stressed by minor occurrences, he or she will have more resources to deal with major dangers and stresses. They suggest that there are many factors to be considered in the individual preparation of a child for emergency surgery, including previous stress experiences, previous hospital experiences, the developmental stage of the child, and his or her current physical and psychological state.

Siegel (1977) is also beginning to explore the effect of past hospitalization and experience on children's anxiety in discrete medical situations such as laboratory blood drawing procedures. He is also attempting to determine the importance of modeling, sensory information, and procedural information on children with no previous experience with blood tests. Thus, future research may not only expand the area of prevention to many different medical situations but may also more clearly delineate the importance of a variety of interacting subjective and environmental variables.

Other Medically-Related Prevention Programs

In addition to treating the at-risk population in the hospital setting, primary prevention of anxiety induced by medical procedures may ultimately be accomplished efficiently with population-wide interventions with children. Primary Children's Medical Center in Salt Lake City, for example, now has an outreach program in which nurses go into public schools and offer information about hospital procedures, allow children to handle and become familiar with medical equipment, and show the children a filmed coping model undergoing medical procedures. An optimal future preventive program might involve comprehensive treatment, beginning with information and in-vivo desensitization prior to hospitalization, and continued individual evaluation and treatment during the entire hospitalization.

The prevention of anxiety in hospitalized children is only one example of future trends in preventive research. Psychological intervention in the fields of health and medicine need not be limited to psychological distress. As the American Psychological Association Task Force on Health Research (1976) has recently reported, psychologists have been underinvolved and underutilized in the study of general health maintenance, of illness prevention, and of health care delivery. Yet, there are many highly preventable health problems such as failure to immunize children against infectious diseases, failure to use discretion in the household storage of toxic substances, and failure to comply with therapeutic dietary regimes in infants, all of which could benefit from behavioral intervention strategies. Familiar techniques such as modeling, information provision, self-control, and reinforcement can be used successfully in the prevention of many health problems. Past prevention efforts utilizing behavioral control procedures range from the prevention of children's seizures using punishment (Zlutnick, Mayville, & Moffat, 1975) to the use of a token economy to prevent induced congestive heart failure in child dialysis patients (Magrib & Papadopoulou, 1977).

Future health related problems to which psychologists might address themselves include increasing exercise, and decreasing obesity and smoking. With a growing understanding of obesity in children (e.g., Aragona, Cassady, & Drabman, 1975; Weiss, 1977), prevention of obesity becomes possible. Also, a large number of teenagers begin to smoke cigarettes each year, despite the well publicized linkage between smoking and a number of lethal diseases. Recently, Evans and his associates (Evans, Rozelle, Mittelmark, Hansen, Bane, & Havis, 1978) have reported a modest degree of success in deterring young people from smoking through an informational program which emphasized: (1) knowledge of immediate unfavorable physiological effects, and (2) methods of coping with peer and media pressure to smoke, and with modeling effects from parental smoking habits. Although the Evans program was not as successful as we might wish, it opens a new and promising field of investigation, and one which might benefit large numbers of people.

The previously mentioned problem of decreasing immunity levels in the population due to failure to get childhood immunizations provides a striking example of the usefulness of behavioral intervention in health care maintenance. Despite the availability of safe and effective vaccines to prevent many infectious diseases, some of which may be fatal, distressingly large numbers of children remain unprotected. This is not because of the expense involved, which is minimal, but rather because parents neglect to bring their children to clinics or to private physicians for immunization. In some impoverished neighborhoods in New York City, diptheria immunization levels among six- to ten-year-olds are as low as 8%, and new cases of diptheria began to occur there in 1977 (Imperato, 1977). Such methods as telephone and postal reminders, home visits to help families overcome transportation problems and other difficulties, and provision of small monetary incentives may prove helpful in increasing the use of medical and dental services, and may be useful in improving immunization levels (Corley, 1978). However, the existing medical care services are too often disorganized and unresponsive to the psychological and social needs of their clientele. Here, too, social scientists may be of service (APA Task Force on Health Research, 1976), because of their special expertise in the area of human relations.

Social scientists might also be profitably involved in preventing medical problems which result from accidents. The use of seatbelts, for example, has been regarded as a psychosocial rather than a medical problem. In one exemplary demonstration of the use of behavioral prevention, Allen and Bergman (1976) demonstrated that self-reported rates of purchase and use of infant restraint devices in automobiles were increased in families who had received descriptive literature or seen filmed demonstrations of the use of these devices. Since highway accidents are the leading cause of death among children between one and 14 years of age, and since more children are injured or killed inside vehicles than as pedestrians (Shelness & Charles, 1975), any measures that would increase the use of child restraint devices in automobiles would save many lives. Thus, preventive efforts by psychologists could be directed toward a wide variety of problems, ranging from purely medical problems to psychological and social-psychological issues.

Conclusion

We cannot stem the tide of child problem behaviors by simply engaging in more treatment. Psychologists and other child mental health workers must adjust their priorities—must undergo a change in lifestyle so as to emphasize *preventing* new disorders in addition to treating existing ones. To further that end, we have described the steps required to mount a prevention program and have discussed programs for training parents, the educationally disadvantaged, teachers, and anxious children. Other potential targets for the preventionist exist in health-related fields.

Prevention may not be an easy task for traditionally trained behavioral psychologists. We may not be able to use some old and trusted repertoires of responses, such as portions of our single subject methodology. We will have to reorient our reinforcer systems. For example, the gratitude of a child or the child's caretaker is unlikely to be forthcoming when the preventionist and the beneficiary never meet, and when the decrement in performance is prevented rather than remediated as it is in treatment. And we will have to acquire new behaviors, including epidemiological, longitudinal, and group experimental design skills.

The effort required to make these changes seems insignificant in comparison to the potential magnitude of the results we may achieve. In assisting in the prevention of children's emotional, neurological, and learning disturbances, we will be promoting one of the most fundamental of children's rights, the right to physical health and psychological well-being (Berlin, 1975).

REFERENCES

Allen, V. L.: *Children as teachers: Theory and research on tutoring.* New York: Academic Press, 1976.

Allen, D. B., & Bergman, A. B.: Social learning approaches to health education: Utilization of infant auto restraint devices. *Pediatrics,* 1976, *58,* 323-328.

APA Task Force on Health Research: Contributions of psychology to health research: Patterns, problems, and potentials. *American Psychologist,* 1976, *31,* 263-274.

Aragona, J., Cassady, J., & Drabman, R. S.: Treating overweight children through parental training and contingency contracting. *Journal of Applied Behavior Analysis,* 1975, *8,* 269-278.

Baer, D. M., Wolf, M. M., & Risley, T. R.: Some current dimensions of applied behavior analysis. *Journal of Applied Behavior Analysis,* 1968, *1,* 91-97.

Ballard, K. D., & Glynn, T.: Behavioral self-management in story writing with elementary school children. *Journal of Applied Behavior Analysis,* 1975, *8,* 387-398.

Bandura, A., & Perloff, B.: Relative efficacy of self-monitored and externally imposed reinforcement systems. *Journal of Personality and Social Psychology,* 1967, *1,* 111-116.

Berlin, I. N.: Some models for reversing the myth of child treatment in community mental health centers. *Journal of the American Academy of Child Psychiatry,* 1975, *14,* 76-94.

Bloom, B. L.: The evaluation of primary prevention programs. In L. M. Roberts, N. S. Greenfield, & M. H. Miller (Eds.), *Comprehensive mental health: The challenge of evaluation.* Madison: University of Wisconsin Press, 1968.

Bowlby, J., Robertson, J., & Rosenbluth, D. A.: A two-year-old goes to the hospital. In R. S. Eissler, A Freud, H. Hartmann, & E. Kris (Eds.), *The psychoanalytic study of the child* (Vol. 7). New York: International Universities Press, 1952.

Bronfenbrenner, U.: Is early intervention effective? In M. Guttentag & E. L. Struening (Eds.), *Handbook of evaluation research,* (Vol. 2). Beverly Hills, Cal.: Sage, 1975.

Caplan, G.: *Principles of preventive psychiatry.* New York: Basic Books, 1964.

Cassell, S.: Effect of brief puppet therapy upon the emotional responses of children undergoing cardiac catheterization. *Journal of Consulting and Clinical Psychology,* 1965, *29,* 1-8.

Chapman, A. H., Loeb, D. G., & Gibbons, M. J.: Psychiatric aspects of hospitalizing children. *Archives of Pediatrics,* 1956, *73,* 77-88.

Chilman, C. S.: Programs for disadvantaged parents. In B. M. Caldwell & H. N. Ricciuti (Eds.), *Review of child development research,* (Vol. 3). Chicago: University of Chicago Press, 1973.

Cochrane, R., & Sobol, M. P.: *Myth and methodology in behavior therapy research.* In M. P. Feldman & A. Broadhurst (Eds.), *Theoretical and experimental bases of the behaviour therapies.* London: Wiley, 1976.

Cook, T., Appleton, H., Connor, R., Shaffer, A., Tamkin, G., & Weber, S.: *Sesame street revisited.* New York: Russell Sage, 1975.

Cooper, B., & Shepherd, M.: Epidemiology and abnormal psychology. In H. J. Eysenck (Ed.), *Handbook of abnormal psychology,* (Vol. 2). San Diego: Knapp, 1973.

Corley, M. J.: *A research proposal for encouraging parents to comply with immunization schedules.* Unpublished paper. University of Utah, 1978.

COWEN, E. L.: Social and community interventions. *Annual Review of Psychology,* 1973, *24,* 423-472.

DEFFENBACHER, J. L.: Relaxation in vivo in the treatment of test anxiety. *Journal of Behavior Therapy and Experimental Psychiatry,* 1976, 7, 289-292.

EVANS, R. I., ROZELLE, R. M., MITTELMARK, M. B., HANSEN, W. B., BANE, A. L., & HAVIS, J.: Deterring the onset of smoking in children: Knowlege of immediate physiological effects and coping with peer pressures, media pressure, and parent modeling. *Journal of Applied Social Psychology,* 1978, *8,* 126-135.

GELFAND, D. M.: *Prevention: Why we must change our priorities.* Invited paper presented at the annual meetings of the Association for the Advancement of Behavior Therapy Atlanta, December, 1977.

GELFAND, D. M., & HARTMANN, D. P.: Behavior therapy with children. A review and evaluation of research methodology. *Psychological Bulletin,* 1968, *69,* 204-215.

GELFAND, D. M., & HARTMANN, D. P.: The prevention of childhood behavior disorders. In B. B. Lahey & A. E. Kazdin (Eds.), *Advances in clinical child psychology* (Vol. 1). New York: Plenum Press, 1977.

GLASGOW, R. E., & ROSEN, G. M.: Behavioral bibliotherapy: A review of self-help behavior therapy manuals. *Psychological Bulletin,* 1978, *85,* 1-23.

GOLDFRIED, M. R.: Systematic desensitization training in self-control. *Journal of Consulting and Clinical Psychology,* 1971, *31,* 228-234.

GOLDFRIED, M. R., DECENTECEO, E. T., & WEINBERG, L.: Systematic rational restructuring as a self-control technique. *Behavior Therapy,* 1974, *5,* 247-254.

GOLDSTON, S. E.: Primary prevention: A view from the federal level. In G. W. Albee & J. M. Joffee (Eds.), *Primary prevention of psychopathology* (Vol. 1). Hanover, N.H.: University Press of New England, 1977.

GUERNEY, B. G. (ED.): *Psychotherapeutic agents: New roles for nonprofessionals, parents and teachers.* New York: Holt, Rinehart and Winston: 1969.

HALL, R. V., & COPELAND, R. E.: The responsive teaching model: A first step in shaping school personnel as behavior modification specialists. In F. W. Clark, D. R. Evans, & L. A. Hamerlynck (Eds.), *Implementing behavioral programs for schools and clinics, Proceedings of the third Banff International Conference on Behavior Modification.* Champaign, Illinois: Research Press, 1972.

HALL, R. V., COPELAND, R., & CLARK, M.: Managment strategies for teachers and parents: Responsive teaching. In N. Haring & R. L. Schiefelbusch (Eds.), *Teaching special children.* New York: McGraw-Hill, 1975.

HALLER, J. A., TALBERT, J. L., & DOMBRO, R. H.: *The hospitalized child and his family.* Baltimore: Johns Hopkins, 1967.

HARTMANN, D. P., ROPER, B. L., & GELFAND, D. M.: An evaluation of alternative modes of child psychotherapy. In B. B. Lahey & A. E. Kazdin (Eds.), *Advances in clinical child psychology* (Vol. 1). New York: Plenum Press, 1977.

HELLER, K., & MONAHAN, J.: *Psychology and community changes.* New York: Dorsey Press, 1977.

HOROWITZ, F. D., & PADEN, L. Y.: The effectiveness of environmental programs. In B. M. Caldwell & H. N. Ricciuti (Eds.), *Review of child development research* (Vol. 3). Chicago: University of Chicago Press, 1973.

IMPERATO, P. J.: Immunization for children: Issues and recommendations. *New York State Journal of Medicine.* 1977, *53,* 1788-1793.

IZARD, G. E.: Anxiety: A variable combination of interacting fundamental emotions. In C. D. Speilberger (Ed.), *Anxiety: Current trends in theroy and research.* New York: Academic Press, 1972.

JACKSON, K., WINKLEY, R., FAUST, O. A., & CERMEK, E. G.: Problem of emotional trauma in hospital treatment of children. *Journal of the American Medical Association,* 1952, *149,* 1536-1538.

JANIS, I. L.: *Psychological stress.* New York: Wiley, 1958.

JENSEN, R. A.: The hospitalized child: Round table. *American Journal of Orthopsychiatry,*

1955, *25,* 293-318.

Jessner, L., Blom, G. E., & Waldfogel, S.: Emotional implications of tonsillectomy and adenoidectomy on children. In R. S. Eissler, A. Freud, H. Hartmann, and E. Kris (Eds.), *The psychoanalytic study of the child.* (Vol. 7). New York: International Universities Press, 1952.

Kanfer, F. H., & Duerfeldt, P. H.: Motivational properties of self-reinforcement. *Perceptual and Motor Skills,* 1967, *25,* 237-246. (a).

Kanfer, F. H., & Duerfeldt, P. H.: Effects of pretraining on self-evaluation and self-reinforcement. *Journal of Personality and Social Psychology,* 1967, *7,* 164-168. (b)

Kazdin, A. E.: Assessing the clinical or applied importance of behavior change through social validation. *Behavior Modification,* 1977, *1,* 427-451.

Kristein, M. M., Arnold, C. B., & Wynder, E. L.: Health economics and prevention care. *Science,* 1977, *195,* 457-462.

Landes, H. R.: Treatment of anxiety in the families of children undergoing tonsillectomy. (Doctoral dissertation, Northwestern University, 1973), *Dissertation Abstracts International,* 1973, *34* 2938B-2939B. (Xerox University Microfilm N. 73-30, 640).

Lazarus, A. A., & Abramovitz, A.: The use of "emotive imagery" in the treatment of children's phobias. *Journal of Mental Science,* 1962, *108,* 191-195.

Levine, M., & Graziano, A. M.: Intervention programs in elementary schools. In S. E. Golann & C. Eisdorfer (Eds.), *Handbook of community mental health.* New York: Appleton-Century-Crofts, 1972.

Lovitt, T. C., & Curtiss, K. A.: Academic response rate as a function of teacher and self-imposed contingencies. *Journal of Applied Behavior Analysis,* 1969, *2,* 49-53.

Magrib, P. R., & Papadopoulou, Z. L.: The effect of a token economy on dietary compliance for children on hemodialysis. *Journal of Applied Behavior Analysis,* 1977, *10,* 573-578.

Mannino, F. V., & Shore, M. F.: The effects of consultation: A review of empirical studies. *American Journal of Community Psychology,* 1975, *3,* 1-21.

Mash, E. J., Handy, L. C., & Hamerlynck, L. A. (Eds.): *Behavior modification approaches to parenting.* New York: Brunner/Mazel, 1976.

Mash, E. J., & Terdal, L. G.: After the dance is over: Some issues and suggestions for follow-up assessment in behavior therapy. *Psychological Reports,* 1977, *41,* 1287-1308.

McReynolds, P. (Ed.): *Advances in psychological assessment.* Palo Alto, California: Science and Behavior Books, 1968.

Meichenbaum, D., & Cameron, R.: Stress inoculation: A skills training approach to anxiety management. Unpublished manuscript, University of Waterloo, 1973.

Meichenbaum, D. H., & Goodman, J.: Training impulsive children to talk to themselves: A means of developing self-control. *Journal of Abnormal Psychology,* 1971, *77,* 115-126.

Melamed, B. G. & Siegel, L. J.: Reduction of anxiety in children facing hospitalization and surgery by use of filmed modeling. *Journal of Consulting and Clinical Psychology,* 1975, *43,* 511-521.

Melamed, B. G., Hawes, R., Heiby, E., & Glick, J.: Use of filmed modeling to reduce uncooperative behavior of children during dental treatment. *Journal of Dental Research,* 1975, *54,* 797-801.

O'Dell, S.: Training parents in behavior modification: A review. *Psychological Bulletin,* 1974, *81,* 418-433.

Patterson, G. R., Reid, J. B., Jones, R. R., & Conger, R. E.: *A social learning approach to family intervention* (Vol 1). Eugene, Oregon: Castalia Publishing Co., 1975.

Peterson, L.: *The use of a self-control procedure to minimize pain and anxiety in hospitalized children,* Unpublished Doctoral Dissertation, University of Utah, 1978.

Peterson, L., & Hartmann, D. P.: Some treatment methodological problems in current child behavior therapy. Paper presented at the annual meetings of the Association for the Advancement of Behavior Therapy. San Francisco, December, 1975.

Poser, E. G.: Toward a theory of "behavioral prophylaxis". *Journal of Behavior Therapy and*

Experimental Psychiatry, 1970, *1,* 39-43.

Poser, E. G.: Strategies for behavioral prevention. In P.O. Davidson (Ed.), *The behavioral management of anxiety, depression and pain.* New York: Brunner/Mazel, 1976.

Poser, E. G., & King, M. C.: *Primary prevention of fear: An experimental approach.* Unpublished manuscript, McGill University, Montreal, 1975.

Powers, E., & Witmer, H.: *An experiment in the prevention of delinquency.* New York: Columbia University Press, 1951.

Powles, J.: On the limitations of modern medicine. *Science, Medicine, and Man,* 1973, *1,* 1-30.

Prugh, D. G., Staub, E. M., Sands, H. H., Kirschbaum, R. M., & Lenihan, E. A.: A study of the emotional reactions of children and families to hospitalization and illness. *American Journal of Orthopsychiatry,* 1953, *23,* 70-106.

Reisinger, J. J., Ora, J. P., & Frangia, G. W.: Parents as change agents for their children: A review. *Journal of Community Psychology,* 1976, *4,* 103-123.

Report of the Joint Commission: *Crisis in child mental healh: Challenge for the 1970's.* New York: Harper & Row, 1969.

Report of the Joint Commission: *The mental health of children: Services, research and manpower.* New York: Harper & Row, 1973.

Rogers-Warren, A., & Warren, S. F.: *Ecological perspectives in behavior analysis.* Baltimore: University Park Press, 1977.

Russell, R. K., & Sipich, J. F.: Cue-controlled relaxation in the treatment of test anxiety. *Journal of Behavior Therapy and Experimental Psychiatry,* 1973, *4,* 47-49.

Russell, R. K., & Sipich, J. F.: Treatment of test anxiety by cue-controlled relaxation. *Behavior Therapy,* 1974, *5,* 673-676.

Sarason, S. B., Levine, M., Goldenberg, I. I., Cherlin, D. L., & Bennett, E. M.: *Psychology in community settings: Clinical, educational, vocational, social aspects.* New York: Wiley, 1966.

Shelness, A., & Charles, S.: Children as passengers in automobiles: The neglected minority on the nation's highways. *Pediatrics,* 1975, *56,* 271-275.

Shigetomi, C., & Barrios, B. A.: *Coping skills training: Potential for prevention of fears and anxieties,* Manuscript submitted for publication, 1978.

Siegel, L. J.: *Therapeutic modeling as a procedure to reduce the stress associated with medical and dental treatment.* Paper presented at the meeting of the annual convention of the Association for Advancement of Behavior Therapy. Atlanta, December, 1977.

Skipper, J. K., & Leonard, R. C.: Children, stress, and hospitalization: A field experiment, *Journal of Health and Social Behavior,* 1968, *9,* 275-287.

Stallings, J.: Implementation and child effects of teaching practices in Follow Through classrooms. *Monographs of the Society for Research in Child Development,* 1975, *40* (Nos. 7-8).

Stuart, R. B.: Teaching facts about drugs: Pushing or preventing. *Journal of Educational Psychology,* 1974, *66,* 189-201.

Suinn, R. M., & Richardson, F.: Anxiety management training: A nonspecific behavior therapy program for anxiety control. *Behavior Therapy,* 1971, *2,* 498-510.

Tavormina, J. B.: Basic models of parent counseling: A critical review. *Psychological Bulletin,* 1974, *81,* 827-835.

Vernon, D. T. A., & Bailey, W. C.: The use of motion pictures in the psychological preparation of children for induction of anesthesia. *Anesthesiology,* 1974, *40,* 68-74.

Vernon, D. T. A., Foley, J. M., Sipowicz, R. R., & Shulman, J. L.: *The psychological responses of children to hospitalization and illness.* Springfield, Illinois: Thomas, 1965.

Wade, T. C., & Baker, T. B.: Opinions and use of psychological tests: A survey of clinical psychologists. *American Psychologist,* 1977, *32* 874-882.

Wade, T. C., Baker, T. B., & Hartmann, D. P.: Behavior therapists' self reported views and practices. *The Behavior Therapist,* 1979, *2,* 3-6.

Weiss, A. R.: A behavioral approach to the treatment of adolescent obesity. *Behavior Therapy,* 1977, *8,* 720-726.

WHITE, S. H., DAY, M. C., FREEMAN, P. K., HARTMAN, S. A., & MESSENGER, K. P.: Federal Programs for young children: Review and recommendations (Vol. 3). *Recommendations for federal program planning.* Department of Health, Education, and Welfare, 1973.

WOLFER, J. A.: Definition and assessment of surgical patients' welfare and recovery: selected review of the literature. *Nursing Research,* 1973, *22,* 394-401.

WOLFER, J. A., & VISINTAINER, M. A.: Pediatric surgical patients' and parents' stress responses and adjustment. *Nursing Research,* 1975, *24,* 244-255.

WOLFER, J. A., & VISINTAINER, M. A.: *Studies in the Psychological Care of the Pediatric Patient.* Nursing research colloquia, University of Utah, Salt Lake City, January, 1978.

ZLUTNICK, S., MAYVILLE, W. J., & MOFFAT, S.: Modification of seizure disorders: The interruption of behavioral chains. *Journal of Applied Behavioir Analysis,* 1975, *8,* 1-12.

8

Lifestyle Change on the Campus: Pilot Test of a Program to Improve Student Health Practices

AUREA CORMIER, MARIELLE PREFONTAINE,
HELEN MACDONALD,
and RICHARD B. STUART

THE HEALTH CARE CRISIS

Much has been written about the role of modern medical technology in efforts to prolong life and to ease the pains of living. Indeed, great strides have been made in extending average life expectancy, but these gains are in certain respects more illusory than real. Some technological efforts such as advances in the control of pain may actually contribute to a deterioration in the strength of health behaviors.

This research was supported by a grant from the Research Program, Health Programs Branch, Health and Welfare Canada.

Between 1900 and 1966, average life expectancy in the United States advanced from 49.2 to 70.1 years. But most of this gain can be explained by a decrease in infant and child mortality rather than by the conquest of the diseases affecting adults. Indeed, while the twentieth century has witnessed an extension of 15 years of life expectancy for newborns, the average person of 65 has gained only 2.7 years during these eight decades of technological advance. Moreover, this increased life expectancy owes more to advances in the control of infectious diseases through inoculation, to improved water and milk supplies and to improved living conditions and sewage disposal systems than to the eradication of the most common diseases (Knowles, 1977b). For example, in 1974, 39% of all deaths were attributable to cardiovascular disease. But with the exception of the antibiotic control of rheumatic heart disease and the surgical remedy of certain congenital heart problems, most of the medical advances in this area have been of a secondary preventive nature and have taken the form of high-technology coronary care units and specialized ambulances to convey patients to these units (Thomas, 1977). In the same vein, no methods have yet been discovered for reversing the development of neoplasms which accounted for 19% of the deaths in 1974; no methods have been developed for reliably reducing the recurrence of cerebrovascular diseases which accounted for 11% of the 1974 deaths; methods for coping with kidney disease (10.4% of the 1974 deaths) are limited to compensating for the loss of renal function rather than to reversing the disease process (Thomas, 1977). Medical science has therefore done little to control many of the diseases affecting adults and has turned, instead, to a less than wholehearted effort to promote health maintenance behaviors through lifestyle change.

The role of lifestyle forces in promoting ill-health has been strikingly noted by John Knowles, President of the Rockefeller Foundation, with the observation that: ". . . over 99% of us are born healthy and made sick as a result of personal misbehavior and environmental conditions" (Knowles, 1977b, p. 58). Patterns of malnutrition (including eating an excess of poorly chosen foods), of pathogenic inactivity, of excessive use of drugs (from caffeine and alcohol to stimulants and depressants), and passivity with regard to environmental hazards (such as poor air, contaminated water and noise pollution) constitute the major known causes of avoidable illnesses in Western societies (Haggerty, 1977). Data from the Alameda County, California studies have shown that self-reported health status is significantly related to such health practices as regularity in mealtimes and hours of sleep, moderation in smoking and drug use, and adequate patterns of physical activity (Belloc & Breslow, 1972). The same observations in the famed Framingham Study led to the conclusion that:

> the *only* hope for a major impact on coronary mortality lies in primary prevention . . . by the development of public health measures which will favorably change environmental and host factors . . includ(ing) improved regimens of both diet and exercise, elimination of cigarette smoking, and reduction of weight and blood pressure (Dawber & Kannel, 1972, p. 400). (Italics added)

The habit disturbances that contribute to ill health are not merely a matter of individual misbehavior. In his often quoted "tale of two states," economist Victor Fuchs noted that Utah and Nevada are:

> contiguous states that enjoy about the same levels of income and medical care and are alike in many other respects but their levels of health differ enormously. The inhabitants of Utah are among the healthiest individuals in the United States, while the residents of Nevada are at the opposite end of the spectrum . . . What, then, explains these huge differences? . . . The answer almost surely lies in the different lifestyles of the residents of the two states (Fuchs, 1974, p. 16).

While differential breeding and age compositions can account for some of the difference in health between these two locales, culturally influenced individual lifestyle decisions about diet, exercise and drug use (as well as differing environmental qualities) are surely important contributors to the health superiority of residents of Utah.

Despite repetition of such findings in virtually every serious investigation, members of our Western societies continue to eat as though our bulging waistlines will never bring on the many varied and crippling coronary and related diseases; we smoke as though our blackening lungs will not spawn neoplasms; we alter the chemistry of our brains as though our neurological systems were endlessly forgiving of our excesses, and we avoid activity like a plague as though to lull our resting hearts into premature eternal rest.

The absence of health behaviors is attributable to many different causes. The first of these is an at best ambivalent commitment by both the medical and general communities to health maintenance. Again, Knowles (1977a, p. 5) observed that "the health industry is pluralistic, competitive and essentially committed to the tenets of a laissez-faire ethos." Among the expressions of this disinterest are the following facts:

(1) Of a total expenditure of over 128 billion dollars for health

care in the United States in 1976, less than 2.5 percent was spent on prevention (American College of Preventive Medicine, 1976, pp. 6-7);

(2) While the American Hospital Association includes health education as an "integral part of high quality health care . . ." only a handful of the nation's 7,000 hospitals maintain even a token health education program (ibid., p. 22);

(3) While the "Forward Plan for Health for FY 1976-80," the master plan for health cost reimbursement for the United States, proclaims that prevention is the highest order of health priorities, reimbursement for preventive care is specifically prohibited by the plan;

(4) While the National Heart and Lung Institute was allocated 175 million dollars in 1975, the United States Department of Agriculture placed its highest "prime" rating on the beef with the highest fat content (U.S. Office of Management and Budget, 1975, p. 395);

(5) While one in four children examined in a national survey has been found to be in need of care for dental caries (Weinberger, 1975), the American government paid 91.5 million dollars as subsidies for sugar production in this country in 1975 (U.S. Office of Management and Budget, 1975, p. 142); and

(6) While as early as 1964, the U.S. Surgeon General identified the health hazards of smoking, the United States Government continues to encourage tobacco growth through direct subsidies for farmers, price supports, tobacco grading, and research programs aimed at increasing crop yields.

With paradoxes such as these endemic in our medical and governmental institutions, it is not surprising that the proverbial "man on the street" is more likely to weaken his health than to take any steps to enhance it.

The dramatic breakthroughs made by the pharmacologists in the conquest of polio and the spectacular advances in surgery for such things as heart repair and kidney transplant are other forces behind the weakening of our health care practices. These advances have contributed to the belief that the medical profession can take care of all that ails us. This, coupled with the development of a medical establishment employing over 4.5 million people in America, an establishment which polemicist Ivan Illich has termed a "medical nemesis" (1974), has conspired to lull Americans into giving up responsibility for their own health and into relying, instead, on ever-ready drugs to painlessly overcome the problem. Illich (1974) notes that the management of pain has been a cultural imperative since the dawn of civilization, and that the containment of pain is an important stimulant to constructive behavior.

However, when society organizes to render pain unnecessary it thereby makes pain unbearable. With pain culturally defined as an unsupportable stress, flight from pain at any cost (e.g., addiction) seems warranted. Moreover, when the burden of pain for one's excesses is lifted through a gesture as slight as the taking of a pill, the motivation to avoid the illnesses that culminate in discomfort all but vanishes.

Along with the culture of the "wonder drug" and the "miracle of science" and the relative abolition of pain, individual responsibility for personal health has been weakened by two additional forces: the proliferation of health insurance and broad spectrum changes in cultural attitudes.

Between 1963 and 1975, the cost of an average 7.7 day stay in an American hospital rose from $270.35 to $1,030.34 (American Hospital Association, 1977). During this time, the percent of American citizens whose hospitalizations were paid for by third-party carriers rose over threefold, to between 80 and 90% of all those under 65 years of age (Mueller & Piro, 1976). This has lead to a situation in which:

> about 90% of all hospital-care expenditures was paid by third-party payers (37% was covered by private health insurance; 53% was paid for by the government); 60% of payments for physicians' services came from third parties, leaving 40% to direct payment by consumers (Knowles, 1977b, p.2.).

Increased technology of care and increased labor and material costs have certainly contributed to the rising cost of hospitalization, but so, too, has the removal of the consumer as an interested monitor of the cost of care (Klarman, 1977). Even more serious, however, is the fact that the removal of much of the financial burden of illness has served to weaken just one more source of motivation to preserve health. In effect, full health care coverage creates a condition in which the individual can play now and allow Blue Cross to pay later.

Weakened by the expectation that medicine will come through with a cure-all and with freedom from the threats of physical and financial pain, many of us are small match for the pressure of a culture that is madly in pursuit of pleasure, cheered on by an unprecedented increase in discretionary income, and full-voiced advertising campaigns that point the way to unending excess (American College of Preventive Medicine, 1976). We are urged to ride where we could walk, to press a button to complete tasks that could be done as well with the application of small effort, and to watch rather than to participate ourselves in many recreational pursuits. Moreover, when these pastimes fail to bring us to the level of expected pleasure, we are promised instant emotional release through the use of drugs in smoke, drink, and multi-colored capsules.

Means for Promoting Better Health Practices

Several changes have been suggested as means for promoting healthier lifestyles. Consistent with the admonition that, "The society which can reduce professional intervention to the minimum will provide the best conditions for health" (Illich, 1975, p. 167), several writers have advocated the use of " 'managerial prevention' through external controls, laws, and technological 'bypass' " (Haggerty, 1977, p. 283). For example, the reduction in deaths caused by auto accidents following the lowering of the speed limit, the reduction of dental caries following the introduction of fluoridation, and the reduction in poisoning deaths following introduction of child-proof caps for medicine bottles are all indications of positive outcomes from such managerial decisions (Haggerty, 1977; Dawber & Kannel, 1972). Other programs such as the restricted use of carcinogenic dyes in food and cosmetics, federally supervised standards for the testing of new drugs and air quality-control measures have a rather high probability of producing further productive lifestyle changes. These varied procedures can be classified according to whether they limit the *production* of potentially harmful agents, and/or prohibit or restrict the *use* of these agents. While the proponents of the methods are quick to point out that any such measures limit individual freedom and may promote better health through an intolerable compromise of individual freedom, other writers such as Knowles (1977b, p. 59) have pointed out the vast social costs of many of these individual decisions. He writes:

> The cost of sloth, gluttony, alcoholic intemperance, reckless driving, sexual frenzy, and smoking is now a national and not an individual responsibility. This is justified as individual freedom—but one man's freedom in health is another man's shackle in taxes and insurance premiums.

When the costs of one person's exposure to another's exhaled smoke and exhaust fumes, the costs of exposure to loss of life and limb through imprudent driving, as well as the cost of delayed medical attention for unavoidable problems (made necessary by the over-utilization of medical facilities from demands for treatment of the avoidable illnesses), are added to the financial costs, a stronger argument can be made that managerial intervention may be necessary to protect the rights of the careful to a quiet and healthful enjoyment of their lives.

The provision of a range of commercially sponsored health care resources—from centers training clients in meditation (Marlatt & Marques, 1977) through health spas, to skilled training in weight management (Stuart, 1977a)—is evidence for an expanding popular awareness of the need for greater attention to personal health care. So, too, is the proliferation of self-help manuals for which there appears to be an ever-growing market, best exemplied by *Our Bodies, Ourselves* which has been produced by the Boston Women's Health Collective (1973). In addition, increased pressure upon all levels of government to provide added park and recreation space, and increased pressure by labor for job-site resources for physical activity are further indications of the popular growth of health behavior awareness. All of these programs, however, depend upon the success of a very generalized program of health education.

In terms of the scope of its potential effects, health education is a close second to managerial intervention in the promotion of healthy lifestyles. Health education is important for at least three major reasons: (1) it has been observed that as many as 90% of those who think that they are well actually suffer from some treatable illness (Zola, 1973); (2) many of the problems that lead to serious adult illnesses are the result of lifestyles that develop early in childhood; and (3) education can, in principle, help to train individuals to self-diagnose many deficiencies in lifestyle so that training can be expected to generalize across newly occurring health stresses. "Health education" has been defined as including activities which:

> (1) inform people about health, illness, disability, and ways in which they can improve and protect their own health, including more efficient use of the delivery system;
> (2) motivate people to want to change to more healthful practices;
> (3) help them to learn the necessary skills to adapt and maintain healthful practices and lifestyles; . . . (American College of Preventive Medicine, 1976, p. 3).

Health education can be provided in varied formats; it can be offered to the healthy public, the "worried well," and to the ill, directly or through the education of significant others (such as family members). It can be provided by primary health care workers or through auxiliary lifestyle-influencing programs in schools, libraries, public health settings and other community settings. Unfortunately, most of those who have studied the effects of health education programs have rated them somewhere between being merely "unsuccessful" (Haggerty, 1977, p. 279), to being "nothing more than a slogan" (American College of Preventive

Medicine, 1976, p. 12), to being: "abysmal at best, confining themselves to preemptory sick calls and posters on brushing teeth and eating three meals a day . . (with) no examinations to determine if anything has been learned" (Knowles, 1977b, p. 61). Indeed, when measurement has been undertaken to assess the effects of well-intended programs, the data have sometimes indicated that the programming was actually iatrogenic rather than merely missing the mark (e.g., Stuart, 1974).

To be useful, health education aimed at lifestyle change seems to require several characteristics:

(1) The program should be targeted to the "worried well," those who have become aware of their vulnerability to certain of their own behaviors (Gochman, 1972).
(2) Because many health oriented behaviors are counter-cultural (Mettlin, 1976), group presentations are often helpful as a means of providing social support for attitudinal changes that may be necessary precursors for changes in health behaviors (Janis & King, 1958).
(3) Because the simple offering of advice has rarely been associated with changes in behavior, the group techniques should encourage active participation by learners (Lewin, 1947).
(4) In addition, the group procedure should maximize participants' perceptions of their own developing self-mastery, a feat often well accomplished in self-help group contexts (Stuart, 1977b).
(5) Finally, there is some evidence that programs are more effective when they ask for changes of behaviors in several areas, possibly because this permits greater opportunity for individual commitment to an area of change that is personally meaningful (Meyer & Henderson, 1974), and partly because an opportunity for generalization training is afforded when the core principles are applied across several behaviors.

When these service delivery techniques are utilized in a program that disseminates the rapidly evolving technology of behavioral self-management (e.g., Katz & Zlutnick, 1975; Stuart, 1977a), and when the programs are offered to participants before their behavioral patterns have become rigid—e.g., college age or earlier—there is good reason to be hopeful about the long-range impact of well designed and carefully evaluated health education programs.

Rationale of the Present Program

The present program sought to promote changes in health behaviors among students at the University of Moncton, using a guided group discussion method. Five clusters of health behaviors were included in the program. The rationale and specific procedures for each of these clusters are presented below.

Management of Stress

Beginning in the mid-1950s, Friedman and Rosenman (1971) noted that there are many exceptions to the familiar bromides that dietary excesses, excessive serum lipids, chronic inactivity, and smoking were inevitably followed by the occurrence of coronary heart diseases (CHD). They further noted that the apparent immunity of white American females from the high risk of CHD faced by males could not be attributed to either dietary or hormonal differences and that higher rates of CHD were common in some, as opposed to other, cultures. They reasoned that the same force could explain both the sex and cultural differentials in vulnerability to CHD: a greater exposure to a high stress environment. They then differentiated two different modes of response to these environmental pressures: Type A responders engaged in a chronic struggle to achieve maximally despite very tight deadlines and considerable opposition, while Type B responders were far less likely to struggle against the barriers that would slow their productivity (Friedman & Rosenman, 1974). They found, for example, that Type As worked 54 hours weekly as opposed to the 42-hour work week of the Type Bs, that the Type As were far more physically active than the Type Bs, in addition to smoking more, and having generally far more "hard driving" life styles (Rosenman & Friedman, 1963). For example, when compared with Type Bs, Type As were far more impatient and worked to capacity despite the futility of meeting deadlines (Carver, Coleman, & Glass, 1976). They further demonstrated that while the Type As were more likely than the Type Bs to suffer from blood lipid abnormalities (e.g., Friedman, Rosenman, & Byers, 1964), even with lipid levels controlled, Type As were more likely to suffer from CHD than were Type Bs (Rosenman, Friedman, & Jenkins, 1966). Moreover, they were able to demonstrate that the presence of Type A behavior patterns was an effective predictor of the incidence of CHD (Rosenman, Friedman, Straus, Wurm, Kositchek, Hawn & Werthesen, 1964; Rosenman, Friedman, Straus, Wurm, Messinger & Jenkins, 1966). Given the weight of this evidence, and the fact that prototypic behavioral differences have been observed in children as young as 10 years of age (Butensky, Faralli, Hubner & Waldron, 1976), a decision was made to attempt to train participants in this program in stress reduction techniques. At this stage,

FIGURE 1
Relaxation Session

1. DISCUSS BENEFITS OF RELAXATION

2. EXPLAIN RELAXATION PROCEDURE
   A. TAKE COMFORTABLE POSITION, CLOSE EYES
   B. RELAX THROUGH ALTERNATE MUSCLE CONTRACTION
   C. BREATHING EXERCISE REPEATING ONE SYLLABLE WORD
   D. ALLOW 10-20 MINUTES PER RELAXATION

3. PRESCRIBE RELAXATION PRACTICE ONE OR TWO TIMES DAILY AT LEAST TWO HOURS AFTER MEALTIMES

participants were taught relaxation techniques as a means of coping with stress reactions; later, participants were taught means of avoiding stress by reprogramming their social environments and by planning for leisure activities.

Relaxation procedures developed by Jacobson (1970) during the 1930s have been used to treat a variety of problems including asthma, migrane headaches, seizures, and tics (Katz & Zlutnick, 1975). In the present context it was believed that relaxation training could serve both to ease tension levels at the start of the students' days and to help them to respond with less tension to the stresses encountered during the day. The procedures used have been fully described elsewhere (Stuart, 1978) and are briefly summarized in Figure 1.

Increased Physical Activity

Data from projects such as the Framingham Study have repeatedly noted that: "physical inactivity . . . appears to promote higher mortality in coronary attacks independent of associated risk factors . . ." (Dawber & Kannel, 1972, p. 507) (see, too: Frank, Weinblatt, Shapiro & Sager, 1960; Cassel, 1971). While these correlational data cannot establish a positive link between inactivity and elevated risk for CHD, they certainly support the possibility that inactivity contributes significantly to higher risk levels. Inactivity rather than hyperphagia was also believed to account for differences in the weight status of participants in the nationwide Nutrition Canada survey (Nutrition Canada, 1975). Two reviews (Fox & Haskell, 1968; Stuart, 1975) have summarized the findings of many studies concerned with the effects of increased activity on factors associated with elevated CHD risk and other problems. For example, increased exercise can increase capacity for coronary flow and oxygen delivery (Schever, Penpargkil, & Bhan, 1974); it can lower heart rate (Redwood, Rosing, & Epstein, 1972); it can decrease triglyceridemia (Holloszy, Skinner, Toro & Cureton, 1964); it can lower blood pressure in both hypertensives and normotensives (Boyer, & Kasch, 1970); it can mildly reduce cholesterol levels (Mann, Garrett, Farhi, Murray & Billings, 1969); it can improve psychological mood (Folkins, 1976); and it can improve fitness in general (Bonanno & Lies, 1974). While the results of evaluations of exercise programs have not always been consistent, there is nonetheless a preponderance of evidence that increased physical activity can lower the risk of cardiovascular disease, and that the risk factors are as much a problem for young adults as for those of middle or advanced age (Wein & Wilcox, 1972). Therefore, considerable support exists for inclusion of efforts to increase physical activity in programs offered to college students.

This program made use of a low intensity, long duration exercise program that would adapt to the rigorous schedules of most students' lives, that would require no special equipment and that could be practiced every day. The specific rationale for the program has been described elsewhere (Stuart, 1978; Stuart & Davis, 1972) and the techniques used are summarized in Figure 2.

Assertiveness

Friedman and Rosenman (1971) differentiate the stress reactions of the Type A from anxiety reactions found in most people in the general population at some time. In their words: "The Type A person usually confidently advances to grapple with his challenges; the subject with true anxiety neuroses despondently retreats before his . . ." (p. 302). If this distinction is valid, then a different set of techniques is needed for stress management (relaxation in the present program) than is needed for the control of anxiety. In the present program, training in assertiveness was chosen because it could help to reprogram social forces that are anxiety producing, could specifically train the students in behaviors that are directly contrary to anxiety responses, and could promote actions that would combat the inactivity of mild depressive reactions as well.

Mood problems—both anxiety and depression—have been found to be associated with heightened risk for varied cardiovascular diseases in many studies in both the United States and abroad (e.g., Eastwood & Trevelyan, 1971; Friedman, Ury, Klatsky, & Seigelaub, 1974; Greene, Goldstein, & Moss, 1972; Medalie, Paier, Goldbourt, & Herman, 1975;

FIGURE 2
Exercise Session

1. DISCUSS ADVANTAGES OF EXERCISE (e.g., coronary vascular conditioning, changing of blood chemistry and mood, and decrease in appetite).

2. EXPLAIN EXERCISE PROCEDURE:
   A. RATE OF EXERCISE IMPORTANT FOR CARDIOVASCULAR CONDITIONING
   B. DISTANCE IMPORTANT FOR ENERGY EXPENDITURE
   C. REVIEW PARTICIPANTS' NORMAL EXERCISE PATTERN
   D. SUGGEST WALKING OR OTHER LOW INTENSITY, LONG DURATION EXERCISE DAILY IN ADDITION TO NORMAL ACTIVITY.

3. DISCUSS BARRIERS TO FOLLOW-THROUGH (e.g., use of cars, spectator sports, exercise as counter-cultural).
4. SUGGEST USING BUDDY SYSTEM, SELECTION OF FIT TIME DAILY FOR EXERCISE, AND OTHER MEANS OF INCREASING FOLLOW-THROUGH.

Perlman, Ferguson, Bergum, Isenberg & Hammersten, 1975; Theil, Parker, & Bruce, 1973; Weiss, Dlin, Rollin, Fisher, & Bepler, 1957). Typically, these investigators and others like them have found both chronic and acute anxiety and depression to be prodromal signs of coronary disease and possibly to have played a key role in its etiology. One explanation for this connection might be the role of anxiety and depression in catalyzing anger reactions which in turn may precipitate cardiac stress (Johns, 1973; Romo, Siltmen, Theorell, & Rahe, 1974). In addition, tension, depression, anger and boredom (the control of which is sought in our fourth step) were all moods that have consistently been observed to serve as antecedents of problem eating (Stuart, 1978). For these health reasons, as well as in an effort to help to improve the psychological climate of the students' lives, training was offered in assertive behavior. The rationale for the program and greater detail concerning its operation can be found elsewhere (Stuart, 1978), with the major points summarized in Figure 3.

Management of Leisure and Sleep

Some years ago, it was noted that the risk factors to which college students were exposed included: inadequate sleep, poor use of leisure time, excessive psychological tension, inactivity and a general lack of self-fulfillment through opportunities for achieving discernable success (Johnson, Terry, Gaines, & Humphrey, 1962). Indeed, the management of leisure time, defined as activities "to which the individual turns at will

FIGURE 3
Self-assertiveness Session

1. DISCUSS BENEFITS OF ASSERTIVENESS: (e.g., can lower emotional tension and prompt behavior that changes life-experience for lasting mood control).

2. DISCUSS DEFENSE MECHANISMS AGAINST CRITICISM AND MANIPULATION.
   THAT SUBVERT ASSERTIVENESS OR HELP IT:
   A. Broken Record
   B. Workable Compromise
   C. Self-Disclosure
   D. Fogging
   E. Negative Inquiry
   F. Negative Assertion

3. DESCRIBE BELIEFS ESSENTIAL TO ASSERTIVENESS:
   A. Excuses not needed to justify behavior.
   B. Determine whether it is your job to solve other's problems.
   C. Changing your mind is okay when you accept responsibility for having done so.
   D. It's okay to make mistakes so long as you take responsibility for having done so.
   E. Decisions must be made logically.
   F. You must accept the responsibilities that are rightfully yours.

4. PARTICIPANTS TOLD TO PRACTICE ASSERTIVE BEHAVIOR TO CHANGE SITUATIONS THAT ARE TROUBLING TO THEM.

for either relaxation or diversion" (Newman, 1976), has been viewed as a problem for people of all ages: for many, passive leisure time pursuits have become as monotonous and as unfulfilling as poorly selected jobs. The impact of the commitment to passive *versus* active, and to pleasing *versus* dull leisure time pursuits is clearly reflected in the self-rated level of physical health reported by large segments of the adult population (Belloc & Breslow, 1972). While psychological energy level may help to determine who does and who does not seek out active leisure time pursuits, it is also reasonable to assume that, like physical health, emotional health would also be strongly influenced by pleasing participation in leisure time activities.

Sleep regularity has also been shown to be associated with improved levels of physical and emotional health. Belloc and Breslow (1972) found that among both men and women, those who slept an average of seven to eight hours per night were somewhat more likely to report themselves as healthy than those who slept an average of nine or more hours per night, and they were significantly more likely to perceive themselves as healthy when compared with those sleeping six or fewer hours nightly. Evidence reviewed by Stuart (1978) similarly showed that while mini-

FIGURE 4
Leisure and Sleep Session

1. LEISURE
   A. DISCUSS BENEFITS OF LEISURE (e.g., association between actions and emotions, role of relaxation in fostering emotions that are positive, role of leisure in overcoming boredom and improving work performance
   B. POINT OUT NEED TO SCHEDULE LEISURE BREAKS PLANNING BOTH WHEN THEY WILL BE TAKEN AND HOW TIME WILL BE SPENT IN PERSONALLY SATISFYING MANNER
   C. PRESCRIBE LEISURE PLANNING FOR THE WEEK.

2. SLEEP
   A. DISCUSS BENEFITS OF SLEEP TO COMBAT DEPRESSION, IMPROVE GENERAL PERFORMANCE
   B. DISCUSS INDIVIDUAL DIFFERENCES IN SLEEP PATTERNS, IMPROVE GENERAL PERFORMANCE
   C. PRESCRIBE FOR WEEK
      1. Decision of retiring, waking time ± 30 minutes.
      2. Set stage for uninterrupted sleep by omitting tea and coffee after 4 p.m., cutting down on all fluids before bedtime, avoiding the evening consumption of alcoholic beverages and avoidance of daytime naps.
      3. Avoid reading in bed.
      4. Use soft music to mask disturbing sounds at bedtime.
      5. Try to concentrate on neutral thoughts at bedtime.
      6. Practice relaxation just prior to retiring.

mum sleep needs were highly variable across individuals, those who slept from seven to eight hours per night were more likely than others to report positive moods and less likely to report themselves to be given to fatigue-motivated overeating and emotional distress.

Because college students are very likely to be highly irregular in their pursuit of satisfying leisure time activities, and to endure highly irregular sleep patterns, inclusion of these two dimensions of lifestyle management in our program seemed highly desirable. An outline of the procedures used is presented in Figure 4.

Management of Eating Patterns

While the data are only correlational, there are strong indications that weight control has a place of critical importance in all programs aimed at promoting health behavior. For example, it has been found that for every 100 average weight young men who die, only 71 underweight, 151 moderately overweight and 212 severely overweight men will die (Berkowitz, 1972). While overweight per se may not be a cause of death, few overweight adults escape the risk of suffering a life-shortening ill-

FIGURE 5
Nutrition Session

1. PRESENT RATIONALE FOR WISE FOOD SELECTION.
2. ENUMERATE MAJOR NUTRIENTS INCLUDING THEIR ROLE IN MAINTAINING HEALTH AND THEIR SOURCES.
3. STRESS IMPORTANCE OF REGULAR MEALTIME PATTERNS INCLUDING BREAKFAST.
4. DISCUSS SNACK FOODS INCLUDING COMPARISON OF 100 KCAL. PORTIONS OF DIFFERENT FOODS INDICATING COST, NUTRITIONAL CONTENT AND ADDITIVES IN EACH.
5. LAST SESSION—THEREFORE NO PRESCRIPTION WAS GIVEN.

ness. For example, men who are as little as 20% overweight have more than ten times the normal risk of becoming hypertensive (Kannel, Brand, & Skinner, 1967) and over four times the normal probability of becoming diabetic (Medalie et al., 1975). Moreover, it has long been known that the chances of developing hypertension and diabetes return to normal when the overweight lose their extra pounds (Berkowitz, 1964; Newburgh, 1942; Terry, 1923).

Because obesity increases with age (Wein & Wilcox, 1972), it is important to intervene as early in the life cycle as possible to reduce exposure to risk factors. This intervention should ideally include training in food selection, portion control, regulating meals and reducing the urge to eat excessive quantities of the correct foods or any amount of problem foods. Health status, as measured by Belloc and Breslow (1972) was shown to be associated with the regularity of eating breakfast and with the relative avoidance of snacking, while Meyer and Henderson (1974) found that overcoming the difficult challenge of substituting fish and chicken for meat could lead to substantial improvements in weight and other CHD risk factors. The method through which this program addressed change in dietary habits is summarized in Figure 5.

FORMAT OF THE PROGRAM

The lifestyle change modules were introduced to participants who met as a group for 75 minutes. During an introductory session, participants were informed about the general content of the program, they were asked to agree to the pre- and postreatment data collections as well as to keeping some daily compliance data, they were asked to attend all sessions and to make a $5.00 deposit which would be returned contingent upon their meeting all of the above requirements. Finally, they were offered a rationale for participating in a program aimed at modifying lifestyles and were promised the opportunity to receive feedback about their own and the group outcome following completion of the program.

Beginning with the second session, an entire meeting was devoted to the presentation of each of the modules. Participants were asked to complete daily compliance records (see Appendix A) for each of the modules, with the exception of that devoted to dietary habits, as this was the final meeting of the group. Results of these daily records were discussed in subsequent sessions.

Sessions were begun mid-way into the fall semester, 1976, at the University of Moncton. Between the second and third weeks students were off campus for a semester break and the final session was held during the week just prior to final examinations. Both of these factors had an impact upon compliance and possibly upon outcome, as will be discussed below.

Participants

The entire freshman class of the University of Moncton was eligible for participation in this program. Of a total population of 794, 125 names were selected at random: 61 males and 64 females. Those who had telephones were called; those who had no telephones were reached by a personal visit. Twenty-six (42.6%) of the males contacted and 46 (72.0%) of the females contacted agreed to participate. These 68 students comprised the experimental group. A control group was selected by drawing 70 additional names at random from the freshman class. The students in the control group were asked to complete the pencil-and-paper questionnaire also completed by those in the experimental group, but were not asked to participate in the biomedical measurements made of that group. Forty-five of those approached agreed to cooperate in this way: 21 males and 24 females.

Dependent Variables

Following the first session, students were asked to appear between 6:00 and 7:00 a.m. following a fast begun at 6:00 p.m. the preceding evening. They were asked to recline for a period of 45 to 60 minutes prior to the taking of a pulse rate and systolic and diastolic blood pressures. Blood was drawn through venous punctures in vacutainer tubes and the following determinations were made: nonestrified fatty acids by the titrimetic method of Trout, Estes and Friedberg (1960); and serum cholesterol and serum triglycerides by the enzymatic methods devised by Abbott Laboratories (1976, 1977). Skinfold thickness was measured over the iliac crest and at the triceps for females and subscapularly and at the triceps for males using a Harpenden caliper. Percent body fat was calculated through use of the Jetté (1977) method for females and the Brozek and Keys (1951) method for males. Weights were taken on a balance beam scale with participants wearing light clothing without shoes. At the same time, height was recorded. Vital lung capacity was measured using a dry spirometer, the highest of three measurements being the recorded measure.

Participants also completed a 41 item pencil-and-paper test. This test included: a mood adjective self-rating task (Lorr, Daston, & Smith, 1967); the Restrained Eating Scale developed by Herman and Mack (1975); questions concerning health behaviors (including regularity of eating breakfast, walking, smoking and the occurrence of strong moods), and age and sex. Students included in the control group completed this questionnaire during the final week of the experimental procedure.

Results

Attrition. Of the 68 students who attended the organization sessions, only two failed to attend any subsequent sessions. Eight, six, five, four and three students, respectively, discontinued after the second through fifth sessions, making a total of 26 dropouts, or 38 percent of the original sample. All of the dropouts were reached by telephone or personal visit. They offered the following reasons for discontinuance: 11 could not free themselves for the Wednesday 12:00-1:15 p.m. meeting; five discontinued because of schoolwork pressures; three each discontinued because they considered the lifestyle change program too demanding or because they were hospitalized for some illness; and two each discontinued because the posttest conflicted with their final examination schedule or because they dropped out of school. Of these discontinuers, all but 8 dropped out for reasons unrelated to the program with only the "lack of time due to workload" or the "lifestyle program too demanding" groups indirectly or directly expressing dissatisfaction with the program. Data for the drop-outs were consolidated into a third group.

TABLE 1
Characteristics of Participants in the Experimental, Drop-out and Control Groups

Characteristic	Group		
	Experimental	Drop-out	Control
Sex			
male (n)	13	13	21
female (n)	29	13	24
Age ($\bar{x}$ ± sd)	18.9± 3.4	19.8± 3.2	18.6± 1.4
Weight (kg)			
male	67.0± 6.5	67.2± 5.8	(a)
female	55.2± 5.7	55.5± 5.3	(a)
Body fat (%)			
male	10.5± 1.1	11.6± 2.7	(a)
female	22.2± 3.5	23.4± 3.2	(a)
Smoking habits			
non smokers (n)	31	21	30
smokers (n)	11	5	15
Breakfast habit			
had it previous day (n)	30	22	31
skipped it previous day (n)	3	4	14

(a)No measurements were made; control group only answered questionnaire.

Characteristics of Participants. The characteristics of participants in the experimental, drop-out and control groups are summarized in Table 1. Fifty percent of the males dropped out as opposed to 28.3 percent of the females. Drop-outs were also less likely to be smokers while members of the control group were more likely, than either experimentals or drop-outs, to have skipped breakfast the previous day. On balance, however, the groups were quite comparable.

None of the volunteers had a ponderal index of less than 11.6, the demarcation line for elevated risk due to obesity used in the Nutrition Canada Survey (1975). The mean percent body fat of the volunteers corresponds to the values for the 45th and 55th percentiles reported by Yuhasz (1966) for men and women between the ages of 20 and 26. The volunteers were therefore well within the normal weight range and the students in general tended to have a regular breakfast habit and were nonsmokers.

Physiological Measures

Results of the physiological measures for the experimental group before and after the program, and for the dropout group before the program (the only physiological measures available) are presented in Table 2. Systolic and diastolic blood pressures were low and well below the hypertension demarcation lines of 140 mmHg for systolic pressure and 90 mmHg for diastolic pressure. The fact that the pulse rates were measured after a one-hour rest period probably accounts for the low averages.

No explanation can be given for the significantly lower pulse rate in the drop-out group. Vital capacity did increase significantly ($p<.001$) between pre and posttreatment. However, at least part of this difference may be due to learning how to use the spirometer. Briscoe (1965) reports a tendency for the mean vital capacity to increase when the maneuver is performed repeatedly over several weeks. The mean values for cholesterol are close to the 159 and 161 mg percent reported as the 50th percentile figure for 10- to 19-year-old Canadian males and females (Nutrition Canada, 1975). Serum tryglyceride averages also coincide well with the 50th percentile values of 77 and 95 mg percent reported for 10- to 19-year-old Canadian females and males (Nutrition Canada, 1975). The mean non-esterified fatty acid values of 0.70, 0.66 and 0.68 /μeq/ml are close to those reported by Taylor, Shoemann, Lovlin, & Lee (1971) for healthy males from 20 to 33 years of age. Non-esterified fatty acids levels are governed by catecholamine levels and also by exercise. However, the complex mechanism of control is not clear. The posttreatment non-esterified fatty acids level was significantly lower than the pretreatment level ($p<0.05$). This result could possibly reflect a decrease in level of stress but this interpretation must be given with caution and would need further testing to be solidly established. Neither the weight nor the percent body fat were significantly altered during the intervention.

Psychological Measures

Table 3 presents a summary of the mean scores of the mood level. An increase in score on the cheerful, energetic, and composed moods signify an improvement in these moods; a decrease in score on the angry, tense-anxious, depression and inert-fatigue moods signify an improvement in these moods. In all of the moods, there was a slight improvement between pre- and post-measurements for the experimental

TABLE 2
Results of Physiological Measures at Pre- and Posttreatment and for Drop-outs

Measure	Groups: Experimental Pretreatment	Groups: Experimental Posttreatment	Groups: Drop-out	t-value: Pre- *vs* Post-treatment[1]	t-value: Pre- *vs* drop-out
Systolic blood pressure	111.8± 13.1	111.6± 10.7	117.6± 13.4	1.05	1.49
Diastolic blood pressure	69.5± 9.3	72.9± 7.8	68.9± 7.6	1.95	0.26
Pulse at rest	68.5± 8.8	69.2± 10.5	63.8± 9.2	0.53	2.12*
Vital capacity (cc)	3664± 766	3892± 751	3863± 525	4.22***	0.95
Serum cholesterol mg%	161.9± 22.8	155.2± 26.1	160.7± 30.0	1.16	0.18
Triglycerides mg%	82.5± 36.9	76.9± 28.5	75.4± 34.6	0.79	0.66
Non esterified fatty acids (μeq/ml)	0.70± 0.15	0.66± 0.13	0.68± 0.13	2.21*	0.52
Weight (kg)	60.4± 8.1	59.0± 7.6	62.9± 8.2	0.49	1.25
% body fat	18.6± 6.2	18.4± 6.0	17.1± 6.7	0.10	0.94

(1) Student's t-test for paired observations
* $p<.00$. *** $p<.001$

TABLE 3
Mean Score of Mood Levels of Pre- and Post- Experimental Subjects, of Control Subjects and of Drop-out Subjects

Mood factor with adjectives used	Experiemental Group		Control group	Drop-out group	*t*-statistics		
	Pre	Post			Pre- *vs* post[1]	Post- *vs* control	Pre- *vs* dropout
Cheerful (elated, on top of the world, excited)	6.0±1.7	6.1±1.8	6.3±1.8	5.7±1.7	0.25	0.56	1.04
Energetic (active, energetic, full of pep)	8.0±1.8	8.6±1.8	8.0±2.3	8.4±1.9	1.63	1.24	0.68
Angry (furious, annoyed, angry)	4.7±2.0	4.4±1.6	5.4±2.2	3.8±2.9	0.87	2.41*	1.81
Tense-anxious (nervous, anxious, shaky)	5.5±1.7	5.4±1.5	6.2±1.8	5.0±1.3	0.01	2.44*	1.25
Depression (hopeless, helpless, worthless)	4.2±1.8	3.9±1.2	4.8±2.1	3.8±1.0	1.19	2.65**	1.57
Inert-fatigue (weary, tired, sluggish)	5.8±1.8	5.5±1.6	6.8±1.9	5.8±2.0	1.00	3.29**	0.16
Composed (calm, at ease, relaxed)	7.6±1.8	8.2±1.7	7.7±2.4	8.2±1.6	1.93	1.40	1.35

(1)Student's *t*-test for paired observations
* $p<.02$
** $p<.01$

group although none of these mood differences taken singly reached statistical significance. The drop-outs did not differ from the experimental subjects at the beginning of the intervention.

Interesting differences were observed between the post-experimental and the control groups. There were four moods which were more deteriorated in the control group than in the group of subjects who had undergone the program. The controls showed more anger-hostility, were more tense-anxious, were more depressed and more inert-fatigued. Given that the post-experimental group and the control group were both tested during the same week, exam week, it seems that the treated subjects coped better with the stressful event of exam time. The control group reacted in the same direction as Lorr et al.'s (1967) group of university students who were tested in an anxious condition.

The questionnaire administered pre- and posttreatment to the experimental and control subjects included three questions concerning the students' generalized self-evaluations. The subjects' responses to these questions are presented in Table 4. Compared to the control group, the posttreatment experimental group perceived themselves as being more emotional ($x^2 = 7.0$; $df = 4$; $P<.05$). No definite explanation can be offered for this. It is possible, however, that having been exposed to sessions which mentioned feelings and emotions, the post-experimental subjects were more aware of their emotions and responded accordingly. In addition, it can be noted that there was a trend for the post-experimental subjects to feel more satisfied with life than the other groups. However, this difference did not reach statistical significance. No differences were found in the responses to the question concerning the frequency of anger although the number of experimental subjects getting angry "very often" or "often" decreased from seven to four. The overall impression conveyed by Table 4 is that the practice of relaxation, of self-assertiveness and of planning sleep and leisure did not strikingly alter the psychological dimensions touched upon by the three questions appearing in Table 4.

Finally, no significant differences were found in participants' responses to the Restrained Eating Scale after their involvement in the lifestyle change program. The pretreatment mean score for these students (6.02 ± 2.12) was somewhat lower than the mean score of 8.24 for 45 female college students studied by Herman and Mack (1975), suggesting that dietary tension was less a problem for the Canadian students than for their American peers. This may have contributed to the failure of the Scale to reflect treatment-induced differences. Dropouts prior to program participation did not differ significantly from experimentals, but control subjects did have small but still statistically

TABLE 4
Responses of Experimental, Control and Drop-out Subjects on Three Questions Related to Feelings and Emotions

Question	Experimental group				Control group		Drop-out group	
	Pre-treatment		Post-treatment					
	Frequency	%	Frequency	%	Frequency	%	Frequency	%
Compared with friends, are you								
More emotional	15	36	19	45	11	24	5	19
Just as emotional	19	45	15	36	29	64	13	50
Less emotional	8	19	8	19	5	11	8	31
			$x^2 = 7.0$; $p<.05$					
Are you satisfied with life?								
Always	5	12	12	29	8	18	6	23
Almost always	12	29	12	29	13	29	10	38
Satisfied	15	36	14	33	15	33	7	27
More or less or no	10	24	4	10	9	20	3	12
Do you get angry about things that happen to you?								
Very often or often	7	17	2	7	8	18	3	12
Sometimes	16	38	22	52	16	36	12	46
Rarely or never	19	45	17	40	21	47	11	42

TABLE 5
Summary of Report Return and Compliance

Completeness Of Return	PRESCRIPTION: Relaxation — % of subjects	Relaxation — x days per week of practice	Exercise — % of subjects	Exercise — x days per week of practice	Self-Assertiveness — % of subjects	Self-Assertiveness — x days per week of practice	Planned Leisure — % of subjects	Planned Leisure — x days per week of practice	Planned Sleep — % of subjects	Planned Sleep — x days per week of practice
All returned	35.7	5.3	50.0	4.69	47.6	3.37	38.1	5.16	38.1	4.97
Missing 1	21.4	4.53	11.9	4.32	26.2	3.95	40.5	4.71	40.5	4.65
Missing 2	21.4	4.82	19.0	5.04	14.3	2.10	21.4	none reported	21.4	none reported
Missing 3	7.2	4.10	4.8	4.67	11.9	none reported				
Missing 4	4.8	4.50	2.4	5.00						
Missing 5	2.4	4.00	11.9	none reported						
Missing 6	7.1	none reported								

significantly less dietary tension than the experimentals ($t = 3.15$; $df = 85$; $p < .01$).

Report Return and Compliance. During four of the five weeks of the program, participants in the lifestyle change sessions were asked to keep track of their success in altering the behavioral targets under discussion each week, as well as recording their continued practice of the changes called for in prior weeks. Perfect completion of these records would have called for the submission of six relaxation records, five records of exercise, four of self-assertiveness, and three each of planned leisure and planned sleep. As will be seen in Table 5, approximately half of the participants completed all of the requested exercise and self-assertiveness records while slightly over one-third of the subjects completed all records of the remaining behavior changes. Given the fact that no pressure was brought to bear upon submission of records—only a casual request was made—these results indicate a rather high level of willingness to self-monitor by examination-harried college freshmen.

Completion of the records did appear to be associated with a greater likelihood of student practice of relaxation but did not appear to affect the other behaviors. With the exception of self-assertiveness, which may be the most situation-specific response, compliance with the remaining three expectations may have been at the highest level compatible with the students' schedules.

Discussion

Rather than being intended as a controlled evaluation of a lifestyle change program, this project was undertaken as a pilot test of the feasibility of delivering lifestyle change services to a group of Canadian college students. As a pilot test, it suffers from a number of very important limitations. For example: (1) it utilized a post-test only rather than a more rigorous pre-test, post-test control group design; (2) because of the necessity of fitting the entire program into the time constraints of a college semester, virtually no time was available to measure the impact of latter stages of the program, such as the nutrition-education segment which preceded by only one week the post-test assessment; (3) as a further reflection of this time constraint, follow-up data are not yet available, these data being far more important in interpreting outcome than pre-post differences; and (4) time constraint did not permit sampling students' interests, then preparing program units that suited these interests and thereby evaluating a program that had empirically demonstrated relevance to its participants. For these, among other reasons, the results of the present project can be taken as no more than mildly suggestive of the reasonableness of offering a lifestyle change program to students in campus settings.

As a pilot project, this investigation was addressed to certain procedural questions rather than to a strong evaluation of program effects. First, it sought to determine whether such a program would be accepted by college students. Table 1 illustrates the finding that those who volunteered to participate did so despite the fact that they apparently were not at risk for physiological consequences of any maladaptive health behaviors that might be present. While the overall drop-out rate was 38 percent, this includes all students who volunteered without knowing the as-yet-not-selected meeting time. Schedule conflicts are obviously not a direct reaction to exigencies of the program, nor are changes in the students' status in the university. Deleting those dropping out of the program for these reasons, the actual drop-out rate was 15.4 percent. This compares with drop-out rates of four (Wollersheim, 1970) and eight (Harris, 1969) percent for students discontinuing other programs reported in the literature. However, in these programs, students sought out the program because of concern with their overweight while the present students were selected at random and asked to volunteer without reference to a personal health stress. It is also important to note that while males were less likely than females to volunteer for program participation, and while they were also more likely to discontinue, some 31 percent of the participants were male. Although prior studies (e.g., Stuart & Jacobson, in press) have shown that a vast percentage of volunteers for weight management programs are women, college men in reasonable numbers can be recruited for participation in programs aimed at change in lifestyle. Therefore, experience with the present program appears to be quite promising with respect to the possibility that students might be successfully involved in a lifestyle change program *before* they develop risk factors associated with any problem behaviors.

This project also sought to determine whether students would be willing to undergo the rigors of a multi-dimensional evaluation protocol—one that involved a 12-hour fast, the drawing of blood, and the answering of probative questions concerning their psychological state. Clearly their willingness was evident in the present project, with only two of 44 eligible students refusing to undergo the procedure for the second, post-test evaluation.

The fact that significant change was not noted in several of the physiological measures—e.g., blood pressure, pulse rate and serum lipids—as well as body weight can be explained by two factors; virtually every participant in the experimental group was well within normal limits for each of these parameters and therefore offered little opportunity for change; and the interval between measurements may have been too brief to permit the appearance of change in parameters that are known to be not immediately reactive. The observed change in vital capacity might have been reflective of the impact of increased physical activity but was more likely attributable to the students' habituation with the test apparatus. The significant change in the level of unesterified free fatty acids is noteworthy because this measure is generally understood to be a physiological index of the level of stress (Balasse, 1968; Cahill, 1974; Issekutz, Bortz, Miller, & Wroldsen, 1967) and the students were known to be under considerable external pressure due to the concurrence of examinations with the time of post-test data collection. Therefore, the relaxation procedures which were taught early in the program may indeed have had an important and positive effect upon the students' abilities to manage their tension levels.

This finding was further confirmed when it was observed that program participants improved somewhat (albeit not significantly) in the level of some of their negative moods (i.e., anger, tension, depression and fatigue) and that they differed significantly from the controls on these dimensions during the high stress examination period. Indeed, the greater emotionality reported by program participants (see Table 4) may have indicated an alertness to their own emotions, an important precursor to the control of these feelings. The failure to show changes in the Restrained Eating Scale may be attributable to the possibilities that this Scale measures a trait which is not promptly reactive to behavioral shifts, or that the program that was offered did not address the issues implicit in this Scale with sufficient specificity to produce detectable change.

Finally, as a measure of participants' interest in the program, 57, 62, 74, 79 and 79 percent of the students returned either all or all but one of the self-monitoring sheets for the relaxation, exercise, self-assertiveness, planned leisure and planned sleep units of the program, respectively. As is clear from this progression, the longer each program dimension was in use, the less likely it was that participants would be completely faithful to the self-monitoring task, but this was as likely to indicate their mastery of the task with no need for further self-monitoring as it was possibly indicative of their discontinuing practice of each set of instigations.

Application of the materials developed for the present project in future research would yield more valuable data if certain experimental procedures not used here were introduced. First, complete data should be collected from experimental and control group participants at all data collection times. Second, a broad spectrum behavioral measure should be administered weekly to all participants to measure changes in each relevant category of behavior in what would amount to a multiple baseline design. Third, follow-up data should be collected in order to assess the delayed effects of intervention and the stability of those changes that are observed. Fourth, participants' evaluation of the difficulty and utility of each unit of the program should have been solicited as a means for the termination of the reasons for complying with or ignoring each set of instigations (see: Yates, in press). In addition, more data should have been available concerning participants' perception of the extent to which they were at risk for each cluster of behaviors, their willingness to undertake change in each set of responses, and other factors such as social isolation, family support and social stability (Baekeland & Lundwall, 1975) that might have helped to predict who would, and would not, persist in program participation. Future research should also begin with an assessment of students' health concerns and of the frequency of unhealthy behaviors as a means of selecting program content empirically, and future researchers would do well to empirically evaluate the utility of meeting duration, spacing, and number as measured by the dual criteria of an acceptable level of participation by students and a desirable level of behavior change.

Preventive health efforts will depend greatly upon the results of these further investigations. In light of our earlier discussion which highlighted the fact that medical control of life shortening illnesses is more hope than reality, it is a first line of defense to prevent or to delay the occurrence of these illnesses to the fullest possible extent. This goal can be achieved by success in training healthy individuals to manage their moods effectively, to participate in at least a moderate amount of physical activity daily, to effect successful management of their social interactions, to plan for enjoyable leisure breaks, to regulate their sleep and eating patterns—all of which were targets in the present project—as well as to moderate their use of tobacco, alcohol and other drugs, to adopt safe driving habits, to utilize safety technologies such as seat belts and to generally choose safe as opposed to more risky behavioral alternatives. The present project suggests that college students may be susceptible to efforts of this sort. While health maintenance training should correctly be undertaken at the earliest possible age, clearly reemphasis of the earlier messages is appropriate for college youth as an adjunct to the introduction of new health behaviors that are age appropriate for young adults. Success in efforts such as these will be a crucial step towards the conquest of disease.

APPENDIX A

RECORD KEEPING FORMS

Record of Daily Relaxation			
Day	Number of times you practiced relaxation	How many minutes?	How did you feel after relaxing?
1			

Record of Daily Exercise			
Day	Number of times you walked 5 min.	Number of times you walked 10 min.	Number of times you walked 20 min.
1			

Record of Self-Assertiveness		
Day	Number of times you practiced assertiveness with someone	Number of times you utilized self-assertiveness with someone
1		

Record of Leisure and Sleep			
	Day		
Prescription	1	2	3 etc.
How many planned breaks did you take?			
Did you go to bed at a predetermined time?			
Did you get up at the predetermined time?			
Did you omit napping?			
Did you reduce your intake of fluids after 4 p.m.?			
Did you avoid coffee or tea after 4 p.m.?			
Did you decrease your intake of alcoholic beverages?			
Did you avoid reading in bed?			
Did you practice physical relaxation before going to sleep?			
Did you concentrate your mind on neutral thoughts?			

REFERENCES

ABBOTT LABORATORIES: *A-Gent clinical chemistry reagent for the determination of cholesterol.* Pasadena, California, 91030. Booklet 07-9873-F2, 1976.

ABBOTT LABORATORIES: *A-Gent clinical chemistry reagent for the determination of triglycerides.* Diagnostic Division, Pasadena, California 91030. Booklet 07-9974-F6, 1977.

AMERICAN COLLEGE OF PREVENTIVE MEDICINE: *Preventive Medicine USA.* New York: Prodist, 1976.

AMERICAN HOSPITAL ASSOCIATION: Hospital costs in community hospitals. *CBS News Almanac, 1978.* Maplewood, N.J.: Hammond Almanac, 1977, p. 251.

BAEKELAND, F., & LUNDWALL, L.: Dropping out of treatment: A critical review. *Psychological Bulletin,* 1975, *82,* 738-783.

BALASSE, E.: Influence of norepinepherine, growth hormone and fasting on free fatty acid mobilization in lean and obese subjects. *Diabetologica,* 1968, *4,* 20-25.

BELLOC, N.B. & BRESLOW, L.: Relationship of physical health status and health practices. *Preventive Medicine,* 1972, *1,* 409-421.

BERKOWITZ, D.: Metabolic changes associated with obesity before and after weight reduction. *Journal of the American Medical Association,* 1964, *187,* 399-403.

BERKOWITZ, D.: Obesity: Biological mechanisms. In L. Lasagna (Ed.), *Obesity: Causes, consequences and treatment.* New York: Medcom Press, 1972.

BONANNO, J. A., & LIES, J. E.: Effects of physical training on coronary risk factors. *American Journal of Cardiology,* 1974, *33,* 760-764.

BOSTON WOMEN'S HEALTH COLLECTIVE: *Our bodies, ourselves.* New York: Simon & Schuster, 1973.

BOYER, J. L., & KASCH, F. W.: Exercise therapy in hypertensive men. *Journal of the American Medical Association,* 1970, *211,* 1668-1671.

BRISCOE, W. A.: Lung Volumes in *Handbook of Physiology, Section 3: Respiration,* Volume II, American Physiological Society, Washington, D.C., 1965, 1359-1360.

BROZEK, J. & KEYS, A.: The evaluation of leanness-fatness in man: Norms and interrelationships. *British Journal of Nutrition,* 1951, *5,* 194.

BUTENSKY, A., FARALLI, V., HUBNER, D., & WALDRON, I.: Elements of the coronary prone behavior pattern in children and teenagers. *Journal of Psychosomatic Research,* 1976, *20,* 439-444.

CAHILL, G. F.: Obesity and the control of fuel metabolism. In G. A. Bray & J. E. Bethune (Eds.), *Treatment and management of obesity.* Hagerstown, Md.: Harper & Row, 1974.

CARVER, C. S., COLEMAN, A. E., & GLASS, D. C.: The coronary-prone behavior pattern and the suppression of fatigue on a treadmill test. *Journal of Personality and Social Psychology,* 1976, *33,* 460-466.

CASSELL, J.C.: Summary of major findings of the Evans County cardiovascular studies. *Archives of Internal Medicine,* 1971, *128,* 887-889.

DAWBER, T. R., & KANNEL, W. B.: Current status of coronary prevention: Lessons from the Framingham Study. *Preventive Medicine,* 1972, *1,* 449-512.

EASTWOOD, M.R., & TREVELYAN, H.: Stress and coronary heart disease. *Journal of Psychosomatic Research,* 1971, *15,* 389-392.

FOLKINS, C. H.: Effects of physical training on mood. *Journal of Clinical Psychology,* 1976, *32,* 385-388.

FOX, S. M., & HASKELL, W. L.: Physical activity and the prevention of coronary heart disease. *Bulletin of the New York Academy of Medicine,* 1968, *44,* 950-967.

FRANK, C. W., WEINBLATT, E., SHAPIRO, S., & SAGER, R. V.: Myocardia infarction in men: Role of physical activity and smoking in incidence and mortality. *Journal of the American Medical Association,* 1960, *198,* 1241-1245.

FRIEDMAN, G. D., URY, H. K., KLATSKY, A. L., & SEIGELAUB, M. S.: A psychological questionnaire predictive of myocardiac infarction. *Psychosomatic Medicine,* 1974, *36,* 327-343.

FRIEDMAN, M. & ROSENMAN, R. H.: Type A behavior pattern: Its association with coronary heart disease. *Annals of Clinical Research,* 1971, *3,* 300-312.

FRIEDMAN, M., & ROSENMAN, R. H.: *Type A behavior and your heart.* New York: Alfred A. Knopf, 1974.

FRIEDMAN, M., ROSENMAN, R. H., & BYERS, S. O.: Serum lipids and conjunctival circulation after fast ingestion in men exhibiting type A behavior pattern. *Circulation,* 1964, *29,* 874-886.

FUCHS, V.: *Who shall live?* New York: Basic Books, 1974.

GOCHMAN, D. S.: The organizing role of motivation in health beliefs and intentions. *Journal of Health and Social Behavior,* 1972, *13,* 285-293.

GREENE, W. S., GOLDSTEIN, S., & MOSS. A. J.: Psychosocial aspects of sudden death. *Archives of Internal Medicine,* 1972, *129,* 725-731.

HAGGERTY, R. J.: Changing lifestyles to improve health. *Preventive Medicine,* 1977, *6,* 276-289.

HARRIS, M. B.: Self-directed program for weight control: A pilot study. *Journal of Abnormal Psychology,* 1969, *74,* 263-270.

HERMAN, C. P., & MACK, D.: Restrained and unrestrained eating. *Journal of Personality,* 1975, *43,* 647.

HOLLOSZY, J. O., SKINNER, J. S., TORO, G., & CURETON, T. K.: Effects of a six month program of endurance exercise on the serum lipids of middle aged men. *American Journal of Cardiology,* 1964, *14,* 753-760.

ILLICH, I.: Medical nemesis. *The Lancet,* 1974, May 11, 918-921.

ILLICH, I.: *Medical nemesis: The expropriation of health.* London: Newman, 1975.

ISSEKUTZ, B., BORTZ, W. M., MILLER, H. I., & WROLDSEN, A.: Plasma free acid response to exercise in obese humans. *Metabolism,* 1967, *16,* 492-502.

JACOBSON, E.: *Modern treatment of tense patients.* Springfield, Ill.: Charles C Thomas, 1970.

JANIS, I. L., & KING, B. T.: The influence of role playing in opinion change. In E. E. Maccoby, T. M. Newcomb, & E. L. Hartley (Eds.), *Readings in social psychology.* New York: Holt, Rinehart & Winston, 1958.

JETTÉ, M.: Technical operations manual: Standardized tests of fitness in occupational health. Ottawa: *Canandian Public Health Association,* 1977.

JOHNSON, W. R., TERRY, D. E., GAINES, J. J., & HUMPHREY, J. H.: *Health concepts of college students.* New York: Roland Press, 1962.

JOHNS, M. W.: Stress and coronary heart disease. *Ergonomics,* 1973, *16,* 683-690.

KANNEL, W. K., BRAND, N., & SKINNER, J. J.: Relation of adiposity to blood pressure and development of hypertension: Framingham study. *Annals of Internal Medicine,* 1967, *67,* 48-59.

KATZ, R. C., & ZLUTNICK, S. (Eds.): *Behavior therapy and health care: Principles and applications.* New York: Pergamon Press, 1975.

KLARMAN, H. E.: The financing of health care. In: J. H. Knowles (Ed.), *Doing better and feeling worse: Health in the United States.* New York: W. W. Norton, 1977.

KNOWLES, J. H.: Introduction. In J. H. Knowles (Ed.), *Doing better and feeling worse: Health in the United States.* New York: W. W. Norton, 1977(a).

KNOWLES, J. H.: The responsibility of the individual. In J. H. Knowles (Ed.), *Doing better and feeling worse: Health in the United States.* New York: W. W. Norton, 1977(b).

LEWIN, K.: Group decision and social change. In: Committee on the teaching of social psychology, *Readings in social psychology.* New York: Henry Holt & Co., 1947.

LORR, M., DASTON, P., & SMITH, I. R.: Analysis of mood states. *Educational and Psychological Measurement,* 1967, *27,* 89-96.

MANN, G. V., GARRETT, H. L., FARHI, A., MURRAY, H., BILLINGS, F. T. SHUTE, E. & SCHWARTERN, S.: Exercise to prevent coronary heart disease. *American Journal of Medicine,* 1969, *49,* 12-17.

MARLATT, G. A., & MARQUES, J. K.: Medication, self-control, and alcohol use. In R. B. Stuart (Ed.), *Behavioral self-management: Strategies, Techniques and Outcome* New York: Brunner/Mazel, 1977.

MEDALIE, J. H., PAIER, C. M., GOLDBOURT, U., & HERMAN, J. B.: Major factors in the development of diabetes mellitus in 10,000 men. *Archives of Internal Medicine,* 1975, *135,* 811-817.

METTLIN, C.: Occupational careers and the prevention of coronary-prone behavior. *Social Science and Medicine,* 1976, 10, 367-372.

MEYER, A. J., & HENDERSON, J. B.: Multiple risk factor reduction in the prevention of cardiovascular disease. *Preventive Medicine,* 1974, *3,* 225-236.

MUELLER, M. S., & PIRO, P. A.: Private health insurance in 1974: A review of coverage, enrollment, and financial experience. *Social Security Bulletin,* 1976, *39,* 3-20.

NEWBURGH, L. H.: Control of the hyperglycemia of obese 'diabetics' by weight reduction. *Annals of Internal Medicine,* 1942, *17,* 935-942.

NEWMAN, O.: Leisure and life style. *Ontario Psychologist,* 1976, *8,* 28-34.

NUTRITION CANADA: *New Brunswick Report.* Ottawa: Health & Welfare Canada, Information Canada, 1975.

PERLMAN, L. V., FERGUSON, S., BERGUM, K., ISENBERG, E. L., & HAMMERSTEN, J. F.: Precipitation of congestive heart failure: Social and emotional factors. *Annals of Internal Medicine,* 1975, *75,* 1-7.

REDWOOD, D. R., ROSING, D. R., & EPSTEIN, S. E.: Circulatory and symptomatic effects of physical training in patients with coronary-artery disease and angina pectoris. *New England Journal of Medicine,* 1972, *286,* 959-965.

ROMO, M., SILTMEN, P., THEORELL, T., & RAHE, R. H.: Work behavior, time urgency, and life dissatisfactions in subjects with myocardia infarction: A cross-cultural study. *Journal of Psychosomatic Research,* 1974, *18,* 1-8.

ROSENMAN, R. H., & FRIEDMAN, M.: Behavior patterns, blood lipids, and coronary heart disease. *Journal of the American Medical Association,* 1963, *184,* 934-938.

ROSENMAN, R. H., FRIEDMAN, M., & JENKINS, C. D.: The prediction of immunity to coronary heart disease. *Journal of the American Medical Association,* 1966, *198,* 1159-1162.

ROSENMAN, R. H., FRIEDMAN, M., STRAUS, R., WURM, M., KOSITCHEK, R., HAWN, W., & WERTHESEN, N. T.: A predictive study of coronary heart disease. *Journal of the American Medical Association,* 1964, *189,* 15-22.

ROSENMAN, R. H., FRIEDMAN, M., STRAUS, R., WURM, M., MESSINGER, H., & JENKINS, C. D.: Coronary heart disease in the western collaborative group study: A follow-up experiment of 2 years. *Journal of the American Medical Association,* 1966, *195,* 86-92.

SCHEVER, J., PENPARGKIL, S., & BHAN, A. K.: Experimental observations on the effects of physical training upon intrinsic cardiac physiology and biochemistry. *American Journal of Cardiology,* 1974, *33,* 744-751.

STUART, R. B.: Drug education: Pushing or preventing? *Journal of Educational Psychology,* 1974, *66,* 189-201.

STUART, R. B.: Behavioral control of overeating: A status report. In George A. Bray (Ed.), *Obesity in perspective.* Washington, D.C.: U.S. Government Printing Office, 1975.

STUART, R. B.: *Behavioral self-management: Strategies, techniques and outcome.* New York: Brunner/Mazel, 1977(a).

STUART, R. B.: Self-help group approach to self-management. In R. B. Stuart (Ed.), *Behavioral self-management: Strategies, techniques and outcome.* New York:Bunner/Mazel, 1977(b).

STUART, R. B.: *Act thin, stay thin.* New York: W. W. Norton, 1978.

STUART, R. B., & DAVIS, B.: *Slim chance in a fat world.* Champaign, Ill.: Research Press, 1972.

STUART, R. B., & JACOBSEN, B.: Sex differences in obesity. In E. Gomberg & V. Franks (Eds.), *Gender and psychopathology: Sex differences in disordered behavior.* New York: Brunner/Mazel, 1979.

TAYLOR, A. W., SHOEMANN, D. S., LOVLIN, R., & LEE, S.: Plasma free fatty acid mobilization with graded exercise. *Journal of Sports, Medicine and Physical Fitness,* 1971, *11,* 234-240.

TERRY, A. H., JR.: Obeisty and hypertension. *Journal of the American Medical Association,* 1923, *81,* 1283-1284.

THEIL, H. F., PARKER, D., & BRUCE, T.A.: Stress factors and the risk of myocardiac infarction. *Journal of Psychosomatic Research,* 1973, *17,* 43-57.

THOMAS, L.: On the science and technology of medicine. In J. D. Knowles (Ed.), *Doing better and feeling worse: Health in the United States.* New York: W. W. Norton, 1977.

TROUT, D. L., ESTES, H., & FRIEDBERG, S. J.: Titration of free fatty acids of plasma: A study of current methods and a new modification. *Journal of Lipid Research,* 1960, *1,* 199-202.

U. S. OFFICE OF MANAGEMENT AND BUDGET: *The budget of the United States Government, FY 1975.* Washington, D.C.: U.S. Government Printing Office, 1975.

WEIN, E. E. & WILCOX, E. B.: Serum cholesterol from pre-adolescence through adulthood. *Journal of the American Dietetic Association,* 1972, *61,* 155-158.

WEINBERGER, C. W.: The role of the federal government in educating the public about health. *Journal of Medical Education,* 1975, *50,* 138-142.

WEISS, E. DLIN, B., ROLLIN, H. R., FISHER, H. K., & BEPLER, C. R.: Emotional factors in coronary occlusion. *Archives of Internal Medicine,* 1957, *99,* 628-641.

WOLLERSHEIM, J. P.: Effectiveness of group therapy based upon learning principles in the treatment of overweight women. *Journal of Abnormal Psychology,* 1970, *76,* 462-474.

YATES, B. T.: Improving the cost-effectiveness of obesity programs: Three basic strategies for reducing the cost per pound. *International Journal of Obesity,* in press.

YUHASZ, M. S.: *Physical fitness and sports appraisal.* London, Ontario: The University of Western Ontario, Department of Physical Health and Recreation, 1966.

ZOLA, I. K.: Pathways to the doctor—from person to patient. *Social Science and Medicine,* 1973, *7,* 677-685.

9

Preventive Strategies in the Treatment of Alcohol Abuse: A Review and a Proposal

LYNN ALDEN

Excessive alcohol consumption is one of the major factors involved in hazardous lifestyles (Berg, 1976; Haggerty, 1977). Chronic alcohol abuse has been linked, directly or indirectly, with a variety of physical problems including cirrhosis of the liver, heart dysfunction and, with less certainty, to certain forms of cancer (Schmidt & Popham, 1975; Vincent, Marchetta, & Nigogosyan, 1964; Fuchs, 1974; Berg, 1976). Those who consume excessive amounts of alcohol are far more likely to suffer injury or death from automobile accidents, homicide, or suicide. Overall, the mortality rate due to alcoholic disorders has been increasing sharply (deLint, 1974). Alcohol consumption has also been held responsible for such things as job absenteeism and impaired job performance. Increasing costs to health care delivery systems, to business and industry, and to the individual involved have led health researchers and practitioners to focus attention on the question of whether alcohol-related problems can be prevented.

Researchers have attempted to adapt the traditional public health model of prevention to the prevention of alcoholism. This model, with its emphasis on the epidemiology of a disorder, agent-host-environmental relationships, and large-scale treatment of populations, proved successful in the eradication of a number of infectious diseases and the hope was that social problems such as alcohol abuse could be handled within the same framework. While some have recently questioned whether such a model can be applied to a social problem whose etiology remains unspecified and whose environmental inter-relationships remain unclear (Blane, 1976; Kalb, 1975), aspects of the model still influence the development and classification of preventive programs. Within the model, three levels of prevention are distinguished: primary prevention, removal of the causes of a disorder to prevent its occurrence; secondary prevention, the early identification and treatment of a disroder; and tertiary prevention, generally taken to correspond with treatment of the developed disorder. Preventive programs can be roughly divided into primary and secondary types.

Primary Prevention

To date, three techniques have been used as primary preventive strategies: alcohol education, public information campaigns, and the modification of government policies for the distribution of liquor.

Alcohol education programs are by far the most common form of primary preventive service offered. In general, the goal of such programs is to increase knowledge about the effects of alcohol on the body and about the consequences of alcohol abuse, producing changes in attitudes toward consumption and in consumption itself. Most education programs have focused on school systems, high school or university, in an attempt to reach youth, their parents, or their teachers. Although professionals have presented arguments in favour of alcohol education, the effects of such programs are far from clear.

One major difficulty is that adequate research is lacking. A recent review of over 200 articles revealed that only 23 studies reported any systematic evaluation. Of these, only 15 involved a pre/post-assessment design coupled with a control group to allow for a true comparison of effects (Randall & Wong, 1976). Several studies involved post-assessment only; others lacked any form of control group. A number of studies shared the additional limitation of using attitude change as the sole dependent measure. Unfortunately, attitude change only indirectly reflects changes in actual consumption.

It can be concluded from these studies that students make significant gains in their knowledge of alcohol as a result of program participation. Attitude and behavior change do not always follow. A number of studies found no change in attitudes following program completion (Tennant, Weaver, & Lewis, 1973; Swisher & Crawford, 1971; Thomas, 1971; Swisher, Warner, & Hern, 1972). Several even reported that attitudes toward drug consumption became more positive. In a study of drug-related knowledge, Hoffman (1971) concluded that the more knowledge students possessed about drugs, the more their attitudes favored drug use. Of the studies which attempted to measure alcohol use, several found decreases in consumption (Kline, 1972; Blauat & Flocco, 1971; Tennat et al., 1973). Unfortunately several of these involved post-assessment only and lumped alcohol with other drugs so that specific changes in alcohol were masked. Two of the studies did not include a control condition. Several studies have found no change in alcohol use upon program completion (Tennant et al., 1973; Swisher & Crawford, 1971; Swisher et al., 1972). More interestingly, three studies have reported that alcohol use actually increased after students completed an educational program (Smart, Bennett, & Fejer, 1976; Stuart, 1973; Lewis, Gossett, & Phillips, 1972). In summary, it appears that alcohol education programs are successful in increasing knowledge about alcohol, but are less consistently successful in producing attitude change or behavior change. Some researchers have concluded that alcohol education programs require modification.

Mass media public information campaigns have been considered integral parts of primary preventive efforts (Wilkinson, 1970). Certainly it is believed that the media plays a powerful role in shaping public opinion. It is also clear that such campaigns have the potential for reaching large segments of the population. While there have been very few systematic evaluations of such campaigns, their effectiveness has been judged to be slight (Blane, 1976). Haskins (1969) has discussed the research design problems common to the few studies that do exist. The evidence indicates that information campaigns are more likely to generate awareness than to motivate people to take steps to solve the problem. For example, Dickman and Keil (1977) in a recent attempt to evaluate a series of alcohol related public television shows found that few people watched the series. Of those who did watch, about 40% reported gaining awareness of alcohol as a problem either for themselves or someone they knew. Unfortunately, this awareness was seldom followed up with a decision to seek treatment. Media campaigns focusing on other health habits have produced equally discouraging results (Haggerty, 1977; Cartwright, Martin, & Thompson, 1960). While recent media efforts such as the Stanford Heart Project are encouraging, the effectiveness of media information campaigns in reducing alcoholism remains to be demonstrated.

Researchers at the Addiction Research Foundation in Ontario have proposed a distribution of consumption model which states that the rate of alcoholism is influenced, to some extent, by the pattern of consumption in the population as a whole (Popham, Schmidt, & deLint, 1976b; Room, 1971; Blane, 1976). It follows from this model that the modification of policies regulating the availability and distribution of alcohol might produce changes in general consumption and, eventually, in the rate of alcoholism. While aspects of the distribution of consumption model have been questioned (O'Neill & Wells, 1971; Edwards, 1973; Blane, 1976), policy modification has been judged to have potential for primary preventive efforts.

A number of policy variables have been found to produce little effect on the rate of consumption. The type or location of alcohol outlets is one such variable. Popham, Schmidt, & deLint (1976a) found few changes in consumption when Ontario beverage houses were converted to cocktail lounges. Similarly, implementing liquor-by-the-drink policies produced few changes in consumption (Bryant, 1954; Dewar & Sommer, 1962). The hours and days that alcohol outlets remain open also appear unrelated to consumption. However, it has been found that the pattern of alcohol-related accidents and arrests covary with the hours of sale (Popham, 1962; Raymond, 1969). Another policy variable with few demonstrable effects is government monopoly instead of licensed private distribution (Jellinek, 1947; Popham et al., 1976a).

The number of alcohol distribution outlets has been found to display a more complex relationship with consumption and alcoholism. There is some evidence to suggest that severe restriction of outlets, such as occurred during prohibition, results in lowered rates of consumption and alcoholism (Popham, 1970; Schmidt & Popham, 1975; Terris, 1967). Similarly, Scandinavian researchers have reported that alcohol-related accidents and arrests decreased when liquor store workers went on strike (Bruun, Edwards, Lumio et al., 1975; Mäkelä, 1974). [On the other hand, strikes in liquor stores in Newfoundland and Nova Scotia did not produce similar effects (Smart, 1977b)]. It seems that with extremely low accessibility alcohol-related problems do decrease. However, above a certain minimal level, outlet frequency has little noticeable effect. Several studies have even suggested that the number of arrests for drunkenness increases as the frequency of outlets decreases (Popham et al., 1976a; Popham, 1962).

Two other policy variables, price of liquor and reduction in legal drinking age, have been more directly related to consumption and alcoholism. Lau (1975) found that price was a significant predictor of demand for alcohol. Seeley (1960) related price to rate of alcoholism. Although alcoholism and consumption are tempered by community attitude toward drinking, most researchers agree that price affects consumption (Popham et al., 1976b).

Studies of modification of the legal drinking age have found that teenagers report increased consumption after drinking age is lowered (Smart & Schmidt, 1975). Similarly, there are reports that on-premise sales of alcohol have increased after such changes (Schmidt, 1972). While these studies suggest that lowering the legal age increases consumption, none included control jurisdictions where drinking policies remained unchanged. Smart and Finley (1975), in one of the few controlled studies, found no striking increases in consumption of beer in jurisdictions where the legal age was lowered as compared with control jurisdictions. Similarly, Barsby and Marshall (1977) found no differences between states in which policies were changed and control states. In terms of consumption, then, there is evidence for and against lowering the legal age.

The effects of lowering the legal drinking age on traffic accidents and fatalities is more clear cut. Five separate studies have reported that alcohol-related collisions and fatalities have increased among youthful drivers following policy changes (Douglass & Filkins, 1974; Smart & Goodstadt, 1977; Schmidt & Kornaczewski, 1973). One study reported an increase in the number of young drinkers in treatment for alcoholism after a similar policy change (Smart & Finley, 1975).

One difficulty in evaluating changes in policies regulating alcohol distribution is that multiple complex factors influence alcohol consumption and rates of alcoholism. Few studies have attempted to take more than one such variable into account. Smart (1977a) recently conducted a study in which a global measure of availability was computed (based on legal age, hours of sale, number of outlets, etc.) and related to per capita consumption and alcoholism rate when average income and degree of urbanism were controlled. Under these conditions, he found that both income and urbanism were related to consumption and to alcoholism, but that availability was not. This study points to the need for further multifaceted investigations. While more investigation of policy factors is clearly needed, the Addiction Research Foundation has proposed that prices of alcohol and legal restrictions be manipulated to reduce consumption.

In summary, most primary preventive efforts have not been well evaluated. The bulk of the studies in the literature are limited by research design flaws such as lack of adequate controls, or post-assessment only procedures. Reliance on indirect indicies of consumption is another problem. The literature that does exist suggests that primary preventive strategies have yet to demonstrate a high level of effectiveness. Alcohol education and public information programs do not always produce the desired behavior change. While several alcohol distribution policy factors (price, legal drinking age) have been linked to levels of consumption and alcoholism, a variety of social norms and pressures make it unlikely that prices or the legal drinking age will be raised.

A number of writers have suggested that primary prevention may be premature at this point since there is a lack of information about the causes of alcoholism. This lack and the scarcity of effective primary prevention techniques have led this group to suggest that preventive efforts be directed toward secondary preventive programs, at least until such time as more effective primary prevention can be developed (Cross, 1967; Philp, 1967; Kalb, 1975; Blane, 1976).

Secondary Prevention

Secondary prevention programs focus on populations judged at high risk for alcoholism. Populations so identified have included drinking drivers, children of alcoholics, delinquents, and employees displaying absenteeism from work or job impairment (Roman & Trice, 1976; Blane, 1968, 1976; Schneiderman, 1975). To date the most common target populations have been drinking drivers and drinking employees.

Impaired drivers have been judged appropriate targets for secondary prevention programs since such individuals generally display elevated blood alcohol concentration levels upon arrest and are likely to be rearrested at a future date. One recent report suggested that impaired drivers fall between normal drinkers and alcoholics on measures of consumption and on psychological problems, i.e., such individuals consume larger amounts of alcohol, drink more frequently, and report more stress or depression than normals, but less than hard core alcoholics (Selzer, Vinokur, & Wilson, 1977).

Impaired driver programs generally follow an educational format. As with other education programs, such courses have been reported to increase the driver's knowledge of alcohol (e.g., Eddy, 1976). Whether such programs also produce behavior change remains an open question.

Several reports have suggested that recidivism rates for impaired driving are reduced after such courses. For example, Eddy (1976) reported that 20% of his impaired drivers had been charged with impaired driving offenses in the years prior to program participation, while only 2% were charged in the year following program completion. Several other studies report similarly small, but significant changes in recidivism rates (Malfetti & Simon, 1975; Pollack, 1973). On the other hand, Zelhart (1973) did not find a reduction in recidivism. Thus, the results are inconsistent. In addition, most studies have lacked control groups. Further, the use of recidivism rate as a dependent measure has been criticized (Hayslip, Kapusinski, Darbes, & Zeh, 1976; Scoles & Fine, 1977). Annual recidivism rates are quite low in general. In addition, poor record keeping and differences between jurisdictions in law enforcement add error to the measure.

The conclusions of two controlled studies employing more rigorous evaluation procedures have been less encouraging. Blumenthal and Ross (1973) found their intervention produced no greater change than the traditional fine for impaired driving. Scoles and Fine (1977) studied changes in alcohol consumption after completion of an educational program. They found that successful program completers reduced their alcohol intake no more than members of a no-treatment control group. They concluded that any decrease in consumption that occurred was probably a function of the aversive nature of the arrest process and they have called for experimentation with different program contents. In particular, they suggested that such programs should take the form of individually tailored treatment, rather than following the traditional educational format.

Although industrial alcoholism programs have more often concentrated on treating the alcoholic employee than on prevention, such programs have several characteristics that make them good avenues for secondary prevention efforts. First, it has been estimated that between three and five percent of all employees have drinking problems (Roman & Trice, 1976), and that few of these workers seek help through traditional programs. Second, it has been suggested that alcohol abuse can be readily detected through job impairment early in the course of the disorder (Maxwell, 1972). Further, early intervention based in industrial settings is likely to be viewed as legitimate. While social norms often preclude active intervention into the private life of another individual, it is generally conceded that an employer has the right to approach an employee if his drinking results in impaired job performance. Alcohol-related problems cost employers much in the way of absenteeism, impaired performance, lowered morale, and sick benefits. It has also been suggested that alcoholism programs belong in industry because job-related problems may be in part responsible for the drinking of employees (Roman & Trice, 1976).

Occupational programs typically involve training supervisors or managers to recognize the drinking employee, and through constructive confrontation, to refer the worker to an established treatment facility. Many businesses will support the worker by providing sick leave, illness benefits, or job security while he seeks treatment. Most programs back up such supportive behaviors with the threat of dismissal if the problem is not corrected.

Evaluation of occupational programs has been scarce and has primarily employed the single group time-series analysis design. Most of the studies in the literature have reported that the establishment of an early identification and referral program is accompanied by such positive changes as drops in absenteeism, increased supervisor satisfaction, and job maintenance by the drinking employee. Franco (1957, 1960) reported that 72 percent of the employees who remained in treatment maintained their jobs as opposed to 61 percent of those who refused or dropped out of treatment. Four years later approximately half of the treated employees were maintaining their jobs. He also found significant decreases in absenteeism after treatment. Hilker (1972) found that 57 percent of treated employees reported abstinence. Positive changes were also found in supervisors' ratings of treated employees, absenteeism, and on-the-job accidents. Several other studies, although less rigorous in design, have reported similar findings (Kammer & Dupong, 1969; Clyne, 1965; Hamilton, 1976). While the studies that do exist are encouraging, the lack of controls makes it difficult to rule out extra-treatment factors as the agents responsible for change. It may be that the process of being confronted by a supervisor produces change or that spontaneous remission occurs.

Several researchers have compared occupational referrals with other groups of drinkers. Smart (1974) compared the treatment outcomes of clients coerced by employers with those of self-referred clients. He found no differences between the two groups when decrease in consumption was considered. However, self-referred clients improved more on overall behavior ratings. Similarly, Moberg (1974) found no differences in treatment outcome between occupationally referred clients and clients referred by other sources. He did find, however, the industrial referrals were in earlier stages of their drinking careers. Alander and Campbell (1973) found few differences between employees who actively participated in treatment and those who refused treatment although improvements were noted in both groups. It appears then that occupational referrals do at least as well in treatment as other types of clients, although possibly no better. There is some suggestion that industrial programs may reach clients who would not otherwise seek help or who are in the earlier stages of a drinking career. The factors responsible for the changes that occur remain to be identified.

It is clear from a survey of the literature that systematic evaluation procedures and experimentation with different program content are necessary if prevention is to be a viable alternative to treatment. The difficulties involved in modifying policies for alcohol distribution (e.g., price, legal drinking age) have been discussed. Public information campaigns, alcohol education programs, and programs for drinking drivers all rely on the premise that an awareness of facts about alcohol and the consequences of abuse will lead to changes in drinking. This premise has yet to receive strong support, and increasingly, educators are calling for new types of programs. Occupational alcoholism programs have generally relied on traditional facilities to treat referred employees. While such programs do seem of benefit to alcoholics, it has been suggested that traditional forms of treatment, with their emphasis on abstinence, may not be appropriate for employees in the early stages of problem drinking (Roman & Trice, 1976). It appears there is a need for investigation of new models of prevention, new treatment techniques, and different treatment goals.

Several writers have recommended that behavioral techniques be employed in prevention programs (Berg, 1976; Haggerty, 1977; Miller & Mũnoz, 1976). Because behavioral approaches have shown promise with alcoholics (Sobell & Sobell, 1973; Caddy & Lovibond, 1976; Miller, 1978), there is every reason to think they might work with problem drinkers as well. The recent work of Miller (1978) on behavioral self-management techniques seems readily applicable to preventive programs. The self-management model proposes teaching problem drinkers how to drink (i.e., self-control of the drinking response) and skills to cope with life stresses. A preventive self-management program would go beyond the traditional educational format, which attempts to modify attitudes toward consumption, by providing the drinker with concrete techniques he can employ. Behavioral researchers, as well as others, have proposed that programs for problem drinkers experiment with a different form of treatment goal, controlled social drinking. It has been suggested that drinkers may seek treatment earlier if they have options other than complete abstinence (Miller & Mũnoz, 1976).

Evaluation of a Behavioral Preventive Program

The present research was an investigation of the use of behavioral self-management techniques in a secondary preventive context. The goal of the project was to teach problem drinkers skills to aid them in achieving controlled drinking. The research addressed four general questions. The first question was whether the application of behavioral self-management techniques would lead to a reduction in alcohol consumption. A second consideration was whether such reductions, if obtained, would be maintained. The third question concerned the most effective form of self-management program. In a preliminary attempt to determine the optimal self-management regimen, two types of programs were developed and compared: a program which focused only on reduction of drinking behavior and a program which focused on both reduction of drinking and on mastery of skills to manage life stresses. The objective of the comparison was to determine whether the inclusion of the additional skills augmented the results obtained from the basic drinking self-management strategies alone.

The final question addressed by the research was whether problem drinkers would be readily attracted to such a preventive program. Some preventive programs have reported difficulties attracting and holding clients. This question was assessed indirectly through the number of calls, referrals, and clients who attended the program as compared with the number of clients interested in attending other behavioral programs offered through the same clinic.

In keeping with the preventive emphasis of the current study, the program was conducted in a public health unit in a Department of Health as part of a larger lifestyle change program. The initial research was designed as a pilot study for a larger lifestyle change project for problem drinkers.

Clients

The project was publicized through the media (newspaper articles, radio and TV shows) and through visits to health and mental health agencies. Clients had to meet the following criteria in order to enter the program: (1) at least 19 years old, (2) able to pass a medical examination to rule out health problems incompatible with further alcohol consumption, (3) not currently psychotic or seriously suicidal, (4) not in need of detoxification or intensive inpatient treatment, (5) displaying a pattern of problematic drinking, either in terms of total consumption or drinking pattern.

A total of 70 clients contacted the program to express interest. Of these, 63 actually attended the first scheduled interview. Twenty-seven clients were referred elsewhere for treatment. Eight were judged in need of either detoxification or intensive inpatient treatment. An additional four were long-term alcoholics currently abstinent who wanted to begin drinking again. These four were judged inappropriate for a preventive program. Five clients were excluded because they were judged to be psychotic or seriously suicidal. Five clients were judged by their physicians to display medical problems incompatible with continued drinking. Five additional clients were excluded because they were not drinking in any "problematic" fashion. Of the 36 clients entering the first treatment session, 31 completed all 10 treatment sessions. Five clients dropped out prior to completion, four from the basic program, one from the enriched.

The majority of the clients (78 percent) were self-referred. The remainder (22 percent) were referred by community agencies or private physicians. No clients were court-referred. The average age of the sample was 39 years, the average education, 12.8 years. The sample consisted of 17 men and 14 women. On the average, clients reported drinking the equivalent of 58 ounces of distilled spirits per week. Subjects were randomly assigned to the basic self-management (B) or enriched self-management (E) condition.

Counselors

Six psychology graduate students served as counselors, four Masters candidates, one Ph.D. candidate, and one post-doctoral fellow.

Dependent Measures

All clients monitored their drinking throughout the 12 week program. On the basis of client monitoring, a variety of drinking indices were computed: (1) total consumption per week reported in standardized ethanol units (one "drink" is the amount of beverage containing ½ oz. pure ethanol), (2) peak blood alcohol level during the week, (3) the number of days when the client's blood alcohol level equalled or exceeded 80 mg%, (4) the number of days per week when the client exceeded his absolute drinking goal.

Significant others' reports of total consumption per week were gathered during the intake period and again at completion of treatment. Twenty-one significant others were able to provide an estimate of client consumption. Of the remaining significant others, one died prior to post-assessment, and one other divorced the client and moved away. Eight significant others reported great difficulty estimating the client's total consumption. These eight, in general, reported improvement on the part of the client, but felt unable to provide an accurate estimate.

In order to judge the clinical significance of the changes observed in drinking behavior, "hazardous" drinking criteria were established. The first criterion was whether a client's weekly consumption exceeded 12.5 ounces of absolute alcohol. This average consumption level was selected because it was comparable to that used in other studies and because consumption in excess of this amount has been observed to increase the likelihood that an individual will experience liver dysfunction (Schmidt & Popham, 1975).

The second criterion was a measure of pattern of consumption, the distribution of alcohol intake over time. In previous studies, a maximum expected blood alcohol level has been selected for clients and the number of violations of this blood alcohol level has been used as a reflection of drinking pattern. In the present study, clients selected their own maximum expected blood alcohol levels. The number of violations of the self-imposed goal was therefore used as a drinking pattern measure. This measure also had the advantage of reflecting the success of the client's attempts at self-control.

All clients completed a test battery prior to and after the program. This battery consisted of the Beck Depression Inventory (Beck, 1967), the State/Trait Anxiety Inventory (Speilberger, Gorsuch, & Lushene, 1970), and a measure assessing marital and job satisfaction (McLachlan & Walderman, 1976).

The Treatment Procedures

Treatment for all clients consisted of two intake interviews and ten treatment sessions. Each client met for one hour weekly with his individual counselor.

Basic Self-management Condition (B)

Clients in the basic condition were taught the following skills: (1) to record their drinking in standard ethanol units (one "drink" equals ½ oz. pure ethanol), (2) to discreetly monitor ongoing drinking and to assertively handle questions about monitoring, (3) to compute his/her blood alcohol concentration level using the external cues of body weight, number of "drinks", and time elapsed, (4) to establish an absolute blood alcohol level as a goal to remain below, (5) a series of drinking skills including a social drinking style (sipping drinks, ordering mixed drinks, interspersing nonalcoholic beverages with alcoholic beverages), and how to space drinks, (6) assertive ways to refuse social pressure to drink, (7) to determine the settings and feelings which accompany overdrinking and to modify such factors. This program was patterned after the work of Miller and Mũnoz (1976).

Most clients mastered the above techniques in six sessions and spent the remaining sessions recording drinking, practicing skills, and discussing overdrinking episodes with their counselors.

Enriched Self-management Condition (E)

The first five or six sessions in the enriched condition were devoted to learning the drinking techniques listed above. In the remaining four or five sessions, clients were taught specific skills designed to help them reduce general stress and social anxiety without drinking. A variety of stress-management techniques were described to the client. In keeping with the self-management framework of the program, clients were asked to select one or two techniques they felt would be useful to them. Techniques presented included: progressive relaxation training (Bernstein & Borkovec, 1973), the relaxation response technique (Benson, 1975), self-instructional training for stress-management (Meichenbaum, 1972), and assertiveness training for social anxiety (Lange & Jakubowski, 1976). The majority of clients selected the relaxation response or self-instructional training with two clients selecting progressive relaxation and one client choosing assertiveness training.

Follow-up Contacts

Clients were contacted at six months after program completion and asked to attend a half hour interview focusing on "how things are going." Clients were asked to bring their significant other with them if possible. Clients or significant others who could not or would not come in for the interview were interviewed by phone and mailed the test battery forms for completion. Clients were asked to monitor their drinking for a week following the follow-up contact and to mail their monitoring to the clinic.

RESULTS

Comparability of Groups

In order to insure group comparability prior to treatment, *t*-tests were performed between the two groups on all pre-assessment measures. None of these tests achieved statistical significance. The random assignment procedure was therefore judged to be effective.

Drinking Measures

The means and standard deviations for both groups on the measures of drinking can be seen in Table 1.

Drop-out rate. The drop-out rates for the two conditions were compared using Fisher's Exact Test. The difference did not achieve statistical significance.

Program effectiveness. Prior to treatment all clients were drinking in excess of the hazardous drinking criteria. At post-assessment 70 percent of those subjects completing the program were drinking in a nonhazardous, controlled fashion. When drop-outs were included as treatment failures, the rate of success was 60 percent. At six-month follow-up, the overall success rate was about the same, both for the program completers (67 percent) and for the total treatment population including drop-outs (57 percent).

Fisher's Exact Test was used to compare the two conditions. At post-assessment a higher rate of success was observed for the enriched condition, both for subjects completing the program and for the total sample (drop-outs included).*

At the six-month follow-up contact, the enriched condition again displayed a higher success rate, both for program completers and for the total sample. However, these differences fell short of statistical significance (p = .27 and .12 for program completers and total population, respectively).

Multivariate analyses of variance. Because the measures of drinking pattern and total consumption were moderately correlated, multivariate techniques were selected for data analysis. Two multivariate analyses of variance for repeated measures were conducted, one to assess pre- to

---

*When only program completers were considered, the differences in success rate fell short of statistical significance (p = .11). However, when drop-outs rates were included as treatment failures, the enriched condition was found to have a significantly higher level of success (p = .04).

TABLE 1
Means and Standard Deviations on Measures of Alcohol Consumption

	Basic		Enriched	
	Mean	S.D.	Mean	S.D.
Total Consumption (in Standardized Ethanol Units)				
pre	38.39	17.50	36.55	19.70
post	25.85	18.40	18.57	9.93
6 months	25.40	14.21	15.35	12.42
Peak Blood Alcohol Level				
pre	.12	.07	.15	.05
post	.08	.03	.10	.07
6 months	.07	.03	.10	.08
Days over limit				
pre	1.3	2.0	1.8	1.5
post	.2	.6	.8	.6
6 months	.8	.9	.3	.8
Days equal to .08				
pre	2.3	2.4	3.3	1.9
post	.9	1.0	1.2	1.2
6 months	1.1	1.8	.8	1.2
Significant Other's Estimate of Client Drinking in Standardized Ethanol Units				
pre	27.45	16.44	27.34	10.54
post	15.70	9.49	15.52	9.38
6 months	16.03	7.36	13.55	7.19

TABLE 2
Multivariate Analysis of Variance
Pre to Post Drinking Indices

Source	*df*	*F*
Between Groups	5,52	1.70
Total consumption	1,56	1.11
Days x .08	1,56	2.01
Peak Blood alcohol level	1,56	3.22
Days > limit	1,56	1.78
Significant others' reports	1,56	0.00
Pre-post	5,52	4.79*
Total consumption	1,56	12.78*
Days > .08	1,56	15.18*
Peak Blood alcohol level	1,56	9.35*
Days > limit	1,56	7.65*
Significant others' reports	1,56	15.21*
Interaction	5,52	0.28
Total consumption	1,56	0.40
Days > .08	1,56	0.54
Peak Blood alcohol level	1,56	0.00
Days > limit	1,56	0.01
Significant others' reports	1,56	0.00

* $p \leq .01$

posttreatment change, the other to assess pre- to six months change (Finn, 1972).

The results of the first multivariate analysis of variance indicated that there was a significant overall pre to posttreatment change ($F = 4.79$, $p < .001$). All five dependent variables showed a significant change. None of the treatment by time interactions was significant (see Table 2.)

The results of the second analysis indicated that there was a significant overall pre to six month change with all five dependent variables displaying a significant change. No treatment by time interactions were significant (see Table 3).

Lifestyle Measures

A series of analyses of variance for repeated measures were performed on the remaining dependent measures to assess pre- to posttreatment change and pre- to six month change.

TABLE 3
Multivariate Analysis of Variance
Pre to Six-Month Drinking Indices

Source	*df*	*F*
Between Groups	5,52	3.00*
Total consumption	1,56	2.00
Days < .08	1,56	0.53
Peak Blood alcohol level	1,56	3.28
Days over limit	1,56	0.00
Significant others' reports	1,56	0.21
Pre-Post	5,52	5.93**
Total consumption	1,56	17.19**
Days < .08	1,56	15.32**
Peak Blood alcohol level	1,56	11.20**
Days over limit	1,56	6.49*
Significant others' reports	1,56	20.28**
Interaction	5,52	.68
Total consumption	1,56	.96
Days < .08	1,56	1.51
Peak Blood alcohol level	1,56	.00
Days over limit	1,56	.14
Significant others' reports	1,56	.18

* $p<.05$
**$p\leq.001$

Marital Satisfaction. The analysis revealed a significant overall pre- to post increase in marital satisfaction, $F(1,28) = 15.89$, $p < .001$. There was a tendency for clients in the basic condition to report greater increases in satisfaction. The six month analysis revealed a significant overall pre- to six month increase, $F(1,28) = 8.83$, $p < .01$. Clients in the basic condition were found to change significantly more than the enriched clients, $F(1,28) = 6.73$, $p = .02$.

Job Satisfaction. The pre-posttreatment analysis revealed no significant changes in job satisfaction. The pre-six month analysis revealed a significant overall improvement in job satisfaction, $F(1,28) = 5.62$, $p = .02$. No significant differences between conditions emerged.

Depression. The analyses revealed a tendency for reported depression to decrease both at post-assessment, $F(1,28) = 2.96$, $p = .10$, and at six months, $F(1,28) = 3.57$, $p = .07$.

Anxiety. The analyses revealed neither significant changes in anxiety over time nor significant time by treatment interactions.

Discussion

The results indicated that the majority of the drinkers involved in this study were able to reduce their alcohol consumption level. Seventy percent of the client population was drinking below the criterion considered to be hazardous after treatment. The reduction in treatment was corroborated by the responses of significant others. Clients were also successful in modifying their pattern of consumption toward a more social style of drinking. They drank to lower blood alcohol levels and were able, in general, to remain below self-selected goals.

Most clients were able to maintain the reduction in drinking for a six month period. Two thirds of the client population was drinking below the criterion hazardous drinking level (12.5 oz. absolute alcohol weekly) at the six month follow-up contact. The maintenance was also generally confirmed by significant others.

Some changes were observed to occur in major life areas other than drinking, most notably, marital satisfaction. Both following treatment and at the six-month point, marital satisfaction was significantly greater than prior to treatment. Changes in job satisfaction and in level of depression were not visible immediately after program completion, but did emerge at the six month point. While the change in these measures may be due to such factors as life events occurring during the months following treatment, it is possible that such changes resulted from lowered alcohol consumption throughout this period. It seems reasonable that satisfaction with work might increase as the client gradually begins to cope with job pressures without reliance on alcohol. The lack of significant improvement in level of anxiety is puzzling given the fact that the enriched program specifically focused on stress management.

The majority of clients in each condition were judged to be drinking in a controlled fashion following treatment. However, a greater number of clients in the basic condition either dropped out of treatment or were found to be drinking at hazardous levels at follow-up and hence were judged treatment "failures." Thus, in terms of global success/failure tabulations, the addition of the stress management techniques appeared to have some benefits.

In terms of the specific drinking and lifestyle measures, however, the differences between the two conditions were far from striking. Although enriched clients displayed better performance on four drinking measures at six month follow-up, the differences did not achieve statistical significance. In fact, there was some suggestion that basic clients were more satisfied with their marital relationships than were enriched clients. The results of the present study were quite similar to those obtained by

Miller (1978). The inclusion of additional treatment techniques did little to augment the effects of the basic self-management drinking skills.

The lack of clear-cut differences between the two programs raises the interesting question of the factors responsible for producing client improvement. It may be that change was largely due to mastery of the drinking self-management skills, and that the stress management techniques were not powerful enough to produce improvement above and beyond these skills. Another possibility is that four to five weeks may have been insufficient to learn stress management. Perhaps with more time devoted to the mastery of the stress management techniques, the enriched program would have improved to a greater extent.

It is also important to consider the so-called "nonspecific" factors involved in treatment. It is certainly possible that the results observed were largely due to such things as the experience of being in treatment, the warm, supportive concern of the counselor, or client motivation to change. An important second step in developing an effective preventive program is to determine whether the improvements observed were a function of the specific self-management techniques or whether other program contents would prove equally effective.

The question of demand for a self-management preventive program was addressed indirectly. Although the recruitment procedures used in the drinking program were the same as those used to recruit clients for stress management and assertiveness programs, the number of calls and clients expressing interest was approximately 25% of the number calling for the other two programs. It appears that attracting clients for preventive programs may in fact be a slow process if traditional recruitment methods are employed. Further, about half of those who contacted the program displayed severe drinking problems requiring more than preventive efforts. Research is necessary to determine how to attract problem drinkers at earlier stages of their drinking careers.

In summary, it appeared that the self-management preventive program was reasonably effective in producing initial reduction and maintenance of alcohol consumption. The drinkers involved in the program will be followed over a five year period to determine whether the program effects will continue without further aid, or whether maintenance interventions are necessary. While additional studies are clearly essential, it appears that a self-management model of prevention is worth further consideration.

REFERENCES

ALANDER, R., & CAMPBELL, T.: *One organization's approach: An evaluative study of an alcohol and drug recovery program.* Oldsmobile Division, General Motors Corp., East Lansing, Michigan, 1973.

BARSBY, S. L., & MARSHALL, G. L.: Short-term consumption effects of a lower minumum alcohol-purchasing age. *Journal of Studies on Alcohol,* 1977, 38, 1665-1679.

BECK, A.: *Depression: Clinical, experimental, and theoretical aspects.* New York: Harper & Row, 1967.

BENSON, H.: *The relaxation response.* New York: Avon, 1975.

BERG, R. L.: The high cost of self-deception. *Preventive Medicine,* 1976. 5, 483-495.

BERNSTEIN, D., & BORKOVEC, T.: *Progressive relaxation training: A manual for the helping professions.* Champaign, Illinois: Research Press, 1973.

BLANE, H.T.: Trends in the prevention of alcoholism. *Psychiatric Research Report,* 1968, 24, 1.

BLANE, H.T.: Education and the prevention of alcoholism. In B. Kissin & H. Begleiter (Eds.), *The biology of alcoholism, Volume IV.* New York: Plenum Press, 1976.

BLAUAT, H. & FLOCCO, W.: A survey of a workable drug abuse program. *Phi Delta Kappan,* 1971, 52, 532-533.

BLUMENTHAL, M., & ROSS, H.L.: Two experimental studies of traffic law. Volume I. The effect of legal sanctions on DUI offenders, DOT Publ. No. HS-800, 825, United States National Highway Traffic Safety Administration, Washington, D.C., 1973.

BRUUN, K. EDWARDS, G., LUMIO, M., MÄKELÄ, K., PAN, L., POPHAM, E., ROOM, R., SCHMIDT, W., SKOG, O., SULKUNEN, P., & ÖSTERBERG, E.: Acohol control policies in public health perspective. *Finnish Foundation for Alcohol Studies,* Vol. 25, Helsinki, 1975.

BRYANT, C.W.: Effects of sale of liquor by the drink in the State of Washington. *Quarterly Journal of Studies on Alcohol,* 1954, 15, 320-324.

CADDY, G., & LOVIBOND, S.H.: Self-regulation or discriminated aversive conditioning in the modification of alcoholics' drinking behavior. *Behavior Therapy,* 1976, 7, 223-230.

CARTWRIGHT, A., MARTIN, F.M., & THOMSON, J.E.: Efficacy of an anti-smoking campaign. *Lancet,* 1960, 327.

CLYNE, R.M.: Detection and rehabilitation of the problem drinker in industry. *Journal of Occupational Medicine,* 1965, 9, 265-268.

CROSS, J.N.: Epidemiological studies and control programs in alcoholism. I. Public health approach to alcoholism control. *American Journal of Public Health,* 1967, 57, 955.

DELINT, J.: The prevention of alcoholism. *Preventive Medicine,* 1974, 3, 24-35.

DEWAR, R., & SOMMER, R.: The consumption of alcohol in a Saskatchewan community before and after the opening of a new liquor outlet. Bureau on Alcoholism, Regina, Sask., 1962.

DICKMAN, F. B., & KEIL, R.J.: Public television and public health. *Journal of Studies on Alcohol,* 1977, 38, 584-592.

DOUGLASS, R.L., & FILKINS, L.D.: *The effect of the lower legal drinking ages on youth crash involvement; final summary report.* Washington, D.C.; U.S. National Highway Traffic Safety Administration; 1974.

EDDY, J.: A DWI Educational program. *Journal of Drug Education,* 1976, 6, 137-139.

EDWARDS, G.: Epidemiology applied to alcoholism: A review and examination of purposes. *Quarterly Journal of Studies on Alcohol,* 1973, 34,28.

FINN, J.D.: *Multivariance: univariate and multivariate analysis of variance, covariance, and regression. Version V. Release 3.* Chicago: National Educational Resources, 1972.

FRANCO, S.C.: Problem drinking in industry: Review of a company program. *Industrial Medicine and Surgery,* 1957, 26, 221-228.

FRANCO, S.C.: A company program for problem drinking: A ten year follow-up. *Journal of Occupational Medicine,* 1960, 2, 157-162.

Fuchs, V.: *Who shall live? Health economics and social health.* New York: Basic Books, 1974.

Haggerty, R.J.: Changing lifestyles to improve health. *Preventive Medicine,* 1977, 6, 276-289.

Hamilton, M.: Treatment of working alcoholics. *Occupational Health,* 1976, 28, 398-399.

Haskins, J.B.: Effects of safety communication campaigns: a review of the research evidence. *Journal of Safety Research,* 1969, 1, 58.

Hayslip, B., Kapunsinski, D., Darbes, A., & Zeh, R.: Evaluation of driving-while-intoxicated programs: Some methodological considerations. *Journal of Studies on Alcohol,* 1976, 37, 11, 91-104.

Hilker, R.R.J.: A company-sponsored alcoholic rehabilitation program. *Journal of Occupational Medicine,* 1972, 14, 769-772.

Hoffman, A.: Information, the irrelevant variable in drug education. Paper presented at the American Personnel and Guidance Association annual convention, Atlantic City, N.J., 1971.

Jellinek, E.M.: Recent trends in alcoholism and in alcohol consumption. *Quarterly Journal of Studies on Alcohol,* 1947, 8, 1-42.

Kalb, M.: The myth of alcoholism prevention. *Preventive Medicine,* 1975, 4, 404-416.

Kammer, M.E., & Dupong, W.G.: Alcohol problems: Study by an industrial medical department. *New York State Journal of Medicine,* 1969, 88, 3105-3110.

Kline, J.A.: Evaluation of a multimedia drug education program. *Journal of Drug Education,* 1972, 2, 229-239.

Lange, A., & Jakubowski, P.: *Responsible assertive behavior: Cognitive/behavioral procedures for trainers.* Champaign, Illinois: Research Press, 1976.

Lau, H.H.: Cost of alcoholic beverages as a determinant of alcohol consumption. In R.J. Givvins, Y. Israel, H. Kalant, R.E. Popham, W. Schmidt, & R.G. Smart (Eds.), *Research Advances in Alcohol and Drug Problems.* New York: Wiley, 1975.

Lewis, J.M., Gossett, J.T., & Phillips, V.A.: Evaluation of a drug prevention program. *Hospital and Community Psychiatry,* 1972, 23, 124-126.

Mäkelä, K.: Types of alcohol restrictions, types of drinkers, and types of alcohol damages; the case of the personnel strike in the stores of the Finnish Alcohol Monopoly. Proceedings of the 20th International Institute of Prevention and Treatment of Alcoholism, 1974, 16-26.

Malfetti, J.L., & Simon, K.J.: A comparison of changes in knowledge and attitude between problem drinkers and non-problem drinkers follwoing a reeducation program. *Proceedings of the 6th International Conference of Alcohol, Drugs, and Traffic Safety,* 1975, 737-748.

Maxwell, M.A.: Alcoholic employees: Behavior changes and occupational alcoholism programs. *Alcoholism,* 1972, 8, 174-180.

McLachlan, J.F., & Walderman, R.L.: Brief scales for evaluating assertiveness, marital communication, and work satisfaction. *Journal of Community Psychology,* 1976, 4, 303-305.

Meichenbaum, D.: Cognitive modification of test anxious college students. *Journal of Consulting and Clinical Psychology,* 1972, 39, 370-380.

Miller, W.R.: Behavioral treatment of problem drinkers: A comparative outcome study of three controlled drinking therapies. *Journal of Consulting and Clinical Psychology,* 1978, 46, 74-86.

Miller, W.R., & Muñoz, R.F.: *How to control your drinking.* Englewood Cliffs, New Jersey: Prentice-Hall, 1976.

Moberg, P.: Follow-up study of persons referred for inpatient treatment from an industrial alcoholism program. Paper presented to the Occupational Section of the Alcohol and Drug Problems Association, San Francisco, California, 1974.

O'Neill, B., & Wells, W.T.: Blood alcohol levels in drivers not involved in accidents. *Quarterly Journal of Studies on Alcohol,* 1971, 32, 798.

Philp, J.R.: Epidemiologic studies and control programs in alcoholism. IV. Discussion. *American Journal of Public Health,* 1967, 57, 971.

POLLACK, S.: Drinking driver and traffic safety: Final report. Los Angeles, University of Southern California, Public Systems Research Institute, 1973.

POPHAM, R.E.: The urban tavern: Some preliminary remarks. *Addictions,* 1962, 9, 16-28.

POPHAM, R.E.: Indirect methods of alcoholism prevalence estimation: A critical evaluation. In R.E. Popham (Ed.), *Alcohol and alcoholism.* Toronto: University of Toronto Press, 1970.

POPHAM, R.E., SCHMIDT, W., & DELINT, J.E.: The prevention of hazardous drinking: Implications for research on the effects of government control measures. In J.A. Ewing and B.A. Rouse (Eds.), *Drinking.* Chicago: Nelson-Hall, 1976(a).

POPHAM, R.E., SCHMIDT, W., & DELINT, J.: The effects of legal restraint on drinking. In B. Kissin & H. Begleiter (Eds.), *The biology of alcoholism, volume IV.* New York: Plenum Press, 1976(b).

RANDALL, D., & WONG, M.R.: Drug education to date: A review. *Journal of Drug Education,* 1976, 6, 1-21.

RAYMOND, A.: Ten o'clock closing—the effect of the change in hotel bar closing time on road accidents in the metropolitan area of Victoria. *Australian Road Research,* 1969, 3, 3-17.

ROMAN, P.M., & TRICE, H.M.: Alcohol Abuse and work organizations. In B. Kissin & H. Begleiter (Eds.), *The biology of alcoholism, Volume IV.* New York: Plenum Press, 1976.

ROOM, R.: The effects of drinking laws on drinking behavior. Paper presented at the annual meeting of the Society for the Study of Social Problems. Denver, Colorado, 1971.

SCHMIDT, W.: A note on the effect of lowering the legal drinking age on the consumption of alcoholic beverages. Addiction Research Foundation, Substudy No. 525, Toronto, 1972.

SCHMIDT, W., & KORNACZEWSKI, A.: A note on the effect of lowering the legal drinking age on alcohol related motor vehicle accidents. Addiction Research Foundation, Substudy, No. 552, Toronto, 1973.

SCHMIDT, W., & POPHAM, R.E.: Heavy alcohol consumption and physical health problems: A review of the epidemiological evidence. *Drug and Alcohol Dependence,* 1975, 27-50.

SCHNEIDERMAN, I.: Family thinking in prevention of alcoholism. *Preventive Medicine,* 1975, 4, 296-309.

SCOLES, P., & FINE, E.W.: Short-term effects of an educational program for drinking drivers. *Journal of Studies on Alcohol,* 1977, 38, 633-637.

SEELEY, J.R.: Death by liver cirrhosis and the price of beverage alcohol. *Canadian Medical Association Journal,* 1960, 83, 1361-1366.

SELZER, M.L., VINOKUR, A., & WILSON, T.D.: A psychosocial comparison of drunken drivers and alcoholics. *Journal of Studies on Alcohol,* 1977, 35, 1294-1312.

SMART, R.: Employed alcoholics treated voluntarily and under constructive coercion: A follow-up study. *Quarterly Journal of Studies on Alcohol,* 1974, 35, 196-209.

SMART, R.G.: The relationship of availability of alcoholic beverages to per capita consumption and alcoholism rates. *Journal of Studies on Alcohol,* 1977, 38, 891-896(a).

SMART, R.G.: Effects of two liquor store strikes on drunkenness, impaired driving and traffic accidents. *Journal of Studies on Alcohol,* 1977, 38, 1785-1789(b).

SMART, R.G., BENNETT, C., & FEJER, D.: A controlled study of the peer group approach to drug education. *Journal of Drug Education,* 1976, 6, 305-311.

SMART, R.G., & FINLEY, J.: Increases in youthful admissions to alcoholism treatment in Ontario. *Drug and Alcohol Dependency,* 1975, 1, 83-87.

SMART, R.G. & GOODSTADT, M.S.: Effects of reducing the legal alcohol-purchasing age on drinking and drinking problems. *Journal of Studies on Alcohol,* 1977, *38,* 1313-1323.

SMART, R.G., & SCHMIDT, W.: Blood alcohol levels in drivers not involved in accidents. *Quarterly Journal of Studies on Alcohol,* 1970, 31, 968-971.

SMART, R.G., & SCHMIDT, W.: Drinking and problems from drinking after a reduction in the minimum drinking age. *British Journal of the Addictions,* 1975, 70, 347-358.

SOBELL, M.B., & SOBELL, L.C.: Individualized behavior therapy for alcoholics. *Behavior Therapy,* 1973, 4, 49-72.

SPEILBERGER, C.D., GORSUCH, R.L., & LUSHENE, R.E.: *The State-Trait Anxiety Inventory test manual for Form X.* Palo Alto, Cal.: Consulting Psychologists Press, 1970.

STUART, R.B.: Teaching facts about drugs: Pushing or preventing. *Journal of Educational Psychology,* 1973, 66, 189-201.

SWISHER, J.D., & CRAWFORD, J.L.: An evaluation of a short-term drug education program. *School Counselor,* 1971, 18, 265-272.

SWISHER, J.D. WARNER, R.W., & HERN, J.: Experimental comparison of four approaches to drug abuse prevention among 9th and 11th graders. *Journal of Counseling Psychology,* 1972, 19, 328-332.

TENNANT, F.S., WEAVER, S.C., & LEWIS, C.E.: Outcomes of drug education: Four case studies. *Pediatrics,* 1973, 52, 246-251.

TERRIS, M.: Epidemiology of cirrhosis of the liver: National mortality data. *American Journal of Public Health,* 1967, 57, 2076.

THOMAS, P.: An evaluation of parent drug education. *Mental Hygiene,* 1971, 55, 456-460.

VINCENT, R.G., MARCHETTA, R.C., & NIGOGOSYAN, G.: Incidence of cirrhosis in oral cancer. *New York State Journal of Medicine,* 1964, 2174-2176.

WILKINSON, R.: *The prevention of drinking problems: Alcohol control and cultural influences.* New York: Oxford Press, 1970.

ZELHART, P.F.: The Alberta Impaired Drivers Program. Final report, phase 1. Edmonton: Department of Psychology, University of Alberta, 1973.

10

Ideal Mental Health Services for Alcoholics and Problem Drinkers: An Exercise in Pragmatics

PETER E. NATHAN

A few months ago, I was asked by the Director of Research at a nearby private psychiatric hospital to consult on a project in which he had become interested. A behavioral psychiatrist from a nearby state, in the course of a recent visit, had offered to establish an outpatient behavior therapy program at the hospital which would give alcoholics and problem drinkers the opportunity to choose either abstinence or controlled social drinking as a treatment goal. Because the latter goal is a most controversial one and the methods to be employed relatively unknown to the Director of Research, a friend and colleague of mine, he had asked me to attend the meeting at which the specifics of the treatment plan and the logistics for its implementation would be presented in greater detail. At this meeting, to which the out-of-state psychiatrist brought a colleague, it rather quickly became clear that the psychiatrist's interest in the project was only as a consultant, that he did not really want to become involved himself in such a controversial, untested enterprise. Instead, he proposed that his colleague, a rehabilitation counselor, be hired to establish the program and to consult with him when, as, and how needed—for a substantial consultancy. Questioned about the procedures and techniques he planned to implement, the psychiatrist dismissed the queries with the off-hand comment that he would use methods he had developed for this purpose in his private practice. Asked to be more specific, he refused, saying only that his experience would provide a methodology that would work.

In fact, it shortly became obvious that the doctor had never actually employed behavioral treatment to modify the drinking behavior of any patient, alcoholic or problem drinker, and that his knowledge of its extensive literature was skimpy and ill-informed. Unfortunately, his enthusiasm for the endeavor during his initial visit had succeeded in rousing the interest and support of the Chairman of the hospital's board, himself a member of Alcoholics Anonymous. Convinced that AA was not the only answer to alcoholism, the Chairman also believed that the problem drinker, long ignored by the alcohol establishment, needed intervention services designed specifically for him/her fully as much as does the alcoholic.

So now the Director of Research had an innovative program, an enthusiastic and influential supporter for it—but no one to do the job!

When the Research Director turned to me to develop the treatment program, he did so because he was under pressure to get the job done, because he thought I knew what needed to be done, and because he was desperate. To the time of his request, no psychologist had directed a clinical endeavor at the hospital. Instead, it had been strongly and identifiably a bastion of private practice psychiatry. It is a measure of how much the hospital and the Research Director felt they needed the program that they turned to a psychologist to do it. Because I felt that development of the program would be a worthwhile service and that a great deal of valuable data on the kinds of alcoholics and problem drinkers responding positively to controlled drinking treatment could be gathered, I agreed to develop the program.

Because I was convinced that an enormous outpouring of interest in the program would be shown by the countless problem drinkers in and around Central New Jersey, resulting in a multitude of clients I would be unable to handle by myself, I enlisted the aid of my colleague Terry Wilson, Co-Director of the Alcohol Behavior Research Laboratory and an accomplished behavior therapist. Together we wrote the following description of the treatment plan, as well as a lengthy research protocol.

Treatment Plan

Following a medical examination, each patient will participate in a total treatment program consisting of 20 therapy sessions distributed over the course of a year. The program blends individual with group therapy sessions in order to accomplish specific treatment objectives. While deliberately structured in accordance with rationally developed treatment guidelines, the program is not inflexible and can be tailored to meet the needs of particular patients.

The Treatment Phase

The treatment phase consists of 12 approximately weekly sessions over an initial three-month period. The first five sessions will be on an individual basis, the primary emphasis being on comprehensive behavioral assessment and the development of a personalized treatment program. Thereafter two sessions will be devoted to group behavior therapy in small groups of three patients each, followed by an individual session, three additional group sessions, and a final individual session. Group sessions will be an hour and a half in duration.

The Maintenance Phase

During the three months following the initial treatment phase, patients will participate in four additional sessions. The first two are scheduled at fortnightly intervals, the others at monthly intervals. The final four sessions will be held at approximately monthly intervals. Sessions 13, 15, 17, and 19 will be group meetings.

Discussion of Treatment Program

The treatment program is designed to develop controlled drinking in problem drinkers. However, the final decision to accept a patient into the program will be based on: (1) a medical examination with appropriate laboratory tests, and (2) behavioral assessment of the patient's drinking problem. In the event that either of these evaluations indicates that abstinence is the more appropriate treatment goal, the program will be modified to this end.

Behavioral Assessment

The primary purpose of the first few sessions, is to establish an ongoing behavioral assessment process that continues throughout treatment and the maintenance phase. As a result, treatment interventions will be continually modified to meet the specific requirements of each patient. Behavioral assessment will be based on several sources of information: (1) intensive interviews with the patient aimed at identifying the specific antecedant, mediational, and consequent variables that are currently maintaining problem drinking. The patient's spouse might be interviewed to obtain clarification or additional information about the patient's drinking problems; (2) information from the pretreatment standardized assessment battery, specifically the Marlatt Drinking History Questionnaire (1975); (3) self-monitoring of daily alcohol-related thoughts, feelings, and behaviors. Patients will be asked to keep daily diaries in which they record amount of any alcohol consumed, the drinking situation (e.g., location and presence of other people), its antecedants, and its consequences; (4) specific imagery and role-playing procedures during therapy sessions.

Treatment Package

Therapy will consist of a multifaceted behavioral approach emphasizing the development of self-regulatory functions and coping skills. The following are core components of the package that will be administered with modifications in timing and emphasis as individual patient assessments dictate.

Self-Regulation

Self-Monitoring. Self-monitoring designed to increase awareness of amount of alcohol consumed under a range of conditions may prove to be reactive in its own right.

Self-evaluation. Patients will learn to set specific target levels of consumption under carefully delimited circumstances. Self-evaluation of adherence to these target levels on a daily basis will be encouraged.

Self-reinforcement. Patients will be instructed to self-reinforce themselves to the extent that they adhere successfully to treatment goals.

Stimulus control. Problem drinking is rarely indiscriminate; it has a higher probability under some circumstances than others. Patients will learn to identify and avoid high risk situations for drinking.

Relaxation Training

Patients will be trained in progressive relaxation as a self-control skill that they can substitute for alcohol intake in situations that previously induced drinking (Goldfried & Trier, 1974). Patients will be provided with cassette audio tapes that they can use to practice relaxation at home.

Cognitive Coping Strategies

Ellis' (1970) rational-emotive(RET) therapy and Meichenbaum's (1977) self-instructional training will be adapted to modify the various cognitive elements of patients' drinking problems.

Guided Imagery Methods

Related to the verbal coping strategies referred to above are imagery based methods such as covert modeling (Kazdin, 1974), in which the patient cognitively rehearses adaptive rather than maladaptive drinking responses to problem situations.

Assertiveness and Social Skills Training

These methods will focus on developing adequate communication competencies and the ability to express genuine feelings (cf., Bower, 1977). Substantial evidence attests to the fact that problem drinkers are deficient in interpersonal skills and the ability to cope behaviorally with conflict or frustration-inducing situations. These interpersonal inadequacies are often centered around the marital relationship. Accordingly, the spouse might be included during this phase of the treatment and considerable emphasis given to behavioral marital therapy. Assertion training is particularly well-suited to group treatment and will constitute a major part of the group sessions.

Maintenance Program

Several explicit maintenance strategies will be employed:

(1) Eight treatment sessions that are distributed over the nine months following the end of the initial three month therapy phase;

(2) Patients will be required to mail in self-monitoring records on a systematic, decreasing schedule over the course of the year. Failure to comply will prompt a telephone inquiry from the therapist;

(3) Patients will be explicitly prepared during therapy to cope with any transgressions from the treatment regimen during follow-up (cf. Marlatt, 1978; Wilson, 1978).

The knowledgeable reader will doubtless recognize the extent to which this plan derives from prior research on broad-spectrum behavioral treatment approaches to chronic alcoholism. A brief review of this literature, designed to highlight its impact on the treatment plan outlined above, follows.

An Overview

Almost 15 years ago, at a time when virtually all behavioral approaches to alcoholism focused solely on modifying the maladaptive drinking response itself, Arnold Lazarus, then and now an influential behavior therapist, suggested instead that a "broad-spectrum" approach to alcoholism might work far better (1965). Among the separate elements of Lazarus' evolutionary treatment package were the following: (1) Medical attention to alcohol-related physical problems; (2) Aversion conditioning, to modify or eliminate abusive drinking; (3) Behavioral assessment, to identify "specific stimulus antecedents of anxiety preparatory to systematic desensitization"; (4) Assertive training, to better equip the patient to respond more appropriately to interpersonally-stressful social situations; (5) Behavioral rehearsal, to develop more adaptive and effective interpersonal skills; (6) Hypnosis, "to counter-condition anxiety-response habits"; (7) Marital therapy, to help the patient's spouse modify his/her central role in the patient's alcoholism. It is striking that the broad-spectrum behavior therapy packages evaluated here, all developed years after Lazarus' conceptual paper, correspond so closely to his suggestions, even though the evaluation component accompanying each renders them much more amenable to validation.

Although a variety of broad-spectrum behavioral treatment packages have been proposed in recent years, only the three most carefully and completely evaluated will be reviewed here. The first of these programs, developed and evaluated by Sobell and Sobell (1973a, 1973b, 1976), is reviewed both because it was the first broad-spectrum package designed specifically to explore the efficacy of controlled drinking treatment and because the follow-up procedures it employed were exceptionally well-planned. Evaluation of the second package, completed more recently by Vogler and his colleagues (1975, 1977a, 1977b), is instructive to review here because a treatment package offered both to alcoholics and to problem drinkers was evaluated. The third broad-spectrum approach overviewed here (Pomerleau, et al., 1976; in press) represented the first behavioral effort to identify and treat middle and upper-middle class alcoholics, a group previously ignored by behavior therapists involved in alcoholism treatment.

The IBTA Study

Guided by the conviction that alcoholism, like other voluntary behaviors, is under the control of its environmental consequences, Linda and Mark Sobell evolved a broad-spectrum behavioral treatment package they called "individualized behavior therapy for alcoholics (IBTA)." The treatment evaluation study of IBTA they subsequently carried out at the Patton (California) State Hospital has become extremely well-known—and very controversial—because it revealed that, regardless of assigned treatment goal (abstinence or controlled-drinking), experimental patients (those receiving IBTA) one and two years posttreatment, were drinking in controlled fashion significantly more frequently than control patients. Specifics of IBTA included the following:

> Irrespective of a subject's assigned treatment goal, all experimental treatment sessions focused directly on drinking behavior, tailoring the treatment as specifically as possible to meet each individual's needs, and emphasizing helping the subject identify the functions of excessive drinking and develop alternative, more beneficial ways of dealing with those situations . . . The only explicit difference in treatment between the non-drinker and controlled drinker experimental groups was that the controlled drinker subjects were trained in methods of non-problem drinking and allowed to practice these behaviors during sessions . . . The vast majority of IBTA treatment sessions can most accurately be termed "behavior change training sessions." The sequence of these sessions incorporated a four-stage process: (1) Problem Identification—Subjects were trained to identify the specific circumstances which had in the past and were likely in the future to result in drinking that would have adverse consequences for the individual; (2) Identification of Alternative Responses to Drinking—Subjects were assisted in generating a series of behavioral options to be used when confronted with problem situations; (3) Evaluation of Alternatives—Subjects were taught how to evaluate each of these behavioral options in terms of their short-term and, especially, long-term effects; (4) Preparation to Engage in the Best Behavioral Alternative—Subjects then practiced the alternative responses which could reasonably be expected to incur the least self-damaging long-term consequences in each instance. Various procedures and behavioral techniques, specific to each individual case, were used to accomplish this objective (Sobell, M.B., 1978, pp. 158-159).

First-year outcome data, reported in 1973 (Sobell & Sobell, 1973b), revealed that both experimental treatment groups (non-drinkers and controlled drinkers) achieved levels of functioning, including levels of alcohol ingestion, superior to their respective control groups. These data were based on follow-up information from 69 of the study's original 70 subjects, an impressive follow-up retention rate. At the end of the second follow-up year, experimental subjects with the assigned treatment goal of controlled-drinking were continuing to function better than their controls while the experimental, nondrinker subjects were doing better, but not significantly better, than their controls (Sobell & Sobell, 1976). Among the most interesting, unexpected features of these data is that subjects in the controlled drinker-experimental group reported significantly more abstinent days than non-drinker experimental subjects—for whom abstinence was the sole treatment goal!

The study's experimental design, conceptual basis, and fundamental aims have been both roundly criticized and widely lauded; both varieties of response to the study have merit. Those who criticize do so by questioning the ethics of controlled drinking treatment in the absence of data attesting to its efficacy, by lamenting the dual status of the lone follow-up worker (L.C. Sobell) as co-investigator, by querying reliance on patient self-reports as principal sources of follow-up information, and by pointing to non-random assignment of patients to treatment groups. Those who consider the study to have been an important contribution, on the other hand, point to the unusually large number of alcoholic subjects selected, treated, and followed to the end of the two-year follow-up mark, to the innovative nature of the behavioral treatment program that was employed, and to the courage of two young investigators in choosing to study as controversial a subject as controlled drinking. Greater detail in criticism of this study is provided by Emrick (1975), Hamburg (1975) and Nathan and Briddell (1977).

But what was of greatest interest to us about this study, as we set about designing a treatment package with similar goals, was why the IBTA treatment package was as successful as it appears to have been. To begin with, the comparative youth of the Sobells—and the enthusiasm and hard work they brought to the project—must be considered as assets of inestimable importance to the study. Beyond these factors, three treatment elements unique to the IBTA program almost certainly also played important roles in its apparent success: (1) Setting out to train one group of alcoholics to be controlled drinkers gave those subjects two new strengths: some of the skills necessary to maintain this changed pattern of drinking *and* the conviction that, even were they to resume drinking after a period of sobriety, they would not have failed either themselves or the program since continued moderate drinking was expected of them. Contrast this attitude toward drinking with that of alcoholics and therapists whose goal is abstinence—that any drinking posttreatment represents crucial failure—and one can appreciate the psychological advantage controlled drinker subjects must have enjoyed as a consequence of this aspect of their treatment; (2) The bulk of IBTA treatment involved an individualized search for the behavioral determinants and correlates of each subject's drinking: the psychological, social, and environmental stimuli associated with each patient's usual drinking circumstances. As a result, patients in the experimental treatment groups received individual behavioral treatment designed to provide them with a whole new repertoire of social behaviors inimical to continued drinking. A minor focus of most therapy for alcoholism, changing attitudes towards drinking and providing the skills for translating changed attitudes into changed behaviors, was a major focus of this treatment; (3) As part of the intensive follow-up of the IBTA program, patients were contacted every two or three weeks to enable the follow-up worker to keep track of their whereabouts for the formal follow-up interviews scheduled at six-month intervals. What the frequent follow-ups also brought about, however, was the following:

> . . . the frequent, continued follow-up contacts were perceived by the majority of subjects, both experimental and control, as beneficial and desirable . . . such frequent follow-up contacts have several advantages over one-time follow-up contacts: (1) They provide extremely low cost "continuing care" after formal treatment which may reduce the likelihood of recidivism; (2) Follow-up as a "continuing care" process may help consolidate gains first made in the treatment program (Sobell, L.C., 1978, p. 179).

Integrated Behavior Change Techniques for Problem Drinkers and Alcoholics

Three recent reports (Vogler, Compton, & Weissbach, 1975; Vogler, Weissbach & Compton, 1977; Vogler, Weissbach, Compton, & Martin, 1977) describe the same set of "integrated behavior change techniques" used with apparent success to treat groups of alcoholics and problem drinkers. One of the most interesting aspects of this work is that a set of procedures first applied to a group of inpatient alcoholics (Vogler et al., 1975) was then used to modify the drinking of a group of problem drinkers who were outpatients. Also of interest is that the several techniques incorporated within Vogler's treatment package bear strong resemblance to those used by the Sobells in the IBTA study. That Roger Vogler and Mark Sobell worked together for a time at the Patton State Hospital accounts for the similarity in their treatment packages; what is more important is that Vogler's findings support the therapeutic potential of the combination of broad-spectrum treatment procedures first assembled by the Sobells. In principle, the Vogler studies make an additional important contribution; their "unpackaging" research design was to permit assessment of the relative contribution to treatment success of the several components of the total treatment package. In practice, however, the actual pattern of findings did not allow these planned comparisons.

Vogler's "integrated behavior change techniques" included the following: videotaped self-confrontation of drunken behavior (to increase motivation for therapy); discrimination training for blood alcohol concentration (to enable subjects to judge with increased accuracy their level of intoxication, in order to maintain their drinking at more moderate levels); aversion training (to establish a conditioned aversion to alcohol); discriminated avoidance practice in which shocks were given for overconsumption (to sharpen the conditioned aversion to alcohol so that it became specific to overconsumption); alternatives training and behavioral counseling (to help patients develop alternative incompatible responses to the setting events that previously occasioned overdrinking); and alcohol education. Most of these procedures were also components of the Sobells' IBTA, though the manner in which they were introduced into therapy and the sequencing of their introduction differed in the Sobell and Vogler studies.

In the first investigation of the efficacy of "integrated behavior change techniques" (Vogler et al., 1975), two matched groups of hospitalized chronic alcoholics were treated. One group of 23 men received the full treatment package over a period averaging 45 days; a second group of 19 men, whose treatment lasted an average of 22.5 days, received only alternatives training, behavioral counseling, and alcohol education. Subjects in both groups attended booster treatment sessions once a week during the month following treatment, then once a month for a year. Data on drinking was also gathered during these visits.

A gross measure of outcome—number of subjects who had maintained abstinence or were drinking in controlled fashion during each follow-up interval—failed to reveal differences between the two treatment groups (65% of patients in both groups met the criterion.) A more discrete measure of outcome, however, revealed that patients in the first group had consumed significantly less ethanol, reflected in ounces per month, than those in the second group over the one-year follow-up period. Other outcome indices, including preferred beverage, preferred locus of consumption, and number of days lost from work pre- and posttreatment, failed to reveal additional differences between the two groups. Essentially the same pattern of group differences in outcome was observed at the 18-month follow-up mark (Vogler, Weissbach, & Compton, 1977).

Four groups of problem drinkers participated in a second trial of Vogler's integrated behavior change techniques (Vogler, Weissbach, Compton, & Martin, 1977). Referred by various community agencies or responding to newspaper advertisements, subjects were considered problem drinkers, not alcoholics, if they had never been diagnosed alcoholic or been hospitalized for alcohol-related problems but had consumed alcohol in sufficent quantities to cause legal, marital, and/or vocational problems. From an original pool of 409 subjects, 80 were followed through to the one-year follow-up mark. Sixty percent of the 409 either failed to meet selection criteria or were unwilling to participate in the program after an initial contact. Another 14% either dropped from treatment or could not be located for follow-up, leaving only 26% of the original subject pool (N=80) available for complete follow-up. Of these subjects, 23 received the full complement of integrated behavior change techniques (Group 1), 19 were given blood alcohol level discrimination training, behavioral counseling, alternatives training, and alcohol education (Group 2), 21 received only alcohol education (Group 3), and 17 were provided behavioral counseling, alternatives training, and alcohol education (Group 4).

The treatment goal for subjects in all groups was moderation. Fifty of the 80 subjects completing treatment and follow-up were considered moderate drinkers at the one-year follow-up mark; three additional subjects had maintained abstinence over the same period. Overall, subjects had decreased their consumption of absolute ethanol by between 50 and 65%. Membership in treatment groups was not associated with differential outcomes. There was no significant difference among groups on any outcome variable. Vogler and his colleagues explain these unexpected findings by pointing to variability among subjects in pretreatment drinking rates and social characteristics, to dependence upon self-reports by subjects for most of the outcome data, and to the fact that subjects in all four groups were given a strong learning orientation to treatment which may have increased the motivation of all to change drinking patterns. The latter explanation, in turn, calls into question whether the specialized behavioral treatment procedures provided subjects in Groups 1 and 2 added anything to overall outcome; if not, one must ask whether they deserve to be maintained in broad-spectrum treatment regimens since they are expensive and require skilled workers for their application. For that matter, one must also question the clinical viability of any set of treatment procedures associated with an 80% attrition rate to the one-year follow-up mark. If subjects must be exceptionally highly motivated to remain in treatment, would not the subjects who do remain respond positively to almost any intervention? One might also ask, in the same context, whether sufficient attention was paid to the problems of maintaining subjects in treatment and active follow-up, given the dramatic subject losses experienced over the course of the study? While one important determinant of these losses was doubtless the subjects' status as "problem drinkers"—men not yet as concerned about their drinking as are many alcoholics—another may have been insufficient attention to efforts to maintain subjects' motivation during and after treatment.

Nonetheless, one must also be impressed by the numbers of subjects in this study drinking more moderately at the one year follow-up mark, even if many or most of them would not have progressed to frank alcoholism. Success in helping such individuals develop more moderate patterns of alcohol consumption is significant. It represents "secondary prevention (Caplan, 1964) in a field that has had to settle for "tertiary prevention"—the least effective, most expensive kind—almost exclusively. The apparent extent of this success was important to us as we planned our own intervention program.

Broad-Spectrum Behavioral Treatment for Middle-Income Problem Drinkers

The problem drinkers to whom Pomerleau and his colleagues at the University of Pennsylvania School of Medicine recently offered broad-spectrum behavior therapy were as different from those treated by Vogler and his colleagues as Vogler's subjects were from the chronic alcoholics to whom the Sobells offered IBTA. Middle-class alcoholics who had to meet strict criteria which guaranteed their membership in this sociocultural category, Pomerleau's patients were almost certainly more highly motivated for treatment, more intact intellectually, socially and emotionally, and possessed of greater familial, vocational, and economic resources than the other groups of broad-spectrum behavior therapy patients studied. As a consequence, both the specifics of the treatment plan outlined by Pomerleau (Pomerleau, Pertschuk, Adkins, & Brady, in press) and its outcome were of interest to us in our own planning.

Pomerleau's problem drinkers came to him via physician referrals and announcements in local media. Subjects were selected on expressing willingness to attend regular treatment and follow-up sessions and to follow detailed treatment protocols and on proving free from serious psychopathology. Thirty-two subjects were ultimately selected for the first trial of the new treatment package. Of these problem drinkers, 18 were randomly asisgned to behavioral treatment and 14 to a traditional treatment package. Treatment, behavioral and traditional, was conducted in groups of three to seven problem drinkers for 90 minutes once a week for three months, then for five additional sessions programmed at increasing intervals for another nine months.

Behavioral treatment consisted of four overlapping phases.

(1) *Baseline*: After an interview designed to elicit a detailed drinking history and to provide information on the treatment program, a prepaid treatment fee (which ranged, on a sliding scale, from $500 to $85, based on ability to pay) was collected. A "commitment fee" of up to $300 was also requested; this sum could be earned back if the subject followed all treatment instructions concerning record keeping, regular treatment attendance, regular sobriety, performance of designated non-drinking activities, and commitment to follow-up contacts. At this time subjects were also instructed on how to keep a detailed record of consumption, drink by drink, as well as how to identify situations which characteristically led to excessive drinking; no effort was made to induce a change in normal drinking during this initial phase of the treatment program.

(2) *Reduction in drinking*: Subjects designated daily quotas for a week's worth of drinking at a time, as well as final treatment goals. Emphasis was placed on gradual, steady improvement rather than abrupt, rapid change. Moderate drinking rather than abstinence was allowed if a subject requested it, he had shown some control over his drinking during the recent past, and there were no medical contraindications to continued drinking. For these subjects, the final goal of the reduction phase of the study was three days a week of abstinence and consumption of no more than three ounces of ethanol on days when drinking was permitted and no more than 10 ounces of ethanol a week overall. Subjects selecting abstinence set similar interim goals but aimed to achieve abstinence within two weeks. Methods taught subjects attempting to alter their customary drinking patterns included stimulus control and contingency management techniques to enable subjects to identify appropriate and inappropriate drinking circumstances (e.g., by drinking with family at dinner rather than with coworkers at a tavern after work), to delay or interfere with maladaptive drinking patterns (e.g., by keeping a glass filled with a soft drink in one's hand at a social gathering), and to increase the likelihood of not drinking in designated situations (e.g., by choosing to attend only those gatherings at which drinking would not take place).

(3) *Behavior therapy for associated behavioral problems*: During this phase of the program emphasis was placed on identifying and altering asso-

ciated behavioral problems with the capacity to affect drinking behavior. Among the behavioral techniques employed (to deal with such behaviors as anger, anxiety, depression, and marital and vocational dysfunction) were assertion training, systematic desensitization, and deep muscle relaxation. Behavior rehearsal and modeling, along with family counseling, were also employed in this effort to confront problems associated with the patient's maladaptive drinking.

(4) *Maintenance of therapeutic gain*: To help patients maintain gains in drinking behavior and in social and vocational spheres, they were encouraged to develop interests in activities (hobbies, physical exercise, academic work) which can be pursued alcohol-free. New friends, rather than old drinking companions, were also to be found. Toward the end of the phase of formal treatment, contact with the therapist was gradually phased out in order to maintain the thrust of therapy for as long as possible.

The traditional treatment offered in this comparative study was designed to last as long and be as intensive as the behaviorally-oriented treatment. Scheduled to cost from $5 to $30 a session for 17 sessions, it did not require prepaid commitment fees nor were refunds available. Stages in the traditional treatment regimen included an introductory phase, lasting three sessions, devoted to development of a sense of group cohesion and mutual trust among group members. Total abstinence was strongly encouraged at the same time that denial patterns were identified. The second, confrontation phase of this therapy, lasting six or seven sessions, also focused on denial patterns, as well as on development of insight into the nature of personal denial mechanisms. The third, resolution phase, lasting two or three sessions, undertook to channel the intense emotions generated in the preceding phase of treatment into productive, future-directed activity; during the same phase, adjunctive psychotherapy for depression, anxiety, family problems, etc. was provided. During the five remaining sessions of this treatment, supportive therapy for nondrinking continued.

Both traditional and behavioral treatment were provided by professionals experienced in the treatment mode they were offering. Of 18 patients treated by behavioral techniques, 16 remained in treatment throughout; by contrast, of 14 patients treated by traditional procedures, only eight remained to the end of the treatment. (Significantly fewer behavioral participants dropped out of treatment.) Drinking rates decreased significantly from screening to the end of the follow-up year in both treatment groups.

These data suggest an advantage for behavioral over traditional treatment: Even though subjects in both groups decreased their drinking rates, more behavioral than traditional subjects stayed with treatment. On the other hand, it is impossible to identify the variable or variables in behavioral treatment responsible for this outcome difference since the two treatments differed so completely, such extra-treatment factors as prepaid commitment fees and monetary penalty for dropping from treatment were not a part of traditional therapy, and subjects in the traditional group could only aspire to abstinence while those in the behavioral group could aim either for abstinence or controlled drinking.

Unlike data from the other two studies reviewed here, these data do not uphold the superiority of behavioral over traditional treatment for alcoholism. On the other hand, the "traditional" treatment offered subjects in this study was undoubtedly superior to the standard hospital milieu "treatment" offered subjects in most other comparative treatment studies. What behavioral treatment did do more effectively than traditional treatment, however, was to keep subjects in treatment through the follow-up period; this achievement was probably brought about both by specific contingencies (e.g., a penalty for dropping from treatment) and by a greater flexibility in permissible drinking behavior posttreatment (e.g., controlled drinking as a treatment goal permits some drinking while abstinence permits none). It is also likely that the prepaid commitment fee required of behavioral subjects yielded subjects who were more highly motivated than those in the traditional group.

Fate of Treatment Program

Along with procedures adapted from these three treatment programs for integration into our treatment package, we also included some promising techniques and procedures whose utility with alcoholics has not yet been fully established. To this end, we planned to teach a variety of self-regulation techniques, including self-monitoring, self-evaluation, self-reinforcement, and stimulus control, because all have been promising as components of innovative behavioral programs to treat obesity (e.g., Mahoney & Arnkoff, in press). Similarly, our decision to include discussion and development of cognitive coping strategies in our treatment program stems from our growing recognition of the importance of cognitions as determiners of both adaptive and maladaptive behavior. In this context, stress will be placed on efforts to identify, then separate, pharmacologic and attitudinal/expectancy effects of ethanol on the alcoholic's behavior; this emphasis derives in part from Wilson's research in our laboratory suggesting that expectations about the impact of alcohol on behavior often determine that behavior, at moderate levels of intoxication, more importantly than the pharmacologic impact of alcohol (Wilson, 1977; Wilson & Abrams, 1978).

Our treatment plan was submitted to the Research Director who, we assumed, would make the final decision about implementation. Instead, the document wended its way through layers and layers of hospital bureaucracy—including the hospital's legal council, medical staff, and Board of Trustees—for clearance. A series of minor but annoying changes were requested; our personal view of this process was that it reflected the hospital's ambivalence about initiating a program that might be, on the one hand, a service to the community, a possible moneymaker, and a public relations coup while being, on the other, a potential source of misunderstanding and conflict with sources which referred members (e.g., AA) to the hospital's large in-patient alcoholism treatment facility. That is, the treatment plan permits patients to pursue a course of treatment designed to convert them from uncontrolled problem drinkers to controlled social drinkers, a treatment goal totally at variance with the abstinence goal of Alcoholics Anonymous.

To "defuse" the potentially fatal impact of this clash of treatment models, a clash made more dangerous by the fact that the inpatient detoxification unit of the hospital was strongly AA-oriented, the hospital's Director met with influential local members of Alcoholics Anonymous and the National Council of Alcoholism, as well as with staff of the detoxification unit, in an effort to reassure them as to our intent to restrict access to the new treatment program to problem drinkers, not alcoholics, and our associated desire to investigate determinants of successful and unsuccessful treatment of problem drinkers, not alcoholics.

The next issue confronted was how to publicize the program. Since the hospital staff—not to say Wilson and Nathan as prospective therapists/researchers—valued their reputations for professional probity and scientific sensitivity, all of us considered very carefully just how to bring the program's availability to the attention of potential patients. Should the hospital take out advertisements in local newspaper, flood the airwaves with announcements, hire billboards, all to announce the exciting new service? Obviously not. What was needed, instead, was a low-keyed, dignified approach that would convince potential clients that the proposed treatment might be more helpful than anything they had tried before, without either overselling an incompletely-tested set of procedures and attracting patients for whom the treatment was clearly inappropriate or underselling it and ending up with few or no appropriate clients. The ultimate decision was to lean over backwards to avoid overpromotion: The program was billed, in a carefully-written press release, as a research project whose ultimate aim was to test out a new set of procedures with a new patient population in order to investigate demographic and drinking history determinants of treatment success or failure. To describe the program as research reduced its appeal to problem drinkers concerned about their drinking and softpedalled its commerical component; in so doing, however, we also ran the risk of offending people when they discovered that the treatment cost money and of failing to reach others who wanted to be treated rather than studied.

Even the final media piece—a press release which simply but accurately described the proposed project largely from its research perspective and identified the program's two principals (Wilson and myself)—had to wend its way through the decision-layers of the hospital; in the process, words, sentences, phrases, and paragraphs came and went as each party to the procedure saw something different in what was being said and, accordingly, changed it according to that perception. When the amended document returned to us, almost unrecognizable, we had to convince the ultimate decisionmakers that what we had originally written remained valid; research was *not* the only purpose of the program and choice of treatment goals *was* necessary to mention.

Sent to some 300 newspapers statewide, the resultant media blitz generated an avalanche—of six telephone calls! A subsequent informational meeting was held, at which projected staff (three) exactly equalled interested potential patients. Moreover, of the latter, one was diagnosed, within five minutes, as both alcoholic and, very likely, psychotic to boot. Of the two remaining subjects, both relatively young, intact, healthy, and probably not alcoholic, one had been a successful AA member for several months, maintaining sobriety during that time via close ties with both his AA sponsor and AA group. As a result, he saw abstinence as his sole treatment goal, a choice with which the program directors heartily agreed. The remaining subject, then, was the only person who could be considered for controlled-drinking oriented treatment!

An Epilogue

While Wilson and I were debating our next step—to go ahead and begin the treatment phase of the program with one abstinence-oriented and one controlled-drinking-oriented patient or to try to add to their number by more aggressive advertising—the debate was resolved by a telephone call from the Research Director, who informed us that the decision to terminate the program had been made. Reasons, he said, included that there was obviously little public interest in behavioral treatment for problem drinkers and that representatives of Alcoholics Anonymous had threatened to stop referring patients to the hospital's inpatient service and its industrial alcoholism program. He also mentioned, in passing, that he had been relieved of his assignment as coordinator of research and was planning to return to full-time clinical work on the hospital's inpatient service.

What Have We Learned?

While we have not given up on the notion of offering a needed public service to a neglected segment of the nation's drinking population, we are nonetheless both surprised and disappointed at the initial response we received from both colleagues and potential clients to what we were convinced was an enormously attractive, ideally-designed treatment approach to a problem all of us had neglected through the years. But, somehow, we either failed to get our message across the first time—or the message was perceived but not believed.

What pragmatic lessons have we learned that could prove useful to others? The following come to mind quickest.

(1) Do not assume that others will recognize the value of what you are offering. Above all, do not assume that the mantle of science will suffice to convince others of the merits of your endeavors. Substance, good public relations, and the success that breeds success are also needed.

(2) Do not assume that an ideal mental health effort, whether directed to assessment, prevention or treatment, will sell itself to a public—or to colleagues—hungry for what is most sound empirically.

(3) Above all, do not assume that an ideal mental health service for alcoholics and problem drinkers can survive the pragmatics of the marketplace simply by force of its empirical justification.

REFERENCES

Bower, G.: Cognitive psychology and behavior modification. Invited address, Association for Advancement of Behavior Therapy, Atlanta, Georgia, 1977.

Caplan, G.: *Principles of preventive psychiatry.* New York: Basic Books, 1964.

Ellis, A.: *The essence of rational psychotherapy: A comprehensive approach to treatment.* New York: Institute for Rational Living, 1970.

EMRICK, C.D.: A review of psychologically oriented treatment of alcoholism. *Journal of Studies on Alcohol,* 1975, *36,* 88-108.

GOLDFRIED, M.R., & TRIER, C.S.: Effectiveness of relaxation as an active coping skill. *Journal of Abnormal Psychology,* 1974, *83,* 348-355.

HAMBURG, S.: Behavior therapy in alcoholism; a critical review of broad-spectrum approaches. *Journal of Studies on Alcohol,* 1975, *36,* 69-87.

KAZDIN, A.E.: Effects of covert modeling and model reinforcement on assertive behavior. *Journal of Abnormal Psychology,* 1974, *83,* 240-252.

LAZARUS, A.A.: Towards the understanding and effective treatment of alcoholism. *South African Medical Journal,* 1965, *39,* 736-741.

MAHONEY, M.M., & ARNKOFF, D.: Cognitive and self-control therapies. In S.L. Garfield & A.E. Bergin (Eds.), *Handbook of psychotherapy and behavior change,* 2nd Ed., New York: Wiley, in press.

MARLATT, G.A.: The drinking profile: A questionnaire for the behavioral assessment of alcoholism. In E.J. Mash & L.G. Terdal (Eds.), *Behavior therapy assessment: Diagnosis and evaluation.* New York: Springer, 1975.

MARLATT, G.A.: Craving for alcohol, loss of control, and relapse: A cognitive-behavioral analysis. In P.E. Nathan & G.A. Marlatt (Eds.), *Alcoholism: New directions in behavioral research and treatment.* New York: Plenum Press, 1978.

MEICHENBAUM, D.: *Cognitive behavior modification.* New York: Plenum Press, 1977.

NATHAN, P.E., & BRIDDELL, D.W.: Behavior assessment and treatment of alcoholism. In B. Kissin & H. Begleiter (Eds.), *The biology of alcoholism.* New York: Plenum Press, 1977.

POMERLEAU, O.F., PERTSCHUK, M., ADKINS, D., & BRADY, J.P.: A comparison of behavioral and traditional treatment for middle income problem drinkers. *Behavior Therapy,* in press.

POMERLEAU, O.F., PERTSCHUK, M., & STINNETT, J.: A critical examination of some current assumptions in the treatment of alcoholism. *Journal of Studies on Alcohol,* 1976, *37,* 849-867.

SOBELL, L.C.: A critique of alcoholism treatment evaluation. In G.A. Marlatt & P.E. Nathan (Eds.), *Behavioral assessment and treatment of alcoholism.* New Brunswick, NJ: Rutgers Center of Alcohol Studies, 1978.

SOBELL, M.B.: Empirically-derived components of treatment for alcohol problems: Some issues and extensions. In G.A. Marlatt & P.E. Nathan (Eds.), *Behavioral assessment and treatment of alcoholism.* New Brunswick, NJ: Rutgers Center of Alcohol Studies, 1978.

SOBELL, M.B., & SOBELL, L.C.: Individualized behavior therapy for alcoholics. *Behavior Therapy,* 1973, *4,* 49-72(a).

SOBELL, M.B., & SOBELL, L.C.: Alcoholics treated by individualized behavior therapy: One-year treatment outcome. *Behaviour Research and Therapy,* 1973, *11,* 599-618(b).

SOBELL, M.B., & SOBELL, L.C.: Second-year treatment outcome of alcoholics treated by individualized behavior therapy: Results. *Behaviour Research and Therapy,* 1976, *14,* 195-215.

VOGLER, R.E., COMPTON, J.V., & WEISSBACH, T.A.: Integrated behavior change techniques for alcoholics. *Journal of Consulting and Clinical Psychology,* 1975, *43,* 233-243.

VOGLER, R.E., WEISSBACH, T.A., & COMPTON, J.V.: Learning techniques for alcohol abuse. *Behaviour Research and Therapy,* 1977, *15,* 31-38.

VOGLER, R.E., WEISSBACH, T.A., COMPTON, J.V., & MARTIN, G.T.: Integrated behavior change techniques for problem drinkers in the community. *Journal of Consulting and Clinical Psychology,* 1977, *45,* 267-279.

WILSON, G.T.: Alcohol and human sexual behavior. *Behaviour Research and Therapy,* 1977, *15,* 239-252.

WILSON, G.T.: Booze, beliefs, and behavior: Cognitive processes in alcohol use and abuse. In P.E. Nathan & G.A. Marlatt (Eds.), *Alcoholism: New directions in behavioral research and treatment.* New York: Plenum Press, 1978.

WILSON, G.T. & ABRAMS, D.: Effects of alcohol on social anxiety and physiological arousal: Cognitive versus pharmacological processes. *Cognitive Therapy and Research,* 1978, *1,* 195-210.

11

Considerations in Developing a Treatment Program for the Coronary-Prone (Type A) Behavior Pattern

ETHEL ROSKIES

The rushed, competitive, achievement-oriented lifestyle subsumed under the Type A label provides both a novel opportunity and a unique challenge to the emerging discipline of behavioral medicine. The behaviors that make up the pattern are not usually categorized as being socially deviant, psychopathological or physically harmful; on the contrary, ambition, goal-directedness and time-urgency are precisely those qualities which our society encourages and rewards. Nevertheless, a growing body of evidence points to the Type A Behavior Pattern (TABP) as a major independent risk factor for coronary heart disease (Rosenman, Brand, Jenkins, Friedmen, Straus & Wurm, 1975; Rosenman, Brand, Sholtz & Friedman, 1976). For what may well be the first time in the history of medicine, a purely behavioral method not tapping subclinical signs and symptoms has successfully and independently predicted future emergence of a somatic disease (Dembroski, Caffrey, Jen-

This paper was written during a sabbatical leave spent as a Visiting Scholar, University of California at Berkeley, partially supported by a Canada Council Leave Fellowship.

kins, Rosenman, Spielberger & Tasto, 1977). Now the test is whether behavioral methods can effectively treat the health problem they have uncovered. If proponents of behavioral medicine can meet this challenge, we shall indeed be opening new vistas in the prevention and treatment of disease.

Researchers and clinicians have recently become aware of Type A intervention as an exciting new area of investigation. The first studies reporting results are just beginning to appear (Roskies, Spevack, Surkis, Cohen & Gilman, 1978; Suinn, 1975; Suinn & Bloom, 1978), but others are in progress or being planned (Friedman, 1977a; Roskies, 1978). Other straws in the wind are workshops on Type A modification at the most recent annual meetings of the American Psychological Association and the Association for the Advancement of Behavior Therapy, as well as a chapter on the topic in a new book on behavioral approaches to medical problems (Suinn, 1977). The addition of this paper to the deliberations of a conference on changing health lifestyles is another indication of the growing interest in the area.

Unfortunately, the very characteristics that make the TABP a tempting therapeutic target also make it an elusive one. If nothing else, our modest success to date in permanently modifying eating, drinking and smoking behavior should have alerted us to the difficulties inherent in attempting to change habits that are deeply rooted in the individual's lifestyle (cf. Bernstein & McAllister, 1976; Marlatt, this volume; Stunkard, 1977). In the case of the TABP these difficulties are intensified by the fact that it is the general lifestyle itself, rather than any specific behavior, that is the focus of our intervention. Moreover, neither the individual nor his or her environment is likely to consider the lifestyle in question as pathological. Thus the behavior change technology developed in the last two decades for "disorders of self-control" (Brady, 1977) cannot simply be generalized to this new area. Instead, the usual problems of designing an intervention program, selecting and recruiting a sample, and evaluating the effects of treatment all have to be considered anew in the light of the unique characteristics of the TABP as a health problem.

In addition to these technical considerations, the attempt to treat the TABP also raises some difficult social and ethical issues. Because the TABP is congruent with the values of our society, it may be impossible to permanently change the pattern in individuals unless we first change the environmental conditions that elicit and maintain this type of behavior. If this is so, classifying certain people as Type A and offering them treatment for the condition may simply create anxiety about this new health problem without providing the means of remedying it. The potential for harm is demonstrated in a longitudinal study of hypertensive Canadian steelworkers (Mossey, 1975; Sackett, Taylor & Haynes, 1977) which showed that becoming aware of one's hypertension, if not followed by effective treatment, was associated with increased absenteeism from work and a decline in psychosocial functioning.

Even if we can directly change the Type A individual's behavior, this may conflict with other goals that are individually and socially valued. For instance, the TABP has often been associated with work involvement and occupational success. In fact, Mettlin (1976) has suggested that the Type A pattern may be "integral to the modern occupational career." Whatever the reality of the relationship between the Type A pattern and occupational success, any treatment program will have to deal with the possibility, or at least the fear, of diminished achievement in participants. And should treatment, in fact, lead to a reduction in work effort, positive gains for the individual may have to be balanced against possible negative effects for his or her family and the society at large.

This paper is not intended as a cookbook approach to overcoming the theoretical and practical problems involved in Type A intervention. Although new areas of research tend to give rise to instant experts, it would be presumptuous in the present embryonic state of our knowledge for anyone to claim to possess the truth, or even the path that will lead us to it. In fact, the major conclusion to be drawn from reading what has been written to date on Type A intervention is that thoughtful people studying the same questions can arrive at very different answers. And as yet, no one has generated good enough results to provide an empirical basis for choosing between alternatives.

But even if we cannot yet know which, if any, of the current approaches to intervention will eventually prove its effectiveness, it is important that we try to be as clear as possible about the conceptual and methodological decisions that underlie our treatment paradigms. Only to the degree that we are able to specify what we are trying to do, how and why, are we likely to generate findings meaningful enough to lead to progress in understanding. This paper hopes to provide some of the clarification needed, first by conceptualizing the process of developing a treatment program as a series of decision points, and second by examining the general Type A literature for its bearing on these points. For those who are already engaged in modifying Type A behavior, it is hoped that the conceptual framework developed here will help to sharpen our thinking about purposes and methods. For those who are just beginning to work on Type A intervention, it is hoped that this attempt at systematization will serve as an introduction, facilitating access to a literature that is scattered in a large number of behavioral and medical journals.

Type A as a Research Concept

If past experience is any indication of future probabilities, then those embarking on Type A intervention research would do well to anticipate a high level of controversy. The field of cardiovascular epidemiology in general has been distinguished by the sharpness of its debates (e.g., the role of diet in hypercholesterolemia), but even within this context the emergence of the TABP as a risk factor has been marked by claims and challenges of unusual intensity. Among the major risk factors for coronary heart disease (CHD), it is the TABP that has had the hardest time gaining the acceptance, or even the serious attention, of the epidemiological community.

Paradoxically, some of the earliest observations made about coronary heart disease concerned the characteristic behavior of those afflicted with it. Beginning with Osler in the last decade of the 19th century, clinicians repeatedly pointed to the hard-driving, goal-directed, aggressive qualities of coronary patients (cf. Rosenman, 1974 and 1977a for reviews of some of this early literature). Nevertheless, when the growing pandemic of CHD in the 1930s and 1940s gave rise to a series of long-term prospective studies of CHD risk factors (e.g., the Framingham Study, the Los Angeles Study, the Chicago Study, the Albany Study), personality factors were largely ignored in favor of medical history, biochemical indices and smoking behavior. As late as 1973, the actuarial tables of coronary risk published by the American Heart Association listed only seven variables: age, sex, cigarette smoking, elevated systolic blood pressure, serum cholesterol, LVH, and diabetes measured by biochemical procedures (Insull, 1973).

Nevertheless, the notion that coronary patients might be distinguished by "personality attributes or behavior traits" (Rosenman, 1977a) did not disappear completely. In the 1950s, two cardiologists, Drs. Meyer Friedman and Ray Rosenman, were sufficiently impressed by what they observed in their own post-coronary patients to begin a series of small scale investigations of the possible role of emotional factors in heart disease (Friedman & Rosenman, 1959; Friedman, Rosenman & Carroll, 1958). Fortunately for the evolution of the concept, neither Friedman nor Rosenman was formally trained in psychosomatic medicine. Thus instead of providing the conventional complex analysis of the coronary-prone individual in terms of his or her unconscious conflicts (Alexander, 1950) or characteriological reaction formations (Dunbar, 1943), they presented a purely phenomenological portrait of a small number of observable behaviors that the Type A individual was likely to manifest in a challenging situation. Even more important, this typology was so simple that at the end of a 15 minute stress interview, designed to elicit the critical behaviors, most individuals could be unambiguously classified either as coronary-prone Type A, or as noncoronary-prone Type B* (Rosenman, Friedman, Straus, Wurm, Kositchek, Hahn & Werthessen, 1964). What they had done, in essence, was to cast the personality hypothesis in a form where it could now be used to predict disease, rather than simply to explain it once it had occurred.

This novel application of behavioral analysis to cardiology did not arouse the enthusiasm either of cardiologists or of psychiatrists. It was not until 1960, much later than most of the other large prospective studies, that the Type A hypothesis was given a full scale test. The Western Collaborative Group Study (WCGS), mounted for this purpose, classified 3,154 initially well, middle-aged, predominantly middle-class men in California according to behavior type, and then followed them for 8½ years to determine their subsequent cardiac morbidity and mortality (Rosenman et al., 1964). The results indicated that, even controlling for the effect of other risk factors, Type A men had double the risk of developing, or dying from, coronary heart disease than did Type B men (Rosenman, Brand et al., 1975, 1976). In addition, the presence of the TABP increased the virulence of other risk factors; at each level of risk for serum cholesterol, blood pressure, cigarette smoking, etc., Type A men had a higher incidence of CHD then did Type B men (Brand, Rosenman, Sholtz & Friedman, 1976). Following a first myocardial infarction, the risk of a subsequent one for Type A men was also higher, being approximately twice that experienced by Type B men (Jenkins, Zyzanski, & Rosenman, 1976).

Although the WCGS remains the cornerstone of Type A epidemiol-

---

*To be more precise, there were originally five categories ranging from extreme A (A_1) through moderate A (A_2), even distribution of A and B characteristics (X), moderate B (B_3) to extreme B (B_4). No convincing dose-response relationship was found in the WCGS between intensity of A or B behavior and level of risk. Subjects classified as A_1 and A_2 had comparable risk, while those classified as B_3 and B_4 had comparable risk at about half the A level (Feinleib, Brand, Remington & Zyzanski, 1977). Most recent publications simply use two categories—Type A and Type B.

ogical research, its findings have been corroborated by others. Citing over 20 retrospective and prospective studies in his recent major review of the literature, Jenkins (1976) concluded that the evidence for the TABP as a causal factor in CHD was stronger than for any other psychosocial variable. The growing recognition of the importance of the behavior pattern as a risk factor for CHD was given concrete expression in the decision of the (U.S.) National Heart Lung and Blood Institute to convene a conference devoted to this specific topic (Dembroski, 1977).

The conference on coronary-prone behavior, held in June 1977, also served to begin a new chapter in the development of the concept. Up to then, most of the debate concerning Type A had focused on the validity of its statistical association with CHD, and the psychometric properties of the methods used to assess it. While these issues were fully discussed at the conference, the program was broadened to encompass consideration of biochemical and neuroendocrine mechanisms, as well as the cultural and familial settings that give rise to the pattern. There was even a section on intervention. A rather slim one it is true, but enough to indicate the shift in focus from debating the risk associated with Type A behavior to discussing how best to go about changing it.

Prevalence of the Type A Behavior Pattern

A basic prerequisite for designing a Type A intervention program is to have some idea of the expected frequency of the target behavior pattern. Most of our knowledge concerning the Type A behavior pattern, both its capacity to predict heart disease and its relationship to demographic variables, comes from the study of middle-aged, predominantly middle-class, white American males. In fact, the two major methods used for assessing Type A, the Structured Interview and the Jenkins Activity Survey, were developed and validated on precisely such a sample in the Western Collaborative Group Study. A few large scale prospective studies tapping more varied populations* have been launched

*Almost all the studies assessing samples other than white, middle-class, middle-aged American males have relied on the Jenkins Activity Survey, a multiple choice, self-administered, computer-scored questionnaire. The Jenkins Activity Survey (JAS) was developed by Jenkins, in collaboration with Rosenman and Friedman (Jenkins, Rosenmen & Friedman, 1967), to provide an objective, convenient and inexpensive method of assessing large samples. Instead of the dichotomous classification of the Structured Interview, it was standardized on the WCGS sample to yield a mean of 0 and a standard deviation of 10. In the WCGS study, 98% of the subjects had scores ranging from -20 on the Type B end to +20 on the Type A end.

(e.g., the Chicago Heart Association Detection in Industry Study whose sample of 5,347 contains substantial numbers of women, blacks and blue collar workers, the Belgian Multi-factorial Prevention Project with a sample of over 7,000 European men aged 40-59, and the Honolulu Heart Project which assessed Type A characteristics in 2,000 Japanese-Americans living in Hawaii), but to date only the Hawaii project has reported on cardiac morbidity and mortality (Zyzanski, 1977). For this reason, statements about coronary-prone behavior in women, Europeans, blue-collar workers, and so on are necessarily incomplete and possibly inaccurate.

In the WCGS study begun in 1960, 50 percent of the sample was initially classified as Type A on the basis of the Structured Interview. Rosenman (1974) has claimed that since then the pressures of our industrialized society have pushed the prevalence of Type A to 75 percent of the population and, in fact, Howard, Cunningham and Rechnitzer (1976, 1977) did categorize 76 percent of their sample of Canadian managers as Type A. It is difficult to know whether the higher percentage found in the more recent study reflects a real shift over time or simply a peculiarity of this specific sample.

Most of the studies that have gathered occupational data have found a positive association between occupational level and Type A scores. A similar positive relationship exists between Type A scores and level of education (Zyzanski, 1977). This does not mean that Type Bs cannot be found in top management and Type As in the laboring occupations. Nevertheless, there is some tendency for individuals in professional and managerial occupations to have a higher frequency of Type A behavior. It is possible, however, that the relationship between occupation and Type A behavior is curvilinear with Type As found most frequently at the middle levels. Howard, Rechnitzer and Cunningham (1977) report that in their sample of Canadian managers the percentage of Type As decreased at the very top levels, in contrast to their heavy clustering in middle management. Similarly in the WCGS, the middle level salesmen had higher mean Type A scores on the JAS than did managers, or professional and technical staff (Zyzanski, 1977).

In general, Type A behavior is more common among men than among women in the United States, though differences between the sexes de-

---

Concern has been expressed (Feinleib et al., 1977) that earlier versions of the questionnaire might include items that are not valid for housewives, students, retired people and certain categories of the self-employed. Recent revisions of the questionnaire (Jenkins, 1977; Waldron, 1977) have provided a form that is valid for both sexes (B) and separate versions for the employed (E) and the non-employed (N).

cline drastically when factors of occupation, age and socio-economic status are taken into account. Women who work, particularly those in the labor force past the age of 25, have Type A scores that are closer to those of men (Waldron, 1977; Waldron, Zyzanski, Shekelle, Jenkins & Tannenbaum, 1977). In fact, when differences in occupational level and education were controlled for statistically in the Chicago Heart Association Detection in Industry Study, women's Type A scores did not differ significantly from those of the men (Shekelle, Schoenberger & Stamler, 1976). The expected frequency of Type A behavior in a sample of women, therefore, would depend on the demographic characteristics of the specific sample being studied.

An issue of prime importance is whether the Type A behavior pattern as it is currently assessed has the same predictive relationship to CHD in women as in men. As yet, there are no findings for women from a large prospective study of the calibre of the WCGS, but a few small studies that have examined the prevalence of CHD in extreme Type A women (Rosenman & Friedman, 1961) and the prevalence of Type A characteristics in women with heart disease (Bengtsson, Hallstrom & Tibblin, 1973; Kenigsberg, Zyzanski, Jenkins, Wardwell & Licciardello, 1974) do provide positive evidence of a relationship. Recently, Haynes, Levine, Scotch, Feinleib and Kannel (1978) extrapolated a Type A scale from items administered in the Framingham Study and found that women rated Type A in this fashion had a significantly higher prevalence of CHD than Type Bs, the differences becoming more marked with advancing age. The Framingham data have also provided the first findings concerning incidence of CHD in Type A women; in the sample of initially well women under 65 followed for 8 years, the risk for those classified as Framingham Type A compared to Type Bs was 5:2 in the 45-54 age range, and twofold in the 55-64 range (Haynes, Feinleib & Kannel, 1978). Although the comparison between the Framingham study and the WCGS is a rough one, Type A appears to increase risk in women as much as, or even slightly more than, it does in men.

Within restricted age groups, such as the 39- and 59-year-old sample of the WCGS, no relationship has been found between age and Type A scores. In studies encompassing men of a wider age range, however, a modest inverse relationship to age is found (Howard, Cunningham & Rechnitzer, 1976; Mettlin, 1976; Shekelle, Schoenberger & Stamler, 1976; Zyzanski, 1977). In contrast to employed women whose Type A scores rise with age, men show a slight slowing down with age. Even in the most extreme example, however (the Boston study of 390 air traffic controllers reported in Zyzanski, 1977), age does not account for more than 4% of the variation in Type A scores.

All non-white and non-American samples studied to date manifest JAS scores that are closer to the B end of the continuum than the mean score established for the criterion WCGS sample. For the European samples, this difference has ranged from a mean of -1.3 in a sample of 12 towns in England (compared to the mean of 0 in the WCGS) to a mean of -4.7 in the Belgian project. Both black males and black females in the U.S. score substantially in the Type B direction (the mean scores in the Chicago study were -3.04 and -5.79 respectively) though in this case the differences are compounded by a disproportionate distribution of age and occupational level within the four sex-race subsamples (Zyzanski, 1977). The largest difference shown to date was in a sample of Japanese-Americans living in Hawaii where only 15% of the men were classified within the Type A range, compared to 50% in the WCGS (Cohen, 1974).

Even more significant than the differences in mean scores is the possibility that the coronary-prone behavior pattern may take very different forms in different cultural settings. For instance, the JAS Scale in the United States has been factor analyzed to yield three sub-scales, Speed and Impatience (S), Hard driving and Competitive (H), and Job Involvement (J) (Zyzanski & Jenkins, 1970). In the Japanese-American sample, however, there was a clear distinction between the hard-driving and hardworking components of the H scale, presumably because only the latter is congruent with Japanese cultural expectations (Cohen, 1977). For blacks in the U.S., too, Waldron et al. (1977) found that hardworking was a more adequate description of the H scale, while Job Involvement was better interpreted in this group as striving to advance. How Type A behavior is expressed in a particular cultural group, therefore, may depend to a considerable extent on the general norms and values of the group.

Deciding What to Change

The Type A person has been described by Rosenman (1974) as "an individual engaged in a relatively chronic excessive struggle to obtain a usually unlimited number of things from his environment in the shortest period of time or against the opposing effects of other things or persons in this same environment." The spate of recent studies using the A-B classification as a variable has added further details to this behavioral portrait: Type A individuals speak louder and faster than persons characterized as Type B (Schucker & Jacobs, 1977); they report less contentment on their jobs, but also feel more able to make a change should they desire it (Howard, Cunningham & Rechnitzer, 1977); on a treadmill task, they work at a level closer to the limits of their endurance, but, even as they do so, they are more likely to suppress feelings of fatigue (Carver, Coleman & Glass, 1976); they prefer to wait with others prior to working on a stressful task, but while actually doing the task they prefer to work alone (Dembroski & MacDougall, 1978), and so on. Unfortunately, this catalogue of presumed Type A characteristics provides no guidelines for distinguishing between those characteristics which are simply chance findings in the specific sample under study, those which are generalizable to most Type A people but are irrelevant to increased risk of CHD, and those which are the true pathogenic ones. *Not all Type A behavior is necessarily coronary-prone behavior, and the distinction between the what is and what is not is crucial if we hope to develop effective and efficient intervention programs.*

One possible method of teasing out the pathogenic elements in the Type A pattern is to isolate what specifically in the Structured Interview or the Jenkins Activity Survey predicts CHD. This analysis was tried first with the JAS, but the results were disappointing in that none of the three factors identified (Hard Driving and Competitive, Speed and Impatience, Job Involvement) successfully predicted CHD in the WCGS sample (Zyzanski & Jenkins, 1970). Using a sub-sample of 186 men drawn from the total WCGS sample, Matthews, Glass, Rosenman and Bortner (1977) were able to extract two factors from the Structured Interview—Competitive Drive and Impatience—that successfully distinguished men who eventually developed CHD from matched pairs who did not. These findings still require cross-validation, of course. An even more ambitious attempt to subject the Type A/B behavior pattern to a multidimensional analysis has recently been launched by a group at the Stanford Research Institute (Tasto, Chesney & Chadwick, 1977), but here, too, work is only beginning.

One solution to the dilemma of specifying a therapeutic target is to attack the TABP at its source by seeking to change the general philosophy of life that gives rise to the specific behaviors. The guidelines for Type A intervention developed by Friedman and Rosenman (1974) appear to be based on such an approach, stressing a radical philosophical reorientation, as much as specific behavior drills. In a recent article on the topic (Rosenman & Friedman, 1977), they state the case clearly:

> We believe that Type A behavior cannot be changed unless patients are sufficiently motivated to do so, by being helped to achieve a certain level of philosophical awareness of their total life structure. This awareness should lead them to recognize perhaps for the first

> time, that they had been falsely attributing many of their past successes to a behavior pattern which has not truly advanced their socio-economic career. Indeed, such a pattern may have done just the opposite. They must be helped to recognize that unless altered, this pattern will continue to impede their socio-economic advance and might also bring on a cardiac catastrophe (p. 325).

The behavioral consequences of this new philosophical outlook would involve a widening of cultural and intellectual horizons, an increased openness to friendship, and greater appreciation of myth, ritual and tradition (Friedman & Rosenman, 1974).

A life filled with good books and good friends is probably closer to the personal ideal of most therapists than one devoted to the solitary reading of financial statements. More relevant, it is possible that this type of maximal therapeutic intervention may prove to be the only effective way of reducing the coronary risk associated with the TABP. Such an approach, however, confronts us with a host of ethical and practical difficulties. Radical re-engineering of an individual's lifestyle can have far-reaching consequences not only for the person him or herself, but also for the family and even the society at large. Until we have stronger data than we currently do about the necessity and efficacy of such changes, the would-be therapist might be justifiably cautious about embarking on such a venture. Practically, too, this type of approach would be restricted to the small fraction of Type A individuals willing to undertake such an extensive change in their lives. And for those who do volunteer, costs can be expected to be high. The pilot project described by Rosenman and Friedman (1977) had 12 men meeting with a psychoanalyst over a period of 18 months.

A very different alternative from seeking to modify Type A behavior at its source, is to attempt to pinpoint the common pathway by which the specific manifestations of the pattern lead to increased atherosclerosis, and to increased risk of CHD. Here we are looking not at what causes the pattern, but at the mechanisms by which it exerts its harmful effects (Williams, Friedman, Glass, Herd & Schneiderman, 1977). A number of recent studies have suggested that Type A individuals are distinguished from Type B persons by their psychological and physiological hyperreactivity to challenge. Individuals with the endogenous predisposition to Type A behavior not only create much of their own stress by perceiving challenge where others do not, but also, compared to Type B persons, show a sharper rise in autonomic and neuroendocrine responses under challenge and are slower to return to baseline (Dembroski, MacDougall & Shields, 1977; Frankenhaeuser, 1977b;

Friedman, Byers, Diamant & Rosenman, 1975; Glass, 1977a). This hyperreactivity is considered particularly important because of the relationship postulated between sympathetic arousal, with its associated endocrine activity, and the development of atherosclerosis (Davis, 1974; Gilmore, 1974; Obrist, 1976; Williams, 1975).

The hypothesis of hyperreactivity as the pathogenic element in the Type A pattern leads us to consider whether the damage is caused by too frequent nonspecific general mobilization, or, rather, whether there is a specific type of emotional response that is particularly harmful. There are a number of studies that suggest both that hostility is an emotion often found in Type A individuals under challenge (cf. Glass, 1977a; Glass, Snyder & Hollis, 1974), and that high levels of hostility are positively associated with degree of coronary atherosclerosis (Williams, 1978) and risk of heart disease (Matthews et al., 1977). What we don't know at this point is the nature of the relationship between hostility, the general Type A behavior pattern, and CHD. It is possible that individuals with the coronary-prone pattern are more likely to be aroused by stimuli that produce anger or, conversely, they may simply have a tendency to label any arousal they experience as anger. It is also possible, however, that there is a somatic response pattern produced by anger that is more damaging than the response patterns produced by other emotions. The issue of generality vs. specificity of emotional response is a complex and highly controversial one (cf. Lazarus, Cohen, Folkman, Kanner and Schaefer, in press, and Schachter, 1966, for opposing views). For treatment purposes, however, it may be sufficient simply to recognize that arousal in Type A individuals is more likely to be manifested as hostility than as fear, guilt, sadness, joy, love, or exhilaration and, therefore we should pay specific attention to anger management (cf. Novaco, 1977; in press) in our intervention programs.

If changing the frequency, intensity and duration of stress responses in the Type A individual will indeed lower his or her risk for CHD, then we have found a treatment target that has a number of practical advantages. For one, individuals can be taught to lower their internal thermostats without necessarily making any radical changes in the external circumstances of their lives. Second, this form of stress management is likely to be acceptable to a wide range of consumers. Third, programs that teach stress management skills are traditionally of short duration and hence economical. Both Suinn (1975; Suinn & Bloom, in 1978) and I (Roskies et al., 1978; Roskies, 1978) are currently testing variations of this approach in our respective intervention programs.

The discussion to this point has focused on changes in the individual.

Instead of, or in addition to, modifying Type A behavior in individuals, one can also seek to change those elements in the environment which encourage or force the individual to behave in a time-urgent, competitive manner. Rosenman and Friedman have repeatedly reiterated their belief that Type A behavior is not simply the expression of an innate personality disposition, but instead reflects a response to environmental pressure (Friedman & Rosenman, 1974; Rosenman, 1974; Rosenman, 1977a). Confirmatory empirical evidence for this viewpoint is provided by Howard, Cunningham and Rechnitzer (1976, 1977), who describe the features of the work environment that are associated with Type A behavior, and emphasize that it was the fast growing companies within their sample which attracted or created the highest percentage of Type As. In contrast, the example of Japan clearly demonstrates that it is possible for a country to be heavily industrialized and highly productive without necessarily fostering individual competitiveness (Cohen, 1977; Matsumoto, 1970). It is unlikely that anyone seeking to modify the coronary-prone behavior pattern will be given the chance to change American society as a whole, but one can envision seeking to change the social environment of a particular office, factory or school (cf. Frankenhaeuser, 1977a; Insel & Moos, 1974). To date this interesting avenue of intervention remains virgin terrain.

Deciding Who to Change

Intervention programs for Type A individuals can be directed towards reducing any one of three levels of risk. Tertiary prevention programs seek to modify coronary-prone behavior in individuals who have already experienced a myocardial infarction with the aim of preventing a subsequent one; secondary prevention programs seek to prevent acute clinical events in individuals without manifest heart disease, but who already exhibit a well-established Type A pattern; while primary prevention is aimed at preventing the development of the coronary-prone pattern itself. Secondary prevention covers the widest range of potential samples since it embraces anyone from an 18 year old in the early stages of the atherosclerotic process to a 50 year old with one or more necrotic plaques.

Working at the level of tertiary prevention makes it much easier to evaluate the effects of Type A intervention. In a representative sample of men under 60 who survived their first myocardial infarction (MI) by at least a month, 13.5 percent died during the subsequent four years

(Mulcahy, Hickey, Graham & McKenzie, 1975). In contrast, in the total WCGS sample of 3,154 initially well subjects under 60, only 1.6 percent (50) died from cardiac-related causes during a follow-up period that was twice as long (Rosenman, Rahe, Borhani & Feinleib, 1975). Obviously, the expected death rate is greatly increased in a population of post-MI patients, making it possible to show a significant treatment effect with a smaller sample and in a shorter time period.

Men who have already experienced an MI may also be more motivated to enroll in and follow a treatment program. In fact, Friedman (Friedman & Rosenman, 1977) recently declared that the only individuals who are likely to make the required changes, and therefore benefit from intervention efforts, are those who have experienced the rude awakening of a heart attack. Empirically, Suinn was more successful in lowering lipid levels in a sample of post-MI patients (Suinn, 1975) than in a nonclinical group (Suinn & Bloom, 1978).

The disadvantage of restricting Type A intervention to those who have already experienced an acute clinical event is that approximately 36 percent of first MI patients under 65 die within the month following their attack (Weinblatt, Shapiro, Frank & Sager, 1968). Even if we ignore the individual and social cost of a heart attack, for many of those stricken there is no second chance. Our own experience (Roskies et al., in press) with 27 healthy, middle-aged managerial and professional men is that intervention with a non-clinical population is feasible and appears to be beneficial, at least in terms of short-term reduction of lipid levels and increased feelings of well-being.

What has not been attempted to date is the extension of secondary prevention programs to a broader age and socio-economic range, as well as to Type A women. Suinn and Bloom's (1978) non-clinical sample of 14 did contain two women and ranged in age from 24 to 55, but we do not know the demographic characteristics of the seven people among them who actually received treatment and hence cannot draw any conclusions on this score. From the public health point of view, a strong argument in favor of directing our attention towards younger samples is Mann's (1977) contention, based on examination of the data from the Framingham experience, that risk factors for coronary disease do not count after the age of 55 and hence it is futile to fuss with them.

Even more serious from the public health standpoint, are the questions that are increasingly being raised about the value of secondary prevention in general. The case was strongly stated recently: "Epidemiologists (and others) must come to terms with the futility of secondary prevention and concentrate on primary prevention where most successes have been gained in the past" (Holland, 1975, p. 390). In terms of Type A intervention, this would involve working with individuals who do not yet manifest the coronary-prone pattern in a stable fashion. While traces of Type A behavior have been identified in children as young as six-years-old (Matthews, 1976, 1977), some evidence suggests that many teenagers and young adults still fluctuate widely in the extent to which they display features of the coronary-prone pattern, increasing during periods of external pressure, such as exams, and returning to a more relaxed, easy-going style when this pressure is removed (Butensky, Faralli, Heebner & Waldron, 1976). Adolescents and college students, therefore, could be considered suitable candidates for primary prevention. Another avenue for primary prevention is to conduct Type A intervention programs for individuals who are just entering situations that are likely to foster Type A behavior, such as housewives returning to employment outside the home (Waldron, 1977), newly-hired managers in a fast-growing company (Howard, Cunningham & Rechnitzer, 1977), or accountants approaching tax time (Friedman, Rosenman & Carroll, 1958). In these cases Type A intervention would take the form of "stress inoculation," helping individuals to anticipate and prepare for high tension situations or periods.

Regardless of the level of risk at which one chooses to work, all intervention programs that wish to evaluate the results of their efforts must include some baseline assessment of the existence or extent of coronary-prone behavior in individuals entering treatment. In general, standard measures of personality (e.g., MMPI, Cattell 16-PF Questionnaire, CPI, Gough Adjective Check List) do not reliably discriminate between Type A and Type B individuals (Glass, 1977a; Rosenman et al., 1975). The choice for those working with middle-aged men, therefore, lies between the Structured Interview (Rosenman, 1977b) or the questionnaire, Jenkins Activity Survey (Jenkins, 1977). The interview classification shows high interrater reliability (as high as 90% between Rosenman and the two auditors in the Multiple Risk Factor Intervention Trials), and in the WCGS study proved the best predictor of CHD (Brand, Rosenman, Jenkins, Sholtz & Zyzanski, in preparation). Its major disadvantages are the expense of training interviewers (via a four-day course at the Harold Brunn Institute in San Francisco) and the time and cost of screening participants individually. Some attempts have been made recently to develop simplified scoring systems for the interview, thereby making it possible to use less highly trained interviewers (Scherwitz, Berton & Leventhal, 1977; Schucker & Jacobs, 1977), but these are still in the experimental stage. The questionnaire method obviously has the edge in terms of cost and convenience, and does provide a reliable measure over time. (Test retest correlations run generally between .60 and .70 when measured at one-year intervals, similar to those obtained with the Wechsler.) It did, however, show lower predictive power than the interview in the WCGS study, and using the interview A/B classification as a criterion, misclassified at least one third of the subjects (Brand et al., in preparation). Rosenman (1977b) and Jenkins (1977) currently disagree about the advisability of using the JAS for classification purposes. Whatever their respective merits, both assessment techniques are currently regarded solely as research instruments and neither is recommended for general clinical use (Dembroski et al., 1977).

The problem of assessing Type A behavior becomes a more difficult one as our samples diverge from the criterion group on which both the interview and the JAS were validated. The JAS does currently exist in a version suitable for both sexes, as well as separate versions for employed and non-employed persons, but the predictive capacity of these editions remains to be established. Similarly, a student version of the JAS developed for college students (Glass, 1977); a ten-question interview for latency-aged children and adolescents (Butensky et al., 1976); a series of performance tasks for children (Bortner & Rosenman, 1967; Bortner, Rosenman & Friedman, 1970); and a rating scale for children as young as six (Matthews, 1977), all require validation. While predictive validity becomes increasingly difficult to establish as the age of the sample decreases, one could seek to establish concurrent validity via behavioral and physiological measures, as Glass (1977) has begun to do.

An additional problem in selecting a sample is whether or not to include individuals who, in addition to Type A behavior, show high levels of traditional risk factors. If one seeks to show that changes in mortality or biochemical indices are solely due to modification of Type A behavior, it would be advantageous, of course, to have "pure" Type A samples. The clinical standpoint, in contrast, would dictate selecting individuals as representative as possible of the general population of Type A individuals, even if this meant that the sample would manifest many other risk factors besides Type A. In any case, it is difficult to pinpoint accurately the relationship between the TABP and standard risk factors. Based on the Structured Interview and the JAS, the correlation for large samples is low, ranging from .01 to .09 (Brand, 1977; Zyzanski, 1977), but the WCGS did show a higher frequency of heavy cigarette smokers and hypercholesterolemia among individuals classified as Type A (Roseman et al., 1975), while in the Canadian managers' study the same higher frequencies were found only in extreme Type As (Howard, Cunningham & Rechnitzer, 1976). In his large-scale intervention project for post-MI patients, Friedman has decided to screen out cigarette smokers on the grounds that the increased risk for CHD of smokers is so great, that even successful modification of their coronary prone behavior will not be reflected in a significant decrease in morbidity or mortality.

The final issue in sample selection concerns the choice between recruiting volunteers and seeking to intervene with all the Type A people in a given environment, such as one or more classrooms in a school, or specific departments in a firm. Working with all the Type As in one or more specific settings has a number of distinct advantages. Most important, by comparing the effects of treatment on groups whose environments differ in degree of pressure, it is possible to investigate the limits placed on individual change by situational determinants. This paradigm would also permit us to test the generalizability of Type A intervention to others besides self-selected and presumably highly motivated volunteers. For our proposed project (Roskies, 1978), we are trying to overcome problems of acceptability, confidentiality and scheduling in negotiating an agreement for an intervention program of this kind with a large public company. In spite of the advantages of using a complete work unit as a sample, however, one should probably not summarily dismiss samples composed of volunteers. In the present state of our knowledge, it would be a distinct advance to show clearly that Type A intervention reduces cardiac risk in anyone, regardless of how representative that individual is of the entire population of Type A persons.

Deciding How to Change Type A Behavior

Glass and his associates (Glass, 1977a, 1977b; Glass, Snyder & Hollis, 1974) have conceptualized the Type A individual as one who has internalized all too well Western society's emphasis on the ability to master and control the environment and, consequently, is continuously challenged and threatened by the numerous potentially uncontrollable events that he or she encounters. In this context the furious pace and aggressiveness of the Type A pattern can be seen as a coping style which seeks to ward off the anxiety aroused by loss of control through ever stronger efforts to reassert control. If one accepts this explanation of coronary-prone behavior, and to date no one has proposed any other, there are at least two ways in which one could seek to modify Type A reactions in the individual. The first would be to change directly the individual's perceptions of and emotional responses to potentially threatening situations with the aim of making it less necessary for him or her to mobilize. The second is to teach the person new, less harmful ways of coping and, by thus strengthening resources, also reduce the intensity of the emotional and physiological response to challenge (cf. Roskies & Lazarus, this volume).

Both rational-emotive and psychoanalytically-oriented therapies are designed to explicitly modify distorted perceptions, the first by directly attacking the irrational belief system that gives rise to them (Ellis, 1962), the second by exhuming the unconscious conflicts that lead to defensive misinterpretations of reality. The rationale underlying the psychoanalytic approach is that once the individual has insight into the reasons for his or her neurotic responses, then he or she will be free to act differently. One of the treatment groups in our pilot project (Roskies et al., 1978) was based on the psychoanalytic approach and it is probable that the psychoanalyst-led group sessions described by Rosenman and Friedman (1977) also followed this model.

In the case of our sample, the therapists involved developed specific treatment hypotheses from their clinical impressions of the results of a number of psychological tests, such as a group Rorschach. Type A behavior was seen by them as originating in a family constellation of an aggressive, demanding mother (Matthews, 1977 provides some corroborative evidence for this from her observations of mothers and young Type A children) and a psychologically passive or absent father. The constant striving characteristic of Type A individuals represents the effort to obtain the mother's love, while the guilt concerning ambition is the result of a projective identification with the father. The aim of therapy was to provide both a corrective emotional experience—using a male and a female therapist as role models—and an awareness in the men that their current behavior was the replaying of an outdated family script. The assumption was that once the men achieved understanding of why they became so anxious in situations that threatened loss of control, they would no longer do so and hence have less need for the Type A coping style.

Rosenman and Friedman (1977) report that in their experience the mere detection, ventilation and even solution of emotional problems did not lead to enduring diminution of Type A behavior until the treatment was supplemented by behavioral drills. Our own results are more ambiguous and suggest that some Type A individuals may well benefit from this type of approach. It should be noted, though, that this highly verbal therapy is more likely to be acceptable to college-educated managers than to grade-school laborers.

An alternative treatment is to leave the basic need for mastery untouched, but instead to provide a less harmful method for coping with threat. A number of techniques ranging from muscular relaxation to yoga, meditation, biofeedback, autogenic training, anxiety management and stress inoculation are currently being used to help individuals lower their levels of cognitive, emotional and physiological arousal (cf. Goldfried, 1977; Meichenbaum, 1977; Suinn & Richardson, 1971; White & Fadiman, 1976). Although these therapies differ in rationale and specific techniques employed, they are all based on the assumption that with sufficient training the beneficial effect of a low-arousal state in a stressful situation can become habitual, with hyperreactivity to stress being supplanted by a new pattern marked by a lessening of sympathetic arousal in the face of threat (Stoyva & Budzynski, 1974).

In spite of apparent similarites, this approach is very different from the often given but seldom heeded advice to "slow down" or "take it easy." Attempts to simply relinquish habitual coping styles render the person passive and helpless, and hence are likely to arouse the very anxiety the individual is seeking to avoid (cf. Suinn, 1974). Treatment based on tension-reducing techniques, in contrast, emphasizes active coping efforts, but of a more adaptive, less harmful sort.

The treatment approach of Suinn (Suinn, 1975; Suinn & Bloom, 1978) is based on a form of anxiety management training in which the individual is first instructed in relaxation procedures and the use of imagery to arouse anxiety. The client then deliberately arouses anxiety via appropriate imagery and controls it with relaxation activities, such as relaxation imagery and deep breathing. This procedure of pairing anxiety arousal with anxiety control is intended to train the patient in the self-management of anxiety, regardless of the source of the anxiety (Suinn & Richardson, 1971).

In contrast to Suinn, our pilot project (Roskies et al., 1978) heavily emphasized *in vivo* practice of the relaxation techniques learned. Our aim was not only to teach a new skill but, even more important, also to weave it into the fabric of the individual's daily life. The preliminary training in relaxation followed a definite sequence beginning with a modified version of Jacobsonian muscular relaxation (Jacobson, 1938), followed by a shortened version of muscular relaxation, and proceeding to specific neck and shoulder and breathing exercises. Two 15 minute practice sessions daily were assigned as homework. Record keeping was used to make the men aware of the variations in their tension levels and of the situations associated with increases and decreases in tension level. At the beginning of treatment the men had claimed to be operating at a consistently low level of tension, and an important aim of treatment was to increase discrimination. With practice, the individual was expected to become adept at regularly monitoring his tension level and keeping it at a comfortably low level. For this purpose, both cue-related relaxation techniques (e.g., relaxation every time the phone rang) and emergency relaxation procedures (e.g., calming down during a business disagreement) were used. The basic thrust of treatment was that, even if the individual could not always control the environment, he did have the power to control his reactions to it.

A major benefit of this approach to intervention is that it led almost immediately to feelings of increased control and increased well-being. Even at the first practice of the relaxation exercise, some men noticed a change in their tension level and as treatment proceeded there were numerous examples presented during the weekly sessions of improved physical, social, and sexual functioning. Far from interfering with their work productivity, the new coping techniques were judged to increase efficiency and ease. In short, this form of stress management was seen not only as a means of preventing future heart disease, but also as an enhancer of present well-being.

Although muscular relaxation proved to be an acceptable and effective coping technique for a wide variety of stressful situations, we believe that the treatment program can be strengthened by adding cognitive and social tension-reducing techniques (cf. Bower & Bower, 1976; Meichenbaum, 1977). In contrast to Ellis and the psychoanalytic approach, the emphasis here would not be one simply of eliminating the irrational beliefs and distorted perceptions that mediate disruptive emotions, but rather one of training the person in the use of more adaptive coping self-statements (e.g., "That foreman is heckling me, but I don't have to get hot under the collar. Stay cool and answer his criticisms one at a time."). Similarly, training in communication skills, particularly the ability to express feelings, needs and wants directly, can be used to provide Type A individuals with an alternative to their habitual hostile and competitive manner of relating to others who block their path. Going beyond a "pure" muscular relaxation program might have the disadvantage, should the program prove beneficial, of making it difficult to pinpoint what exactly in the treatment was helpful. At this stage, however, the most urgent priority is to design an effective intervention program. Component analysis to increase efficiency would constitute a subsequent step.

Some concern has been expressed concerning the professional and personal qualifications required for helping people to modify their coronary-prone behavior. Specifically, Blankenhorn, Jenkins, Insull & Weiss (1974) have questioned whether "Super A" physicians might not be so impatient and perfectionistic as to lead patients to become discouraged and abandon treatment. The solution they propose is to train A- or B paramedical personnel who could then work under the supervision of a physician. Our own bias is that the professional skills required would depend in large measure on the content of the specific program. However, unless the person who actually administers the treatment has a job that is recognized by the client to be as demanding and pressured as his or her own work situation, the therapist's assertion that Type A behavior need not be situation-determined is likely to lack force. And in our society equivalent job demands are most clearly demarcated by equality of status. Delegating treatment responsibility to lower status personnel, therefore, may not affect competence, but will likely lessen credibility.

Whether a therapist who is Type A him or herself can effectively modify the coronary-prone behavior of others is another relevant problem. It is also an issue of considerable practical importance because many of the people who are in a professional position to design and implement intervention programs are themselves Type A. Unless we follow Blankenhorn et al.'s (1974) solution and create a new breed of therapists, we are likely to be faced with the situation of a Type A therapist seeking to change a Type A client. Contrary to what we might expect, however, the findings of a number of studies suggest that modeling of the therapist's active coping efforts can be even more effective than a simple demonstration of mastery in teaching a new skill (cf. Meichenbaum, 1977, pp. 125-129). This would suggest that Type A therapists could treat others effectively, if they were actively engaged in and achieving at least moderate success toward modifying their own behavior.

Except for Suinn (Suinn, 1975; Suinn and Bloom, 1978) who does not specify whether his anxiety management training sessions were directed towards individuals or groups, all the Type A intervention programs proposed or carried out to date (Friedman, 1977a; Rosenman and Friedman, 1977; Roskies, 1978; Roskies et al., 1978) have been group treatment efforts. Therapist economy is an obvious advantage of a group approach, but there appear to be treatment advantages as well in providing a new reference group to support participants in their efforts to change (Henderson & Enelow, 1976; Meyer & Henderson, 1974). Both Rosenman and Friedman (1977) and we have noted the importance of this factor for Type A men, many of whom reported finding greater emotional contact in the group experience than they did in their habitual environments. An additional benefit of group treatment is that it serves as a spur to therapeutic progress. No self-respecting Type A man, even a reformed one, is going to allow others to benefit from treatment while he does not!

Intervention programs for Type A individuals have ranged in duration from five or six sessions in two or three weeks (Suinn, 1975; Suinn & Bloom, 1978) to approximately 60 sessions spread over five years (Friedman, 1977a). Our own pilot program (Roskies et al., 1978) was intermediate in length with 14 sessions over 14 weeks. The feasible duration of a program depends not only on treatment resources, but also on the specific sample one is working with. It is probably more realistic to expect a post-MI patient, who in any case must have regular medical surveillance, to agree to a five-year program than it would be to structure a similar regime for a healthy college student. Friedman's program, however, does contain one feature that might be incorporated into less extensive interventions, the gradual phasing out of sessions. In his scheme, weekly sessions are gradually reduced to fortnightly ones and eventually to once a month sessions. This essentially would provide the client with periodic booster shots.

The question of timing raises the whole issue of recidivism. As Marlatt (this volume) shows so convincingly, efforts to influence diet, smoking and alcohol consumption have typically resulted in some initial success followed by recidivism. It would be naive not to expect a similar pattern in coronary-prone individuals, particularly during periods of high environmental pressure. One wonders, however, whether there are not ways of preventing temporary tumbles off the wagon from becoming permanent ones. A particularly innovative approach to relapse has been described by Marlatt (in press) in his work with alcoholics. On the basis of a cognitive-behavioral analysis of those situations that frequently led to relapse in alcoholics (e.g., negative emotional states, social pressure), Marlatt incorporated such high risk situations into the intervention process itself, and had clients anticipate and train for managing them. A similar approach could easily be incorporated into a Type A intervention program.

In addition to helping participants avoid relapse, it may be even more important to provide a conceptual framework for dealing with it when it occurs. Instead of therapist and client conceptualizing any reversion to former ways as treatment failure, in this way dismissing the temporary improvement shown as valueless, might not our intervention programs prepare the individual for the ebb and flow of his or her coronary-prone behavior, and provide the means of coping with this, too. Just as we use "stress inoculation" (Meichenbaum, 1977) to prepare the individual to anticipate and cope with difficult situations, so might we use "slip inoculation" to prepare the person to anticipate and cope with temporary or partial recidivism.

What we are suggesting here, essentially, is that Type A intervention programs might increase their chances of success by adopting modest goals and by making these goals explicit right from the beginning of treatment. Not only might we accept that Type As are unlikely to be transformed into Type Bs, but also, and even more important, the fact that the most we can hope for is modulation, rather than complete eradication, of the pathogenic elements in the pattern. The amount of behavioral change required to produce a 'just noticeable difference' in cardiac morbidity and mortality can only be determined by trial and error. Unless we are willing to conduct these experiments, however, we may be condemning therapists and clients to needless frustration and failure. We may also lose the chance of helping most of the people who have not yet been confronted with the crisis of overt heart disease, as well as those recalcitrant heart patients who would literally rather die than completely renounce cherished pursuits.

All the treatment possibilities discussed in this section have been based on a model of face to face interaction between therapist and client. The Stanford Heart Disease Prevention Project suggests an alternative model, the use of the media (T.V., radio, newspaper) to provide health education to an entire community (Maccoby, Farquhar, Wood & Alexander, 1977). This innovative approach warrants further investigation. It may be more difficult to teach Type A modification in this fashion than it is to provide instruction for the more familiar targets of diet, smoking and exercise, but we shall not know the limits of our ingenuity until we test them.

Recruiting the Sample

Even the best designed intervention program is doomed to failure unless a way can be found to convince the people you want to treat to enroll and remain in the program. When the target for change is the Type A pattern, this involves confronting obstacles such as the lack of public recognition of this lifestyle as a health hazard, the fear that "becoming Type B" might diminish occupational success, and the lack as yet of any proof that undergoing the painful process of changing behavior will, in fact, result in a significant lowering of coronary risk. In short, motivating people to participate in a Type A intervention program involves persuading individuals to change a deeply rooted, gratifying and socially approved lifestyle for the sake of health benefits that are still very uncertain.

The writings on Type A intervention to date have largely ignored this issue except for Friedman's assertion that only post-MI patients are likely to be sufficiently motivated to make treatment possible. It appears, however, that even restricting intervention attempts to this clinical group does not automatically solve the problem of sample recruitment. A recent column in a San Francisco newspaper (*San Francisco Chronicle,* April 5, 1978), revealed that Dr. Friedman's project had easily succeeded in recruiting the 450 Type B individuals sought, but had only succeeded in recruiting 300 Type As because of numerous refusals in this group on the grounds of being "too busy."

Our own experience in seeking to recruit a sample of 30 healthy, occupationally successful, middle-aged Type A men suggested that there is a large pool of individuals who would be willing to undertake this form of treatment if they were approached appropriately. On the basis of a single experience there is no way of knowing, of course, which of the techniques used could be generalized successfully to other samples, particularly those differing in age, sex, cultural background and occupational level. Nevertheless, as the only information we have on the topic, the description of sample recruitment in our pilot project (Roskies et al., 1978) will at least serve to open the discussion.

Initially, we tapped two different referral sources, top executives of a number of large companies, and physicians affiliated with executive health clinics. Unfortunately, after a month of effort, we succeeded in obtaining much verbal expression of interest, but almost no concrete referrals. It was therefore decided to appeal directly to potential consumers. The program was promoted in a newspaper article and a radio interview in which would-be volunteers were asked to phone the hospital under whose auspices the study was taking place. This time the response was overwhelming with over 150 calls in three days. Even more impressive, almost all of these self-referrals were appropriate in terms of demographic criteria.

The media appeal that called forth this enthusiastic response stressed a few basic points. First, there was a brief description of the Type A behavior pattern and of its association to substantially increased risk of heart disease. The finding of a shifting ratio in favor of Type Bs at the summit of the occupational ladder (Howard, Rechnitzer & Cunningham, 1977) was also mentioned. Then the aims and requirements of this project were clearly spelled out. The aim of this project, it was stressed, was not to make Type As into Type Bs, but simply to make them into more efficient Type As by teaching them how to control and modulate their undifferentiated expenditure of energy. By learning how to pace himself—the promise held out by the program—the individual was likely to accomplish more with less psychological and physiological strain. However this experimental program, under the auspices of the city's largest university and a prestigious teaching hospital, could only accommodate 30 men and they would have to meet stringent criteria regarding age, occupational success, health and so on.

In retrospect, it appears that we had succeeded in formulating a "sales pitch" that appealed as much to participants' needs for control, efficiency and success as to their fear of illness. Even the format of the program reinforced this theme by being prestigious, innovative, restricted to men identified as healthy and successful, and only open to a limited few. In short, a perfect Type A challenge.

The media appeal attracted a pool of potential participants, but the real work of motivation began during the lengthy screening process and continued throughout the program. At the time of the initial phone call, many subjects expressed doubt about whether they were really Type As with increased risk of heart disease, as spouses and business colleagues claimed, or whether they simply had a few Type A characteristics. Not surprisingly, too, these Type A men were extremely concerned about the time commitment required by the program. Each of these two issues was dealt with differently.

Individuals' concerns about whether they were really Type A were handled mainly by going through the assessment interview and then discussing with the potential participant the characteristics of his responses that led to his classification as Type A. This was then followed by a description of the purposes and methods of the two treatment programs to be tested. Although the exploratory nature of the program was stressed, by the end of this session all but two of the men who had been classified as suitable were prepared to enroll. In terms of predicting successful treatment, it is perhaps significant that, although the two laggards did eventually enroll, one was the sole voluntary drop-out in the sample and the other was a clear treatment failure.

On the subject of time requirements, in contrast, we were adamant. The program consisted of 14 1½-hour early evening sessions, as well as pre- and posttesting, and participants had to agree to attend a minimum of 12 of the 14 sessions. In fact, a $100 deposit was required that would only be returned if attendance requirements were met. The rationale given for this intransigence was that this program required a heavy investment of the therapists' time and effort, and we did not wish to risk our investment. The time requirements were a serious problem for many potential participants, because of business travel and vacation plans, but only two prospective participants, of 36 classified as Type A, eventually decided against enrolling on this ground. In fact, many participants remarked approvingly that the procedure was "businesslike."

The final phase in the motivational process was the gradual build up of trust and confidence in the therapists during the course of treatment. This was accomplished mainly by the men's own perceptions that they were feeling better and coping with stress more effectively. This high level of motivation was reflected in good attendance with only two men missing more than the permitted two sessions. In fact, we were impressed by the efforts the men made to attend, including arriving directly from the airport or rescheduling a business trip.

One problem that was not successfully resolved in our initial project was that of finding a way to convince busy Type A men to constitute a control group, that is to submit to the extensive testing required without receiving treatment. Frankly, we doubted our ability to keep men of this type involved in an attention-placebo group for 14 sessions. Friedman (1977a) has constituted a control group and will see its members yearly during the 5 years of the program. It will be interesting to see whether the controls will, in fact, remain in the program during the full five years, and how many of those who do remain will be motivated to change their Type A behavior, either through their own efforts, or by seeking professional help elsewhere. An alternate solution that we plan to use in our next attempt is the designation of a delayed treatment group as controls.

Evaluating the Effects of Treatment

For the therapist who hopes to clearly demonstrate the beneficial effects of his or her Type A intervention program, the history of past efforts in psychotherapy evaluation is not particularly encouraging (Mahoney, 1977):

> The demonstration of an unequivocal success is rare in psychotherapy research. The demonstration of a success which can be

> logically attributed to the therapy in question is extremely rare. The demonstration of a successful intervention and an identified therapeutic source plus long term maintenance of improvement has been about as common as a mute politician (p. 9).

In the case of Type A intervention, the habitual difficulties are compounded by the ambiguity surrounding the target. Unlike treatments for obesity, smoking and alcoholism, Type A intervention does not possess a self-evident criterion by which to judge improvement. Reduction in cardiac morbidity and mortality would obviously constitute acceptable goals from the clinical standpoint, but only large samples followed for a number of years are likely to generate sufficient cases to make significant differences possible. This has the disadvantage of restricting research in an area which is still in the exploratory stage to only a few large, well-funded projects. To date, only Friedman's (1977a) study is large enough to use cardiac morbidity and mortality as criteria, and even this study can only do so by selecting a sample of very high risk.

For researchers who wish to work with younger and/or healthier samples, other criteria are required. One possibility is to use the screening instruments themselves for evaluation of change in Type A behavior. In fact, Suinn & Bloom (1978) have used change in the participants' JAS scores as one of their criteria. Unfortunately, neither of the screening instruments is in itself adequate as a measure of treatment effectiveness. The Structured Interview appears to capture Type A behavior best in terms of predicting CHD, but as it is currently used its predictive ability is based solely on a dichotomous classification (Type A vs. Type B). Hence, it is not sensitive to change less marked than the conversion of a Type A into a Type B. In contrast, the JAS as a continuous measure is able to register smaller degrees of change, but a simple shift in numerical score does not tell us much about the clinical significance of what is changing. Analyzing changes in the scores of the various sub-scales of the JAS would help to pinpoint what is changing, but the poor showing of these sub-scales as predictors of CHD in the WCGS makes it difficult to equate any change in them with a real reduction in coronary-prone behavior.

A third possibility is to study the effect of Type A intervention on standard biochemical risk factors, such as serum total cholesterol, ratio of low density lipoproteins, serum triglycerides and blood pressure. Only a single study has found a higher level of blood pressure in the resting state for Type As compared to Type Bs (Howard, Cunningham & Rechnitzer, 1976), but the differences in serum lipid levels have been corroborated in a number of studies (Friedman, 1977b; Rosenman et al., 1975). Nevertheless, the validity of serum cholesterol as an outcome measure is clouded somewhat by the doubts expressed whether lowering cholesterol level does, in fact, result in decreased morbidity and mortality from CHD (cf. Ahrens, 1976; Cornfield & Mitchell, 1969). In spite of the deficiencies of resting blood pressure and serum cholesterol as indices of effective change in the TABP, both we and Suinn have used these measures to evaluate outcome in our respective exploratory studies, probably because they are among the most easily obtained and widely accepted measures of coronary risk. Whatever the usefulness of including these variables, to measure them properly requires multiple baselines, standardized procedures, repeated measures over time and, in the case of lipids, careful control over the quality of the laboratory analyses.

More interesting in terms of the mechanisms by which Type A behavior leads to heart disease, is the assessment of changes in endocrine and automatic reactivity to challenge. We have already referred to some of the data showing that Type As are more labile in their responses to challenge, both as experienced in the course of their working day and also during individual competitive activity (Dembroski, MacDougall & Shields, 1977; Frankenhaeuser, 1977b; Friedman et al., 1975; Friedman & Rosenman, 1959; Friedman, Rosenman & Carroll, 1958; Friedman, St. George, Byers & Rosenman, 1960). In fact, one of the suggested targets for change was decreasing the frequency, intensity and duration of autonomic and endocrine responses. In view of the many different forms that arousal can take, however (cf. Lacey, 1967; Williams, 1977), this in turn raises the issue of which parameters are the crucial ones.

In a study by Keys, Taylor, Blackburn, Brozek, Anderson and Simonson (1971) of Minnesota businessmen followed for 20 years, the rise in diastolic blood pressure following the cold pressor test was found to be the best single predictor of CHD. Friedman (1977b), in contrast, has suggested that, because of their potential artery-damaging and thrombogenic propensities, fluctuations in catecholamine levels, in particular norepinephrine, deserve more thorough investigation. In our proposed study (Roskies, 1978), we hope to test changes both in blood pressure and norepinephrine lability as measures of change in the coronary-prone pattern. The major disadvantages of incorporating endocrine measures, particularly plasma norepinephrine, are the practical difficulties involved in obtaining uncontaminated samples, and the complexity and cost of analysis.

Behavioral ratings, too, can be used to assess change in competitiveness, time pressure and so on. Family and business associates would be particularly good informants for this purposes. As in all behavioral ratings, validity can be greatly improved by making them as specific and concrete as possible. Rather than asking for a global rating of irritability, it is better to ask for the rating of the number of temper outbursts in a given situation on a given day.

The individual's subjective assessment of his behavior also deserves consideration. The Type A person is usually believed to lack insight into his or her own behavior and, consequently, to constitute an unreliable witness. Whatever their deficiencies as an objective criterion of change, however, the participant's feelings about what is happening are of definite clinical significance. To paraphrase an old adage, unless the patient feels better, the operation is definitely not a success.

In the present state of our knowledge, no single one of these evaluation procedures is likely to be adequate in itself. The investigator, therefore, may have to settle for combining a number of imperfect measures. As we learn more about the components of Type A and how they lead to CHD, hopefully, we shall also learn more about how to measure change.

Concluding Comment

In the tradition in which I was initially socialized, inconclusive debates were habitually terminated with the pious hope that Elijah the Prophet would someday provide the wished-for resolution. In the graduate school where I underwent my professional socialization, the appeal to Elijah was replaced by calls for additional data. Time has eroded my faith in the second arbiter as much as in the first one. Elijah has not yet appeared, and the addition of new data is more likely to intensify controversy than to resolve it. For all its limitations, however, empirical testing of hypotheses remains the scientist's best protection against the tyranny of dogma. It is time now to supplement our speculations about Type A intervention with findings derived from well-designed and carefully-executed studies in the field.

REFERENCES

Ahrens, E. H.: The management of hyperlipidemia: whether, rather than how. *Annals of Internal Medicine,* 1976, 85, 87-93.

Alexander, F.: *Psychosomatic medicine: Its principles and applications.* New York: W.W. Norton & Co., 1950.

Bengtsson, G., Hallstrom, T. & Tibblin, G.: Social factors, stress experience, and personality traits in women with ischaemic heart disease, compared to a population sample of women. *Acta Medica Scandinavia,* 1973, (Suppl.) 549, 89-92.

BERNSTEIN, D.A., & MCALLISTER, A.L.: The modification of smoking behavior: Progress and problems. *Addictive Behavior,* 1976, 1, 89-102.

BLANKENHORN, D.B., JENKINS, C.D., INSULL, W., & WEISS, L.: Letters to the Editor: Type A physicians and coronary risk education. *Annals of Internal Medicine,* 1974, 81, 700-701.

BORTNER, R.W., & ROSENMAN, R.H.: The measurement of pattern A behavior. *Journal of Chronic Diseases,* 1967, 20, 525-533.

BORTNER, R.W., ROSENMAN, R.H., & FRIEDMAN, M.: Familial similarity in pattern A behavior. *Journal of Chronic Diseases,* 1970, 23, 39-43.

BOWER, S.A., & BOWER, G.H.: *Asserting yourself.* Reading, Mass.: Addison-Wesley, 1976.

BRADY, J.P.: Concluding remarks. In R.B. Williams, Jr. & W.D. Gentry (Eds.), *Behavioral approaches to medical treatment.* Cambridge, Mass.: Ballinger, 1977, pp. 249-252.

BRAND, R.J.: An examination of the association between A-B behavior and coronary heart disease incidence. In T. Dembroski (Ed.), *Proceedings of the Forum on Coronary-Prone Behavior.* Washington, D.C.: Dept. of Health, Education and Welfare Publication No. (NIH) 78-1451, 1977, pp. 29-46.

BRAND, R.J., ROSENMAN, R.H., JENKINS, C.D., SHOLTZ, R.I., & ZYZANSKI, S.J.: Comparison of coronary heart disease prediction in the Western Collaborative Group Study using the structured interview and the Jenkins Activity Survey assessments of the coronary-prone Type A behavior pattern. In preparation.

BRAND, R.J., ROSENMAN, R.H., SHOLTZ, R.I., & FRIEDMAN, M.: Multivariate prediction of coronary heart disease in the Western Collaborative Group Study, compared to the findings of the Framingham Study. *Circulation,* 1976, 53, 348-355.

BUTENSKY, A., FARALLI, V., HEEBNER, D., & WALDRON, I.: Elements of the coronary prone behavior pattern in children and teen-agers. *Journal of Psychosomatic Research,* 1976, 20, 439-444.

CARVER, C.S., COLEMAN, A.E., & GLASS, D.C.: The coronary-prone behavior pattern and suppression of fatigue on a treadmill test. *Journal of Personality and Social Psychology,* 1976, 33, 460-466.

COHEN, J.B.: Sociocultural change and behavior patterns in disease etiology: An epidemiological study of coronary disease among Japanese-Americans. Unpublished Ph.D. thesis. University of California, Berkeley, 1974.

COHEN, J.B.: The influence of culture on coronary-prone behavior. In T. Dembroski (Ed.), *Proceedings of the Forum on Coronary-Prone Behavior.* Washington, D.C.: Dept. of Health, Education and Welfare Publication No. (NIH) 78-1451, 1977 pp. 243-253.

CORNFIELD, J., & MITCHELL, S.: Selected risk factors in coronary disease. *Archives of Environmental Health,* 1969, 19, 382-291.

DAVIS, R.: Stress and hemostatic mechanisms. In R.S. Eliot (Ed.) *Stress and the heart.* New York: Futura, 1974, pp. 97-122.

DEMBROSKI, T. (Ed.): *Proceedings of the Forum on Coronary-Prone Behavior.* Washington, D.C.: Dept. of Health, Education and Welfare Publication No. (NIH) 78-1451, 1977.

DEMBROSKI, T.M., CAFFREY, B., JENKINS, C.D., ROSENMAN, R.H., SPIELBERGER C., & TASTO, D.L.: Summary statement: Assessment of coronary-prone behavior. In T. Dembroski (Ed.), *Proceedings of the Forum on Coronary-Prone Behavior.* Washington, D.C.: Dept. of Health, Education and Welfare Publication No. (NIH) 78-1451, 1977, pp. 73-78.

DEMBROSKI, T., & MACDOUGALL, J.: Stress effects on affiliation preferences among subjects possessing the Type A coronary-prone behavior pattern. *Journal of Personality and Social Psychology,* 1978, 36, 23-33.

DEMBROSKI, T., MACDOUGALL, J., & SHIELDS, J.: Physiologic reactions to social challenge in persons evidencing the Type A coronary-prone behavior pattern. *Journal of Human Stress,* 1977, 3, No. 3, 2-9.

DUNBAR, H.F.: *Psychosomatic diagnosis.* New York: Paul B. Hoeber, Inc., 1943.

ELLIS, A.: *Reason and emotion in psychotherapy.* New York: Lyle Stuart, 1962.

FEINLEIB, M., BRAND, R.J., REMINGTON, R., & ZYZANSKI, S.J.: Summary statement: Association of the coronary-prone behavior pattern, and coronary heart disease. In T. Dembroski (Ed.), *Proceedings of the Forum on Coronary-Prone Behavior.* Washington, D.C.: Dept. of Health Education and Welfare, Publication No. (NIH) 78-1451, 1977, pp. 19-28.

FRANKENHAEUSER, M.: Job demands, health and well being. *Journal of Psychosomatic Research,* 1977(a), 21, 313-323.

FRANKENHAUESER, M.: Dept. of Psychology, University of Stockholm, personal communication, 1977(b).

FRIEDMAN, M.: Harold Brunn Institute, Mt. Zion Hospital, San Francisco, personal communication, 1977(a).

FRIEDMAN, M.: Some pathophysiologic phenomena observed in subjects exhibiting Type A behavior. In T. Mason (Ed.), *Advances in heart disease,* vol. 1. New York: Grune & Stratton, 1977(b), pp. 73-83.

FRIEDMAN, M., BYERS, S., DIAMANT, J., & ROSENMAN, R.H.: Plasma catecholamine response of coronary-prone subjects (Type A) to a specific challenge. *Metabolism,* 1975, 24, 205-210.

FRIEDMAN, M., & ROSENMAN, R.H.: Association of specific overt behavior pattern with blood and cardiovascular findings. *Journal of the American Medical Association,* 1959, 169, 1286-1295.

FRIEDMAN, M., & ROSENMAN, R.H.: *Type A behavior and your heart.* Greenwich, Conn.: Fawcett, 1974.

FRIEDMAN, M., & ROSENMAN, R.H.: Modification of the Type A Coronary Prone Behavior Pattern. Paper presented at the annual meeting of the American Psychological Association, San Francisco, August, 1977.

FRIEDMAN, M., ROSENMAN, R.H., & CARROLL, V.: Changes in serum cholesterol and blood clotting time in men subjected to cyclic variation of occupational stress. *Circulation,* 1958, 17, 852-861.

FRIEDMAN, M., ST. GEORGE, S., BYERS, S.O., & ROSENMAN, R.H.: Excretion of catecholamines, 17-ketesteroids, 17-hydroxy-corticoids and 5-hydroxyindole in men exhibiting a particular behavior pattern (A) associated with high incidence of clinical coronary artery disease. *Journal of Clinical Investigation,* 1960, 39, 758-764.

GILMORE, J.P.: Physiology of stress. In R.S. Eliot (Ed.), *Stress and the heart.* New York, Futura, 1974, pp. 69-90.

GLASS, D.C.: *Behavior patterns, stress and coronary disease.* Hillsdale, N.J.: Erlbaum, 1977(a).

GLASS, D.C.: Pattern A behavior and uncontrollable stress. In T. Dembroski (Ed.), *Proceedings of the Forum on Coronary-Prone Behavior.* Washington, D.C.: Dept. of Health, Education and Welfare, Publication No. (NIH) 78-1451, 1977b, pp. 192-202.

GLASS, D.C., SNYDER, M.L., & HOLLIS, J.F.: Time urgency and the Type A coronary prone behavior pattern. *Journal of Applied Social Psychology,* 1974, 4, 125-140.

GOLDFRIED, M.R.: The use of relaxation and cognitive relabeling as coping skills. In R.B. Stuart (Ed.), *Behavioral self-management: Strategies, techniques and outcome.* New York: Brunner/Mazel, 1977, pp. 82-116.

HAYNES, S.G., FEINLEIB, M., & KANNEL, W.B.: Psychological factors in coronary heart disease incidence in Framingham: Results from an 8 years follow up. Paper presented at the annual meeting of the American Psychosomatic Society, Washington, D.C., April, 1978.

HAYNES, S.G., LEVINE, S., SCOTCH, N.A., FEINLEIB, M., & KANNEL, W.B.: The relationship of psychosocial factors to coronary heart disease in the Framingham Study. II. Prevalence of Coronary Heart Disease. *American Journal of Epidemiology,* 1978, 107, 384-403.

HENDERSON, J.B., & ENELOW, A.J.: The coronary risk factor problem: A behavioral perspective. *Preventive Medicine,* 1976, 5, 128-148.

HOLLAND, W.W.: Letters to the Editor: Screening for disease. *Lancet,* February 15, 1975,

No. 7903, 390.

HOWARD, J.H., CUNNINGHAM, D.A., & RECHNITZER, P.A.: Health patterns associated with Type A behavior: A managerial population. *Journal of Human Stress,* 1976, 2(1), 24-33.

HOWARD, J.H., CUNNINGHAM, D.A., & RECHNITZER, P.A.: Work patterns associated with Type A behavior: A managerial population. *Human Relations,* 1977, 30, 825-836.

HOWARD, J.H., RECHNITZER, P.A., & CUNNINGHAM, D.A.: The 'Type A' manager. *The Business Quarterly,* 1977, 42, 42-47.

INSEL, P.M., & MOOS, R.H. (Eds.): *Health and the social environment.* Lexington: Heath & Co., 1974.

INSULL, W. (Ed.): *Coronary risk handbook.* New York: American Heart Association, 1973.

JACOBSON, E.: *Progressive relaxation.* Chicago: University of Chicago Press, 1938 (2nd ed.).

JENKINS, C.D.: Recent evidence supporting psychologic and social risk factors for coronary disease. *New England Journal of Medicine,* 1976, 294, 987-994, 1033-1038.

JENKINS, C.D.: Assessment of the coronary-prone behavior pattern. In T. Dembroski (Ed.), *Proceedings of the Forum on Coronary-Prone Behavior.* Washington, D.C.: Dept. of Health, Education and Welfare, Publication No. (NIH) 78-1451, 1977, pp. 104-126.

JENKINS, C.D., ROSENMAN, R.H., & FRIEDMAN, M.: Development of an objective psychological test for the determination of the coronary-prone behavior pattern in employed men. *Journal of Chronic Diseases,* 1967, 20, 371-379.

JENKINS, C.D., ZYZANSKI, S.J., & ROSENMAN, R.H.: Risk of new myocardial infarction in middle-aged men with manifest coronary heart disease. *Circulation,* 1976, 53, 342-347.

KENIGSBERG, D., ZYZANSKI, S.J., JENKINS, C.D., WARDWELL, W.I., & LICCIARDELLO, A.T.: The coronary-prone behavior pattern in hospitalized patients with and without coronary heart disease. *Psychosomatic Medicine,* 1974, 36, 344-351.

KEYS, A., TAYLOR, H.L., BLACKBURN, H., BROZEK, J., ANDERSON, J.T., & SIMONSON, E.: Mortality and coronary heart disease among men studied for 23 years. *Archives of Internal Medicine,* 1971, 128, 201-214.

LACEY, J.: Somatic response patterning and stress: Some revisions of activation theory. In M.H. Appley & R. Turmbull (Eds.), *Psychological stress.* New York: Appleton-Century-Crofts, 1967, pp. 14-37.

LAZARUS, R.S., COHEN, J.B., FOLKMAN, S., KANNER, A., & SCHAEFER, C.: Psychological stress and adaptation: Some unresolved issues. In H. Selye (Ed.), *Guide to stress research.* New York: Van Nostrand, in press.

MACCOBY, N., FARQUHAR, J.W., WOOD, P.W., & ALEXANDER, J.: Reducing the risk of cardiovascular disease: Effects of a community-based campaign on knowledge and behavior. *Journal of Community Health,* 1977, 3, 100-114.

MAHONEY, M.J.: Cognitive therapy and research: A question of questions. *Cognitive Therapy and Research,* 1977, 1, 5-16.

MANN, G.V.: Diet-heart: End of an era. *New England Journal of Medicine,* 1977, 297, 644-650.

MARLATT, G.A.: Craving for alcohol, loss of control, and relapse: A cognitive-behavioral analysis. In P.E. Nathan & G.A. Marlatt (Eds.), *Experimental and behavioral approaches to alcoholism.* New York: Plenum, in press.

MATSUMOTO, Y.S.: Social stress and coronary heart disease in Japan. A hypothesis. *Milbank Memorial Fund Quarterly,* 1970, 48, 9-36.

MATTHEWS, K.A.: Mother-child interactions as a determinant of Type A - Type B behavior. Unpublished doctoral dissertation, University of Texas, Austin, 1976.

MATTHEWS, K.A.: Assessment and developmental antecedents of Pattern A behavior in children. In T. Dembroski (Ed.), *Proceedings of the Forum on Coronary-Prone Behavior.* Washington, D.C.: Dept. of Health, Education and Welfare, Publication No. (NIH) 78-1451, 1977, pp. 261-277.

MATTHEWS, K., GLASS, D.C., ROSENMAN, R.H., & BORTNER, R.W.: Competitive drive, Pattern A, and coronary heart disease: A further analysis of some data from the Western Collaborative Group Study. *Journal of Chronic Diseases,* 1977, 30, 489-498.

MEICHENBAUM, D.: *Cognitive behavior modification: An integrative approach.* New York: Plenum, 1977.

METTLIN, C.: Occupational careers and the prevention of coronary-prone behavior. *Social Science and Medicine,* 1976, 10, 367-373.

MEYER, A.J., & HENDERSON, J.B.: Multiple risk factor reduction in the prevention of cardiovascular risk. *Preventive Medicine,* 1974, 3, 225-236.

MOSSEY, J.M.: The psychosocial and behavioral consequences of blood pressure intervention. Ph.D. Dissertation, University of North Carolina School of Public Health, Chapel Hill, N.C., 1975.

MULCAHY R., HICKEY, N., GRAHAM, I., & MCKENZIE, G.: Factors influencing long-term prognosis in male patients surviving a first coronary attack. *British Heart Journal,* 1975, 37, 158-165.

NOVACO, R.W.: Stress Inoculation: A cognitive therapy for anger and its application to a case of depression. *Journal of Consulting and Clinical Psychology,* 1977, 45, 600-608.

NOVACO, R.W.: A stress inoculation approach to anger management in the training of law enforcement officers. *American Journal of Community Psychology,* in press.

OBRIST, P.A.: The cardiovascular-behavior interaction—as it appears today. *Psychophysiology,* 1976, 13, 95-107.

ROSENMAN, R.H.: The role of behavior patterns and neurogenic factors in the pathogenesis of coronary heart disease. In R.S. Eliot (Ed.), *Stress and the Heart.* New York: Futura, 1974, pp. 123-141.

ROSENMAN, R.H.: History and definition of the Type A coronary-prone behavior pattern. In T. Dembroski (Ed.), *Proceedings of the Forum on Coronary-Prone Behavior.* Washington, D.C.: Dept. of Health, Education and Welfare, Publication No. (NIH) 78-1451, 1977(a), pp. 13-18.

ROSEMAN, R.H.: The interview method of assessment of the coronary-prone behavior pattern. In T. Dembroski (Ed.), *Proceedings of the Forum on Coronary-Prone Behavior.* Washington, D.C.: Dept. of Health, Education and Welfare, Publication No. (NIH) 78-1451, 1977(b), pp. 83-104.

ROSENMAN, R.H., BRAND, R.J., JENKINS, C.D., FRIEDMAN, M., STRAUS, R., & WURM, M.: Coronary heart disease in the Western Collaborative Group Study: Final follow-up experience of 8½ years. *Journal of the American Medical Association,* 1975, 233, 872-877.

ROSENMAN, R.H., BRAND, R.J., SHOLTZ, R.I., & FRIEDMAN, M.: Multivariate prediction of coronary heart disease during 8.5 year follow-up in the Western Collaborative Group Study. *American Journal of Cardiology,* 1976, 37, 902-910.

ROSENMAN, R.H., & FRIEDMAN M.: Association of specific behavior pattern in women with blood and cardiovascular findings. *Circulation,* 1961, 24, 1173-1184.

ROSENMAN, R.H., & FRIEDMAN, M. Modifying Type A behaviour pattern. *Journal of Psychosomatic Research,* 1977, 21, 323-333.

ROSENMAN, R.H., FRIEDMAN, M., STRAUS, R., WURM, M., KOSITCHEK, R., HAHN, W., & WERTHESSEN, N.T.: A predictive study of coronary heart disease. *Journal of the American Medical Association,* 1964, 189, 15-22.

ROSENMAN, R.H., RAHE, R.H., BORHANI, N.O., & FEINLEIB, M.: Heritability of personality and behavior pattern. Paper presented at the meeting of the American Psychosomatic Society, New Orleans, March, 1975.

ROSKIES, E.: Changing the Type A behavior pattern in a non-clinical population. Research proposal submitted to Health and Welfare, Canada, January, 1978.

ROSKIES, E., SPEVACK, M., SURKIS, A., COHEN, C., & GILMAN, S.: Changing the coronary-prone (Type A) behavior pattern in a non-clinical population. *Journal of Behavioral Medicine,* 1978, 1, 201-217.

SACKETT, D.L., TAYLOR, D.W., & HAYNES, R.B.: Increased absenteeism among working men following the labeling and treatment of their hypertension. Paper presented at the annual meeting of the Society for Epidemiological Research, Seattle, June, 1977.

SCHACHTER, S.: The interaction of cognitive and physiological determinants of emotional state. In C.D. Spielberger (Ed.), *Anxiety and behavior.* New York: Academic Press, 1966, pp. 193-224.

SCHERWITZ, L., BERTON, K., & LEVENTHAL, H.: Type A assessment and interaction in the behavior pattern interview. *Psychosomatic Medicine,* 1977, 39, 229-240.

SCHUCKER, B., & JACOBS, D.R.: Assessment of behavioral risk for coronary disease by voice characteristics. *Psychosomatic Medicine,* 1977, 39, 219-228.

SHEKELLE, R.B., SCHOENBERGER, J.A., & STAMLER, J.: Correlates of the JAS Type A behavior pattern score. *Journal of Chronic Diseases,* 1976, 29, 381-394.

STOYVA, J., & BUDZYNSKI, T.: Cultivated low arousal—an anti-stress response. In L.V. DiCara (Ed.), *Limbic and Autonomic Nervous Systems Research.* New York: Plenum, 1974, pp. 370-393.

STUNKARD, A.J.: Behavioral treatment of obesity: Failure to maintain weight loss. In R.B. Stuart (Ed.), *Behavioral self-management: Strategies, techniques and outcome.* New York: Brunner/Mazel, 1977, pp. 317-351.

SUINN, R.M.: Letters to the Editor: Behavior therapy for cardiac patients. *Behavior Therapy,* 1974, 5. 569-571.

SUINN, R.M.: The cardiac stress management program for Type A patients. *Cardiac Rehabilitation,* 1975, 5, 13-15.

SUINN, R.M.: Type A behavior pattern. In R.B. Williams Jr. & W.D. Gentry (Eds.), *Behavioral approaches to medical treatment.* Cambridge, Mass.: Ballinger, 1977, pp. 55-65.

SUINN, R.M., & BLOOM, L.J.: Anxiety management training for Pattern A behavior. *Journal of Behavioral Medicine,* 1978, 1, 25-37.

SUINN, R.M., & RICHARDSON, F.: Anxiety management training: A nonspecific behavior therapy program for anxiety control. *Behavior Therapy,* 1971, 2, 498-510.

TASTO, D.T., CHESNEY, M., & CHADWICK, J.: Multi-dimensional analysis of Type A/B behavior. In T. Dembroski (Ed.), *Proceedings of the Forum on Coronary-Prone Behavior.* Washington, D.C.: Dept. of Health, Education and Welfare, Publication No. (NIH) 78-1451, 1977, pp. 142-155.

WALDRON, I.: Sex differences in the coronary-prone pattern. In T. Dembroski (Ed.), *Proceedings of the Forum on Coronary-Prone Behavior.* Washington, D.C.: Dept. of Health, Education and Welfare, Publication No. (NIH) 78-1451, 1977, pp. 253-261.

WALDRON, I., ZYZANSKI, S.J., SHEKELLE, R.B., JENKINS, C.D., & TANNENBAUM, S.: The coronary-prone behavior pattern in employed men and women. *Journal of Human Stress,* 1977, 3, No. 4, 2-19.

WEINBLATT, E., SHAPIRO, S., FRANK, C.W., & SAGER, R.S.: Prognosis of men after first myocardial infarction: Mortality and first recurrence in relation to selected parameters. *American Journal of Public Health,* 58, 1968, 1329-1353.

WHITE, J., & FADIMAN, J. (Eds.): *Relax.* U.S.A.: Confucian Press, 1976.

WILLIAMS, R.B.: Physiological mechanisms underlying the association between psychosocial factors and coronary disease. In W.D. Gentry & R.B. Williams (Eds.), *Psychological aspects of myocardial infarction and coronary care.* St. Louis: Mosby, 1975, pp. 37-50.

WILLIAMS, R.B.: Psychophysiological differences between Type A and Type B individuals that may lead to coronary heart disease. In T. Dembroski (Ed.), *Proceedings of the Forum on Coronary-Prone Behavior.* Washington, D.C.: Dept. of Health, Education and Welfare, Publication No. (NIH) 78-1451, 1977, pp. 185-192.

WILLIAMS, R.B.: Arousal, relaxation and biofeedback. Paper presented at the symposium on Concepts of Stress/Stress Management, Houston, April, 1978.

Williams, R.B., Friedman, M., Glass, D.C., Herd, J.A., & Schneiderman, N.: Summary statement: Mechanisms linking behavioral and pathophysiological processes. In T. Dembroski (Ed.), *Proceedings of the Forum on Coronary-Prone Behavior.* Washington, D.C.: Dept. of Health, Education and Welfare, Publications No. (NIH) 78-1451, 1977, pp. 157-169.

Zyzanski, S.J.: Associations of the coronary-prone behavior pattern. In T. Dembroski (Ed.), *Proceedings of the Forum on Coronary-Prone Behavior.* Washington, D.C.: Dept. of Health, Education and Welfare, Publication No. (NIH) 78-1451, 1977, pp. 46-67.

Zyzanski, S.J., & Jenkins, C.D.: Basic dimensions within the coronary-prone behavior pattern. *Journal of Chronic Diseases,* 1970, 22, 781-795.

12

Physical Activity in a Healthy Lifestyle

SANDY KEIR and RICHARD LAUZON

The potential benefits of increased physical activity can be manifested in two different ways: from the direct benefits of the activity itself and from the use of activity as a vehicle to modify other behaviors (see Figure 1). The more obvious inherent benefits can include the control of body weight while permitting the intake of nutritionally adequate diet; improved body efficiency and appearance, including cardio-pulmonary and general body function; reduction of stress and tension; and most important, an overall sense of well-being or "joie de vivre." Equally important in today's society, is the improved outlook on health that often accompanies increased physical activity, which may stimulate other lifestyle changes such as quitting smoking, modifying the diet or reducing alcohol intake. In addition, it is fairly obvious that the situational conditions required for physical activity are just not compatible with many maladaptive behaviors.

Much of the behavior modification literature to date in the health arena illustrates techniques to minimize or eliminate negative behaviors such as smoking and obesity. Yet all these intervention techniques and the philosophy behind them apply equally as well to the maximization of a positive behavior. Educators have traditionally opted for "positive

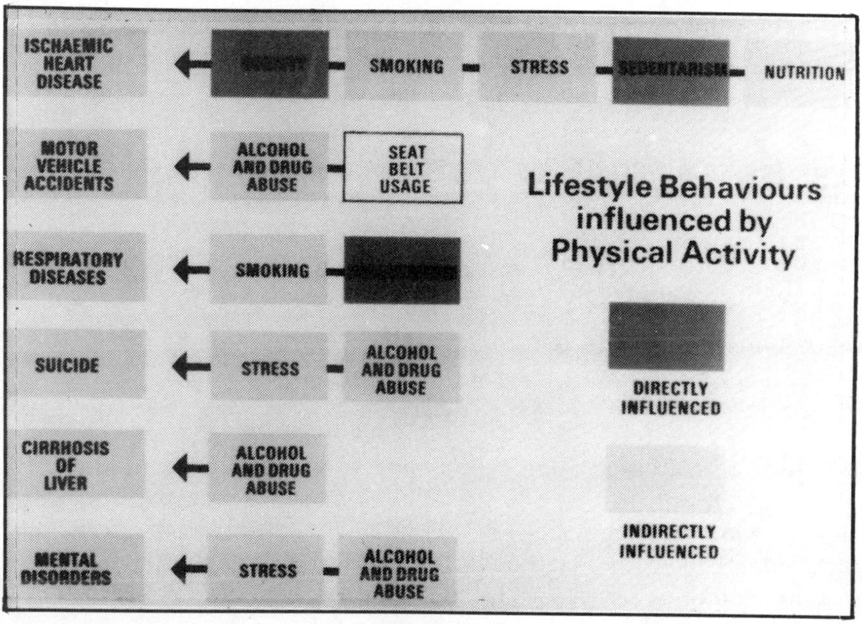

FIGURE 1

suggestion over negative command" or to paraphrase a popular song of the late thirties, "Accentuate the positive, eliminate the negative, and don't fool with Mr. In-between" (Mercer).

It is soon apparent when one reads the behavior modification literature that long-term compliance with most health-related lifestyle behaviors continues to elude most practitioners (Ziffenblatt & Wilburn, 1977). Unfortunately, the target behaviors do not possess the same "addictive" qualities as the maladaptive behaviors. Two English medical researchers, however, have found that exercise-induced adrenal secretions stimulate the pleasure center in the hypothalamus producing a distinct enjoyment as a result of the exercise (Taggart, Parkinson, & Carruthers, 1972). Perhaps physical activity is the drug-less pill we've searched for. Moreover, the fact that physical activity tends to reduce or subliminate tension and aggression may also influence long-term compliance to exercise programs. Certainly the world is ready for a non-chemotherapeutic cathartic.

There are a number of principles of behavior modification which have been incorporated into the development of strategies to encourage a greater personal commitment to increase physical activity.

(1) *Planned behavior change is best applied in a group setting as opposed to a one-on-one interaction. The group increases both the interaction phase of learning and the amount of feedback available to the individual (Jacobson & Pellegrino, 1977).*

Although some successful activity programs take place with individuals, our experience in physical education tends to support this theory of socialization and a great many individuals remain in group programs. Women especially rate the opportunity for social interaction as the most important feature of their exercise classes (Bannister, 1972).

(2) *Intervention programs are based on several principles of learning, i.e., learning new behaviors must be made pleasurable if the unlearning of old behaviors is to take place (Jacobson & Pellegrino, 1977).*

There is an increased awareness among physical educators today that fitness is not only achieved and maintained "by running to exhaustion at 5:00 a.m. every morning," or "doing 500 push-ups in the gym," but by getting out with your family or friends on a weekend and cross-country skiing or bicycling, and enjoying not only the exercise but the surroundings and the companionship.

(3) *People learn from each other and model their behavior after those they most admire (Jacobson & Pellegrino, 1977).*

Activity certainly lends itself to this principle and we do not lack for sport heros although our most significant disciples in recent years have not necessarily been from the sport world, i.e., President Eisenhower (golf and walking); Governor-General Mitchener (jogging and calisthenics); President Kennedy (50 miles walk and informal sports); Dr. Dudley White (bicycling); Prime Minister Trudeau (jogging and all round sportsman); Dr. Hans Selye (stair climbing and bicycling); and so on.

(4) *Change is facilitated when the advocated measures are both available and accessible (Jacobson & Pellegrino, 1977).*

Again activity of some type is readily available to most individuals and more recently less sophisticated forms of exercise have become the vogue, (i.e., walking, cycling, swimming, jogging, cross country skiing, snow shoeing, etc.). While many of today's popular activities are no more or less accessible than heretofore, they appear to be because of the massive marketing and promotion programs as well as their practice by growing segments of the population.

(5) *Education for a new behavior must emphasize the new gains rather than what is lost (Jacobson & Pellegrino,* 1977).

Again, increasing one's physical activity is usually thought of as a plus in one's life rather than a loss. Physical activity programs have strongly promoted the physiological and psychological benefits associated with exercise, namely, weight control, cardio-respiratory efficiency, strength, balance, flexibility, and increased ability to tolerate stress and tension.

Although exercise and other behavior changes can be introduced at any time, there are certain identifiable periods of the year, or what could be called "teachable moments," where greater chances of success may be possible. For example, January first, although New Year's resolutions are perhaps best known for their short duration, is an opportune time to build on the guilt feelings resulting from Christmas over-indulgence. Many cultures and religions highlight their year by festival periods (i.e., Mardi Gras) which precede a 40-day period of restraint or self-control and religious observance. Again, healthy lifestyle behaviors can be featured, such as a fifteen minute walk every day for 40 days as well as abstaining from alcohol or cigarettes. At the change of seasons, especially in Northern climates, people change their lifestyles. Thus, spring and fall are particularly opportune times to introduce changes in physical activity patterns. In the spring, people think about getting in shape to wear their summer clothing or swimwear; in September people sign up for special self-improvement courses and could schedule their evenings and weekends to attend exercise classes.

The following project reports, and personal experiences illustrate, the physical activity in four different target audiences.

PARTICIPaction—The Canadian Movement for Personal Fitness

In 1971, a private non-profit organization was incorporated in Canada called PARTICIPaction, formed to employ marketing methods to promote fitness. Funded primarily by the Federal Health Department, this agency produces messages to promote physical activity and delivers them through extensive public service campaigns as well as corporate involvement. It borrowed the ideology of the marketing of goods and services in a free enterprise society whereby demand is created by the employment of a variety of marketing tools. Marketing theorists agree on a series of steps (Kisby, 1978) which inform the public of the existence of a product and then promote the products use.

The first step was to make consumers aware of the product and this was done through signs in public transit.

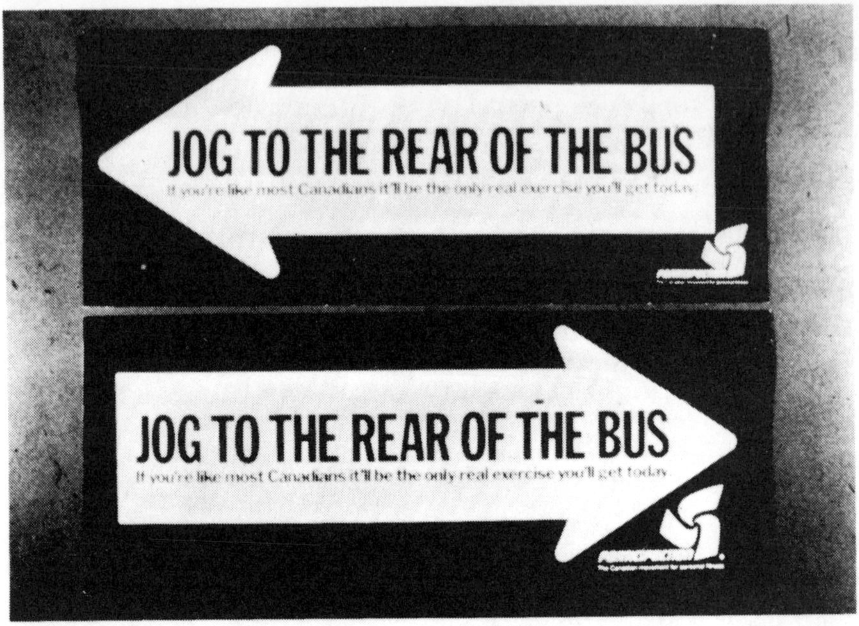

FIGURE 2. Signs in public transit are used to make people aware of the benefits of physical activity.

> Jog to the back of the bus. If you're like most Canadians, it will be the only real exercise you get today.
>
> *or*
>
> A 30 year-old Canadian is in the same shape as a 60 year-old Swede.

Although the benefits of physical activity are well-known, the average Canadian has been either ignorant of the amount and kind of activity needed to maintain health, or has been deluded into believing that he or she gets enough.

The next step for the marketing agent was to change the attitude of the audience or at least to educate them about their alternatives. This was done through messages such as:

> Fitness: In your heart you know it's right.
>
> *or*
>
> Three times a week I take my body out and give it a good run—wind her up and let her go. It's good for your heart and lungs and everything.

Then, the consumers must be induced to buy the package by committing themselves to take the first step to change activity habits. Examples of the motivational campaign are:

> Walk a block a day. It won't make you fit, but it's a start and you'll feel better for it.
> PARTICIPaction salutes Sam Fuller on his greatest moment in Sport. (Sam Fuller has just been convinced by his wife to walk around the block.)

When the campaign has finally managed to attract the consumers, the marketing agent must persuade them to try the product. If it lives up to its promises then the consumers may become regular users, but pressure must be kept up to keep the converts, since competitors will always be trying to win them back. It is at this point that the physical activity marketer can easily be in trouble. If that vital first experience is unpleasant, it will be difficult to get the consumers to repeat. If the facility is crowded, if the beginner is ridiculed, if muscles are stiff and ache after the first jog, the consumer may give up and may not try again. Finally, the last step is regular usage. This is the ultimate goal of any marketer be it a product or some form of behavior.

There is considerable evidence to show that the PARTICIPaction campaign is working. The most dramatic project would have to be the PARTICIPaction Saskatoon project, which was an intensive marketing and media campaign in a moderate sized western city to prove the viability of a community-oriented campaign and to serve as a model for future national programs.

Some of the facts that were learned from Saskatoon are:

> There is no question that advertising works—virtually everyone in Saskatoon is fitness conscious and a great many have become active.
>
> About 94 percent of the Saskatoon population were aware of PARTICIPaction's campaign. In addition to the 25 percent of the population who reported being physically active prior to the PARTICIPaction project, an additional 16 percent were encouraged to adopt regular physical activity habits (Jackson, 1974).
>
> In a survey, over 50 percent claimed to have increased their physical activity. This was supported by a national survey which reported a participation rate of 67 percent in Saskatoon, the highest of all Canadian metropolitan centers surveyed.
>
> It was learned that a general campaign to increase physical activity can also promote specific sports, i.e.:

—YMCA fitness classes are filled and the attendance rate is better than ever;
—evening badminton classes enrollment has doubled and redoubled;
—cross-country ski equipment sales have more than doubled.

—contrary to popular belief in sport and fitness circles, not everyone who takes up a physical activity wants to be "managed." In fact over 75% of the people in Saskatoon who claim to be active now, chose activities that require no leadership, no teams, no set hours, no specific facilities, and usually no equipment.

The Fit-Kit

A second project which utilized some of the principles of behavior modification, and yet was quite different from the PARTICIPaction media campaign, was the development of the *Fit-Kit.* The Fit-Kit is a self-contained fitness testing and information package presently sold in book stores and other retail outlets and by professional, recreational, and health associations. In the design of the Fit-Kit, an attempt was made to address four stages in encouraging behavioral change, namely awareness, education, a readily available solution, and reinforcement (Lauzon, 1976).

The most unique component of the kit is the Canadian Home Fitness Test which allows individuals to determine their level of aerobic fitness in the privacy of their own home (Bailey, Shephard, & Mirwald, 1975). The Canadian Home Fitness Test is essentially a progressive, double-step test of cardio-respiratory fitness performed in two or three stages. Each stage is composed of a sub-maximal workload adjusted for the individual's sex and age group. The individual's ten second pulse rate after stepping determines whether or not the subject should advance to the subsequent more vigorous stage and ultimately determines the individual's fitness status. The step height of eight inches (20.3 cm) was determined from specifications in the Canadian Building Code for residential homes.

Rather than exercising to a metronome, the tempo for the stepping, which varies with age and sex, is provided by a long-play record of musical cadences. Each musical tempo attempts to match the taste of the particular age group—slow, pleasant melodies for the over 60s to rock-type rhythms for the teens and twenty-year-olds.

Concern for the safety of the participants was reflected by the inclusion of a self-administered screening questionnaire, the Physical Activity

FIGURE 3. The Fit-Kit.

Readiness Questionnaire (PAR-Q), as part of the Canadian Home Fitness Test (Chisholm, Collis, Kulak, Davenport, & Gruber, 1975). This tool attempts to identify the vast majority of adults who do not require a medical examination prior to a submaximal test or before entering supervised physical activity programs. Again, it was imperative to remove as many obstacles as possible if we hoped to encourage the adoption of a new lifestyle. The Canadian Home Fitness Test was designed to be used by all persons from 15 years of age to over seventy. An interesting observation from the test market results (a market survey conducted in two representative Canadian cities) indicated that of the 54% who actively took the test upon receiving it gratis in the mail, 96% of them had four or more other persons use the test (Recreation Canada, 1975). This demonstrated that besides developing the "users," the test had created a group of "pushers" of the fitness message.

To satisfy the education component of the program the popular booklet Health and Fitness authored by Dr. P.O. Åstrand (1974) was provided with an up-to-date foreword on the Canadian scene.

The solution phase of the kit comprised three items: a glossy wall chart entitled Fit-Tips which provided a series of simple calisthenics exercises; a prescription pad, outlining five important elements necessary for a physically active lifestyle; and a Walk-Run Distance Calculator which allowed each individual to work out a walking or jogging program based on their personal needs (determined by age, sex, weight, height, and fitness level as determined by the Canadian Home Fitness Test (Jette, 1975a, 1975b; Jette, Thoden, & Gauthier, 1975).

The fourth stage of the model, reinforcement, included a Progress Chart which allowed individuals to measure their own progress and adherence to the program, a series of crests identifying the user as a convert, and an advanced version of the Canadian Home Fitness Test to be used only by those person who achieved the highest fitness category on the first test.

Although the Fit-Kit and the Canadian Home Fitness Test were designed to function as a self-contained unit for families, they have had wide use in a variety of other settings. Laboratory research related to the Canadian Home Fitness Test has contributed encouraging information. A correlation between the Canadian Home Fitness Test predicted maximal oxygen uptake results and the direct gas analyses—treadmill results—produced a Pearson r of .902 suggesting that the Canadian Home Fitness Test is indeed not only a motivational fitness testing tool, but a sophisticated instrument when pulse rates are monitored accurately. This latest information has led to the use of the

Canadian Home Fitness Test by Statistics Canada and the Federal Health Department in the Canada Health Survey, as well as the aerobic testing procedure in the national Standardized Test of Fitness presently being developed.

The Fit-Kit has been utilized and marketed to support other behavior change programs, i.e., each air traffic controller in a Lifestyle Intervention Program at the Toronto International Airport receives a Fit-Kit for home use; various testing campaigns utilise the Fit-Kit for reinforcement of their counseling sessions; and even the private sector has successfully integrated the Fit-Kit into a salad and salad dressing campaign (Kraft).

Employee Physical Fitness

Our involvement in the field of employee physical fitness has presented us with the opportunity for utilizing various behavioral strategies to reintroduce physical activity into the daily lives of our work force. It was felt that people commit eight hours or more a day, five days a week to the job and that many might be persuaded to initiate changes in their lifestyle during that period rather than after work or on their weekends. One study indicated that a change to a four-day work week to produce a three-day weekend resulted in one more day of watching television and drinking beer.

In particular, when employees are involved in inservice or professional development courses (either prior to employment or during employment), the curriculum should include information related to their lifestyle and how this may affect their jobs in addition to the training specific to their particular job. If we hope to increase physical activity or change other lifestyle behaviors, there seems to be greater potential for success if the intervention is introduced at a time when the target group has already disrupted their normal routine. Furthermore, these training programs provide the opportunity to take advantage of a communications monopoly in which conflicting messages could be minimized.

An interesting study which illustrates the disruption principle is based upon a group of people from a middle management training course within the Canadian Federal government called the Career Assignment Program (Recreation Canada, 1974). These people are selected from different government departments to be trained as Senior Administrators within the government. Their initial training requires their attendance in a residential training course for three months. As a start, we tried to assess what kind of lifestyle these 25 or 30 people were exposed to in the three months they were on the course.

The organizers of the course felt that to make up for being away from home, the participants should get very, very good food. Thus, they have a gourmet menu, prepared by an excellent chef, wine with their meals, and a bar conveniently open at all times. Generally the work week is from Monday to Friday noon, when they go home for the weekend. Each day they study and work from early morning, break for lunch, work to 4:30, and resume each evening from 7:00 until nearly midnight.

It was obvious that over the years the Career Assignment Program courses had been held, there had been no attempt to relate the role of the candidate's "lifestyle" to his effectiveness on the job. In fact, the types of lifestyles developed and accentuated in the previous courses showed that the candidates ate too much of too many kinds of foods, drank too much and too often, gained excessive amounts of weight, moved around too little (they didn't even play with their kids each evening or put out the garbage), and worked under high stress loads for long periods of time in a fairly competitive situation. This lifestyle was the opposite of one desirable for the most effective work performance and personal health.

In September 1973, a pilot project relating a physical fitness program to lifestyle change was incorporated into the Career Assignment Program course. The program included a regularly scheduled physical activity session each day at 4:30, an extensive pre- and post-fitness appraisal, and the introduction of various materials and information on the role of lifestyle and its relationship to personal health and job performance.

The final appraisal of the program which included the feelings and observations of the participants, revealed that the lifestyle component was *the* most significant aspect of the three months and that the majority of the group had made significant changes in their lifestyle. Several months after the course, a follow-up interview confirmed that the changes were generally not transient, but permanent. The lifestyle component, by the way, was made a continuing part of all future Career Assignment Program courses.

Although there are many examples of employee fitness programs across Canada and the U.S., it is still difficult to identify the factors that are necessary for success.

> To be successful, an employee fitness programme must be broadly-based and embrace a significant percentage of its target group. Most importantly, an employee fitness program must attract people who would otherwise not be engaged in regular physical activ-

> ity. Unless a programme can attract and hold such people along with their more athletic colleagues, it will not make an impact on the overall health and fitness of the employee community. Fitness programmes can take many forms, but must provide opportunity for vigorous, sustained cardiovascular exercise in addition to activities which promote general muscle tone and flexibility. Virtually all successful programmes feature some form of initial health and fitness assessment. However, it is not the fitness assessment that is important, but the activity that follows it. Characteristics of good programmes include: gradual progression beginning with a level of activity suited to the initial condition of participants; enjoyable vigorous exercise; individual daily recording of activity; exercise counselling; feedback relating to changes in fitness performance; and most important of all, stimulating leadership (Collis, 1976).

This winter our Fitness and Amateur Sport Branch has adopted a program idea from other countries and has begun to introduce the concept of the exercise break into business and industry in Canada. Although an active break has been popular for years in European companies, the "coffee break" has traditionally represented the time for passive relaxation from work in our society. It is often time for a cigarette or donut to perk up lagging spirits. An interesting and certainly healthier alternative would be to do some simple exercises during a break in the work day (Exercise Break Manual, 1978). A brief exercise break does not constitute an employee fitness program, but it will improve circulation, relax tense muscles, and perhaps reintroduce activity back into what would otherwise be a sendentary day.

FIGURE 4. Employees on an "exercise break."

As stated earlier, there is a tremendous variety of approaches to implementing fitness and lifestyle intervention in business and industry, ranging all the way from simple information giving, to awareness programs, through introductory programs such as the exercise break, to sophisticated fitness centers with professional leadership.

Many of the programs that were initiated as pilot projects as far back as 1972 are still very active and flourishing, and although lacking formal evaluation, they indicate the importance and relevance of these programs to the company. There is, however, a real need to measure and document the benefits that might accrue to companies and to individuals by involving them in activity programs at the place of work. The Federal Health Department is involved in such a controlled research and demonstration project in the Toronto area which will be completed in September of 1978. This study may provide some of the data that are sorely needed for economically justifying employee fitness programs. The first part of this project was the design and implementation of a model fitness and lifestyle intervention program with the employees of a large company. The company has built a small fitness facility including change and shower rooms, and converted storage space into a group fitness room. A fitness program has been designed, leaders trained, and classes for both individuals and groups have been scheduled in the exercise area. Throughout the six-month program, lifestyle information relating to nutrition, drug and alcohol abuse, tobacco use, safe driving, reduction of stress, etc. will be provided to the employees. Speakers, films, nutritional programs through the cafeteria, home programs for weekends, and many other activity experiences that have been successful in other programs will be presented to the employees (Employee Fitness, 1979).

The second part of this project was to measure the effects of such a lifestyle intervention and compare the results with a control company. Some of the parameters measured, in addition to fitness levels of both groups of employees, included health care costs, absenteeism and tardiness, productivity, job satisfaction, and various attitudinal measurements, especially those related to the lifestyle of the employees involved. The problem in past studies of this type have been the large number of drop-outs from the experimental group, such that there is a serious attempt in this project to minimize recidivism by concentrating as much effort on the program itself as on the research.

Environmental Control

One's environment may dramatically determine one's personal lifestyle decisions such as the decision to increase physical activity. Strong-willed persons can often overcome environmental factors but most people require an environment that supports their efforts to become healthy. In other words, it is very difficult to get people physically active in the absence of opportunities which permit or demand physical activity, especially in an environment dominated by television sets, telephones, convenient bus service, and other easy transportation. It is not enough to merely encourage people into changing their activity patterns. Attention must be given simultaneously to the nature of the individual, the problem and the environment in which the interacting forces exert their influence. One situation where this principle has been successfully conducted has been at conferences similar to the Banff Conference. As has been mentioned earlier, the temporary dislocation of an individual while attending a conference could be used to dramatically modify their lifestyle and is potentially a great opportunity to expose that person to a variety of healthy lifestyle alternatives and environments. Moreover, conferences are attended by decision makers in a variety of fields who have the power to affect changes in their own occupational environment. To date, our Branch has been involved in a number of national and provincial conferences, in which environmental change programs have been integrated into the conference day: the National Conference on Fitness and Health in December of 1972; the Canadian Nurses Association Annual Meeting in June 1974; the Canadian Public Health Association Annual Meeting in May 1975; the Ontario Public Health Association Meeting of October 1975; and the Canadian Public Health Association Meeting of May 1976.

Similarly, a number of other conferences have adopted lifestyle modification activities as integral parts of their programs. Some of the activities that were included are:

(1) A nutrition break rather than merely coffee (fresh fruits, juice, skim milk, and even raisins and carrot sticks);
(2) an exercise break (between long sessions);
(3) controlled smoking areas;
(4) exercise testing available to delegates;
(5) information on calorie balance during a typical conference day;
(6) lunch hour walk;
(7) Health Hazard Appraisal (a computerized personal evaluation);
(8) breathalizers at cocktail hour and information regarding alcohol;
(9) morning jogs;
(10) swim/exercise programs at the end of the day;
(11) scheduled dances or square dances;
(12) a conference located in a rural setting rather than in a large city, walk to various meetings, and social events; and

FIGURE 5. Exercise programs are being used at conferences.

(13) conference menus which are low in calories, low in animal fat and identification of the nutritional components of the various meals.

Several years after these conferences, individuals have forgotten who the major speakers were or even key recommendations from the workshops, but they still remember that there are eighty calories in four black olives or they remember that they had their blood pressure assessed at this particular conference. Meetings or conferences, whether for health professionals or others, lend themselves to this type of environmental influence.

A very dramatic example of modifying the environment and subsequently changing the behavior of a large group of people, was the clearing of the snow from the Rideau Canal which runs through the center of the city of Ottawa, the capital of Canada. Several years ago (and I wish I could say it was a behavior modification person or a health educator but I am afraid it wasn't), someone in the National Capital Commission, the office responsible for this canal, decided to clear the snow from the canal during the winter months rather than using the canal as a receptical for excess snow cleared from the streets. Within a very short period of time, the availability of this eight-mile skating rink which runs through the center of the city stimulated thousands of Ottawans to change their leisure time activities from sitting in front of television to skating on the canal. Coupled with the availability of such a facility, there is the chance of seeing our Prime Minister or a federal Deputy Minister or perhaps your own boss skating, which reinforces the possibility that more and more government officials who work in Ottawa will don the blades from time to time, to see and be seen.

Other examples of environmental changes that have produced an increase in physical activity would have to include the lighting of cross-country ski trails in city parks; the increase in the number of bicycle paths available not only for weekend bicycling but to be used to cycle to and from the workplace; the closing of major streets especially parkways on weekends for the use of bicycles; the fact that building planners are making stairways more available and attractive, so that people are encouraged to walk up and down the stairs rather than wait for the elevator; and perhaps the epitomy of environmental control, the programming of an office building elevator to stop only on the odd floors in the morning and the even floors in the afternoon ensuring that at least once a day, everybody in that building walks one flight of steps.

In conclusion, a quote from a recent editorial in the Canadian Medical Association Journal highlights the important influential role of physical activity:

> Interest in fitness has insinuated itself into public consciousness far more effectively than one could possibly have hoped, when public education concerning its importance first began in earnest. As a byproduct of this changing social atmosphere, emphasis on physical activity can be used as a component of all programmes designed to minimize destructive lifestyles—for example, use of alcohol, habits of indolence and development of obesity, as well as smoking. Stress can be placed on the advantages or positive ben-

efits of these pleasurable and invigorating alternatives. Their realization that both benefit and pleasure can be incorporated into a productive lifestyle explains the relative ease with which these programmes can be effectively pursued and why the changes induced tend to be incorporated into permanent patterns (Delarue, 1978).

REFERENCES

ASTRAND, P.O.: *Health and fitness.* Ottawa.: Minister of State for Fitness and Amateur Sport, 1974.

BAILEY, D.A., SHEPHARD, R.J., & MIRWALD, R.L.: *Validation of a self-administered home test of cardio-respiratory fitness.* Ottawa: Department of National Health and Welfare, 1975.

BANNISTER, R.: Sport, physical recreation, and the national health. *British Medical Journal,* 1972, 4, 711-715.

CHISHOLM, D., COLLIS, M., KULAK, L., DAVENPORT, W., & GRUBER, N.: Physical activity readiness. *British Columbia Medical Journal,* 1975, 17, 375-378.

COLLIS, M.L.: *Employee fitness.* Ottawa: Department of Supply and Services, 1976.

DELARUE, N.C.: Join the majority, be a non-smoker. *Canadian Medical Association Journal,* 1978, 118, 7-8.

Employee Fitness and Lifestyle Project, Tornoto 1977-78, Ottawa: Minister of State for fitness and Amateur Sport, 1979.

Exercise break manual. Ottawa: Minister of State for Fitness and Amateur Sport, 1978.

JACKSON, J.: Diffusion of an innovation: An exploratory study of the consequences of sport participation Canada's campaign at Saskatoon. Ph.D. dissertation, University of Alberta, 1974.

JACOBSON, L. & PELLEGRINO, E.: Forum: The role of allied health professionals in prevention. *Preventive Medicine,* 1977, 6, 379-385.

JETTE, M.: An exercise prescription program for use in conjunction with the Canadian Home Fitness Test. *Canadian Journal of Public Health,* 1975, 66, 465-467, (a).

JETTE, M.: The Canadian Home Fitness Test as a predictor of aerobic capacity. *Canadian Medical Association Journal,* 1976, 114, 680-682.

JETTE, M., THODEN, J.S., & GAUTHIER, R.: Aerobic exercise prescription intensity in terms of maximal working capacity. *Canadian Journal of Public Health,* 1975, 66, 465-467.

KISBY, R.: Notes from discussions on PARTICIPaction, Jan. 1978. Personal communication.

LAUZON, R.: Fit-Kit for fat-cats. *Canadian Journal of Public Health,* 1976, 67, 95-100.

MERCER, J.: Song Writer.

Recreation Canada: *Report on physical fitness and lifestyle included in Career Assignment Program (C.A.P.) Management Course, Fall 1973.* Ottawa, 1974.

Recreation Canada: *The Canadian Home Fitness Test: Summary of the test market report.* Ottawa 1975.

TAGGART, P., PARKINSON, T., & CARRUTHERS, M.: Cardiac response to thermal, physical and emotional stress. *British Medical Journal,* 1972, 4, 71-76.

ZIFFENBLATT, S., & WILBURN, C.: Maintaining a healthy heart: Guidelines for a feasible goal. *Preventive Medicine,* 1977, 6, 514-525.

13
Use of Media in Lifestyle Programs

NATHAN MACCOBY and
JANET ALEXANDER

LIFESTYLE AND CARDIOVASCULAR DISEASE

In the past two decades, psychologists have made important advances in applying their professional skills to human psychosocial problems. Therapeutic procedures have been developed to help people learn how to change their behaviors from antisocial to pro-social, from self-damaging to health-promoting, from dysfunctional to functional. These new techniques for modifying behavior have some important implications for dealing with one of the developed world's most important public health problems, cardiovascular disease. This chapter discusses the California Three Community Study where the elements of successful behavior change provide the basis for an intervention program aimed to help adults to make lifestyle changes that will reduce their risk of premature cardiovascular disease.

Heart disease is the single greatest killer in the United States, and in most other highly industrialized societies throughout the world. Although, in the last few years, the death rate due to heart disease has abated slightly in the United States, it is still largely responsible for the fact that the life expectancy of the average U.S. male at age 40 is only slightly better than was his forebearers at the beginning of this century (Lew & Seltzer, 1970). While once considered a disease of old age in North America and other highly developed areas, the prevalence of coronary heart disease is now increasing in younger and younger age groups. It might be said that the American way of life (adopted by many other developed countries) is hazardous to your health.

Although there is some disagreement about the relative contribution of the various risk factors to heart disease, the Framingham longitudinal study (Truett, Cornfield & Kannel, 1967), and other reports (Inter-Society, 1970) make it clear that smoking, high blood pressure, and high blood fats (cholesterol and triglyceride) are involved. Other factors related to lifestyle, such as excess body weight, lack of exercise, stress, and inadequate diet, are highly suspect as contributors. Further evidence that lifestyle factors are strongly implicated is provided by the epidemiological observations that in general, as lifestyle factors vary from one country to another, so do cardiovascular disease rates. For example, when serum cholesterol levels are compared for people in countries with differing disease rates (e.g., children in Wisconsin and in Mexico), there is almost no overlap in the distributions (Golubjatnikov, Paskey, & Inhorn, 1972). Similarly, Japanese in Japan have a much lower death rate from heart disease than age-comparable Americans. However, Japanese who now live in California have approximately the same rates as other Americans (Robertson, Kelley, O'Neill, Wixom, Eisworth & Haddon, 1974), indicating that as the Japanese adopt facets of the "American" lifestyle their disease rates tend to increase.

Apparently, it is this affluent but unhealthful lifestyle that is the basis for our greatly increased risk of premature cardiovascular disease. If these habits can be changed to more healthful ones, there is good reason to believe that morbidity and mortality due to cardiovascular disease can be substantially reduced, although this has not yet been fully demonstrated. Currently, several large-scale intervention trials and several international studies are testing the hypothesis that reducing these risk factors, either singly or in combination, can delay or prevent cardiovascular disease.

Given a successful completion of these trials in the early 1980s, there will be a need to devise means to educate large numbers of Americans about lifestyle change for risk reduction in a cost-effective way. In the Three Community Study, the research objective was to begin to investigate the kinds of large-scale primary prevention programs that might be mounted community-wide to accomplish this goal.

Elements of Project Design

The central objectives of the project were to observe the changes in information, attitudes and risk-related behaviors that occurred as a consequence of the intervention. The overall goal was to achieve a clinically meaningful reduction in overall risk of heart disease. This ultimate endpoint, the "risk score," is the estimated probability that a person will be the victim of a cardiovascular event over the next twelve-year period. The score is derived from an equation based on the results of the Framingham longitudinal study (Truett, Cornfield & Kannel, 1967). Factors entered into the equation are age, sex, individual and family history of heart disease, systolic blood pressure, relative weight, amount of cigarette smoking, and level of cholesterol in the blood. Consequently, the behavior change aims were for subjects to achieve their ideal weight, cut down or stop smoking, increase physical activity, and to reduce or moderate their consumption of refined sugar, salt, cholesterol, saturated fats, and alcohol.

In the Three Community Study, one major consideration was the choice of a target population. Resource constraints demanded selectivity; the epidemiological evidence provided direction. A medical model focusing on the 10-15 percent at the highest risk within the general adult population was not deemed the wisest course of action. We reasoned that since risk factors are widely distributed across age and sex groups, almost everyone has some "risk." Thus, even though the rate of heart attack is lower among 85 percent of the adult population at lesser risk, it is among this apparently healthy segment of the population that the larger absolute share of heart attacks will occur. Coupled with the fact that half of all the first sudden heart attacks are fatal ("sudden death" syndrome), the implication is clear that for prevention to be successful, a total adult population, however apparently healthy, is the logical target audience. Thus, we chose as the target audience all adults ages 35-59 in the two treatment communities.

Another concern at the design stage was the problem of randomization in the selection of treatment and control groups. Since the intervention was to be directed at adults in entire communities, random assignment of individuals was not feasible. The level of resources available made it impractical, if not impossible, to consider an equally rigorous experimental method, that of treating a large number of entire geographically-defined populations as single units and randomly assigning some of them to treatment or control. Thus, we concluded that the best choice was a compromise between feasibility and rigor, a "quasi-experimental" design (Campbell & Stanley, 1966) with three experimental units.

The clinical and epidemiological evidence suggested the behavioral approach to risk factor modification. The community interventions were also based on a number of theoretical and research findings about how change can be achieved in human behavior and the factors that influence the change process.

One research finding which greatly influenced the project design was a formulation of Cartwright. Analyzing household sample survey data on the purchasing of United States Savings Bonds, Cartwright (1949) found data suggesting that mass media alone were not effective in achieving sales, but that personal solicitation, in the context of the campaign, was. To account for this finding, he posited that in order to influence behavior, it was necessary to stimulate action or behavioral structures in addition to informational and motivational ones. Thus from this perspective, it was seen that the intervention might be enhanced by the addition of an interpersonal element designed to stimulate or "trigger" specific behavior changes linked to cardiovascular health, through interpersonal influence and group process.

Another of the primary theoretical orientations guiding intervention planning was derived from Bandura's social learning theory (1969, 1971). In a recent formulation, Bandura (1978) describes a reciprocal interaction model. According to this conceptual approach, human behavior is regulated by immediate situational influences and by the person's performance skills and his anticipations of the consequences for different courses of action, rather than by such global constructs as personality traits. Bandura views the interplay between environment and behavior as a reciprocal influence process in which the environment shapes the individual behavior, but the person also shapes his environment. Thus, the person's relationship with his or her environment is an open system, always modifiable by providing the individual with appropriate skills for self-management and motivating him or her to make use of them.

Social learning theory and research—particularly with the introduction of cognitive training for self-control—offers a promising conceptual framework for stimulating community-wide behavior change. We noted, however, that the techniques employed in behavior change typically have involved live face-to-face training either one-on-one, or, at most, one instructor with a class. Although effective, these training methods are extremely costly when one considers the size of the clientele served and compares it to the numbers of highly skilled instructors required. Such procedures are potentially viable only when the target population is limited to the 10 to 15 percent at "highest risk." But, as noted above, a community model rather than a medical model was adopted by the Three Community Study; not 15 percent, but the entire adult population in the towns was to be the "target audience." For total communities clearly the one-on-one or group treatment modes are totally impractical. However, theoretically the mass media has the potential to offer substantial improvements over individual or group treatment in terms of the numbers of people who can be reached by the efforts of a small group of highly skilled individuals. On this basis, in the Three Community Study, we decided to rely upon a mass media program as the major intervention mechanism by which to foster lifestyle changes leading to cardiovascular risk reduction, supplemented in one town by face-to-face intensive instruction for a subset of those at higher risk.

Social learning theory appeared to have application both to mass-mediated communications as well as to face-to-face learning. The person-to-person behavior modification protocols in the Three Community Study for the face-to-face contact treatment were directly based on social learning theory as explicated by Bandura. As for the application to media, since it is evident that skills can be learned by modeling or the practice of observed behavior, it seemed clear that audio-visual portrayals (film and television) and, to a lesser extent, audio alone (radio and recordings), or visual alone (slides, pamphlets, billboards, posters, etc.) could constitute the appropriate models. Another problem for media, of course, is whether or not the acquired skills will be practiced in the appropriate circumstances. Again the learning of appropriate cueing for acquired behavior can be learned via mass media. A family picnic scene on film can serve via imagery as a cue for utilizing acquired knowledge of what kinds of foods to pack in the basket when preparing to go on a family picnic. Listening to a radio statement warning the listener about how to respond to the advertising of unhealthy products helps remind the listener of such ads of the need to discount false claims. Self-management of behavior involves precisely such self-cueing in the appropriate situation at the appropriate time. If then, the problem of helping people to learn healthier habits is thought of as involving not only new knowledge and increased incentive but also the acquisition of skills and the maintenance of such new behavior in the appropriate settings, media if properly planned, produced and exhibited, ought to have an excellent chance of being effective.

The literature in persuasion or attitude change also contributed to elements of project design (Katz and Lazarsfeld, 1955; Katz, 1957; McGuire, 1969). Much of the experimentation in this field has been concerned with temporary rather than stable change. Festinger (1954) postulated that pressures to conformity exist in groups and are brought to bear on the individual group member in such a way that he or she will tend to conform to the opinions and behavioral patterns of the other group members. Research has generally supported this proposition. More recently, Roberts and Maccoby (1973) have formulated and tested some hypotheses on counterarguing and persuasion aimed at discovering the bases for stable change.

Within these perspectives, the project was designed to observe the nature and magnitude of the changes that might be stimulated by the use of mass media alone. Several other auxiliary objectives were woven into the design fabric. For purposes of comparison, we wanted to utilize the powers of interpersonal communication and group treatment for a subset of individuals in one of the two communities. Given some uncertainty as to what media could and couldn't be expected to do, we wanted to be able to compare the effects of media alone with a combined treatment which we expected to be maximally effective, regardless of its ultimate adaptability to wider use. We selected a face-to-face method of instruction as the method that might be maximally effective, especially when carried out with high risk people in a milieu of a mass media campaign. Comparison of the effects generated by these two treatment conditions should define a range of programs with potential practical effectiveness and varying cost-effectiveness. Also, this situation should reveal any potential shortcomings of a mass media treatment by comparing the relative effectiveness of mass media alone (a highly exportable procedure) with a maximally effective method as well as with a control.

The research design compares two California towns (Gilroy and Watsonville) over a three-year period with one control town (Tracy). All were independent communities rather than bedroom towns. They were matched to the extent possible with respect to such characteristics as socio-economic status, minority/majority distribution and population size. The populations of the towns ranged from 13-15,000. Agriculture, agricultural marketing and retail trade comprised the main economic base of all three towns. The treatment and control towns had mutually exclusive media services. For example, the two treatment communities were within one television coverage area, but the control community was well removed from its reach. A narrow range of low mountains separated the two treatment towns, thus diminishing the intercommunication between the two.

A description of the response rates and the composition of the twelve study groups observed over the course of the three years can be found in Farquhar et al. (1977), and in Maccoby, Farquhar, Wood, & Alexander, (1977). An intervention program was developed for delivery through mass media and interpersonal communication. Gilroy received the mass media only treatment; in Watsonville, this campaign was supplemented by a program of intensive instruction for a subsample of those assessed at the baseline survey to be at highest risk of cardiovascular disease. A probability sample of residential addresses was drawn (Stern et al., 1976). The study then went through the following stages: (1) About 550 subjects per town, ages 35-59, were recruited into the study during the initial or baseline survey (in autumn of 1972). (2) A mass media campaign in English and Spanish began directly after the baseline survey(s), and continued through August, 1973. It was followed by the second survey of the same sample (S_2) in the autumn of 1973. This pattern repeated itself through 1974 and 1975. To observe the effects of the measurement process itself, a smaller "after-only" subsample was interviewed only at the second survey in 1974. The Tracy sample was also interviewed at baseline and annually thereafter but no further intervention took place.

Individuals falling into the top risk quartile, stratified by age-decade, were defined as high risk. In Watsonville only, in the first year two-thirds of such individuals were randomly selected and offered "intensive instruction," in group sessions or individual home counseling over a ten-week period. The remaining one-third were treated exactly like the non-high risk portion of the treatment samples, i.e., they received the mass media treatment only. Spouses also participated if they wished, even though their risk status did not qualify then for inclusion. The high risk counterparts in Gilroy and Tracy were identified and observed as subgroups over the course of the study; however, no further action was taken with respect to them. The full design over three years is displayed in Figure 1.

Elements of Media Design

Any campaign aimed at inducing specified attitudes, knowledge and behavior change involves a number of processes. We conceptualized the interface between behavior change and mass media management in

	1972	1973		1974		1975	
Watsonville (W)	Baseline Survey (S1)	*Media campaign *Intensive instruction (II) for ⅔ of high risk participants	Second Survey (S2)	*Media campaign *Intensive instruction (II) for ⅔ of high risk participants	Third Survey (S3)	*Maintenance (low-level) Media campaign *II: Summer Follow-up	Fourth Survey (S4)
Gilroy (G)	Baseline Survey (S1)	*Media campaign	Second Survey (S2)	*Media campaign	Third Survey (S3)	*Maintenance (low-level) Media campaign	Fourth Survey (S4)
Tracy (T)	Baseline Survey (S1)		Second Survey (S2)		Third Survey (S3)		Fourth Survey (S4)

FIGURE 1. Three Community Study Design

terms of the number of steps that are required to move the target population from initial awareness of, and interest in, the problem to the adoption and maintenance of the advocated attitudes or behavior (McGuire, 1969; Rogers with Shoemaker, 1971). While, for any individual, depending on his or her pre-campaign state, some steps may be more or less important than others and although for some individuals the sequence which the processes are engaged in may vary, across a total population it is possible to characterize the general processes to be engaged. By doing so, we specify the major stages of the campaign design:

(1) *Agenda-setting*: By agenda-setting, we mean the process by which an individual's attention is obtained and focused on specified issues and problems. It has been shown that while the mass media may be limited in their ability to persuade, they can be effective in setting agendas, i.e., for bringing specified matters to the public's attention (McCombs and Shaw, 1972) for discussion or debate. As political scientist Bernard Cohen (1963) put it: "The press may not be successful in telling people what to think, but it is stunningly successful in telling its readers what to think about (p. 13)."

(2) *Informing*: Once a particular topic or subject matter is on the public agenda and is perceived as a salient issue, a campaign must present the logical set of propositions, in laymen's terms, that brings the issue home and sets the stage for individual action. This self-appraisal through information and analysis is a crucial stage in furthering long-range objectives.

(3) *Training*: Once members of the population understand their personal relationship to the problem, they must be taught how to modify risk-related behaviors including how to handle barriers and personal costs.

(4) *Motivation and Reinforcement*: The population must be given positive incentives to change their behavior, and support and encouragement in maintaining their new behavior.

(5) *Self-Maintenance*: If newly acquired habits are to be maintained, they must be under self-control. Prompting or self-cueing at the appropriate time and place can be critically important in this maintenance process.

These five stages are by no means definitive nor mutually exclusive. No doubt messages may serve different functions for different receivers, e.g., a message which provides information to one person may perform an agenda-setting function for another. Messages may serve different functions for the same receiver, e.g., a message may simultaneously persuade, inform, and motivate a single receiver (Cartwright, 1949).

Nevertheless, it is clear that there is a certain sense in which these processes occur in a time sequence. In terms of a large aggregate population, it is necessary to promote a new behavior before promoting actions designed to reinforce and maintain it. In general before new behavior occurs, motivation and training must take place. Prior to that, information transfer and persuasion processes are at work. And, initially, in order to set the stage, that issue must appear on each person's individual agenda as a matter of concern and interest.

Changes in overt human behavior are known to occur through the basic series of intermediary processes outlined above; however, a number of other contributing variables such as age, sex, socioeconomic status, current health beliefs and previous education are important influences on the accomplishment of these basic processes. These influences are complex; often they are contradictory or negative. Our design of a community-wide intervention strategy attempted to take into account the full range of potential influences operating at the individual level, the primary group level, and at the social or macro-environmental levels (DeFleur and Ball-Rokeach, 1974).

Although agenda-setting must be the initial objective of any mass media campaign, it cannot be thought of in isolation from the latter objectives—persuasion and behavior change. Putting heart health communications into the public agenda was seen as only the first step for the public to begin to learn useful information and ways to act effectively upon it. To develop and create messages and designs which not only put the heart health issue into the public agenda but also change attitudes and behaviors, it is necessary to draw upon research findings in several areas related to the communication process.

Taken as a whole, communication research findings ask the media planner to deal with a configuration of interacting factors from which different effects on attitude, information gain, and behavior can be predicted. Acknowledgement of the audience as a full partner in the communication process makes a developmental approach to campaign planning necessary to the successful prediction of the specific factors influencing the acceptance or rejection of campaign messages. Research also suggests that when the task is to communicate specific information about complex issues to demographically varied audiences for measurable behavior purposes, formative or process evaluation of media products and schedules is essential. Situational differences across topics, audience, locales, etc., all interact in unpredictable ways. From the extensive body of research that the empirical tradition in communication studies has produced, the main conclusion the experienced practitioner must reach is that the strategy with the highest probability of success is to pretest multiple approaches. The primary method by which research findings and established psychological principles are applied to campaign design is an iterative process of audience analysis, trial runs, formative evaluation for feedback, finally utilizing the evaluation results to reshape and restructure messages and campaign plans. Only through this process can the most positive approaches to presenting the intervention strategy be located and refined and some assurance provided that they will be effective with the intended audience.

The media campaign consisted of a variety of media (e.g., TV spots, bus cards, etc.) that were released to the target audience through the most generally available media channels. A broad range of materials were produced: for example, about 50 television spots, three hours of television programming, over 100 radio spots, several hours of radio programming, weekly newspaper columns, newspaper advertisements and stories, billboards, printed material sent via direct mail to participants, calendars, and other assorted materials. The media campaign began two months after the initial survey and continued for nine months in 1973, stopped during the second survey, and then continued for nine more months in 1974. A very reduced campaign continued in 1975. Given a sizable Spanish-speaking population, a specially tailored campaign was presented in Spanish.

The campaign messages were distributed to target audiences through the most generally available and widely used mass media channels in the towns. The media campaign was pre-packaged in that all of the communications were sent by us directly to the distribution channels. The campaigns differed only insofar as the local media gatekeepers varied their overall placement, publication or broadcast of the materials made available to them.

The design precluded the use, in the media-only treatment, of any direct interpersonal or quasi-interpersonal communications with the target audience. Thus, many types of events often associated with such public education programs (appearances at public forums, speeches to community groups, participation in celebrations or fairs, etc.) were not undertaken within this campaign. The campaign also avoided the use of communication opportunities that were idiosyncratic to one town (a popular radio talk show, a TV news feature interview) to keep the media output reaching each town as comparable as was practically possible.

A central element of the campaign was the use of various kinds of survey data to guide the design, production and distribution efforts. The initial plan grew out of the profile of the target population relative to the study objectives that emerged from information available prior to the beginning of the campaign. The main pre-campaign data sources were: a pretest of the survey questionnaire on a similar population in Modesto, California; the baseline survey; the results of formative evaluation and audience testing; a series of interviews with scientific, professional and political figures in the towns; marketing data on media usage patterns; results of talks with the owners and managers of local media channels; also, consideration of the very practical limitation imposed by the budget and available time.

Once the campaign was underway, it became necessary to supplement these preliminary data sources with a series of occasional, informal interviews and observations (dubbed "mini-surveys" as compared to "surveys"). These were designed to provide media planners with immediate feedback on public response to a particular media event or set of events in order that the ongoing production and distribution process could benefit from the information. For example, in March 1973, we conducted what we then termed an informal survey in Gilroy and Watsonville. We interviewed a total of about 80 adults in the two towns in their homes. The aim was to find out about their exposure to, awareness of, and information gained from the campaign to date. Our purpose was to get some indication of the penetration of our materials and in the experimental sense, to find out whether or not a "treatment" was being applied from the individual subject's point of view. The data gathered, albeit an informal gathering, led us to conclude that much of the campaign was visible to the individuals, and therefore we had passed a "threshhold" level of awareness. Further, we believed that we were detecting indications of increased awareness and comprehension of the specific causes of heart disease.

The overall campaign activities could be seen as an orchestration of discrete media events that occurred in many channels with common themes, styles and content; a monitoring mechanism was occasionally activated to provide feedback on both the efficiency and reliability of the distribution system and the public response to current media events. In this way, flexible planning within practical limits was possible to refocus priorities, reset directions, and, in general, to modulate the course of the campaign in directions likely to promote further progress.

Results of the Three Community Study

In general, we found that both the media-only town (Gilroy) and the town with media plus intensive face-to-face instruction of a set group at high risk (Watsonville) showed general improvement in contrast to the treatment community (Tracy). Let us take a look at some of the main findings. We first examine the effects of the various treatments on the learning of information about cardiovascular risk reduction (Table 1). A test of 24 items was developed in order to assess knowledge effects of the campaigns.

All three intervention groups gained substantially in knowledge over the two-year period. The non-intervention town's gains are minor by comparison. It should also be noted that the media-only town of Gilroy, while demonstrating substantial gains at the end of the first year, did not show as much of an increase as the intensive instruction town (Watsonville). However, by the end of the second year of campaigning, Gilroy's gains were much more impressive. This phenomenon may also be noted in subsequent comparisons.

We turn to behavior. What if any changes in behavior occurred?

Reduction of egg yolk consumption was one of the specific targets of the dietary aspect of the overall campaign (Table 2). Here again the change in media-only towns lags a little (but is substantial compared with the control town) during the first year but gains in the second year. In any case, the drop in egg consumption was not only statistically significant ($p<.01$), but also substantial.

TABLE 1
Knowledge of Risk of Cardiovascular Disease

		Baseline Scores on Knowledge Test	End Year 1 % change	End Year 2 % change
Gilroy (397)	Media Only	11.16	+18.1	+26.5
Watsonville* Reconstituted (424)	Media Only	11.15	+30.9	+36.0
Watsonville (423)	Media plus Intensive Instruction	11.15	+36.3	+40.8
Tracy (384)	No Treatment	11.42	+ 1.7	+ 6.3

*Intensive instruction omitted and samples reconstituted so as to represent entire town.

TABLE 2
Egg Yolk Consumption

Behavior - Eggs Consumed per Day

		Baseline	End Year 1 % change	End Year 2 % change
Gilroy (397)	Media Only	0.84	−27.5	−33.3
Watsonville Reconstituted (423)	Media Only	0.79	−37.1	−42.2
Watsonville (423)	Media plus Intensive Instruction	0.78	−41.8	−44.4
Tracy (384)	No Treatment	0.76	−14.9	−15.9

Other important behavior measures include dietary cholesterol, saturated fat consumption and smoking. Again, substantial decreases in cholesterol consumption were reported for the intervention communities. In the mass media only treatment town, there was a 24.6 percent reduction from baseline to end of one year and 28.0 percent from baseline to end of year two. In the maximum intervention town, there was a 26.3 percent reduction from baseline to end of one year, and a 28.7 percent reduction from baseline to end of two years of education in Watsonville. In saturated fats, similar reductions took place. For all differences, $p<.01$.

The percentage of smokers who quit tells a less encouraging story. While the percentage who reported cutting down is substantial, only among the intensive instructees did a really substantial proportion of smokers stop smoking. Fifty percent were non-smokers at the end of three years. Small reductions on the order of 7 percent and 8 percent did take place in the mass media-only treatments, but these are barely significant ($p<.05$), and not of sufficient clinical importance.

Next, let us examine some physiological measures such as serum cholesterol and systolic blood pressures (Tables 3 and 4).

There are statistically significantly smaller increases in serum cholesterol as compared with the normal expected increase that occurs in the no treatment town, but clearly these are disappointingly small. There are highly statistically significant differences in blood pressure which are of clinical importance.

TABLE 3
Physiology—Plasma Cholesterol

		Baseline (mg/100ml) mean	End Year 1	End Year 2	Year 3
Gilroy (397)	Media Only	212.3	+0.1	0.0	+1.4
Watsonville Reconstituted (423)	Media Only	211.5	−0.3	+1.5	+2.6
Watsonville (423)	Media plus Intensive Instruction	212.8	−1.4	+1.1	+1.8
Tracy (384)	No Treatment	209.0	+1.4	+3.8	+5.0

TABLE 4
Physiology—Blood Pressure

		Baseline mean blood pressure	End Year 1 % change	End Year 2 % change	End Year 3 % change
Gilroy (391)	Media Only	131.8	−2.2	−7.3	−4.3
Watsonville Reconstituted (423)	Media Only	133.0	−0.5	−4.6	−4.4
Watsonville (423)	Media plus Intensive Instruction	133.4	−1.3	−4.6	−3.8
Tracy (384)	No Treatment	128.6	+3.2	+1.3	+0.9

Generally, in all of the above measures, when high risk samples are examined, the same pattern of differences emerge, but there are almost always larger ones.

Finally, let us look at an overall measure of risk, risk equation developed by Truett, Cornfeld and Kannel (1967) in the Framingham longitudinal study (Table 5). There are not only highly significant drops in risk (all differences are $p<.01$) but they are of clear-cut importance clinically since risk equation predicts the probability of a cardiovascular incident within 12 years.

TABLE 5
Risk Score/Total Participants

		Baseline risk score	End Year 1 % change	End Year 2 % change	End Year 3 % change
Gilroy- (391)	Media Only	0.076	−4.7	−17.3	−8.8
Watsonville Reconstituted (423)	Media Only	0.094	−4.3	−16.2	−12.8
Watsonville (423)	Media plus Intensive Instruction	0.092	−12.9	−18.4	−15.2
Tracy (384)	No Treatment	0.080	+7.7	+6.5	+ 3.3

TABLE 6
Risk Score: High Risk Subjects

		Baseline risk score	End Year 1 % change	End Year 2 % change	End Year 3 % change
Gilroy (94)	Media Only	0.160	−10.7	−24.0	−16.1
Watsonville Control (40)	Media Only	0.199	− 7.8	−24.7	−23.1
Watsonville (77)	Intensive Instruction	0.183	−29.0	−30.3	−29.0
Tracy (95)	No Treatment	0.172	+ 4.4	− 2.0	− 8.0

If we examine the high risk subject comparisons, the reductions in risk scores are even more dramatic (Table 6). These are the subjects at highest risk—those most in need of reduction. Here, even though the secular trend accounts for some lowering of risk, the reductions for all intervention groups are gratifyingly substantial.

Discussion and Conclusions

Changes that we have observed must be considered in the context of the samples in which they were obtained. Unlike the subjects of previous smoking cessation (Bernstein and McAlister, 1976) and weight reduction studies (Stunkard, 1975), our samples were randomly selected from open populations, thus providing a better basis for generalization to future public education efforts. But since we were able to recruit only about two-thirds of the total sample of eligible participants selected in the three surveys, the generalizability of our results may be limited by that ratio. Also, some of the print media materials were available only to the sample groups. Further analysis of the characteristics of refusals and drop-outs will help pinpoint biases introduced by our response rate. Some of the observed changes in blood pressure may be due to measurement bias, especially in Gilroy where diastolic blood pressure may have been initially underestimated despite our best efforts to standardize the measurement procedure. Realizing the high variability of blood pressure determinations, we must be cautious in interpreting these data. Finally, we must acknowledge that we did not produce, or were unable to measure accurately, any increase in physical activity in the treatment communities, nor were we able to help participants learn to achieve sustained weight loss, although significant reductions in relative weight were present in the intensively instructed high risk Watsonville cohort after the end of the first year.

In our Three Community Study, we attempted to generate behavior change as well as information and attitudinal change both via mass media alone and through a combination of mass media and intensive personal instruction with a subsample of high risk subjects. Consistent with the Cartwright formulation, we had considerable success when our mass media programs were supplemented by intensive instruction. However, we also found that in many instances our mass media efforts were quite successful even in the absence of supplemental personal instruction. It now seems evident that certain kinds of behavior associated with risk reduction can be learned through exposure to mass media (Farquhar, 1975; Maccoby, 1975; Maccoby and Farquhar, 1975; Farquhar, et al., 1977; Maccoby, et al., 1977); while others require a different constellation of media events which contain a considerable amount of skills training (e.g., cigarette smoking cessation). However, we believe that, if access to media can be secured, mass media can be designed to provide some of that training and to organize personal instructions systems to augment that mediated training.

We tentatively attribute much of the success of the community education campaigns to the quality of the media campaign and to the synergistic interaction of multiple educational inputs and to interpersonal communication stimulated by application of these inputs in a community setting. We are especially gratified to find that, in general, the changes in knowledge, behavior and physiologic endpoints observed in the first year of treatment were maintained and even improved in the second year of intervention.

These results provide evidence that behavior change for better health can be accomplished through sustained community-based education, but we have only begun to define the optimal strategy for conducting that education. Intensive face-to-face instruction and counseling seem important for changing refractory behavior such as cigarette smoking and for inducing rapid change in dietary behavior. But we must learn how to use these methods to correct obesity as well and to employ them effectively with limited resources (i.e., by training volunteer instructors). It is clear that the mass media can increase knowledge and change dietary behavior. However, we believe that the power of the media can be enhanced if we can find ways to use them to stimulate and coordinate programs of interpersonal instruction in natural community groups, such as facets of the existing health care system or employee groups, and to deliver some forms of specialized training and counseling (e.g., training in improved eating habits to achieve weight loss or skills for avoiding smoking).

One of the problems in the use of mass media for helping people to achieve changes, such as quitting smoking or reducing saturated fat consumption, is that learning how to modify complex habitual behaviors can be as difficult as learning to perform well in athletic competition or learning not to lose one's temper under provocation. Acquisition of such skills is enhanced when there is feedback of the results of practice. Ideally, there is initial modeling and then guided practice at the appropriate time tailored for individuals, and an individual perception of accomplishment or rewards. Mass media may not readily provide all of this. They can, however, effectively provide the initial modeling (Lumsdaine, 1961) and encourage the development of community organization and support systems to deliver the necessary individual guided practice.

In the Three Community Study, however, a number of principles were developed based upon behavioral theory and research. These principles were integrated into the development of the two intervention strategies and, we believe, can be applied with even more positive results to the formulation of the overall strategy for the cardiovascular disease prevention program for our forthcoming larger communities project.

We also believe that their application and testing in the future project will help us understand more clearly which principles can be made effective for general community use.

As for media, a campaign plan that can successfully integrate the concepts of goals, social support, and social controls and that uses existing interpersonal networks as channels for the diffusion of health information, albeit a more complex media campaign, can be successful. Such a strategy does not use mass communications exclusively; however, media are central to the plan. Although it is possible that in the future the entire effort might be accomplished via media, our current view is that the prudent choice of the "best" strategy for optimum efficiency of community-based risk reduction is a matrix plan which blends a minimal, but focused amount of face-to-face instruction with an extensive media campaign that is strong enough to create the desired outcomes, in part, by itself.

The potential significance of these findings is considerable. Cartwright (1949) had implied that mass media campaigns are futile unless supported by direct interpersonal intervention. On a mass scale, interpersonal intervention is labor-intensive, expensive, and often very hard to organize, coordinate, and monitor. If mass media alone, however, can lead to results in behavior change, then there is far more hope for health campaigns than was previously suspected. It would seem imperative, therefore, that our findings from the Three Community Study be tested further and elaborated. If indeed mass media alone can be effective, we need to understand more clearly under what conditions.

REFERENCES

BANDURA, A.: *Principles of behavior modification.* New York,: Holt, Rinehart and Winston, 1969.

BANDURA, A.: *Social learning theory.* Morristown, N.J.: General Learning Press, 1971.

BANDURA, A.: The self system in reciprocal determinism. *The American Psychologist,* 1978, *33,* 344-358.

BERNSTEIN, D. A., & MCALISTER, A. L.: The modification of smoking behavior: Progress and problems. *Addictive Behaviors,* 1976, 1, 89-102.

CAMPBELL, D. T., & STANLEY, J. C.: *Experimental and quasi-experimental designs for research.* Chicago: Rand McNally, 1966. (Reprinted from: *Handbook of research in teaching,* American Educational Research Association, 1963.)

CARTWRIGHT, D.: Some principles of mass persuasion. *Human Relations,* 1949, *2,* 253-267.

COHEN, B. C. *The press, the public, and foreign policy.* Princeton: Princeton University Press: 1963, 13.

DEFLEUR, M. L., & BALL-ROKEACH, S.: Mass communication and persuasion. In *Theories of mass communication,* Third Edition, New York: David MacKay, 1974, 237-254.

FARQUHAR, J. W.: Interdisciplinary approaches to heart disease prevention (results of community-based risk reduction campaign using mass media). Paper presented at AAAS meetings, 1975. Reprinted in *Hearing on disease control and health education and promotion* before the Subcommittee on Health (Edward Kennedy, Chairman) of the Committee on Labor and Public Welfare, U.S. Senate, 94th Congress, 1975.

FARQUHAR, J. W., MACCOBY, N., WOOD, P. D., ALEXANDER, J. K., BREITROSE, H., BROWN, B. W., JR., HASKELL, W. L., MCALISTER, A. L., MEYER, A. J., NASH, J. D. & STERN, M. P.: Community education for Cardiovascular health. *The Lancet,* June 4, 1977, *4,* 1192-1196.

FESTINGER, L.: Theory of social comparison processes. *Human Relations,* 1954, 7, 117-140.

GOLUBJATNIKOV, R., PASKEY, T., & INHORN, S.L.: Serum cholesterol levels of Mexican and Wisconsin school children. *American Journal of Epidemiology,* 1972, 96(1), 38.

Inter-Society Commission for Heart Disease Resources, Atherosclerosis Study Group, and Epidemiology Study Group: Primary prevention of the atherosclerotic diseases. *Circulation,* 1970, *42,* A55. (Revised, April 1972).

KATZ, E.: The two-step flow of communication: An up-to-date report on an hypothesis. *Public Opinion Quarterly,* 1957, *21*, 61-78.

KATZ, E. & LAZARSFELD, P. F.: *Personal influence.* New York: The Free Press, 1955.

LEW, E. A. & SELTZER, F.: Uses of the life tables in public health. In *Milbank Memorial Fund Quarterly,* 1970, *48*, 15-37.

LUMSDAINE, A. A. (Ed.): *Student response in programmed instruction.* Washington, D.C.: National Academy of Sciences, National Research Council, publication, 943, 1961, 471-500.

MACCOBY, N.: Achieving behavior change via mass media and interpersonal communication. Paper presented at AAAS Meetings, New York, 1975. Reprinted in *Hearings on disease control and health education and promotion* before the Subcommittee on Health (Edward Kennedy, Chairman) of the Committee on Labor and Public Welfare, U. S. Senate, 94th Congress, 1975.

MACCOBY, N., & FARQUHAR, J. W.: Communication for Health: Unselling Heart Disease. *Journal of Communication,* 1975, *25*(3), 114-126.

MACCOBY, N., FARQUHAR, J. W., WOOD, P. D., & ALEXANDER, J.: Reducing the risk of cardiovascular disease: Effects of a community-based campaign on knowledge and behavior. *Journal of Community Health,* Winter, 1977, *3*, 100-114.

MAHONEY, M. J.: The behavioral treatment of obesity. In A.J. Enelow & J.B. Henderson, (Eds.), *Applying behavioral science to cardiovascular risk,* Heart Association, Inc., 1975, 121-131.

MCCOMBS, M., & SHAW, D.: The agenda-setting function of mass media. *Public Opinion Quarterly,* 1972, *36,* 176-187.

MCGUIRE, W. J.: The nature of attitudes and attitude change. In G. Lindzey, & E. Aronson, (Eds.), *The handbook of social psychology,* Reading, Mass.: Addison-Wesley, 1969, 136-314.

ROBERTS, D. F., & MACCOBY, N.: Information processing and persuasion: Counterarguing behavior. In P. Clarke, (Ed.), *New models for mass communication research,* Beverly Hills, Ca,: Sage Publications, 1973, 269-307.

ROBERTSON, L.S., KELLEY, A. B., O'NEILL, B., WIXOM, C. W., EISWORTH, R. S., & HADDON, W.: Epidemiology of coronary heart disease and stroke in Japanese men living in Japan, Hawaii, and California. *Am. J. Publ. Hlth,* 1974, *64,* 1971.

ROGERS, E. M., with SHOEMAKER, F. F.: *Communication of innovations: A cross-cultural approach.* New York: Free Press, 1971.

STERN, M. P., FARQUHAR, J. W., MACCOBY, N., & RUSSELL, S.H.: Results of a two-year health education campaign on dietary behavior: The Stanford Three Community Study. *Circulation,* 1976, *54,* (5), 826-833.

STUNKARD, A. J.: From explanation to action in psychosomatic medicine: The case of obesity. *Psychosomatic Medicine,* 1975, *37,* 195.

TRUETT, J., CORNFIELD, J., & KANNEL, W.: Multivariate analysis of the risk of coronary heart disease in Framingham. *Journal of Chronic Disease,* 1967, *20,* 511-524.

14

Mass Media, Self-Management, and Smoking Modification

J. Allan Best

Few individuals in our society achieve the ambitious goal of maintaining a healthy lifestyle. As a consequence, those concerned with health-behavior change face a problem of massive proportion. Mass media approaches to smoking modification deserve serious consideration for several reasons.

First, from the service delivery perspective, there's the problem of manpower. Nine of ten smokers have tried to quit or claim they would if effective means were available (USPHS, 1976). Clearly, the traditional health care system would be overtaxed if smokers sought to make good this threat by seeking help. Furthermore, major training efforts would be required before health care personnel could competently address the difficult task of smoking modification. While smoking clinics in research settings have gradually become more effective (Bernstein & McAlister,

The stimulating collaboration of KVOS-TV personnel in the production of the television series is gratefully acknowledged. Lois Owen and Maurice Bloch provided valuable assistance in the development of program content. Funding for evaluation was made available by KVOS-TV and through a contract (No. 1200-4-1) from the Non-Medical Use of Drugs Directorate, Health and Welfare Canada.

1976; Best & Bloch, in press; Lichtenstein & Danaher, 1976), dissemination of this technology to service settings has not kept pace (Best, Bass, & Owen, 1977). Greater use of the mass media might eliminate the middleman, making effective smoking modification procedures directly available to the consumer.

Mass media programming has three further advantages from the consumer's perspective. It tends to influence greater numbers at any given time, creating a social milieu more supportive of behavior change (Allen, 1977; Delarue, 1973). In addition, the mass media help may be preferred by many consumers. While most smokers apparently want to quit, only a third say they would like a face-to-face clinic (Gallup, 1974; Schwartz & Dubitzky, 1968). Thus, mass media programming may reach a large population of smokers who otherwise would not receive assistance. Finally, the mass media may assist changes for which the smoker can feel largely responsible. It has been argued that change attributed to one's own efforts may be more likely to endure than change attributed to external causes (e.g., Davidson, 1976; Kopel & Arkowitz, 1975).

The desirability of mass media approaches is one thing; their viability is another matter. The potential effectiveness hinges on two distinct sets of factors—those affecting the impact of the medium itself and those affecting content. Despite McLuhan's (1964) classic argument that the medium is the message, a close look at possible uses of television in smoking modification suggests an alternative view.

The Medium

Most discussions of television's potential effectiveness confuse the medium/message distinction. Thus, even as Mendelsohn (1976) distinguishes between "mass education" and "mass persuasion," he argues that persuasion is the major potential for the medium. Indeed, most mass media applications have relied too heavily on information combined with fear arousal. Such interventions may serve to motivate behavior change but do little to shape it. Measured against what might be expected of such limited persuasion interventions, the mass media have been reasonably effective (Hochbaum, 1976; Warner, 1977). But is "mass education" an unreasonable aim for the medium? Maccoby and Alexander present one model for utilizing the mass media to educate or train behavior change skills (see Chapter 13). Another approach was used in the project reported here. Basically, questions about the use of mass media for behavior change should be empirical questions and evaluations of the more varied uses now emerging provide such tests.

The Message

If behavioral research is to provide a basis for the message, the most relevant data to consider are those describing self-management approaches to smoking modification, since the smoker's response to mass media will almost by definition involve self-management.

A variety of conceptual models has guided researchers in this area. Rather general definitions of self-management are typical. For example, Lichtenstein and Danaher's (1976) review considers self-management to include "those procedures which the client applies *in situ* to change some aspect of his own behavior." This broad definition is necessitated by the varied, usually implicit and simplistic assumptions about self-management processes which underlie technique development. More systematic models are available and a brief review may serve to highlight problems with self-management of smoking research.

Logan (1973) viewed smoking behavior as an operant and concerned himself with the issue of motivation for change. If smoking is reinforcing, either intrinsically or on the basis of past learning, what is to reinforce the act of self-control? Logan postulated a learned self-control drive which develops from a history of *lack* of control in fear and frustration situations. Thus, an individual becomes motivated to exercise self-control to avoid aversive consequences. Self-control can be learned through "the periodic practice of possible self-control techniques in particular situations, with the goal being to determine an effective method for that situation so that incentive motivation is developed" (Logan, 1973, p. 135). Note the situational specificity of self-management behavior from this perspective, consistent with Marlatt and Gordon's model for relapse.

Ferraro (1973) elaborated Logan's model with a discussion of the covert self-control behaviors commonly used in the smoking area, including Homme's (1965) coverant control, Cautela's (1970) covert sensitization, covert self-punishment as described by Bandura (1969), and "contingent humiliation" as proposed by Premack (1970). Again, the major hurdle for self-management concerns motivation. How do we initially motivate smokers to apply these primarily aversive techniques to themselves and what will ensure that they continue to apply the procedures repeatedly and consistently in an ongoing effort to manage smoking urges? In this context, Logan (1973) noted that ineffective punishment increases persistence and that a smoker thus may actually increase her tendency to smoke by trying to eliminate it through self-punishment. An alternative approach to self-management would include techniques designed to increase the net positive incentive for non-smoking.

The Logan/Ferraro model is nicely complemented by Kanfer's (1975, 1977) model for self-regulation. Kanfer outlined three stages which describe the processes by which a smoker's motivation to exercise self-control over his behavior might be translated into practice: a) *self-monitoring,* the act of carefully attending to one's own behavior, b) *self-evaluation,* the discrimination response of comparing one's behavior to some standard, and c) *self-reinforcement,* contingent upon the degree to which performance approximates the relevant standard. The model calls attention to such practical considerations as the potential importance of self-monitoring procedures; the structuring of treatment through contracting; the roles of attribution, expectancy, cognitive antecedents to behavior, etc.; and the need to strengthen alternative responses. The latter two points provide mechanisms for increasing the net positive incentive, as Ferraro suggested. Kanfer also clarified our emerging conceptualization of self-managed non-smoking by distinguishing between the generic term of self-management and the more specific concepts of self-regulation and self-control. The process by which self-regulation affects behavior, and through which self-mangement techniques can operate has been described. Self-control refers to the special case where a behavior (like smoking) has both positive and aversive consequences, and the individual emits a controlling response at a point in the behavior chain prior to the act (of smoking) such that the probability of the behavior's occurrence changes. This self-control response must be initiated by self-generated cues; it should not be under the direct control of the social or physical environment. This distinguishes self-control from many self-management smoking techniques which require the smoker to engineer her physical and social environment so as to affect the occurrence of subsequent smoking behavior. The Logan/Ferraro model applies most directly to *self-control,* although it can be extended to self-management more generally.

Another self-control model worth mentioning is D'Zurilla and Goldfried's (1971) problem-solving approach which provides a systematic strategy for producing changes in Kanfer's self-regulation process. The model does not suggest specific self-control behaviors appropriate to smoking but it does provide a vehicle whereby the smoker can take an active and central role in applying self-management models and techniques to his own idiosyncratic circumstances. This ingredient seems key in a self-management program for the mass media. Problem-solving has assumed a central role in programs for the control of weight (Mahoney & Mahoney, 1976) and alcohol (Miller & Munoz, 1976).

The final model is particularly germane to the present project. Bernstein (1974) proposed an approach to smoking modification based on programmed "symptom substitution": the development of both generalized and situation-specific non-smoking skills. As operationalized in our previous work (Best et al., 1977; Best, Owen, & Trentadue, 1978), this implies systematic functional analysis of an individual's smoking, followed by training in a variety of tailored alternative behaviors which may be of two types. First, to the extent that smoking is an operant in a given situation, the primary alternative should be functionally equivalent. For example, smokers apparently smoke to produce relaxation, stimulation, and rewards (cf., Best & Hakstian, 1978); therefore, alternative responses should produce similar effects. Second, to the extent that smoking is a respondent or to the extent that control is required over and above that provided by a functional alternative in a given situation, the alternative should involve a more general self-management technique as conceptualized above. Taken together, these self-management models provide a complex, but hopefully reasonably comprehensive and complete, recipe for effective self-management programming with smoking. Smoking behavior has both operant and respondent characteristics to consider in treatment. Motivational problems are endemic to the self-control of smoking and undue reliance on aversive self-control procedures can compound this. "Non-smoking" is a set of situation-specific alternatives to smoking which must be shaped and practiced like any skill. Change efforts occur through self-regulatory processes, perhaps guided by problem-solving strategies which consider environmental, cognitive, and motivational factors as well as existing relevant behavioral repertoires.

Research on smoking modification has varied both with respect to the kind and number of self-management techniques used. A selective review will illustrate some important issues. Stimulus control techniques were popular in early work (e.g., Bernard & Efran, 1972; Frederiksen & Peterson, 1973; Harris & Rothberg, 1972; Levinson, Shapiro, Schwartz, & Tursky, 1971, Shapiro, Tursky, Schwartz, & Snidman, 1971; Upper & Meredith, 1970). The relatively poor results highlight a recurrent problem in the literature: stimulus control techniques address only one small aspect of the conditions for behavior change which seem to follow from our self-management models. For example, stimulus control techniques do little to address the motivational considerations addressed by Logan (1973). In a similar way, although self-monitoring is a key component in Kanfer's model, use of the associated recording technique in isolation produces negligible effects (Kantorowitz & Walters, 1977; McFall & Hammen, 1971; McGrath & Hall, 1976; Rozensky, 1974). Cognitive control techniques alone are relatively ineffective (Danaher & Lichtenstein, 1974; Dericco, Brigham, & Garlington, 1977; Katz, Heiman, & Gordon, 1977).

In contrast, there are trends towards multifaceted treatment programs and towards the specific provision of alternative responses (Best et al., 1977; Best et al., in press; Brengelmann & Sedlmayr, 1977; Brockway, Kleinmann, Edleson, & Gruenewald, 1977; Chapman, Smith, & Layden, 1971; Conway, 1977; Danaher, 1977; Delahunt & Curran, 1976; Flaxman, 1978; Lando, 1977; McAlister, Meyer, & Maccoby, 1976; Morrow, Sachs, Gmeinder, & Burgess, 1973; Pechacek, 1976; Pomerleau & Ciccone, 1974). The results are not entirely consistent but they often rival the best in the smoking literature. Conclusions must be tempered by the fact that good results have often been achieved by combining self-management with aversion procedures.

What then is the present status of the self-management "message"? While tests of single self-management techniques generally show no significant long-term impact on smoking, a variety of recent programs have relied heavily on combinations of self-management techniques and achieved good results. The existing data do not allow us to form conclusions about either the outcome levels which might be expected from entirely self-managed cessation programs or the specific role and relative importance of individual self-management techniques.

This picture is quite consistent with the self-management models outlined. Self-management processes are complex and, if a coordinated and comprehensive treatment program is not provided, limited success is to be expected. At the present time, the viability of a self-management message for mass media depends more on our ability to profitably apply theoretical considerations than on data.

The Program

The project was designed as a feasibility study to provide preliminary data on the effectiveness of comprehensive self-management programming for a television/print format. Program content was primarily adapted from self-management components in our previous face-to-face clinics (cf., Best et al., 1978), supplemented by the more promising techniques in the literature. In addition, some components such as a problem-solving strategy were included on the basis of conceptual considerations. The television series was produced and broadcast by KVOS-TV, a CBS affiliate in Bellingham, Washington. The companion self-help guide is available upon request (Best, 1977). There were three objectives for the research:

(1) to evaluate the overall effectiveness of the program, with respect to maintained smoking modification;
(2) to describe the sample with respect to characteristics such as age, sex, education, occupation, smoking rate, and success expectations and to relate these characteristics to program effectiveness so as to facilitate future program development and promotion;
(3) to assess subject perceptions of the relative utility of various program components and of situational factors associated with relapse.

Method

Sampling

The series was broadcast on six consecutive Saturdays between 7:00 and 7:30 PM, beginning on April 16, 1977. The average KVOS-TV audience during this broadcast time included approximately 20,000 adults.

Viewers were invited to phone or write in, following the first two shows, to request the self-help guide. They thereby registered for the evaluation of the series. Station telephone lines were open for two hours following each of these first two shows. A total of 1448 persons requested the guide. Non-smokers and smokers who had already quit were excluded from the sample, yielding a final sample size of 1403. All subjects provided age, sex, and current smoking rate information in addition to an address and telephone number, at the time that they made their request for the guide.

The final sample was 60.1% female. Mean age was 40.1 years (SD=13.57). Subjects began smoking at a mean age of 17.8 (SD=4.83), and before the program reported smoking a mean of 26.9 cigarettes per day (SD=11.49). They reported an average of five previous attempts to quit (SD=13.08).

These sample characteristics are similar to those reported by many face-to-face clinics, except for the overrepresentation of females. The sample seems relatively large considering the expected adult viewing audience of 20,000. As a rough estimate, if 46.0% of the males and 33.6% of the females in the normal audience were smokers (Non-Medical Use of Drugs Directorate Technical Report #1, 1976), this sample might represent 18% of the potential smoking audience. On the other hand, while the sample is large, it is also biased by virtue of the self-selection factor in recruitment. The prudent course is to limit generalizations from present data to similarly constituted samples.

Procedure

Each television show was linked to a specific chapter in the self-help guide. The first show and chapter provided an introduction and called for an explicit decision to quit. Behavior change strategies were not introduced until the second session, allowing time for viewers to receive the self-help guide by mail.

A social learning theory model of smoking behavior was provided. Subjects were instructed to record time, place, activity, and perceived reason for smoking each cigarette throughout the program. On the last day of the first recording week, they were to summarize their reasons for smoking in preparation for the third television show, yielding an initial functional analysis of smoking behavior. Urges to smoke for the duration of the program were to be similarly analyzed using a "problem-solving" technique. Each time an urge occurred, subjects were to (1) pinpoint controlling antecedents and consequences, (2) identify possible alternative responses, (3) perform the alternative response in future similar urge situations, and (4) once good alternatives had been identified, consistently practice these alternatives in the urge situation. During the last television show, a stock-taking procedure for reviewing current status and formulating future coping efforts was elaborated.

A major emphasis was placed on the development of situation-specific coping strategies which might be either functional or more general self-management techniques, as conceptualized above. Both functional and nonfunctional alternatives may require three phrases of development. First, if the skill is not in the subject's repertoire, skill development is required. For example, a program of progressive deep muscle relaxation training was included in the self-help guide. Second, alternatives may need to be rehearsed prior to their performance in the urge situation. For example, clients were encouraged to rehearse specific phrases for declining preferred cigarettes. Third, alternatives must be consistently and repeatedly practiced in urge situations.

A variety of learning aids were used. Actors simulated right and wrong ways of coping on the television shows. Techniques were introduced on television shows, described in detail in the self-help guide, and often accompanied by specific learning exercises. Each show included a simulated brief interview with an individual going through the program. The interviews modeled the decision making and typical problems at each point in the program.

All subjects were encouraged to quit smoking abruptly on the day of the fourth television show. However, an optional system for gradually reducing between shows three and five was included. Subjects were encouraged to develop two kinds of social support: a) a buddy system, and b) friends and family. A variety of cognitive behavior modification techniques were included in the fifth show: a) thought stopping, b) coverant control, c) self-instructional training, and d) covert rehearsal. Weight management techniques were suggested throughout the series.

Data Collection

From the 1403 subjects in the sample, 812 (57.9%) of the pre-program questionnaires mailed with the treatment guide were returned. A post-program questionnaire was mailed to all subjects two days before the final broadcast. A prompt was mailed five days later. If the questionnaire had not been returned within ten days of the initial mailing, a minimum of five telephone calls were made in an attempt to contact each subject. Telephone contact required only minimal response from the subject, i.e., average smoking rate during the preceding seven days and the total number of television shows watched.

Three and six months following the final broadcast, all subjects were again sent a brief questionnaire. Nonrespondents were again telephoned ten days following the initial mailing and asked to report on smoking rate during the preceding seven days. If a subject could not be reached with five telephone calls, a second questionnaire was sent.

It should be noted that these data collection procedures essentially generated two sets of data. Data are relatively complete at a given point in time for those subjects returning the questionnaires. However, only smoking rate data are available for other subjects. As a consequence, results for analyses involving other than smoking rate must be viewed with caution since they are based on smaller, possibly biased samples. It is noteworthy that smoking rate did not vary as a function of method by which follow-up data were obtained, perhaps suggesting that the sample is not unduly biased.

Results

Treatment Outcome

Post-program incidence of abstinence is summarized in Table 1. Each follow-up point requires some comment. The end of series figure may underestimate short-term success. The final show was broadcast only two weeks after the scheduled "quit date." As a consequence, there may have been too little time for non-smoking to stabilize: A significant proportion of the nonabstinent subjects may have smoked a nominal number of cigarettes during the final week and subsequently achieved abstinence. The three month follow-up point suffers from a relatively low response rate because contract funds were approved too late to permit long-distance telephone follow-ups. However, since there is no reason to think that the viewers not reached by telephone would be less successful, this should not have influenced the abstinence figure. Finally, six month follow-up data collection was hampered by a continuing strike of telephone maintenance workers. As a result, telephoners were unable to obtain new numbers from information for viewers who had moved since the end of the series. It may be that the more transient viewers were less successful and, as a consequence, the six month abstinence figure may be artificially inflated to a slight degree. Despite these qualifications, the trend in the data remains clear—there is relatively little reduction (if any) in success levels over time.

The issue of maintenance can be approached in another way. Hunt and Bespalac (1974) reviewed 89 smoking cessation studies and reported that approximately 70% of initial abstainers relapsed within the first six months. This finding is contrasted in Figure 1 with results from the present program and the face-to-face clinic reported by Best et al. (1978). Rate of relapse is remarkably consistent for the face-to-face and television/print versions of the program. In both cases, maintenance appears

Table 1
Response Rates and Post-Program Smoking

	end of series	three month	six month
Percent Responding	86.5	64.2	71.4
Percent Reporting Abstinent	11.5	14.7	17.6

FIGURE 1: Rate of Relapse for Initial Abstainers

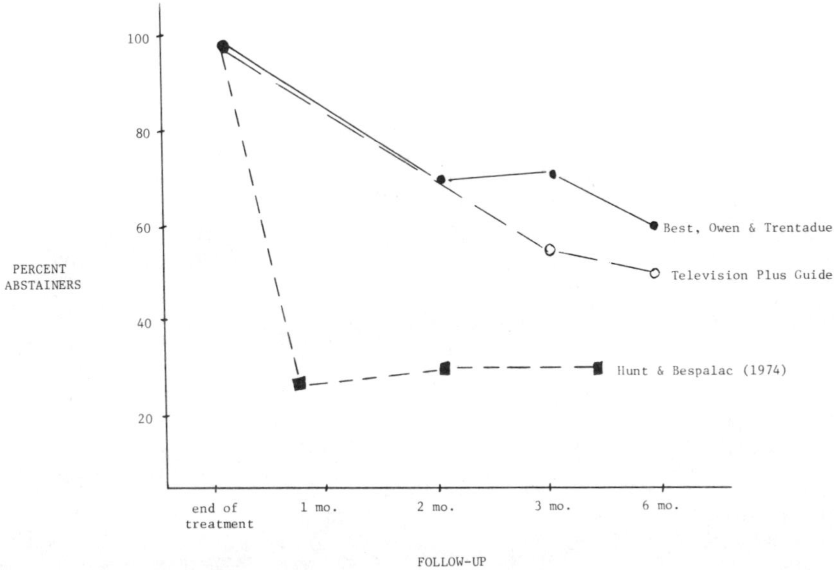

to be relatively good, suggesting that the alternatives training model for treatment may indeed promote better maintenance.

What are we to make of these levels of success? In the absence of appropriate controls, inferences must be drawn with caution. A comparison can be made with the spontaneous quit rate in the population, which is in the order of 5% (Horn, 1971). Russell (1977) reported a similar rate for no treatment controls. Alternatively, the results can be compared to those obtained by group cessation programs as commonly offered in the community by voluntary organizations. Long-term success rates here are typically in the order of 15-20% (Best and Bloch, in press). By these standards, the present outcome levels seem relatively good. In contrast, 50% of the clients seen individually in our face-to-face program are abstinent at six months (Best et al., 1977; Best et al., 1978).

The results can also be evaluated with respect to cost/benefit considerations. The estimated service cost in our face-to-face clinic is approximately $100 per client or $200 per client per success. Programs in the community are either commercial, where the average cost is about $250 or more, or staffed by volunteers, in which case cost is difficult to estimate. KVOS-TV estimates production cost for the series at $8,500, including $3,000 for evaluation, or $48 per documented abstinence at six months. In evaluating cost for the television/print program, it's important to note that nonregistrants may also have quit, that production costs

TABLE 2
Pre-Program Individual Differences as a Function of Six Month Abstinence Versus Nonabstinence

	mean for abstinent Ss	mean for non-abstinent Ss	t	df	P
Age	40.9	40.8	−0.12	920	.903
Pretreatment Smoking Rate	23.5	27.2	3.82	906	<.001
Nicotine	1.42	1.51	1.89	531	.059
Tar	10.0	10.6	1.61	531	.180
Age Start	18.5	18.0	−0.99	607	.321
Attempts to Quit	5.9	4.7	−0.96	576	.335
Months Since Last Attempt	36.9	37.9	0.14	464	.888
Perceived Likelihood of Success	3.3	3.2	−0.75	587	.451
			x^2		
Education			4.34	7	.740
Previous Methods			11.80	5	.038
Previous Weight Gain			4.59	6	.598

are one time only, and that the series might in the future be sold as entertainment and thus actually generate a profit. Clearly, these very rough calculations do not substitute for the careful cost/effectiveness analysis which needs to be done. Nevertheless, it would seem that the cost/effectiveness potential is considerable, especially given the impact on the population and the possibility of ripple effects through changes in social norms (cf., Allen, 1977; Delarue, 1973).

Predictors of Outcome

Subjects were classified according to abstinence vs. nonabstinence status at six months and pre-program variables compared to test for individual differences which might relate to outcome. As can be seen in Table 2, few variables predicted six-month success. Demographic variables such as age, sex, and education were not related. Smoking history with respect to age of starting smoking and previous attempts to quit did not relate. Pre-program smoking status did have some relationship to outcome. Successful subjects tended to have smoked less initially and there was a trend towards consumption of lower nicotine cigarettes being predictive of success. Previous methods for quitting also related: those subjects who had previously tried to quit unaided, rather than

TABLE 3
Post-Program Variables and Six-Month Abstinence Versus Nonabstinence

	mean for abstinent *Ss*	mean for non-abstinent *Ss*	*t*	*df*	*P*
Cigarettes Yesterday	6.9	17.4	7.30	411	<.001
Nicotine	1.40	1.53	1.73	296	.085
Tar	9.9	10.7	1.60	296	.111
Rate Past Week	11.2	20.0	7.38	831	<.001
Perceived Likelihood of Success	3.7	3.1	−4.35	395	< .001
Number of Shows watched	2.8	2.7	x^2 4.14	7	.764

with a program or pharmacological aid, tended to be more successful in the present program.

Measures taken at the end of the program were better predictors of long-term success (Table 3). Smoking behavior towards the end of the series was highly predictive, as was the subject's (related) perceived likelihood of future success. Somewhat surprisingly, the number of shows watched was not related to six month success.

Especially since number of shows watched did not relate to success, it's important to ask whether or not success was specifically related to the techniques included in the program. The post-program questionnaire asked subjects to rate six program components, both with respect to their perceived frequency of use and their perceived usefulness:

a) writing down reasons for smoking;
b) problem solving where you (1) pinpoint the problem, (2) plan an alternative, (3) try alternatives, (4) practice alternatives;
c) actively practicing things to do instead of smoking;
d) getting other people to help you;
e) changing the way you think about smoking;
f) reading the guide which was mailed out.

Results are shown in Table 4. First, note that the mean rated use on a five-point scale is not great. There would seem to be problems of adherence with this kind of programming. Nevertheless, both rated use and usefulness do discriminate successful from unsuccessful subjects at six months. Usefulness in contrast to use seems to be a slightly better

TABLE 4
Rated Use and Usefulness of Program Components as a Function of Six Month Abstinence Vs. Nonabstinence

Use	mean for abstinent	mean for nonabstinent	*t*	*df*	*P*
(a) writing down	2.4	2.3	−0.35	395	.727
(b) problem solving	2.8	2.5	−2.07	373	.040
(c) active practice	2.8	2.5	−2.04	373	.042
(d) others help	1.9	1.7	−2.14	380	.033
(e) changing thinking	3.1	2.9	−1.42	370	.156
(f) guide	3.1	2.8	−1.95	364	.052

Usefulness	mean for abstinent	mean for nonabstinent	*t*	*df*	*P*
(a) writing down	2.8	2.7	−0.62	317	537
(b) problem solving	3.3	2.7	−4.20	343	<.001
(c) active practice	3.2	2.8	−2.72	342	.007
(d) others help	2.4	1.9	−3.12	309	.002
(e) changing thinking	3.4	2.7	−4.58	336	<.001
(f) guide	3.7	3.4	−2.40	362	.017

discriminator. The data tempt one to conclude that the program does produce specific effects but it's important to realize that the data are open to response bias. Better motivated, more competent subjects are more likely to be successful in any program and, as a consequence of their success rather than the program per se, they may be more likely to rate the program as useful. Future research should address this issue by collecting actual recordings of program adherence and technique utilization.

Relapse

The three and six month follow-ups asked relapsed subjects to specify the circumstances under which initial relapse occurred. Responses were coded for reason and place of relapse. Results are shown in Tables 5 and 6. In general, subjects seem not to have relapsed because of physical cessation problems or because of special, unexpected situations. Rather, nearly 70% of the relapse occurred in the specific situations which the change program was designed to address. This is both encouraging and discouraging. On the one hand, relapse does seem to be situation-specific and associated with failure to perform alternative non-smoking behaviors. On the other hand, the results show that the program was

TABLE 5
Reasons for Relapse
Percent Relapse by Category for Three and Six Month Reports

Habit	3 mo.	6 mo.	*Cessation Problems*	3 mo.	6 mo.	*Special Situations*	3 mo.	6 mo.	*Other*	3 mo.	6 mo.
Boredom	9.7%	4.3	Withdrawal	7.9	6.4	Holiday and Business Trips	8.8	2.1	Low Will Power	.9	0
Alcohol	7.0	6.4	Weight Gain	3.5	6.4	Depression	4.4	0	Unknown	3.5	6.4
Stress	38.6	55.3		11.4	12.8	Return to Work From Illness	1.8	4.3		4.4	6.4
Coffee	1.8	0					14.9	6.4			
Social	8.8	2.1									
Alcohol + Social	.9										
Coffee + Social	.9										
Coffee + Stress	1.8										
	69.3	68.1									

Table 6
Place and Social Context of Relapse

THREE MONTH

SOCIAL CONTEXT	PLACE: out	in	can't tell
social	19.7	9.9	2.8
alone	1.4	12.7	0
can't tell	21.1	29.6	2.8

where context is known, 80.5% relapse when with other people

where place is known, 44.8% when not at home

SIX MONTH

SOCIAL CONTEXT	PLACE: out	in	can't tell
social	28.6	6.5	2.6
alone	0	11.7	0
can't tell	13.0	23.4	14.3

where context is known, 71.1% relapse when with other people

where place is known, 50% relapse when not at home

not entirely successful in preparing individuals to deal with the situations.

The high incidence of relapse associated with stress is noteworthy. While this result is quite consistent with Marlatt and Gordon's data (see Chapter 16), it contrasts with a relatively low stress involvement recently reported by Lichtenstein, Antonuccio, and Rainwater (1977). On the other hand, the high incidence of failure in a social context is consistent with the data of Lichtenstein and his colleagues. These data serve to underscore the importance of focusing on social situations in treatment programs. They also suggest that treatment procedures which mobilize social support may be particularly important.

Discussion

The outcome data are encouraging and clearly justify further research. Several issues need to be addressed empirically. First, the effectiveness of the television/print format needs to be evaluated against appropriate controls. These should include probability samples of both unselected smokers and those currently motivated to quit through their own efforts. In addition, results should be compared to those obtained when the same program is offered in a large group, face-to-face format. The long-term population impact of television/print programming also needs to be evaluated. Second, careful cost/effectiveness comparison of television/print programs with other service delivery options is needed. Third, we need to address factors affecting utilization of these programs and perhaps develop promotional approaches which improve utilization. Fourth, the problem of low adherence must be addressed and appropriate methodological innovations added to programs. Fifth, in a similar way, program development research is needed to provide more effective assistance with relapse problems associated with stress and social factors. Finally, we need much more systematic and detailed data on factors associated with relapse.

Three research strategies arise. The first would aim to improve the effectiveness of such programs, addressing the identified adherence and relapse problems, refining program materials, etc. The second would provide outcome evaluation of a variety of service delivery options, including, for example, (a) the present program, (b) the present program plus community-based maintenance groups, (c) a large group face-to-face variation of the program, and (d) the present program plus back up, face-to-face programs for relapsing subjects. The third line of research would be process evaluation, focusing on a relatively small group of subjects and intensively evaluating response to programs with respect to adherence, factors affecting relapse, etc.

The results of this project are clearly preliminary but, just as clearly, they are promising. The potential uses of mass media in health lifestyle change deserve much greater attention in the future.

REFERENCES

Allen, R.F.: A culture-based approach to the improvement of health practices. In *Proceedings of the Thirteenth Annual Meeting, Society of Prospective Medicine.* Bethesda, Md.: Health and Educational Resources, 1977.

Bandura, A.: *Principles of behavior modification.* New York: Holt, Rinehart & Winston, 1969.

BERNARD, H.S., & EFRAN, J.S.: Eliminating vs. reducing smoking using pocket timers. *Behaviour Research and Therapy,* 1972, *10*, 399-401.

BERNSTEIN, D.A.:The modification of smoking behavior: Some suggestions for programmed "symptom substitution." Paper presented to the annual meetings of the Association for the Advancement of Behavior Therapy, Chicago, 1974.

BERNSTEIN, D.A., & MCALISTER, A.: The modification of smoking behavior: Progress and problems. *Addictive Behaviors,* 1976, *1*, 89-102.

BEST, J.A., BASS F., & OWEN, L.E.: Mode of service delivery in a smoking cessation programme for public health. *Canadian Journal of Public Health,* 1977, *68*, 469-473.

BEST, J.A., & BLOCH, M.: Compliance in the control of cigarette smoking. In R.B. Haynes, D.W. Taylor, & D.L. Sackett (Eds.), *Compliance with therapeutic and preventive regimens.* Baltimore: John Hopkins University Press, in press.

BEST, J.A., & HAKSTIAN, A.R.: A situation-specific model for smoking behavior. *Addictive Behaviors,* 1978, *3,* 79-92.

BEST, J.A., OWEN, L.E., & TRENTADUE, B.L.: Comparison of satiation and rapid smoking in self-managed smoking cessation. *Addictive Behaviors,* 1978, *3*, 71-78.

BRENGELMANN, J.C., & SEDLMAYR, E.: Experiments in the reduction of smoking behavior. In J. Steinfeld, W. Griffiths, K. Ball, & R.M. Taylor (Eds.), *Smoking and health, Volume II: Health consequences, education, cessation activities, and governmental action.* Washington, D.C.: U.S. Department of Health, Education, and Welfare, 1977.

BROCKWAY, B.S., KLEINMANN, G., EDLESON, J., & GRUENEWALD, K.: Non-aversive procedures and their effect on cigarette smoking. *Addictive Behaviors,* 1977, *2*, 121-128.

CAUTELA, J.R.: Treatment of smoking by covert sensitization. *Psychological Reports,* 1970, *26*, 415-420.

CHAPMAN, R.F., SMITH, J.W., & LAYDEN, T.A.: Elimination of cigarette smoking by punishment and self-management training. *Behaviour Research and Therapy,* 1971, *9*, 255-264.

CONWAY, J.B.: Behavioral self-control of smoking through aversive conditioning and self-management. *Journal of Consulting and Clinical Psychology,* 1977, *45*, 348-357.

DANAHER, B.G.: Rapid smoking and self-control in the modification of smoking behavior. *Journal of Consulting and Clinical Psychology,* 1977, *45*, 1068-1075.

DANAHER, B.G., & LICHTENSTEIN, E.: An experimental analysis of coverant control: Cueing and consequation. Paper presented at the annual meeting of the Western Psychological Association, San Francisco, 1974.

DAVIDSON, P.O.: Therapeutic compliance. *Canadian Psychological Review,* 1976, *17*, 247-259.

DELAHUNT, J., & CURRAN, J.P.: Effectiveness of negative practice and self-control techniques in the reduction of smoking behavior. *Journal of Consulting and Clinical Psychology,* 1976, *44*, 1002-1007.

DELARUE, N.C.: A study in smoking withdrawal. *Canadian Journal of Public Health,* 1973, *64*, Smoking and Health Supplement, S5-S19.

DERICCO, D.A., BRIGHAM, T.A., & GARLINGTON, W.K.: Development and evaluation of treatment paradigms for the suppression of smoking behavior. *Journal of Applied Behavior Analysis,* 1977, *10*, 173-181.

D'ZURILLA, T.J., & GOLDFRIED, M.R.: Problem solving and behavior modification. *Journal of Abnormal Psychology,* 1971, *78*, 107-126.

FERRARO, D.P.: Self-control of smoking: The amotivational syndrome. *Journal of Abnormal Psychology,* 1973, *81*, 152-157.

FLAXMAN, J.: Quitting smoking now or later: Gradual, abrupt, immediate and delayed quitting. *Behavior Therapy,* 1978, *9*, 260-270.

FREDERIKSEN, L.W., & PETERSON, G.L.: Short- and long-term effects of three methods of smoking cessation. Paper presented to the annual meeting of the South Eastern Psychological Association, New Orleans, 1973.

Gallup Opinion Index, Report #108, June, 1974, 20-21.

HARRIS, M.B., & ROTHBERG, C.: A self-control approach to reducing smoking. *Psychological*

Reports, 1972, *31,* 165-166.

HOCHBAUM, G.M.: Focus and introduction: In J.W. Cullen, B.H. Fox, & R.N. Isom (Eds.), *Cancer: The behavioral dimensions.* New York: Raven Press, 1976.

HOMME, L.E.: Perspectives in psychology: XXIV. Control of coverants, the operations of the mind. *Psychological Record,* 1965, *15*, 501-511.

HORN, D.: Epidemiology and psychology of cigarette smoking. *Chest,* 1971, *59*, 225-245.

HUNT, W.A., & BESPALEC, D.A.: An evaluation of current methods of modifying smoking behavior. *Journal of Clinical Psychology,* 1974, *30,* 431-438.

KANFER, F.H.: Self-management methods. In F.H. Kanfer & A.P. Goldstein (Eds.), *Helping people change: A textbook of methods.* New York: Pergamon, 1975.

KANFER, F.H.: The many faces of self-control, or behavior modification changes its focus. In R.B. Stuart (Ed.), *Behavioral self-management: Strategies, techniques, and outcome.* New York: Brunner/Mazel, 1977.

KANTOROWITZ, D.A., & WALTERS, J.: Positive versus negative self-monitoring in the self-control of smoking. Paper presented to the annual meeting of the Western Psychological Association, Seattle, 1977.

KATZ, R.C., HEIMAN, M., & GORDON, S.: Effects of two self-management approaches on cigarette smoking. *Addictive Behaviors,* 1977, *2,* 113-119.

KOPEL, S.A. & ARKOWITZ, H.: The role of attribution and self-perception in behavior change: Implications for behavior therapy. *Genetic Psychology Monographs,* 1975, *92,* 175-212.

LANDO, H.A.: Stimulus control, rapid smoking, and contractual management in the maintenance of nonsmoking. *Behavior Therapy,* 1978, *9*, 962-963.

LEVINSON, B.L., SHAPIRO, D., SCHWARTZ, G.E., & TURSKY, B.: Smoking elimination by gradual reduction. *Behavior Therapy,* 1971, *2*, 477-487.

LICHTENSTEIN, E., ANTONUCCIO, D.O., & RAINWATER, G.: Unkicking the habit: The resumption of cigarette smoking. Paper presented to the anual meeting of the Western Psychological Association, Seattle, 1977.

LICHTENSTEIN, E., & DANAHER, B.G.: Modification of smoking behavior: A critical analysis of theory, research and practice. In M. Hersen, R.M. Eisler, & P.M. Miller (Eds.), *Progress in behavior modification: Volume 3.* New York: Academic Press, 1976.

LOGAN, F.A.: Self-control as habit, drive and incentive. *Journal of Abnormal Psychology,* 1973, *81*, 127-136.

MCALISTER, A., MEYER, A., & MACCOBY, N.: Long-term results of education to reduce smoking: Stanford Three-Community Study. Presented to the American Heart Association meetings. Miami Beach, November, 1976.

MCFALL, R.M., & HAMMEN, C.L.: Motivation, structure, and self-monitoring: Role of nonspecific factors in smoking reduction. *Journal of Consulting and Clinical Psychology,* 1971, *37*, 80-86.

MCGRATH, M.J., & HALL, S.M.: Self-management treatment of smoking behavior. *Addictive Behaviors,* 1976, *1*, 287-292.

MCLUHAN, H.M.: *Understanding media: Extensions of man.* New York: McGraw-Hill, 1964.

MAHONEY, M.J., & MAHONEY, K.: *Permanent weight control: A total solution to the dieter's dilemma.* New York: W.W. Norton, 1976.

MENDELSOHN, H.: Mass communications and cancer control. In J.W. Cullen, B.H. Fox, & R.N. Isom (Eds.), *Cancer: The behavioral dimensions.* New York: Raven Press, 1976.

MILLER, W.R., & MUNOZ, R.F.: *How to control your drinking.* Englewood Cliffs, N.J.: Prentice-Hall, 1976.

MORROW, J.E., SACHS, L.B., GMEINDER, S., & BURGESS, H.: Elimination of cigarette smoking behavior by stimulus satiation, self-control techniques, and group therapy. Paper presented at the meeting of the Western Psychological Association, Anaheim, Calif., 1973.

Non-Medical Use of Drugs. *Smoking Habits of Canadians, 1965-1974:* Technical Report No. 1. Ottawa: Health and Welfare Canada, 1976.

PECHACEK, T.F.: Specialized treatments for high anxious smokers. Paper presented to the annual meeting of the Association for Advancement of Behavior Therapy, New York, 1976.

Pomerleau, O.F., & Ciccone, P.: Preliminary results of a treatment program for smoking cessation using multiple behavior modification techniques. Paper presented at the annual meeting of the Association for Advancement of Behavior Therapy, Chicago, 1974.

Premack, D.: Mechanisms of self-control. In W. Hunt (Ed.), *Learning mechanisms in smoking.* Chicago: Aldine, 1970.

Rozensky, R.H.: The effect of temporal location of self-monitoring behavior on reducing cigarette consumption. *Journal of Behaviour Therapy and Experimental Psychiatry,* 1974, *5*, 301-303.

Russell, M.A.H.: Smoking problems: An overview. In M.E. Jarvik, J.W. Cullen, E.R. Gritz, T.M. Vogt, & L.J. West (Eds.), *Research on smoking behavior.* Rockville, Md.: National Institute on Drug Abuse, 1977.

Schwartz, J.L., & Dubitzky, M.: Requisites for success in smoking withdrawal. In E.F. Borgatta & R.R. Evans (Eds.), *Smoking, health, and behavior.* Chicago: Aldine, 1968.

Shapiro, D., Tursky, B., Schwartz, G.E., & Shnidman, S.R.: Smoking on cue: A behavioral approach to smoking reduction. *Journal of Health and Social Behavior,* 1971, *12*, 108-113.

United States Public Health Service: *Adult use of tobacco: 1975.* Washington, D.C.: United States Department of Health, Education and Welfare, 1976.

Upper, D., & Meredith, L.: A stimulus control approach to the modification of smoking. *Proceedings of the XVIIth American Psychological Association Convention,* 1970, *5,* 739-740.

Warner, K.E.: The effects of the anti-smoking campaign on cigarette consumption. *American Journal of Public Health,* 1977, *67,* 645-650.

15
Evaluating Lifestyle Change Programs

PARK DAVIDSON

INTRODUCTION

Program evaluation is becoming almost as faddishly popular these days as sex therapy but it isn't quite as easy to document progress in the state of the art. These are some similarities: They both start out many interventions with what I call "the contraceptive question"—in program evaluation it is phrased something like this: "Can I continue to 'seduce' my funding source without producing any long-term outcome?" They both encounter and have to deal with feelings of impotence—on the part of the client in the case of sex therapy but on the part of the intervener in many program evaluations! (There are some squeeze techniques available in program evaluation but they can't be taught with a half-hour video presentation.) I don't wish to push the analogy into premature ejaculations but I would note that sex therapists have an easy life when it comes to presenting their technology. The first half of such a presentation is spent viewing a film or collection of slides, and the second half in convincing you that what you have seen is science and not just pornography! Program evaluators, alas, have no films but still must convince you that their technology is more than "hustler" material.

While I can't present any *dirty* pictures on program evaluation, the current literature is certainly replete with *gloomy* pictures. A nonrandom but representative sample:

> Good program evaluation studies fail more often than they succeed in having any impact on subsequent programs (cf. Fairweather, Sanders, & Tournatzky, 1974).
>
> Evaluation studies showing that a program failed to reach its goals seem to never have any effect on the particular program or even the field in general. (cf. Lester, 1974; Polak, Egan, & Vander Bergh, 1975; Zusman & Bissonette, 1973).
>
> Program evaluation studies seem to be limited to minor programs or minor aspects of major programs. Policy makers seem to be concerned with evaluating only those programs that can be easily dispensed with (Zusman, 1976).
>
> The assumption that all you need to do to improve professionals' work is to inform them of earlier poor results is psychologically naive and organizationally simplistic (cf. Bolin & Kivers, 1974).
>
> Evaluators have damaged the credibility of their techniques by surrounding them with an aura of complexity and a jargon that mitigates against their use (Lund, 1978).

Problems in Program Evaluation

It may be worthwhile trying to assess what is going wrong in the program evaluation field. It appears that there are major pragmatic, conceptual, and tactical problems to be faced in setting up any evaluation effort. A few frequently encountered examples should be noted:

(1) The first major problem is a pragmatic problem. Many programs are initially set up on the basis of holding out a promise (usually implicit) that they will solve problems or produce outcomes which are far beyond what can be empirically documented for such a program. In other words they oversell their success. Such an agency or program is apt to be punished (psychologically if not fiscally) by doing a program evaluation since, no matter how favorable, it will show that the program outcome falls far short of what was promised or expected. On the other hand many such programs may be punished these days by loss of funding if they refuse to do a program evaluation!

In other words many program evaluation attempts represent a classic noncontingent conditioning paradigm (signalled emission punishment combined with signalled omission punishment - Tyron, 1976). Clinicians will immediately recognize this as the *learned helplessness* paradigm (Abramson, Seligman, & Teasdale, 1978) the behavioral effects of which include;

a) very low response rates
b) inability to learn from past mistakes
c) occasional nonfunctional aggressive outbursts.

Does that sound like any program evaluators you know? As a matter of fact, reading the program evaluation literature can be fascinating to the clinician. Much of it could be recast as accurate self-monitored descriptions of professionals learning to be helpless!

(2) The second major problem is a conceptual problem. Most health professionals have not been trained to do program evaluation. They have been trained to do experimental research and to do therapy. When asked to do program evaluation they put on their research hats and start looking for *reliable data, causal conditions, controls, truth, internal validity,* and all those other outgrowths of the research tree of knowledge. (They are thought to flower in abundance—during the summer at least—in our groves of academe. The necessary kind of fertilizer doesn't seem to be as abundant in treatment agencies.) Failure to achieve randomization, reliability, control, or internal validity is often viewed as a technological problem we should strive to overcome. I would like to argue that more often it is a conceptual problem we should strive to look beyond.

I think we professionals grabbed the wrong hat when we rushed out to embrace program evaluation. Let me illustrate this conceptual problem with an example. When we do behavioral therapy we are *systematic* and try to be *objective* about what we are doing—and in that sense we are scientific. We don't concern ourselves overmuch with general causal laws, control groups, test-retest reliability, internal validity, etc. While we don't turn a blind eye to these important aspects of our science, they are procedures that don't seem to fit when we move from trying to measure behavior to trying to change it. But, the counter argument might run, surely you need accurate measurement and a clear knowledge of causes in order to change behavior—whether it be that of an individual or an organization? There is some validity to this counter argument but it contains a large trap (one in which clinical psychology floundered until almost the present decade).

Remember when the major clinical role of psychologists was to do just psychodiagnostic testing? At the time that I quit, in the early sixties, I was seeing a 19-year-old girl who had been referred by an orthodontist because of thumbsucking. There were serious problems of malocclusion but the dentist was reluctant to do anything because the dental literature clearly indicated that preventing thumbsucking caused all sorts of serious psychological problems—including masturbation (cf. Pearson, 1948)! I had completed an extremely comprehensive assessment of the girl's intelligence, personality, self-concepts, social relations, etc.—all the dynamics of her behavior that might possibly be related to the thumbsucking. During the extensive and careful interpretation of these dynamics to her, it became obvious to me that I had her complete attention because I knew that any time she became engrossed in something her thumb inevitably crept up into her mouth! She sat there nodding and at the end she said: "For the first time, I really understand what my problem is." (All said with thumb firmly in mouth. Try it sometime—it is much more difficult than with your foot.) It occurred to me at this insightful (?) moment that I was dealing with a problem of habit and not of psychodynamics. The orthodontist and I went on to successfully treat 365 thumbsucking children and adults knowing little more about them than the shape of their teeth, name, age, address and telephone number (Haryett, Hansen & Davidson, 1970; Davidson, 1970).

You would think we should learn from our mistakes! Ten years later I was sitting in the office of a senior government administrator presenting a detailed and complex assessment of one of his agencies, at the end of which he said: "For the first time in this position I really understand. . . ." I had this déjà vu (except that the administrator's thumb may have been in a different orifice!). I would argue that, similar to my young client, some administrators' behaviors may also simply be learned habits that are in no way affected by elaborate evaluation reports—no matter how accurately interpreted. The point to be made is that improvement in programs does not necessarily, or even usually, follow from the presentation of comprehensive data about that program regardless of how reliable, valid, or true those data may be.

To the extent that the raison d'être of program evaluation is to improve the quality of programs, then we may extrapolate from this analogy an idea that we are more apt to succeed in that endeavor if we approach it with a (organizational behavior) therapeutic orientation rather than a (diagnostic) measurement orientation. I will elaborate on the implications of this conceptual shift in a later section.

(3) The third major problem, a tactical one that derives from the previous problem, relates to faulty criteria of data collection. Cronbach (1977) maintains that there is only one test of an evaluation: Does the system function better as a consequence of the evaluation effort? Clearly,

if this test is to be passed we had better focus on the *utility* of the data, not just the *quality* of the data.

> Data are no good if the report on them is ready too late. They are of precious little good if the relevant audience does not comprehend them. They may have negligible impact if the evaluator, limiting himself to what he can measure well, winds up with nothing to say about some critical outcomes. Excellent data may lead to wrong social action if they report on a specially controlled treatment that cannot be duplicated when the program is disseminated (Cronbach, 1977, p. 2).

If we accept Cronbach's utility criterion for program evaluation, a number of interesting tactical decisions follow. Evaluations have to be planned as they go. The fixed design experiment is usually too inflexible to answer new questions as they arise or to account for new variables as they are introduced. Evaluations ought to use early returns regarding a new treatment to help those who run the treatment to improve it. The criterion of utility introduces the concept of accountability to the evaluation and not just to the treatment program. The best evaluation presumably delivers the most useful information at the least cost. A critical issue in designing evaluations, therefore, is the cost effectiveness of alternative evaluations. Will the improvements in function that follow from a particular kind of evaluation be worth the costs of conducting that evaluation? Since improvement in agency function usually involves some change, what is the benefit of collecting data on things that can't be changed—or more data than you need on things that can be changed? There are opportunity costs as well as dollar costs to these kinds of excess data collection. The amount of time staff spends collecting these extra or unneeded data might better be spent doing more treatment.

Experimental or Therapeutic Approach to Evaluation

I would like to give an example from my early experience in program evaluation that demonstrates the differences between an experimental and a therapeutic approach to the kind of data necessary for effective program evaluation. About 15 years ago—long before program evaluation became fashionable—I was hired one summer by an agency to do an evaluation of their treatment program for them. The agency was a private alcohol treatment agency whose funding was being taken over by a provincial government. A condition of the takeover was to have an evaluation done (nobody seemed concerned about the outcome of the evaluation—only that the process occur). In my initial negotiations with the agency I wanted to know what kind of data base I could work with and so I asked if I could see some patient files. "Oh, we don't keep any files on our patients," was the reply, "each therapist keeps his own therapy notes on his own patients." I then suggested that I would have to interview the clients directly myself. "Oh, no, we assured our patients of complete confidentiality and that there would be no contact with them except by their own therapists." As a last attempt to get some kind of client data I raised the possibility that I therefore talk to the therapists themselves—"in general terms of course and not about any specific client." "A good idea but unfortunately with summer holidays etc., the available staff workloads preclude any such interviews until early fall."

A question I ask my graduate students in their program evaluation seminar: "Would you accept the consultant position to begin a program evaluation with this kind of data base?" The answers to this question indicate the extent to which the students see evaluation as experimental or therapeutic, and the extent of their concern with validity vs. utility in a data base. What I actually did probably derived more from the context of what assistant professors' salaries were in those days than from any context of preferential data bases. I accepted the consultation and advised the agency that, since I did not have to waste time wading through files and interviewing people, I could have a preliminary report available in three weeks and we could decide where to go from there. Three weeks later I wrote a letter to the deputy minister with a copy to the agency director that said in effect "I have been unable to find any evidence that this program is of any benefit to anyone!" I threw away the original, took the copy to the director, told him it was a draft and asked if there was anything else he would like added before the final report was sent. As one might anticipate, I spent the rest of the summer helping the agency to establish a client monitoring system. At the end of the summer the agency funding was picked up before any outcome data were available from the monitoring system. Given that the content of the earlier preliminary report was still essentially correct, how successful had the evaluation been? A clear failure in terms of obtaining valid data *about the clients* that would lead to improved agency function. Perhaps a modest success in terms of obtaining data *about the agency* that would lead to changed (improved?) agency function. These data were essentially:

(1) The agency could not document what kinds of patients were seen, what was done to them, or what effect the treatment had; because

(2) the agency had no systematic record keeping system; and
(3) the agency did not wish to have the above points reported to its funding source.

These findings were relevant, replicable, and sufficient for the planning and monitoring of a suggested improvement in agency function.

I do not wish to imply from the above discussion that we should abandon the experimental paradigm of program evaluation and convert everyone to a therapeutic paradigm. As Kuhn (1962) has pointed out, cross-paradigm controversies tend to be quite sterile, since it is certain that neither party to the controversy can convince the other—unless one or the other is prepared to abandon its paradigm. I think it would be foolish to suggest that either paradigm be abandoned. They have different orientations, methods, goals, and uses. Kuhn has also cautioned against the futility of criticizing the problems, procedures, or results of research guided by one paradigm, using values from a different paradigm. What we can do, however, is to recognize that there is more than one program evaluation paradigm and make careful decisions about which one is appropriate for a specific evaluation situation. We must also exercise care in insuring that we don't mix our paradigms—using the methods of one when we wish to achieve the goals of the other.

There have been some attempts to categorize various kinds of evaluations. For example, the time at which an evaluation is carried out can be distinguished by the terms formative or summative (cf. Glaser & Backer, 1972). Formative evaluations often conform to the therapeutic paradigm and are carried out during the life of a program. Summative evaluations usually follow program termination and hence tend toward the research paradigm. Who carries out the evaluation can be indicated by the distinction between in-house evaluations and external evaluations (Windle & Ochberg, 1975). In-house evaluations are more likely to be conceptualized therapeutically while external evaluations more frequently adopt the research conceptualization. (There is no particular reason why the opposite could not be the case.) We are faced with a blitzkrieg of acronyms distinguishing various methods of program evaluation including: ATGON (Automated Tri-informant Goal Oriented Progress Note; Wilson, 1974), PASS and PEP (Program Analysis of Service Systems; Wolfensberger & Glenn, 1975; Performance Evaluation Procedure; Joint Commission on Hospital Accreditation, 1975), to SCL-90 (a 90-item symptom check list; Derogatis, Lipman & Covi, 1975). The gabble of jargon emanating from these evaluation methods may detract from their value or usefulness (Lund, 1978), and they certainly violate the most fundamental acronym of program evaluation methodology—KISS (Keep It Simple, Stupid; Wilson, 1976). These and other evaluation methodologies have been described in detail elsewhere (Struening, & Guttentag, 1975; Epstein & Tripodi, 1978) and will not be reviewed here. Many of them are derived from a (quasi-experimental) research orientation and require some greater or lesser degree of "fiddling" (the model not the data) to make them fit the therapeutic evaluation orientation.

Evaluation Strategies for Health Lifestyle Change Programs

Since health lifestyle change programs are a relatively recent innovation in the preventative health field, we will certainly require a great deal more experimental research to develop and improve these programs. We will also require summative research studies to compare alternative approaches to dealing with health hazards. Figure 1 illustrates kinds of summative evaluation studies that are needed in behavioral medicine. It should be noted that such studies may do much more than compare clients treated by a single program to appropriate control clients. We should also do summative studies on the outcome effects of multiple agency treatment, multiple program treatment, and repeated treatment. Figure 1 also indicates the primary role of epidemiological studies (cf. Susser, 1975). We need to know much more about the incidence and prevalence of faulty health lifestyles; the factors which influence whether such clients will seek treatment; what kinds of treatment programs they enter and why; and the kinds of treatment programs needed.

Many professionals in the behavioral medicine field will be involved in setting up and operating health lifestyle programs without the opportunity or resources to do extensive epidemiological need assessment or summative evaluation studies. They will, however, want to collect data relevant to program operation that will allow them to determine the kinds of clients who are being seen, what is being done to them, and what effect it has. Since the purpose of such data is to supply feedback to facilitate program change, what is needed is a formative study using the therapeutic evaluation paradigm. What methodology best meets this need? I would suggest that we adopt the methodology that appears to be particularly efficient for changing individuals' behaviors—applied behavior analysis—and adapt it for organizational behavior. Back in the dark ages of behavior modification when Og Lindsley was peddling log-log paper to ward off evil Rorschachs, he developed the pinpoint-record system, (Lindsley, 1965) that formed the basis of applied behavioral

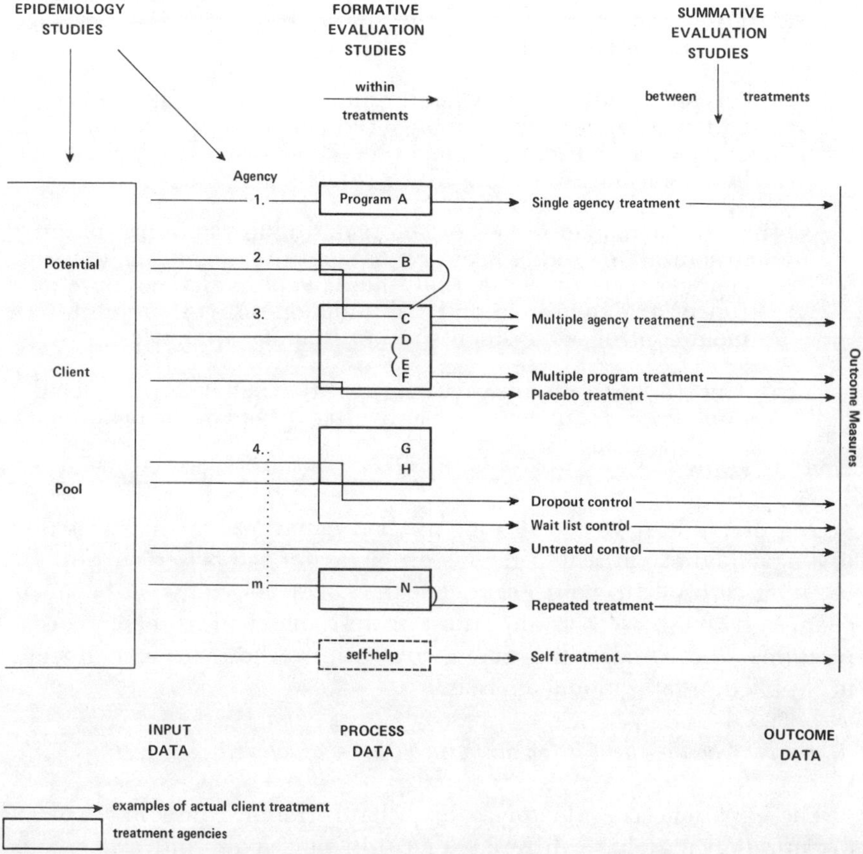

FIGURE 1. Conceptual Framework for Program Research

analysis. Let's take those procedures and update them for working with troubled agencies rather than troubled individuals. There are some important similarities and differences between the principles governing the behaviors of organizations and individuals. It is clearly beyond the scope of this chapter to explain principles of organization development (cf. Argyris & Schon, 1978; Dunnette, 1974; Etzioni, 1969; Franklin, 1973; Katz & Kahn, 1966) but a few oversimplified principles should be noted.

(1) Organizations seal off their technology and resist change.

(2) Organizations do not change simply because new knowledge or procedures are made known.

(3) Organizations change when input to the organization changes and that input cannot be buffered (stockpiling excess input is one kind of buffer—in human service organizations this is done by establishing a waiting list or referral system).

(4) Social or human service organizations, unlike industrial/business organizations, don't seem to be sensitive to output demand changes (like a free operant, these agencies change more as a function of environmental manipulation rather than reinforcement control—antecedents rather than consequences).

(5) Uncertainty is disruptive to organization behavior (in much the same sense as anxiety is for individuals). One of the major goals of a program evaluation should be the reduction of uncertainty.

One of Lindsley basic rules for applied behavioral analysis was that if you wanted to pinpoint a client's problem you had better start out by listening carefully to your client. Let the client tell you what behavior changes he or she sees as important or desirable. Unfortunately, organizations don't speak with a single voice and so there are several steps in "applied organizational analysis."

A. Decide who the client is for purposes of this evaluation.

The experienced evaluator realizes that different components of an organization may have different or conflicting goals, and evaluations that are beneficial at one level may be useless or costly at a different level of the organization (Hiebert, 1974). A typical health agency may be divided into the following levels:

i) Funding source,
ii) Board of Directors,
iii) Administrator,
iv) Program or Clinical Director,
v) Front line therapist, and
vi) Recipient of service—patient or client, from a
vii) Referral source

Which "level" is the evaluation designed to benefit—and be accountable to? Which "level" is going to pinpoint the problems for which data are required to plan change? Spivak, St. Clair, Siegel and Platt (1975) have clearly indicated that the decisions about what evaluation topics should or should not be studied depend upon the level of the person asking the question and on when and where it is being asked. For example, funders prefer evaluations that focus on program costs, staff morale, or internal audits. Community board members may be more interested in consumer knowledge about and satisfaction with the program. The administrator typically wants cost effectiveness or cost benefit studies of service delivery and evaluations of public image of the agency. The clinic director wants to know differential effectiveness of therapists' and *program* goal attainment. The therapists may be unanimously opposed to therapist effectiveness evaluation but want to know alternative treatment effectiveness and *client* goal attainment.

It would be a gross oversimplification, therefore, to claim that "the agency" is the client and that the evaluation will be directed at the problems identified by "the agency." By the same token it is often a gross overcomplication to try to design the evaluation to satisfy the conflicting goals of all the components of the agency. Unless the evaluation is very adroit and the agency organizationally simple, such attempts often end up confusing rather than clarifying problems, and satisfying no one in the agency.

In addition to making a conscious decision about which level of the organization you will define as the client, I think there is probably an ethical requirement that you insure that all other levels of the organization know what that decision is. When an evaluator is reporting to the administrator and collecting data relevant to that administrator's decision needs, then information collected from the therapists and clients must have their informed consent (i.e., they must be informed about whom the information is being given to and consent to its being given).

There are no rules about which level of an agency is best for the evaluation intervention. Some evaluators prefer to orient their evaluation toward the administrative or board level since program changes are officially approved at that level. Other evaluators prefer the evaluation to be set up closer to the front line therapist level since that is where the changes are often initiated. Perhaps the best guideline currently available for a therapeutic evaluation is to gear that evaluation effort to the level of the organization that seems the least rigid and most willing to plan for or accept change.

Once you have accepted your client, the next step in applied behavior analysis is to "pinpoint" or specify the goals or objectives.

B. Specification of evaluation objectives.

The concept of pinpointing is particularly useful for this stage of evaluation. Many agencies or programs have stated goals that are vague platitudes ("improve mental health") or tautologies ("the goal of our alcohol treatment programs is to treat alcoholism") which give no direction to the program evaluator. Goal attainment scaling (Kiresuk & Sherman, 1968) is a procedure that is frequently used to identify program or client objectives. Goal identification and measurement should be the start of program evaluation in our conceptualization—it shouldn't be the end. Use of goal attainment scaling as an evaluation procedure by itself is coming under increased criticism (cf. Marsh, 1978). Stated goals may not be real goals, and Scriven argues (Salasin, 1974) that evaluations should evaluate what a program actually does rather than what it says it is trying to do. Too often goals are identified using only the criterion of how easy they are to measure. Goal attainment scaling often has problems in delay of feedback which makes the results more useful for decision justification than decision making. It is tempting to manipulate the results by specifying goals that are either impossible to achieve or already obtained. Trying to attain goals once they have been specified is somewhat analogous to shooting arrows in a crosswind. Programs seldom end up where they were originally aimed. (I could push the analogy even further and suggest that too often the function of goal attainment evaluators is to wander out in the woods, find the arrows and paint bulls eyes around them!) The main fault with goal attainment procedures is that they are non-contingent, i.e., they don't indicate what program changes will or will not occur with goal attainment or with goal failure.

While most evaluations will have as an objective the changing of treatment outcome toward some desired goal, it must be recognized that this is not the only objective for evaluations. Many agency-change decisions which require data involve problems other than outcome goals. If we are to pinpoint organizational behaviors to be changed, then perhaps our evaluation objective is to pinpoint the decisions for which further data are required, or to pinpoint the uncertainty condition that needs to be changed.

The next step is problematic. In applied behavior analysis you record the stimulus environment and the potential reinforcers for the terminal behavior of the pinpointed problem.

C. Record relevant data.

What you record depends very much on the nature of the pinpointed problem and in many health lifestyle change programs we can't specify what the target behavior should be. The pinpointed problem for program evaluators is probably some program decision to be made. When this is the case, the target is probably reduction of uncertainty relating to that problem (Santa-Barbara, 1977).

At the organizational level it is extremely difficult to identify the parameters that might relate to the types of consequences that maintain the current program, or the types of reinforcements necessary to introduce a new program. Much further research needs to be done on identifying the reinforcers that operate in human service programs where the outcomes are not governed strictly by dollar values.

We have progressed further in identifying the discriminative stimuli that set the occasion for specific program decisions or program changes. However, collecting data on the stimulus environment of programs is time consuming and costly. Furthermore, administrators have a time lag which tends to be very short between pinpointing a program problem and making a change in that program. If evaluators are to supply data to reduce uncertainty about the planned change, then the data must be currently available (stockpiled as it were). There is no time (and usually no money either) to set up and collect a specific data base for each identified problem. This time constraint implies that if our data are to be generally useful they must be continuously available—i.e., the program should have some form of ongoing data collection system. In the earlier discussion I argued that these ongoing data should be limited to variables that are likely to relate to program change decisions and that the KISS (Keep it Simple, Stupid) principle should guide the development of this data base. Extremely elaborate data acquisition tends to be cumbersome, expensive, and difficult or slow to retrieve. Too many facts can be almost as difficult to use for decision making as too few. Many data systems that opt for simplicity collect data only on client characteristics (usually demographic, and usually required by some government agency). While these data can answer a few simple questions (for example: "Does marital status relate to amount of smoking?"), the program has to add some information about client outcomes before evaluation kinds of questions can be answered. The behavior sequence we are analyzing goes something like this; clients enter an agency for treatment which has some outcome. There are characteristics of each component of this sequence that can be measured and there are also processes relating to each component. The stimulus environment for formative evaluations relating to program decisions can be conceptualized as shown in Figure 2. (The data base examples in this figure are for an alcohol treatment program.)

The particular data that are collected on an agency or program should

	Clients (enter)	*Agency/ Program* (for)	*Treatment*	*Client Outcome*
Characteristics of	1. age marital status chronicity drinking patterns locus of control self attribution etc.	2. organizational structure physical & social environment rural/urban size orientation goals funding etc.	3. therapist characteristics procedures inpatient/outpatient professional orientation treatment goals structure of group etc.	4. drug use (frequency, pattern, etc.) physical and psychological health interpersonal relationships problem-solving abilities vocational adjustment legal/judicial involvement maintenance generalization etc.
Processes relating to . .	5. record systems intake processes waiting lists dropouts etc.	6. *between agencies* referral network *within agency* client processing decision making staff relations etc.	7. length intensity extent actually used by client model coherency use of volunteers etc.	8. direct vs. indirect measures frequency of follow-up duration of follow-up involvement of significant others preceding and intervening treatments etc.

FIGURE 2. Conceptual Framework for Formative Evaluation

be decided by examining the value of each of the cells to the decision processes of the agency. To the extent that evaluation decisions are concerned with improving the agency or program, the criteria will usually be identified as some change in the characteristics of client outcome. Hence, there should always be some data in cell four. Usually there are data collected for cell one, as well, which give a base for answering the archetypical evaluation question, "Do changes in input affect changes in outcome?" But evaluation questions can be formulated between any variable within any cell or across any combination of cells (a within cells example: "Does establishing a waiting list affect outcomes by increasing drop-outs?"—client processes affecting client outcomes through different client processes). An example of an across cells question might be "Will a change in our agency orientation from remediation to prevention, resulting in less intensive treatment, still give us the same long-term client outcomes if we increase frequency of follow-up?" (agency characteristic to treatment process to client outcome process and characteristic). One thing to notice about the above examples is that they all include client outcomes in the formulation of the problem. Having this kind of data base for evaluation purposes would not preclude addressing it for management decisions that don't involve evaluation of outcomes (examples would include questions such as, "Did change in the referral network result in changes in the treatment procedure?", or "Do younger therapists spend proportionately less time doing therapy with older clients?"). A second aspect of all these sample problems is that they involve reduction of uncertainty by making some comparison.

In traditional applied behavior analysis the next step is to introduce change and compare effects of that change to the previously established data baseline.

D. Compare the value of alternatives.

In formative evaluation of organizations, this step is usually similar to individual therapy as the comparison is over time (pre—post, baseline to intervention, old program to new). It is often difficult to systematically introduce changes in agencies. Program evaluation does not always require planned change since one can and probably should compare the baseline conditions with those produced by some unplanned changes! Fortunately, in many agencies it is not necessary to introduce specific changes since many of the alternatives that are of interest already exist so that the comparisons can be made. Santa-Barbara (1977) maintains that this comparison procedure is central to the evaluation process since it helps determine the value or worth of alternative policies, programs or interventions. In comparing one set of information with another, the decision-maker can determine whether that program or intervention is to be increased, reduced or altered.

There is still, however, a final step to be completed in our "applied program analysis" that never occurred in applied behavior analysis (in the early years there was too little money and now perhaps there is too much).

E. A cost-benefit monitoring of the evaluation procedures.

If we are not bound by a fixed-design experimental procedure, there is no reason for the program evaluation system to be rigid and inflexible. With a therapeutic orientation to program evaluation we should expect that the procedures will be constantly refined as we find changes in the benefits and costs of the evaluation procedures. The most likely candidate for change is the data base being monitored. As decision processes change, there may be interest in collecting new data (from different cells of Figure 2, for example). With a cost-benefit orientation, however, the data that are collected should not be governed by "more is better," and the data-monitoring system may need to be pruned by deleting or simplifying the amount of information collected on variables that are seldom used in decision making or are unhelpful for reducing uncertainty. In a field that is as undeveloped but as dynamic as behavioral medicine, program evaluation procedures cannot be set up on a one-shot basis and then allowed to run unchanged for the duration of the program if they are to meet the criterion of utility. Particular emphasis should be paid to minimizing the time cost of collecting evaluation data. If the required forms are repetitive, difficult to fill out and time consuming, agency staff are apt to use some implicit cost benefit decision process regarding the forms. If the data output back to staff members is not perceived *by them* to be particularly beneficial, they are unlikely to put a great deal of (time) cost into completing forms. Hence, the reliability and completeness of the data deteriorate, which further reduces the benefit of the data and sets the stage for a vicious circle of decreased benefit—decreased care in accuracy of input—decreased reliability —decreased benefit. The effect of this spiral is either stagnation of the evaluation process or artificial inflation of the input time (reliability checks, increased form monitoring, etc.). These are problems that are easier to prevent than to cure! Data forms should be planned carefully with as much concern for costs as completeness. They should be designed so that there is minimal time required to complete them and no unnecessary duplication. In lifestyle change programs, many of the intake forms can be designed so that clients can take them away and complete the form by themselves. There are several advantages to this procedure: It frees the front-line staff to spend more of their time on the treatment program itself; it can be useful therapeutically in getting the clients to view themselves as active participants in the program; and they may begin conceptualizing more clearly their lifestyle problems when answering the questions on the intake form. Having the clients monitor and record their own behavior changes during the course of the program has similar cost and therapy benefits. Learning to monitor can be an important component of self-management of lifestyle change and may be critical to maintenance of change.

In collecting client outcome information, telephone contact may be far more cost beneficial than personal interviews with former clients—particularly if they come from widely scattered locations. We have found in some preliminary pairwise comparisions between personal interviews, telephone interviews and mail follow-up, that telephone and personal interviews don't differ noticeably from each other in terms of reliability, validity checks, completeness of information and percentage of former clients seen. Both are consistently superior to mail follow-up on percentage of former clients that respond and completeness and reliability of response. Telephone contact is, of course, far cheaper than sending a follow-up worker out to interview clients in their own homes. (We have no data on personal interview follow-up where the client is asked to return to the agency.) Some thought needs to be given to the timing and frequency of collecting follow-up information. While programs are interested in short- and long-term effects, the nature of lifestyle change contemplated, the intensity of the program, and the kind of clients all determine what kind and duration of outcome might be reasonably expected. More is not necessarily better. Too frequent a follow-up may alienate the former client or, conversely, continue his/her dependence on the program too long. A too frequent follow-up may interfere with the client attributing maintenance of effects to his or her own efforts and reduce the likelihood of self-managed maintenance (Davidson, 1976). Obviously, frequency and timing of follow-up, like all other components of the evaluation effort, must be decided from a cost-benefit perspective, keeping in mind that follow-up can be extremely important therapeutically and not just scientifically.

Program evaluation results, if they are useful, are probably going to have major influence on how lifestyle change programs develop. I have argued that program evaluations which have a therapeutic orientation analagous to applied behavioral analysis are more likely to be useful than those based on models (diagnostic or experimental) that are oriented to simply describing or explaining the program successes and failures.

REFERENCES

ABRAMSON, L. Y., SELIGMAN, M. E. P., & TEASDALE, J. D.: Learned helplessness in humans: Critique and reformulation. *Journal of Abnormal Psychology,* 1978, *87*, 49-74.

ARGYRIS, C., & SCHON, D.A.: *Organizational learning: A theory of action perspective.* Reading, MA: Addison-Wesley, 1978.

BOLIN, D. C., & KIVERS, L.: Evaluation in a community mental health centre. *Evaluation*, 1974, *2*, 26-35.

CRONBACH, L. J.: Remarks to a new society. *Evaluation Research Society Newsletter*, 1977, *1*, 1-3.

DAVIDSON, P. O.: Thumbsucking. In C.G. Costello, (Ed.), *Symptoms of psychopathology: A handbook*. New York: Wiley, 1970.

DAVIDSON, P.O.: Therapeutic compliance. *Canadian Psychological Review,* 1976, *17,* 247-259.

DEROGATIS, L. R., LIPMAN, R. S., & COVI, L.: SCL-90: an outpatient psychiatric rating scale—preliminary report. *Psychopharmacology Bulletin,* 1975, *9*, 13-28.

DUNNETTE, M. D.: *Handbook of industrial and organizational psychology.* Chicago: Rand McNally, 1974.

EPSTEIN, I. & TRIPODI, T.: *Research techniques for program planning, monitoring and evaluation*. New York: Columbia University Press, 1978.

ETZIONI, A.: *A sociological reader on complex organizations.* New York: Holt, Rinehart & Winston, 1969.

FAIRWEATHER, G., SANDERS, D. H., & TOURNATZKY, L. G.: *Creating change in mental health organizations*. New York: Pergamon, 1974.

FRANKLIN, J. L.: *Organization development: An annotated bibliography*. Ann Arbor: Institute for Social Research, 1973.

GLASER, E. M., & BACKER, T. E.: Outline of questions for program evaluations utilizing clinical approaches. *Evaluation*, 1972, *1*, 56.

HARYETT, R. D., HANSEN, F. C., & DAVIDSON, P. O.: Chronic thumbsucking. *American Journal of Orthodontics*, 1970, *57,* 164-178.

HIEBERT, S.: Who benefits from the program? Criteria selection. In P.O. Davidson, F. W. Clark, & L. A. Hamerlynck, (Eds.), *Evaluation of behavioral programs*. Champaign, IL: Research Press, 1974.

Joint Commission on Accreditation for Hospitals: *The PEP primer for psychiatry.* Chicago, IL: Joint Commission on Accreditation for Hospitals, 1975.

KATZ, D., & KAHN, R. L.: *The social psychology of organizations*. New York: John Wiley, 1966.

KIRESUK, T. J., & SHERMAN, R. E.: Goal attainment scaling: A general method for evaluating comprehensive community mental health programs. *Community Mental Health Journal*, 1968, *4,* 443-453.

KUHN, T. S.: *The structure of scientific revolutions*. Chicago: University of Chicago Press, 1962.

LESTER, D.: Suicide prevention centers: Data for 1970. *Journal of the American Medical Association*, 1974, *229*, 394.

LINDSLEY, O. R.: Direct measurement and prosthesis of retarded behavior. *Journal of Education*, 1965, *147,* 62-80.

LUND, D. A.: Mental health program evaluation: Where you start. *Evaluation and Program*

Planning, 1978, *1*, 31-40.

MARSH, J. C.: The goal-oriented approach to evaluation: Critique and case study from drug abuse treatment. *Evaluation and Program Planning*, 1978, *1*, 41-51.

PEARSON, G. H. J.: The psychology of finger sucking, tongue sucking, and other oral habits. *American Journal of Orthodontics*, 1948, *34*, 589-598.

POLACK, P. R., EGAN, D., & VANDER BERGH, R.: Prevention in mental health: A controlled study. *American Journal of Psychiatry*, 1975, *132*, 146-149.

SALASIN, S.: Exploring goal-free evaluation: An interview with Michael Sariven. *Evaluation*, 1974, *2*, 9-16.

SANTA-BARBARA J.: Can evaluation be cost-effective. *The Ontario Psychologist*, 1977, *9*, 21-30.

SPIVAK, G., ST. CLAIR, C. H., SIEGEL, J., & PLATT, J. J.: Differing perspectives on mental health evaluation. *American Journal of Psychiatry*, 1975, *132*, 1295-1299.

STRUENING, E. L., & GUTTENTAG, M.: *Handbook of evaluation research*. Beverly Hills, CA: Sage Publications, 1975.

SUSSER, M.: Epidemiological studies. In E.L. Struening & M. Guttentag, (Eds.), *Handbook of evaluation research* (Vol. I). Beverly Hills, CA: Sage Publications, 1975.

TYRON, W. W.: Models for behavior disorder. *American Psychologist*, 1976, *31*, 509-518.

WILSON, N.: An information system for clinical and administrative decision-making research and evaluation. In J. Crawford, D. Morgan, & D. Giantruco (Eds.), *Progress in mental health information systems*. Cambridge, MA: Ballinger, 1974.

WILSON, N.: *The Kiss principle*. Paper presented to the HEW/NIMH State Level Program Evaluation Conference, Windsor, CT, 1976.

WINDLE, C., & OCHBERG, F. M.: Enhancing program evaluation in the community mental health centers program. *Evaluation*, 1975, *2*, 31-36.

WOLFENSBERGER, W., & GLENN, L.: *Pass 3: A method for quantitative analysis of human services* (3rd ed.). Toronto: National Institute for Mental Retardation, 1975.

ZUSMAN, J.: Can program evaluation be saved from its enthusiasts? *American Journal of Psychiatry*, 1976, *133*, 1300-1305.

ZUSMAN, J., & BISSIONETTE, R.: The case against evaluation. *International Journal of Mental Health*, 1973, *2*, 111-125.

16

Determinants of Relapse: Implications for the Maintenance of Behavior Change

G. Alan Marlatt and
Judith R. Gordon

Introduction

Few would doubt that the techniques of behavior therapy or behavior modification are capable of bringing about meaningful changes in behavior. In the past two decades, we have developed a plethora of intervention procedures that have proven effective in modifing a wide variety of target behaviors ranging from snake phobias to sexual dysfunctions. Despite our successes in being able to initiate changes in behavior, we are still grappling with the difficulties involved in *maintaining* behavioral change over time and across situations.

To date, there have been two major directions in our attempts to deal with the problem of maintaining change. One approach, sometimes referred to as the "shotgun" method, involves the development of bigger and better treatment packages, beefing them up to the point where we now refer to them as "broad spectrum" or "multi-modal" programs.

There seems to be an underlying assumption here that if we have enough variable components built into the initial behavior change program, the effects on treatment outcome will somehow last longer. An analogous situation is the advertising claim made for certain brands of gasoline: with the addition of new (or sometimes "secret") active ingredients to the "basic" gas, we can expect to travel more miles per gallon than we did before. The second major approach has been the development of self-control procedures, in which the client is trained to self-administer a program of assessment and intervention procedures. A key assumption in this approach is that the client can be trained to become his or her own therapist, and will be able to implement procedures to maintain changes in behavior long after the initial treatment program has ended. A successful graduate of a self-control program might be described as a "maintenance man," someone who is handy with the tools of behavior modification, and can "fix things up" on his own when signs of trouble appear. Despite the advances in knowledge and the increase in long-term treatment successes associated with the development of both broad-spectrum intervention programs and self-control strategies, we still have a long way to go in understanding and applying the principles associated with the maintenance of behavior change.

In this chapter, we would like to describe a third approach to the maintenance question. The focus of this new approach differs from the first two described above on at least one important dimension. Rather than asking the question of how we can make treatment more effective and long-lasting in its effects, we are turning the tables to ask: Under what conditions do the effects of treatment fail? What processes underlie the "breakdown" of treatment effectiveness, the point at which the maintenance of change gives way? From this perspective, we are focusing on the determinants of recidivism, the tendency to relapse into a previous condition or mode of behavior. The rationale for pursuing this approach is straightforward. By obtaining information about the process of relapse, we may be able to derive important implications for prevention and treatment programs. It may be the case, for example, that there are some common denominators or principles associated with relapse (especially in terms of antecedent and consequent events) which apply regardless of the particular behavior involved. In this paper, we will present data supporting this contention, and attempt to develop a theoretical model of the relapse process that bears directly on the problem of maintenance.

The study of addictive behaviors provides ample opportunity to observe the relapse process in action. One might conclude that those who

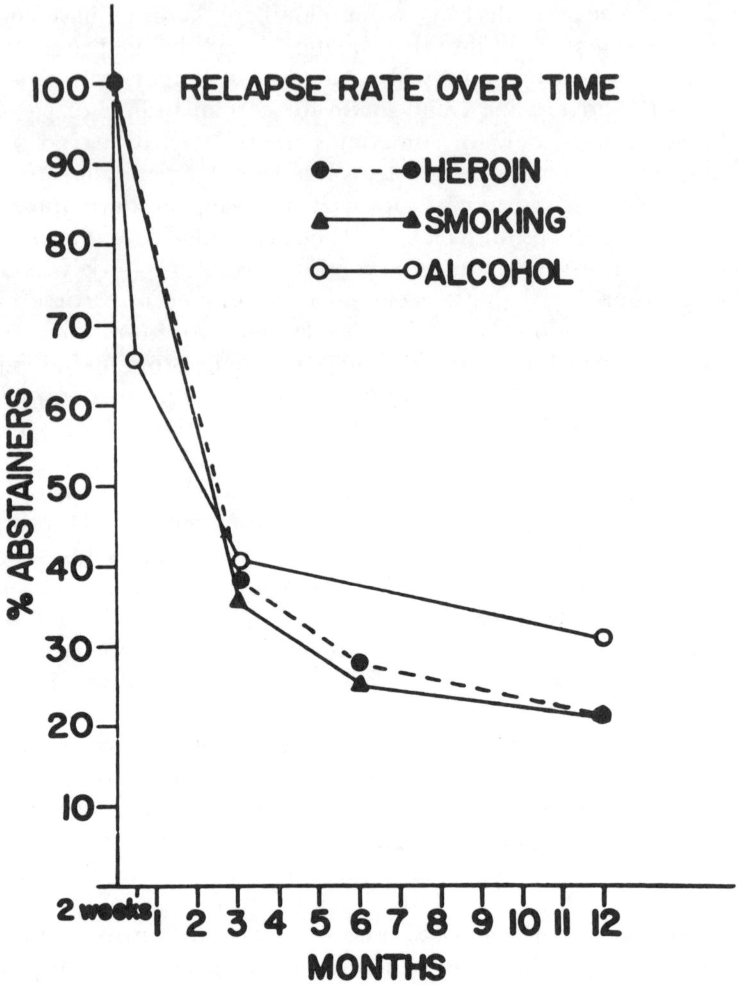

FIGURE 1. Relapse Rates for Smokers, Alcoholics, and Heroin Addicts from Hunt, Barnett, & Branch (1971).

work in the area of addictions have already acquired a reputation in dealing with the maintenance problem, based on the observations that maintenance is already a key component in many of our treatment programs—such as methadone maintenance, heroin maintenance, and controlled drinking. While one may play with the word maintenance in this regard, the fact that we rely so heavily on programs such as methadone maintenance in the treatment of heroin addiction underscores the highly recalcitrant nature of addictive behaviors. Recidivism rates are notoriously high across the spectrum of such behaviors. The temporal characteristics of the relapse process also show a pattern of consistency across addictive substances, as illustrated in Figure 1. This graph is taken from an article by Hunt, Barnett, and Branch (1971), showing the temporal pattern of relapse across treatment programs for smokers (this curve is based on an averaging of data from 84 separate smoking treatment studies), alcoholics, and heroin addicts. The commonality of relapse rates across these problem behaviors is striking: About two-thirds of all relapses occur within the first 90 days following treatment. These data strongly suggest the possibility of common elements underlying the mechanism of relapse itself.

The traditional interpretation of the observed similarity in relapse rates across substances, as illustrated in Figure 1, has been that these substances are roughly equivalent in addictive properties. The temporal similarities in relapse rates for individuals treated for habitual smoking, alcoholism, and heroin addiction would seem to indicate that tobacco, alcohol, and heroin are equally addicting in their effects, as viewed from this perspective. Acceptance of this view has led investigators to search for the biochemical substrate that may underlie the addictive mechanisms involved. Although quality research in this vein continues (with mixed success), a different conceptualization of the relapse data yields an alternative approach. We would like to suggest that there may be common behavioral and cognitive components associated with relapse, regardless of the particular "addictive substance" involved. While the importance of the individual properties of various substances cannot be ignored, particularly as they affect the development of abuse patterns within user groups, the approach we have adopted seeks to understand the determinants and reactions to the relapse episode itself, viewed as a discrete behavioral entity.

Our approach applies specifically to the study of relapse in human subjects, where cognitive factors play a paramount role as they interact with other behavioral and physiological factors. As such, we have defined relapse as any discrete violation of an imposed rule or set of rules governing the rate or pattern of consumption behaviors. The criterion of abstinence, the most stringent and absolute rule one can adopt in this regard, is violated by a single occurrence of the target behavior. While violation of the abstinence rule is the primary form of relapse we have studied to date, other forms of relapse would also fall under this analysis; the violation of rules governing caloric intake for someone on a strict diet would qualify as a relapse under our definition, for example.

The plan of this chapter is as follows. We will begin by presenting a comparative analysis of a large number of relapse episodes, drawn from individuals who have received treatment for problems associated with the use of alcohol, tobacco, and heroin. Rather than focusing on the internal, physiological factors associated with the addictive properties of these three substances, we will base our analysis on the situation or environmental determinants and on the individual's cognitive interpretation of the relapse episode. As we are primarily interested in investigating the potential relation between the initial relapse episode (the first "slip") and subsequent use of the substance (whether or not the "slip" is followed by a return to habitual or uncontrolled use), we will describe a theoretical model that attempts to predict reactions to the relapse, based on cognitive-behavioral theoretical principles. The theoretical model will then be illustrated in detail through an in-depth analysis of one primary determinant of relapse, the experience of frustration and/or anger. We will conclude the chapter with a description of the model's implications for maintenance of behavior change in general, and for the prevention and treatment of relapse.

Determinants of Relapse

Our research in this area began with a study evaluating the effectiveness of aversive conditioning procedures with chronic alcoholics (Marlatt, 1973). In this study, 65 male alcoholics were exposed to an aversive conditioning program comparing several methods of applying electric shock as the aversive stimulus. Follow-up assessment was conducted at periods of three and fifteen months following discharge from the hospital. In summary, the results showed that the conditioning program produced significant decreases in drinking rates at the three-month follow-up period, but that these differences tended to be of a lesser magnitude at the fifteen-month follow-up. It became clear that something extra needed to be added to the conditioning program itself in order to augment and maintain the treatment effects obtained. The clue to that "extra" ingredient became apparent in a close examination of the relapse data for all patients who began drinking again following discharge from the treatment program (78% of the sample had consumed at least one drink in the first 90 days following release from the hospital). An attempt was made to determine the exact circumstances for the situation that immediately preceded the consumption of the first drink for each patient who relapsed. Each patient was interviewed regarding the relapse situation in order to ascertain such facts as: time of day, detailed description of the situation, presence or absence of others, self-reported feelings at the time, and the occurrence of significant environmental events. The descriptions of each situation were categorized using a reliable scoring system we developed for the purpose. The scoring system was based on the content-analysis procedures developed to score our behavioral assessment questionnaire for use with alcoholics, the *Drinking Profile* (Marlatt, 1976a).

The results of this analysis revealed that over 50% of all relapse situations fell into one of the following two categories: a) situations in which the patient was frustrated or angered, usually in an interpersonal or social situation; and b) situations in which the patient was confronted by social pressures to resume drinking, usually from a drinking partner or family member. The important implication of these findings is that although the treatment program relied upon the development of a conditioned aversion to alcohol itself (based on the principle of classical aversion conditioning), analysis of the relapse data showed that the majority of patients began drinking again in the presence of powerful interpersonal forces, thus highlighting the salience of *social* factors as determinants of relapse. The influence of social factors on relapse in alcoholics (as opposed to the role of internal, physiological determinants, such as "craving" for alcohol and resultant loss of control over drinking) has recently been discussed in a review paper (Marlatt, 1978a).

The results from this preliminary analysis encouraged us to expand the classification system for relapse situations, and to evaluate its effectiveness over a larger sample of subjects. Accordingly, we obtained detailed accounts of relapse episodes from a total of 137 individuals, all of whom were involved in treatment programs for either alcoholism, smoking, or heroin addiction.* The alcoholism sample consisted of 70 subjects, all male chronic alcoholics (average age in the mid-forties) drawn from two inpatient treatment programs (48 subjects from a state hospital inpatient program, and 22 from an inpatient Veterans Administration hospital program). All alcoholics participated in programs with abstinence as the primary goal of treatment. Data on smoking relapses were obtained from 35 subjects, college-age males and females, who partici-

---

*We would like to express our apreciation to Dr. Edmund Chaney of the Seattle Veterans Administration Hospital, for giving us access to relapse data from his alcoholic subjects, and to Professor Roger Roffman, School of Social Work, University of Washington, for providing us with relapse data for the heroin addicts.

pated in a smoking cessation program conducted by the second author as part of her doctoral dissertation (Gordon, 1978). Descriptions of relapse were also obtained from 32 heroin addicts (both male and female young adults), who were assessed following termination of treatment (in either abstinence-oriented therapeutic communities or in methadone-maintenance programs) as part of a statewide evaluation of services. A relapse was defined as the first use of illegal heroin or other opiates for this group of subjects. For the alcoholics and the smokers, the first drink or the first use of tobacco constituted the relapse episode.

All subjects were contacted within 90 days of the termination of each subject's treatment program for follow-up assessment. The alcoholics and heroin addicts were interviewed in person at this time, whereas the smoking subjects filled out a detailed questionnaire that was designed to obtain the same information. Most of the questions asked were patterned after the follow-up version of the *Drinking Profile* (Marlatt, 1976a). Information was sought concerning the circumstances associated with the *first use* of the substance following completion of the treatment program. Each subject was asked to give the date and time of the relapse episode and to describe the setting in which the episode occurred (place and presence/absence of other individuals). In addition, the following open-ended questions were asked, to provide the descriptive basis for the subsequent content-analysis ratings: a) "When I took my first drink [or cigarette, or fix of heroin], the situation was as follows (briefly describe the important features of the situation which led you to take the first drink)"; b) "What would you say was the *main reason* for taking that first drink?"; c) "Describe any inner thoughts or emotional feelings (things *within* you as a person) that triggered off your need or desire to take the first drink at that time,"; and d) "Describe any particular circumstances or set of events, things which happened to you in the outside world, which triggered off your need or desire to take the first drink." Other questions were asked concerning the subject's reactions to the relapse episode, including whether or not the first "slip" was followed by subsequent use of the substance on the same or on following occasions.

The next step involved the development of a classification system to enable the assignment of each relapse episode to an independent category. The original classification system developed by the first author (Marlatt, 1973) to categorize relapses from the aversion study was revised and enlarged, using the basic principles of content analysis (cf. Kiesler, 1973). The final set of categories, with descriptive definitions for each subcategory, is presented in Table 1. Inspection of Table 1 reveals that the relapse episodes are first categorized in one of two major classes. The first category, *intrapersonal/environmental determinants*, is used whenever the relapse episode involves a response to primarily psychological or physical events (e.g., coping with intrapersonal emotional states, giving in to "internal" urges, etc.), or a response to a nonpersonal environmental event (e.g., misfortune, accident, financial loss, etc.). Here, the emphasis is on precipitating events in which another person or group of individuals is *not* a significant factor. The second major category, *interpersonal determinants,* applies whenever the relapse episode does involve the significant influence of other individuals (e.g., coping with interpersonal conflict, social pressure, etc.). The eight subcategories (five within the intrapersonal/environmental determinants classification, and three within the interpersonal determinants category) are described in detail in Table 1.

TABLE 1
Categories for Classification of Relapse Episodes

I. *Intrapersonal/Environmental Determinants*
Includes all determinants which are primarily associated with intrapersonal factors (within the individual), and/or reactions to nonpersonal environmental events. Includes reactions to interpersonal events in the relatively distant past (i.e., in which the interaction is no longer of significant impact).

A. *Coping with Negative Emotional States*
Determinant involves coping with a negative (unpleasant) emotional state, mood, or feeling.

(1) *Coping with Frustration and/or Anger*
Determinant involves an experience of frustration (reaction to a blocked goal-directed activity), and/or anger (hostility, aggression) in terms of the self or some nonpersonal environmental event. Includes all references to guilt, and responses to demands ("hassles") from environmental sources or from within the self which are likely to produce feelings of anger.

(2) *Coping with Other Negative Emotional States*
Determinant involves coping with emotional states other than frustration/anger, which are unpleasant or aversive, including feelings of fear, anxiety, tension, depression, loneliness, sadness, boredom, worry, apprehension, grief, loss, and other similar dysphoric states. Includes reactions to evaluation stress (examinations, promotions, public speaking, etc.), employment and financial difficulties, and personal misfortune or accident.

B. *Coping with Negative Physical/Physiological States*
Determinant involves coping with unpleasant or painful physical or physiological reactions.

(1) *Coping with Physical States Associated with Prior Substance Use*
Coping with physical states which are specifically associated with prior use of drug or substance, such as "withdrawal agony" or "physical craving" associated with withdrawal (Note: references to "craving" in the absence of withdrawal are classified under Section E below).

(2) *Coping with Other Negative Physical States.*
Coping with pain, illness, injury, fatigue, specific disorders (e.g., headache, menstrual cramps, etc.), which are *not* associated with prior substance use.

Table 1 (continued)

C. *Enhancement of Positive Emotional States*
Use of substance to increase feelings of pleasure, joy, freedom, celebration, etc. (as when traveling, or on vacation, etc.). Includes use of substance for primarily positive effects, e.g., to "get high", or to experience the enhancing effects of a drug.

D. *Testing Personal Control*
Use of substance to "test" one's ability to engage in controlled or moderate use; to "just try it once" to see what happens; or in cases in which the individual is testing the effects of treatment or a commitment to abstinence (including tests of "will power").

E. *Giving in to Temptations or Urges*
Substance use in response to "internal" urges, temptations, or other promptings. Includes references to "craving" or intense subjective desire, in the absence of interpersonal factors. (Note: references to "craving" which are associated with prior drug use or withdrawal are classified under Section B-1 above)

(1) *In the Presence of Substance Cues*
Use occurs in the presence of cues associated with substance use (e.g., running across a hidden bottle or pack of cigarettes, passing by a bar, seeing an ad for cigarettes, etc.). (Note: where other individuals are using the substance, refer to Category II-B below)

(2) *In the Absence of Substance Cues*
Here, the urge or temptation comes "out of the blue", and is *followed* by the individual's attempt to procure the substance.

II. *Interpersonal Determinants*
Includes determinants which are primarily associated with interpersonal factors: reference is made to the presence or influence of other individuals as part of the precipitating event. Implies the influence of present or recent *interaction* with another person or persons, who exert some influence on the user (reactions to events which took place in the relatively distant past are classified in Category I). Just being in the presence of others at the time of the relapse does not justify an interpersonal classification, unless some mention is made or implied that these people had some influence or were somehow involved in the event.

A. *Coping with Interpersonal Conflict*
Coping with a current or relatively recent conflict associated with any interpersonal relationship, such as marriage, friendship, family patterns, employer-employee relations.

(1) *Coping with Frustration and/or Anger*
Determinant involves frustration (reaction to blocked goal-directed activity), and/or anger (hostility, aggression) stemming from an interpersonal source. Emphasis is on any situation in which the person feels frustrated or angry with someone, including involvement in arguments, disagreements, fights, jealousy, discord, hassles, guilt, etc.

(2) *Coping with Other Interpersonal Conflict*
Determinant involves coping with conflicts other than frustration and anger stemming from an interpersonal source. Feelings such as anxiety, fear, tension, worry, concern, apprehension, etc., which are associated with interpersonal conflict, are examples. Evaluation stress in which another person or group is specifically mentioned would be included.

B. *Social Pressure*
Determinant involves responding to the influence of another individual or group of individuals who exert pressure (either direct or indirect) on the individual to use the substance.

(1) *Direct Social Pressure*
There is direct contact (usually with verbal interaction) with another person

Table 1 (continued)

or group who puts pressure on the user or who supplies the substance to the user (e.g., being offered a drug by someone, or being urged to use a drug by someone else). Distinguish from situations in which the substance is obtained from someone else at the request of the user (who has already decided to use).

(2) *Indirect Social Pressure*
Responding to the observation of another person or group who are using the substance or who serve as models of substance use for the user. If the model(s) puts any direct pressure on the individual to use the substance, it should be categorized under II-B-1, above.

C. *Enhancement of Positive Emotional State*
Use of substance in a primarily interpersonal situation to increase feelings of pleasure, celebration, sexual excitement, freedom, etc. Distinguish from situations in which the other person(s) is using the substance *prior to* the individual's first use (classify these under Section II-B, above).

Scoring Rules
For each relapse episode, only one category can be used for scoring. When multiple categories seem to apply, choose the most significant precipitating event for scoring (the event *immediately* preceding the relapse). When it is impossible to decide between two equally-likely categories, assign the score on a priority basis: Category I takes precedence over Category II; within each major category, the ordering of categories (A before B, etc.) indicates the priorities.

After the classification system was derived, two students were trained to assign category scores for the relapses described in the questionnaires mentioned above.* Training continued until a high degree of agreement between raters was obtained: In an independent test of reliability, the inter-rater agreement was 88 percent for category assignment. Each rater was then asked to score approximately half of the 137 relapse episodes given by subjects in the alcoholism, smoking, and heroin addiction treatment groups. The results of this classification system are presented in Table 2. For purposes of clarity only the major categories are presented in this table; subcategory differences of interest will be described below.

The data in Table 2 indicate that over three-quarters (76 percent) of all the relapse episodes fall into just three categories: coping with negative emotional states (I-A, with 37 percent of all relapses), social pressure (II-B, 24 percent), and coping with interpersonal conflict (II-A, 15 percent). For the remaining 24 percent of all relapses, the distribution was as follows: giving in to temptations or urges (I-E, 7 percent), enhancement of intrapersonal positive emotional states (I-C, 6 percent), negative physical states (I-B, 4 percent), testing personal control (I-D, 4 percent), and enhancement of interpersonal positive emotional states (II-C, 3 percent).

---

*Thanks are due to Claudette Adams and Lisa Friedman who served as raters in assigning relapse episodes to categories.

TABLE 2
Analysis of Relapse Situations with Alcoholics, Smokers, and Heroin Addicts

Situation	Alcoholics (N = 70)	Smokers (N = 35)	Addicts (N = 32)	All Subjects (N = 137)
Intrapersonal Determinants	61%	57%	53%	58%
Negative Emotional States	38%	43%	28%	37%
Negative Physical States	3%	—	9%	4%
Positive Emotional States	—	8%	16%	6%
Testing Personal Control	9%	—	—	4%
Urges and Temptations	11%	6%	—	7%
Interpersonal Determinants	39%	43%	47%	42%
Interpersonal Conflict	18%	12%	13%	15%
Social Pressure	18%	25%	34%	24%
Positive Emotional States	3%	6%	—	3%

The majority (58 percent) of all relapses involved intrapersonal/ environmental determinants (Category I), with 42 percent involving primarily interpersonal determinants (Category II). For the major categories at least, there appear to be more similarities than differences across the three subject groups. For alcoholics and smokers, for example, the ordering of the three categories associated with greatest number of relapses is the same: negative emotional states (38 percent of the alcoholic relapses, 43 percent of the smokers), social pressure (18 percent of the alcoholics, and 25 percent of the smokers), followed by interpersonal conflict (18 percent of the alcoholics and 12 percent of the smokers). The ordering of the first two categories was reversed for the heroin addicts, with 34 percent of their relapses falling in the social pressure category, followed by 28 percent for negative emotional states, and 16 percent for enhancement of positive emotional states.

Examination of the subcategory scores reveals some interesting patterns. Categories I-A (coping with negative emotional states) and II-A (coping with interpersonal conflict) both were subdivided into coping with frustration and/or anger (I-A-1 and II-A-1) and coping with other negative emotions or interpersonal conflict (I-A-2 and II-A-2). Here, the findings seem primarily influenced by whether the relapse occurred in either the intrapersonal or interpersonal context. In the *interpersonal* settings, almost all (82 percent of the relapses within category II-A) relapse episodes involved coping with frustration and/or anger. The results were reversed in the *intrapersonal* category, where emotional states other than frustration and anger accounted for 85 percent of the relapses in category I-A. These results seem to indicate that frustration and anger associated with relapse stem primarily from interpersonal sources (arguments with others, etc.), whereas other negative emotions (fear, anxiety, etc.) seem to predominate as determinants of relapse when significant other individuals are not involved. Again, these findings are consistent for each of the three subject groups in our sample.

Coping with negative physical states accounted for only 4 percent of all relapses. Most of these cases involved the heroin addict group: Nine percent of the addicts relapsed in category I-B-1, coping with physical states associated with prior substance use (e.g., withdrawal symptoms). None of the alcoholics or smokers cited physical withdrawal as a determinant of relapse (although 3 percent of the alcoholics cited coping with *other* negative physical states, in category I-B-2), a finding which casts doubt on theories which posit withdrawal symptoms as the primary precipitating factor in relapse (cf., Marlatt, 1978a). Temptations or urges may be related to the subjective experience of craving, sometimes posited as a conditioned response to cues associated with prior withdrawal (Ludwig & Wikler, 1974). Yet this category (I-E) accounted for only 7 percent of all relapses. Most of these relapses occurred in the alcoholic group (11 percent of their relapses), with relatively few smokers (6 percent) and none of the heroin addicts citing this as a determinant. When giving in to urges or temptations was mentioned, most of these feelings were experienced in the absence of substance cues (category I-E-2).

The use of a substance to enhance positive emotional states, whether in an intrapersonal or interpersonal situation (categories I-C and II-C), also accounted for relatively few relapses (9 percent of the total). Wanting to get "high" in the absence of any identifiable stress accounted for 16 percent of all relapses reported by the heroin addict group (all within the intrapersonal category). Only 8 percent of the smokers and none of the alcoholics relapsed in this category (I-C). For the parallel interpersonal category (II-C), only 3 percent of all relapses were attributed to this source. These findings suggest that coping with stress (whether it is associated with negative emotional states, interpersonal conflicts, responding to social pressure, etc.) is a much stronger determinant of relapse than simply giving into the desire to "feel good" or using a substance to enhance already existing positive emotional states.

Only among the alcoholic sample was testing personal control (category I-D) given as a determinant of relapse. For a small subgroup of the alcoholics (9 percent), the desire either to test one's ability to have a drink or two and then stop, or the intention to test the effects of the abstinence-oriented treatment program, was given as the precipitating event. As none of the smokers or heroin addicts cited tests of personal control as the primary determinant, it seems likely that some alcoholics are particularly susceptible to this temptation. Perhaps the prevailing notion of alcoholism as a disease, with the additional assumption that an alcoholic cannot take a single drink without experiencing loss of control drinking ("one drink away from a drunk"), contributes to the alcoholic's tendency to pit his or her own "willpower" against the supposedly involuntary nature of the disease.

Approximately one-fourth of all relapses were classified under the social pressure category (II-B). Whether the influence of social pressure was direct (category II-B-1) or indirect (II-B-2) in nature interacted in an important way with the substance or drug used. For alcoholics and heroin addicts, the predominant relapse situation involved *direct* social pressure, or actual contact between users (e.g., meeting an old drinking buddy who put pressure on the person to begin drinking again; or the addict running across someone who offers some of his/her stash). For the addict sample (where 34 percent relapsed in social pressure situations, the highest of all categories for this group), 28 percent relapsed under conditions of direct social pressure, whereas only 6 percent relapsed under indirect pressure (simple observation of others using). Similarly, for the alcoholic sample (18 percent relapse rate for social pressure), most began drinking again under direct pressure (14 percent), and only a few under indirect pressure (4 percent). For the smokers, on the other hand, the pattern was reversed. For the smokers taken as a group, 25 percent of the relapses were categorized as incidents of social pressure, with the bulk (19 percent) classified as *indirect* pressure and a minority (6 percent) as direct pressure. Smokers showed a greater tendency to succumb in situations where others were smoking (observation of models), even though the other smokers put no direct pressure on the observers to join in the indulgence. This finding may reflect the fact that smoking is a far more public behavior (exhibited across a wide variety of situations) than is drinking, or the illicit use of narcotics.

In addition to the classification of relapse episodes presented in Table 2, a number of other points of interest emerged from our questionnaire data. The setting, or physical location where the relapse occurred, is an important consideration, particularly in terms of treatment implications (to be discussed in a later section of this chapter). Physical setting varied as a function of the drug used. Alcoholics, as might be expected, took their first drink most frequently in a bar or tavern (63 percent of all alcoholic relapses for our sample). The next largest grouping (12 percent) began drinking in their own homes, or in the homes of friends or relatives (9 percent). The remainder of relapses in this group was spread over a wide variety of settings (e.g., hotel rooms, outdoors, while driving, etc.). For the smokers, one's own home was the primary setting for relapse (44 percent), followed by the work environment (19 percent), restaurants and bars (13 percent), and at parties (6 percent). Because of the illegal nature of heroin addiction, the setting for relapse with this drug is much more limited: Twenty-two percent first used illegal narcotics in their own homes, with the large majority (78 percent) relapsing in other locations (presumably other residences, although these details were not available from the addict sample). For the addict group, the heroin was obtained primarily in one of two ways: by purchase from a sought-after connection (56%), or obtained without cost from friends or other users (41%).

Time of day when the relapse occurred was obtained from the alcoholic and smoking group subjects. For purposes of summary, subjects were grouped in accordance with whether they took their first drink or smoke in the morning, afternoon, or evening hours. As might be expected, relatively few subjects relapsed in the morning period (13 percent of the alcoholics, and 22 percent of the smokers). For the alcoholics, the relapses were about evenly divided between afternoon (42 percent) and evening (46 percent) periods. The smokers showed a greater tendency to relapse in the evening (61 percent) than in the afternoon period (17 percent). Data on time of relapse were not available for our heroin addict sample.

Consistent with the data presented in Figure 1, the subjects in our three groups relapsed within a relatively short time of completing their respective treatment programs. For our sample, the average number of days between beginning abstinence (for the smokers) or completion of a treatment program (for the alcoholics and addicts) and the subsequent date of relapse was 17 days for the smokers, 30 days for the alcoholics, and 32 days for the heroin addicts. These figures must be interpreted with caution, however, because of differences among the treatment programs involved. For the alcoholics and addicts, for example, abstinence was enforced from the start of the inpatient program (sometimes many weeks prior to release). Some of the addicts were maintained on methadone during treatment while others took part in abstinence-oriented therapeutic community programs. The smokers in our sample took part in a program in which rapid smoking was a key component of treatment (and was used as a self-control intervention procedure during the posttreatment phase by some subjects), thus making it difficult to define a period of "pure" abstinence (Gordon, 1978). Since our data are limited to the analysis of relapses that occurred within a few weeks of the completion of treatment (usually the majority of cases in any similar program), we cannot generalize these results to apply to individuals who have relapsed after much longer periods of abstinence. We are currently following up subjects who have maintained longer periods of abstinence (more than six months), to see if their relapse episodes, if any, fall into the classification of categories described above.

Finally, we have some data from our alcoholics and smokers showing that the "single slip" (the first drink or cigarette) is usually followed by a "full blown" relapse. Subjects were first asked if they took at least one additional drink or smoke following their initial slip during the same time interval or occasion. Almost all (90 percent) of the alcoholics reported that they continued drinking on that occasion, and only a few (10 percent) were able to stop after a single drink. Smokers were somewhat more successful on this first occasion, with 26 percent stopping after the first cigarette, and 74 percent continuing to smoke. By the next distinct occasion (separated by at least some period of abstinence), however, the situation was reversed. Almost a third of the alcoholics (31 percent) were able to regain abstinence following the first occasion of use, whereas 69 percent of the sample continued to drink. Far fewer smokers (9 percent) were able to stop again after their first smoke, and the rest (91 percent) were soon smoking again on a regular basis. Why do most users seem unable to quit again following a single fall off the wagon? We feel that the individual's cognitive reaction to a "single slip" is crucial to the understanding of the relapse process. An analysis of this reaction, along with a theoretical model of the overall pattern of relapse, is presented in the following section.

The Relapse Process: A Cognitive-Behavioral Analysis

Drawing upon the data on determinants of relapse described above, we have constructed a theoretical model of the relapse process based on a cognitive-behavioral orientation. A schematic representation of this model is presented in Figure 2. The main points of this analysis will be discussed in reference to the branching flow-chart presented in this diagram.

The model applies to cases in which the individual has made a commitment to a period of abstinence, following voluntary termination of

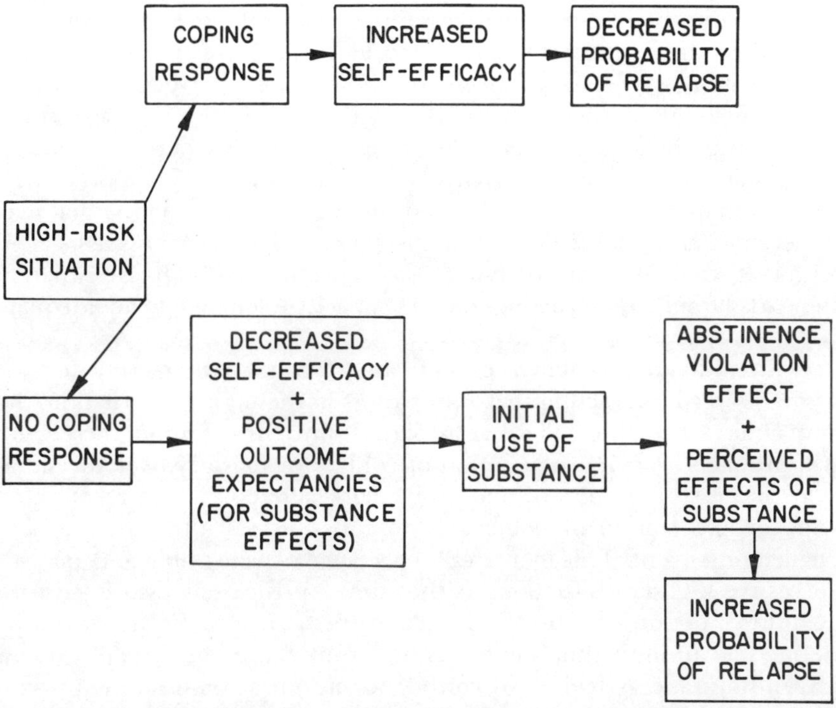

FIGURE 2. Cognitive-behavioral model of the relapse process.

the use of a substance such as alcohol, cigarettes, or illicit narcotics. Aspects of this analysis also apply to those situations in which the individual sets a firm rule or set of rules governing any consumption behavior, such as adhering to a strict dietary regimen or refraining from illicit sexual activities. An important condition of the theory is that it applies only to those cases in which the individual has made a voluntary choice or decision to change a target behavior (e.g., to stop drinking or to begin a dietary program). The implications of the theory for enforced or involuntary abstinence (associated with incarceration, etc.) have yet to be determined.

We also assume that the individual, while maintaining abstinence (or complying with other absolute rules governing behavior) experiences a perceived sense of personal control over the target behavior. The perception of control will continue until the individual encounters a *high-risk situation* (see Figure 2). A high-risk situation is defined broadly as any situation that poses a threat to the individual's sense of control and increases the risk of potential relapse. In terms of the present discussion, all of the relapse categories presented in Table 1 are considered high-risk situations since they were the ones most closely associated with relapse. In many of these situations, it seems likely that the person experiences a challenge to his or her ongoing sense of personal control. Since many of these situations involve a confrontation with another person or environmental event "beyond one's control," the individual may experience an initial feeling of helplessness or powerlessness associated with the event. Whether or not a relapse occurs in a high-risk situation depends largely upon the individual's capacity to engage in an adequate coping response.

If the individual is able to execute an effective *coping response* (e.g., is assertive in counteracting social pressures) in the high-risk situation, the probability of relapse will decrease significantly. In addition, the person will probably regain a perception of control or mastery over the situation. Successful mastery of one problematic situation is often associated with an expectation of being able to cope successfully with the next challenging event. This increased expectancy of being able to cope with successive high-risk situations as they develop is closely associated with Bandura's notion of self-efficacy (Bandura, 1977). Self-efficacy can be defined as an individual's expectations concerning performance on an impending task. A feeling of confidence in one's abilities to cope with a high-risk situation is associated with an elevated perception of self-efficacy—a kind of "I know I can handle it" feeling. On the other hand, if the person does not expect to do well in coping with these problematic situations, a sense of decreased self-efficacy develops. As the duration of the abstinence period increases, and the individual is able to cope successfully with more and more high-risk situations, the perception of control and self-efficacy will increase in a cumulative fashion.

What happens if a coping response to the high-risk situation is not performed? It may be the case that the person has never learned the coping skills involved, or that the appropriate response is inhibited by fear or anxiety. Or, perhaps the person fails to recognize and respond to the risk involved in a particular situation before it is "too late." For whatever the reason, if a coping response is not forthcoming, the person is likely to experience a decrease in self-efficacy, coupled with an increased sense of helplessness and a tendency to "give in" to the situation. The mode of behavior shifts from one of active coping to one of passive yielding. "It's no use, I can't handle this," is a common reaction. As self-efficacy drops in the precipitating high-risk situation, it is likely that one's expectations for coping with subsequent problematic situations will drop accordingly. If the next situation involves dealing with the "temptation" to take a drink or smoke a cigarette, the stage is set for a probable relapse.

The temptation or urge to succumb will increase even further if one harbors positive *expectancies* about the effects of the substance or activity involved. The person may selectively recall the positive aspects of substance use in the past, and anticipate these effects in the high-risk situation. For many individuals, taking a drink or smoking a cigarette has long been associated with coping with stress. "If only I could have a cigarette, I could feel relaxed," or, "A drink would help me get through this," are typical expectations of this type. Despite having experienced many of the negative consequences for excessive drinking or other drug use in the past (e.g., nausea, hangovers, and social disapproval), users often tend to anticipate only the positive consequences or effects when faced with the opportunity to indulge (cf., McGuire, Mendelson, & Stein, 1966; Tamerin, Weiner, & Mendelson, 1970). Expectation of positive effects from a drink or a cigarette, particularly if drinking or smoking has been used as a means of coping with stress in the past, is a powerful additional determinant of relapse.

We now have a loaded situation for relapse, and a double-barreled one at that. On one side, the individual is faced with a high-risk situation with no coping response available. Self-efficacy decreases as the person sinks lower into a sense of helplessness and loss of perceived control. On the other side, there is the lure of the old coping response, the drink, cigarette, or whatever. To the extent that this behavior has been used as a means of dealing with stress in the past, the attractiveness of that substance or activity will increase considerably in the current high-risk situation. If the individual also believes that the effects of the substance will enhance feelings of control or power, and the high-risk situation has contributed to a sense of powerlessness and decreased self-efficacy, the temptation to give in may become extremely intense. At this point, barring the possibility of a last-minute coping response or a sudden change in circumstances, the trigger of relapse may be pulled.

The requirement of abstinence is an absolute concept. Once someone has crossed the line, there is no going back. Just as one cannot be a "little bit pregnant," so also one cannot be a little bit nonabstinent. Only one drink or one cigarette is enough to break the rule of abstinence: The deed cannot be undone. To account for the reaction to this transgression of an absolute rule, we have postulated a mechanism called the *abstinence violation effect* (AVE). The intensity of this cognitive and affective reaction will vary as a function of several factors, including the prior degree of effort or personal commitment to maintain abstinence, the duration of the abstinence period (the longer the duration, the greater the effect), and the overall value or importance of the behavior to the individual involved.

In our analysis (Marlatt, 1978a), there are two primary components of the abstinence violation effect. First, there is a *cognitive dissonance* component (Festinger, 1964), in which the behavioral act associated with the initial use of the substance (the first drink, etc.) is in direct conflict with the individual's self-image as an abstainer. This conflict between one's behavior and the cognitive definition of oneself as abstinent is a classic example of cognitive dissonance, according to Festinger's theoretical model. The second component of the AVE is a personal *attribution* effect (Jones, Kanouse, Kelley, Nisbett, Valins & Weiner, 1972) in which the user attributes the "cause" of the transgression to internal weakness or personal failure. Rather than attributing the first "slip" to a lack of coping abilities in a high-risk situation, the individual may assume that the behavior is due to personal shortcomings, such as a lack of "willpower" or insufficient control over temptations or urges arising from within.

To illustrate the potential effects of the AVE in the relapse process, let us examine the hypothetical case of an alcoholic who has pledged himself to abstinence, and at some point in time experiences a slip and takes a drink. This analysis was reported in an earlier paper describing the determinants of relapse in alcoholism (Marlatt, 1978a):

> Although the dissonance and attribution components of the AVE may overlap to a degree, the additive effects of both reactions will greatly increase the probability of repeating the restricted behavior, according to our theoretical model. The dissonance state will vary in intensity depending on the duration of the abstinence period and the degree of personal and public commitment to the role of an abstainer. A member of Alcoholics Anonymous, for example, who refers to himself as a "recovering alcoholic," and has made a public pledge never to take another drink, is particularly susceptible to an intense dissonance reaction upon consuming a single drink. According to classical cognitive dissonance theory, dissonance is experienced as a negative emotional drive state, and can serve as a motivating force to engage in behaviors (or changes in cognition) which serve to reduce dissonance. Consumption of more alcohol, following the first drink, is a particularly effective behavior in this regard, because (a) to the extent that alcohol reduces tension or anxiety, it should also be effective in reducing feelings of dissonance and guilt; and (b) the alcoholic can modify his self-image to achieve consonance with his drinking behavior

> (e.g., "I guess I still haven't fully recovered; the disease has got me again."). From the perspective of dissonance theory, it is very difficult to "undo" the act of taking the first drink: A single drink is enough to shatter the image of oneself as an abstainer.
>
> Most abstinent alcoholics are justifiably proud of their continued sobriety. Although they may partially attribute their success to a specific experience, such as involvement in a particular treatment program or A.A., it seems likely that they also feel personally responsible for having taken the "first step" towards a new life, totally free from alcohol. As each day of abstinence passes, "one day at a time," their self-confidence and feelings of personal control over the temptations to drink increase. How is this self-image affected by taking the first drink? To the extent that the individual feels personally responsible for "giving in" and consuming that drink, attribution theory would predict that he or she would attribute this "failure" to internal, personal causes (cf., Weiner, Frieze, Kukla, Reed, Rest & Rosenbaum, 1971). Even though an objective observer of the relapse might ascribe the causes to environmental stressors beyond the individual's control, the individual concerned will frequently attribute the event to personal weakness or other shortcomings. People often draw inferences about their own personal states through the observation of their behavior (Bem, 1972). Thus, if a relapse occurs, the alcoholic is likely to infer a lack of will power or personal control as the determinant of the relapse. If the relapse is viewed as a personal failure in this sense, the individual's expectancy for continued failure will increase as a result. An expectancy of failure is likely to mediate decrements in actual performance. If one feels weak-willed and powerless for giving in to the temptation of the first drink, the expectation of resisting the second or third drink is correspondingly lower: "once a drunk, always a drunk."

A final factor to be considered in the relapse process is the subjective effect of the substance, as experienced by the user. While these effects will differ with the type of drug or other activity, many drugs act in such a way as to produce an initial "high" or state of arousal which is interpreted as a pleasant or euphoric state by the user. Both alcohol and tobacco, for example, produce an initial state of physiological arousal (increased heart rate and other autonomic reactions) which may be subjectively experienced by the user as an increase in energy or power. Many psychoactive drugs seem to have a biphasic effect in this regard, in which the first state is experienced as an excitatory "high" or "upper" (cf., Docter, Naitoh & Smith, 1966; Garfield & McBrearty, 1970). This initial increase in physiological arousal may be labeled by the user as a feeling of enhanced power or control (cf., McClelland, Davis, Kalin, & Wanner, 1972). If this reaction occurs, the use of the substance to counter the individual's prior feelings of decreased self-efficacy or personal powerlessness in the high-risk situation is strongly reinforced. Taken together, the cumulative effects of the AVE coupled with the reinforcing perceived effects of the drug or the user's response greatly increase the probability that the first slip will be followed by a full relapse or return to habitual patterns of use within a relatively short period of time.

Frustration and Anger as Determinants of Relapse in Alcoholics

In order to provide a concrete example of the relapse process presented in the preceding section, we will examine frustration and anger as potential determinants of relapse for the alcoholic patient. The highlights of this example are presented in the flow chart depicted in Figure 3. In our earlier review of the determinants of relapse for our overall sample, it was noted that the experience of frustration and/or anger was one of the major relapse situations: About one of every five relapses was assigned to this category within the major divisions of intrapersonal (category I-A-1) and interpersonal (category II-A-1) determinants. For

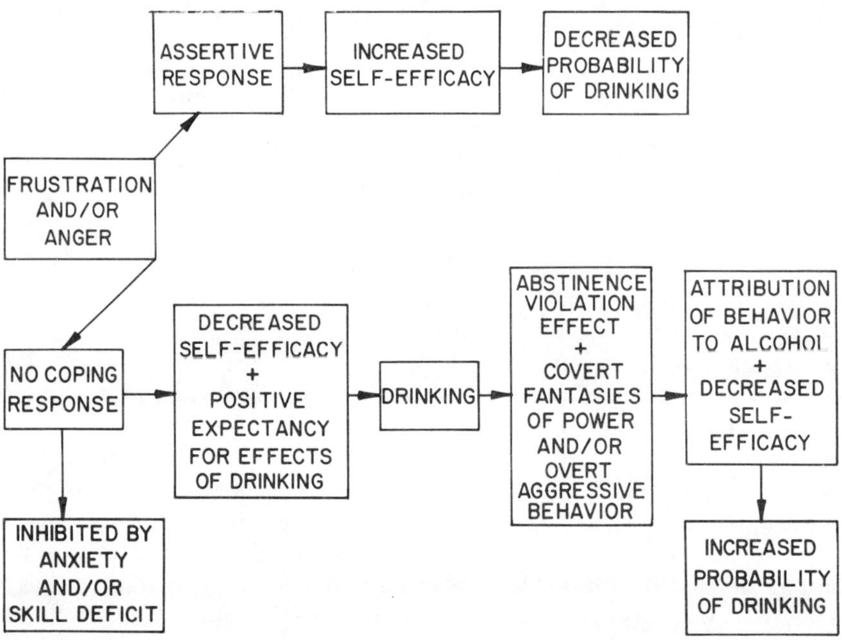

FIGURE 3. Frustration and/or anger as a determinant of relapse of alcoholics.

the alcoholic sample, frustration and/or anger accounted for almost one-fourth (24 percent) of all relapses. Clearly, frustration and anger constitute a difficult high-risk situation for drinkers who have pledged themselves to abstinence.

The majority of relapses attributed to frustration and anger occur in an interpersonal situation, frequently involving a disagreement or argument between the individual and a significant other. For many of the alcoholics in our sample, the chain of events was similar. The individual would first report feeling frustrated and angry about an event involving another person. Rather than expressing this anger or engaging in a constructive assertive response, the alcoholic turned to a drink instead. In one case, a man reported that he tried to contact his estranged wife after he had been out of the hospital for a week or so, to make arrangements to see his children. Once his wife recognized his voice on the telephone, she hung up on him. When asked about his reaction to this frustrating event, he told us that he felt furious and overcome with anger toward "that bitch." How did he respond to this high-risk situation? After the abrupt termination of the telephone call, he went down to the corner liquor store and bought himself a fifth of vodka. Frequently in such cases, it seems as though drinking takes the form of a symbolic act of aggression, a "slug of booze" coupled with an "I'll show you" attitude of defiance.

An assertive response would provide an alternative coping response to drinking in many of these situations. Our model predicts that an assertive response which enables the individual to cope effectively with the provocation involved will decrease the probability of drinking. Successful coping with frustration and anger will increase one's sense of self-efficacy, and will bolster one's perception of ongoing control. For many alcoholics, however, an adequate coping response may be unavailable (never acquired as part of their behavioral repertory) or may be inhibited by anxiety or some other blocking emotion. Research with this population has shown, in fact, that alcoholics are frequently deficient in assertive response skills (Miller, 1976).

The results of an analogue drinking study provide some support for the theoretical predictions described above. This experiment (Marlatt, Kosturn, & Lang, 1975) was one of a series to investigate determinants of alcohol consumption in heavy drinkers. In this study, subjects were first placed in a situation in which they were deliberately angered and provoked by a confederate subject prior to taking part in a drinking task where alcoholic beverages were freely available. Some subjects were allowed the opportunity to respond assertively against the subject who had provoked them, thus allowing us the opportunity to assess the effects of this alternative coping response on subsequent drinking.

Both male and female college students classified as heavy social drinkers were told that the study was designed to assess the role of intellectual functioning on the ability to make taste discriminations among various wines. Subjects were randomly assigned to one of three groups. In two of these conditions, the subjects were insulted and criticized by a confederate subject while both were ostensibly taking part in a difficult anagrams task, presented as a measure of intellectual abilities. Subjects in the third control condition experienced a neutral interaction with the confederate during the anagrams task. In one of the provocation to anger groups, subjects were provided with the opportunity of "retaliating" against the confederate subject. In this condition, the angered subject was allowed to deliver a fixed number of electric shocks to the confederate in a standard "teacher-learner" paradigm. While no shocks were actually delivered, the procedure was rigged in such a way that the real subject believed he or she was actually aggressing against the other subject. Following this initial procedure, all subjects were presented with the drinking task in which they were asked to make a number of discriminative ratings of the taste qualities of three different wines. This "taste-rating task" (Marlatt, 1978b) provides an unobtrusive measure of alcohol consumption, and has been used as the dependent variable for assessing drinking in a series of experimental studies.

The results of this study supported our predictions. Angered subjects who were not given the opportunity to retaliate against the confederate (no coping response) consumed the most wine in the taste-rating task. Subjects who were allowed to express their anger by shocking the confederate showed a significant *decrease* in drinking relative to the no-retaliation group. The consumption level for the non-angered control subjects fell between the other two groups. The findings support the hypothesis that heavy drinkers who are provided with a means of coping with a problematic social situation frequently associated with drinking will show a drop in alcohol consumption.

In the case of an alcoholic who fails to respond assertively or cope effectively with feelings of frustration and anger, it is likely that he or she will experience a decreased sense of self-efficacy. If the individual feels helpless or powerless to cope with this high-risk situation, the thought of drinking may occur as an alternative coping response. Positive expectancies about the effects of alcohol will heighten the probability of drinking under these circumstances. It may be the case, for example, that the alcoholic feels unable to express anger or engage in an overt act of aggression without the assistance of alcohol to "fortify" his courage. Alternatively, drinking may be seen as a suitable justification or excuse for expressing anger, since the individual may be able to avoid the responsibility for his actions by attributing his aggression to the effects of alcohol. In either case, it is the individual's beliefs or expectations about the effects of alcohol which are of primary importance in this analysis.

Research on cognitive determinants of drinking behavior have shown that expectancies about the effects of alcohol may have a greater impact on behavior than the actual physiological effects associated with drinking (cf., Marlatt, 1978a; Marlatt, Demming & Reid, 1973; Wilson, 1978). In terms of aggressive behaviors, there exists a common belief system in our society that alcohol facilitates the expression of anger, perhaps through its "disinhibiting" effect on behaviors which are ordinarily under social control. It may be the case, however, that one's expectations about alcohol's effects on aggression play a more significant role in this relationship than the actual physical effects of alcohol. In order to evaluate this possibility in an experimental setting, it is necessary to independently vary the expectation or belief that a drink contains alcohol with the actual alcoholic content of the drink consumed. Four groups are compared in this experimental design: expect alcohol/receive alcohol; expect alcohol/receive no alcohol; expect no alcohol/receive alcohol; and expect no alcohol/receive no alcohol. In a recent study (Lang, Goeckner, Adesso, & Marlatt, 1975), we utilized this four-group design to evaluate the relative contributions of cognitive and pharmacological factors as potential mediators of the relation between drinking and aggressive behavior.

The subjects in this study consisted of 96 male heavy drinkers drawn from a college population. Half of the subjects were led to believe that they would be drinking alcohol (a mixture of vodka and tonic) and half believed they would be consuming only tonic water. Within each of these two groups, half of the subjects actually received alcohol, but half were given only tonic. We had found on the basis of previous research (Marlatt, Demming & Reid, 1973), that with a mixture of one part vodka to five parts tonic water, subjects could not detect whether or not the drink contained alcohol on better than a chance basis. Subjects who received alcohol in the study were given a dose to bring their blood-alcohol levels to .10 percent, the lower limit of legal intoxication in most states. Following the beverage administration, half the subjects were provoked to anger by exposing them to an insulting confederate, whereas control subjects experienced a neutral interaction with the confederate subject.

Aggression was assessed by the intensity and duration of shocks administered to the confederate on a modified Buss aggression apparatus (again, although subjects believed they were giving shocks to the other subject, no one was actually shocked in the procedure). The findings showed that the only significant determinant of aggression was the *expectation* factor. Subjects who believed they had consumed alcohol were more aggressive than subjects who believed they had consumed a nonalcoholic beverage, regardless of the actual alcohol content of the drinks received. This study, along with others showing the influence of expectancy factors associated with drinking behavior (cf., Engle & Williams, 1972; Maisto, Lauerman, & Adesso, 1977; Wilson & Lawson, 1976), provides empirical support for the notion that what one believes about the effects of drinking must be taken into consideration along with the actual pharmacological effects of alcohol. For a recent review of the expectancy effect literature in alcohol research, see Marlatt & Rohsenow (in press).

Let us return now to the relapse model presented in Figure 3. The alcoholic who is faced with the high-risk situation of frustration and anger, and who fails to perform an adequate coping response, is likely to experience an increased sense of helplessness and lack of perceived control. Decreased self-efficacy, coupled with positive expectations about the effects of alcohol as described above, may combine to set the stage for relapse. If the alcoholic does take a drink under these circumstances, two outcomes may add together to further increase the probability of a full-blown relapse and the return to habitual drinking behavior. The first drink will trigger off the guilt and conflict associated with the Abstinence Violation Effect, as described in the previous section. Secondly, the act of drinking may serve to increase the individual's potential for engaging in aggressive behavior, either at the covert or overt level. There is some empirical evidence to suggest that the consumption of alcohol may give rise to covert fantasies of increased power or strength, at least for male heavy drinkers (McClelland et al., 1972). Perhaps this ideational reaction is the cognitive counterpart to the increase in autonomic arousal associated with the initial energizing phase of the biphasic physiological response to alcohol. On the other hand, it is possible that drinking may be associated with the overt expression of aggression, as discussed above. Here, drinking may provide a means of avoiding responsibility for acting in a violent or hostile manner, since the drinker can attribute this behavior to the effects of alcohol: "It's not my fault—I didn't know what I was doing because I was drunk."

Whatever the exact mechanism involved, if the drinker *believes* that alcohol has enabled him to feel stronger or more powerful (through the process of covert fantasy), and/or that alcohol has enabled him to engage in overt aggressive behavior, it seems likely that he will attribute these effects to alcohol rather than to himself. The potency of alcohol as the magic elixir will be enhanced as a result. Just as in the children's tale of Dumbo the elephant, who believed he could fly only if he held the magic feather in his trunk, so will the alcoholic come to believe that he cannot behave assertively or aggressively without the assistance of alcohol. By attributing the "cause" of his behavior to booze, his sense of self-efficacy will suffer accordingly. The probability of drinking as a response to future high-risk situations will increase because of this misattribution effect.

Implications for Prevention and Treatment

Most traditional treatment programs for addictive behaviors, including those for alcoholism, smoking control, and heroin addiction, tend to ignore the relapse issue altogether in their intervention procedures. Almost all of the customary treatment procedures are geared toward the goal of abstinence, regardless of the theoretical orientation adopted. Treatment success is evaluated in terms of the number of clients who maintain abstinence over a given period of time, and those who "relapse" are counted as treatment failures. In the alcoholism and narcotic addiction fields, the traditional approach to evaluating the effectiveness of treatment is to group clients into one of two groups: those who have maintained total abstinence, and those who have relapsed. The dichotomous all-or-none approach to assessing outcome has reinforced the clinical myth that all relapses are "total"—that patients are drinking or using illicit narcotics to the same extent as they were prior to treatment. Recently, in the alcoholism area, a government-funded study of a wide variety of abstinence-oriented treatment programs went beyond the traditional follow-up procedures by including rates or amounts of drinking as one of the evaluation measures for patients who had relapses subsequent to treatment. The findings of the now infamous "Rand Report" (Armor, Polich, and Stambul, 1976) sent shock-waves through the traditionally-oriented alcoholism community, because the data showed that a sizable proportion of the sample (about one-fourth) were drinking in a "normal" or controlled manner at the 18-month follow-up period.

Those who have conducted research in the area of smoking have usually reported follow-up data in more detail than their counterparts in the alcoholism and heroin addiction fields. Smokers who have relapsed are frequently described in terms of percent reduction in smoking rate relative to pretreatment baseline levels. This approach, which views smoking as a continuous rather than a dichotomous behavior, is a preferable one, since it permits the investigator to make fine-grained analyses of the relative effectiveness of various treatment components on overall smoking rates. This willingness of investigators to view smoking relapses in this manner reflects the underlying assumption that smoking is a habitual behavior and not a uniform disease.

When it comes down to treatment intervention procedures, however, programs for smoking, drinking, and other addictive behaviors are equally deficient in their neglect of anticipating and planning for the possibility of relapse with their clients. There seems to be a kind of consensus involved that to talk about relapse is tantamount to giving one permission to indulge in the taboo behavior. Recently, one of the authors attended a two-hour lecture given to alcoholics who were participating in a traditional hospital treatment program. Almost all of the time was spent covering the various deleterious effects of alcohol on all of the body's physiological systems from the liver to the brain. The captive audience was told in no uncertain terms that alcoholism was a disease, and that they would be back on the road to recovery only by abstaining from alcohol for the rest of their lives. As a concluding comment, the lecturer advised the audience what to do if someone were to offer any of them a drink after they had left the hospital. "Just tell them that your liver is shot, and that you can't drink," was the only suggestion given. All that input about alcoholism as a disease, and only one brief suggestion about how to handle the many high-risk situations patients are likely to experience upon release from the treatment program! It reminds one of those programs in which volunteers are dropped somewhere in the wilderness and left on their own for several days, with only a single match to light fires with—except in the latter case, the volunteers are usually already trained in the basic skills of survival. With most alcoholics, the single match is the moral imperative: *don't drink*.

Teaching skills that may help an individual to cope successfully with a relapse, either in terms of preventing one from occurring altogether or by minimizing the extent of the relapse if it does occur, would seem to be a matter of common sense. In our society, we have regulations which require us to prepare for the possibility, no matter how remote, of a wide variety of problematic and dangerous situations. We have fire drills to help us prepare for what to do if a fire breaks out in public buildings or schools. For those who travel by ship, there are lifeboat drills to teach the passengers what to do in the remote possibility that the ship may run into trouble at sea. Certainly no one believes that by requiring people to participate in fire drills or lifeboat drills, the possibility of future "accidents" will increase; quite the contrary, in fact, as the aim is to minimize the extent of personal loss and damage if an accident occurs. The same argument would seem to apply in the case of relapses. Why not have a "relapse drill" as a prevention strategy to be included as part of an ongoing treatment program? Skills offer more help to the individual than relying on vague constructs such as "willpower" or trying to adhere to the advice implied by various slogans (e.g., "one drink leads to a drunk"). In fact, we might offer a slogan of our own to emphasize this point:

SKILLS INSTEAD OF SLOGANS!

In the material to be discussed below, some possible components of such a prevention strategy will be outlined briefly. The discussion will follow the diagram presented in Figure 4. In this figure, the stages of the relapse process as described earlier are represented in rectangles, and the points of intervention are listed in the circles.

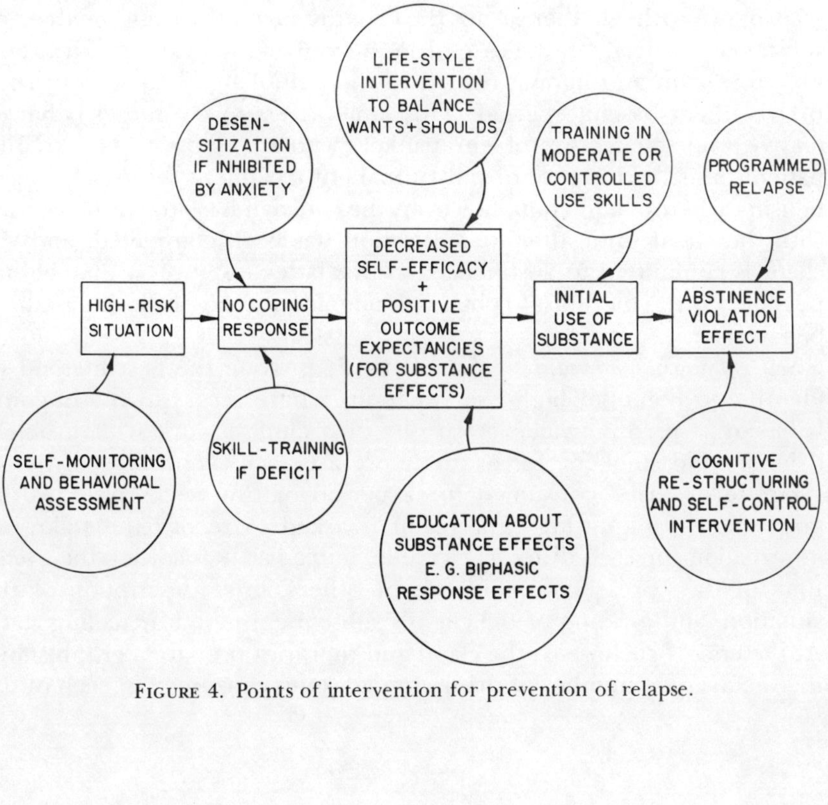

FIGURE 4. Points of intervention for prevention of relapse.

High-Risk Situations

The first step to take in the prevention of relapse is to train the client to recognize those high-risk situations which are likely to increase the likelihood of relapse. Here, the earlier one becomes aware that one is involved in a chain of events which can be identified as high-risk, the sooner one can intervene by engaging in an appropriate coping skill. The goal would be to teach the client to recognize the discriminative stimuli that are associated with "entering" a high-risk situation, and to use these warning signals as cues to implement an alternative sequence of behavior. These discriminative stimuli may involve environmental cues (e.g., entering a bar or restaurant where individuals are smoking and drinking), cognitive strategies (e.g., making "mini-decisions" which may lead the individual closer to the brink, such as deciding to visit a friend who may have some illicit drugs), or physiological state changes (e.g., feelings of frustration or arousal which the person labels as "craving" for a particular drug). How can we teach the individual to recognize and respond to these early warning signals before it is too late?

The procedures available to help identify high-risk situations vary in accordance with whether or not the client is currently using the drug or substance involved. In the case of most smokers, for example, it is possible to obtain an ongoing record of their smoking behavior during a pretreatment baseline period. This same access to the target behavior may be available from problem drinkers who are being seen on an outpatient basis. In the case of most inpatient treatment settings for alcoholism or heroin addiction, however, the clinician has little or no contact with the client until after detoxification has been completed, and the client is committed to abstinence. In this latter instance, it may be impossible for the therapist to obtain an ongoing record of the drug-taking behavior.

Self-monitoring procedures (McFall, 1977) provide the best method of identifying potential high-risk situations where access to the ongoing behavior is readily available. In our own clinical work with problem drinkers and smokers, for example, we ask each client to record each cigarette or drink consumed for a period of two weeks prior to the target date for quitting. The client is asked to record the following information for each drink or cigarette, immediately following the event: time of day, presence or absence of others, brief description of the situation, and a rating of the client's subsequent mood or feeling state. At the end of each week, the client and therapist prepare a graph showing the average number of drinks or cigarettes consumed in each of the major situational categories (e.g., while working alone, after meals, at parties, etc.,). A thorough examination of the self-monitoring data frequently reveals a pattern of situations in which the behavior occurs with the highest frequency and is associated with the greatest psychological payoff. These situations are often the ones most associated with urges or temptations to relapse during the abstinence period.

Other assessment procedures are available to identify high-risk situations in those cases where self-monitoring is not possible. In our own laboratory we have developed two assessment techniques which have proved quite successful in identifying high-risk situations for alcoholics or problem drinkers. A structured interview guide has been prepared for use with drinkers who are undergoing initial evaluation for treatment planning purposes. The *Drinking Profile* (Marlatt, 1976a) is a questionnaire designed to obtain a wide variety of information from problem drinkers during a treatment intake interview. In addition to sections dealing with information concerning the client's demographic status, drinking history, rates and patterns of drinking, etc., the questionnaire contains a number of items dealing with situational and personal antecedents for the client's typical drinking behavior. A sample item: "Are there any particular situations or set of events, things which would be most likely to make you feel like having one or more drinks?" Careful use of the *Drinking Profile* as part of a thorough behavioral assessment procedure can provide a wealth of information concerning potential high-risk situations for relapse.

In a recent treatment study with male alcoholics who participated in an inpatient abstinence-oriented program, Chaney and other members of our research team (Chaney, 1976; Chaney, O'Leary, & Marlatt, 1978) investigated the effectiveness of a social skill training program designed to help patients cope with high-risk relapse situations. As part of the assessment battery developed to evaluate this program, Chaney developed a test called the Situational Competency Test.* In this test, administered both prior to and following the training program, each subject is asked to respond verbally to a high-risk situation presented by a narrator on an audiotape. A variety of situations are presented on the tape (each equated in terms of perceived difficulty), drawn from the high-risk categories discussed earlier in this chapter. The subject's response

---

*Requests for information concerning the Situational Competency Test should be addressed to Dr. Edmund Chaney, Veterans Administration Hospital, 4435 Beacon Avenue South, Seattle, Washington, 98108.

is tape-recorded and is later scored along a number of dimensions (latency and duration of the response, degree of compliance, and specification of alternative behaviors). A sample item from the Situational Competency Test: "You are eating at at a good restaurant on a special occasion with some friends. The waitress comes over and says, 'Drink before dinner?' Everyone orders one. All eyes seem to be on you. What would you do?" This test has shown itself to be a useful assessment procedure for identifying the most problematic situations for individual clients, as an aid in treatment planning, and as a pre- and posttreatment measure in treatment outcome studies. Other behavioral assessment procedures which have been developed for use with alcoholics and problem drinkers, many of which could be adopted for use with smokers, heroin addicts, and others, can be found in a recent review chapter (Marlatt, 1978b).

Once the high-risk situations have been identified, the client can be taught to respond to the cues as discriminative stimuli for behavioral change. In some cases, it might be best to simply avoid risky situations if this is easily possible (e.g., to avoid going to bars). In most cases, however, the situations cannot be easily avoided, and the client must rely on coping skills or alternative behaviors to "get through" the situation without a relapse.

Coping Responses

A thorough behavioral assessment of the client's responses to a spectrum of representative high-risk situations will yield a profile of the individual's relative strengths and weaknesses for various coping responses. It is the clinician's responsibility to determine the extent to which deficient responding represents actual deficits in the initial acquisition of skilled behaviors, or represents responses which have been blocked or inhibited by anxiety, fear of evaluation, or other emotional reactions. If the client has never learned the appropriate coping response, the emphasis should be on teaching the requisite skills involved. On the other hand, if the response is available in the client's repertory but is blocked by an inhibiting influence, the therapist must first deal with the client's reactions so that the response can be performed with minimal anxiety. Desensitization or a related procedure might be selected for clients who seem immobilized by anxiety when confronted by social pressure, for example. The therapist must combine skill training with the use of such fear-reducing techniques, to maximize the effectiveness of the intervention program. Teaching relaxation in the absence of skill training may produce nothing more than a "relaxed incompetent," to borrow a phrase from Bandura (1969).

Skill training should be related specifically to the client's profile of proficiency, as determined by the results of the assessment phase, focusing on those behaviors which fail to meet the therapist's standards of adequacy. In the skill training program for alcoholics developed by Chaney and his coworkers (Chaney, O'Leary, & Marlatt, 1978), the client's responses to the Situational Competency Test were taken into consideration when planning the specific intervention procedures. For one client, the problem may involve an inability to resist social or peer pressure to indulge; for another, the problem may involve a deficit in coping with feelings of loneliness or depression. If the clients can be treated in a group setting, the skills can be taught most readily by adopting role-playing methods (cf., Flowers, 1975). In Chaney's research, alcoholics in treatment met together in a small group format for a series of skill training sessions. Each group was led by two therapists, who began by describing a particular high-risk situation. The group then discussed the situation, and generated various ways of responding to it. The therapist and cotherapist then modeled an appropriate coping response and probable consequences. Each client then rehearsed a particular response to a related form of the situation, and practiced it in front of the group. By this procedure, each client received individualized feedback from group members and specific coaching and instructions from the therapists. The client was required to repeat the coping response until it matched the therapists' criteria for adequacy. The skill-training condition proved more successful than either a control group, who spent an equivalent amount of time discussing their emotional reactions to the same high-risk situations, or a no-treatment control procedure, on a number of outcome measures related to relapse (Chaney, O'Leary, & Marlatt, 1978).

One suggestion that may increase the generalization of newly acquired coping skills is to require the client to practice the adaptive behavior in the actual high-risk situation. The therapist who is working with smokers or drinkers who have recently pledged themselves to abstinence could, for example, take a group of clients to an actual bar or nightclub for a "dry run" experience. The responses suggested by the group could serve as the focus of discussion, while clients meet together for a coffee or soft-drink in a setting where they are surrounded by other people who are modeling the target behavior. A simulated party setting could provide another "dry run" practice session. The literature on social skill training and assertiveness training provides a wealth of suggestions for the therapist to draw upon in developing additional procedures (cf., Goldfried & Davison, 1976; Kanfer & Goldstein, 1975; Rimm & Masters, 1974).

Self-Efficacy and Lifestyle Intervention

In addition to providing the client with a set of specific skills, each designed as a coping response to a particular high-risk situation, the therapist can also impart a number of global strategies or procedures which provide a broader framework for the relapse prevention program. Simply instructing the client to respond mechanically to one high-risk situation after another is not enough. For one thing, it is impossible for the therapist to identify or work with all of the possible high-risk situations the client may experience. For another, the training sessions are, by necessity, quite specific in content and generalization to other, somewhat different situations may not always occur. In this section, we would like to discuss several global intervention strategies which may help the client to develop a general approach to problematic situations, coupled with an attitude of "I can handle it." Although we may be stretching the concept beyond the author's original intention, Bandura's notion of self-efficacy seems to be an appropriate term for this generalized attitude. The following procedures are worthy of investigation as methods of increasing the client's self-efficacy in dealing with the numerous problems of life, any one of which may be capable of precipitating a relapse.

One obvious approach is to teach the client to first identify high-risk situations, and then apply a general *problem-solving strategy* in coping with the situation. Goldfried and his coworkers (D'Zurilla & Goldfried, 1971; Goldfried & Davison, 1976) have described an effective application of problem-solving procedures for a variety of behavioral problems. The client is taught the specific skills involved in a "trouble-shooting" approach to any problem that may arise. The stages of this approach include initial problem definition and formulation, generation of alternatives, decision making, and action followed by verification of the outcome. Use of the problem-solving approach as a component of a relapse prevention program is highly recommended in that it teaches the client to become his or her own therapist in dealing with future problematic situations.

A key component of the problem-solving approach with particular relevance to the issue of relapse is the *decision-making* stage. In this regard, the client could be trained to view the relapse as a decision in itself. By doing so, the therapist can emphasize the client's individual sense of choice or autonomy involved in the relapse, rather than viewing it as an act which occurred beyond the individual's control. By applying a decision-making analysis to the issue of whether or not to resume smoking, for example, the client is forced to consider all the potential positive and negative outcomes of such a decision prior to engaging in the behavior. The therapist may also point out "danger signs" or early indications that the client is moving toward making a decision to resume use of the substance. The client may be relatively unaware that he or she is making "mini-decisions" that may lead him/her closer to the brink of relapse (e.g., an ex-smoker who suddenly "decides" to sit in the smoking section of an airplane, and finds himself next to a passenger who offers him a cigarette the moment the "No Smoking" sign goes off after takeoff). The application of decision theory to the control of addictive behaviors has received relatively little attention to date.

On a global level, excessive drinking, smoking or other addictive behaviors may represent ways of coping with stress. Taking time out for a smoke, or for a relaxing double martini after a hard day's work, may represent the only times when some individuals are able to take a break from a busy daily schedule of responsibilities. For a hassled "workaholic," engaging in indulgent habitual behaviors such as smoking may be a means of taking *some* time (even if only a moment or two) for oneself. For these individuals, taking away a pleasurable habit without giving them something back in return is tantamount to setting the stage for relapse.

In our own clinical work with drinkers and smokers, we have found that the potential for relapse increases for those individuals whose daily schedule of activities fails to include periods of "time out" for some form of self-rewarding or pleasurable activity. For these clients, a feeling of personal deprivation begins to build up once the drinking or smoking has been eliminated as a form of indulgence. This feeling of deprivation may make it increasingly difficult for the individual to cope with high-risk situations. The client may say, "But I need to do something for *myself* for a change," and may view a drink or a smoke as a kind of reward for hard work and sacrifice ("I owe myself a drink," etc.).

We have developed a rough index of the potential for relapse associated with this sense of increased deprivation that we call the *want/should ratio*. The client is asked to keep a record of all daily activities, and to assign a rating to each activity on a seven-point scale. On one end of the scale are activities the client feels obligated to perform, and these are labeled as "shoulds." Paying household bills, performing household chores or menial tasks at work, would rate highly on the "should" side for many individuals. At the other end of the scale are the "wants," the activities the individual likes to perform and gains some personal satisfaction from engaging in (e.g., going fishing, taking time off for lunch with a friend, engaging in a creative work task, etc.). Other activities, representing a mixture of "wants" and "shoulds" are given an intermediate rating. By examining the daily want/should ratio, representing a measure of how balanced the client's lifestyle is, the therapist is better able to assess the potential risk for relapse. If the want/should ratio is strongly weighted in the direction of "shoulds," the probability of relapse may be high. Taking a drink or having a cigarette may be viewed by the client as the only "want" available after a day full of "shoulds." Here, the therapist must assume the role of lifestyle engineer, providing the client with alternative forms of "indulgence," without recourse to drugs. The overall aim is to provide a better *balance* in the want/should ratio.

In recent years, a number of procedures have been developed which seem to increase one's sense of inner perceived control and "response-ability" in dealing with stressful life situations. Foremost among such procedures are relaxation training, meditation, and physical exercise (e.g., jogging). These activities also represent alternative forms of "self-indulgence," in the sense that the individual is taking time out to engage in a personally rewarding experience. In a recent study (Marlatt & Marques, 1977), we investigated the effects of participating in a daily relaxation program on the ongoing drinking behavior of heavy social drinkers. Subjects who volunteered for the study agreed to keep a daily record of their drinking behavior (self-monitoring) for a period of 15 weeks. We chose heavy drinkers instead of alcoholics as our subjects because we wanted to determine if the relaxation training would lead to a change in alcohol consumption for individuals who had expressed no particular desire to cut down or stop their drinking. After two weeks of pretreatment baseline recording, subjects were randomly assigned to one of four groups: progressive muscle relaxation, meditation training (Benson's 1975 procedure), a "bibliotherapy" control group, or a no-treatment control condition. Subjects in the progressive relaxation and meditation groups were asked to practice their techniques twice daily (morning and late afternoons) for a period of six weeks. The bibliotherapy group, intended as an attention-placebo control condition, was asked to spend their daily relaxation periods quietly sitting and reading material of their own choosing. After the six-week training period, subjects were followed up for a period of seven weeks, during which time subjects were free to continue or discontinue practice of their techniques. The results showed a significant reduction in alcohol use (approximately a 50% drop from pretreatment rates) for subjects in all three relaxation conditions, in comparison to the no-treatment control group. Subjects in these three groups also showed a significant shift towards a greater internal locus of control during the treatment period. During the follow-up period, almost all of the subjects discontinued practice of the procedures, and drinking rates tended to increase toward baseline levels.

These results seem to indicate that taking regular "time out" periods to relax, even if only for a short 20-minute period twice a day, is associated with decreased rates of drinking. The locus of control data obtained from our subjects suggests that this decrease in alcohol consumption may be mediated by an increase in perceived internal control over one's behavior. The implications for prevention of relapse seem clear-cut. By teaching our clients a relaxation technique such as meditation or progressive relaxation, we are providing them with a *global* coping strategy that can be meaningfully combined with the specific skills we teach as means of coping with high-risk situations. The ability to cope adequately with the myriad of problematic situations encountered in day-to-day living depends not only on the individual's behavioral response capacity (the repertory of specific skills) but also on a general sense of perceived control or positive self-efficacy. A positive self-image is associated with an overall sense of being able to cope with whatever comes along, in a more or less adequate manner. Mistakes or "slips" can be viewed positively as learning experiences, an impetus for further self-awareness, rather than as indices of setback or relapse.

Outcome Expectancies for Substance Use

After someone has been abstinent for some period of time, a shift in attitudes and beliefs about the effects of the taboo substance often occurs. As time passes and the individual recovers from any deleterious effects associated with prior drug use, the negative aspects of the past drug-taking experiences may begin to lose their impact. The individual may selectively recall more of the positive effects associated with use of the substance, as the memories of the harmful effects begin to wane. Positive expectancies for the effects of a drink or a cigarette may be especially influential when the individual is faced with a high-risk situation and has no other coping response available.

Education about the actual effects of the drug or substance involved may help offset this tendency to see the "grass as greener" on the other side of the abstinence fence. Information about the long-range effects of excessive drinking or smoking on physical health and social well-being may help counter the tendency to think only of the initial pleasant short-term effects of indulging. In the case of alcohol, for example, knowledge of the biphasic response associated with the effects of drinking would be valuable in this regard. The drinker may expect that a drink will make one relaxed or high, and may conveniently overlook the second phase of the reaction, characterized by an increase in unpleasant emotional and physical reactions (withdrawal and hangover). Smokers could be reminded of the initial unpleasant reactions: the dizziness and coughing and the other negative effects one experiences with the first cigarette after a prolonged period of abstinence. The aim of such educational programs is to provide the individual with a list of reminders about the actual physiological effects of the drug involved, to counter the tendency to look at the substance through "rose-colored glasses," tinted by positive expectations about the anticipated effects.

Initial Use of Substance: What to Do if a Slip Occurs

What if all else fails, and a slip occurs? The client can be prepared in advance to cope with this possible outcome, and to try to apply some "brakes" so that the slip does not escalate into a full-blown relapse. Here again, a combination of specific skills and cognitive intervention strategies would seem to offer the greatest advantage for relapse prevention. On the one hand, we need to teach the client behavioral skills to moderate or control the indulgent behavior, once it has occurred. On the other hand, if the controlled use skills are to be successful, we must instruct the client to cope with the Abstinence Violation Effect, using cognitive restructuring procedures.

There are numerous behavioral procedures that the therapist can teach the client to help him or her stop after the first drink or cigarette. Many of these techniques have been introduced by behavioral investigators who have been developing controlled drinking programs as an alternative to abstinence as treatment goal for alcoholics. Although the original purpose of such techniques was to teach the individual how to moderate or exert control over alcohol consumption over prolonged periods of time, the principles involved also have application to the relapse situation. In addition, whereas almost all of these techniques have been used to date with alcoholics or problem drinkers, many of the procedures can be adapted with some modifications to other target behaviors such as smoking, eating, or illicit drug use.

A complete description of the techniques which can be used to control or moderate substance use is beyond the scope of this presentation. The interested reader may wish to consult some of the following sources which provide detailed descriptions of procedures that have been developed in the area of controlled drinking programs: Marlatt and Nathan (1978), Miller (1976), Miller and Mastria (1977), Miller and Mũnoz (1976), and Sobell and Sobell (1978). In the case of a drinker who slips and takes a drink, for example, a relapse prevention program might involve some or all of the following components:

(1) The client may be asked to sign a contract with the therapist, stating that the slip will end after the first drink; a second drink will cost the drinker an agreed-upon fine or other penalty which exceeds the costs for the first drink (e.g., the first drink carries a fine of $25, and the second drink a fine of $50).

(2) The client may be taught that if a slip occurs, he/she should order a drink which has a low alcoholic content (e.g., a beer vs. a martini), and "nurse" the drink over a period of at least 30 minutes. Similarly, the client can be requested to purchase only one drink, and to agree not to buy a larger supply from a liquor store or other source.

(3) The client can be taught to delay taking the first drink for at least 20 minutes after the initial temptation to "give in." This delay may give the client time to reconsider the situation, and to see it as a clear choice or decision rather than as a passive yielding to external pressures or internal urges. A delay also decreases the probability that the first drink, if it occurs at all, will occur at the peak of a high-risk situation.

One Swallow Doesn't Make a Summer

The effectiveness of any of the skills designed to moderate or control initial use of the substance may be undermined, however, unless some provision is made to prepare the client to cope with the guilt and sense of failure associated with the Abstinence Violation Effect. In this case, the therapist can first instruct the client about the components of this reaction, followed by methods which enable the client to cognitively restructure the chain of events. In teaching the client to anticipate the reaction which may follow the first slip, the therapist could pass on the following rationale: "A slip is not all that unusual. It does not mean that you have failed or that you have lost control over your behavior. You will probably feel guilty about what you have done, and will blame yourself for having slipped. This feeling is to be expected; it is part of what we call the Abstinence Violation Effect. There is no reason why you have to give in to this feeling and continue to drink (or smoke). The feeling will pass in time. Look upon the slip as a learning experience. What were the elements of the high-risk situation which led to the slip? What coping response could you have used to get around the situation? Remember the old saying: One swallow doesn't make a summer? Well, one slip doesn't have to make a relapse, either. Just because you slipped once does not mean that you are a failure, that you have no willpower, or that you are a hopeless addict. Look upon the slip as a single, independent event, something which can be avoided in the future by the use of an appropriate coping response."

By providing the client with an alternative cognitive interpretation to the Abstinence Violation Effect, the therapist may be able to forestall or minimize the sense of personal failure associated with a slip. In addition, by teaching the client to examine the sequence of events which led up to the slip, and to cognitively rehearse alternative coping strategies to similar high-risk situations, the client's sense of efficacy may be restored. Rather than passively concluding that all is lost and that nothing can be done if a slip occurs, the client can be taught to interpret the slip as an opportunity to intervene and initiate an effective self-control response.

The Programmed Relapse

At the time of this writing, the authors are working with a client who came to us for help with his smoking. He is a cigar smoker, and during the pretreatment baseline period, his self-monitoring record showed that he was smoking approximately 15 cigars per day. After the baseline period, he signed a contract with us to stop smoking for a period of at least six weeks. When the contract was signed, he deposited six $30 checks with us, one of which was to be returned to him for each week he maintained abstinence. Smoking a cigar (or any other tobacco smoking) would cost him a $30 fine, with the check being sent to his ex-wife (the person he disliked most at the time), along with a note saying something like, "Good luck on your new life, dear; here's a little something to help out." To date, the contract has worked exceedingly well, and he has maintained abstinence for the first four weeks. As the expiration date on the contract approaches, however, he has started to have some "second thoughts" about whether he wants to sign a second contract to maintain abstinence for another six-week period. As the unpleasant effects of smoking begin to fade in his memory, the positive lure of having a cigar has increased.

This client may be a good prospect for a programmed relapse. As the term implies, a programmed relapse is scheduled by the therapist, at a time and place set in advance. With this particular client, for example, the "relapse" will be scheduled to occur on the same day when the original six-week contract expires. There are several potential advantages to the programmed relapse. By setting the terms for the relapse, the therapist may be able to minimize the intensity of the Abstinence Violation Effect, since it is the therapist, not the client, who is "responsible" for the first use of the substance. By being present at the time, the therapist can monitor the reactions of the client and suggest alternative ways of conceptualizing the event. A programmed relapse, set in the neutral context of the therapist's office, avoids the possibility that the client will attribute magical powers to the smoke or drink as a means of being able to cope with a high-risk situation. Since the actual effects of the substance are usually disappointing in contrast with the client's positive expectancies, the therapist can discuss the sequence of events which led up to the "relapse," and can work out a plan for the future. Hopefully, the client will find it easier to "climb back on the wagon" and resume abstinence following this experience. Although the use of the programmed relapse has yet to be evaluated in a controlled study, the authors have found it useful as a "last ditch" effort with clients, particularly with those cases where the client has indicated a strong desire or tendency to resume use of the substance.

Conclusion

This concludes our discussion of suggested procedures to prevent or minimize the impact of the relapse process. In the future, we hope to extend our research on determinants of relapse to include other problem behaviors, including eating (going off a dietary regimen), compulsive gambling, and other habits which lend themselves to this analysis. A similar theoretical model could be developed for those cases in which the individual is attempting to *start* a new behavior pattern (as opposed to stopping an already ongoing behavior), such as initiating a regular program of exercise, or learning new skills which require adherence to a fixed schedule of practice. In these latter cases, a "relapse" would be defined as a failure to engage in the target behavior (e.g., dropping out of an exercise program). By examining the determinants and reactions to violations of self-imposed rules governing any target behavior, we will extend our understanding of the mechanisms involved in the "breakdown" of self-control programs. Careful application of this knowledge in the development of new treatment programs may enable us to further increase the maintenance of change with addictive behaviors.

REFERENCES

ARMOR, D. J., POLICH, J. M., & STAMBUL, H. B.: *Alcoholism and treatment.* Report #R-1739-NIAA; Santa Monica, Calif: Rand Corporation, 1976.

BANDURA, A.: *Principles of behavior modification.* New York: Holt, Rinehart & Winston, 1969.

BANDURA, A.: Self-efficacy: Toward a unifying theory of behavioral change. *Psychological Review,* 1977, 84, 191-215.

BEM, D. J.: Self-perception theory. In L. Berkowitz (Ed.), *Advances in experimental social psychology,* Vol. 6. New York: Academic Press, 1972.

BENSON, H.: *The relaxation response.* New York: William Morrow & Co., 1975.

CHANEY, E. F.: Skill training with alcoholics. Unpublished doctoral dissertation, University of Washington, 1976.

CHANEY, E. F., O'LEARY, M. R., & MARLATT, G. A.: Skill training with alcoholics. *Journal of Consulting and Clinical Psychology,* 1978, 46, 1092-1104.

DOCTER, R., NAITOH, P., & SMITH, J.: Electroencephalographic changes and vigilance behavior during experimentally induced intoxication with alcoholic subjects. *Psychosomatic Medicine,* 1966, 28, 605-615.

D'ZURILLA, T. J., & GOLDFRIED, M. R.: Problem solving and behavior modification. *Journal of Abnormal Psychology,* 1971, 78, 107-126.

ENGLE, K. B., & WILLIAMS, T. K.: Effect of an ounce of vodka on alcoholics' desire for alcohol. *Quarterly Journal of Studies on Alcohol,* 1972, 33, 1099-1105.

FESTINGER, L.: *Conflict, decision and dissonance.* Stanford: Stanford University Press, 1964.

FLOWERS, J. V.: Simulation and role playing methods. In F. H. Kanfer & A. P. Goldstein (Eds.), *Helping people change.* New York: Pergamon, 1975.

GARFIELD, Z., & MCBREARTY, J.: Arousal level and stimulus response in alcoholics after drinking. *Quarterly Journal of Studies on Alcohol,* 1970, *31,* 832-838.

GOLDFRIED, M. R., & DAVISON, G. C.: *Clinical behavior therapy.* New York: Holt, Rinehart & Winston, 1976.

GORDON, J. R.: The use of rapid smoking and group support to induce and maintain abstinence from cigarette smoking. Unpublished doctoral disseration, University of Washington, 1978.

HUNT, W. A., BARNETT, L. W., & BRANCH, L. G.: Relapse rates in addiction programs. *Journal of Clinical Psychology,* 1971, 27, 455-456.

JONES, E. E., KANOUSE, D. E., KELLEY, H. H., NISBETT, R. E., VALINS, S., & WEINER, B. (EDS.): *Attribution: Perceiving the causes of behaviors.* Morristown, N. J.,: General Learning Press, 1972.

KANFER, F. H., & GOLDSTEIN, A. P. (Eds.): *Helping people change.* New York: Pergamon, 1975.

KIESLER, D. J.: *The process of psychotherapy: Empirical foundations and systematic analysis.* Chicago: Aldine-Atherton, 1973.

LANG, A. R., GOECKNER, D. J., ADESSO, V. J., & MARLATT, G. A.: The effects of alcohol on aggression in male social drinkers. *Journal of Abnormal Psychology,* 1975, 84, 508-518.

LUDWIG, A. M., & WIKLER, A.: "Craving" and relapse to drink. *Quarterly Journal of Studies on Alcohol,* 1974, 35, 108-130.

MAISTO, S. A., LAUERMAN, R., & ADESSO, V. J.: A comparison of two experimental studies investigating the role of cognitive factors in excessive drinking. *Journal of Studies on Alcohol,* 1977, 38, 145-149.

MARLATT, G. A.: *A comparison of aversive conditioning procedures in the treatment of alcoholism.* Paper presented at the meeting of the Western Psychological Association, Anaheim, Calif., 1973.

MARLATT, G. A.: The Drinking Profile: A questionnaire for the behavioral assessment of alcoholism. In E. J. Mash & L. G. Terdal (Eds.), *Behavior therapy assessment: Diagnosis, design, and evaluation.* New York: Springer, 1976. (a)

MARLATT, G. A.: Alcohol, stress, and cognitive control. In I. G. Sarason & C. D. Spielberger (Eds.), *Stress and anxiety.* Vol. 3, Washington, D.C.: Hemisphere Publishing Co., 1976. (b)

MARLATT, G. A.: Craving for alcohol, loss of control, and relapse: A cognitive-behavioral analysis. In P. E. Nathan, G. A. Marlatt, & T. Loberg (Eds.), *Alcoholism: New directions in behavioral research and treatment.* New York, Plenum, 1978. (a)

MARLATT, G. A.: Behavioral assessment of social drinking and alcoholism. In G. A. Marlatt & P. E. Nathan (Eds.), *Behavioral approaches to alcoholism.* New Brunswick, N. J.,: Center of Alcohol Studies, 1978. (b)

MARLATT, G. A., DEMMING, B., & REID, J.: Loss of control drinking in alcoholics: An experimental analogue. *Journal of Abnormal Psychology,* 1973, 81, 233-241.

MARLATT, G. A., KOSTURN, C. F., & LANG, A. R.: Provocation to anger and opportunity for retaliation as determinants of alcohol consumption in social drinkers. *Journal of Abnormal Psychology,* 1975, 84, 652-659.

MARLATT, G. A., & MARQUES, J. K.: Meditation, self-control and alcohol use. In R. B. Stuart (Ed.), *Behavioral self-management: Strategies, techniques, and outcomes.* New York: Brunner/Mazel, 1977.

MARLATT, G. A., & NATHAN, P. E. (Eds.): *Behavioral approaches to alcoholism.* New Brunswick, N. J., : Center of Alcohol Studies, 1978.

MCCLELLAND, D. C., DAVIS, W. M., KALIN, R., & WANNER, E.: *The drinking man.* New York: Free Press, 1972.

MCFALL, R. M.: Parameters of self-monitoring. In R. B. Stuart (Ed.), *Behavioral self-management: Strategies, techniques, and outcomes.* New York: Brunner/Mazel, 1977.

MCGUIRE, M. T., MENDELSON, J. H., & STEIN, S.: Comparative psychosocial studies of alcoholic and non-alcoholic subjects undergoing experimentally-induced ethanol intoxication. *Psychosomatic Medicine,* 1966, 28, 13-25.

MARLATT, G. A. & ROHSENOW, D.: Cognitive process in alcohol use: Expectancy and the balanced placebo design. In N.K. Mello (Ed.) *Advances in Substance Abuse: Behavioral and Biological Research.* Greenwich, Conn.: JAI Press, in press.

MILLER, P. M.: *Behavioral treatment of alcoholism.* Oxford, U.K.: Pergamon, 1976.

MILLER, P. M. & MASTRIA, M. A.: *Alternatives to alcohol abuse: A social learning model.* Champaign, Illinois: Research Press, 1977.

MILLER, W. R., & MUÑOZ R. F.: *How to control your drinking.* Englewood Cliffs, N. J., : Prentice-Hall, 1976.

RIMM, D. C., & MASTERS, J. C.: *Behavior therapy: Techniques and empirical findings.* New York: Academic Press, 1974.

SOBELL, M. B., & SOBELL, L. C.: *Behavioral treatment of alcohol problems.* New York: Plenum, 1978.

TAMERIN, J. S., WEINER, S., & MENDELSON, J. H.: Alcoholics' expectancies and recall of experiences during intoxication. *American Journal of Psychiatry,* 1970, 126, 1697-1704.

WEINER, B., FRIEZE, I., KUKLA, A., REED, L., REST, S., & ROSENBAUM, R. M.: *Perceiving the causes of success and failure.* Morristown, N. J.,: General Learning Press, 1971.

WILSON, G. T.: Booze, beliefs, and behavior: Cognitive processes in alcohol use and abuse. In P. E. Nathan, G. A. Marlatt, & T. Loberg, (Eds.), *Alcoholism: New directions in behavioral research and treatment.* New York: Plenum, 1978.

WILSON, G. T., & LAWSON, D. M.: Expectancies, alcohol, and sexual arousal in male social drinkers. *Journal of Abnormal Psychology,* 1976, 85, 587-594.

Name Index

Subject Index